The Invention of Prophecy

Hopi Elder Thomas Banancya with Elizabeth Taylor and Jon Voight at a Hollywood press conference. Photo by Janet Gough, © Celebrity Photo.

The Invention of Prophecy

Continuity and Meaning in Hopi Indian Religion

Armin W. Geertz

UNIVERSITY OF CALIFORNIA PRESS
Berkeley Los Angeles London

University of California Press
Berkeley and Los Angeles, California

University of California Press
London, England

Library of Congress Cataloging-in-Publication Data
Geertz, Armin W., 1948-
The invention of prophecy: continuity and meaning in Hopi Indian religion / Armin W. Geertz.
p. cm.
Includes bibliographical references and index.
ISBN 0–520–08181–1 (alk. paper)
1. Hopi Indians–Religion and mythology. 2. Prophecy. 3. Hopi Indians–Philosophy. 4. Hopi Indians – Social conditions. I. Title.
E99.H7G446 1994 93–39975
299'.784–dc20 CIP

Printed in the United States of America

1 2 3 4 5 6 7 8 9

The paper used in this publication meets the minimum requirements of American National Standard for Information Sciences–Permanence of Paper for Printed Library Materials, ANSI Z39.48-1984 ♾

CONTENTS

ILLUSTRATIONS

FIGURES

CHARTS

PLATES

MAPS

PREFACE

This book is about the Hopi Indians of Arizona, their religion, and their internal and foreign affairs. Since these matters are often controversial among Hopis today, it may justifiably be asked what right I have to pursue a study of this kind. I have two answers to this question: The first is that the Hopi Indians have played a significant role in ethnographic science and in the imagination of the general public both in the United States and in Europe. Both of these audiences have tendered images and stereotypes about the Hopis which many Hopis find reprehensible and therefore subject to criticism. My second reason for writing the book is that my Hopi colleagues and consultants stipulated that if I wished to pursue academic projects on the reservation, I would have to return the favor by explaining to Americans and Europeans how things there really are. They did not require that I present a certain point of view, but they did require, quite reasonably, that I tell the truth and that I share my insights.

The implications of the Hopis' request are in my opinion 1) that most outsiders have false views about the Hopis, and 2) that outsiders should correct those views. The request is further based on the sophisticated insight that knowledge about other people is primarily rooted in the pursuit of knowledge about oneself. Hopis know as well that the control and proliferation of knowledge is a political matter, and that they have been on the bad end of the bargain for most of Hopi-U.S. history. Although Hopis disagree about many things, most of them agree on the following paraphrase: "You helped us get into this mess, so you should help get us out of it!"

I do not claim that this is *the* true story of the Hopis. Any point of view is subjective. But after years of interviews and discussions, study, and reflection, I have developed ideas about Hopi religion and history which Hopis recognize, but which at the same time go against the grain of most popular and some academic assumptions. I take issue with a whole series of falsehoods about the Hopis held by environmentalists, activists, artists, hobbyists, literature pandits, and some Americanists. As I wrote in my article "A Container of Ashes," I am taking issue as well with crazy Whites "who claim that the Hopis are beyond all expectations of sacredness, harmony, and peace, a people where women reign in true harmony with 'Mother Earth' and where the men are 'High Priests' of North America guarding the occultistic 'spiritual' centers of the continent until the Great Spirit chooses to return. And, besides all of this wonderful stuff, they speak a timeless, spaceless, and obviously alien (which is somehow admirable) language" (1989*b*:1). In other words, I specifically reject the misrepresentation of other people for ideological, existential, or any other reasons. If we wish to pursue the representation of other cultures, then it should at least be recognizable to the people being represented.

The criticisms raised here are not criticisms of the Hopi people. My admittedly skeptical stance is in fact a criticism of Americans and Europeans through the medium of a sobering reexamination of Hopi history. I have kept various political representatives informed about the progress and results of my research both during my stays on the reservation and during the writing stages of my work. These representatives include Abbott Sekaquaptewa, the chairman of the Tribal Council during my stay in 1978–1979; Patrick C. Dallas, former director of the Hopi Lands Office and present vice-chairman of the Tribal Council; Leigh Jenkins, former assistant director of the Hopi Health Department and present director of the Cultural Preservations Office; Leon A. Nuvayestewa, the present director of the Hopi Health Department; Alph Secakuku, superintendent of the Bureau of Indian Affairs, Hopi Agency, until 1988; the Hotevilla Village Committee (during 1978–1979, as well as in 1982) and its advisors the late Percy Lomakwahu and Charley Sekenooyoma; and James Pongyayawma, the late village chief of Hotevilla. Some have found uses for my documents and others have graciously given me access to theirs. Furthermore, I have received permission to do research and to publish from the consultants and elders who kindly provided me with the oral evidence that is presented here.

Having said all of this, it must be made absolutely clear that although many Hopis have been kept informed about my work and many have supported it, I make no claims to final representational authority. The opinions, evaluations, and conclusions of this book are entirely my own and should in no way be construed as being the opinion of the Hopi people. I have tried to answer a number of challenging questions in good faith and I hope that some of my insights will be of use to the Hopi people as well.

My original intentions were to pursue a study of Hopi religion in contemporary affairs. I had no interest in politics and certainly not in the continual stream of movements and individuals who have used and still use the Hopis as symbols and/or more-or-less active participants in their own ideological, political, or religious activities, who define how Hopis should be and thereby what Hopis *ought* to be. But it was impossible for me to avoid getting involved simply because my Hopi friends and neighbors were talking about it all the time.

After my first field trip I spent the next several years in sublime isolation meticulously transcribing and translating my Hopi tapes. I was well on the way to producing traditional ethnographic material on a little-known aspect of Hopi religion.

But by 1981 the trouble began. A group of European supporters of the Hopi Traditionalist Movement in Denmark produced a political exhibition at a local museum in which the Hopis were portrayed in exactly the manner that the majority of the Hopis on the reservation abhor. I wrote a critical editorial in the local newspaper which brought on a furor. I sent an English version of the editorial to the Hopi newspaper *Qua' Töqti*, which was published in 1982. My intention in sending the editorial had been to let the Hopis know that I was keeping my side of the bargain. A short trip to the reservation that year confirmed this approach by the many positive responses from my Hopi consultants and colleagues as well as the villagers of Hotevilla who had held a public meeting about the article.

However, angry reactions from White readers of the editorial continued coming in. Somehow I had challenged some dearly held myths that non-Hopis considered to be essential to their own existential well-being. The next year I wrote a short article in *Anthropos* (A. W. Geertz 1983) which was highly critical of Frank Waters' *Book of the Hopi* (1963). I had come to the conclusion that many American and European misconceptions about the Hopis stem from this book. The responses to that article are still coming in from Europe and the U.S.

In 1986, when the deadline for the removal of recalcitrant Navajo families who resided on the wrong side of the Joint-Use-Area boundaries was scheduled, representatives of the American Indian Movement staged lecture tours, demonstrations, and rock concerts throughout Europe and the U.S. in opposition to the relocation program which they perceived to be the genocide of the Navajo people by the U.S. government. I wrote a critical editorial in the local newspaper calling for a stop to Navajo histrionics. Nobody had bothered to mention the fact that the relocation had been requested by the Hopi tribe in order to remove the Navajos from Hopi lands. The Hopis were not interested in having the relocation plans stopped, except for Traditionalist Movement spokesmen. Those plans had been avoided by the Navajos for several decades already. After pointing this out, I was promptly labeled a liar and racist. So I wrote two essays in appeal to the international community which further explained my views on the matter: One was "Hopi-Forschung und literarische Gattungen" for Hans Peter Duerr's book on anthropology and authenticity (A. W. Geertz 1987*b*), and the other was "Prophets and Fools," which was written for our new journal in Budapest (now in Vienna), *European Review of Native American Studies* (A. W. Geertz 1987*c*).

"Prophets and Fools" was an attempt to impart some insight into the complexities of the Hopi situation for a nonspecialist audience. It is critical of the Hopi Traditionalist Movement mainly because the article expresses the viewpoints of non-Traditionalists who, by the way, are no less "traditional" than the Traditionalists. But in the process of trying to sort things out as I understand them, I was unavoidably pursuing a critique of our own culture and of the desperate romance and nostalgia that for various reasons accompany our present cultural disorientation. Hopis who have read the article recognize this immediately, and even though it puts the Traditionalists in another light than they are used to, it is even more so a criticism of their White supporters who have uncritically and primitively been causing havoc out on the reservation. This book, then, is a systematic examination of the whole issue of the Hopi Traditionalist Movement and its activities at home and abroad.

My explanations notwithstanding, this study raises some fundamental questions about the ethnographic pursuit and its literary expressions. It also raises questions about ideology and the pursuit of knowledge that should challenge all of us to reflect on what we are doing and why we are doing it, scientist and tourist alike.

This book also addresses academic readers who are interested in American Indian studies in particular and religious studies in general since it raises issues relevant to ongoing theoretical discussions in sociology, anthropology, the history of religions, and the philosophy of religion. The topics addressed are prophecy, meaning, politics, and the mechanisms of change, especially changing prophecies and changing meanings. Besides trying to trace and explain the complexities of the situation on the reservation today, this book also attempts to describe what that situation can tell us about prophecy and religion in general.

In the following I attempt to analyze a set of religious ideas and the changes they undergo through time and in relation to different groups. It is an analysis of the history of a set of ideas promulgated by certain groups of people. The analysis is not based on quantity statistics, political and economic theory, sociology, linguistics, theology, or kinship theory. The stringency of the analysis is to be found in its uncompromising focus on a set of ideas and the influence these ideas have had on individuals and groups; and, vice versa, the influence that psychological and sociological factors have had on these ideas. Numerous methods are employed and the data and sources are of varying types and genres. But the goal governs the means, the goal being to correlate the living religious reality of a people with the factors that move them: cognitive environments, personal and political motivations, fortuitous historical situations, and the perennial human desire to find the meaning of it all.

Hopi religion is viewed against the kaleidescopic backdrop of changing political, social, and historical factors. The development of Hopi religion is plotted from local, mainstay agricultural concerns, through the confrontation between cultures, to the rise of the universal, missionizing aspirations of the Traditionalist Movement. Cultural confrontation has led to a complicated symbiosis between the Traditionalists and various Euro-American ecological movements, new religious movements (such as New Age), and other special-interest groups. The interactions between the Hopis and these various interest groups are specifically set out.

In an attempt to explain what causes prophets to change their apparent revelations, traditionalists to change their traditions, and believers to keep on believing, I maintain that the answer is to be found by rethinking what we know about prophecy, tradition, and religion and how we should study them. In focusing on human beings as culturally competent social agents continually engaged in negotiating, inventing, and reinventing meaningful interpretations of their worlds, we come to see and understand the contradictions of human life not so much as contradictions, but more as the effervescence of creative genius.

ACKNOWLEDGMENTS

For permission to publish, grateful acknowledgment is extended to: Cline Library, Special Collections Department, Northern Arizona University, Flagstaff, Arizona, for illustrations from the Louis A. Hieb field notes; Genealogy Library, Department of Library, Archives and Public Records, Phoenix, Arizona, for articles from the *Arizona Republic*; Dr. Louis A. Hieb, University of Arizona, Tucson, for quotes from his unpublished dissertation *The Hopi Ritual Clown* (1972); the Hopi Health Department, Kykotsmovi, Arizona, for quotes and illustrations from the Hopi Mental Health Conference reports; the Mennonite Library and Archives, Information and Research Center, North Newton, Kansas, for quotes from the John P. Suderman manuscript "A Hopi Indian Finds Christ" (n.d.); Professor Shuichi Nagata, University of Toronto, Ontario, Canada, for quotes from his unpublished paper "Political Socialization of the Hopi 'Traditional' Faction" (1968); Abbott Sekaquaptewa for quotes and illustrations from *Qua' Töqti*; the Smithsonian Institution, National Anthropological Archives, Washington, D.C., for illustrations from the G. K. Gilbert archives; Special Collections Library, University of Arizona, Tucson, Arizona, for quotes and illustrations from several archival sources; Viking Penguin, New York, New York, for quotes and illustrations from Frank Waters, *Book of the Hopi* (1963); the University of Arizona Press, Tucson, Arizona, for permission to quote from Peter Whiteley, *Deliberate Acts: Changing Hopi Culture through the Oraibi Split* (1988); the University of Nebraska Press, Lincoln, Nebraska, for permission to quote from *Maasaw: Stories of Maasaw, a Hopi God* by Ekkehart Malotki and Michael Lomatuway'ma (1987); and *Maasaw: Profile of a Hopi God* by Ekkehart Malotki and Michael Lomatuway'ma (1987); the

University of New Mexico Press, Albuquerque, New Mexico, for quotes from *Big Falling Snow. A Tewa-Hopi Indian's Life and Times and the History and Traditions of His People*, by Albert Yava (1978) and *Hopi Voices. Recollections, Traditions, and Narratives of the Hopi Indians* edited by Harold Courlander (1982); Mrs. Ingrid L. Bak, Copenhagen, for the use of two maps by A. G. Bak from *"Og da blev jeg en sky" - tekster om hopiindianernes religion* by Armin W. Geertz (1986); *New Age Journal*, Brighton, Massachusetts, for permission to reprint illustrations from *The 1988 Guide to New Age Living*; Acoma Books, Ramona, California, for permission to quote from *Continuities of Hopi Cultural Change* by Richard O. Clemmer (1978); *East West Natural Health: The Guide to Well-being*, Brookline Village, Massachusetts, for quotes and illustrations from "The Hopi Prophecy," (Banyacya 1975) and "The Hopi: At the Heart of the World," (Tarbet, Jr. 1975).

For research funding and facilities I wish to thank the Danish Research Council of the Humanities, the Research Fund of the University of Aarhus which awarded a grant from the 60th Anniversary Fund, and the Faculty of Theology at the same university. This publication is a revised and abridged edition of my thesis submitted for the acquisition of the post-doctoral degree (Doctor Philosophaeia) at the University of Aarhus in Denmark.

I am grateful to the following Hopi friends, colleagues, and officials, some of whom have sadly passed away: Patrick C. Dallas, George Hamana, Leigh Jenkins, Karl Johnson, the late Percy Lomakwahu, the late Michael Lomatuway'ma and his wife and family, Leon A. Nuvayestewa, the late James Pongyayawma, Alph Secakuku, Abbott Sekaquaptewa, Emory Sekaquaptewa, Charley Sekenooyoma, Herschel Talashoma, the Hotevilla Village Committee, Mrs. Yaiva-BigPond, the members of the Kwan Kiva of Hotevilla, my hosts and other friends who wish to remain anonymous.

I am also grateful for assistance from William H. Mullane, head of the Cline Library at Northern Arizona University, Flagstaff, Arizona, Louis A. Hieb, head of Special Collections at the University of Arizona, Tucson, Arizona, John D. Thiesen and David A. Haury, director and archivist at Mennonite Library and Archives, North Newton, Kansas, Mrs. Rosemund B. Spicer in Tucson, Arizona, Donald Bahr at Arizona State University, Tempe, Arizona, William Merrill formerly at National Anthropological Archives, Washington, D.C., and the Historical Department at the Church of the Latter-Day Saints in Salt Lake City, Utah, the Utah State Historical Society in Salt Lake City, and the Library Department at Phoenix Newspapers Inc. in Phoenix, Arizona.

For inspiration and critical comments to portions of the manuscript special thanks are extended to Clifford Geertz at the Institute for Advanced Study in Princeton, New Jersey, Ekkehart Malotki at Northern Arizona University, Flagstaff, Arizona, Peter Whiteley at Sarah Lawrence College, Bronxville, New York, Alice Schlegel at the University of Arizona, Tucson, Arizona, E. Thomas Lawson at Western Michigan University in Kalamazoo, Michigan, Shuichi Nagata at the University of Toronto, Toronto, Ontario, and my colleagues Tove Tybjerg at the University of Copenhagen and Per Bilde and Jeppe Sinding Jensen at the University of Aarhus in Denmark. Thanks go as well to my artist and friend Poul Nørbo at the University of Aarhus, Denmark. My gratitude is further extended to the adjudication committee consisting of Louis A. Hieb, Tucson, Arizona, Søren Giversen at the University of Aarhus, Denmark, and Torben Monberg at the University of Copenhagen, Denmark.

For their patience and cooperation, I would like to thank Stanley Holwitz, Rebecca Frazier, Eran Fraenkel, and Diana Feinberg at the University of California Press, Los Angeles.

Finally, my wife Rita's critical comments have been an important factor in many ways because her experiences during our first field trip were different than mine. Her support during the writing stages as well as the patience and love of our children Njal, Astrid, and Ida have helped me through some difficult moments.

INTRODUCTION

PROPHECY AND ONTOLOGY

At a conference held on the theme "mental health" under the auspices of the Hopi Health Department in 1981 at Kykotsmovi, Third Mesa, the following observation was made by a keynote Hopi speaker:

> A major theme of Hopi culture that winds its way like a thread through all Hopis' lives–young and old alike–and has a dramatic impact on the peoples' capacity to deal with mental health needs is *Hopi Prophecy*. . . . Hopi prophecy and underlying beliefs of mental health and illness are very important in determining peoples' attitudes to individuals experiencing problems. Everyday members of the Hopi community can be found who are discussing the present state of Hopi society, religion, and culture and why we have serious problems. Almost always the words "Hopi Prophecy" can be heard during the course of conversation. To more fully understand mental-health conditions on Hopi, we must turn our attention to Hopi prophecy. (Hopi Health Department n.d.: 49)

This observation, made by a Hopi to Hopis of all ages and political persuasions, is a major step forward by the Hopi people to secure the resiliency of their collective mental health and their culture. It is at the same time a simple observation, pregnant with ontological and cognitive significance, which until recently has hardly been touched on in the scholarly literature about the Hopis.

The quotation above represents a conscious articulation made by the subjects of a culture based on a difficult and at times heart-rending process. But the Hopis have been talking about prophecy (at least as far as the sources indicate) since 1858,[1] and with increasing frequency since 1906. And yet, for all our scientific acumen, we have hardly taken notice!

With all the thousands and thousands of pages written about the Hopis, few have attempted to understand and interpret the people being described. We have two main types of anthropological literature on the Hopis. The major type is simply descriptive ethnography: data, observations, archaeological and other reports, and some texts, with very little interpretation. Second is a smattering of ethnological analyses often attempting to prove or disprove some universal theory. The requirements of an ever more theoretical development in anthropology, linguistics, archaeology, and comparative religion demand more contemporary analyses of the ethnographic material—and not only that, we need *relevant* analyses, especially if we truly want to understand anyone other than ourselves.

There are a number of studies that have provided fruitful analyses: on the corn metaphor in Hopi ideology,[2] witchcraft,[3] concepts of death,[4] the *katsina* cult,[5] the ritual clown,[6] the concept of person,[7] ritual and ceremonialism,[8] ritual objects,[9] ritual knowledge,[10] mythology,[11] and gender ideology.[12] All of these matters can ultimately be explained in terms of the central religious ideology of the Hopi people. And this ideology is found most fully articulated in the "emergence myths" that are freely told and retold to anyone who cares to listen. A careful analysis of the emergence myths will in due time unravel any central problem in Hopi studies which we might wish to solve and will at the same time be relevant and recognizable to the Hopis themselves. It is therefore surprising

1. There is good reason to believe that prophetic motivations played a role in Hopi confrontations with the Spaniards from the 16th century on, but the sources cannot prove this unequivocally. See my arguments in chapter 1.

2. Kennard 1972; Black 1984.

3. Parsons 1927; Beaglehole and Beaglehole 1935:5–10; Titiev 1943.

4. Beaglehole and Beaglehole 1935: 11–14; Kennard 1937.

5. Colton 1949; Kennard 1938; Dockstader 1954.

6. Parsons and Beals 1934; Hieb 1972.

7. A. W. Geertz 1986, 1990*a*.

8. Parsons 1933, 1939; Beaglehole 1936; Titiev 1944; Bradfield 1973; A. W. Geertz 1977, 1986, 1990*a*.

9. A. W. Geertz 1977, 1982*a*, 1986, 1987*a*; Geertz and Lomatuway'ma 1987.

10. Whiteley 1987, 1988.

11. Goldfrank 1948; Tyler 1964, 1975; F. Eggan 1967; Nagata 1978; Malotki 1983*a*; Malotki and Lomatuway'ma 1985, 1987*b*; A. W. Geertz 1983, 1984, 1987*b*, 1987*d*, 1989*a*, 1990*b*.

12. Schlegel 1973, 1977, 1979; A. W. Geertz and Lomatuway'ma 1987:177–189.

that so few analyses of the emergence mythology have appeared during the last century of research on the Hopis.[13]

I understand myth to be narrated tradition that codifies, coordinates, and sometimes systematizes interpretive frameworks and categories in terms of stories about beings and events that are of primary significance to a given culture. By this definition, I come close to folklorist Pierre Maranda's formulation:

> Myths display the structured, predominantly culture-specific, and shared, semantic systems which enable the members of a culture area to understand each other and to cope with the unknown. More strictly, *myths are stylistically definable discourses that express the strong components of semantic systems.* (Maranda 1972:12–13)

Myth is of course more than Maranda's literary definition seems to allow. There are many other proposals from which to choose, but a recent one by the historian of religions William G. Doty, from the University of Alabama, covers most of what can be succinctly said about myth:

> A mythological corpus consists of (1) a usually complex network of myths that are (2) culturally important (3) imaginal (4) stories, conveying by means of (5) metaphoric and symbolic diction, (6) graphic imagery, and (7) emotional conviction and participation, (8) the primal, foundational accounts (9) of aspects of the real, experienced world and (10) humankind's roles and relative statuses within it. Mythologies may (11) convey the political and moral values of a culture and (12) provide systems of interpreting (13) individual experience within a universal perspective, which may include (14) the intervention of suprahuman entities as well as (15) aspects of the natural and cultural orders. Myths may be enacted or reflected in (16) rituals, ceremonies, and dramas, and (17) they may provide materials for secondary elaboration, the constituent mythemes having become merely images or reference points for a subsequent story, such as a folktale, historical legend, novella, or prophecy. (Doty 1986:11)[14]

In my 1984 paper, I concentrated on the spatial orientation evident in emergence mythology. In this study, I will attempt to formulate the nature of Hopi prophecy and prophetic mentality. With our starting point in the emergence myth, I will delineate the development and use of Hopi prophecy by the Hopis, followed by a study of the use of Hopi

13. Exceptions to this are Goldfrank 1948, F. Eggan 1967, Clemmer 1987*b*, A. W. Geertz 1984, Vecsey 1983, and Malotki and Lomatuway'ma 1987*b*.

14. See my review of Doty's book in A. W. Geertz 1990*c*.

prophecy by Hopis and non-Hopis in interaction, thereby imparting a sense of the dynamism involved.[15]

THE ANALYSIS OF HOPI PROPHECY

In this study I will argue the following:

Proposal 1: Hopi prophecy is indigenous and it stems from the core narrative which is called the emergence myth by scholars. A subsidiary point is that this narrative is simultaneously stable and changing.

Proposal 2: The rhetoric of traditionalism is not equivalent to the reality it portrays. A subsidiary point is that "tradition" is a strategic resource for all the members of a society.

Chapter 1 illustrates the dynamic tapestry of Hopi prophecy in history and suggests that Hopi prophecy is indigenous, in other words, that it is not a cultural borrowing (i.e., from biblical prophecy), but is a genuinely indigenous response to culture contact. Hopi prophecy is rooted in the emergence myth, which is the "core narrative" embodying what is of ultimate significance to all Hopis. Chapter 2 attempts to define Hopi prophecy and identify its distinguishing characteristics. Chapter 3 will examine the core narrative paying special attention to exactly what changes in the core narrative and what does not. It will be demonstrated that the emergence myth is simultaneously stable, thus securing continuity, and accommodative (or malleable), thus securing meaning. In other words, the emergence myth and the prophecies that are purported to stem from it demonstrate fixity, on the one hand, and fluidity on the other. Chapters 3 and 4 will demonstrate the relationships between genre and change.

Numerous theories have been produced to account for the inherent tension between tradition and change. But whereas most theories have tried to account for change, I will also attempt to account for persistence. As sociologist Robert A. Nisbet wrote, "Nothing is more obvious than the *conservative* bent of human behavior, the manifest desire to preserve, hold, fix, and keep stable" (1969:271). Seen from this point of view, the maxim that "tradition is change" erroneously assumes that change is more "natural" than persistence. I hold that persistence and change are aspects of the same social phenomenon, namely, tradition.

In order for a tradition to remain viable it must be both resilient and malleable. It must change in order to retain meaning in the face of

15. Cf. A. W. Geertz 1987*c*, 1989*b*, 1989*c*.

changing social and political circumstances.[16] It must draw on the central narrative to account for change. It must objectify and symbolize agents of change, whether foreign peoples or ideas, internal mechanisms, or factional interests, in order to identify and ultimately assimilate these agents in terms of indigenous theory.

Proposal 2 is the Gordian knot which the rest of the book tries to unravel. The story of the Traditionalist Movement is fairly easy to tell historiographically, but it is not so easy to unravel in terms of interpretation. Not only that, the interpretation involves political and ideological issues that are still relevant on—and off—the reservation today. My reasons for pursuing this topic are that even though the issues have been volatile, they are no longer so, since the Traditionalist Movement has all but died out and the Tribal Council has taken over the initiative in matters of cultural preservation. Secondly, the processes and structures that an analysis of the issues reveals are relevant both to contemporary Hopis and to analytical theory.

Those who have lived with and studied the Hopis seriously know that the Traditionalists have changed their story over the years, but no one ever considered it worth the trouble to prove it. And yet, if there is to be any hope in cutting through the Gordian knot, it must be systematically shown that the Traditionalists have been engaging in what common sense tells us traditionalists never do, namely, changing their traditions! The story of pretence and posture is, of course, the basic human story the world over, but the ultimate goal of this analysis is not to debunk. The inevitable debunking in this study is an argumentative strategy mostly in relation to Euro-American activists and non-Hopi supporters of the Traditionalist Movement, academic or otherwise, as well as to the doubters, of whatever persuasion they might be.

What I have considered more important to prove is that the Traditionalist Movement has not just changed its story; it has, in fact, been a major agent of cultural change on par with the Tribal Council. Now, this is nothing new in social theory. But it is new in Hopi studies, and in fact goes against the grain of those who have written about the Traditionalist Movement, especially Richard Clemmer. Sociologists Edward Shils, S. N. Eisenstadt, and Milton Singer have all argued not only that "traditionalism" is not the same as "tradition," but also that the traditionalist is both innovator (Shils 1971:146), and a major instrument of modernization (Singer 1971:162).

The term "traditionalist" does not automatically imply the continuity

16. The Dutch anthropologist van Baaren argued similarly about the flexibility of myth in his article of that title (Baaren 1984).

of tradition. It implies the opposite in fact. It implies the pursuit of tradition, which again implies that the traditionalist neither stands in nor accepts the tradition of his contemporaries. In other words, the traditionalist is an innovator, one who intensely promotes sacred matters that are perceived as having been "displaced" by contemporary tradition. This book will show that the Traditionalist Movement was not only innovative in this sense of the word, but also by introducing foreign elements in support of the reinstitution of displaced tradition. As Shils wrote, "Both those who recommend the displacement of the once recommended traditional belief and those who recommend its observance in purified form are innovators" (1971:146). Thus, Progressives and Traditionalists are two sides of the same coin.

This point alone might have served as sufficient cause for a study of this kind. There are, after all, quite a number of basic misconceptions concerning the Traditionalist controversy which will be cleared up in the process. During the years devoted to this study I have discovered a number of interesting things in the archives, and these small discoveries will be revealed in their proper place.

But there is much more to the job! Proposal 2 also contains a subsidiary element which, as commonplace and uninteresting as it may seem, nevertheless represents the more important discovery. Namely, it was not just the Traditionalists who have changed their story—everybody has!

This insight raises a number of questions about the nature of prophecy both in the Hopi context and in religion in general. One could ask with typical Western cynicism, "What moves people to claim in the name of religious truth things that are neither falsifiable nor even empirically true? What needs are behind this universal activity?" The answer or answers to these kinds of questions must inevitably lead to social and psychological determinisms, so, I will not ask those kinds of questions.

The problem seems to be inextricably enmeshed in our own argumentative metaphors. While talking about concepts and mechanisms we have forgotten about agents. We forget that tradition and prophecy are a way of thinking, a way of speaking, and a way of acting that articulates in myriad ways the webs of significance produced by human cultures. Prophecy is not prediction, even though it purports to be so. Prophecy is a thread in the total fabric of meaning, in the total worldview. In this way it can be seen as a way of life and of being.[17]

I am in good company in this matter. In 1979 Johannes Fabian edited

17. Cf. Wagner 1972, Fabian ed. 1979, Herzfeld 1981, Kaplan 1990.

a volume of papers which were published in the journal *Social Research* under the title "Beyond Charisma: Religious Movements as Discourse." As the title indicates, the participants were formulating a departure from earlier causal explanations, typologies, and theories of charisma. The sort of study they had in mind does not "elaborate timeless codes of prophetic thought but retrace[s] events and give[s] accounts of the inevitably 'temporal' articulations of prophetic messages" (Fabian 1979*a*: 27). Like Foucault, Fabian emphasized that the study of "discourse" in this sense does not consist of discovering the rules that have generated some discursive fact or other; rather, it consists of describing the events of discourse where the question is why one particular statement was made rather than another (Foucault 1976:27; Fabian 1979*a*:28). Thus, discourse is social praxis and it occurs both in temporal and spatial contexts as "unfolding in a process of internal differentiation, and of openness to response and argument from an audience" (Fabian 1979*a*:28).

It will be demonstrated in this study that Hopi prophecy is a social, narratological phenomenon: It is tradition that is spoken by someone to someone else for specific purposes, whether for moral, ideological, or political reasons. Prophecy is not static, but is and always has been used in response to internal and external conditions. It is a way of articulating and defining contemporary events within the context and language of "tradition." Prophecy, being understood in this manner as a cultural strategy, gives us a major key to understanding not only our pueblo neighbors but also ourselves.

My approach to the pragmatics of prophecy follows insights which the American sociologist Peter Berger and the German sociologist Thomas Luckmann presented in their study of the social construction of reality (Berger and Luckmann 1966). Drawing especially on the thinking of Edmund Husserl and Alfred Schutz, Berger and Luckmann developed the idea of "sedimentation," which posits that human experiences congeal in recollection as sediment. This sediment becomes social when objectivated in a sign system, that is, when the reiterated objectification of shared experiences becomes possible. They argued that its transformation into a generally available object of knowledge allows it to be incorporated into a larger body of tradition "by way of moral instruction, inspirational poetry, religious allegory and whatnot" (ibid.:86).

The argument runs further that this aggregate of collective sedimentations can be acquired monothetically, that is, as cohesive wholes,

> without reconstructing their original process of formation. Since the actual origin of the sedimentations has become unimportant, the tradition might invent quite a different origin without thereby threatening what has been objectivated. In other words, legitimations can succeed each other, from

> time to time bestowing new meanings on the sedimented experiences of the collectivity in question. The past history of the society can be reinterpreted without necessarily upsetting the institutional order as a result. (ibid.:87)

This body of tradition is transmitted as "knowledge" by specified "knowers" to others in the social network. All three instances–knowledge, knowers, and nonknowers–are defined in terms of what is socially defined as reality. It is especially in the realm of the definition, transmission, and maintenance of social meaning that control and legitimation procedures become paramount. Thus:

> To understand the state of the socially constructed universe at any given time, or its change over time, one must understand the social organization that permits the definers to do their defining. Put a little crudely, it is essential to keep pushing questions about the historically available conceptualizations of reality from the abstract "What?" to the sociologically concrete "Says who?" (ibid.:134)[18]

It is precisely this social aspect of Hopi prophecy that is relevant to this study. In studying Hopi sacred history, I ask with Graeme MacQueen *whose* sacred history are we talking about? (MacQueen 1988).

Like Roy Wagner, I do not mean by the title of this book, "The Invention of Prophecy," to restrict its meaning to "bolt-from-the-blue" stereotypes (Wagner 1975:xvi) or even conscious inventions. I am instead referring to the creative interaction between paradigm and agent, where the agent continuously reworks pieces of the cultural repertoire in order to construct, adjust, and reconstruct interpretations of experience. The term "invention" also implies replication and representation. It implies the living into reality of what is perceived about reality.

On a larger scale, Victor Turner's processual approach to a "social drama" is a useful instrument in interpreting the contexts that mobilize the paradigms or premises of a culture and which in turn produce meaning. In this book, I consider the ideological conflict between the Traditionalists and the Tribal Council to be the overarching "social drama" (or F. G. Bailey's "arena," 1960:243–248), and the actual historical conflicts as episodes in that drama. Thus, with Fabian, I hold that probing into the historical depths–as opposed to the naive explanatory models of social anomie and psychological pathology–results in a "widening appreciation of the contemporary significance of movement activities" (Fabian 1979*a*:33). In other words, movements are not a priori

18. See Wisdom 1973, Jarvie 1972, and Radford 1985 for critiques of Berger and Luckmann's approach.

deviant, marginal, or disturbing; they can, and usually are, "creative, constructive, and universally appealing" (Fabian 1979*b*:169).

Meaning takes on a functional, emergent quality in this perspective. With Wagner I agree that meaning is involved in every cultural act and cannot be detached from the contexts of those acts. Meaning is therefore not a closed system, but is "open-ended and ongoing" (Wagner 1972:8). And yet, in tune with the inherent tension between persistence and change, meaning takes on explicitly residual form as well. It becomes emergent only in the hands of social actors.

It is along these lines that a detailed analysis of the historically specific case study will entail consequences of general theoretical significance. I agree with James Beckford's observations in reference to the study of new religious movements that studying them has less to do "with what they represent in themselves and more to do with what they indirectly reveal about the state of society, other religious bodies, or structures of meaning" (Beckford 1987:392).

Following this line of thought, this book ends with a chapter that introduces an interpretive model of tradition and change in Hopi prophecy which should find applicability in other contexts as well.

A DEFINITION OF RELIGION

The term religion is notoriously impervious to definition attempts. Many have tried, but it is beyond the scope of this book to review them.[19] Some have even denied the usefulness of a priori definitions.[20] One of the problems with existing definitions of religions is that they consist of various types. They can be substantive, functionalist, family-resemblance, monothetic, operational, or essentialist (cf. Byrne 1988) or they can be stipulative, ostensive, nominal, or real (cf. Wahlström 1981). Another problem is that they often function programmatically for academic schools and traditions and are therefore inextricably intertwined with school polemics.

I have no pretensions about solving the problem. My approach to the problem consists of a combination of an empirical definition based on indigenous terms and an analytical definition based on areas emphasized in this study. The Hopi term *wiimi* comes closest to our term religion and is often translated by Hopi consultants that way (cf. A. W. Geertz

19. See discussions in Leuba 1912, Goody 1961, Birnbaum 1964, Spiro 1966, C. Geertz 1966*b*, Alston 1967, Baird 1971:17–27, Guthrie 1980, Baal and Beek 1985.

20. Cf. Nadel 1954, Bianchi 1972, 1975:1–3; however, see 30–33, Eister 1974, Machalek 1977, Wahlström (1981).

1986:41–42). The term is also used to designate ceremonials, ritual objects, and the knowledge, songs, and traditions about them. Thus, in the Hopi context, religion is that part of Hopi reality that deals with activities, beliefs, and institutions which are anchored in conceptions about presumed relationships between nonhuman, human, and superhuman beings. These relationships were initiated in primordial times and they consist of a network of human, animal, mineral, geophysical, and divine forces which are causally linked. These relationships are of such a fundamental and pervasive nature that Hopi religion encompasses all of Hopi culture and society.

For the purposes of this study, an analytical definition of religion will necessarily encompass symbolic systems as well as action systems. My working definition of religion is that it is a formalized social institution that governs, informs, and interprets the ultimate meanings and capacities of human existence. On the cognitive side, religion deals with and promotes ideal interpretations. And, on the action side, it deals with and promotes ideal praxis. I realize that the same definition can be applied to philosophy, ideology, or even art. But in a culture where religion is not compartmentalized in relation to other ultimate interpretive and social strategies, this is not a problem.

My definition comes close to that of the historian of religions R. J. Zwi Werblowsky, who wrote that

> there is almost general agreement that religions endow human existence with a "sense of meaning," or that they articulate the sense of meaning (of life, existence, the cosmos, or history) which has been "shown" or "revealed" to them. They do so by means of symbolic expression. (Werblowsky 1975:149)

Whether or not he would agree with my definition is another matter. At any rate, the simplicity of my definition does not deny the many dimensions of religion, such as the six dimensions for which historian of religions Ninian Smart has argued so well, namely, the ritual, mythological, doctrinal, ethical, social, and experiential dimensions (cf. Smart 1969:15–25; 1973:15).

THE ETHNOHERMENEUTICAL APPROACH

The texts and the data presented here raise issues and problems which only a plurality of approaches can deal with. As a consequence, I have tried to apply methods from comparative religion, historical science, political anthropology, ethnography, ethnohistory, and social-science theory. One could ask what kind of approach this might be. I draw on the position advanced by Donald Levine and Wayne Booth which they call "methodological pluralism." They hold that "two or more conflicting positions may be entirely acceptable." (Booth 1979:24; Levine 1986:273) As Levine noted, many social scientists take a pluralist methodological stance "implicitly or embryonically," but only a few have attempted to develop its position. The main argument of methodological pluralism is that "the variance among divergent approaches reflects differences in the weighting of various features" (Levine ibid.:275), which can be realized in a variety of forms.

The methodological approach I promote here is both contrastive and dialectical. It applies a problem-oriented procedure whereby the data are confronted with theories, models, and analytical techniques which seem to be the most productive to a solution. This dialectical approach has the advantage of viewing the data from a variety of frames of reference, which in effect produces new data and new questions and, consequently, new knowledge. Thus, changing lenses coax significance and meaning out of the woodwork.

I can see no other solution since this study raises questions which no one discipline can answer. The questions can be as impossibly broad as, what is religion? what is history? or what is a "text?" Or they can be as impossibly specific as, why were the Hopis and the Mormons attracted to each other in 1858? or why was Awat'ovi burned by the other villages in 1700? The answers to these questions can only be found with the help of philosophy, history, ethnography, and so on. One cannot pretend to answer all of the questions nor even to address all of the relevant issues. Nor can one even claim to treat the issues chosen in a complete manner. One can only suggest possible solutions to the problems raised and hope that nothing of importance has escaped one's attention.

In dealing with the study of religion, I have argued in several publications for a more specific approach that combines anthropological, historical, and linguistic methods. I call this approach "ethnohermeneutics."[21] This approach draws from the development of the ethnosciences and of cognitive anthropology since the early 1960s and from the development

21. A. W. Geertz 1989*d*, 1990*a*, 1990*b*, 1990*d*. I introduced the term at the XVth Congress of the International Association for the History of Religions in Sydney in 1985 (A. W. Geertz 1990*a*). The only other person I know of who has used the term is my Hungarian colleague Mihály Hoppál at a conference in Finland in 1987 (Hoppál 1988). In a section entitled "Towards an Ethnohermeneutics," he wrote,

> A program for an ethnosemiotical hermeneutics is to understand the meaning embedded in the tradition of a given culture. . . . The hermeneutical emphasis on tradition makes its efforts very similar to that of anthropological understanding of alien cultures. (ibid.:28)

of methods for interpreting culturally constructed common sense,[22] all of which more or less draw their inferences from the primary data of "transcribed tapes of interviews or other discourse or other 'hard' records of the behavior of individuals" (R. M. Keesing 1987:376). I am referring especially to the new ethnotheory,[23] ethnosociology,[24] ethnomethodology,[25] ethnosemiotics,[26] and the study of folk models.[27]

This development shares the perennial concern for meaning and interpretation in the history of religions. The pursuit of ethnohermeneutics is more than interpretation because it utilizes models that are derived from indigenous speech and action. As will be clearly demonstrated in this book, the people we are studying are also practicing the art of hermeneutics, especially during the on-the-spot interview situation, but certainly also in a variety of situations both in everyday life and in times of culturally significant confrontations. And this hermeneutical behavior must be drawn into our academic interpretations. As I have written elsewhere:

> 'Indigenous hermeneutics' is the activity of producing meaningful interpretations, the indigenous act of constructing reality. . . . Ethnohermeneutics, on the other hand, is the study and explication of this activity both in its implicit and explicit forms.
>
> There are many aspects involved in the term. The study of the pursuit of meaning is of primary importance, but the entire social, historical, and linguistic context is implied as well. . . . The next level of the job of the historian of religions is to relate the results of the ethnohermeneutic analysis to the general pursuit of the study of religion. In other words, to the construction of theories and models, or the evaluation of such, in relation to the empirical interpretation. (A. W. Geertz 1990*d*)

Roger Keesing has also argued that native participants, like ethnographers, are constructing generalizations and trying to recover "rules" from patterns whereby "meanings are evoked by, not embodied in, cultural symbols." And the depth and coherence of native interpretations are, as with those of the ethnographer, dependent on what they know (R. M. Keesing 1989:463).

22. C. Geertz 1966*a*, 1972, 1973*b*, 1974, 1975.

23. Lutz 1987:291.

24. Whiteley 1988:244, 287.

25. Garfinkel 1967, 1968; Turner 1974; O'Keefe 1979; Heritage 1984; Sharrock and Anderson 1986; Quasthoff 1986; R. M. Keesing 1987:371.

26. MacCannell 1979; Herzfeld 1981; MacCannell and MacCannell 1982; Voigt 1986; Hoppál 1987, 1988.

27. Haviland 1977; Holy and Stuchlik 1981; Holland and Quinn 1987.

Where anthropologist Michael Agar has argued that the goal of the ethnographic pursuit is a "shared implicit commitment to make sense of group meanings" (Agar 1980:269), I consider the history of religions to be explicitly committed to the same thing.

I am also in agreement with Johannes Fabian that the interpretation of meaning involves not only "matching expression and content, bounded provinces of meaning with distinct systems of symbols and then with distinct forms of behaviour," but also, and especially, to understand "the *creation* of meaning, or of a meaningful praxis, in and through events of speech and communication" (Fabian 1985:147).

ON MEANING AND LITERARY STYLE

The study and interpretation of other peoples' meanings is a pursuit which, in James Clifford's words, is situated

> *between* powerful systems of meaning. It poses its questions at the boundaries of civilizations, cultures, classes, races, and genders. . . . [It] decodes and recodes, telling the grounds of collective order and diversity, inclusion and exclusion. It describes processes of innovation and structuration, and is itself part of these processes. (Clifford 1986:2–3)

The new approach to movements *as* discourse (Wagner 1979) implies that the older notion of ethnography as observation and anthropology as description must give way to "a notion of ethnography as *listening* and *speaking* (rather than observing) and an ideal of anthropology as *interpretive discourse*" (Fabian 1979*a*:27).

This notion is equally applicable to the history of religions. What is required is interpretive understanding besides the explanatory and classificatory models. Along with the notion of an interpretive science is the realization that this science is itself interactively situated in fleeting contexts. Not only are the interpretations influenced by the general intellectual climate,[28] it is also influenced by factors such as career possibilities, project funding, and the vagaries of public interests.[29] In other words, the difficulties in studying the meanings of foreign peoples is compounded not only by the nature of meaning, but also by the nature of the interpretation of meaning.

The academic study of other cultures is also a way of writing. In the first place, much of the "objectivity" of science in general is ultimately

28. Cf. Fabian 1979*a*:1983, Maruyama 1980, Stipe 1980, Crick 1982, Van Maanen 1988.

29. Cf. Brannigan 1981, Helm 1985, Van Maanen 1988.

metaphor and rhetorical style confused with content.[30] And secondly, it is literature and thus is involved in the same mechanisms and consequences and, more importantly, the vicissitudes of the literary "text."[31]

Stephen Tyler has recently argued for the deconstruction of ethnographic writing and, like Jacques Derrida, he encouraged the ideal goal of simultaneity in writing (Tyler 1987:xi–xiii). The idea is to simultaneously present all the aspects of a topic in each chapter in an attempt to capture the living in the heavy cloak of the text. This is also the approach practised by Wagner (1979).

It is difficult to capture the simultaneity and complexity of reality and at the same time restrict oneself to the logical structure of a general overarching argument and point of view. Tyler's goal may very well be an impossibility, but the appeal to reflections on the act of writing is itself important and praiseworthy, especially if we wish to interpret the meanings of others. We are not only scholars, we are also writers.

It must be emphasized that it is not just a question of cleaning up our vocabulary or literary style. It is a question of rethinking the nature of our enterprise. Roy Wagner wrote that the way we represent the creativity of a subject-culture in terms of "a fixed, unchanging, 'logical' order or a 'closed' system of timeless determinants"—the static artifacts of creative analysis—affects the way we end up thinking about the people we study. Many scientists mistake the static artifacts for the people (i.e., confuse the map with the territory) and posit convenient *apologia* such as the notion of "hot" and "cold" societies (Wagner 1972:3–4). These representational forms "mask" the subject, and "the *hubris* of the artist or scientist springs from an all-too-thorough 'masking'" (ibid.:4). The important point to remember is that the "representation of representations," that is, the "illuminating of another creativity" through the medium of our own, is itself inextricably bound to culture-specific mechanisms of meaning, such as symbolization and metaphorization.

FURTHER GOALS

Besides trying to apply recent theory to this well-known ethnographic case area, I am also trying to improve the empirical data at our disposal. Besides the introduction of new original texts in the colloquial, which

30. Cf. Fabian 1979*a*:25, Marcus 1980, Lakoff and Johnson 1980, R. M. Keesing 1985, Clifford and Marcus 1986, Lakoff 1987, and Sangren 1988. Spencer 1989 and Roth 1989 are critical of the whole argument.

31. Cf. Clifford 1980, 1988, Marcus and Cushman 1982, Clifford and Marcus 1986, Bruner 1986*b*, Tyler 1987.

cast light on several topics, I also introduce previously unknown archival data. The sources used here are from a spectrum of genres: amateur printed leaflets, archival documents, petroglyphs, ethnographic description, narratives in the native language and in translation, historical works, letters to the editor, and journalistic pieces, just to name a few. My understanding of a "text" is therefore not restricted to classical philological text norms. I include social, oral, and written phenomena in my use of the term "text." It is the topic that dictates the sources used, since it cuts across the boundaries of topics traditionally studied by historians of religions, social anthropologists, ethnographers, and historians.

Much of what is presented in this book is largely an unexplored area. I have tried to systematize the material wherever possible, but have been forced to refrain from going into too much detail in some areas, such as in chapters 4 and 10, and in other areas having had to depend on the work of others, such as the historical framework of chapter 5. I have had to consolidate a focal point within the array of factual detail and documentary material and to stick with that.

My final goal was stimulated by a conference on methodological and theoretical problems in relation to the social sciences which was held in 1989 and attended by scholars representing a number of national bodies of the International Association for the History of Religions (Canada, Denmark, England, Korea, Poland, the United States, and West Germany), several officers of the executive committee of the International Association, and individuals from Western Europe, Czechoslovakia, Poland, and Lithuania. The representative composition of the conference is important because it reflects a shift of attention in method and theory which historians of religions from various parts of the globe wish to pursue.

The participants concluded the conference with the following statement:

> A convergence of opinion became apparent with regard to the nature of "history" that permits reconceiving the history of religions as a human and cultural science. There was also agreement that such a reconceived study of religion would understand "religion" as a reality which interconnects social activities both implicitly and explicitly. Of significance in this respect was a shift in attention to the meaning of religion in social interaction. There was general agreement that analysing social processes which are correlative with religious phenomena would require the evaluation and use of innovative social theories and models as well as those from cognate disciplines. Whether such a methodological orientation will prove fruitful must be judged in the context of future research.[32]

32. Statement agreed upon in the concluding session (September 9, 1989) of the conference on "Studies of Religion in the Context of the Social Sciences: Methodological and

This book is an attempt to comply with the Warsaw statement.

A NOTE ON ORTHOGRAPHY

I follow the Hopi orthography developed by Ekkehart Malotki. Short vowels (a, e, i, o, ö, u) are in single letters and long vowels (aa, ee, ii, oo, öö, uu) are in double letters. The Hopi language also contains diphthongs with w-glide (aw, ew, iw, öw, uw) and y-glide (ay, ey, iy, oy, öy, uy), consonants including stops (p, t, k, kw, ky, q, qw, '), nasals (m, n, ng, ngw, ngy), affricate (ts), fricatives (h, r, s, v), lateral (l), and glides (w, y). Stress and falling tone are not marked in the natural text nor are glottal stops (') which automatically precede vowel-initial words. The latter is, however, marked according to its second main function as glottal catch.

I have departed from using the proper orthographic renderings of the names of the Hopi villages by adopting the usage of the Tribal Office. In other instances, I have compromised between orthographic accuracy and common usage in connection with certain personal names, when and if they are close enough to the proper pronunciation.

A more serious problem and a potential source of misunderstanding is in the fact that during the hundred years of communications and reports about the Hopis, the student is confronted with a jungle of mutually exclusive orthographies and long traditions of misspellings. I have not attempted to correct the resultant inconsistencies and have instead retained them in their quoted settings as well as in the reference and bibliographic system. Readers who wish to find the correct spelling of a name or Hopi term can find their equivalents in appendix E. This can be supplemented by the chart of names (c) in chapter 8, page 240.

Theoretical Relations," under the auspices of the Polish Society for the Study of Religions, Institute for Philosophy and Sociology of the Polish Academy of Sciences, and the International Association for the History of Religions (cf. A. W. Geertz 1989*e*).

PART I

Prophecy and Discourse

ONE

The Story of the Mysterious Mr. Johnson

ON THE BURNING OF ALTARS AND THE ADVENT OF THE APOCALYPSE

A male member of the Aawatngyam (Bow Clan) by the name of Tuwaletstiwa challenged a companion one day to a leg-breaking contest, so the story goes, while they were out horseback riding. The idea was to test the powers of healing which their ceremonial offices gave them, Tuwaletstiwa being chief of the Aa'alt (Two-Horn) Brotherhood at Oraibi. His companion refused, and fate would have it that Tuwaletstiwa's horse bolted and threw him off so that his leg was broken; and it never healed properly. We know nothing about how this event affected Tuwaletstiwa psychologically, but later events seem to indicate that the experience was traumatic.

The man became a Mennonite convert and is described by Frank Waters (1963:382) as the mysterious Mr. Johnson, "an old, crippled man with a tortured face—a strange man, still believed to have mystic powers, who limps down the street with a cane." He will always be remembered as the man who burned the Aa'alt altar in 1922.[1]

Albert Yava, a Tewa man from First Mesa, witnessed the occasion:

> He was in charge of those objects, and when he became a Christian he took the Wuwuchim and Two Horn altars and all the other ritual objects of those two kiva societies and burned them. He made a big public display of it, announcing in advance what he was going to do. Quite a few people assembled and watched the bon-fire. I was in Oraibi the day it happened. I

1. I wish to thank Dr. Peter Whiteley of Sarah Lawrence College, New York, for information on the exact date.

> had to take a wagonload of supplies to New Oraibi from Keam's [Canyon], and when I arrived I saw the crowd over on the north side watching Johnson destroy the altars and other paraphernalia. He took the responsibility on himself because it was his people, the Bow Clan, who had brought those traditions from Awatovi. (Courlander, ed. 1982:128; Yava 1978:115)

Waters adds a little more colorful detail to the story:

> Then a strange and dreadful thing happened: he was seen carrying into the street, publicly exposed to everyone's view, the Bow Clan altar, the two huge elkhorns, the six-foot-long *mongko,* the one foot-long *mongko,* and the most sacred tiny *mongko* made of wood in the preceding Third World. Heedless of the gathering Hopis and the whites and Navajos watching from the trading post, he set up the altar and all of its ritual paraphernalia in perfect order in the middle of the street. Then he lit a match to it.
>
> Lorenzo Hubbell burst out of his trading post and offered him five hundred dollars for the altar. Tuwaletstiwa refused. Hubbell then offered him three hundred dollars for permission to photograph it. Again he refused. The fire by now was taking hold. All the Hopis, frightened and horrified, rushed home and closed their doors. The flames mounted and died, changing to a pillar of smoke, all that remained of an altar and a ritual that had been at once the most famous and infamous in all Hopi ceremonialism. (Waters 1963:381–382; 1969:127–128)[2]

This could suffice as a good story, however tragic it may be. But we do not fully understand the point of Tuwaletstiwa's controversial action. Was it because he became a Christian that he burned the paraphernalia? Harry C. James, in his book on Hopi history, seems to think so, judging by his reference to the period of the early 1920s where "many Christian converts became zealots and in fanatic zeal gathered up priceless ceremonial objects and burned them before the horrified eyes of fellow Hopi" (James 1974:191). Whether or not there were other arsons, are we justified in assuming that Tuwaletstiwa's act was that of a zealous convert?

Yava quotes Tuwaletstiwa as having referred to his clan tradition, and, indeed, the reference to Awat'ovi has deep-lying and painful significance on the cognitive order of the Jewish diaspora.[3] This should alert us to the possibility of a much more meaningful interpretation.

Tuwaletstiwa's motives were not as simple as the convert/traditionalist dichotomy suggests. As with anything Hopi, complexity lies directly

2. Cf. A. W. Geertz and Lomatuway'ma 1987:148, n. 4, and Titiev 1944:208.

3. See the curious story of White Bear's reactions to "the professor" in Waters 1969:91–96. Further details on the nature of the history of Awat'ovi will be dealt with below.

beneath the serene surface of things. Fortunately for us, we have access to other sources on this remarkable man which more than compensate for the behavioristic statements quoted above, and which allow us to identify the significance and meaning of Tuwaletstiwa's deed.

In the archives of the Mennonite Library and Archives is lodged a small document entitled *A Hopi Indian Finds Christ. The Experience of Mr. K. T. Johnson and His Judgment on Idolatry*, prepared by Rev. John P. Suderman, missionary to the Hopi Indians at Oraibi.[4] It is dated in pencil 1901, but this must be a mistake since the matters described in the booklet deal precisely with the affairs of 1922. The booklet contains two chapters: "The Experience of Mr. K. T. Johnson, Native Christian, Oraibi, Arizona (As Told to Missionary J. P. Suderman)," and "The Judgment upon Idolatry (Written by Otto Lomavitu)." Otto Lomavitu was later to become instrumental in establishing the Tribal Council (cf. Bureau of Indian Affairs 1955, 40).

As a result of the missionary activities of John B. Frey during the early 1920s, Tuwaletstiwa began to think about Hopi prophecy:

> It is said that some one from the East should come to deliver us from our enemies and set us free. He would also bring a looking-glass with him and in it we could find out what kind of a man we are. He would be somebody who would have great power. So I began to think that the prophecy is like the Bible which says that when He comes, everybody would be free. . . . I also began to realize that this was the One the Hopis were waiting for. (Suderman n.d.:2–3)

Thus, the point is not one of simple conversion, which purists and cultists would, if they could, dismiss as the actions of just one more benighted soul. On the contrary, Tuwaletstiwa's words are loud and clear: He became a Christian in fulfillment of his own indigenous religious tradition![5] As he said in connection with his deliberations on just how public he should go on the matter of his conversion, "then I began to think, why should I not make it public, because it was time to fulfil Hopi prophecy" (ibid.:4).

Of course he was filled with zeal too. Being a habitual smoker, he burned all of his cigarettes and all of the thirty or so Bull Durham sacks he had as decoration on the walls. Then he began burning his prayer feathers and other ceremonial articles. However, the burning of the Two-Horn altar proceeded in the same deliberate and meditative frame of mind that characterizes any other Hopi ritual activity.

4. Once again, thanks to Dr. Peter Whiteley for the reference. See Whiteley's text edition and analysis of this document (Whiteley 1992).

5. Whiteley draws the same conclusion in Whiteley (1992).

On the evening of August 22nd, in striking resemblance to Hopi ceremonial day counting, where the announcement to fellow members occurs on the night before a full four-day period leading up to the ritual event, Tuwaletstiwa told Otto Lomavitu the following:

> My aunt died today and the fire of our clanship is extinguished. We have in our possession the Al-vo-na . . . and I have been minded to burn them. I have thought of bringing these things down from the upper village and have them displayed before the public on this coming Sunday afternoon prior to burning them. Before doing this, however, I would be glad to know whether it would be scriptural or not. (ibid.:7)

The fact that his clan was dying out must have considerably strengthened his eschatological forebodings. He had, at any rate, decided to burn the altar *before* he sought biblical counsel.

After a heated discussion at a prayer meeting with the rest of the Mennonite congregation, it was decided that Tuwaletstiwa should proceed. On August 25th he went to Yukiwma, the village chief and leader of the Hostile faction up at Hotevilla, where the paraphernalia were kept. Yukiwma was not willing at first to let Tuwaletstiwa have the paraphernalia. However, neither having the authority nor the right to keep the altar pieces, Yukiwma had to give in, and he said "in tones of deepest feeling":

> Alas! it has come, but so must it be. By destroying these things you will have DESTROYED the very foundation of our ceremonies. The conflagration must spread. Take these and do as you have said. (ibid.:10)

If we accept the face value of this apparent quotation, then the fact that Yukiwma allowed a Christian convert to take these esoteric and powerful instruments from him indicates that Yukiwma, who was the symbol of traditionalism, also believed in the prophetic rightness of Tuwaletstiwa's intended action and, in tune with Hopi social psychology, he resigned himself to the fate that awaited him and his people.[6]

It is also significant that Tuwaletstiwa and his partner Otto Lomavitu did not treat the altar pieces and idols lightly. It is obvious that they were treated with respect and as living creatures—again, in accordance with traditional Hopi thought. For example, Lomavitu wrote that, after bringing the paraphernalia home, they were lodged in a back room until the upcoming event. "We left them to wait for their trial on serious charges of murder! These helpless creatures, helpless, though gods, in the house of Almighty God" (ibid.:11).

6. Yukiwma was the rebel leader who was the direct cause of the split of Oraibi in 1906.

On Sunday, August 27, 1922, the following occurred, in the words of Lomavitu:

> After the service missionaries from other stations arrived to witness the judgment upon the wretched idols. At half past two o'clock in the afternoon, we loaded our booty and hauled them upon a hill which is the center of the lower village. The bell was rung and a good number from other villages were assembled. We sang several songs in Hopi. A brother missionary from Hotevilla offered prayer. (ibid.)

The name of the hill in question, according to my sources, is Nayavutsomo, "Clay Hill."

While Tuwaletstiwa was arranging the altar and the idols, Lomavitu addressed the White tourists who had come out to witness the Snake Dance, which has attracted tourists in droves ever since the latter half of the 19th century. He scolded them, first of all, for forcing civilization on the Hopis and then, secondly, for coming around to witness and encourage barbarous aboriginal ceremonies.

Tuwaletstiwa then read Psalm 115, verses 4–8 to the audience—a text aptly chosen.

> Their idols are silver and gold, the work of men's hands. They have mouths, but they speak not; eyes have they, but they see not; they have ears, but they hear not; noses have they, but they smell not; they have hands, but they handle not; feet have they, but they walk not; neither speak they through their throat. They that make them shall be like unto them; yea, everyone that trusteth in them.[7]

Then he looked at the audience and said:

> We are this day gathered around these idols for the purpose of burning them. Permission will be granted you to examine them in due time. Look at the idols before you. They are made of wood. They have eyes but they see not. They have noses but should you pour out perfume before them they will not be able to smell it. They have hands but should you come up to them and offer them your hand they will not respond. They have ears, but they will not hear your greeting; feet have they, but they cannot walk.
>
> And yet these have kept me from coming to Christ for many years. They have sent hundreds of my people into perdition and, though wood, they will yet be the means of sending countless numbers of souls into hell under the power of Satan. Shall we save them? They that make them and keep them are like them. . . . I lay myself open to the consequences if there be

7. The King James Version, Oxford University Press, 1898. David A. Haury provided references and a copy of the text.

> any. I will gladly sacrifice myself in saving our people from perdition through these. (Suderman n.d.:13–14)

After a long speech, the audience was allowed to look but not to take pictures. By this time a heavy wind was bringing a lightning storm from the east.

> Quickly we piled the idols and the altar pieces. After pouring some gasoline on the pile Johnson lit it. Soon the smoke arose from these wretched prisoners and amidst their smoke we sang in Hopi, "When the Roll Is Called Up Yonder" the words in Hopi being appropriate for the occasion. As the idols were reduced to ashes the storm also ceased, resulting in a particular calm as though God would have it thus. (ibid.:16)

Thus, in line with traditional thought, ritual action, accompanied by ritual song, is the culmination of careful preparation and deliberation, and it clearly affects geophysical dynamics.[8] This particular ritual act contained the added dimension of prophetic finality and was consummated with the Hopi flair for colorful drama.

The hymn that was chosen was indeed aptly apocryphal. The first verse of the hymn by James M. Black runs:

> When the trumpet of the Lord shall sound, and time shall be no more,
> And the morning breaks, eternal, bright, and fair;
> When the saved of earth shall gather over on the other shore,
> And the roll is called up yonder,
> I'll be there.[9]

Karl Nasewytewa, also known as Karl Johnson, the former tribal chairman and governor of Kykotsmovi in 1988, told me that his stepfather, Tuwaletstiwa, had explained to him many years ago that what he had done was to "act out the meaning of Hopi religion." Tuwaletstiwa told him once:

> You see that tree trunk lying out there on the ground? You can go out there and water it and water it, but it will never grow again. I cut the Hopi religion at the root. It will never live again, and you must not become a member.[10]

The apparently zealous act struck at the very heart of Hopi religion, and, as time went on, Tuwaletstiwa's reflections on the meaning of his

8. See A. W. Geertz 1977, 1987*a*. Pongyayawma, the former chief of Hotevilla, described Tuwaletstiwa's action to me in the same ceremonial terminology.

9. This text was provided by David A. Haury. It is taken from the *Baptist Hymnal* (1956). The Hopi text is found in *Hopiykwa Lomatuawh Tatawwi* (*Hopi Gospel Songs*) (1918).

10. Related to me on April 7, 1988 at Kykotsmovi.

act became more subtle, yet always remaining within the framework of Hopi traditional thought, despite the fact that he was an active Mennonite and helped in translating the Bible and hymns into Hopi as well as composing his own hymns.

A full thirty-three years after the event, in 1955, Tuwaletstiwa presented his more mature reflections on the significance and meaning of his act during the hearings conducted on the reservation by a team appointed by Glenn L. Emmons, then commissioner of Indian Affairs.

After explaining Yukiwma's actions in the split of Oraibi and the subsequent founding of Hotevilla, Johnson told his own story. His speech is four pages long (Bureau of Indian Affairs 1955:171–174) and so I will paraphrase where needed.

> I would like to speak to you now of the little knowledge that I have acquired. I once had a position. I also had a tradition. This goes back to the life below and the position I there had. . . . I am of the Bow Clan. . . . When this bow was first given it was given only with the center of the bow painted white. There was no other painting on this bow. This white symbolizes the pure, clean, holy authority of the ruler. The one who brought this bow made these remarks: Here take this bow. This is yours forever. No one will take it from you and do not give it away to anyone else. Along with the bow he gave specific instructions of how I was to continue in my walk of life. He said this is yours, take it with you. The time will come when the people who have great ideas, great thoughts, will misconduct themselves; they will disrespect you as leaders. You are not to hurt anyone. You are not to cause any one to weep. You are . . . to encourage the discouraged . . . take the child by the hand and lead him back to his home . . . take care, good care, of the people.

Then follows a description of how things became worse and worse until the prophecy was fulfilled, and the people were forced to leave the underworld and flee up to the surface of the present world.

> I was told that I had my clan distinction given to me below. . . . The purpose of these clan classes was supposed to be for the purpose of respecting one another. Because of such a life of evil, disrespect, hatred, and fighting division came. This was the dividing point in the life below, and it seems it was the life that was to be followed in the life above. We, today, are again following that pattern. We are divided.

Then follows a description of the emergence[11] and the subsequent clan migrations. The Bow clan was given the task of watching over the people and especially of keeping an eye on the rulers of the people. Rulers were to be criticized and their deeds recorded on the bow, the

11. More information on the emergence myth will follow in the next two chapters.

colors of which "were to serve as a record for the day of judgment." Then he recited the differences between the Hotevilla leaders who were against the Euro-American ways and the Kykotsmovi leaders who were for the Euro-American ways. He pointed out the contradictory behavior of the Hotevilla resistance, and then he addressed the Bureau of Indian Affairs team directly:

> You have heard them ask for the Hopi way of life and in your thinking you hope there may be some hope of unity, but as for me I see absolutely no way of becoming united. We know the time has come, as was foretold by our forefathers, that there would be wars among nations. Therefore, they said when that time came the world would be upside down, and that the Hopi way would be underneath and the white man's way on top.

He envisioned a time when the significance of the Hopi way of life would be lost:

> It was told to us by our forefathers that this religious setup was to disintegrate the people here at Oraibi and the time would come when we as Hopis would all come to the point of following the Holy One. This is yet to be fulfilled. Hotevillay is trying to pick up the remains of what is left, something that is supposed to be disintegrating or supposed to be vanishing, according to prophecy. They are being encouraged by many white people. This is wrong not only to the Hopis but also to the white people, and it has a bad end.
>
> I was once in the position of authority, the authority of this clan. Its leadership was once in my hand and those who passed it on to me that this was ours to use in this village and that it would be up to me to decide in what manner this should be destroyed. When this leadership, the authority, was placed into my hands, knowing what has been handed down to me, knowing that this which had been placed into my hand was the root of this religious pattern, knowing of its evils and all that was involved, I took them and burned them. I felt sorry for the people of this future generation. We know that the Bible says Thou shalt have no other gods before me for I am a jealous God . . . visiting the inequity of the Father upon the children unto the third and fourth generation of them who hate me and showing mercy unto thousands of them that love me and keep my commandments. Perhaps we have been here almost two thousand years and yet there are only a few of us people. Is this another testimony to the fact that what God stated is true? This whole religious setup has its weapons and its curses, as I learned about that, and because I wanted my people to live, and seeing the evil purpose of these ceremonies, I burned these religious rituals which had been handed down to me.

The respectful manner in which Tuwaletstiwa recited his indigenous traditions in 1955 and the clear explanation of why he did what he did—seen always within the context of Hopi traditional logic—show us that his action and his testimony are valuable tools in trying to understand the multifaceted significance of Hopi prophecy. The half-mystical descriptions of "the mysterious Mr. Johnson" which Frank Waters presented do an injustice to a brave and tragic man who bore the burden of a dark prophecy and who tried to find the beacons of his own clan destiny.

As I stated in my study of Hopi altar iconography (A. W. Geertz 1987*a*:vii), ritual objects are highly significant because religious as well as secular power resides almost completely in the possession and use of these objects. This possession and use imply, of course, the knowledge, songs, and rituals that go with the objects. And, as I have noted, and as Peter Whiteley has demonstrated,[12] leadership in Hopi social life is based on control over ritual knowledge rather than over economic factors such as land and agricultural products. Thus, it is no coincidence that we find Tuwaletstiwa present at the highly important 1955 hearings. He felt that it was his duty and that he, and only he, had the authority to correct the eclectic and uninformed interpretations of the significance of Bow clan paraphernalia which one of the leaders of the Traditionalist Movement, David Monongya, was presenting at the hearings (Bureau of Indian Affairs 1955:47).

As he said, "You gentlemen also know that David showed you a bow and he explained to you the symbols on that bow. I am of the Bow clan. Being of the Bow clan I have been instructed what to do and what these symbols mean, and I would like at this time to pass on to you this information" (ibid.:171). After explaining the significance of his clan paraphernalia, he stated, "it seems that the wrong person was trying to explain the significance of the various colors to you" (ibid.:173).

We do not meet a deviant, Christianized convert in 1955, rather, we meet the voice of traditional clan authority, a leader who had lived his life in accordance with his clan destiny and who had tried to choose a way out of the contradictions of Hopi eschatological thinking.

Others were, of course, in disagreement about the choice Tuwaletstiwa had made. Rumors were, and still are, rife that he had burned the altar in order to become a Christian, and that shortly thereafter his two sisters died because of his action. Any Hopi will tell you that the desecration of ritual paraphernalia or even the mere transgression of ritual space in ritual contexts can lead to illness and death. But the accusation about the death of his sisters implies that Tuwaletstiwa was a sorcerer—sorcery being defined in Hopi terms as the ritual murder of close relatives whereby the life of the murderer is prolonged (cf. Titiev 1943; A. W. Geertz and Lomatuway'ma 1987:114–119).

12. A. W. Geertz and Lomatuway'ma 1987:119, 143, n. 94; and Whiteley 1985, 1986, 1987, 1988:249.

Having asked the nephew of Yukiwma, the recent chief of Hotevilla, James Pongyayawma, in 1988, whether he thought that Tuwaletstiwa had done the right thing, he answered with a resounding "Qa'a!" (No!). He also accused Tuwaletstiwa of sorcery, but his application of the term was meant to be understood in a much wider context than that of mere witchcraft.

Pongyayawma explained what he meant by beginning with the emergence myth. The schematic lines were identical with all the other versions, but certain details were emphasized. He explained how the leaders of the clans and secret societies also had occult power like sorcerers do. Providing the mechanism of escape from the underworld (which is the starting point of the emergence myth) was in itself evidence of such power. He insisted, just as Tuwaletstiwa did at the hearings in 1955, that the ceremonies and ritual paraphernalia were brought up from the underworld. As he said, "They came here searching for life and they brought their *wiimi* [in this case, ritual paraphernalia] and set it all up."[13]

According to Pongyayawma, it was the Bow clan who led the emergence, followed by his clan, Kookop, in second place. The emergence myth related in Appendix A confirms this statement, since the narrator is of the Piikyas clan in Hotevilla, which feels itself closely related to the Kookop people. Other versions change the clan affiliation of the leaders of the emergence depending on contemporary political factors. Pongyayawma's uncle, Yukiwma, did not say that the Bow clan was the leader, but Yukiwma's son, Qötshongva, did.

Although I consider Qötshongva's versions as being unreliable for reasons made obvious in chapters 6, 7, and 8, it is interesting to note that Qötshongva considered the activities of the Bow clan leader, shortly after the emergence, to be directly responsible for the intrinsic mechanisms of prophecy and its relation to and cause of the present state of affairs in the world. He claimed that the Bow clan leader disappeared during the post-emergence migrations and secretly made his way to the "Earth Center" where

> clever, ingenious people from all nations meet to plan the future. . . . Until today, we do not know the significance of this action. It had to do with the future. By this action, he caused a change to occur in the pattern of life as we near the end of the life cycle of this world, such that many of us would seek the materialistic world, trying to enjoy all the good things it has to offer, before destroying ourselves. (Katchongva 1973:7)

He claimed that the Bow clan chief died the day after he had set the great cycle in motion. His two sons, upon learning of his misdeed, de-

13. Related to me on April 8, 1988 at Hotevilla. For the implications of "they go to seek life," (*qatsihepwisa*) see chapter 2, as well as A. W. Geertz 1986:48–49.

cided to develop a mechanism of escape from the consequences of their father's action. And these two brothers, therefore, developed the Pahaana sequence of prophecies, described in chapter 3, wherein the Younger Brother awaits the apocalyptic return of his Elder Brother, Pahaana, who lives in the east. The brothers are of the Sun clan and therefore by extension, Qötshongva (who is also of the Sun clan) conceived of himself as being the waiting younger brother.

However tantalizing this story may be, where we find one layer after another being compounded into a portrait of the Bow clan, it is significant that neither Qötshongva nor Monongya mentioned these particular details at the 1955 hearings where Tuwaletstiwa also was present.[14] In the face of the paucity of evidence, I cannot confirm the Traditionalist version and presume it to be either an example of misinformation or of scapegoating.

At any rate, Pongyayawma was of the opinion that the Bow clan must have been wicked. Without further qualification, he stated to me:

> Tuwaletstiwa found another belief. Even though he already had his belief, he went over to another belief *in order to live longer*. In this manner, he left his Hopi beliefs behind; he burned his own. They are finished now. Now they are worth nothing. If they were not wicked, they would have never abandoned it. But they were wicked so they destroyed their paraphernalia.

Pongyayawma saw Tuwaletstiwa's action in the context of the whole tragedy of Oraibi, and he believed, as did his uncle Yukiwma, that the conflagration would spread to all the Hopi people. It was the Oraibians who, in his opinion, brought an end to Hopi religion. It was they who discarded it, and that is why Tawakwaptiwa (the chief of Oraibi at the time of the split) lost his power. As he concluded,

> I have received the power from Maasaw in my stone tablets, and I still believe in Him. But it's finished here. The only thing we lack now is to be purified.

That purification will come with the apocalypse.

Chief Tawakwaptiwa was of the same opinion. During the last years of his life, he had the *Soyalangw* altar on display–like Tuwaletstiwa–but in his home. When he died in 1960, he was buried as instructed in his Ewtoto costume and with the altar parts which

> meant the end of Oraibi's history and rituals, and an end of the clans' control over the fields and lands around Oraibi. Masauwu had given out those

14. It is, however, mentioned in Banancya's 1960 letter to M. Muller-Fricken (cf. chapter 6 and Appendix B). Tuwaletstiwa's own version, which was related during the 1955 hearings, makes no mention of this, and, in fact, it follows the consensus of most versions, i.e., that the emergence was led by the Bear clan (Bureau of Indian Affairs 1955:172).

> lands, and the chief being buried that way signified that the gift was revoked, that henceforth the Oraibis were on their own without any ceremonial connections to the past. Tawaquaptewa made his meaning clear before he died. Shortly before his death I heard him say to a group of elders, "Now anyone can select his land anywhere he wants. The clans don't control the land any more." In those days the words of the Kikmongwi were law. He said that the chieftainship was coming to an end. He designated Myron Poliquaptewa of the Parrot Clan to perform the duties of the chief for four more years, and after that Oraibi wasn't supposed to have a traditional Kikmongwi. I know this to be true because I was present when he made this declaration! (Yava 1978:115–116)[15]

Clearly, Pongyayawma conceived of Tuwaletstiwa's action in the same eschatological terms as had Tuwaletstiwa himself, and, as will be shown in later chapters, any knowledgeable Hopi would concur in this viewpoint.

THE AWAT'OVI CONSPIRACY

A brief excursion into the conceived history of the Bow clan will give us the remaining evidence concerning the significance of Tuwaletstiwa's dramatic bonfire.

It seems to be a reasonable assumption that a man like Tuwaletstiwa, who conceived of himself and his clan within a clearly delineated cosmohistory, would also be highly aware of the significance of his act in relation to perhaps one of the most infamous Hopis known to researchers and Hopis alike, namely, his forefather, Tapolo, chief of Awat'ovi who, like his perhaps less-infamous descendant, was faced with a strikingly similar situation in 1700. The difference between these two clan leaders, who although separated in time and space were evidently united by a common clan destiny, is that they apparently chose mutually exclusive, absolutely converse solutions to the same problem. I write "apparently" because the data we have at our disposal are contradictory and require reevaluation.

According to the published oral tradition,[16] Chief Tapolo, due to reasons mentioned below, enlisted the help of a number of other Hopi villages—particularly Walpi and Oraibi—to kill all of the men of his own village, kidnap the women and children, and take over the Awat'ovi landholdings. In November 1700, the men were killed by fire in their kivas during the Wuwtsim ceremonial, and the captives, except for those who were willing to impart their ritual knowledge, were tortured and killed at

15. For the meaning of these changes, see Whiteley 1988:243–284.

16. Voth 1905:202, 246–255; Yava 1978:88–97; Fewkes 1893:363–375; Curtis 1922: 84–89; Mindeleff 1891:33–38; Courlander, ed. 1982:55–60; and Bourke 1884:90.

a knoll in the valley known as Mastsomo, "Maasaw, or Death Hill." The ceremonials purportedly transferred in this manner to the other villages were Maraw, Lakon, Owaqöl, and three of the four main rituals of the Wuwtsim ceremonial, namely Tawwimi, Wuwtsimwimi, and Alwimi.

The various reasons that are given for this horrifying event are: sorcerers incited the people to sexual immorality, including the chief's wife (Courlander, ed. 1982:55ff): sorcerers incited the people and there were fights during ceremonies (Curtis 1922:85–86); the Awat'ovi men were criminally inclined (Fewkes 1893:364); the daughter of the chief was accidently killed during a hunting expedition (Voth 1905:246–247); the son of the chief was angry because the Awat'ovi girls did not like him (ibid.:254); and finally, the chief was a mad sorcerer (ibid.:252).

These reasons seem to be so insubstantial that other answers must be sought. Indeed, Parsons considered the reasons to be "too frivolous to be credible" and thought that the real marauders were nomad raiders, and that the Hopis were too proud to admit it (1936:559, n. 32; cf. 1939:916 n.*). But this explanation does not harmonize with the data at our disposal, as Brew noted (1949:23).

Excavations confirm the fact that the kivas of Awat'ovi were gutted by fire and that a massacre had taken place. As Fewkes wrote:

> There is good evidence that a massacre of Awatobians occurred in the southeastern angle of the eastern part of the pueblo, just east of the mission. If so, it is probable that many of the unfortunates sought refuge in the outbuildings of the church. Suspecting that such was the case, I excavated a considerable space of ground at these places and found many human skulls and other bones thrown together in confusion. The earth was literally filled with bones, evidently hastily placed there or left where the dead fell. These bodies were not buried with pious care, for there were no fragments of mortuary pottery or other indication of burial objects. Many of the skulls were broken, some pierced with sharp implements. . . . According to the legends, the hostiles entered the pueblo through the adjacent gateway; their anger led them especially against those of the inhabitants who were regarded as *powako* or sorcerers, and their first acts of violence would naturally have been toward those who sought refuge in the buildings adjacent the church. Near this hated "Singing-house" the slaughter began, soon extending to the kivas and the whole of the eastern section of the village. There was no evidence of murderous deeds in the rooms of the western section of the old pueblo, and the legends agree in relating that most of the men were in kivas, not far from the mission, when the village was overthrown. There is no legendary evidence that there were any Spanish priests in the mission at the time of its destruction, and there is no record extant of any Spaniards losing their lives at Awatobi at the time of its destruction, although the fact of the occurrence . . . was recorded. (1898:610)

Excavations also confirm that bodies lie at Mastsomo (James 1974: 64). The interesting fact that both archaeology and Spanish chronicles document, but which is underplayed in Hopi oral tradition, is that Awat'ovi was the focal point of Franciscan Catholicism under the thriving aegis of the mission of San Bernardo de Aguatubi, which was established by Francisco Porras, Andrés Gutiérrez, and lay brother Cristóbal de la Concepción on August 20, 1629 in Awat'ovi.[17]

Porras was evidently an exceptional personality. Spanish sources claim that Porras performed a miracle at Awat'ovi in which a blind boy was made to see again. This led to many conversions, and Porras, who quickly learned the language, established a thriving Christian community at Awat'ovi. Hopi leaders were so concerned over the success Porras enjoyed that they poisoned him in 1633, but this did not stop the influence of the mission. The mission buildings, standing at the edge of the mesa, provided the home base for an active mission and presented an "imposing appearance from the plain below . . . making a conspicuous structure for miles across Antelope valley" (Fewkes 1898:607). Spanish sources indicate that the friary was in active use; that

> the local friars and guests from the great world—Santa Fe, Mexico City, even Spain—[were] seated side by side at the refectory table, strolling afterward in the courtyard garden, and repairing finally to a friar's cell for a good talk. The friaries of New Mexico were not built for one or two lonely friars. (Brew 1949:14)

Scandal and brutality at the hands of other, less-gifted padres led to the death of all resident Spanish clergy during the Pueblo Rebellion of 1680. The large church at Awat'ovi was razed, as were the missions and *visitas* of the other villages.

When Governor Captain-General Don Diego de Vargas Zapata y Luján Ponce de León reconquered the New Mexico pueblos in 1692 and moved on to Awat'ovi in November of that same year, the chief of Awat'ovi, called Miguel in the chronicles, not only capitulated to an exhausted and vulnerable expedition, but allowed the reconsecration of the church and baptism of infants. In fact, he asked Vargas to become the godfather of his grandchildren! Not only that, he joined Vargas in his campaign against Walpi. The Walpi chief reacted immediately in the same manner as his Awat'ovi colleague had, even to the point of asking Vargas to become godfather to his grandchildren. The other villages capitulated during the next few days as well.

The point here is, if Miguel was in fact the tragic Tapolo who eight years later destroyed his own people, then his capitulation, extraordinary

17. The rest of this section draws on Brew 1949:3–43.

gestures of Christian fellowship, and calculated treachery against Walpi were merely political expediency. If, on the other hand, these actions were not sham, then we must reevaluate Miguel's actions. Perhaps he was Christian and therefore in political difficulties due to hostilities from anti-Spanish villages and hostile factions in his own village.

Oral tradition seems to support the idea that the Awat'ovians were better off than the others and were given to roving the valleys on their ponies, killing, ravishing, and pillaging individuals and groups from other villages.[18] The fact that the spoils of the destruction of Awat'ovi were land for the Walpians and women for the Oraibians should warn us that the story of a madcapped chief just does not tell the whole story.

From 1692 to 1699 all the towns that still lay at the foot of the mesas were moved to their craigs. Hopi territory was also becoming the gathering place for refugees and rebels from the eastern Pueblos as well as from Utes, Havasupai, and Apaches. They presented a formidable and hostile force against any likely Spanish expedition.

Nevertheless, a request was sent to the Spaniards—perhaps by Miguel—to send a missionary to Hopi land. When Fray Juan de Garaycoechea and Fray Antonio Miranda arrived at Awat'ovi on May 28, 1700, they not only found people waiting to be baptized, but also that the convent had been rebuilt. Archaeological evidence clearly shows that the church had been destroyed in 1680, but that the friary had been transformed into a pueblo house that was later deconstructed and the interior rebuilt into a makeshift church. These were strange activities if their only purpose was political expediency!

Another twist to the story is that, according to Spanish sources, a Hopi by the name of Don Francisco de Espeleta, who had been brought up and tutored by Father José de Espeleta presumably at Awat'ovi—although the possibility exists that this occurred at Oraibi during the 1660s or the early 1670s—had gained a position of leadership (evidently at Oraibi) and was the instigator of hostilities towards the Spaniards during the two decades leading up to the destruction of Awat'ovi. Espeleta and a contingent of twenty companions traveled to Santa Fe in October 1700 to ask the governor for religious toleration, but were refused. Upon returning, an unsuccessful attack was single-handedly launched against Awat'ovi.[19]

Espeleta tried again in November of that year with the help of the Walpians, and this time he succeeded. Father Luís Velvarde wrote in his *Relación de Pimería Alta* in 1716:

18. Voth 1905:246–247; Fewkes 1893:364; Curtis 1922:86–87; and Mindeleff 1891:34.

19. I follow Fewkes's reconstruction here 1898:601. Oral tradition also speaks of the fiasco attack, cf. Fewkes 1893:364. The same myth is recorded in Fewkes 1898:603.

> At this time, his people being infuriated because the Indians of the pueblo of Aguatubi had been reduced to our holy faith and the obedience of our king, he [Espeleta] came with more than one hundred of his people to the said pueblo, entered it, killed all the braves, and carried off the women, leaving the pueblo to this day desolate and unpeopled. (Quoted in Brew 1949:22)

No less than three published oral sources confirm that the chief of Awat'ovi was not the cause of the destruction: John G. Bourke wrote that the town was destroyed by the people of Mishongnovi because Awat'ovi "was full of 'singing men,' whom the Moquis did not like" (1884:90). Mindeleff (1891:34) placed the blame squarely on Walpi because the Awat'ovians plagued the Walpians due to the role of the latter in the destruction of Sikyatki. The third source is Albert Yava, whose quietly critical views on his Hopi neighbors of First Mesa provides surprising insights into a number of matters. He said that the trouble at Awat'ovi was between the traditionals and the Catholics. The Catholics were evidently actively interfering with traditional religious practices (echoes of Tuwaletstiwa's action?). He wrote:

> The basic story they tell says that the Awatovi chief was really responsible for everything that happened after that. I can't tell you if it's true or not. It could be that the other villages added that part to take some of the responsibility off themselves. (1978:91–92)

The evidence, however circumstantial it may be, points more towards a conspiracy plotted and effectuated by outsiders rather than by the chief himself. There was evidently hostility and competition between the two powerful neighbors, and Walpian expansionism succeeded with help from Oraibi and others against the Spanish-backed Awat'ovi. This would also account for the incredible discrepancy between the apparent initial indifference of the Walpi and Oraibi chiefs to Tapolo's plan and the subsequent torture and murder of the prisoners who were promised as booty, especially to Oraibi. Details about beautiful women being killed in order to quell disagreements between the Walpians and Oraibians, about women losing their breasts to conquerors' knives, and old men and women being tortured until they revealed their ritual secrets are present in almost every oral record. One version even describes Tapolo creeping out of his hiding place and pathetically coming upon the mutilated bodies of the victims on his way to Walpi, where he was allowed to stay on the condition that he revealed his ritual knowledge (Curtis 1922:88–89). The fact that the Walpians took over the Awat'ovi lands is also prominently recorded.[20]

20. This is one of the few forms of proof Hopis accede to in land claims issues.

Perhaps the most perplexing and yet revealing point is that *all* the men were killed; not just the Christians, but all of them—even the chief in some versions of the story. Fewkes (1893:366–367) confirms that other versions point to a variety of conflicts between Walpi and Awat'ovi over fields, ownership of springs, accusations of sorcery, and Awat'ovi's many Christians. Fewkes was, however, more convinced that the cause of the destruction was

> the progress Christianity was making in Awatobi. . . . They foresaw that it heralded the return of the hated domination of the priests, associated in their minds with practical slavery. . . . Moreover, after the reconquest of the Rio Grande pueblos, many apostates fled to Tusayan and fanned the fire of hatred against the priests. (1898:605)

If ritual knowledge is truly the main base of power in Hopi society (with land ownership a close second), then this travesty might very well be the result of a conspiracy by outsiders against Awat'ovi, taking the spoils of the attack into due consideration. This would explain the diversion of apparent cause being placed in Tapolo's hands as well as the relative silence in oral tradition concerning Christians and Spaniards.

The Reed clan chief at Walpi reportedly responded to a request by the Catholic Church sometime after the 1930s to make the remains of Awat'ovi into a historical monument,

> Yes, it happened a long time ago and we don't want to remember it. I don't want my people to know anything about it. Leave Awatovi alone till it disappears. (Yava 1978:96)

As Yava noted, the Hopis want to forget because it affects the way they conceive of themselves as being the peaceful people (ibid.:88, 95). Frank Waters (1963:325) wrote that "the ruin of Awatovi is the first great monument to the tragic defeat of the Hopi spirit of universal brotherhood." I disagree. It is neither the first nor the last defeat. There is not a people on this earth who does not meet defeat in the face of its ideals every day. Besides, the so-called universal brotherhood ideal is more that of Frank Waters than of the Hopis. There is nothing more revealing and meaningful in the study of religion and culture than how, when, and why we humans break the very rules we make.[21]

This subchapter on the fate of Awat'ovi may very well show that Tapolo had in fact chosen the same solution to the same problem as his descendent did, and that he was villified in tradition due to the political interests of powerful rivals. This may also explain why Tuwaletstiwa makes no mention of Awat'ovi and instead chooses to emphasize the

21. See Baal 1981 and chapter 7 below on this topic.

function of the Bow clan as keeping an eye on the ambitions of political leadership and protecting the people.

THE TIINGAVI HYPOTHESIS

Let us reconsider the possibility that Tapolo was the instigator of the conspiracy. What would have been his reasons in such a case? Surely not because his son was unpopular with the girls of Awat'ovi!

The answer may be that he also regarded the tense situation at Awat'ovi in eschatological terms and, having the same goals in mind as Tuwaletstiwa, chose punishment as a way out: If Hopi religion is at an end, then let us end it all.

Parallels can easily be found in the split of Oraibi in 1906 and in the use of the mechanism called *tiingavi* in Hopi. Recent works by Hopi and Euro-American scholars present a plausible explanation.

It is not my intention in this book to go into the complexities of the conflicts leading up to the split nor of the convolutions of the aftermath. References will be made to this signal event throughout this book, but interested readers are referred to the large body of literature on the subject.[22]

Based on accounts of a variety of Hopi consultants and historical documents and supported by the work of Emory Sekaquaptewa, Whiteley concluded that the analyses of knowledgeable Hopis of the events leading up to and following 1906 concentrate on four sets of features:

> 1. The split was a deliberate plot, brought into operation by Oraibi's active *pavansinom*, or politico-religious leaders, via the subtle machinations of Hopi political action.
> 2. The split was foretold in a body of prophecies, recorded in ritual narrative and song, and the years prior to the split were recognized as fulfilling the conditions set forth in the prophecies as appropriate for the destruction of the village.
> 3. The split's primary purpose was radical change in the structure of society.
> 4. Such radical change was directed particularly toward the politico-religious order, which was regarded as the central axis of the social system. (Whiteley 1988, 283)

22. Sekaquaptewa 1972, provides an informed native point of view, Titiev 1944 and 1972 provides a sociological point of view, and Whiteley 1988, provides insights previously overlooked by both native and ethnographic approaches. Clemmer 1978*b*, is interesting due to the fact that Clemmer is an apologist for the Hopi Traditionalist Movement. His book is filled with interesting details about the Traditionalists, and I will return to his work

We do not need to accept the theological implications of these features, but we do need to take the emphasis on a deliberate, decision-making element seriously, even though there may have been extenuating circumstances, as Whiteley also acknowledges. Some scholars, such as Richard Clemmer (1978*b*:55), consider it to be post hoc rationalizations, but Whiteley's study presents irrefutable evidence that shows that this element was contemporaneous with the Oraibi split, and that the native theory does, in fact, account for a whole series of otherwise inexplicable events up to, during, and after the split.

According to Gordon Krutz, it is the element of planning, in this case the term *tiingavi*, which is fundamental to Hopi prophecy. In his article on the split of Oraibi in 1906, he stated:

> it was *diingavi* that really set the stage on which actors played out their predetermined roles fulfilling Hopi prophecy; the split was inevitable, preordained and Hopis merely played a part, as had earlier Hopi villages facing similar stresses in the process of segmentation. (1973:85)

Krutz's consultant was Emory Sekaquaptewa, and in his opinion the split was not due to haphazard factional dispute, but to a carefully laid-out plan agreed upon by the leaders of the two factions (Sekaquaptewa 1972:247–248). Sekaquaptewa's brother Wayne expressed this same sentiment in one of his editorials (*Qua' Töqti*, September 9, 1976).

Tiingavi means "religious intent" and it refers to announcing the date of an impending ceremonial. But in this context it is given apocryphal valency and thus refers to a deliberate plot with ultimate or dramatic consequences conceived of as fulfilling prophecy. Whether or not this explains the split of Oraibi is unimportant here. The point is that this way of thinking is specifically Hopi and it informs Hopi social action. There is ample evidence of it in the accounts of other, similar events—which brings us back to Tapolo. Nequatewa, in describing the "true" story of the split of Oraibi, described the mechanism of conspiracy in this manner:

> Lololama [the chief of Oraibi until around 1904] was the only one of the party to think out a plan to move his people and he worked this out in his mind on the way home. Of course, he knew very well that just asking his people to move out would not be enough to get them started. They would have to have some strong reason, like a quarrel or disagreement among themselves. Now Lololama knew that this was a traditional plan or "theory" among his people and that it always had worked. When the leaders found that for some reason it was desirable for their people, either the

in chapters 4 and 7. For references to other works on the subject of the split of Oraibi see Laird 1977, index entry "Oraibi split."

> whole village, or a part thereof, to move away and found a new establishment, they would deliberately get together and plan to foment a quarrel. This would be invariably carried out in such a clever way by the leaders that the people themselves would never suspect the plot, and eventually the separation or move would occur just as it had been planned. However, after such a conspiracy these leaders always considered themselves guilty because of the trouble and distress they had brought upon their people in the process of working out a plan which was to benefit these same people eventually. They often "sacrificed" themselves deliberately, in atonement for the distress caused their people in this process and any misfortune befalling them after such an act, even though for the good of their people, was considered right and just punishment. The Hopi say that this is one of the reasons why there are so many ruins all over the country. (Nequatewa 1936:131–132; cf. Whiteley 1988:259–260)

This description does indeed describe the Hopi way of thinking. The very lack of unequivocal coercive measures in Hopi traditional government gives very few alternatives to impossible situations. In myth, so in history: Hopi chiefs and leaders have either escaped to better places (whether to other worlds or to Riverside, California) or have coerced human or superhuman beings into destroying their enemies (whether the Feathered Serpent, other Hopis, or foreign tribes). The concept of the sacrifice of the chief as a third alternative has recent historical interest in connection with the split of Oraibi. Self-sacrifice by beheading or murder is well known in Hopi folklore and is integrally related to predeterminism.[23]

Peter Whiteley, in focusing on the term *pasiwni* instead of *tiingavi*, summarized perceptively that decisions that are ritually agreed upon and sealed in such a way that their planned consequences are unavoidable

> inhabit a cosmology far from the western conception of an intentionless arrangement of material phenomena in which events often occur at random. Rather, the Hopi universe is filled with intentional forces, of which mankind is a part. *Pavansinom* [people of the highest status] have the capacity to tap these intentional forces to affect the course of events. (1988: 266)

The explanatory scope of the tiingavi/pasiwni hypothesis is undeniable. And it satisfactorily explains why Tuwaletstiwa did what he did. Ac-

23. Cf. F. Eggan 1967:47–48. Of relevance here is the October 25, 1906 entry (one month after the split of Oraibi and the subsequent founding of Hotevilla) of Theodore G. Lemmon, superintendent of the Hopi Agency at Keams Canyon from 1904–1906:

> The next day I took Tewaquaptewa with me to talk to Yokeoma. The latter firmly stood his ground and stoutly maintained that tradition required that the Chief who had departed from the Hopi way should have his head cut off, and again requested that Tewaquaptewa be beheaded. (Cited in Udall 1969:85)

cording to Tuwaletstiwa, his clan was given a task that was closely related to the entire sequence of a world age. When a clan strays from the task it must bear and cannot return to the path, then the leader has the right and authority to decide "in what manner this should be destroyed."

As one of Whiteley's Bacavi consultants stated, "The ritualism, all the songs, the ritual prayers and the knowledge were ritually destined to be forgotten. No one will possess these ever again. This is what was done at the time Oraibi split" (Whiteley 1988:256).

But none of this seems to adequately explain the actions of Tuwaletstiwa's ancestor. As noted above, it is conceivable that Tapolo planned some sort of plot against his village, but a motive seems to be lacking. Here we are talking about the demise of all the men and a considerable number of the women and children, with torture as part of their fate. A plot as intricate and subtle as the designed split of Oraibi evidently was seems to be lacking in Tapolo's case.

Two plausible explanations spring to mind: either Tapolo's actual plot, the content of which we have no way of knowing, went horribly wrong somehow, or Tapolo and his village were the victims of a conspiracy orchestrated by the chief of Oraibi, Espeleta. Whiteley's documentation of the apparent dominance of Oraibi throughout the historical period seems to substantiate the latter possibility. Otherwise we are left with the conclusion that Tapolo for reasons of his own wanted to destroy his village completely.

Other explanations could probably be postulated, but we have exhausted the flexibility of our sources so much that our only answer can be that no definitive answer is to be had. But it is certain that the Hopis themselves have complex feelings about the Bow Clan which has in at least two crucial periods in Hopi history–and perhaps in the very matrix of emergence mythology–stood out as a volatile catalyst spreading a conflagration that the Hopis have been trying to put out for at least 450 years.[24]

The fatal act of Tuwaletstiwa is now more comprehensible. Events on the reservation convinced him that the Hopis were at the threshold of the end of the world, exactly as they stood at the threshold of the end of the prior Third World. He and his clan were warned that that time would come and that it would be their task to soothe the distraught and

24. In Tawakwaptiwa's version of the emergence myth, which supposedly was the version told by Loololma, the Spider and Bow clans were partners in the mischief making in the Third World. Titiev, in commenting on this fact, wrote, "The Bow Clan is frequently called 'crazy' at Oraibi, and at least two of its members were actually psychopathic" (1944:73, and n. 49). This latter may be a reference to Tuwaletstiwa. Other examples of the highly negative public opinion of the Bow clan are documented in Whiteley 1992.

not to hurt anyone. So he chose a peaceful, nonviolent demonstration of his convictions, and he chose to point to what he considered to be a possible "way out," namely, Christianity. There was no turning back, in his opinion, and therefore the rebel elements at Hotevilla were not only hurting themselves, but also the White people who supported them.

THE IMPLICATIONS OF BURNING ALTARS

I indicated in the Introduction that Hopi prophecy is not a matter of cultural borrowing. Rather it is clearly an indigenous response to and a hermeneutical framework for the way cultures meet. Despite the paucity of evidence from the early centuries of contact with the Spaniards, I think it is safe to assume that Hopi prophecy has served as an interpretive strategy since the beginnings of the Euro-American presence.

It is furthermore evident that Hopi prophecy is intimately linked with the indigenous concept of directed cultural and social change. The story of Tuwaletstiwa is the story of a tragic leader who chose to destroy his religion in order to trigger the apocalypse. This action on his part supports the idea of directed cultural change in Hopi thought. Although some believe the so-called tiingavi hypothesis to be a post hoc rationalization, it is enough for us to observe that it is an indigenous interpretive model that not only plays a role in Hopi myth, but which also has been perceived as a causal factor in Hopi political reality.

The tiingavi hypothesis should also alert us to the fact that Hopi tradition, and therefore Hopi prophecy, resides in theory solely in the hands of clan leaders. This means that some narratives are more "authentic" or more "authoritative" than others.

At this point, then, we are confronted with two highly significant variables: 1) There may be indigenous factors of deliberate change whose form and impact we have difficulty measuring and evaluating; and 2) of the many narratives at our disposal, only a handful are authoritative.

Concerning the first point, we have no choice but to examine the factors that explicitly appear in the historical record, on the one hand, and, on the other hand, to be constantly aware of the fact that the evidence we happen to have may simply be the surface layer of a whole labyrinth of other unknown but equally important factors. Such is the case when describing and interpreting the mutually incompatible claims and accusations of chiefly rivals.

One of the more productive methods of analysis is to follow the historical trail of available and easily definable objects or ideas such as the stone tablets or the motif of beheading and to try to make sense of the manner in which the object or idea is treated and interpreted on the basis of what we think we know about Hopi society, religion, and culture. Another trail to follow is that of extraordinary persons or easily recognizable groups. Chapters 6 to 10 represent both types of approach.

Concerning the second point, on the matter of authenticity, if we were to follow the rule in its strictest sense, then most of the narratives at our disposal should be rejected as inauthentic, or at least as inadmissible. This would include, among others, all Traditionalist narratives. Such a rejection would, however, be absurd. There are no indications to suggest the conclusion that the only true, complete, and/or authentic narratives are those held by the heads of the clans. The very nature of the Hopi clan system implies at least two partners in the business of authenticity, namely, the matron of the clan and her brother. And, in practice, clan affairs and clan history are shared in detail with members of one's lineage and, if not in detail, then in broad outline, with other clan members.

In the context of meetings between leaders, disparate clan traditions confront one another in the form of discussions, disputes, coordinated ritual and secular activity, and formal deliberations. In the process, each clan redefines itself in relationship to the other clans, and it can be reasonably assumed that all the clans know at least the general outlines of each other's narratives, duties, and rights. In fact, much of our data stems from informants who also make claims about, and for, other clans. That this has sometimes led to misrepresentation is another matter. Each clan finds itself in the midst of a continual, mutual dialogue where individuals and clans are perceived in terms of a loosely structured hierarchy that must be clarified, modified, and mobilized in relation to each new situation and each new challenge or problem.

Several scholars have noted a puzzling contradiction in Hopi social behavior. According to Titiev, when a Hopi community splits up, the divisions always follow along clan lines because internal clan ties are much stronger than the ties among clans in the same phratry, a unit which purportedly lacks an indigenous term. The contradiction is that "if the phratry is an unnamed unit, and the clan has a name, why should natives rarely err in assigning people to their proper phratries, but make frequent mistakes with regard to clan membership?" (Titiev 1944:58). Titiev suggested three possibilities: 1) It might be due to the fact that phratrial exogamic lines of demarcation between related clans are of little importance; 2) joint phratry ownership of all member clans' totem keeps phratry lines more distinct than clan lines; and 3) it is easier to remember all the totems associated with nine phratries than to remember totem ownership among thirty different clans (ibid.). Titiev's suggestions are incorrect because he misunderstood some important aspects of Hopi social structure.

British anthropologist Richard Bradfield (who wrote one of the few theoretical treatises on Hopi ethnography) held that the reason for the contradiction lies in the functions of the two groupings, clan vs. phratry (1973, II:199, 303–304). On the one hand, the clan is the unit for the "transmission of rights" and the ownership of things. On the other hand, the phratry represents as a whole a grouping of natural phenomena or conceptual categories through which "its members exert an influence on the *event* that lies at the core of that grouping" (ibid.:303; cf. F. Eggan 1950:62–63, 80). Thus, there is the dichotomy between being a member of a body "owning" things and being a member of a body "exerting influence" on the course of events (ibid.:304). Hopis "rarely err in assigning people to their proper phratries" because they accord precedence to exerting influence on events in their habitual thought, and especially in their ceremonial attitudes.

But, again, it is a question of having misunderstood the Hopi social system. As Whiteley has pointed out in several publications (1985, 1986, 1988:162–191), the precise nature of the Hopi clan system has not been adequately accounted for by kinship theory. One of the problems is the alleged lineage-clan-phratry paradigm, which social anthropologists have consistently assumed but which can neither consistently nor unambiguously be demonstrated (1988:49). Conventional accounts have pointed out that there are no Hopi terms for "lineage" or "phratry," and yet, scholars nevertheless insist on these descent-group categories. For linguists, such as the Voegelins, the solution to the Hopi problem lies in the resolution of anthropological typologies and folk taxonomies. In other words, improvement in elicitation techniques will prove the correctness of the anthropological typology (Voegelin 1959; Voegelin and Voegelin 1970*a*, 1970*b*, 1971). But Whiteley suggested that these categories may in fact not fit the Hopi situation too well and may reveal instead the structural-functionalist bias of conventional ethnography (1988: 184–185).

Another interesting fact which most fieldworkers will have noticed is the curiously frequent disagreement between self-designation and another's designation of clan ascription (ibid.:180). Thus, some clan names do not refer to separate isomorphic categories, but to categories of prestige revealing "the notion of negotiable clan identity" (see the excellent phratry-by-phratry discussion, ibid.:180ff). These matters cannot be sufficiently explained by the decline of the subsistence economy and of the ritual order.

Whiteley concludes that phratries are distinct groupings. In fact, he notes two of the ways of referring to them: *naanangaqvim* and *amumumya* (1985:373, n. 3). I have also heard terms such as *pumangyam, himungyam, naanasinom*, and *hiisa'niiqam* (A. W. Geertz and Lomatuway'ma 1987: 142, n. 91). Whiteley concluded further that the smaller units of clans and lineages "operate on a sort of sliding scale between precise differentiations (e.g., the Bear and Spider clans) and rather imprecise conflation (such as in Phratries I, III, and VII)," (1988:184) which are subject to "political and social considerations that have nothing to do with genealogy" (ibid.:183). In fact, the only matrilineal principle the Hopis insist on is exogamy. Economic cooperation, religious-society membership, and even inheritance of high office were and are often based on agnatic and affinal ties (ibid.:186).

What we are confronted with, then, is a relatively contained pluralism in a constant flux of hermeneutical negotiations. The measuring stick of these negotiations is the ideal social and religious structure, but the social reality challenges claims to authority and leads to modifications even in authoritative narratives.[25]

A case in point is the evidence presented in Chicago anthropologist Fred Eggan's enlightening analysis of the modification of mythical narrative and the mythologizing of historical narrative in his article "From History to Myth" (1967). Not only does Eggan's case study document the negotiable nature of the assumption of office, it also documents how the exception to the rules of inheritance can also lead to changes in the details of the paramount Hopi narrative, the emergence myth.

Eggan's example concerns Mashali of the Dove clan in the Snake phratry. The Dove clan is not important in the hierarchy at all, and yet Mashali became chief of the Antelope Society as well as the village chief of Walpi (ibid.:40–41). The situation on First Mesa was that the Bear clan had died out some time before 1850 and the Snake clan had somehow managed to take power. The correct and ideal procedure would have been to find a chief within the ranks of the clans of the Bear phratry, but this did not happen.

After Mashali's death in a tragic conflict with the Navajos, the Horn phratry moved into the political scene, and Simo of the Millet clan was chosen as village chief. Again, a chief from a less important clan was chosen. The reason given for this was that he had close connections with the Navajos and therefore would be better able to keep them at bay. His choice was, therefore, based on intertribal diplomacy and not on the cor-

25. There are many examples of this phenomenon. It has just never been demonstrated in precisely these terms before. Besides the example given below, I will simply refer the reader to the diary literature (Parsons, ed., 1925, 1936; Simmons 1942; Titiev 1972; Waters 1969), the speeches given during the hearings of 1955 (Bureau of Indian Affairs 1955), the analyses of political conflict (Titiev 1944; Whiteley 1987, 1988), and to my own data (A. W. Geertz and Lomatuway'ma 1987:113–146, 171–176; A. W. Geertz 1990*a*).

rect procedures of clan legitimacy. As it turns out, the ploy worked and relations with the Navajos improved.

Eggan noted that the Horn ceremonial, the Blute Flute, increased in importance, and its *tüponi* (e.g., the central clan ritual object) became the symbol of the village chieftaincy at First Mesa. Of significance to this study is the fact that in the narrative of the traditional order of arrival at Walpi, the Horn clans were advanced and the ceremonial dramatization of their mythical arrival was altered in conformity. Thus, Simo finished relating his 1892 narrative to Alexander Stephen in the following way:

> When we got to the entrance of the village all the people had gathered together and they barred the trail with meal, and the chiefs of the Bear and Snake demanded to know where we were going and what we desired to do. Our chief said, "We are Hopi, our hearts and thoughts are good and our speech is straight, and we carry on our backs the *lenûñ poñ'ya ko'hü*, the wood of the Flute altar, and we can cause the rain to fall." Four times they challenged us and we told them the same story, and after the fourth time, A'losaka opened the trail and the chiefs rubbed the meal away from the trail, and we passed in. We set up the Flute altar and sang and the rain fell and the Bear and Snake said, "For a surety your chief shall be our chief." And truly [concluded Simo], I am chief (Kikmoñwi, Town Chief) this day. (Parsons, ed., 1936:810–811)

We know now that it did not happen this way. But, what Simo did was to incorporate the changing social and political realities into the framework of *the* central narrative in Hopi mythology. One can, with Titiev, remark on "the speed with which recent events can be woven into Hopi mythology" (1944:71, n. 28).

I suggest that we draw the following conclusions:

1. Hopi prophecy is indigenous and is intimately linked with clan narratives;
2. "Authoritative" versions of clan narratives are not inviolable in practice;
3. There is therefore good sense in pursuing the study of a pan-clan core narrative; and
4. The study of divergent narratives must pay unswerving attention to the sociopolitical motives and posturings of the narrators.

Esther S. Goldfrank came to conclusions similar to point 4 in her study on four emergence myths. In comparing Talay'ima's account from 1882, Yukiwma's two accounts from 1903 and 1911, and Tawakwaptiwa's account from 1932 (see the texts in Appendix B), Goldfrank concluded that certain politically important themes were subject to reformulation and reinterpretation (Goldfrank 1948:243) and that further study must involve "both a good knowledge of the historical situation and familiarity with the narrator's experience and personality" (ibid.:260). In agreement with her observations, I will attempt to pay close attention to historical, social, political, and (wherever possible) personal factors.

Thus, following in Jan Vansina's footsteps (1961),[26] a series of control measures must be applied through which we can distinguish the chain of transmission and the characteristics of that transmission, the characteristics, structure, and meaning of the testimony, and the social, cultural, and psychological significance of the testimony. Furthermore, we must apply comparative methods in which texts as well as circumstances of transmission are compared. But we must also compare the evidence of the testimonies with archaeological, historical, and linguistic evidence. And, finally, we must pay attention to the relationship between genre and change.

26. Cf. Finnegan 1970.

TWO

Hopi Prophecy Defined

AN INDIGENOUS DEFINITION OF HOPI PROPHECY

The basic elements of Hopi prophecy are integral to the emergence myth. Hopi mythographers postulate a series of worlds through which all humans have passed. Each world begins as a paradise but ends in cataclysm. When mankind emerged from the prior world to this "fourth world," it met its tutelary deity, Maasaw. Before he withdrew from sight he apportioned a tract of land to the Hopis provided that they lived according to his simple way of poverty and humility and that they ruled the land according to their clan system under the leadership of the Bear clan. These precepts are to be followed until the end of the fourth world is heralded by the return from the east of the Hopis' White Brother (who had parted ways with them in primordial times). This return will be signaled by a variety of signs, and when the Hopi people have fulfilled their human (or evil) ambitions, Maasaw will return once again to punish and purify humanity and the earth as a prelude to a new "fifth" world era. The White Brother, called Pahaana, will bring a new way of life with him, and the Hopis were commanded to fulfill the seemingly impossible task of simultaneously clinging to their ancient ways and following the new ways of their White Brother until Maasaw's apocryphal return. It is especially this latter task that has played such an important role in the development and interpretation of Hopi prophecies.

We have seen that Tuwaletstiwa claimed that he had been given indications of the signs of the end of the world by others: "It was told to us by our forefathers that this religious setup was to disintegrate" (Bureau of Indian Affairs 1955:174). In other words, prophecy is in Hopi thought a subcategory of clan tradition ("our forefathers"), called *navoti* in Hopi. As the German linguist Ekkehart Malotki wrote: "'Prophetic statements' given to the Hopi in conjunction with the laws of the *pötskwani* [ethical rules, see below] are commonly known as *navoti*, literally 'knowledge gained from hearing, i.e., not from seeing or experience'" (Malotki and Lomatuway'ma 1987*b*:58). Prophecy is, in other words, spoken by someone to someone else. It is part of the ongoing oral tradition, whether in song, myth, or speech, which thrives within the framework of each clan.

Navoti covers the whole concept of clan history. As the leader of the Traditionalist Movement on Third Mesa, Dan Qötshongva told the Mormons in Salt Lake City: "I know the history of my own people, where they came from and how they got here" (Kotchongva 1936:84).

Wukwnavoti, "great knowledge," carries the connotations of "wisdom, things told to make one aware of how life should be," "history," and "prophecies." *Wukwnavoti* is often used as the modern term for prophecy (Hopi Health Department n.d.:52; Robin 1983:36).

Social anthropologist Peter Whiteley explained that the Hopi term *hopinavoti* expresses what I would call "indigenous hermeneutics." As he wrote:

> *Hopinavoti* is the general category of Hopi ideation that provides thoroughgoing analyses that are comparable to anthropological analyses, in that they stem from a demarcated tradition of interpretation that is specialized, restricted, and "expert." *Navoti* indicates a system of knowledge that includes philosophy, science, and theology and incorporates conceptual models for explaining the past and predicting, or "prophesying," future events. . . . in short, it is a sort of Hopi hermeneutics. (1988:255)

Hopi prophetic cognition is therefore intimately bound up with clan identity and clan ideology. Prophetic statements constantly refer to the activities of the speaker's clan in the past. Prophetic statements are also told in relation to the particular qualities of each clan. For example, the Bow clan was given the task of watching over the rulers and recording their deeds for the day of judgment. Thus the most basic characteristic of Hopi prophecy is that it is clan-based.

The second major characteristic of Hopi prophecy is that it is collective: There is prophecy but there are no prophets (cf. A. W. Geertz 1987*c*:38). Anyone can relate *wukwnavoti*, even though the clan leader has the prominence of authority. This collectivity must be understood, of course, in terms of clan membership.

It was not until 1949 that Hopi prophecies were severed from clan contexts by Hopis, thereby becoming universalistic. But even then the major spokesman of the political movement that initiated the collation of prophecies in 1949 (which is called the Traditionalist Movement in this book) incorporated those prophecies at a later time within the contexts of his own clan traditions, thereby universalizing not only his clan, but himself as well—but more on this in chapter 7.

The third basic characteristic of Hopi prophecy is that it is located in a simultaneous continuum of present perfect, past perfect, and future perfect tenses where the historical present is a constant repetition of the mythical past, and where the speaker can choose at any time to vocalize (thereby incarnate) any moment in that continuum. The speaker can, in fact, use all three tenses at once.[1]

This relation to time is not perceived as metaphorical, but as ontological. There are many statements that prove that the Hopis experience their clan history intimately and realistically. As was evident in chapter 1, Tuwaletstiwa not only realized that his office was given to him in primordial times in the third world, but he also actually believed that he personally was there: "This goes back to the life below and the position I there had"; "along with the bow he gave specific instructions of how I was to continue in my walk of life"; and so on.

Another example of this phenomenon is Ebin Leslie, village chief at First Mesa, who told his listeners at the Third Hopi Mental Health Conference in 1984: "It is a wonder that I was approached by Masauu and given all these instructions to uphold. This is what I realize today" (Jenkins and Kooyahoema 1984:33, 38 [Hopi text]).

Although it may be that this continuum consciousness is restricted to leaders alone, it is sufficient to have demonstrated that it exists among those who have the authority to pass on prophetic tradition. This personalized identification with past events does not mean that the Hopis cannot discern past from present or future, as Whorf and the whole tradition he started would have us believe.[2] It simply means that authority is cognitively established through an experiential encounter with primordial affairs. At the same time the Hopis are quite aware of the fact that tradition is also passed on by uncles and grandfathers: "We know the time has come, as was foretold by our forefathers."

The fourth characteristic of Hopi prophecy is that it is fatalistic. Prophecies are indeed linked to an intricate existential web—most fundamentally expressed in the *pötskwani*—that gives to the Hopis a secure knowledge of their origins, their development, how they are to act, and where they stand in time and space. *Pötskwani* is the Hopi term for "rules for living and maintaining the proper way of life." It is sometimes trans-

1. See, for instance, Mumzewa's statement this chapter, on page 67.
2. See Carroll (1956) and criticisms by Gipper (1972) and Malotki (1979, 1983*b*).

lated as fate, but another term, *qatsimkiwa*, "the kind of life given to someone, destiny," is more in use: "Evidently it is his destiny, that is why he has expired at an early age." *Pay kya pi pam pan qatsimkiway'taqe oovi pay naat tsayniikyangw haqami'i* (provided by Michael Lomatuway'ma, 1982). *Pötskwani* is generally rendered as "life plan" in the English literature, but the term *qatsivötavi*, "life road," recently made its way into the literature (Robin 1983:35). Malotki wrote that younger Hopis who are no longer familiar with the term *pötskwani* often substitute the word *tutavo*, "instructions, teachings" (Malotki and Lomatuway'ma 1987*b*:58).

Voegelin and Voegelin, however, understood *tutavo* in this sense and defined the term as "didactic ethics" (1960:53), or as "advice from ascending generation" (1957:51). Whiteley's consultants used the term *maqastutavo* for the Hopi ethical system, which is considered to be similar to a legal system as a means of maintaining social order (Whiteley 1988:273).

The *pötskwani* has implications that reach beyond the individual's own particular destiny. The term encompasses the clan and ultimately the Hopi people. As I have demonstrated elsewhere (A. W. Geertz 1986:46ff; 1990*a*:317–319), we are in the conceptual realm of what it means to be *hopi*, that is, "well behaved, well mannered."[3] Intimately connected with this behavior is the role of ritual, wherein human life is equated with ritual life (A. W. Geertz 1986:48). *Qatsit aw hintsaki*, "working to achieve life," is a holistic, though primarily ritual activity that is intimately bound up with contemplating the holistic image of reality. This image of reality sees humanity as an important and fateful element in the cycles of nature, where poor weather is equal to unethical and immoral behavior among humans. Personal and societal harmony and balance are necessary ingredients in maintaining cosmic harmony and balance. Therefore, human activity is purposeful and requires concentration. This concentration is characterized by the term *tunatya*, "intention." One who sponsors a ceremony is called *tunatyay'taqa*, "one who has an intention." Although he or she has the responsibility to maintain proper concentration and behavior, the success of a ceremony is nontheless a collective affair.

The norms involved in ritual behavior have their roots in the *pötskwani* given to the clans in primordial times, but they do not only refer to the day-to-day endeavors in maintaining a balance in life and nature. The holistic image of reality also regards humans as being intrinsic to the way things have happened in the past and to how they will happen in

3. This image of the ideal person corresponds with Sherry Ortner's concept of the *key scenario* as idealized action. See Ortner 1973 and Foster 1980:376f.

the future. The fact that the present is continually identified with similar activities in the primordial past underlines the sense of continuity, simultaneity, and coevalness. The past has clearly demonstrated that deviance from the norms leads to *koyaanisqatsi*, "a life of turmoil," which in turn brings on apocalyptical destruction. And, as mentioned earlier, the main reason for the onslaught of *koyaanisqatsi* is not because people have lost their concentration and intentions, but because they have the wrong intentions.

The security that the precognitive epistemology clan knowledge offers carries with it a Janus head: There is always the temptation to "give up" in the face of what is to be.

Anthropologist Edward A. Kennard wrote about the Hopis' precognitive predilections in his article "Metaphor and Magic" (1972). He focused, among other things, on the term *pasiwna*, which he translated as "predetermining future events" whether in ritual or secular contexts (ibid.:469). The element of predetermination does not lie in the term *pasiwna* itself, which simply means "plan it." Kennard based his assumption on the activities during the Soyalangw in December at which the kiva leaders literally plan the ceremonial events of the coming year by acting out those events in abbreviated form, and in this manner predetermine their outcome. This element of planning is evident linguistically in several other ways. *Wuuwa*, "intend, design, plan," *tiingavi*, "plan," *hin yukuya*, "plan it, establish standards for," are all terms that indicate Hopi interest in leaving nothing to chance.

As Kennard wrote: "Even when speaking English, a Hopi does not say (as we would), 'I guess I'll have to change my ways.' Instead, he says, 'I guess I'll come to that,' meaning 'I will arrive in my own path of life at the place where such a change is predestined for me'" (ibid.:470). Ceremonial events are thought of in the same manner; they are predetermined events towards which the organizers move: "So, while we think about it, we will move towards it." *Oovi itam put wuuwankyaakyangw yaapiy hoyoyotani*. Another example: "We came to it on the fourth day." *Paasat naalös talqw pu' itam put aqw pitsinaya* (A. W. Geertz and Lomatuway'ma 1987:62, 272).[4]

Precognition is a common motif in Hopi folklore as well. Many are the stories of the young hero who is about to embark on a journey carrying the right amount of gifts and knowing exactly whom he is to meet and what he is to do. Not only do his parents tell him these things before

4. Parallels can be found in the terminology of paragraph 41 of the emergence myth in Appendix A. Compare as well the precognitive certainty that dominates the raison d'être of the clan migrations in paragraphs 42, 45–46, 62, etc.

the fact, but they also tell him when he will reach his destination and which people, spirits of the dead, or deities are expecting his imminent arrival. Perhaps the significant thing is that very little surprise is expressed when events occur as foretold. This sense of shared omniscience in the adult world or between adults and superhuman beings is so common that I believe it to be more than restricted to the world of folklore. Even though the Hopis believe in the verity of their tales, we must still make comparisons with the nonfolkloristic reality with care. Nonetheless, taken together with the evidence presented in this book, I am convinced that precognition is a basic element in Hopi religious thought.

The fifth characteristic of Hopi prophecy is that it reflects political, social, and ideological contexts. Since this factor needs to be demonstrated, I will spend the rest of this book doing just that.

THE LOGIC OF PROPHETIC RHETORIC[5]

The documents we have make it clear that Hopi prophecy is more (or less, depending on your point of view) than it purports to be. Under the guise of precognitive authority it is more often than not a mechanism that incorporates contemporary affairs into the framework of traditional religious values, evaluates those affairs in terms of conceived tradition, and interprets and judges those affairs on the authority of conceived tradition. Since traditional authority in the Hopi sense is relative in a social system of disparate clans, it is self-evident that authoritative statements can only be absolute within specific clan environments. Prophecies are no exception: Their absolute value is relative, not only concerning the rest of the world, but also within Hopi society itself.

The Hopis are well aware of this factor. Each Hopi reserves the right to decide for him or herself. An oft-heard comment is the conditional "They are most probably true," *Pu' pay antsa pi sonqa panta.* Even in the Mental Health Conference reports, which describe the role of prophecy in relation to Hopi collective mental health, one finds the refrain, "Only time will tell."

Prophecy is therefore more than a connotative device. It is also a rhetorical device constrained by its own rhetorical logic. Prophetic statements are told under the pretence of anterior precognition (i.e., before the fact), even though in actual fact it is posterior "precognition" (i.e., after the fact). Even though posterior precognition is by definition an impossibility, it is nevertheless a useful hybrid of Hopi conception and

5. This subchapter appeared in A. W. Geertz 1989*b*.

historical evidence. My hypothesis is that the inherent logic of the rhetorical process is a self-preserving mechanism that supports and strengthens the belief in anterior precognition. I will attempt to briefly indicate some of the major characteristics of this logic.

It should be said in all fairness that some statements are actually anterior. For example, the prophecies about a coming holocaust are anterior, but they cannot properly be labeled precognitive until the fact occurs. The fact that most of the modern world, at least during the 1950s and 1960s, also believed in the possibility of a coming holocaust does not mean that this belief is ipso facto a prophetic belief. It may also just be commonsense anxiety about the future.

Hopi prophetic rhetoric is authoritative. It consists of a series of dogmatic statements which receive their authoritative status from two main sources, the ancestors and/or Maasaw. A quote from one of Malotki's consultants is instructive:

> These are the elders' instructions. They are derived directly from the teachings and the life plan of Maasaw. Here and there one of us still remembers the words of Maasaw, the god who lives unseen. A few of us actually still follow his directives. We have not strayed from them. (Malotki and Lomatuway'ma 1987*b*:256)

Two elements are worth noting. First, all prophetic statements, no matter how superficially ancient, are given the stamp of authority. Second, there is no distinction evident between the sources. Whether an old uncle, the ancestors, or Maasaw, sources are of equal validity and authority because they bespeak a continuity from the earliest times to the present. But again it must be remembered that the Hopi clan system binds each person only to the authority of his or her own clan traditions. Other clan traditions do not have the same persuasive power or authority.

Hopi prophetic rhetoric is conditional. There is hardly a statement that does not presuppose its opposite or a least one or two alternatives. The present leader of the Traditionalist Movement, Thomas Banancya, presented a quadripartite series of prophecies about the identity of the coming "purifier" (cf. 4.33.0–4.33.4 in Appendix C) which are all conditionally linked with each other. 1) Maasaw commissioned three to bring about the purification day: the true White Brother, one with the swastika symbol, and one with the sun symbol. 2) If these three fail, then one from the west will come like a big storm and cover the land like ants—they will be many and unmerciful. And the Hopis must not go on their rooftops to watch this punisher. 3) If all of these fail, then the Hopi leaders will ask Maasaw to strike the people with lightening and only the righteous will be revived. 4) If none revive, then Maasaw will send a flood, and humanity will have lost the chance to acquire everlasting life. Then only ants will inhabit the earth (Banyacya 1-12-1961).[6]

These statements are highly conditional in many respects. They also end with the further conditional statement that "if the three succeed, and if one, two, or three Hopis remain faithful to the ancient traditions, then Maasaw will appear before all those who will be saved, and the three will lay out a new life plan which will lead to everlasting life" (Banyacya 1-12-1961). The possibilities for adapting to changing conditions are thus endless.

Hopi prophetic rhetoric is open ended. It makes heavy use of metaphors that can be understood, misunderstood, debated, and interpreted. A case in point is the use of the *qöötsaptanga*, "container of ashes" motif. This motif seems to be an old idea associated with the Kookop Clan. The earliest reference I could find is in the 1911 emergence myth told by Yukiwma, former Hostile leader at Hotevilla, in which he stated that his clan was deemed a necessary ally in order to win battles against the Utes, Navajos, and Apaches:

> So the bravest of the warriors then put explosives in pottery, and threw these bombs among the enemy, and scattered them. Then the Ghost-and-Bird clan lived at Oraibi, and were taken into the sacred fraternities, and were known as warriors. (Crane 1925:165-166)

It should be remembered that cannonballs were already an ageold phenomenon at the time, and we know for sure that the Hopis had personal experience with them at least thirty years prior to 1911.

The next reference is from anthropologist Mischa Titiev's 1944 monograph, which is mostly based on information collected during 1932-1934. Titiev quoted Tawakwaptiwa's (chief of Oraibi at the time) version of the confrontation between the Oraibi rebels and the contingent under First Lieutenant L. M. Brett on June 21, 1891. The rebels sent costumed figures out to the soldiers before any armed conflict could occur. One of the figures was Maasaw. As Tawakwaptiwa related, "After Masawu'u had appeared, a woman named Sinimka was supposed to come out with a gourd full of ashes. This she was to dash on the ground, scattering the ashes and so weakening the enemy that they would be helpless to resist being clubbed to death" (Titiev 1944:78). The ashes in the gourd were considered to be "potent war medicine" owned by the Kookop clan.

During an armed conflict between the Oraibians and the "Chimwava,"

6. Banancya is one of the compromises between orthographic accuracy and common usage. White supporters call him Banyacya and he spells his name that way, but no Hopi will recognize it when pronounced accordingly. Phonetically it is written Pangangqwya.

an impersonation similar to the 1891 episode was supposedly enacted, according to Tawakwaptiwa, during which runners crossed each other's paths and "as their paths crossed they threw down their gourds of ashes. Immediately the contents flew up like flames, covering the attackers and making them faint and sluggish" (ibid.:155).

Traditions along these same lines still exist in contemporary folklore. Both Malotki and I have recorded stories of this nature.[7]

Two new developments in the ash-gourd story have occurred since Yukiwma's time.[8] The Traditionalist Movement, which had begun shortly after the end of World War II, now interpreted the idea of the ash gourd as referring to the atomic bomb, cast neither by the Kookop nor their god, but by the White Man. Once they accepted this interpretation of the ash gourd, the subsequent logic inevitably uprooted the idea from its indigenous context and became part of a development that parallelled the Traditionalists' development of their ideas on the nature of the White Man. What in the beginning had been a sign of the coming of the White purifier became in time the weapon of the "evil" White Man. I will return to the Traditionalist Movement in more detail and will therefore simply note here that they have reinterpreted the ash-gourd metaphor. This particular interpretation has fortuitously become famous the world over and has won thousands of non-Hopi supporters to the Traditionalist cause. It should be clear now that the motif has other interpretations as well.

The second new development has its source in the original idea of Kookop ownership. In this development the ash gourd is presently considered by non-Traditionalist Hopis to be the weapon of Maasaw. It is not an atomic bomb, rather it is the instrument of punishment that Maasaw will use against his people in the guise of the coming purifier:

> They say that if in the future we deviate from the teachings given to us by the one who gave us the breath of life, and if we ignore our religious beliefs, thereby bringing ourselves to *koyaanisqatsi* or "a life of turmoil," at that time our father will cast down upon us a jar of ashes as a result of which we will all perish. Thereupon the entire earth will go up in flames and all the seas will boil. At that point life will cease to exist. (Malotki and Lomatuway'ma 1987*b*:256–258)

With this new interpretation, Hopi theologians are confronted with the problem of theodicy: Can a being with such an evil weapon be good himself? One of Malotki's informants answered in the negative:

> A different Maasaw is the clan ancestor of the Kookop group and . . . is thought to be malevolent. He, it is claimed, will reveal himself to a person.

7. See Malotki and Lomatuway'ma 1987*a*:81–85.
8. Comparison with Chart C on page 240 will help in keeping track of the Hopi names.

> The clan deity of the Kookop group is endowed with evil. While he is said to be wearing shoes, the barefooted Maasaw is the one who takes care of us. The evil Maasaw possesses a weapon with which he can harm people. He uses it to make people suffer. (ibid.:200)

But, which of these two will return to purify the earth? This leaves the theologians with the problem of having to deal with two returning purifiers.

James Pongyayawma, the former chief of Hotevilla, told me in an interview in 1988 that Traditionalist leader David Monongya's interpretation of the ash-gourd legend is pure fantasy. The legend is the property of the Kookop clan (i.e., Pongyayawma's clan), and Pongyayawma was emphatic in pointing out that Monongya had therefore no authority to interpret the legend as he did. I will return to the politics of prophecy in chapters 6 and 7.

Hopi prophetic rhetoric is reflective. Because of the use of metaphors and allusions, much interpretive deliberation is involved. A case in point is a statement given by Monongya during a series of hearings conducted by the Bureau of Indian Affairs on the reservation in 1955, which explained his opposition to the activities of attorney John S. Boyden, who was representing the Hopi tribe:

> These are the many things that were told to me by my father. He told me several times that some time there will be a time someone will come and attempt to cut up your land. He did not know when that would take place, but he told me to watch and if we ever come to that time I must support the one who is standing for the Hopi traditional life pattern because with that we are holding this life and land for the Hopi people. . . . So as I go along year by year watching and waiting for the time when this will come before us, then later a Mormon man from Salt Lake City, Utah, John S. Boyden, came along and started work on the land problem of the Hopis and I recognized this as the time when they would be cutting up our land so I began to work and help those leaders who are holding this life plan for us. . . . So I began to work and help in protesting against any plans which appear to cut up our land in any manner. (Bureau of Indian Affairs 1955:52–53)

Although this interpretation seems to be straightforward enough, it is clearly an example of stretching the evidence for political ends. I am sure that neither Monongya nor his father could have had the slightest doubt about the meaning of the stated prophecy. The first part of the statement most certainly refers to the land-allottment program that was already a reality on the reservation in 1890, fully sixty-five years before Monongya's "prophecy." Secondly, the context of the statement clearly refers to the division of the land and not to the mining of the land, thus precluding any claims to visions about the mining activities of the 1960s.

The reference to Boyden shows that prophecy is characterized by reflective interpretations which have the very important function of making it relevant to contemporary needs.

Other examples indicate that the prophecies often justify political tactics. Hermequaftewa related during the above-mentioned hearings that the Whites would bring "metal instruments of power." One would think that this refers to guns, but not so: "For a while I thought it was a gun; however, today we have begun to realize and see that the power of this new law is to be a new organization [referring to the Tribal Council]." (Bureau of Indian Affairs 1955:87–88)

Kennard (1972:471–472) expressed this malleable aspect of Hopi prophecies in the following way: "Like all prophecies and forecasts of the future, they are sufficiently vague so that a certain amount of interpretation is essential in fitting today's events into the pattern of tradition." This brings us to the next characteristic.

Hopi prophetic rhetoric is inflective. This is to be understood as meaning changeable, malleable, and absorbing new details and interpretations, which Kennard called "a living ongoing process" (ibid.:472).

One specific example will make this clear. In 1961, General Herbert C. Holdridge, a Mormon who wanted to move to Utah "where he would be close to active Indian Nations and in the midst of the True Mormons," (Carpenter 3-20-1961) had asked the Traditionalists for permission to move his headquarters and people to St. George, Utah. Holdridge was probably the first White man ever to make such an unusual request. Even though the area is not legally under Hopi jurisdiction, the Traditionalists lay claim to all of North America. Needless to say, their response was positive, and it actually resulted in a slight modification of Banancya's prophecies (quoted above on conditionality, pages 52–53) which are found in a letter written to a woman by the name of Muller-Fricken residing in Frankfurt, Germany (see Appendix B). It looks as if the Traditionalists hoped that Holdridge was the awaited White Brother. In a letter addressed to Holdridge, Banancya now included Holdridge in his prophecies:

> Dear Holdridge:
>
> Re your urgent letter requesting advice and consideration of your proposal to set up a provisional government of the United States and to be administered by you. I have talked to Monongye and his Kiva leaders only so far. At their suggestion I am enclosing for you a copy of my letter to Germany. It's not a very good copy but hope you can read it. I have sent one to Craig, he may already have shown it to you. It gave you a general pattern of life to be played by different nations in this world. Already it is shaping up in this fashion and soon these THREE NATIONS will band to-

gether all or most of the population of the world to help them in bringing about Purification Day in this land of the Red Man. It is so near! Already Hopi faces the two last Attempts to break down the Hopi Way of Life and Land. LAND AND STOCK. By that time it has been foretold that a highway will be forced upon your land. Your land will be forced to be divided and shall be cut up four times each cut smaller than the other one. From the SOUTH a power will rise to come and help when the time comes. When the young men take control of your form of government and at the very end when the white men with Long Dress take control of your lives the end is Very Near.

Then among you a White man, anyone, has a right to rise up and lead his people on the right road to Real Peace, Brotherhood and Everlasting Life. If you are on the right road, a civil strife may break out right here and all people will undermine the White House. Hopis have been warned not to take sides but remain fast to his Ancient Instructions and NEVER take up arms. It will be up to the white man to clean his own house before the TRUE BROTHER COMES to judge, punish and destroy all Evil Ones. This is part of the prophecy told in the Kiva.

Will give you more later.

(signed) Banancya
(SOURCE: Banyacya 1-31-1961)[9]

It seems as though the story has changed only eighteen days after the letter to Muller-Fricken was written! In a letter to Craig Carpenter, Banancya wrote concerning Holdridge: "So far he has traveled on the right road, a hard road, but soon, if he stick to it, MANY good people will come to him for help" (Carpenter 3-20-1961).

Such flexibility may be a mechanism of survival, where symbiosis is a way of simultaneously preserving authority and making it viable for contemporary life.

Hopi prophetic rhetoric is emotive. An aspect that our intellectualized analyses tend to overlook is the emotive side of the issue. Prophecies and traditions use language capable of provoking intensely emotional reactions. One reason for this is the imagery being used. The judicious use of images and references can conjure up ethnic or national identity and thus awaken powerful emotional and volitional resources.[10]

9. The italics are mine. The letter was written in broken English, and I have corrected it for this quote. Carpenter was Holdridge's secretary.

10. Cognitive psychologist William Brewer has developed a hypothesis about the nature of story schema (Brewer 1985; Brewer and Lichtenstein 1981. Cf. Polkinghorne 1988:13ff.). One component of his story theory is his posited relation between particular discourse structures and particular affective states. See also I. M. Lewis' admonitions in his introduction (1977:2).

One of the speakers during the 1955 hearings was one Secquaptewa from Hotevilla. His prologue illustrates the depths of the feelings involved:

> I want to say some things that have been in my heart, and I am glad that you have come to listen to us today. I cannot speak of anything else but of the same things that have been already spoken by other men and that is of the life of the Hopi: where he came from and why he came here. . . . I want to mention this that whenever I speak on these vital problems or the Hopi life I cannot help but cry at times. I cannot control myself because I live with sincere prayer and everything that has been taught me is within me so that when I speak I think of all those things and it makes my heart weak or sad so that I cannot control myself when I speak. (Bureau of Indian Affairs 1955:53–54)

It may very well be that the emotive side of prophetic rhetoric has much to do with the aura of authority it attempts to promote. At any rate, it cements the convictions that posterior precognition invites and upon which it thrives. Belief has deep roots in the emotive side of the cognitive environment where it finds sustenance, inspiration, and a sense of rightness.

PROPHECY AS SOCIAL STRATEGY

Prophecy clearly fulfills deep-seated needs, and it plays a pivotal role in social and political strategies. It is therefore useful for our analysis to characterize the ways in which prophecies are used, to identify interest groups that manipulate the cosmological mythology, and to identify the themes that are meaningful to these groups. I will focus on the use or function of an ideology by various social groups. Thus the framework of this section is sociological, but the heart of the matter revolves around religious ideology. The strategies involved may be catalogued in the following functional categories:

1. Myth as a strategy to establish (or maintain) ethnic identity and/or internal sociopolitical structures;
2. Myth as a strategy to resist the dominant White society;
3. Myth as a strategy to attract subversive interest groups in the dominant White society;
4. The use of Hopi myths by White interest groups as a strategy to search for an identity;
5. The use of Hopi myths by White interest groups as a strategy to resist their own society; and
6. Myth as a strategy to recreate psycho-social stability and meaning.

Thus, categories 1-3 and 6 are strategies employed by Hopis, whereas categories 4 and 5 are strategies employed by Whites. The first category will be exemplified especially in chapter 3. The second category will be found throughout the book because it is all-pervading, but especially in chapter 7. Categories 4 and 5 will be seen in chapters 8, 9, and 10. Category 6 is to be differentiated from category 1 especially in historical terms. Category 6 represents a conscious reflection and regeneration, and is exemplified at the end of chapter 5. All of the categories will be referred to wherever applicable in this study.

In this study, we will see that myth is used by the Hopis not only as a strategy to define themselves but also to define themselves in relation to other peoples. The mythical paradigm grants all the conceivable types of relationships that make sense to Hopi reality and in this manner normalizes actual historical relationships. At the same time, the myth grants all the conceivable contrasts between human types and in this manner differentiates actual historical peoples. Perhaps more importantly, myth provides a vehicle for symbolization that allows the assimilation of potentially dangerous realms or peoples in the Hopi cosmos.

The confusing relationship offered by the European and American presence is normalized by the prophetic return of the White Brother. The disturbingly contradictory behavior of these Whites is explained within the differentiating framework of Hopi cosmology. And, finally, having been defined as relatives (i.e., as brothers) who are intimately sharing a part of Hopi destiny, these Whites are effectively assimilated.

Thus, I question the adequacy of the widely accepted explanation of religious innovation as a redressive mechanism. In this I agree with Manchester anthropologist Richard Werbner who, in his essay "The Argument of Images" (1985), proposed an alternative to the "images of adaptive conversion" argument held by, for example, anthropologists Robin Horton (1967) and James Fernandez (1978). Drawing on Fabian (1979:170ff.), Werbner maintained that imagery can also be directed at spiritual regeneration or at remaking the environment rather than merely adjusting to it. Perceived disorder is thus recognized, or "even embraced for what it is," through disharmonic imagery (Werbner 1985:254). Thus, Werbner demonstrated how the use of locational imagery clearly expressed the quite different tactics of three Zionist churches in Zimbabwe.

Whether or not such might be the case for all emergence-myth imagery, it is at least the strategy adopted in Traditionalist mythic and prophetic imagery. It could also be argued that the early fatalism of prophetic accounts were replaced by the Hostiles and later Traditionalists by a clearly more aggressive rhetoric. The use of dislocational imagery was used to emphasize tactics of dissent. One can, for instance, refer to the frequent use in Traditionalist accounts of the image of the White Man as the *intruding*, uninvited guest of the North American continent, or to the cataclysmic imagery of races or nations *overrunning* the United States (cf. Appendix B).

Most discussions on cultural change are more or less hampered by antiquated beliefs about what happens when a weaker nation or people is confronted by a stronger one. In such cases, cultural assimilation or acculturation is simply assumed as the end result by scholars as well as by colonial administrators.[11] What is hardly understood is the fact that Hopi prophecy mobilizes ethnic identity in terms of cultural confrontation. Hopi prophecy formulates and conceptualizes cultural confrontation in terms of symbols that are highly significant to Hopi identity. Thus, it evaluates confrontation, conceives it, assimilates it, and ultimately defuses it.

These insights are hardly new. Even in the face of the longstanding traditions of acculturation theories (cf. F. M. Keesing 1953), anthropologist Edward Spicer argued during the early 1960s that those theories could not explain how the Indians of the Southwest and Mexico could survive 500 years of conquest and domination (Spicer 1961, 1962). In the early 1970s, he proposed the concept of "persistent identity systems" in two articles (1971, 1972) and until his recent death was working on a massive documentation of his theory in the histories of the Jews, Basques, Irish, Welsh, Catalans, Mayas, Yaquis, Senecas, Cherokees, and Navajos.

Spicer formulated his conceptual framework most clearly in his article "Persistent Cultural Systems" (1971). The concept of "identity systems" he found useful in accounting for the kind of continuity between precolonial and postcolonial entities. An identity system is "an individual's belief in his personal affiliation with certain symbols, or, more accurately, with what certain symbols stand for" (ibid.:795–796). Thus, we are dealing with beliefs and sentiments that are associated with particular symbols. These identity symbols constitute, in Spicer's opinion, "a sort of storage mechanism for human experience, a means for organizing the accumulating experience of people" (ibid.:796), and the subsequent cumulative image that people construct of themselves and which is symbolized by identity symbols serves as the source of collective and individual motivation. Thus, any study of persistence in change should pay attention to:

11. See my criticisms of this belief in chapter 5 of the Danish edition of this book as well as in A. W. Geertz (1993) and the introduction to A. W. Geertz and Jensen (1990).

> (i) the set of identity symbols and their configuration of meanings, (ii) spheres of participation in the common understandings and sentiments associated with these symbols, and (iii) the institutionalized social relations through which participation in the system of meanings is maintained. (ibid.:798)

Spicer was arguing for a study of the "full and clear determination of the cultural logic" of a people; sound ethnography, in other words.[12]

In this book, I attempt to determine the cultural logic behind Hopi prophecy and to explain the contrast between what they and others have believed to have taken place and what the documents and evidence suggest. In the process it will become apparent that we are dealing with a particular style of flexibility and continuity that can tell us much about religion and identity.

FROM THE CRADLE TO THE GRAVE AND BEYOND (VIA THE BRAIN)

The idea of the power of identity symbols implies that people evince competence in relation to their symbolic-cultural systems; in other words, that ideal individuals are culturally competent. Cultural competence constitutes in Lawson's and McCauley's words, "(usually) unconscious representations of cultural and social forms (and their underlying principles) which participants share" (1990:3; cf. McCauley 1986). I will argue below and throughout the book that cultural competence is more dynamic than Lawson and McCauley's definition allows.

Cultural competence is a primary assumption in cognitive studies (e.g., cognitive anthropology, ethnoscience, ethnomethodology, and developmental psychology mentioned in the Introduction). Roger M. Keesing, however, rightly warned against taking the earlier naive view of "an idealized native actor mechanically enacting implicit rules" (1987: 371). It is essential to realize that this competence draws on frameworks of interpretation, what I have called the "cultural repertoire" from which indigenous interpreters produce hermeneutical solutions (A. W. Geertz 1990*d*), thus allowing room in our analyses for processes of "co-creation, negotiation, and contextual shifting."[13]

Recent cognitive study has attempted to map the processes involved in the relationship between symbolization and hermeneutics. Charles Laugh-

12. These insights are now becoming more widely held. See for instance the recent study by E. Thomas Lawson and Robert N. McCauley (1990). Janet Moone (1981) has recently developed and systematized Spicer's ideas in a useful model of the dimensions of maintenance with change in dynamic processes.

13. R. M. Keesing 1987:371. Cf. Boster 1985, Quinn and Holland 1987.

lin, Jr. and Christopher D. Stephens (1980:325) have argued that the principal function of the brain is the modeling of the phenomenal world. Seen from this perspective, a symbol is a stimulus that evokes the total intentionality of a model. This total intentionality is the symbol's meaning (ibid.:327). The symbol thus functions as "an efficient organizer of information within the nervous system" (ibid.:328). Evoking information about whole classes of entities, it simultaneously provides economy of organization and integrity of information.[14]

Symbolism is also more than just efficient information exchange. It also gives coherence to direct experience and allows the communication of experience to others (ibid.:328–329).

> Symbols order and direct the flow of experience. They determine how events are experienced; they focus attention and integrate information sufficient for meaningful re-cognition by organizing the information about events of the moment in terms of knowledge contained with the E_c [e.g., the cognized environment] of E_o [e.g., the operational or phenomenal environment] events experienced in the past. (ibid.:331)

Once a model-symbol connection has been constructed, such models move to a "lower order level outside the purview of consciousness" and become stimulated afterwards by a symbol or symbols in the hermeneutical environment. The response to this stimulation is termed semiotropism, which is further defined as "the automatic response to symbols of great phenomenological salience" (ibid.:332); phenomenology being understood by Laughlin and Stephens as consciousness, or the process of cognizing. It is the semiotropic response that "maintains congruity between the meanings evoked" in the cognized environment of a group's members (ibid.).

Roy Wagner has argued along similar lines. Drawing from his work on the symbols and myths of the Daribi of eastern New Guinea, Wagner was concerned with the cultural dimensions of symbolization more than the cognitive dimensions. But it is nontheless instructive to note the convergence between his cultural theory and the cognitive theory of Laughlin and Stephens. His point of departure (Wagner 1986) is that symbols and the larger orders of symbols (metaphors and tropes) do not stand for something else, but, as the title of his publication indicates, for themselves. By this he meant that symbols are not just points of reference in relation to something else, but they are mechanisms of cultural organization. For him, symbols and especially metaphors expand from "a play on conventional points of reference" to "an organizer of cultural frames" (ibid.:xi). This unit of self-reference "expands the frame of its

14. See Ohnuki-Tierney's parallel theory of icons in her 1981 publication.

self-referentiality by processual extension into a broader range of cultural relevance" (ibid.:9). This phenomenon, which he called "trope," perceives meaning within the framework of cultural reference points. It is coherent and pervasive, and wherever it appears it is the same phenomenon, thus evincing the characteristics of a "holograph" (ibid.:126).[15]

For Laughlin and Stephens, myth is the quintessential form of a conceptualized symbol system. Myth serves to organize experience around a society's "core symbols," which are "invariably oriented upon the zone of uncertainty—that is, the set of events giving rise to significant effects for which there exist no readily perceivable causes for a large number of a society's members" (1980:335). Myth operates, therefore, as a "socially imposed hermeneutic for experience," (ibid.:337) which is transmitted via language, ritualized drama, and art (cf. Manning 1981, Drummond 1981), and which is internalized in the ontogenesis of the child.

Following Ricoeur (1962), Laughlin and Stephens argued that the symbols and symbol systems of myth "invite thought about possible meaning":

> That is, (*a*) they evoke wide fields of intentionality, both within the normal waking phase of consciousness, and within alternate phases; (*b*) they "channel" experience (i.e., 'provide meaning') in the sense that information is processed through the structure of myth; and (*c*) they ensure, through an expanded polysemy, that the myth remains meaningful in spite of the presence or absence of a particular contingency. (1980:337)

An important point to note in Laughlin and Stephens's theory is that it covers the whole range of human signification. This integrative approach has been criticized for example by Sperber (1974) and Bloch (1974, 1977, 1980), but I think it makes good sense to develop integrative theories. My presentation does little justice to the intricacy and preciseness of Laughlin and Stephens's arguments. But, it is sufficient to illustrate that there do exist neurofunctional and cognitive arguments that support my use of the ideas of cultural competence and indigenous hermeneutics.[16]

Cultural competence is learned through a complex interplay between awareness of the actual phenomenal environment, orientation response,

15. Wagner's tropes seem to resemble Edwin Ardener's "*P*-structure" (the *paradigmatic* dimension of symbolism), which is the abstract organizing principle that generates realized syntagmatic sequences (Ardener 1980). The paradigmatic mode is organized around metaphor, that is, a relationship of partial likeness; (cf. Foster 1980:373). The major difference between Ardener and Wagner is that Ardener draws his model from transformational linguistics.

16. See also Colby, Fernandez, and Kronenfeld 1981, Gardner 1984, Collins and Gentner 1987, Freeman, Romney, and Freeman 1987.

stimulus reception, and "several moment-to-moment transformations [e.g., symbolization] of neural subsystems operating upon information" pertaining to the phenomenal environment.[17]

Cultural competence is also learned through socialization and language acquisition, which secure the continuities of group experience in the face of direct experience. The dynamics of ontogenesis consists then of an interplay between the individual cognizing process, the corporate enterprise based on a "shared knowledge of categories," and action sequence. The acquisition of language itself in ontogenesis occurs in the very "context of interacting organisms" and therefore fundamentally influences the way that the child and, later, adult will experience and understand the world.[18]

I have not had the opportunity to conduct research that can reveal the relationship between cognitive development and symbolization among the Hopis. But, the ethnographic data on socialization practices, ceremonialism, initiation, social pressure, narrative style, and so on (cf. A. W. Geertz 1990*a*), and a number of psychological studies such as those on dreaming seem to support cognitive theory. At any rate, given the generally held position that symbolism does play a central role in the ontogenesis of the individual, it can be said that the symbol of the White Brother (and the concomitant referential framework of the apocalypse) is evidently prominently present in Hopi cognitive development.

Apocryphal expectations are intense among contemporary Hopis, and they follow them from the cradle to the grave. Helen Sekaquaptewa explained how these beliefs were inculcated in the children:

> The month of December is sacred and special. . . . This time is set apart for teaching the young. The uncles (mother's brothers) go to the homes of their sisters in the evening to teach her children. An uncle is treated with respect, and the family gathers around to listen as he tells about the advent of the Hopi, recites traditions and prophecies, and give instructions. We call it "Pbutsquani" which is like the Ten Commandments. Besides the universal laws as given in the Ten Commandments, he says:

17. Laughlin and Stephens 1980, 331. Cf. Bates 1979*b*, Lamendella 1980, and especially Ohnuki-Tierney's explication (1981:455–458).

18. Laughlin and Stephens 1980, 333. Cf. Bowerman 1980 and the papers presented in T. Schwartz 1975, Bates 1979, Hinde, Perret-Clermont, and Stevenson-Hinde 1985, Jahoda and Lewis 1988. Seen from the point of view of a culturally competent adult, the complexity of symbol acquisition and use is overwhelming. Psychologist Elizabeth Bates humorously noted that the finished product is nontheless held together with "tape and safety pins":

> If we trace this marvel to its beginning in human infancy, we will see that this particular work of art is a collage, put together out of a series of old parts that developed quite independently. (1979*a*:1)

> Don't add to the already heavy burden of the sun by causing him to have to awaken you; get up before he does. Don't be lazy; don't lie in bed after sunup. When you get up, first thing, run out into the cold air to the water and dash in with your naked body. Don't eat or drink hot stuff. Keeping your body cold will make it strong so you can resist disease. Be industrious. Be courageous. Keep your mind clean.
>
> By keeping these commandments you will be ready to meet your white brother when he comes from the East to destroy the wicked ones, and he will not destroy you. Then destruction will be so terrible that you might just die of a heart attack from seeing it, unless you are strong and good. (Udall 1969:228–229)

As we can see, narrative plays a dominant role in the cognitive environment of the child, a fact that recent cognition and developmental psychology studies have emphasized.[19] In the Hopi case it is evident that myths, tales, and other narrative forms are told in order to serve as a "resource for the culture-acquiring child" and instill community values in the young (Miller and Moore 1989:429).[20] These values are intimately related to the apocalyptical expectations of adult Hopis.

Albert Yava described how the process continues right into the grave and even beyond.

> Anyway, that special Bahana never arrived. He is still expected, though, especially among old, tradition-minded people. For this reason, important personages—village officials, clan chiefs and leaders in the kiva societies—usually are buried facing the east so that they can recognize and welcome the Good Bahana when he makes his appearance. Their bodies are dressed in the proper ceremonial costumes to explain who they were when they were living. Sometimes they are buried sitting up. Or they can be buried lying with their feet toward the east, so that if they were to sit up they would be looking eastward. Even people who aren't important personages can be buried this way if it is known that they wanted it, or if their families want it. Hopis and Tewas alike on First Mesa follow this tradition. How-

19. Cf. Colby and Cole 1973, Ochs and Schieffelin 1984, Brewer 1985, Miller and Moore 1989, Miller et al. 1990.

20. These matters are self-evident. Psychologists Peggy Miller and Barbara Moore have argued that in psychological studies not enough attention has been paid to the socializing potential of "informal, mundane, and often pervasive narrative accounts that people give of their personal experiences." In their opinion ordinary talk "is a pervasive, orderly, and culturally organized feature of social life in every culture" and "a major, if not the major, mechanism of socialization" (ibid.: 429). These insights constitute, by the way, some of the main assumptions of the ethnomethodologists. What Miller and Moore have done is to elucidate these mechanisms through clinical experiment. There is in Miller and Moore's words a "relentless" flow of social and moral messages in "the myriad small encounters of everyday life" (ibid.). It is within the narrative environment that the social construction of self occurs in childhood (cf. Miller et al. 1990). This is indeed the case with the Hopis.

> ever, like other aspects of our ceremonial life, the custom is often ignored among younger people. (1978:105)

COGNITION AND COLLECTIVE MISREPRESENTATION

Perhaps the most poignant indication of the cognitive power of mythical symbols is the curious behavior of the Hopis during actual historical contacts with White people. Their reactions clearly indicate a collective misrepresentation of the "Other."

Like the Jews of Palestine during the 1920s, the Hopis have nurtured a messianic expectation that measures each and every White person who happens to show up on the reservation. There is a whole series of subjects to choose from. Albert Yava mentioned a few:

> Still, we have had a long line of missionaries parading through the villages. First were the Catholics, but they were thrown out—unfortunately not without some sad events, such as the massacre and destruction at Awatovi. Then there were Mennonites, Mormons, Jehovah's Witnesses, Seventh Day Adventists, and Baptists. You will find churches in or close to all the villages now. The missionaries came telling the Hopis and Tewas that the old traditional ways were barbaric, and each one claimed to have the true faith, the only one that paid respect to the Great Spirit. Because of that old tradition that a good bahana would come some day, the Hopis and Tewas listened, some of them wondering if this missionary or that missionary was the right one. (Courlander, ed. 1982:142)

It was unavoidable that the Hopis more than once mistook some persons as the White Brother. Homer Cooyama from Kykotsmovi, for instance, told Harold Courlander in 1970 that many Hopis thought that the missionary at Oraibi at the turn of the century, H. R. Voth, was the White Brother:

> There were two main things the Hopis were looking for in the old days, a promised land and a promised person. These things were prophesied. Religious Hopis are still looking for the promised place where they are supposed to settle. We've discussed these things many times in the kiva. The person they are expecting is said to be a bahana, a white man, who will arrive in great glory. Everybody knows this belief. And so when the first white man came to stay in Oraibi, they were looking for someone who could speak Hopi and all kinds of languages. Well, Voth spoke a little Hopi. And when he came they thought he was a god. He'd studied the Hopi language before he came, but he spoke brokenly. But we thought that was marvelous. That's the man, we thought, that we'd been expecting. But after a while we found out that he wasn't the man. (ibid.:125–126)

Another interesting example is found in the minutes of the 1955 hearings mentioned above. It is clearly evident from the minutes that when the BIA team reached Walpi, Earl Mumzewa believed them to be the awaited White Brother. His speech depicted the primordial bonds between the BIA team and himself:

> My people, I am glad that you have found us. You want to know what we have to offer. I believe that is the purpose of us meeting here. I am only existing. I am taking care of what subjects I have under me, because they are subject to me. I remember how we are to greet each other, and also what we are to do. I realize now at this age you know our plight. We had an agreement to fulfill. This agreement, if you have any record, was made at the place in our language called "Bapchiva", or a rugged place. How we talked over things with one another and how we are to proceed on the way of an agreement. We have agreed on certain things, and before parting, after making the agreement, we shook hands as brothers before we separated. We went our way with the common understanding that some day we might meet one another and greet ourselves again the way we have separated. You told me, because you are intelligent you know how to cope with life by acquiring the true experience, and because of that there would be a different phase after we meet each other again in the future. We are to prepare, then, and you told me if I was burdened with many things that are a detriment to me you ask me to leave it behind. I did so afterwards. You said to me that when we separate you will go to the eastward direction, and you said that is where you will abide. I asked if you settle how are you to let me know. You said, "there is to be a sign in the heavens that you can observe. That would be the sign that I am to return." When I saw that sign in the heavens, I had my hopes and was wishing that I would see you again in the near future. If you return we will have things in common again. You instructed me, the younger brother, to lead my people the best that I know how. You said, "If I come back I might come back speaking a different language. Then I will lead you and deal with you accordingly." Then when you started off to the eastward direction, I, the younger brother, asked you to return as soon as you can. We bade each other farewell. Ever since we have separated I have had hard times, and was on my way to a place called Flower Mountain, on my journey after suffering many things. I arrived at a place where I expected to make my home with the people that I have led. We met a group of people and were received cordially. You said that falling stars would be the sign that you were returning, and when I saw that again I felt in the hope that you would come sooner. The agreement that we made is still intact in my memory. I am still in the position that I was in at the time you left me. Your life is good, as I say. We are to treat one another with the best of love. (Bureau of Indian Affairs 1955:331–332)

This remarkable speech illustrates with painful clarity that, for Mumzewa, there was no doubt that primordial times had converged in contemporary times. His monologue is in the present perfect, past perfect, and future perfect tenses simultaneously, in both time and space. For him, his feet were firmly planted both near the place of the emergence,

Sipaapuni (during the primordial dialogue between the two brothers), and at Walpi, in front of a seated panel (reliving the primordial dialogue). In shaking hands with the committee members, mythical heroes were meeting once again in order to begin life anew.

Anthropologist Shuichi Nagata described another example of mistaken identities. Nagata attended a meeting held by the Traditionalists at Hotevilla in 1962 which was also attended by a Chinese Buddhist priest. Some of the Traditionalists, including their leader Dan Qötshongva, became convinced that the priest was the Pahaana:

> I must add that a Chinese Buddhist priest and an American Japanese interpreter also attended the meeting, both of whom were invited from Los Angeles by the Eskimo Bahai'ist and the Hopi seemed to be rather intrigued by this priest in a standard Mahayana Buddhist monk's costume. But all he did at the meeting was to go around among the Indian audience and shake hands with them. Otherwise he remained silent, without addressing the meeting, sitting quietly and wearing an inscrutable smile.
>
> Soon after the meeting, however, the landlady's father, who also attended the meeting, broke a rather surprising piece of news to her and her husband upon his return to Moenkopi. The old man recounted that Dan [Qötshongva] had decided this Chinese priest was the Pahana and now that Dan had met the real 'White Brother', he was handing over the job of protecting the Hopi to Thomas [Banancya] and others, while Dan himself retired. He further added that the priest as well as his Japanese interpreter were white of skin complexion and that the priest showed tattoo marks of the sun and swastika on his chest and belly. According to the old father, the priest also whispered into Dan's ear, saying that he came to help the Hopi. While recounting all this, the father showed to the landlady and her husband the swastika mark on a Hopi gourd rattle, which was hanging on the wall of our house.
>
> In the afternoon of the day that we were introduced to this amazing news, the old father's sister's son visited us from Hotevilla and told essentially the same story but added that the priest had told the people he would come back in the near future. My landlady was obviously rather agitated with all this and in the next morning, at the breakfast table, she reported the news to her son and asked his opinion, whereupon the son made a rather strong response to her, adding that 'white' means only 'Caucasian'.
>
> A few days afterwards, during which time nothing of consequence happened, Thomas visited our house and the landlady took immediate advantage of it by asking him about the authenticity of the story. Thomas was undisturbed and reassured the landlady by telling her that all Dan meant was only to support Thomas in what the Traditionals had been doing. According to Thomas, the Chinese priest never said he came to help but only that he was friend of the Hopi. (Nagata 1978:78–79)

Dan Qötshongva was convinced at the time that both the Russians and the Chinese were prophesied in Hopi tradition and tried to persuade Nagata to help him write a letter to the Russian and Chinese embassies. Although Banancya persuaded Nagata not to send it, Nagata kept it on file and published it in 1978. As the following excerpt shows, Qötshongva was asking for nothing less than an apocalyptic recollection. He was literally trying to get the Russians and the Chinese or Japanese to re-cognize their part in the primordial plot:

> Those of you across the seas, those of you across the seas, those of you who live on the continents and lands, I look to you. But it is you who are in the centre, who, in our instructions, are called the "red one," whom we came to know as Russia, and also the one who has the Sun for a symbol, whom I do not know the name for, the short people who have the same head and appearance as we, and also this swastika-like symbol (*moeha*), which never ceases to exist on this earth, this cross which the Hopi call *moeha*, which has a useful purpose on this earth, so that the earth may be encouraged on, so that the Hopi shall always go by his faith. This is how it is, this is why I am telling you. And so, if you get my message, you, who are in the centre, the one called "red," will be called upon to work for us. That is why I call on you specifically and so, if you get this message, gather yourself and think it over and see if I am not speaking correctly or similar to your own instructions. I am willing because it is said you would be waiting. This is in our instructions. That is why I am not scared while I am telling you this.
>
> We have suffered much because of this way of the government and so now I tell you this. However, this will not get too far. Those of us who have suffered, remember this brother of ours, who shall come to our aid. This is what we are waiting for, all of us, people, throughout. That is why I ask you this. So gather together and think about this—if there is one thing similar to yours. It does not have to be exactly the same and all to your instructions for they will all come out true. Then, when you gather there and think it over, and if you feel that I who know all these things, should go over there in person and should tell you—if you want this, then I shall do it. (ibid.: 84–85)

The Hopis have been waiting for centuries, first accepting and then rejecting one White group after another as the White Brother. Some Hopis are convinced that the Americans are the White Brother and that the new era has already begun. Others reject the idea and find more meaning in clinging to their eschatological hopes and dreams.

THREE

The Narrative Context of Hopi Prophecy

THE CORE NARRATIVE

The basic elements of Hopi prophecy are narrated as integrated parts of the emergence mythology. Emergence mythology is actually a depiction of a series of events which repeat themselves through four world ages. Each world begins more or less as a paradise that slowly and inevitably becomes disrupted through human inequity. Each world is destroyed by natural catastrophe, thus forcing the faithful to climb up to the next world level, the fundament of which is the sky of the lower level. Through the forced magical growth of a giant reed, the faithful create a means of transportation–an eschatological escape on an *axis mundi* (cf. A. W. Geertz 1984)–and begin life anew at the next level. The life in the present fourth world has already become disrupted and will end in a manner similar to the primordial catastrophes. Thus, the very framework of the narrative is apocalyptic, i.e., it begins and ends with collective destruction.

There are seven characteristics that should be made explicit in our study of the emergence myth and the prophecies:

1. Apocryphal thought has its roots in Hopi conceptions about primordial times;
2. These conceptions are codified in a common narrative;
3. This narrative, called the emergence myth, is the starting point of all clan traditions;
4. This narrative is identical for all clans without exception;
5. This narrative consists of a number of standard features which never change and a number of features which are structurally standard, but highly variable in detail;

6. The susceptibility of certain features to stability or to change can be predicted; and
7. The continuity of this narrative is enhanced through ritual, social, and psychological mechanisms.

I consider the emergence myth to be what Victor Turner called a "root paradigm" (1974:64, 67–68). This is a higher order conglomeration of symbols which form a model for behavior and which express the goals of a people. Root paradigms are fundamental and reach into the very core of the individual.

> Root paradigms are shown in behavior which appears to be freely chosen but resolves at length into a total pattern. They go beyond the cognitive, and even the moral, to the existential domain, and in so doing become clothed with allusiveness, implicitness, and metaphor.[1] They reach down to the irreducible life stances of individuals, passing beneath conscious prehension to a fiduciary hold on what the individual senses to be axiomatic values, matters literally of life and death. Root paradigms emerge at life crises, whether of groups or individuals, whether institutionalized or compelled by unforeseen events. One cannot escape their presence or their consequences. (Turner and Turner 1978:248–249)

The emergence myth is composed of a series of symbols and motifs organized in a hierarchy of episodes structured around stories. Only some of the symbols and episodes are pivotal. The main stories are as follows:

1. The apocalyptical conditions of the primordial third world prior to the emergence;
2. The actual emergence to the fourth world;
3. The post-emergence creations of the heavenly bodies, the distribution of languages and foodstuffs, and the establishment of death;
4. The meeting with Maasaw and/or the story of the two brothers and related prophecies;
5. The migrations of the clans; and
6. The settlement of Oraibi and the meeting between the Bear clan and Maasaw.

Despite slight variations in the order of events the basic narrative structure remains and the pivotal episodes are usually present in all variations.

The resemblances among many versions of the myth are so striking that I do not consider it necessary to prove the point in detail. Nonethe-

1. Turner's understanding of the term "cognitive" is more restricted than its use in this study.

Story No.:	1	2	3	4	5	6
Description:	Third World, birds	Emer-gence	Post-emer-gence	Maasaw and/or Brothers	Migra-tions	Arri-vals/ Maa-saw
First Mesa						
Hoñi 1893		X	X	X	X	X
Second Mesa						
Lomávantiwa 1903	X	X	X	X	X	
Unknown 1912	X	X	X	X	X	X
Nequatewa 1936	X	X	X	X	X	X
Third Mesa: Oraibi						
Talay'ima 1882	X	X	X	X	X	
Yukiwma 1903	X	X	X	X	X	X
Tawakwaptiwa 1932	X	X	X	X	X	X
Third Mesa: Hotevilla						
Yukiwma 1911	X	X	X	X	X	X
Qötshongva 1935	X	X	X	X	X	X
Qötshongva 1970	X	X	X	X	X	X

Hoñi 1893: Cactus lineage of the Snake clan, crier chief, Walpi, First Mesa (Stephen 1929, 7-10).
Lomávantiwa 1903: Shipolovi, Second Mesa (Voth 1905, 10-15).
Unknown 1912: Hopi residing at Carlisle Indian School, Shongopovi, Second Mesa (Wallis 1936, 2-17).
Nequatewa 1936: Sun forehead clan, Kwan Society, Shongopovi (Nequatewa 1936, 7-37, 50-51).
Talay'ima 1882: Spider clan, Momtsit chief, Oraibi, Third Mesa (Cushing 1924).
Yukiwma 1903: Kookop clan, Oraibi, Third Mesa (Voth 1905, 16-26).
Tawakwaptiwa 1932: Bear clan, village chief, Oraibi, Third Mesa (Titiev 1944, 73-74).
Yukiwma 1911: Village chief, Hotevilla, Third Mesa, recorded after split of Oraibi (Scott 1911).
Qötshongva 1935: Sun clan, co-ruler, Hotevilla, Third Mesa (Kotchongva 1936).
Qötshongva 1970: Told two years before his death (Tarbet 1972).

Chart A. Frequency comparison of emergence myth variants.

less, some evidence may be useful to readers who are unfamiliar with the literature. Chart A is based on ten versions of the emergence myth selected according to these principles: 1) they represent all three mesas; 2) they represent different political persuasions; 3) they are examples from chiefs or priests; 4) they include a small selection of variants from the same informant; and 5) they span a relatively large period of time. The chart is not broken into episodes or motifs because this would require an unnecessarily complicated model. Still, this simple chart shows that all six stories are found in all but three of the narratives.

Turning our attention back to the six-story structure of the emergence myth, it is worthwhile to consider what changes in each episode and what does not. We find that the first story is always apocalyptic, but that the details about the disruptions sometimes vary considerably. Most narratives, however, just pass this part over simply by stating that those times were just like today.

The main episode, or series of episodes of the story of the third world concerns how the chiefs discovered that there was another world, how they magically created birds in order to send them up to the new world and find the tutelary of that world, and what passed between Maasaw and the successful bird. The details of these episodes are uniform in all traditional narratives except for which bird met Maasaw (because the bird represents a specific social group that gains considerable prestige through the association) and what passed between them (which is also vulnerable to political manipulation).

Humanity was granted temporary residence by the owner and tutelary of the present fourth world, Maasaw, on the condition that they live his frugal way of life and adopt his religion.

In the second story, the emergence is triggered by the magical growth of the reed that pierces the sky. The actual emergence is then set within ceremonial contexts. Some versions disagree about which ceremonial it was, but most agree that it was the extended Wuwtsim ceremonial. In other words, it was the version of the ceremonial that contains the tribal initiation rituals. This is a fitting ceremonial for such a highly charged, collective flight from one realm to another. The story always ends with the chief shaking the evil people off of the reed and knocking it over. The part that is open to discussion and negotiation is the order of the emergence of the clans.

The third story is standard. Some details may vary, but there is no variance in the main elements of the story: The moon and the sun are created by the priests, languages and foodstuffs are distributed, and the death of the chief's child introduces witchcraft and death to the new world and transforms the third world into the paradisic afterlife of the underworld (cf. A. W. Geertz 1984:221, 223). Changes in detail are associated with the witch, especially concerning the politically volatile detail of which clan she decided to travel with.

The fourth story is oftentimes identical with the Maasaw episode in the sixth story. The greatest variation is found here.

At this point the chronology of events changes according to the storyteller, but most of the Hostile and Traditionalist versions place Maasaw's prophetic statement before the great migrations of the various clans. The main elements of the Maasaw episode, however, are the same: the people ask for land, and they become lease holders; Maasaw tells them that he will return one day and reclaim his rights; they ask him to become their chief; he refuses and points out that they have brought evil ambitions and intentions with them, so he will return one day and punish them.

In both cases it seems that Maasaw's ambivalence stemmed from the presence of human evil. They were only allowed the temporary use of the land on the following grounds:

> You have come to this place having great plans. You emerged from down below with evil schemes. You have grand visions. That is why I cannot turn it over to you. When something finally happens to you [i.e., the end of the world], I will regain its possession. You will progress into the future wishing for different ways at which time you will meet your fate, and then I will get the land back.
>
> *Taq uma a'ni hiita tunatyawkyaakyangw pew nönga. Pay uma hiita qa lomatunatyawkyaakyangw pew nönga. Uma a'ni naat hiita tunatyawyungwa. Noq oovi nu' son umuy naat put maqani. Pay umuy hintotiqw pay nu' naap putni. Uma yep hiihin naawakinwiskyaakyangw uma hiita aw ökiqw pu' pay nu' paasat put naaptini. Pay uma paasat piw inumi itutskway no'ayani. Pay nu' put soosok ahoy naaptini.*[2]

In response to their request that he become their chief, Maasaw replied in a similar vein:

> All of you came with great ambitions. The day you've seen those ambitions through and fulfilled them, I'll assume that leadership position. Once you've realized your plans and lived the life you want to live, I'll return and give some thought to your request. If you're still leading a good life then, I'll consider your suggestion. For the time being, however, you'll be on your own. . . . I'm the first, but I'm also going to be the last. Now I'll go forth from here and head towards the rising sun. But I assure you I'll return. (Malotki and Lomatuway'ma 1987*b*:82–83, Hopi text not quoted here)

How Maasaw is to return and what the signs of his return may be are subject to lively debate among the Hopis, but one more important matter seems to be generally agreed on. There were two brothers present at this significant meeting with Maasaw. The older one was White and the younger one was a Hopi. Maasaw asked Kookyangwwuuti, "Spider Woman," the female tutelary deity of the Hopis, to make two *owatutu-*

2. Related to me by a Hotevilla informant in 1982. He was of the Piikyas clan and an initiated member of the Kwan Society.

veni, "stones with multiple markings," or stone tablets. This she accomplished with the help of her two grandchildren, the Pöqangwhoyat twins. One of Malotki's consultants stated: "What exactly was drawn on the stones is not known. But their markings are said to describe the land in its entirety. They delineate the dimensions all the way to the edge of the sea" (ibid.:74, with Hopi text). Chapter 6 will show that there is very little consensus about what was on the tablets and about their significance.

One was given to the Hopi Brother and the other was given to the White Brother, Pahaana, with the instruction that the clan migrations were to begin. When the first group reached the sun in the east, all migrations were to end. The group living in the east would keep an eye on his Hopi Brother, who, as it turned out, happened at the time to be near the center of the world, Oraibi.

The narrative relates further that if and when the Hopis stray from their life path, the White Brother will return and bring his stone tablet as proof of his identity. Some traditions say that there is only one tablet, which is broken in two, and that the brothers will match their pieces. What occurs after that meeting is highly disputed, giving us plenty of interesting material for speculation and analysis.

Before moving on it is important to reflect briefly on the manner in which the Hopis have incorporated the White man into their core narrative. We must remember that the European and American presence in the Hopi area has stimulated positive as well as negative situations and attitudes. The question is, how does the emergence myth account for the history of Hopi-White relations?

In the first place, it is significant that Hopi narrators chose the motif of "brothers." The motif of the sibling pair (brother/brother, brother/sister, or sister/sister) is one of the most pervasive motifs in Hopi mythology.[3] Each type of pair contains its own valency, but it can be generally stated that the sibling pair plays both a dynamic role in the technique of the narrative as well as in the resolution of the problem addressed by the narrative.

The brother/sister pair seems to represent a central ideal in Hopi matriclan logic. The brother and sister usually enter the beginning of the narrative as helpless and abandoned children, but usually end up becoming, with the help of superhuman agency, bearers of new ritual knowledge. Anthropologist Alice Schlegel (1977, 1979) examined the social roles of two kinds of male/female dyadic relationships in the context of the household, namely, the husband/wife team and the brother/sister team. In her emphasis on the social construction of gender, Schlegel

3. Without going into detailed documentation, I will simply refer to the following story numbers in Henry Voth's 1905 narrative collection: brother/brother (3–5, 12, 18–26, 100); brother/sister (2, 12, 26, 35, 39, 51); sister/sister, or two girls: (18, 27, 39, 49, 80).

concluded that sexual reproduction is through the wife whereas social reproduction is through the sister. Thus, we find a correspondence between mythical narrative and social ideals.

The other types of pairs have other qualities. Setting the sister team aside for present purposes, it can generally be said that the brother team is usually a variant of the Pöqangwhoyat war-twins narratives. One of the most prominent characteristics of those narratives is sibling competition. Thus, the ambivalence, jealousies, and competition of siblings is a seemingly logical framework for the relationship between Hopis and Whites.

Brothers are in principle on equal footing, but older brothers can have a highly significant role in terms of privileges, duties, and rights. Older brothers are significant power factors in the lives of younger brothers. And once again, the ambivalence of Hopi-White relations fits in with the mythical motif. Older brothers are usually protective, however, and are thus admired and emulated, a factor Hopis also include in the brother motif. Almost every mention of the White Brother in Hopi myth not only expresses his protective nature, but also expresses admiration of the technical skills and wealth of the White man. Even in the narratives of the Traditionalists, the admiration is there, and where those very same skills are despised, Traditionalist rhetoric still retains admiration through positing two types of Whites, i.e., the evil, or the false and the good, or the real brother.

At any rate, the end of the world, which is called *nuutungk talöngvaqa*, "the last day," will be heralded by the appearance of the White Brother and carried out by Maasaw who will return as *powataniqa*, "the one who will purify." Some stories are not very specific, but others speak of his weapon *qöötsaptanga*, "container of ashes," and others speak of beheadings. All are in agreement, though, that the purification will result in a new paradise.

This is the "prophecy" in skeletal form. There are many more details, some of which are mutually exclusive, but the basic outline remains the same.

Stories 5 and 6 vary explicitly from version to version due to social, political, and religious factors. The fifth story deals with the details of the wanderings of each clan. In other words, each clan has its own fifth story that explains the route it followed, the specific cultic powers it developed, the animal, human, and divine groups or individuals who entered into relationships with it; and its claims to certain locations, ruins, and shrines. Thus, the pan-clan emergence myth is a prelude to each and every local clan myth.

Story 6 returns to the pan-clan narrative and deals with the order of each clan's arrival at each village. This part of the narrative is mostly a justification for Bear clan hegemony. But, as mentioned in chapter 1, when the political situation calls for it, the clan that first met with the local tutelary (Maasaw at Oraibi or Aalo'saka at Walpi) changes accordingly. Fewkes was the first to note the differing sequences of arrival in a systematic manner (1900:585), but since he was attempting the impossible task of drawing historical conclusions from migration legends, he felt obliged to excuse the discrepancies as being due to misunderstandings between him and his informants. We know better today. As I noted in my analysis of the emergence myth, this part of the narrative serves to justify the cosmographic, urbanographic, sociographic, and agriographic status quo in each village at the time of recording the legend (A. W. Geertz 1984:230).

As I argued in chapter 2, this core narrative is enhanced, mobilized, and reiterated in hundreds of ways in social praxis. One can even postulate that every ceremonial and social drama either refers explicitly to this narrative or assumes it. The narrative and its prophetic framework follow the Hopi individual from the cradle to the grave. It defines his or her worldview and provides the individual with powerful instruments in the creation of meaning and significance. The basic message does not change. It always defines ethnic identity and the Hopi place in the world. The crucial facts about prophetic statements are that they express authority and tradition and that they deal with the evils of war, the risks of ecological catastrophe, and the undeniable interdependency of all humans.

Even when conflicting details prevail, there can be no denying that their confrontation, contradiction, and resolution are meaningful. They are, indeed, the building blocks of meaning. Thus, the core narrative provides a series of major factors of continuity in the following ways: 1) It provides mythological coherence; 2) it provides structural coherence in social and religious domains; and 3) it provides a coherent frame of reference for each individual.

THE TRANSFORMATIVE MECHANISMS OF PROPHETIC MEDIA

One of the keys to understanding the nature of Hopi prophecies and the transformative mechanisms of prophetic utterance and replication is to examine the nature of the medium as well as its content. The rest of this and the next chapter will explore the means of communication and how each medium has influenced prophetic communication.

The Norwegian anthropologist Fredrik Barth wrote in a perceptive essay on religious covariation within a restricted area of New Guinea that "to understand reproduction and historical change we need to understand the functional system which is undergoing reproduction and change" (1987:26). The most appropriate functional system to begin with in the Hopi context is the narrative contexts and genres of prophecy. An analysis of their nature and of their susceptibility to change gives a good indication of how prophecies and traditions actually change. This approach to the problem of change Barth calls a "generative" approach where cultural transmission is perceived as being a creative process and where the detail of the evidence is of utmost importance to the success of the approach. This approach prefers to move away from the digital codes of structuralist analyses to the analogic codes of the empirical data and, in concurrence with S. F. Nadel (1951), to test propositions concerning interconnectedness between certain features of cultural systems without sacrificing the holistic or systemic description of cultures and societies (Barth 1987:9–10).

This type of approach is analogous to Dan Sperber's "epidemiology of representations" where the human mind's susceptibility to cultural representations is comparable to the human organism's susceptibility to diseases. Whereas the science of epidemiology traces in great detail the transmission of diseases, the epidemiology of representations studies the causal chains of mental and public representations. Most discussions of these representations—whether a myth, religious doctrine, ritual technique, etc.—consider them in abstract terms to the neglect of "the psychological processes [they] may undergo or of the interplay of [their] mental and public representation" (Sperber 1985:78). Sperber is more concerned with the distributions of representations than with their content, but I hold with Barth that these two aspects inform each other and therefore require careful study.

THE NARRATIVE CONTEXTS OF HOPI PROPHECIES

There are three basic contexts I choose to delineate in terms of genre in the widest sense of the term. The first is prose narrative (myth and ritual speech), the second is ethnopoetic narrative (ritual song), and the third is modern prose narrative (casual dialogue, letters, and the mass media). Although I am sympathetic to Dennis Tedlock's persuasive arguments about the analytical advantages of considering all oral narrative to be dramatic poetry (1983:51–55), there are other advantages in maintaining, at least for this analysis, a tripartite division of genres (cf. Vansina 1961, Finnegan 1970).

Seen as a category, Hopi myth is a formalized, stylistic, repetitive prose genre that serves as the source that informs the other genres. It is a restricted, collective, cultural treasure. Ritual speech is a subtype that is similar to myth in all aspects except that it does not inform the other genres; rather it contains the same receptivity as they do. Ritual song is a formalized, stylistic, repetitive poetic genre that introduces isolated detail, often with contemporary relevance. It is a product of an individual composer within a ritualized context. The modern prose narrative is informal, nonritual, multistylistic, literary, and geared specifically to contemporary events. It is an expanded, collective, cultural treasure, expanded in the sense that the collective group that possesses the cultural treasure is significantly increased to include other Hopis as well as non-Hopis.

The effect these various media have on their content, in terms of change, can be generalized as follows:

1. Myths provide authoritative contexts, rules, and metaphors to live by. The possibilities for change over shorter periods of time are minimal;
2. Ritual songs replicate these contexts, and although the possibility of individual innovation is available, it is also a highly visible medium and therefore restrictive for individual innovation; and
3. Modern prose narratives recreate the authoritative contexts and develop new contexts through a process of dialogue and exchange between Hopi, between Hopi and non-Hopi, and between non-Hopi and non-Hopi speakers and writers. It is the medium where Hopi pluralism meets Euro-American pluralism.

THE PROSE NARRATIVE CONTEXT

The problem with pinpointing the mode of communication employed in narrating the emergence myth lies in the fact that we know very little about it. The genre is implicitly formal, consisting of a narrative that reproduces motifs and structures commonly recognized and accepted by Hopis as essential to the proper telling of the story. The manner of narration is seldom formal, however, but is usually told in impromptu situations. Someone may ask about some matter that would require telling a part of or the entire myth for clarification, or it would be narrated with the specific goal of telling the whole story as it is, an event that in practice, though not in indigenous theory, can occur at any time. One can, however, only deduce how these narratives are related by Hopis among Hopis without the intrusive presence of researchers who have specifically asked for the story. Reviewing *Hopi Hearings* (Bureau of Indian Affairs 1955) and other sources available to us, it seems that Hopi speakers can turn any problem or theme into the context for narrating the emergence myth. It serves as the starting point, but is certainly also a reservoir from which meaningful contexts and plausible causal relationships can be drawn. In other words, the emergence myth is to a certain extent a pliable, thematic construct that can be applied to changing hermeneutical conditions.

Whether or not the emergence myth is related in formal, ritual contexts is open to question. No proof exists that such is the case. It is said by some that the Wuwtsim ceremonial is a dramatization of the emergence myth. And, indeed, one can deduce from scattered bits of information that certain activities may be understood as metaphorical dramatizations of parts of the myth, such as the removal of the kiva ladder as a metaphor for the toppling of the reed so that no other people could emerge. But how much detailed explanation is related during the ceremonial is unknown. It is hard to believe that new initiates have not already heard the story long before they were initiated. In fact, it is hard to believe that the many interest groups that are involved in the production of such a complicated ceremonial would agree upon one "standard" version of the myth. It is more probable that the brotherhoods have their own conglomerate versions. It would be of great interest to discover how such versions have developed in the face of the multiplex membership of the brotherhoods.

There are so few indications that the emergence myth is reenacted during the Wuwtsim—and no indications exist that it is reenacted in detail—that we must look for other possibilities. It is true that the absence of reported phenomena is not the same as empirical absences, however, so why should so easily accessible facts in some circumstances be well nigh inaccessible in other circumstances? Secrecy is, of course, at play here. But why secrecy in one context and not in another, unless the facts are on a different level of knowledge?

Could it be that it is only the primordial *situation* that is reenacted? In other words, it is not a dramatization with well developed roles, plots, and dialogue, which would go down through human history as lasting monuments, to be emulated for everyone's benefit. My hypothesis is that the most important situations are reenacted—in this case, the council of the chiefs meeting because of the chaos and insecurity of life, making plans for a future life in the new world above, and exercising their ritual powers—by a real council of chiefs meeting because of the same chaos and insecurity in order to make plans for a future life in a coming new age and to exercise their ritual powers. What better medium for the very real apocryphal expectations of Hopi worshippers?

Formalized speeches would, of course, be repeated and the same rituals would be utilized, but this is not a repeat performance of a classical drama. Rather it is a dramatization consisting of structural replication that uses the same actions in structurally similar but temporally dissimilar contexts. As I showed in chapter 2, the Hopis do conceive of the insanity and chaos of primordial times as identical to that of today. It would be a natural consequence to act out the solutions chosen in primordial times, and this is indeed what one of my consultants suggested.

My consultant, who is a member of the Kwan Kiva, having spoken somewhat on the Wuwtsim ceremonial, told me the following:

> And these Kwan members, who are in ceremonial abstinence, initiate the novices and go to the plaza at midnight to dance for them. Then the one who calls out, "Aaaa, iiiiii," sings the following song:
>
> Aa'a, ii'i,
> From the Sipaapuni,[4]
> They will begin life anew.
> The Tsorovi approach their altar water,[5]
> The Taw[6] members are distributing many things to help you grow, the disheveled leaders.[7]
> They would send their powerful ones, the water bird and the sandpiper.[8]
> The mist will help us grow and they will initiate our novice children,
> From the west, our fathers the Kwans, the Tokonaka leaders.[9]
>
> This is what they sing.
>
> *Pay ima kwaaniy'yungqam, pu' puma piw imuy hakimuy hoohoynaya, meh kiisonmi puma suutokihaq tiivawisngwu, hoyoyotangwu. Pu' tsa'timaqa, "Aaaa, iiiiii," kitaqw pu' paasat taawi:*
> *Aa'a, ii'i,*
> *Sipaapunvavee'e,*
> *Qatsitaa yahiinayaani,*
> *Tsoromum ngakuuyiy awii'i,*

4. This is the place of emergence which Hopis locate geographically in one of the side canyons of the Grand Canyon system.

5. This refers to the "medicine altar." See A. W. Geertz 1987*a*:18–20. Tsorovi is the name of a kiva brotherhood; see A. W. Geertz and Lomatuway'ma 1987:123 n. 31.

6. The Taw are one of the four brotherhoods which perform the Wuwtsim ceremonial.

7. It is unclear what "the disheveled leaders" (*mootsenmongwitu*) refers to. Perhaps it is a reference to the *mootsenkatsina* which is one of the warning figures involved in punishing the clowns.

8. This is a highly tentative translation. *Atoko* means "long-legged water bird, mythical bird" according to Albert and Shaul 1985. *Pataaruru* might be construed as being *patro*, "sandpiper." "They would send their powerful ones" (?), *paavalesavahoonikyangw*, is unfamiliar.

9. *Tokonaka* is the characteristically pointed helmet of Sootukwnangw, the lightning deity.

Tawtoykyangaaqö wungwuunangwaata umuuyuu tuuhuylawuu mootsenmongwi-itu,
Paa'atokoo pataaruru paavaalesaavaahoonikyaango,
Itamuy wungwiinayaanii pamöösi kyeleetuy itiimuy hoohooyinanii,
Taavang kwaniivee tookoonaakaamongwiit iinaamuu.
Yan pi taawiy'yungwa.

It is not essential for us to secure a completely intelligible translation of this obscure song. What is important for us to note is that the leaders mentioned in the song are described in the present ceremonial as being gathered around the Sipaapuni, the place of the emergence of mankind—which has a symbolic counterpart in every kiva—and engaged in beginning life anew.[10]

Later, my consultant explained about the initiation night of the Wuwtsim ceremonial:

> On Astotokya they also go somewhere and gather together. And when they get back to the village, they all shout encouragements to each other. I do not know how to explain it really! But they gather together. In the company of the Two Horns, they (the Kwans) ritually plan on how to start a new life. It is really a powerful thing. I do not think that anybody knows about it. Just these initiated ones know about it.
>
> And even these Wuwtsims do not know about it. They are kept inside (their kivas). Only these Two Horns and the Kwans make such plans. They have knowledge about life. And they must give them directions on what to do, so they go off in all directions and take their children with them. So these Wuwtsims tell their children all these things that are prophesied. But they scare them with it. These Kwans and Two Horns do not do that. Because they are the ceremonial leaders.
>
> *Pu' oovi astotokyat ep piw haqe' pi puma nankwusangwu. Pu' puma kiimi ökye pu' puma a'ni na'qalantotangwu. Pay pi hinta pi pasi! Niikyangw puma haqam naanami ökingwu. Aa'altuy amumumniqw pep puma qatsit hin pasiwnayangwu. Pam pi pay piw pas son pavan qa himu. Son oovi hak put tuwiy'tani. Pay imasa wiiwimkyam put tuwiy'yungwa. Noq ima wuwtsimt pi pay put qa tuwiy'yungwa. Puma pi pay huur tangawtangwu. Pay panis ima aa'altniqw pu' kwaakwant put hin yukuyangwu. Pu' it qatsit puma tuwiy'yungwa.*
>
> *Pu' oovi pay kya pi pumuy son pi qa hin ayawtoynayaqw puma naanahoyyakyangw imuy timuy paasya. Pay yaw oovi ima wuwtsimt pay yaw as piw timuy paas hin timuy yungtoynayaqey paas put piw enangya. Niikyangw puma yaw pay pumuy tsatsawinaya. Noq ima kwaakwantniqw pu' ima aa'alt pay qa pantotingwu. Ispi yaw puma momngwitniiqe'e.*

So we see that the various societies are, officially at least, unaware of what each is doing. We also find, as expected, that the ceremonial is effectuated on many levels and infused with many meanings. It is also

10. See A. W. Geertz 1986:48–49 and chapter 2 for discussions of the concept of life in ritual contexts.

interesting that the quoted consultant chose to point out in the open-ended interview that there were two conceptually disparate activities at play: The Kwans and Two Horns "begin a new life" at the Sipaapuni, and the Wuwtsims scare their novices with the prophecies.

Hearkening back to the myth, we can note two important points. As the Piikyas version of the emergence myth shows (Appendix A), the actual emergence occurred during the singing of a Kwan ritual song during the Wuwtsim ceremonial (paragraph 36). And secondly, the first thing the leaders do after the emergence is to create various things that are essential for the proper contexts of life on this earth, such as the heavenly bodies (in the Piikyas version) and plant life (in other versions). But what they really intended to create was a new life in a new paradise, devoid of evil and insanity. As the story goes, they failed at this, and, as the Hopis insist, the primordial chaos is once again evident in human affairs. So both myth and ritual seem to point to a dramatization of sorts.

This ceremonial may be viewed in terms of Barbara Myerhoff's "definitional ceremonies" (1979), which recreate group identity through dramatic narratives about the group, and Victor Turner's "third-phase" ritual processes (Turner 1986). The latter set the stage for "unique structures of experience" in the liminal mode "where structures of group experience (*Erlebnis*) are replicated, dismembered, re-membered, refashioned, and mutely or vocally made meaningful" (ibid.:43). The Hopi evidence seems to suggest that during the *limen* of this collective liminal ceremonial (that is, tribal initiation), the apocalyptic activities of primordial humans are directly reenacted by their twentieth-century incarnations, not theatrically, but literally. Through this ceremonial, the present apocalyptic conditions are identified with the primordial ones, thus fusing past with present. And this fusion not only confronts past conditions with present ones, but it also provides past solutions to present problems.

In the Introduction, I argued that the emergence myth contains the paradigms for all of Hopi religion and culture. Indeed, besides playing a key role in the Hopi cognitive environment, the myth itself is attributed substance in the mechanics of the apocalypse. Wilson D. Wallis's Sun clan consultant from Shongopovi told him in 1912:

> When the story is forgotten, something disastrous will happen. Perhaps the stars will fall down into the ocean, and the ocean will become oil. Then the sun will set fire to it, and the conflagration will consume everyone. Perhaps there will be an earthquake that will kill everyone. That is what my father's father told me. (Wallis 1936:16–17)

The Piikyas version of the emergence myth in Appendix A clearly demonstrates that the emergence myth is an analytical subcategory belonging to the *navoti,* ("clan tradition") category. It is an integral part of the migration story. The fact that each migration tradition is specifically differentiated along clan lines and yet each emergence episode resembles all other emergence episodes to a very high degree seems to indicate that the categories should be reversed.

Indeed this is what I have chosen to do. And yet, the Hopis have no standard term for the emergence myth, which may be an indication of a grey area of collective "survivals" in a historical sense or some other factor that may be conscious or unconscious. The fact that the prophecies belong to the emergence episodes warns us that something unusual is at work here. One could imagine, for instance, that it is the emergence episodes that belong to the pan-clan brotherhoods and the migration episodes which belong to the clans.

The Piikyas narrative has almost all of the standard stories of the emergence. Life was chaotic and immoral in the third world. The chiefs applied their ritual powers in order to escape to a new world, and the emergence was effectuated by the Kwan brotherhood during the initiation night of the Wuwtsim ceremonial. When the song ended the reed was kicked down. Then the leaders created the heavenly bodies together with the Kwan Old Woman. This is followed by the dialogue between Maasaw and the leaders during which the prophecy of Maasaw's return is introduced. Then the migration story begins.

What is most obviously missing from the account is the story of the immanent return of the White Brother. This element was evidently not considered necessary in this particular telling, which instead serves to function as an apology for the Kwan brotherhood, as paragraphs 91–92 illustrate.

This brings us to the question of the degree of change that can be introduced to the narrative. The emergence myths presented in Appendix B clearly indicate a free-wheeling propensity for changing not only details, but also the thrust of the myth. I do not think, however, that the modern versions of the Traditionalist Movement can be used as examples here. Their versions belong to another medium and to other functions set within a radically alien context.

I have two examples to present at this point. The one concerns a retelling of the Piikyas myth by the same speaker six years later and the other concerns the myth of another clan told by two different narrators from the same village.

The narrator of the Piikyas version was in the process of explaining a story to me in 1988 about a beheading that reportedly once took place at Oraibi. This moved her to comment on the nature of the Kookop clan and the Kwan brotherhood. One of her sons, who also was present at the interview, asked her to comment on the landholdings of the brotherhood.

In response she went immediately into the dialogue related in paragraph 41, adding that the dialogue was between the Bear clan, the Kwan chief, and Maasaw. Then she told the migration story. Any changes that were made between 1979 and 1988 were a matter of more details and further amplification. The story itself remained unchanged.

My second example demonstrates the opposite. I obtained a version from the head of the Grey Eagle clan at Hotevilla in 1978. It resembled in part the myth related by another Hotevilla Grey Eagle clan consultant, which Hieb published in his dissertation (1972:146ff), but the former contained elements that were obviously borrowed from Christian mythology. In 1988, I obtained another version from another Hotevilla Grey Eagle clan consultant, which can be said to resemble the 1978 version, but which in major details is quite different. Without going into a documented, detailed analysis, the existence of these covariants is significant for our understanding of the role the emergence myth plays in the transformation of Hopi tradition. It is not without significance that the obvious transformations of Traditionalist narratives are mostly found in their versions of the emergence myth.

It is easy enough to account for differences in versions owned by different clans since each clan is sovereign. Differences within a clan held by members from different villages are also understandable. But differences within a clan in the same village need explanation. Whiteley's observation (1986) that each clan has a core lineage which simply possesses greater knowledge than the other lineages may have been at stake here, but I believe that other extenuating circumstances are involved since the 1972 and 1988 versions were told by two brothers.

My hypothesis is that, as with the Traditionalist versions, the Grey Eagle versions are the result of two factors; influence from non-Hopis—in this case, Christians—and the influence of political factors. The three versions referred to were held by one of Qötshongva's former counselors who was actively against the Traditionalist Movement and a strong supporter of the Tribal Council (the 1978 version), a former chairman of the Council (Hieb's version), and one of the former chairman's brothers (the 1988 version).

The hows and whys of these covariants are just as impossible to define as those of the versions published in Appendix B of this book. It is sufficient for our purposes to note that the emergence myth may be radically transformed in response to certain political circumstances. Several of the later chapters will focus on the politics of Traditionalist narrative for which there is better documentation. It seems, however, that the content of the myth does not change so easily within the traditional prose narrative context.

RITUAL SPEECH

Ritual speech involves speeches spoken in ritual contexts which are formalized and provide no real opportunity for variation. We have so little evidence on this genre, however, that I have relegated it to a subordinate prose narrative context (cf. A. W. Geertz 1986:50–51). Although many instances of ritual speeches with prophetic content must exist, I have only a few examples. The first is found in the *tsukulalwa*, "they are clowning," put on by the *tsutskut* ("the clowns") during the summer katsina dances.

According to the Eagle clan traditions, reported in Hieb (1972), the antics of the brotherhood are closely linked to the emergence myth. Their whole repertoire is to be understood within the schemata of the myth. This means that much of what occurs is a reenactment of the emergence myth, but once again we are speaking about staging primordial situations and not classical dramatizations.

Throughout the day the clowns do all manner of mischief, but as the end draws near their activities and speech take on apocryphal tones. Warning figures begin to appear in the afternoon foreboding ill for the clowns. And, in line with the Hopi belief in *tiingavi*, the clown chief openly makes contact and deliberates with the warning figures so that the other clowns assume that a conspiracy is taking place.

The following example, recorded by Hieb, will suffice as an exemplification of this subcategory:

> Late in the afternoon after the warnings have nearly reached their greatest frequency and intensity, the Chief Clown goes to the *kiva* used by the Owl kachina. Thus when the Owl kachina next appears, he makes contact with the Chief Clown publicly and conspicuously. They kneel and talk together with the other clowns watching suspiciously. The Owl kachina asks, "Why is it you want me in great haste?" The Chief Clown attempts to buy his life with several strands of turquoise beads, the "clowns' wealth": "I recognize that my brothers are deserving of punishment, but I am a chief and deserve to be treated differently. I want you to take these [beads]. Remember, I wish to be spared." These words are not spoken loud enough for them to be heard beyond the Chief Clown and the Owl kachina. In what follows the other clowns assume a conspiracy has taken place, but there are other versions of the significance of this transaction:
>
> The Chief Clown realizes they've reached the end of life and purification is about to occur. Either they will be saved or lost forever. And so the Chief Clown—out of compassion for his people—takes the lesser of two evils. Because of their transgressions, they've not earned salvation. But the Owl gives the Chief Clown a choice regarding the kind of punishment to be given out. He says, "I do not desire the ultimate punishment [death]." So the Owl asks, "What is the punishment of your choosing for your peo-

ple, for your children?" So he gives him wealth as payment for the lesser punishment.

After the transaction has been made, the Owl kachina returns to the *kiva*, followed shortly thereafter, by the Chief Clown. They smoke together and say these prayers:

Chief Clown: If I have done anything to put a smile on the face of our people, I have succeeded.

Owl Kachina: Let there be life. Let everything with being or spirit enjoy life in its fullest to old age. Let there be rain.

The Owl kachina and the Chief Clown then make a covenant. The Owl kachina gives instructions for the punishment. The Chief Clown then says, "Yes, I accept punishment for my people. Have sympathy for us. Do not give us the full count [four] of whips but only one or two. I appeal to the sympathies of the kachinas." Throughout this elaborate conspiracy and transaction, the Chief Clown is understood to take the role of the *kikmongwi* (village chief). The Chief Clown then returns to the plaza. The punishment follows. (1972:201–202)[11]

The second example illustrates a direct relationship between ritual prayer and the return of the White Brother. The following statement by Viets Lomahaftewa from Shongopovi was presented at the 1955 hearings:

> All of us have grandfathers, grandmothers and uncles who have told us about these great teachings and instructions which you have heard here today from these men who have just spoken. These were provided for this time and today we are seeing those things which were told to us by our forefathers. In those days our forefathers, when they would come together, they used to smoke for the rain and also for the white brother of his so that he will come soon, so that he will use some of these things that he will bring to us and to enjoy them when he comes. As we know these teachings, our brother has went off to another place and in order to make him turn back we smoke and pray that he will come back. (Bureau of Indian Affairs 1955:90–91)

This type of ritual narrative is the so-called "smoke-talk."

The final example repeats the above claim and adds a further dimension. Not only do the adults perform ritual prayers concerning the Pahaana, but they also urge their children to do the same during their morning prayers to the sun:

> Most everybody was anxious to see the Bahana come, for they were so afraid that he might not come during their lifetime and they would not be able to enjoy all the benefits that he was to bring back with him. . . . These people were telling their children that the Bahana was wise and with his inventions had reached the rising sun and was coming back to them again. . . .

11. Note the striking resemblance to the examples of *tiingavi* described in chapter 1.

> They would tell their grandchildren to go out in the mornings before sunrise with sacred corn-meal to ask the sun to hurry the Bahana along so that he would come soon. (Nequatewa 1936:50)

This latter example also indicates less-formal opportunities for introducing especially pedagogical, apocryphal detail.

In conclusion, we find positive evidence that prophecies and related subjects do appear in formal prose narrative contexts that are independent of the emergence myth and yet draw their structure and contents from it.

THE ETHNOPOETIC NARRATIVE CONTEXT

Although literary poetry as we understand it has become a new medium for Hopi artists today, and although some reference to prophecies may be found in contemporary Hopi poetry, my concern here is with ritual songs. Music is a frequent mode of communication among Hopis, and composers are in constant demand no matter what social or religious status they may have.

Before the advent of the use of mass media, songs may have been one of the major vehicles of prophetic detail, casual dialogue being the other. Songs are formalized both in genre and in mode of communication. They are composed and owned by individuals who are in the position to transmit their own body of prophetic details to a larger audience than the prose-narrative contexts allow. Thus, content may change, at least until committed to performance. The structure of ritual songs, however, does not change.

An important characteristic of this genre is that it can and does appeal to dimensions of human psychology other than the intellectual. The use of complex metaphors and imagery can produce emotive reactions. Not only do they conjure up ridicule, laughter, shame, and tears, but they also mobilize and reaffirm collective identity in the face of collective tragedy. The nature of poetic effects influences the nature of the generative process of poetic narrative contexts, and therefore it is important for this study to specify exactly what types of changes are possible in this medium.

Sperber and Wilson's description of poetic effect applies to Hopi songs:

> How do poetic effects affect the mutual cognitive environment of speaker and hearer? They do not add entirely new assumptions which are strongly manifest in this environment. Instead, they marginally increase the manifestness of a great many weakly manifest assumptions. In other words, poetic effects create common impressions rather than common knowledge.

> Utterances with poetic effects can be used precisely to create this sense of apparently affective rather than cognitive mutuality. (1986:224)

The result in the case of the richest and most creative poetic effects is that

> the hearer or reader can go beyond just exploring the immediate context and the entries for concepts involved in it, accessing a wide area of knowledge, adding metaphors of his own as interpretations of possible developments he is not ready to go into, and getting more and more very weak implicatures, with suggestions for still further processing. The result is a quite complex picture, for which the hearer has to take a large part of the responsibility, but the discovery of which has been triggered by the writer. The surprise or beauty of a successful creative metaphor lies in this condensation, in the fact that a single expression which has itself been loosely used will determine a very wide range of acceptable weak implicatures. (ibid.:236–237)

The cognitive complexity of poetic effects makes it difficult for us not only to translate and understand the songs, but also to evaluate the degree of transformation the content may be undergoing. This is an important point to which I will return shortly.

TYPES OF RITUAL SONGS

On the formalistic side, Hopi songs are standardized in structure and redundant in style. There is, nonetheless, a wide variety of song types. The category *pavasiwtawi* ("ritual song") contains esoteric songs known only to the members of secret societies. Such songs are designated by the name of the society, such as *wuwtsimtawi* ("Wuwtsim brotherhood song"), *powamuytawi* ("Powamuy brotherhood song"), and *marawtawi* ("Maraw sisterhood song"). Within the contexts of each society ritual, there is a whole range of songs for every important occasion, such as *makwantawi* ("asperging song"), and *navootsiwtawi* ("purification song"), which accompany all major rituals and ceremonials. And on more specific occasions, songs like the *uytawi* ("planting song"), *wungwintawi* ("growing song"), and *tsovalantawi* ("harvesting song") are used in raising the sprouts for the Powamuy ceremonial. Another example is the *tawsoma* ("song tie"), which is sung by the Wuwtsim fraternity to the Maraw sorority and vice versa. An inversion of ceremonial song is found in the lore about the ceremonials of sorcerers and witches, which are called *tuskyaptawi* ("insane song"). The same subcategories as those of ritual songs are used. The difference between ritual songs and sorcerous songs is that the latter are evil.

A second major category of songs is the *katsintawi* ("katsina song"), which is parallel to the *tseletawi* ("social dance song"). Each katsina song is named after the katsina type, such as *maswikkatsintawi* ("Maswikkatsina song") and *angaktsintawi* ("Long-hair katsina song"). For each katsina dance there is a *yungwtawi* ("entering song") and a *nöngantawi* ("emerging song"), which are sung either upon entering or emerging from the kiva or the plaza. Another type of song that occurs within the katsina context, but is not sung by katsinas, is the *tsukutawi* ("clown song").

A third category of songs is the *tuwutstawi* ("myth song"), which are sung in connection with the narration of a myth or folktale. A subcategory is the *titaptawi* ("lullaby"), which often incorporates folkloristic imagery.

A fourth category of songs can be called "work songs." Some contain ritual effect, whereas others are sung to simply pass the time. The *uytawi, wungwintawi,* and *tsovalantawi* are used out in the cornfields, *maktawi* ("hunting song") is used for spellbinding the game, and *ngumantawi* ("grinding song") helps the women through their daily corn grinding.

The structure of ritual and katsina songs is strictly held. Characterized by a consistent repetition of key verses, Hopi songs are so repetitive that a song master, called the "Father of the Katsinas," is required to keep track of where the singers are in the song and to yell this information out to them.[12]

The basic structure of Hopi songs was described by one of my consultants in this manner:

> It begins with the "down" (part). When it ends, the "down" (part) is repeated. So it is performed twice. Then comes its "up" (part). That is also done twice. Now the "down" (part) is done only once, and then the song concludes.
>
> Noq pam pi mooti atkyaqw kuyvangwu. Nen pu' pam so'tiqw pu' paasat naat piw atkyaqningwu. Pam oovi lööstingwu. Pu' paasat i' omiwa'atningwu. Pam piw oovi lööstingwu. Paasat pu' pay suus atkyaqniqw pu' pay pam taawi so'tingwu. (A. W. Geertz and Lomatuway'ma 1987:110, 289)

Verse 1 is called *atkyamiq* ("down"), and verse 2 having the same name is a repetition of verse 1. Verse 3 is called *oomiq* ("up") and verse 4 having the same name is a repetition of verse 3. Verse 5, which is the last verse, is a repetition of verses 1 and 2 and also has the same name. Thus every Hopi song, at least in ritual contexts, consists of five verses: *atkyamiq, atkyamiq, oomiq, oomiq,* and *atkyamiq.* It is the job of the song master to tell the singers when they are to begin a new verse and whether the

12. A more detailed description of this functional side of Hopi song art can be found in A. W. Geertz and Lomatuway'ma (1987:110–111, 133–134). Cf. List (1968).

verse is *atkyamiq* or *oomiq*. In a village with six kivas, a katsina group can easily end up singing its song from twelve to twenty-four times during the course of a Katsina Night Dance, necessitating a song master to direct it. Conversely, the song masters, who remain in one kiva and direct from twelve or more performances, may be familiar with the songs, but must have a dependable structure from which to direct.

Each song type has a single melody or a small choice of melodies at most, with standard preludes and (sometimes) standard choruses, which are often just sounds without semantic content. Thus, innovation within such strict standardization requires the talent of an artist drawing on puns, alliterations, emphatic juxtaposition, symbolic substitution, and metaphors directed toward content, and assonance, onomatopoeia, rhyme, and an array of other techniques directed toward form. By these means a vast environment of connotations is created by the composer for his specific purposes.

The problem of continuity and change in oral song was systematically discussed by Albert Lord, who made epic songs containing thousands of lines the focus of his study. Consequently, his empirical data is of a different order than the Hopi example. Lord's main argument was that oral transmission, composition, creation, and performance are all one and the same (1960:101). A performer in an oral culture is not merely a reproducer but a composer as well (ibid.:13). Each performance is a moment of creation contingent on contextual and interpretive factors. Thus, the singer of tales has a store of formulas, themes, and compositional techniques that are used in each performance. Wording and content may change, but what never changes is "the essence of the story itself" (ibid.:99). Thus, the singer's craft must be understood in terms of fluidity and not in terms of changes in a hypothetical "original text."

In my opinion, Hopi ritual songs are not that fluid. First, they are of a different character than epic songs—shorter and performed collectively. And second, they are, of course, ritual songs that are conceived as being efficacious. Lord wrote that sacred texts are not "oral" in his sense of the word, but in the most literal sense. He claimed this to be so because sacred texts must be preserved word for word (ibid.:280). I think, however, that sacred, oral "texts" are *not* restricted to literal reproduction per se. They are also fluid in Lord's sense. This can be claimed with certainty at least in relation to sacred epic song.

Nevertheless, the types of changes noted by Lord in oral epic songs are most likely at work in Hopi ritual songs as well:

> (1) saying the same thing in fewer or more lines, because of singers' methods of line composition and of linking lines together, (2) expansion of ornamentation, adding of details of description (that may not be without sig-

> nificance), (3) changes of order in a sequence (this may arise from a different sense of balance on the part of the learner, or even from what might be called a chiastic arrangement where one singer reverses the order given by the other), (4) addition of material not in a given text of the teacher, but found in texts of other singers in the district, (5) omission of material, and (6) substitution of one theme for another, in a story configuration held together by inner tensions. (ibid.:123)

But again, Lord emphasized that changes are neither brought about by vaccilation nor chance, "but by an insistent, conservative urge for preservation of an essential idea as expressed in a single theme or in a group of themes" (ibid.:120).

THE PROPHETIC CONTENT OF RITUAL SONGS

During the past decade consultants and friends have sung songs for me which were performed during the Wuwtsim, Maswikkatsina, and Maraw dances. Despite the fact that the owners of these songs considered them to be essential to my analysis of Hopi prophecies, the transcripts will not be presented here. Publishing songs, sacred or not, has become a sensitive issue, and so I will simply summarize the prophetic elements of the songs in question.[13]

The underlying tone of the male Wuwtsimtatawi and Maswikkatsintatawi is of tragedy, despair, and fatalism. Whereas the cause of today's troubles is clearly pinpointed, solutions are random and diffused. In fact, although the religious leaders are considered to be the cause of the apocalypse, the main purpose of the songs is more to enlighten the audience than to suggest concrete solutions. The die is cast, it seems. The actions of the leaders in times past have unavoidable and unequivocal consequences, namely, the end of Hopi culture and the meting out of punishment at the time of purification.

The main causes attributed to the present cultural dissolution are immorality, squabbling, collective insanity, and sorcery. It is especially the latter which is allotted detail in the songs. This is hardly surprising since ritual power was and still is the essence of Hopi religion. When that power is twisted, it becomes the driving force of witchcraft. Medicine men possess this same power, called *tuhisa*, and are just as often suspected of sorcery as of healing.[14]

The logic of the songs is clear: The deliberate evil and immorality of

13. Transcripts of the songs are found in my dissertation, which is presently out of print.

14. Cf. Titiev 1943:552–553, A. W. Geertz 1982*a*:184, A. W. Geertz and Lomatuway'ma 1987:33 n. 27, and chapter 8 below.

the leaders has led them and the people to the brink of cultural and ecological disaster. There is, however, the unshakeable conviction that this state of affairs had been prophesied already in the beginning when humans emerged onto the surface of the fourth world. This conviction, if nothing else, provides a more-or-less clear idea of what is to come, thus giving the consolation of an interpretive framework.

The female Marawtatawi are more specific and more earthy than the men's. They point out individuals and groups by name and describe their shortcomings and crimes in detail. The overriding tone is one of ridicule, but the songs also review tantalyzing glimpses of what had been in order to encourage what might become again.

All of the songs are in no doubt about the cause of the end of the world. But, whereas the male songs are darkly fatalistic and emphasize the abhorrent evils in terms of startling juxtapositions (fertility/decomposition, beauty/horror, love/wantonness, innocence/malice), the female songs pad their concrete accusations with appeals, concrete solutions, and hope. The female songs refuse to give up and they find a source of hope in the possible rehabilitation of Hopi religion. By focusing on ridicule and ribaldry, the Maraw songs move the focal lens from collective despair to individual, human idiosyncracies. When things thus become human again, and individual responsibility is thereby awakened, then the end might possibly be avoided. For example, the Traditionalist leader who threatened to hang himself because his wife refused to feed his hippie girlfriends became the victim of public ridicule in the hope that he might see the foolishness of his behavior, make amends, and help prevent the end of the world. This optimistic vein may be due to the fact that the female ceremonials were the last to disintegrate at Hotevilla.

In sum, ritual songs contain specific details about the end of the world, analyze the exact causes of the apocalypse, express moral indignation and heap ridicule on the responsible parties, and suggest possible solutions to the situation. Furthermore, these songs are performed in paramount male and female ceremonials, with the evident purpose to instill shame and guilt in the young, the leaders, and those who deal in sorcery. The songs give poignant voice to the collective experience of cultural disintegration and immanent oblivion, and they illustrate the painful struggle between despondency and hope.

Ritual songs suggest the plausible possibility that they have the efficacy to combat the forces of evil that are orchestrating the apocalypse. Although there is no concrete proof of this, the ritual nature of the songs secures their efficacy in terms of the collective ritual intentions. As I argued in my paper on Hopi ritual (1986), songs help break the barriers of different realities. In Hopi thought, they increase the efficacy of the ritual and are either malignantly or benificently efficacious in their own right. Ritual songs are called *pöötavi*, "road prayer-feather," which, like the ritual object of that name, provides the participants with a symbolic road to tread. Songs are thought of as providing the performers with the power to control the gods. Furthermore, songs are the necessary magical ingredients of the power wielded by gods, priests, or sorcerers (ibid.:52). So, why not an ingredient against (or even for!) the end of the world?

FOUR

The Modern Prose Narrative Context of Hopi Prophecy

LITERACY VERSUS ORALITY: A CRITIQUE

The modern, prose narrative context of Hopi prophecy was described as being informal, nonritual, multistylistic, geared specifically to contemporary events, and, in most cases, literary. I further noted that it is an expanded cultural treasure in which the collective group becomes ever more inclusive, even to the point of admitting non-Hopis (willingly or unwillingly) into the picture.

What distinguishes this context from the other contexts is both the genre and the mode of communication. This category covers a wide range of genres from oral dialogue to the use of the mass media. I am speaking about casual conversation, speeches, and eyewitness accounts on the one hand, and letters to the editor, newspaper interviews, propaganda literature, government documents, letters in general, books, and radio and television programs on the other hand.

This chapter can hardly deal with all of these genres. I will not deal with broadcast media, not because they are unimportant, but because the bulk of the documents at my disposal are in the print media.[1] Nor will I go into casual conversations, except to express the subjective impression that prophecy is one of the most important topics in contemporary Hopi conversation. My interest is in prophecy and the ways in which prophecy has been affected by the use of the print media. Since the Traditionalists have used the print media for the dissemination of their prophetic corpus more than any other person or group on the reserva-

1. For discussions on the impact of the mass media and especially television on "developing nations" and oral societies see Worth and Adair 1973, Lent 1975 and 1977, Khatri 1976, Katz and Wedell 1977, Katz 1977, Michaels 1986, and Fienup-Riordan 1988.

tion, it is natural to dwell specifically—although not exclusively—on their activities. The Traditionalist Movement will be dealt with historically and sociologically in more detail in the rest of this book, and therefore I will leave such detail aside for the moment.

There are two major problems in evaluating the impact literacy has had on Traditionalist prophecy. The first problem is that the literate language in question is a foreign one. This means there are other social and psychological mechanisms involved which occlude the simple dichotomy of literacy versus orality. The second problem is that a major portion of the literature is literally the oral "writ large"; in other words, it is written discourse. The bulk of the literature consists of transcripts of tape-recorded speeches or verbatim notes of such, and newspaper interviews. The rest of the literature consists of actual "literature," understood here as the composition of messages specifically for the written medium. This involves such things as letters, press statements, and newsletters. But it should be noted that even in this decidedly literate medium, an important portion of it consists of summaries or sometimes even transcripts of oral discourse. Many Traditionalist communiques, for instance, are introduced with the statement, "we have been instructed by the Great Spirit to tell of our traditions and prophecies," after which a summary of those traditions and prophecies is presented. The summaries are, of course, applied to a certain problem, but they are nontheless summaries of oral discourse.[2]

I do not intend to go into the jungle of theories about literacy and orality. The discussions are simply riddled with assumptions about the superiority of literacy, its greater objectivity, logic, and complexity as well as its presumed intimate relationship to our own technologically advanced civilization. I am firmly in agreement with anthropologist Brian Street in his criticism of theories of literacy and the manner in which they are put into practice in educational programs and in literacy campaigns (1984). In his opinion, "the skills and concepts that accompany literacy acquisition, in whatever form, do not stem in some automatic way from the inherent qualities of literacy, as some authors would have us believe, but are aspects of a specific ideology" (ibid.:1).

I will show in this chapter that the main difference between the oral and written traditions of prophecy is that the oral traditions have be-

2. The observation that oral genres are simply carried into writing has been noted, for example, by Mbelolo ya Mpiku (1972) and John Janzen (1985). Janzen also argued for an awareness of the political implications of literacy, such as the "control of text" and which genres are excluded (i.e., in missionary literature) from the texts (ibid.:226ff, 230ff). Like Pentikäinen before him (1979), Janzen also called for flexibility in the use of the term "genre" (1985:233ff).

come frozen into texts that have carried them beyond the reach, understanding, and control of their producers.[3] This circumstance has led to two main consequences: 1) What was once a body of knowledge restricted to more-or-less formalized and ritualized contexts has now, especially with the use of mass media, been made accessible to a broader public—not only to a Hopi public, but more importantly and especially to the Euro-American public. Contrary to stereotypical expectations about the stabilizing effects of the printed word, the enlarged audience has actively stimulated a formerly restricted dialogue. 2) The publication of Hopi prophecies has indeed invited contention since it has left indelible proof that the prophecies and their exegesis have constantly changed.

LITERACY AND ACCULTURATION

I do not think that the Hopi use of the print media has effectuated any cognitive changes, as some theorists might conjecture. But it has definitely led to a number of sociological changes which I hope to demonstrate in this chapter.

The Traditionalist Movement built a political platform based on a number of assumptions and claims, all of which will be dealt with in more detail later in this book. Briefly, these are that the U.S. government has neither legal nor moral rights, claims, or authority over the Hopis; that the Tribal Council is not a traditional institution, but an illegal puppet institution for the U.S. government; that the only rightful leaders are the "traditional chiefs"; and that resistance to Euro-American ways and programs are both implicitly and explicitly present in Hopi prophecy and tradition. Thus, the Traditionalist Movement, which began in 1949 (cf. chapter 5), presented itself as an antigovernment and antiprogressive body with the express aim of fighting for the removal of the Tribal Council and what it stands for.

As Nagata has argued (1968), its rhetoric and ideology notwithstanding, the Traditionalist Movement failed not only to maintain the clear divide between traditionalism and progressivism, but also even to maintain a clear distinction between itself and the Tribal Council in terms of both means and ends. In fact, the movement was just as much a partner in acculturation as the Council was.

The Traditionalists, Nagata claimed, were at a disadvantage in relation to the Tribal Council in two of the three main political arenas available to the Hopis, namely, the village, the reservation, and the nation. In the village arena both groups were on equal footing, but in the latter two arenas the Council had a distinct advantage.

3. See the eloquent discussion on this topic in F. Smith 1985.

Nagata's main point was that in order to offset the advantages of their political opponents, the Traditionalists were forced to adopt their methods. It is at this point that literacy comes into the picture.

In the first place, Traditionalist tactics, especially in the national arena, required that English be adopted as the *lingua politica*. In the beginning it was necessary to depend on bilingual Hopis, who had learned English in government schools, as interpreters. The political problem of depending on potential opponents as interpreters was soon solved by replacing them with Hopi and non-Hopi interpreters who were sympathetic to the movement. But developments led to the natural consequence of introducting a new form of leadership in the Hopi context, namely, secular "spokesmen" whose redeeming qualities were loyalty to the movement and a command of the English language (Nagata 1968: 20–21). One of the best-known of these spokesmen is the present nominal leader of the movement, Thomas Banancya (cf. chapter 9).

In my opinion, the use of English as *lingua politica* brought the important consequence that Traditionalist prophecies were now reprduced in a foreign medium. This has two implications: 1) that the disparate traditions were summarized into a common corpus; and 2) that the prophetic discourse changed languages and, with it, audiences. Both of these implications are powerful acculturative devices.

English was not only used as a *lingua politica,* it had been used as a *lingua franca* since the end of the last century. The Traditionalists simply followed suit by conducting their meetings with Whites and other Indians either with bilingual translators or entirely in English (cf. Nagata 1968:21–22).

The use of English was not restricted to oral modes alone. One of the main political tactics employed by the Traditionalists was the frequent use of letters, petitions, statements, and communiques sent to U.S. government officials as well as to English-speaking support groups. The use of written English gave access to an arena otherwise unattainable for an opposition group that chose not to participate in the democratic system. It enabled them to bypass both the lower echelons of BIA officialdom and the Tribal Council on the reservation and to make direct appeals to the commissioner of Indian affairs, the president of the United States, and the public at large. These appeals were clearly meant to drum up external support for Traditionalist views on a variety of topics.

There are many documents of this nature since the beginning of Hopi and U.S. affairs. The value of such a tactic is clear enough, but it is equally significant to make it explicit that the tactic is in itself an instrument of acculturation. Carrying Nagata's implications further, I will show that ever since Yukiwma sent a letter to President Taft in 1911, the

Hostiles, and the Traditionalists after them, have consistently appealed to the implicit "higher authority" of the president and the commissioner.

Two documents will indicate what I am referring to. The first is the letter written to President Taft by Ray Rutherford Dewanyema from Shongopovi on behalf of Yukiwma in 1911. The letter refers to a journey Yukiwma made to Washington in 1911 in order to present his stone tablets to the president and to protest the forced schooling of the Hotevilla children (cf. chapter 6). After he returned to Hotevilla, a Colonel Scott was sent out to him in order to remove the children. At the same time, Kewanimptewa was establishing himself as a considerable political opponent in the newly established Bacavi right near Hotevilla.

The letter was written ten days after the children were removed from Hotevilla. It is presented here in corrected English:

Dear Sir:

I take great pleasure in writing to you while sitting with Chief Yukiwma as he is talking about his long trip. He said that he was glad to have visited you once and to have spoken to you himself. You now all know him, and you know what is going on—about his people not wanting to send their children to school because they like to keep their children with them so the boys can help their fathers on the farm and the girls can also help their mothers in their homes. Those are the reasons why they don't let them go to school. Of course, we are Indians. The school is not our business. The school belongs to the White people. I think it would be all right if you leave Chief Yukiwma alone. Let them stay home, there are only 600 people who want to keep their children at home and not go to school. Chief Yukiwma does not want his people to become lazy. He wants them to work on the farms and raise corn, oat wheat, potatoes, and vegetables so they can sell them for money and buy clothes for themselves. That is what Yukiwma wanted his people to do. He doesn't want any harm for his people. He wanted to take good care of his people and children.

Yukiwma wants me to tell you about this man Kewanimptewa who is trying to make himself chief even though everyone knows he has never been chief before. So the people think that it was crazy of him to make himself chief and to make trouble with Yukiwma's people. So they are dissatisfied with him staying near Yukiwma's village—by the name of Hotevilla—because they are all trying to be good to one another.

I think we like staying the Hopi Way. I think that it is best for us Indian people. Of course, the Friendly people's children must attend school and the Hostile people's children must not be allowed to go to school, but to stay at home and help their fathers or mothers. That's the way they want it. You American people must stay in your own way and we Hopi Indians must stay in our own way, too.

About a week ago, we were crying because the Superintendent from Keams Canyon, Mr. Leo Crane, took the children to school. Did you send the soldiers to Yukiwma? A company of soldiers came here with Crane. And that man [Colonel Scott] came to Hotevilla to Chief Yukiwma asking what the old people were saying. Then Yukiwma told him everything he knows and then that man wrote it all down and sent it to you. But now this Superintendent Crane and the soldiers caused a lot of trouble, and that man too—I don't know what his name is. He said that he came from Washington D.C.

Did you send that man to Chief Yukiwma? Did you tell him to come out here and make trouble? Yes or no? Yukiwma wants you to answer this letter and send it to me. I will tell what you say to Yukiwma.

Tomorrow I am going to Winslow. You must hurry to answer this letter. I guess this is all I have to say to you.

Goodbye from Ray Rutherford Dewanyema.

(SOURCE: Dewanyema 12-12-1911)

This letter indicates that Yukiwma may not have understood the signals he received from Washington during his visit in March of that year. But, even though he in no way relented from his position of resistance, the letter clearly indicates that he bypassed the local officials in an attempt to deal with a higher authority. It is true that his main message was to leave the Hotevilla people and their children alone, but the letter also contains an unspoken request to: do something about that upstart Kewanimptewa, who, as Whiteley has shown (1988), had become a major factor not only in Third Mesa politics, but also throughout the reservation.

The incompatible positions of maintaining a stance of resistance coupled with invitations to a foreign authority to help remove political opponents are not just glaring contrasts. They are the result of a complicated political situation. That situation will be examined in detail in the following chapters from various angles. In this chapter, it is enough to establish that the Hostiles were accomplices not only to change, but even to acculturation, and that a major vehicle in bringing this about was the use of written English.

All that remains of preliminary matters is to indicate how the Traditionalists carried on with Hostile tactics. But first, I wish to make it clear that being an accomplice to acculturation through the written medium does not mean that acculturation was Yukiwma's ultimate purpose. On the contrary. I do not think, though, that he or the later Traditionalists were aware of the ultimate consequences of maintaining a direct dialogue with the officials in Washington.

In October 1968, Ralph Selina, a Second Mesa spokesman for the Traditionalists, wrote a letter to President Lyndon B. Johnson, who had declined an invitation to a spiritual summit meeting on the reservation. The letter is actually a report on what happened at the meeting:

Dear Sir:

Thank you for your Telegram of Sept. 27th. We regretted very much that you could not be able to come and meet with our Highest Hopi Leaders and Religious Headman at this time. Because we who are initiated Hopis know the Ancient Prophecies and Religious Instructions concerning all life in this land your people called Americas, and because mankind now faces dreadful disaster in the near future, our Highest Black Bear Clan Hereditary Chief is anxious that you make arrangement to meet with him as soon as possible.

As to the meetings held the past week-end I make this report with full knowledge and consent of our Village Chief. The meeting was called and invitations were sent out to all people, Hopis, other Tribal Leaders and white people. Many did come. Both Indians and non-Indians came from State of Washington, California, Nevada, New Mexico and Arizona. The meeting went along fine on the first day which was held outdoor in the morning. In the afternoon it was held in one of the Kivas. Many white people came including some called Hippies. They did not cause any disturbance or trouble. Neither the other white people. But on the second day some of our own Hopi government employees and those who felt that white man should not attend these meetings took it upon themselves and called on the Keams Canyon Agency and Police to come and attempt to stop our peaceful and religious meeting. They kept on interfering with the speakers and created such disturbances that the meeting had to end at noon on Sunday. All the Agency Police were there but make no effort to stop them from interfering with the speakers.

Two Hopi brothers from Hotevilla Village both seemed to be under the influence of liquor and at the behest of Peter Nuvamsa of Shungopavy village who continue to present himself as a Chief when he is not, did called the speakers, troublemakers, liars and did everything to DISRUPT the meeting. It appears to all those present that Peter Nuvamsa, Saul and Charlie and other members of the Shungopavy village called the Police and State Highway Patrols from Holbrook to come on the Traditional Village to support those few Hopis who tried to stop the meeting of the Hopi Traditional and Religious Leaders with other people. Our Interpreter was called a liar and many speakers were unable to complete their expression on religious matters. Our Interpreter told us that you have a Constitution which said there should be or must be Freedom of Speech, assembly and expression of opinions and worship. But these young men with the help of Police tried to suppress this meeting.

Because of these uncalled for actions on the part of some of your government employees and some of our educated Hopi people our Highest Hopi Leaders and all those who were at the meeting urgently call on you to take immediate step to stop those who continue to interfere with our free assemblies and free speech. You wage war in foreign countries to stop such dictatorial actions yet you seemed to allow much to happen in this land, in our own homeland, by your government employees. We will follow this report up with full report as soon as possible. Our Hopi Leaders are being ignored, ridiculed and pushed around by these young educated Hopi men, some members of the so-called Hopi Tribal Council and members of your government employees. They interfere with the village life of our people. Our Leaders demand that they be stopped or moved into towns which they want and let us live in peace and follow the way of life laid down by The Great Spirit.

Sincerely yours,
Ralph Selina
(SOURCE: Selina 10-2-1968)

This appeal to the improvement of democratic principles on the reservation by direct governmental intervention looks like an "about-face" change of Traditionalist policy. But the letter is symptomatic and amply demonstrates the role literacy has played in transforming factionalism into a channel of acculturation.

Turning now to other acculturative consequences in adopting the literate media, Nagata (1968) emphasized that the large amount of information exchange between the Traditionalists and outsiders raised the problem of how to store the necessary information for later retrieval. There were long, highly technical, and often bafflingly obscure official documents from the U.S. government which needed to be kept and incorporated into Traditionalist discourse. They had neither office nor reproducing machines. Although the Traditionalists had no centralized authority, the documents in question were kept in the hands of the "leaders" and in secrecy.

As time went on, however, things changed. Battery-powered tape recorders were brought to meetings and a newsletter was started in the 1970s:

> Battery-run tape recorders turned out to be a perfect and favorite tool for such a purpose. One Traditional has a fantastic collection of the tapes made in various meetings. Another has acquired two. The Hopi Traditionals seldom take notes of their proceedings and it was more than amusing to observe them trying to adjust a Norelco tape recorder in one Hotevilla meeting with the Navajo, while the latter were busily making notes in English in their little pocket notebooks. Recorded tapes are seldom played back in public but are often translated into English and published in obscure circulars run by non-Indian sympathizers. (ibid.:22)

This is not the only change that was introduced. As Nagata noted, engagement in the movement had economic consequences. Stationary, tape recorders, and trips to distant cities involved considerable costs. And although these matters were normally resolved in one way or another (from selling katsina dolls to hitchhiking), sudden crises would sometimes require immediate cash which only sympathetic villagers could provide. Nagata described just such an instance in 1964. Villagers from Shongopovi raised the funds to subsidize the travel expenses of a "Traditional politician from Third Mesa." Without going into details, the fundraising led to a number of accusations and protests within the subsidizing group of villagers. Records of the transactions were kept in a notebook and the remaining capital was placed in a bank. This experience was symptomatic of the changes the movement was succumbing to:

> First, the enterprise itself is an innovation, motivated out of the economic need for coordination of the Traditional politics across the boundary of autonomous village; the people of this Second Mesa village acted on behalf of the Third Mesa Traditional. Secondly, the book keeping as a result of this enterprise was something of a revolutionary nature to these people. In the past, the Traditionals criticized the Council men as *pensilhoyam* (little pencil people) because the latter were preoccupied with taking notes and keeping minutes but now the very Traditionals were doing the same! (ibid.:26)

LITERACY AND KNOWLEDGE

One of the primary sources of political power in Hopi society is the possession of esoteric knowledge. This knowledge is owned by central figures from central lineages in central clans. Esoteric knowledge is rooted in mythical theory and is both demonstrated and reaffirmed in the performance of rituals and ceremonials, the execution of specific activities, and in the administration of clan lands and shrines. Political power is exercised by a council of religious leaders who serve as advisers to the chiefs, who again are headed by the village chief. These leaders and chiefs have attained their positions in principle through heredity and/or initiation, and the whole structure rests upon esoteric knowledge and its "traditions."

The new media have neither changed the style nor the generative process of the oral communication reproduced in print. Knowledge is still imparted by specialists, as in oral circumstances. The main factor is that secrecy was apparently abandoned by the Traditionalist Movement as a political ploy in 1949 when they sent their letter to President Truman (Appendix D). The use of writing, especially the print media, made Hopi knowledge–particularly Hopi prophecies–part of the public domain. This was one of the most significant acts of directed social change in Traditionalist history. It not only placed Hopi prophecy in another context, it removed prophecy from the whole indigenous context and all of the intricate social relationships and postures necessary for obtaining that knowledge. The end result was threefold.

The Impact of Writing on the National Arena

Traditionalists were constantly plagued by legitimate criticisms of their claims to power, which rested on highly questionable grounds, and yet they criticized the members of the Tribal Council on exactly the same grounds. Writing gave them a chance to create the trappings of power through the consistent use of the rhetoric of power. Their audiences were non-Hopis, who by definition were ignorant of Hopi affairs.

The standard opening phrase for almost every Traditionalist communication (whether letters, pamphlets, articles, or interviews) is, "we, the traditional and religious leaders of the Hopi people." The turns of phrase differ, but the claim to power and cultural competence is always made, especially when dealing with officials in Washington. Likewise, the members of the Tribal Council are persistently discredited and cast in the role of swindlers.

But the standard opening is not just a defense of Traditionalist legitimacy, nor even a simple ploy against the Tribal Council. When writing to the president, the Traditionalists never take a subservient role. They do not address him as the Great White Father. They hardly even address him as an equal. In a letter to President Nixon in 1970, Thomas Banancya began in the following way:

> We, the True and Traditional religious leaders, recognized as such by the Hopi People, maintain full authority over all land and life contained within the western Hemisphere. (Banyacya 8-4-1970)

The letter ends with an invitation to the president and to "all spiritual leaders" to come to a summit meeting in order to discuss the "welfare of mankind." The tone of the letter may seem preposterous and presumptuous, but the fact of the matter is that the introduction of writing media has simply led to an expansion of the political arena. Hopi ideology and politics were easily adapted to writing, and it gave the possibility of direct and easy access to the highest governmental echelons. Even President Nixon made sure that Banancya was answered twice.

The Traditionalists increased their political impact by applying two methods normally used by their opponents on the Council: press releases and filing lawsuits. In 1971, the Traditionalists adopted going to U.S. courts as a political strategy for the first time. On May 14th, the Traditionalists filed suit against Secretary of Interior Rogers C. B. Morton, "individually and in his capacity as Secretary of the Interior of the United States," and against the Peabody Coal Company. As their news release stated:

> The lawsuit combined a claim of religious discrimination with claims that the government failed to observe legal procedures required by the Hopi Tribal Constitution. Sixty-two individually named Hopi Indian traditional-

ists are suing to halt the strip mining operations of Peabody Coal Company on lands deemed to be jointly owned by the Hopi and Navajo Tribes. Black Mesa, the area being stripped away, has special significance in the Hopi religion, and the Hopis consider the strip mining a desecration and a sacrilege.

The Indians charge in their complaint that the 1966 lease to Peabody Coal Company from the Hopi Tribal Council was illegal and that consequently the Secretary of the Interior's required approval of the lease was unlawful. The traditionalists assert that the Tribal Council was illegally constituted and was without the power to lease under the Hopi Constitution. The failure of the Secretary to administer the laws correctly has amounted to discrimination against the Hopi traditional people in favor of the "progressive" Hopis who control the Tribal Council, and who accept the white man's way more readily. (Native American Rights Fund 5-14-1971)

The Traditionalists had now set the stage for a national dramatization of their political and religious platform. The "Statement of the Hopi Religious Leaders" was introduced as Exhibit A in the suit filed in the United States District Court, District of Columbia. The statement is a succinct summary of their religious claims, and although the word prophecy is not found in the text, Hopi prophecies are implicit throughout:

Hopi land is held in trust in a spiritual way for the Great Spirit, Massau'u, Sacred Hopi ruins are planted all over the Four Corners area, including Black Mesa. This land is like the sacred inner chamber of a church—our Jerusalem. . . .

This land was granted to the Hopi by a power greater than man can explain. Title is invested in the whole makeup of Hopi life. Everything is dependent on it. The land is sacred and if the land is abused, the sacredness of Hopi life will disappear and all other life as well.

The Great Spirit has told the Hopi Leaders that the great wealth and resources beneath the lands of Black Mesa must not be disturbed or taken out until after purification when mankind will know how to live in harmony among themselves and with nature. The Hopi were given special guidance in caring for our sacred lands so as not to disrupt the fragile harmony that holds things together.

Hopi clans have traveled all over the Black Mesa area leaving our sacred shrines, ruins, burial grounds and prayer feathers behind. Today, our sacred ceremonies, during which we pray for such things as rain, good crops, and a long and good life, depend on spiritual contact with these forces left behind on Black Mesa. . . . If these places are disturbed or destroyed, our prayers and ceremonies will lose their force and a great calamity will befall not only the Hopi, but all of mankind.

Hopis are the caretakers for all the world, for all mankind. Hopi lands extend all over the continents, from sea to sea. But the lands at the sacred center are the key to life. By caring for these lands in the Hopi way, in accordance with instructions from the Great Spirit, we keep the rest of the world in balance.

To us, it is unthinkable to give up control over our sacred lands to non-Hopis. We have no way to express exchange of sacred lands for money. It is alien to our ways. The Hopis never gave authority and never will give authority to anyone to dispose of our lands and heritage and religion for any price. We received these lands from the Great Spirit and we must hold them for him, as a steward, a caretaker, until he returns. . . . The life of all people as well as animal and plant life depend on the Hopi spiritual prayers and song. The world will end in doom.

Water under the ground has much to do with rain clouds. Everything depends upon the proper balance being maintained. The water under the ground acts like a magnet attracting rain from the clouds; and the rain in the clouds also acts as a magnet raising the water table under the ground to the roots of our crops and plants. Drawing huge amounts of water from beneath Black Mesa in connection with the strip-mining will destroy the harmony, throw everything we have strived to maintain out of kilter. Should this happen, our lands will shake like the Hopi rattle; land will sink, land will dry up. Rains will be barred by unseen forces because we Hopis have failed to protect the land given us, as we were instructed. Plants will not grow; our corn will not yield and animals will die. When the corn will not grow, we will die; not only Hopis, but all will disintegrate to nothing.

We, the Hopi religious leaders, have watched as the white man has destroyed his lands, his water and his air. The white man has made it harder and harder for us to maintain our traditional ways and religious life. Now—for the first time—we have decided to intervene actively in the white man's courts to prevent the final devastation. We should not have had to go this far. Our words have not been heeded. This might be the last chance. We can no longer watch as our sacred lands are wrest from our control, as our spiritual center disintegrated. We cannot allow our control over spiritual homelands to be taken from us. The hour is already very late. (Lomayaktewa et al. 5–14–1971)

The statement is a blend of all sorts of assumptions from civil rights secured by the United States Constitution to indigenous cosmotheory applied to the hydraulics of the Black Mesa area. Once again, the Traditionalists emphasized not only their authority but also their claim to power over the entire continent. This claim, its general wording and style, the use of the courts, and the skillful use of writing in both the mass media and in judicial contexts have had a greater political impact than ever before.

The Use of Writing and the Expansion of Extramural Dialogue

The fact that Hopi knowledge became part of the public domain brought with it an implicit invitation to Hopis and especially non-Hopis to participate in a more-or-less conscious orchestration of apocryphal dialogue. This made Hopi thought more easily accessible to other like-minded movements, such as the ecology and civil rights movements, and also to other Indian organizations.

Nagata mentioned the role the Traditionalist use of circulars and newspapers had in this respect:

> While these circulars are biased and limited in circulation, local newspapers have also provided a larger arena for propaganda battle of Hopi factionalism. During the last war, the Third Mesa Traditionals visited a local newspaper office to air their grievances against compulsory draft by the United States government. A number of Traditionals wrote letters to the newspaper editors for publication and reporters visited them on the reservation. (1968:23)

Wider news coverage brought with it a considerable network of interrelationships and outside support. It also brought with it a dialogue with non-Hopis on apocalyptic subjects. And even though the Hopis have maintained the dominant role of "spiritual leaders" revealing the sacred traditions in a one-way communicative flow, they have nevertheless been influenced by the needs, topics, and wording of their White supporters.

The founding of a Traditionalist newsletter in the 1970s was basically an attempt once again to emulate the methods of the Tribal Council and its supporters. This gave them a competitive advantage, at least in the national arena. But it also provided a completely new advantage, namely, the possibility of constructing and controlling their public image. In other words, newsletters were an effective propaganda device, and useful, as well, in manipulating public opinion.

Each issue of the Traditionalist newsletter, *Techqua Ikachi. Land and Life–The Traditional Viewpoint from the Hopi Nation*, begins with a poetic description of one or another aspect of Hopi traditional life. These scenarios leave the reader with a clear impression of a sense of purity, eternity, peace, and mystery. The rest of each newsletter is filled with speeches by Traditionalist leaders or unabashedly biased accounts of various happenings both on and off the reservation. The poetic prelude is therefore juxtaposed with the impure, temporal, unpeaceful, and illogical activities of the opponents of the Traditionalists.

Sometimes the prelude is used to illustrate how perfect the Traditionalists are and how stupid the Progressives are. The following example from the June–July 1976 number is clearly a type of "Everyman" tale:

> One can barely see the three figures moving about in the distance. The land is bare, dry and empty, as if no one could survive there. Not a speck of moisture is visible on the surface. One who expects green meadows would be disappointed. This is Hopi land.
>
> In this large sandy field, the three men are busy working, each with a planting stick, a bag of seeds and thoughts of food for tomorrow and winter months. (This past winter brought less snow, which Hopi depend on for

> spring moisture.) Planting could have been easier, but the wind and hot sun has dried up much of the moisture. So they must go down quite deep to place the seeds below the surface of wet soil. In our traditional way, each hopes and prays it will rain soon so the planting will be quicker and easier. As he works, the eldest softly hums encouragement and blessing to the seeds. Now and then he shyly glances westward where the rainclouds are building.
>
> A short distance west of them, another group is busy working, hurrying to complete their job before it rains. "Stop your rain songs, Joe, until we finish this job," yelled the foreman jokingly, trying hard to be heard above the earth-moving machine. This is the land the Hopi Tribal Council chairman fenced off for his own stock, even though this area is very dry; hardly anyone could call it grazing land. However, there could be wealth underneath, as was foretold in the prophecies, so it has been leased without traditional approval to the oil company for exploration.
>
> Suddenly a cloud burst—workers scramble for cover. It lasted just a few minutes as puddles began to flow. "You should not have stopped me boss," mocked Joe, boastfully adding "drumbeats and foot stomping aren't necessary to make rain so I can drink!"
>
> Outside the fence, the men are disappointed. In spite of traditionals' disapproval, and the blame of themselves and the dam builders, the dam was approved and built at the insisting of the Hopi Tribal Council chairman. The dam greatly disturbs our prayers. Perhaps it will rain much harder next time. These and other earth dams in Hopi land and elsewhere will break down and be a waste of time and money.
>
> So the time passes on into summer and men tend their plants like newly born infants. We will face all the challenges of nature, wind, animals and insects, plus keep the weeds removed, or the soil will be sucked bone dry.

This little essay is a superb piece of political literature. It simultaneously idealizes the Hopi traditional way of life, counters modernist criticisms of its superstitious nature, and elegantly pictures the tribal chairman as a corrupt bumbler and a fool.

The Traditionalists were telling their story just as cleverly as the most sophisticated advertising consultant would. They knew exactly whom they were addressing and what types of images worked best in gaining their support and in persuading them to the points of view expressed in the political tirades in the rest of the issue.

One might ask what their goal was. The answer is that they wished to move their non-Hopi supporters emotionally and intellectually in order that they might physically, economically, and politically join the Traditionalist's battle against the Tribal Council. And it worked! For instance, the myth of the Mormonized "puppet" Council has become standard rhetoric in support-group publications. An ecologist publication had this to say:

> The traditional Hopi are grimly worried that their own tribal council will betray their tradition and the land. They know that the council members have all been trained in the white man's Indian School and have been led, since childhood, away from Traditional Hopi belief by Mormon, Mennonite and other missionaries. (Anonymous 1972, 34)

This statement is filled with so many misconceptions that it would take a book to explain why. Briefly, it can be said that betrayal is on *both* sides, *everyone* has been through the Indian schools, hardly 10 percent of the Hopi population are nominal Christians, and the Tribal Council is *not* a Christian organization nor is it dominated by Christians.

It should be clear now that literacy brought with it a more powerful instrument for propaganda. Earlier pamphlets and circulars had, of course, the same possibilities, but that literature was in the hands of White supporters and, therefore, out of Hopi control in principle. Only through letters, newsletters, and statements was it possible to construct a distinctively Hopi image on their own terms.

The Use of Writing and the Expansion of Intramural Dialogue

The effect that the new availability of secret knowledge had on intramural dialogue, that is, among Hopis of different persuasions, is just as significant a change as the dialogue with non-Hopis.

There are several points to be noted in this connection. In the first place, the availability of Hopi knowledge in the news media helped to alleviate the serious crisis which Hopi youths faced. It gave them a chance to express their views, reject the perceived self-destruction of their elders, and chart their own route in the apocryphal seas ahead. Since initiation is out of the question for a majority of the Hopi youth, letters to the editor were one of the few ways of expressing ethnic identity and exploring ways to accommodate acculturative processes with a minimal loss of cultural specificity. Besides that, the news media opened alternative paths to ethnic knowledge by providing easy access to Hopi traditions. In the second place, the news media allowed opponents one of the few opportunities to express their mutual criticisms to each other. In the third place, the written media served as a meeting place for all parties in the face of perceived cultural crises thus serving to develop an apocryphal consensus.

Nagata noted the effects that the use of the news media had on youth participation:

> More recently, however, the Letters to the Editors column of the Navajo Times, published by the Navajo Tribal Council, became a forum of the Hopi factionalism and the young members of both factions exchanged their viewpoints there for a prolonged period of time over such issues as

the legitimacy of the Council and value of Hopi ceremonies. Such exchange of opinions, vigorously partisan and yet channelled through an established means of communication, had never occurred in public before and once again marks a significant change in factional conduct. (1968:23)

One of the letters, written by a group of younger Hopis to the *Navajo Times*, attacked the Traditionalists in a thirteen-point program. The introduction and the last point are relevant to our discussion on the contexts of Hopi prophecy.

TO: So-Called Traditionalist Leaders
FROM: The Younger Hopi Generation

We have set out in various meetings to explode more than music. We have started to detonate the myth of a soft, self-indulgent and arrogant Hopi Indian Reservation.

We have demonstrated a Hopi enthusiastic in our sacrifice and sweat to help create a better reservation. Rather than sit around and listen to all dogs bark, or riot for so-called Traditionalist Leader's rights, we, the Younger Hopi Generation, have decided to pay a price of discipline in our lives.

We have made our aims:

- to end all hatred and give birth to equality and liberty, and unity for all Hopi People;
- to end moral pacifism and give birth to our recognized government, The Hopi Tribal Council;
- to end violent actions and give birth to a Hopi Nation that speaks out with a true and united voice.

That is why, we, the Younger Generation of the Hopi Indian Reservation, decided to speak out for what we feel is everybody's rights. Hundreds of us have expressed a desire to put our thoughts out, but have not, because of like pacifism.

We have formed and have expressed our thoughts which would give our people a purpose and inspire them with a postive idea.

Then follows their thirteen-point program.

13. Do you know, as Traditional Hopi People, that all these present actions by the younger Hopi People, were prophesied by our elders, that these things were going to be, and did you know that one cannot fight what is going to be? And are you aware, that, we don't believe, any one Hopi Indian is willing to go back and live "EXACTLY" as our elders lived centuries ago? Are you willing to go back and start all over again? We are all aware of these prophesies, so we, the younger generation, have decided to do exactly what was prophesied. We feel that the older people do not think of us, the younger generation, but only of themselves and what they can accomplish. We, the younger generation, cannot live as our forefathers did centuries ago, especially in this day and age. We are in a different world, and we want to live as that in this world.[4]

The news media have served as a public place in which to air grievances which opponents would never listen to at a meeting. The following exchange published in *Qua' Töqti* and *Techqua Ikachi* will suffice as illustration.

By 1976, the non-Traditionalist leaders of Shongopovi had had enough of Traditionalist tactics. On April 29th, they released a statement in *Qua' Töqti* which clearly articulated an anti-Traditionalist policy:

> We must now begin to give serious consideration to correcting and informing our people of Shungopavi the unfortunate situation we are experiencing today. From the very beginning of things down to modern times, we find that it is our duty and responsibility to reveal the truth.
>
> We speak only for our village, Shungopavi, and the majority of our people. Since the welfare of our people is being threatened, it is for that reason we wish to speak.
>
> Recently, we learned and understood that our village is being used for political purposes. Non-Hopis, other Hopis from different villages, and even our kikmongwi is involved in breaking down our ancient customs.
>
> Although our kikmongwi is supposed to look after the welfare of our people, he has become involved with "outsiders" who do not belong to this village. Old men complain of the carelessness of his responsibilities. This is part of the consequent breaking down of our religious structure.
>
> Other people who claim to represent our village under the disguise of "traditional leaders," are not the true leaders. Most of these individuals are from other villages and don't even participate in our sacred ceremonies. These people are selfish people who represent only themselves.
>
> The ones who are from this village seldom participate, or they neglect their duties that are assigned to them. Whenever they assemble here for their meetings, they never inform the people of what they are discussing. They never notify us of these meetings, and the kikmongwi is not supposed to listen to these outsiders for advice.
>
> Instead of helping the village with matters in these difficult days, the kikmongwi listens to a Christian preacher from Winslow and other outsiders who have no business in our village affairs. None of these outsiders who claim to be traditional leaders help us and participate in our sacred ceremonies. Many of them aren't even initiated.
>
> We are fearful, not of them, but of losing our tradition because of what is developing.
>
> We believe that we must continue our beliefs and traditions, and we must determine for ourselves what is best for our people. We know we have to deal with the present way of life today, and we have to deal with this fact for our children's sake.
>
> Only by overcoming the evil and corruption we have to face, can we accomplish and restore our land and people back to health.

4. *The Navajo Times*. The copy available to me was not dated. A valuable index of *The Navajo Times* was compiled by Richard E. Grant (n.d.) and is on file at Special Collections, University of Arizona.

The Christian preacher referred to is Caleb H. Johnson, who is an interpreter and spokesman for the Traditionalist Movement and present interpreter for the chief of Oraibi. The Shongopovi statement was signed by Alfred Joshevama (Piikyas clan), former leader of the Kwan Society; Viets Lomahaftewa (Cloud clan), former leader of the Al Society; and George Nasafotie (Blue Bird clan), former adviser to the Village Chief.

The Traditionalists, following their time-proven tactic of accusing their opponents of what they themselves are doing, responded in their own newspaper, *Techqua Ikachi,* with an article entitled "Shungopavi Sellout and Coverup":

> We feel obliged to comment on a very confusing article in *Qua'toqti,* the weekly newspaper of the "puppet" Hopi who have abandoned their tradition. The April 29 issue ran an article which quoted "leaders" in Shungopavi who claimed that the priesthood in that village is "jeopardized by corruption." This statement would be music to our ears if it were not from the mouth of "Bahanna Traditionalists," who in fact have abandoned their religious purpose.
>
> We regret that we must intervene and defend our traditional brothers in Shungopavi. We've known all along that one day our old songs would become very popular, and our pattern of life would once again be regarded as very beautiful, yet we would have to beware of the danger hidden beneath this show of "tradition." The article stressed that several religious leaders were dissatisfied with the political affairs of the Kikmongwi (chief) of the village, Claude Kewanyawma, claiming that his actions are not in harmony with his responsibility for the "welfare" of the village, and that "tradition" obliges them to reveal the "confusion" now threatening their "religious" way of life.
>
> It went on to say that serious consideration was taken to inform the people of Shungopavi of the "unfortunate situation," and that the Kikmongwi has become involved with "outsiders" and Hopi from other villages who were breaking down the "ancient custom" for selfish political purpose.
>
> In reality the "puppet" Hopi who make these claims are not defending Hopi tradition, though they would like it to look that way! They smear the Kikmongwi because he has taken a stand in opposition to a housing project which is indeed the work of *outsiders breaking down the ancient customs.*
>
> They claim to act from religious obligation, but they would not dare tell the truth, that the Kikmongwi is bound to defend the right of his villagers to own their land in common without allowing it to be leased or sold to the United States.
>
> These so-called Hopi are only looking for hand-outs. The Kikmongwi and the true Hopi in Shungopavi know it is best to survive in freedom as our ancestors have, by their own hands. All true Hopi deeply oppose handouts such as housing, sewers, water and power lines, because we want to remain farmers of the land, not puppets looking for a job. This is what is meant by following the Great Spirit's instructions.
>
> It suits the purpose of these seekers of handouts to make it appear that

> outside "radicals" are interfering and corrupting the religious structure, but it's the other way around. . . .
>
> The article fails to mention that these supposedly Hopi religious leaders are not Hopi, but Mormon! What else could they be, considering the fact that they prefer to follow the Mormon chairman of the Tribal Council rather than their traditional chief! (April-May 1976)

There is a whole series of untruths in the *Techqua Ikachi* piece. It should be noted for the record at this point that the tribal chairman was not a Mormon, that the authors of the *Qua' Töqti* statement are not puppets, but are respected leaders in the traditional Hopi sense of the word, and that Traditionalist meetings were indeed disrupting life at Shongopovi.

Finally, the written media have served to construct a common meeting place for the development of an apocryphal consensus. The increased capacity of the Traditionalists to maintain and replicate a growing list of prophetic statements, together with the increased participation of noninitiated Hopis in the dialectical process due to the use of the mass media, has resulted in perhaps the most curious development in the history of Hopi thought. I am referring to the document, quoted in detail in chapter 5, produced by the Hopi Health Department, which implicitly accepts the forty-year old prophetic corpus of the Traditionalists, and which seeks to explain and prove these statements by applying Western modes of rational argumentation. From the perspectives of this book, the document in question illustrates more than any other the generative process of cultural transmission and thus the relationship between tradition and change in modern Hopi affairs.

LITERACY AND TEXTUALIZATION

Stephen A. Tyler has addressed the relationship between speech and writing in his attempts to provide a postmodern orientation to anthropology (1978, 1987).

> Writing restructures the speech act, for every text is addressed to every reader in every time, carries its own world of reference within itself, and has freed itself from the intentions of its author. A text is timeless, universal, and objective, speaks to anyone who is literate, and reveals to him a self-contained meaning. . . . Yet this objective and universal character can be realized only through the subjectivity of some reader; thus the burden of interpretation. Though a text is always about a world or a possible world, it does not refer directly to a world outside itself, for its world is always created in the dialectic between itself and the reader, the reader supplying a world where the text does not specify one. Nor need a text speak openly of its author or his intentions. Once written, a text assumes an independent existence and acquires meanings of its own quite apart from those

> intended by its author. The author's intentions, like the text's world, are supplied by the reader, not the text, and it is not uncommon for a reader to understand an author better than he could understand himself, as the reader may see in the text implications for a world far wider than that of the author's. He may, for example, see the text in relation to others not even written when the author lived, or have access to learned commentaries, or simply understand it from an existential situation much different from the author's. (1978:378–379)

I am interested in the distinctively emergent and cooperative nature of textualization which not only allows the reader to interpret "a negotiated text," but which also allows "the parties to the originating dialogue" (Tyler 1987:204) to do so as well. I also want to point out that writing bears with it certain consequences that have little to do with reader or writer and yet affects their way of perceiving the topic that is ostensibly being textualized. Writing creates, in Tyler's words, "totalistic illusions" (ibid.:208). For instance, in looking through the emergence myths reproduced in Appendix B, one is left with the impression of continuity, historical rightness, and existential truth. Such is the impression the judicial use of rhetorical devices is meant to impart! But a closer look at the texts reveals fragmentation, historical contingency, chance encounters with chance audiences, and the direct manipulation of purportedly revealed truths.

Qötshongva's texts are a case in point. How do we account for the coherence of the 1935 text (Kotchongva 1936), the incoherence of the 1956 text (Bentley 1956), the almost totally new story of 1970 (Skidmore 1970), and the final return to the original story in 1970 (Tarbet 1972)? The answers to these questions are not found in the texts themselves, but in the emergent and cooperative nature of textualization, where rhetorical devices define historical realities. Our job must be to pursue an interpretive description of the realities of which the text is a product.

The fact that the oral tradition of the Traditionalists has become written tradition is not without serious consequences to both the tradition and its bearers. The written texts impart the illusion of permanence, but they also provide ease of review for the reader. Thus the metaphors of consistency and permanence, upon which prophecy makes its claims to authority and power, seem to disappear in the face of historical and comparative criticism.

One might label such criticism as an exercise in hegemony, but it could also be understood as a means by which to reflect on other meanings beyond the surface realities of things. Is it useful for us to dwell on sham, posturing, and fraud, or are there other mechanisms at work which are fundamental to religious sentiment? This study will indicate that there are.

PART II

Prophecy and Politics

FIVE

Hopi Prophecies in History

Looking at Hopi religion against the kaleidescopic background of changing political, social, and historical factors clearly indicates that the development of Hopi religion can be plotted historically from local, mainstay agricultural concerns, through the confrontation with dominant cultures, to the rise of a universal, missionizing religion promoted by the Traditionalist Movement. The phase of confrontation with White Americans and Europeans has led to a complicated symbiosis between the Hopis and a whole gamut of Euro-American ecological movements, new religious movements (such as New Age), and other special interest groups. A meticulous comparison, however, of Hopi prophetic statements that have been committed to print for one reason or another since 1858 and their in situ historical context clearly shows that important changes have occurred in the contents of Hopi prophecy.

The method used in this chapter is not detailed historiography, although significant events will be mentioned especially in relation to Hopi prophetic expectations. Rather, the method chosen here is comparative: What are the themes of these prophetic statements, how do they stand in causal relationship to historical events, and what, if any, other factors may have been influential in the formulation of these prophetic statements?

The list of prophetic statements from 1858 to 1961 (in Appendix C) is as complete as possible. It does not contain everything because of the nature of the sources. Traditionalist prophecies, for example, are mostly found in out-of-the-way newspapers in several different languages, in unavailable, underground newspapers, any number of unindexed incidental "my life among the Indians" type of books, completely unidentifiable flyers and leaflets, and other fortuitous literature, or radio and television spots. We do, however, have a large number of official and published sources that are easily available and which have never been analyzed, and there are several private and public collections that are invaluable for our purposes.

It should be noted that the prophetic statements are paraphrased for analytical purposes. Many of the original statements are conflations of several different elements which are best analyzed in clearly delineated categories. Other statements contain redundancies, circumlocutions, colloquialisms, and implicit contextualisms that detract from the consistency and utility of the catalogue. The reader can judge whether this approach is justified by comparing fully quoted prophecies in this chapter with the corresponding statements in the typology in the Appendix.

The statements in Appendix C are presented both chronologically and typologically. The main types concern: 1) The White Brother, 2) the Mormons, 3) internal affairs, 4) Maasaw and the purification day, 5) the emergence myth, and 6) the land. Categories 1 and 4 represent over 80 percent of all prophetic statements, category 1 alone representing over half. About 70 percent of the corpus originates from the Hostiles and the later Traditionalist Movement.

Concerning the chronological criteria, I date all statements according to when they were committed to print and have deliberately ignored the postulated age of the statements. Believers, whether Hopis or others, will rightfully criticize me here. On the one hand, the postulated, nondocumented age of a statement is impossible to date, and on the other hand, its postulated age is central to the rhetorical and sociological aspects of Hopi prophecies. These latter factors, I feel, require explanation more than the analytical reasons for ignoring precognitive claims.

My typology of statements stops with the year 1961. One of the reasons for this is that a veritable explosion of prophecies occurred during the period of 1961–1980. The sheer amount of documents involved would overreach the limits of one book. The second reason is that this chapter sets out to prove that no recorded prophecy can be shown to predate the event, and that the prophecies reflect contemporaneous concerns. This can easily be shown for the period in question and so I do not feel that it is necessary to prove that none of the prophecies of the last three decades predates any of the events spoken of, such as space trips to the moon, gene splicing, test-tube babies, and so on. Even though the documentation of prophetic statements in Appendix C ends with 1961, the two last sections of this chapter indicate the themes of the following decades and a more-or-less complete summary of the accumulated prophetic corpus of the 1980s.

THE PROPHECIES OF 1858–1958

There are many accounts describing the history of the Hopis from the first contacts with Europeans to recent times.[1] I intend here only to characterize the themes and concerns of each decade. I have also chosen to skip over the Spanish period because we have no documents that prove the existence of Hopi prophecies at that time, and so there would be no reason for us to begin our review at this early period. I will concentrate instead on the period from the 1830s to the end of the 1950s in this subchapter and then on the 1960s to the 1980s in the next.

The 1830s

During the Mexican control of the area (1823–1848), most of the settlers of the southwest were under constant attack by marauding bands of Ute, Navajo, Comanche, and Apache. The Hopis suffered considerably from the assaults, many being killed or taken as slaves, and their food and goods stolen. The Hopis had met individual Euro-Americans, mostly trappers, as early as 1826. One of the events that is remembered was the ruthless murder of fifteen or twenty Hopis by a group of trappers in 1834. This event, in Titiev's opinion (1944:71), marked the beginning of the many decades of hostility which especially the Oraibians held towards Americans.[2]

The 1850s

In 1850 a deputation of Hopi leaders met with James S. Calhoun, Indian Agent of the Territory of New Mexico (including Arizona), at Santa Fe to determine the purposes of the American government and to ask for assistance in keeping the Navajos out of Hopi territory. A year later they repeated their request and asked for assistance in getting more rain as well. Calhoun was not in any position to help them despite his good intentions. During the mid-1850s the Hopi population, which already

1. James 1974; Brew 1949, 1979; Dockstader 1979; Spicer 1962; Titiev 1944; and Clemmer 1978*b*, 1979. One of the best modern studies of Hopi history is Whiteley 1988.

2. See Sabin 1935. The event is described by Frances Victor: In 1834 a trapping party under Joseph L. Meek was joined by another party of sixty men under Frapp and Jervais, two of the partners in the Hudson's Bay Company. Reaching the pueblos of the Moquis (Hopi)

> these trappers, instead of approaching them with offers of purchase, lawlessly entered their gardens, rifling them of whatever fruit or melons were ripe, and not hesitating to destroy that which was not ripe. To this, as might be expected the Moquies objected, and were shot down for so doing. In this truly infamous affair fifteen or twenty of them were killed. (1870:153)

Meek stated that he "didn't belong to that crowd."

was suffering depletion due to starvation and hostile raiders, was decimated by a severe smallpox epidemic (Donaldson 1893:28). It is also important to note that farming implements were distributed from Fort Defiance to the Hopi villages at this time (Hammond 1957, I:21; Whiteley 1988:32).

The Mormons were very interested in the Indians because, as is well known, the *Book of Mormon* calls them the Lamanites, one of the lost tribes of Israel. According to Mormon eschatology, the ten tribes will be restored, Zion will be built in North America, where Christ will reign personally on earth, and the earth will be renewed and become a paradise. During the gathering of the tribes, the Lamanites, who had been cursed with dark skins, will be converted and become white again (Hoekema 1963:67ff; O'Dea 1957).

After the assassination of Jonathan Smith, the founder of Mormonism, Brigham Young became its leader when the Mormons migrated out west. In 1858, the Mormon missionary Jacob Hamblin was sent to the Hopi area by Brigham Young. He visited Oraibi and was greeted as the long-awaited Pahaana. Hamblin wrote that he received the following information through a Ute interpreter:

> They told us some of their traditions, which indicate that their fathers knew the Mexicans, and something about Montezumas.
>
> A very aged man said that when he was a young man, his father told him that he would live to see white men come among them, who would bring them great blessings, such as their fathers had enjoyed, and that these men would come from the west. He believed that he had lived to see the prediction fulfilled in us. (Little 1881:62 reformulated as 1.0.0.–1.0.2. in Appendix C)

It is interesting to note that the notion of White men coming from the west (statement 1.0.1.) is the only one of its kind in the whole corpus. All other versions state that the White man will come from the east. This inconsistency could reflect any number of things: that all other versions are post-Mormon (meaning that all the Hopi clans changed their story when they discovered the Mormons were not the awaited Pahaana—an explanation that seems unlikely); that Hamblin's consultant changed the details to fit the moment; or that Hamblin himself, or Little, his biographer, changed the details to fit their own considerable eschatological expectations. There is no doubt, at least, that the Mormon party arrived from a westerly direction, having traveled the route from Santa Clara, Utah, with stops at Pipe Springs and the foot of the Kibab mountains and crossing the Colorado River at Ute Ford.

As the quote shows, Hamblin's consultant is reported to have believed that he had lived to see the prediction fulfilled in Hamblin and his party.

But after two months, the missionaries who had remained after Hamblin's departure were forced to leave because "a division arose among the people as to whether we were the men prophesied of by their fathers, who would come among them with the knowledge that their fathers possessed" (ibid.:63).

Hamblin had tried to persuade the Hopis to move to the other side of the Colorado River. The following prophecies were their response:

> They must not cross that river until the three prophets who took them into the country they now occupy, should visit them again. Their chief men also prophesied that the "Mormons" would settle in the country south of them, and that their route of travel would be up the Little Colorado. (ibid.:63–64, cf. 2.0.0.–2.0.1.)

This latter prophecy may be the only instance of apparent precognition in the entire corpus, if we are to believe Hamblin when he says that "this looked very improbable to us at that time, but all has since been fulfilled" (ibid.:64). One could counter that an intimate knowledge of the lay of the land and astute political discernment were integral to the prophecy. Mormon settlement along the Little Colorado River began due south of the Hopi area (where the Little Colorado and the Rio Puerco meet) by the United Order in 1873. The first attempt failed, but the second attempt in 1876 resulted in the establishment of the four colonies of Sunset, Brigham City, Obed, and St. Joseph.[3] Even though it was first published in 1881, Little's diary ends with the year 1877. It is obvious that this particular section of his diary was written in hindsight. Since just exactly how much was hindsight and when it was written are impossible to establish, we also cannot determine the reliability of these particular prophecies.

Although repeated attempts were made to convert the Hopis during the years following, no real inroads were achieved. By 1875 the Mormons had established a community near Moenkopi, due to the friendliness of an Oraibi man called Tuuvi. However, no more than a dozen were converted and after 1880 Mormon efforts lay dormant.[4] But it is not without significance that, as Whiteley put it, "the Hopi developed separate categories of person for these two types of newcomers—*momonam* (Mormons) and *pahaanam* (other Anglos)—and they trusted the former considerably more than the latter" (1988:34). This indicates that the Hopis were constantly engaged in reassessing their ideas about White people.

3. Cf. McClintock 1921:135, Tanner and Richards 1977, Abruzzi 1989.

4. For an excellent summary of Mormon efforts among the Hopis, see Whiteley 1988:33–37.

The 1860s

The 1860s brought famine, drought, and smallpox epidemics, but also the defeat of the Navajos in 1863 by Kit Carson. Material aid to the destitute Hopis finally arrived in 1864.

The 1870s

The Moqui Pueblo Agency, which had been established at Fort Wingate in 1869, was moved to Keams Canyon in 1873 (cf. Donaldson 1893: 36). The decade brought increased government and missionary activity in Hopi territory. In 1876 the agency was discontinued and then reinstated as a subagency of the Navajo Agency at Fort Defiance, administered by the school superintendent. Throughout the 1870s Oraibi was hostile to U.S.-government agents, but was more hospitable to other visitors such as John Wesley Powell's expeditions of 1869–1872 (Whiteley 1988:40–42).

The 1880s

The 1880s brought several dire events and the next spate of prophecies. In 1882 President Chester A. Arthur declared the boundaries of the Moqui Indian Reservation, apparently in a superficial attempt to check the recurring encroachments of the Navajos. The Executive Order Area consisted of 2,500,000 acres which were set aside for Hopis and "such other Indians as the Secretary of Interior may see fit to settle thereon."

One of Alexander Stephen's consultants at Walpi, Müauwutaka, stated what was uppermost in the minds of the Hopis at the time, namely, that the White chief would protect them against their enemies and would give them tools and other goods (1.1.0.–1.2.0.).

Frank Hamilton Cushing, on an expedition to Oraibi in 1882 to collect for the National Museum and to record scientific information, met with other attitudes that were clearly expressed in apocryphal terms. He had evidently been cordially received by the village chief, Loololma, but was hardly prepared for the impertinence and hostility he met at the general council. Cushing handled the situation as best he could, but his opponent postured and blustered more vehemently. Cushing's description of the context of the prophetic statements, which are to follow, gives a good impression of the dynamics of the exchange:

> They said to me, "You are a heap of dung in our plazas; you stink of your race. Leave or we will throw you off the mesas, as we throw dung out of the plazas."
>
> "Oh no; I must know why you hate the Americans, who are your friends."
>
> "We do not hate you; we hate Washington and his American children."

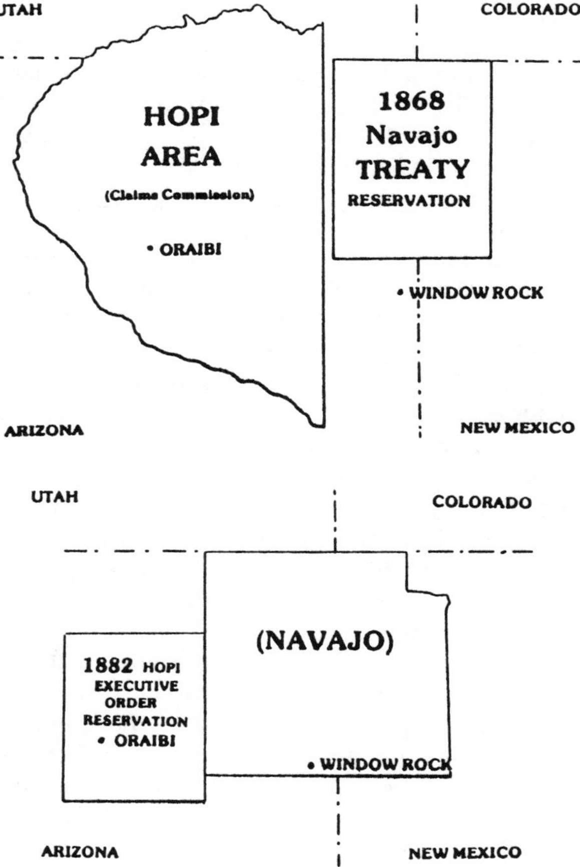

Map 1. Estimated Hopi aboriginal territory and the 1868 Navajo Treaty Reservation, compared with the 1882 Hopi Executive Order Reservation and the 1880 Executive Order Navajo Reservation. SOURCE: *Hopi Tutu-veh-ni,* vol. 1, no. 1, Spring 1986. Courtesy of the Hopi Tribe, Office of Public Relations.

"But you must tell me why you hate Washington, for he it was who, through his chiefs, sent me here."

"Because of the words of our ancients."

"Yes, yes! but how do you know what your ancients said about the Americans?"

"We know their speeches of many years ago, even of the times when the world was new." (Cushing 1922:263)

Incredibly enough, Cushing managed to convince his opponent to relate the emergence myth to him. It is difficult to imagine the absurdity of that moment: The kiva filled with angry Hopis, emotionally whipped up, yet waiting patiently for the interpretor to translate the narrative, while Cushing, who most certainly was just as upset, laboriously wrote down every word on paper by firelight! As he wrote:

> As soon as I had sat down by the fire, they gave me in substance their myth of creation, which for the sake of clearness I have given rather as a myth than as an infuriated argument, interspersed with the most insulting messages to Washington, and demands that he send his soldiers without delay to destroy or attempt to destroy the Oraibi tribe, in the face of their magic and the prophecies of the myth. (ibid.:263–264)

After having written what later became six printed pages, Cushing had to leave with his gun drawn. These were, of course, not the best of circumstances for procuring reliable data. There is even some doubt whether the story was told at all during this confrontation. Parsons mentions in a note that in his report to the Bureau of Ethnology, Cushing "states that he recorded the myth in the days subsequent to the meeting" (Parsons, ed. 1922:264 n.10), which raises questions about the identity of the actual narrator. Evidently Cushing did receive a summary of the emergence myth during the encounter, and what he managed to record over one-hundred years ago is of central importance to this study.

Conventional ethnographic accounts attribute the origin of the conflicting factions, which Cushing noted in 1882 and which ultimately led to the split of Oraibi in 1906, to the policies of Chief Loololma. He had evidently been hostile to the government until he and a number of other Hopis visited Washington in an attempt to find a solution to the Navajo problem. He came back impressed by American affluence and power, and he had promised to allow his children to go to school. He was convinced that the true Pahaana had come, but the conservative groups under the leadership of Lomahongyiwma of the Spider clan disagreed, and thus began the series of conflicts at Oraibi which ultimately led to its tragic split in 1906.[5]

Whiteley has now disproven this theory. No such visit to Washington had occurred prior to 1890, and a careful analysis of those present at the Cushing encounter proves that the lines of conflict were already clearly demarcated and that the leaders of the opposing factions held social and political positions substantially similar to those present at the split in 1906. Whiteley's conclusion is that "although this visit may have been a

5. Cf. Titiev 1944:72ff, James 1974:130–131, Clemmer 1978*b*:39, 54, Dockstader 1979:526.

powerful catalyst of dispute, it was not the originating source of the factions" (1988:73).

Another corrective is that Lomahongyiwma was not the leader of the hostile faction at that time. He first became important in 1894 when he became head of the core lineage segment of the Spider clan (ibid.: 86–88). It is therefore unlikely that Lomahongyiwma was the narrator of the tale recorded by Cushing, as Titiev (1944:76), Goldfrank (1948:244), and others have thought. Cushing wrote in his report that the main hostile leader was "Kui-ian-ai-ni-wa," which Whiteley suggests is another name for Talay'ima, identified by Titiev as head of the Spider clan, chief priest of the Momtsit, and Lomahongyiwma's mother's brother. It is highly probable, therefore, that the narrator of the myth was Talay'ima (Whiteley 1988:320 n. 7).

At any rate, the following prophecies from the narrative clearly indicate a symbiosis between tradition and contemporary events:

> Then you shall turn back to the place of your birth, seeking a country more spacious wherein to dwell. It is then that you will meet me again. You will find me poor, while you will return in the grandeur of plenty, and in the welfare of good food. You will find me hungry and offer me nourishment; but I will cast your morsels aside from my mouth. You will find me naked and offer me garments of soft fabrics, but I will rend your raiments and trample them under my feet. You will find me sad and perplexed, and offer me speeches of consolation and advice; but I will spurn your words, I will reproach, revile and despise you. You will smile upon me and act gently; but I will scowl upon you and cast you aside as I would cast filth from my presence. Then will you rise and strike my head from my neck. As it rolls in the dust you will arrest it and sit upon it as upon a stool-rock. Then, nor until then, may you feed my belly or clothe my body. But a sorry day will it be for you when you sit upon my head as upon a stool-rock, and a glad day for me. For on that day you will but divide the trail of your own life with the knife which severs my head from my body, and give to me immortal life, liberty, and surcease from anxiety. (Cushing 1924:169–170, cf. 1.3.0–1.4.1.)

Here we find that the White Brother is a complex figure. He is heading west because he needs more room, but the Hopis must not just wallow in the grandeur and affluence of their White Brother. This can be understood as a direct criticism of Loololma's open-door policy. The narrator formulated his open rebellion not only against Loololma's policy, but also against his right to remain chief; and all of it is subtly expressed in eschatological terms. The reference to beheading as the transformative process probably meant then, as it did later, that the chief must be beheaded. Whereas later references to beheading were thought to be the punishment for sorcerers and wicked people, in Talay'ima's case it becomes a tool for defeating the Whites and for gaining immortality and peace for the Hopis. In Talay'ima's statements we find the beginnings of the darkly apocryphal tones that characterize the prophetic traditions of the conservative groups and the later Traditionalist Movement. Statements by groups more friendly to the Whites are clearly optimistic and positive and resemble in structure the expectations of millenarian cults the world over.

Things worsened after the Cushing episode. 1887 saw the reestablishment of the Hopi Agency (administered until 1899 as the joint Moqui and Navajo Agency), the establishment of the Moqui Boarding School at Keams Canyon, and the passing of the Dawes Severalty Act, which was an attempt to radically change the system of land allotment.

The 1890s

The 1890s brought the implementation of the Dawes Severalty Act, which was clearly a threat not only to indigenous territoriality, but also to Hopi social patterns. The implementation led to armed confrontation between the hostile Oraibians and the U.S. Cavalry. The Hostiles evidently felt that they had been betrayed by Loololma during his visit to Washington in 1890 and they were convinced that the beheading was at hand. Indeed, the Kookop men announced during the armed (but bloodless) confrontation in 1891: "Now the world is going to end, and if you want to be saved come to Kokop house and join our side" (Titiev 1944: 79). The confrontation ended in arrests, but the allotment program was widely opposed by Hopis and knowledgeable Whites and was abandoned in 1894.

During the following years government troops forced the Oraibi children to move to the school at Keams or to the Mennonite Missionary School below Oraibi. The latter was established in 1893 by the controversial H. R. Voth. More schools were established and from 1899 to c.1903 the Oraibi Day School was directed by the violent and temperamental principal Herman Kampmeier, who played no small part in alienating Hopi parents from the system he represented.[6]

Further confrontations led to further arrests, but, more significantly, Lomahongyiwma was now raised up by the hostile faction as a direct rival to Loololma for the position of village chief. This act led to the establishment of separate observances of certain key ceremonials. Thus, religious affiliation coincided with political allegiance. For example, the Bear clan was opposed by the Kookop and Spider clans, which means

6. Cf. Whiteley 1988:74–86 concerning the issues of schooling and missionaries.

that the village chief was opposed by the war chief, an opposition to which Whiteley ascribes great significance (1988:67, 1987).

A smallpox epidemic during 1898–1899 led to programs of forced segregation, the burning of clothes, fumigation of houses, and vaccinations. These measures led to confrontations with troops at Second Mesa and imprisonment. Several of the imprisoned turned out to be instrumental in the Oraibi split seven years later (Whiteley 1988:90–91).

During the latter half of the 1890s a growing number of tourists began to arrive, especially in response to the colorful and romantic pamphlets issued by the Fred Harvey Company and the Atchison, Topeka, and Santa Fe Railway. As Clemmer wrote,

> the Santa Fe Railroad was issuing elaborate tourist pamphlets full of photographs, advertising colorful Hopi ceremonies and quaint Hopi villages as the best tourist attraction on the route of the Chief. . . . Photos of Hopi ceremonies at Oraibi in 1897 show not only the ceremonial participants, but also other photographers, carefully lining up their tripods smack in the midst of one of the most important and sacred Hopi ceremonies. (1978*b*:56–57)

The activities of the Fred Harvey Company were manifold, and the company developed and/or played a part in restaurant and hotel chains, museums and display rooms, guided automobile tours, stationside "world's fairs," ethnic theme-amusement parks, and so on. More importantly, the Fred Harvey Company "appropriated, displayed, and marketed the cultures of the Native American," not just catering to middle-class taste, but actually forming it (Weigle 1989:115, 121).

One of the most startling of these unwanted guests was the anthropologist Matilda Coxe Stevenson, who had studied the neighboring Zunis. According to the *Illustrated Police News* for March 6, 1886, she forced her way into a Hopi kiva. Since the Hopis could not stop her, they locked her up so that she had to be rescued by Thomas Keam (Fewkes 1922:273; James 1974:109–110). Oraibians had repeatedly warned Whites not to attend their ceremonials. Despite these excesses, government agents and school superintendents were just as anxious to remove not only the tourists, but also the growing number of missionaries and long-term visitors who sided with the Hostiles and who were opposed to the enculturation programs effectuated by the agents and the schools (Whiteley 1988: 93–94).

The 1900s

The first two decades of the twentieth century were probably among the darkest in recent Hopi history. The agent to the "Moqui Reservation," Charles E. Burton, was just as violent and temperamental as

Kampmeier. During the first years of the decade he attempted to have all Hopi men and boys given haircuts, a move that fortunately was stopped by a campaign conducted against Burton by Charles F. Lummis, a friend of Theodore Roosevelt and one of the spokesmen of the Sequoyah League (cf. Lummis 1903).

By this time Oraibians were resigning themselves to their fate. The town was already divided politically and religiously, and it was only a matter of time before the combined forces on the reservation would clash. Yukiwma was now the leader of the anti-American, conservative group, and Tawakwaptiwa was the village chief and leader of the pro-American, progressive group. Drought and harvest failures plagued the Hopis and, in the fateful year of 1906, the springs were failing. The Navajos were encroaching right up to the villages, the school program was being enforced, and the factional leaders were provoking each other more and more. All of these conditions could only be, and were, understood as the result of negligence and witchcraft on the part of the religious leaders.

Whereas some of the prophecies of that time reflect a simple desire for help from the White people (1.5.0., 1.6.0.), the prophecies of the leaders of the factions were specifically oriented to contemporary affairs. Yukiwma, who was now leader of the Hostile faction, introduced a more radical interpretation of what the Elder Brother will do than had his grand-uncle Talay'ima. In his opinion, if the Hopis get into trouble again, as in the lower world, the Elder Brother will come back to them, find the sorcerers who caused the trouble, and behead them (1.8.0.).

The problem then became a question of who the Elder Brother is and who the sorcerers are. Yukiwma distinguished between two types of Whites: the Elder Brother, and those White men who baptize, beat, trouble, and kill the Hopis, and take away their children (1.9.0.), which is a brief but accurate list of U.S.-government and missionary activities during the preceding twenty years. The sorcerers he identified as those Hopis who will join the White men and try to be like them and speak on their behalf (1.9.1.). In other words, the sorcerers who were prophecied are Tawakwaptiwa and his supporters (3.0.0.).

But Yukiwma was not content with prophetic analysis. He also provided a solution to the problem, albeit, clothed in the prophetic tense:

> But we should not listen to them, we should continue to live like the Hopi. We should continue to use the food of the Hopi and wear the clothes of the Hopi. (Voth 1905:26, cf. 1.9.2.)

His policy was, therefore, political opposition as the key to cultural survival. The land issue, which one would expect to find as a central theme already at this time, is only vaguely referred to (4.0.0.).

September 7, 1906, brought the violent confrontation between opposing parties in Oraibi which ended in the split of that village and the subsequent founding of Hotevilla by Yukiwma.

None of the opposing parties actually won anything after the split. Besides all of the bitterness and shame, the Hopis had to contend with the U.S. government now playing a more active role on the reservation. The new chief of Oraibi (Loololma's successor) was Tawakwaptiwa. He was temporarily divested of his chieftainship, and he and his family were sent off to the Sherman Institute in Riverside, California, to learn to become Americans. This experience, however, turned him into a bitter and resentful ally. Yukiwma was serving the first of many prison terms to come, and many other Hostiles were also jailed, leaving about 200 women, children, and younger men to survive the winter.

The statements we have from shortly before and immediately after the split are without exception thinly disguised commentary on contemporary political affairs. Yukiwma's prophecies clearly show that he maintained his two categories of White persons, and that he was waiting for the true Pahaana to come and behead the troublemakers and to establish Yukiwma himself as the legitimate village chief (1.11.0.–1.12.0.). The emphasis on sorcerers is gone. Yukiwma related prophecies about the chief who abandons the old ways and who is to be beheaded, not necessarily by the still-immanent White Brother, but immediately by the already-present Americans (1.13.0.).

Tawakwaptiwa and his supporters agreed with Yukiwma about the Americans, but they were of course of another opinion concerning the identity of the persons to be beheaded. Speaking about the migrations of the Bear clan, Wikvaya from Oraibi stated:

> In all they stopped ten times before arriving at the Americans, where the sun rises. Here they stopped four years. Their children learned a little English. The land being scarce, the Americans told them to go west and hunt land for themselves, and if anybody would be bad to them (núkpana) and cause their children to die, they (the Americans) would come and cut the Núkapana's heads off. (Voth 1905:28)

Thus, there was no doubt in Wikvaya's mind that the Hostiles were to be beheaded.

Another important theme in the prophecies documented at this time concerns the split itself. Both Yukiwma and Tawakwaptiwa agreed that the split of 1906 had been prophecied (3.1.0. and 3.2.0.). New light has been shed by Whiteley on the years following the split, especially concerning the role of the government during the aftermath and the little-known factors intrinsic to the foundation of Bacavi (1988:110–118, 150–161, 198–216). Instead of being founded, as the conventional view holds, by Christian and progressive elements who were supposedly driven out in 1907 by the recently returned and now-resentful Tawakwaptiwa, Bacavi was founded by some of the most powerful leaders of the Hostile faction. They had returned to Oraibi in 1906 through the mediation of government agents after Tawakwaptiwa was sent to Sherman. They resided in Oraibi for three years and, when Tawakwaptiwa returned, a second split occurred in November 1909, which led to the founding of Bacavi.

Other matters contributed to the Hopi misery. The government reinstated the allotment program in 1908 to provide land for Moenkopi and the offshoot villages of the Oraibi split, but unfortunately also for the Navajos.

The 1910s

Tawakwaptiwa also spent the next years driving out all Christian and progressive villagers, which led to the establishment of Kykotsmovi (Titiev 1944:94–95). He evidently wanted the village to die with him, as later statements indicate (cf. statements 3.4.1. and 3.6.0.).

Yukiwma, in contrast, seemed to be in a more moderate mood, judging from his prophetic statements of 1910 (1.14.0.–1.14.2.). The political situation in 1910, with the newly established, nearby, rival village of Bacavi thriving on the assistance and goodwill of the U.S. government, now allowed him to admit that the good things of the Whites may be used, even though the Hopis must still stick to their own way of life.

The allotment program was finally abandoned in March 1911, the same year that agent Leo Crane took over. Political reality for the Hostiles had now changed for the worse. Crane began to encourage policies of forced education and the restriction and prohibition of Hopi ceremonials. That year we find Yukiwma making strident statements to Colonel Scott shortly before Scott forcibly removed the Hotevilla children to the school in Keams Canyon. Yukiwma had visited Washington and was now certain that they were not the Pahaana (1.15.0.; 1.16.0.). In general, his statements are apocryphal, bitter, and political. He blamed the Bear clan for the present troubles of the Hopis (1.15.0.). He once again expected a beheading (1.17.0.–1.17.4.), and also showed signs of a persecution complex (3.3.0.).

Yukiwma truly perceived his situation in apocryphal terms, despite the contemporaneous elements in his prophetic statements. One day Crane visited Yukiwma while he was imprisoned at Keams Canyon. Yukiwma explained his actions in this manner (1.15.2.):

> I am doing this as much for you as for my own people. Suppose I should not protest your orders—suppose I should willingly accept the ways of the

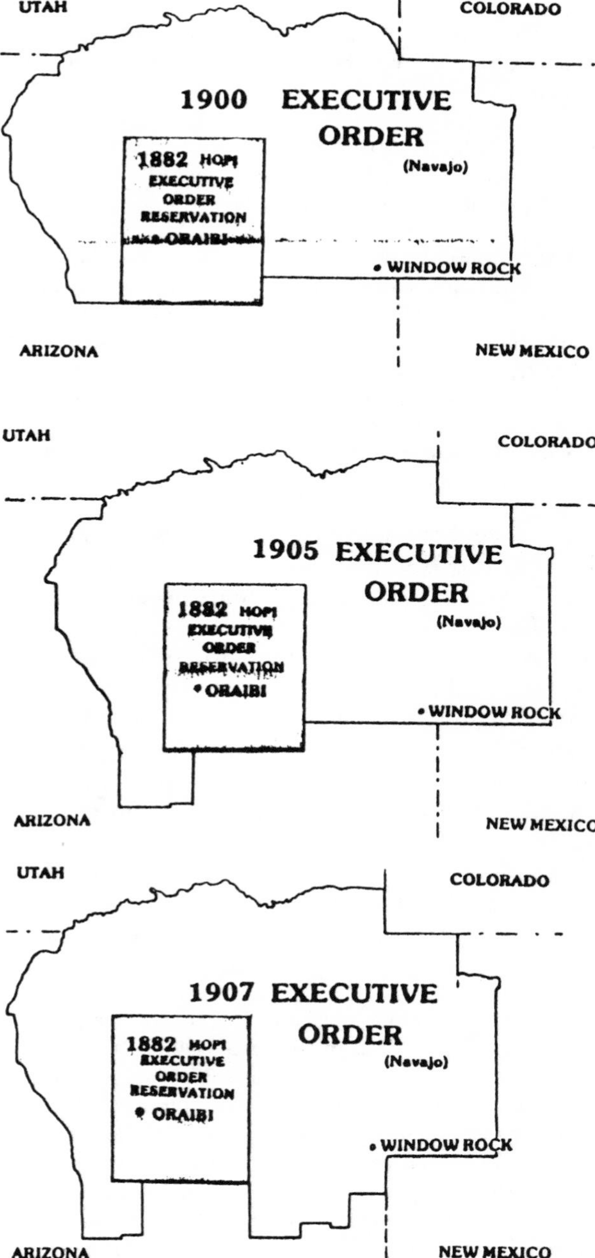

Map 2. Executive Order expansions of the Navajo Reservation, 1900, 1905, and 1907. SOURCE: *Hopi Tutuveh-ni,* vol. 1 no. 1, Spring 1986. Courtesy of the Hopi Tribe, Office of Public Relations.

> Bohannas. Immediately the Great Snake would turn over, and the Sea would rush in, and we would all be drowned. You too. I am therefore protecting *you*. (Crane 1925:188)

Wilson D. Wallis' Sun clan consultant from Shongopovi told him similar things in 1912 (1.18.0.–1.18.3.). He tried to visualize what would happen if the Hopis ever forgot their oral traditions:

> Ma'cawa gave this story [the emergence myth] inscribed on a stone, to the Hopi. He said: "The whole earth is mine. As long as you keep this, it all belongs to you." One piece of the stone is broken off. Ki'oma, the present chief of Shumopovi, has the stone now. "When this story is forgotten, something disastrous will happen. Perhaps the stars will fall down into the ocean, and the ocean will become oil. Then the sun will set fire to it, and the conflagration will consume everyone. Perhaps there will be an earthquake that will kill everyone." That is what my father's father told me. (Wallis 1936:16–17, cf. 5.0.0.)

It is interesting to note that natural cataclysms begin to enter Hopi prophecies several years after the fatal earthquakes in San Francisco (1906), Valparaiso (1906), and Messina (1908), and the devastating typhoon at Hong Kong (1906).

The Shongopovi consultant's attitude towards the Whites is much more positive than Yukiwma's. The Americans are messianic figures with whom the Shongopovian could imagine a more intimate social relationship. It should be noted that this information was provided while the consultant, who was residing off the reservation at the Carlisle Indian School, visited Wallis at the University of Pennsylvania Museum at Philadelphia.

Leo Crane's prisoners at Keams Canyon were avidly interested in developments outside the reservation, especially during the war in Europe, a curiosity that undoubtedly influenced the details of their later prophecies:

> The Hopi interest in war-time methods and inventions could always be aroused through the illustrations in the great dailies. My pictorial sections of the *New York Times* were in great demand. They would pour over them, remarking the vast number of soldiers, and would ask for many explanations. Men were flying as birds through the air, and carrying the war beneath the waters. They had seen locomotives and automobiles; and they could believe in the aeroplane and submarine, because of white man's magic. But at wireless they balked. "No!" said an old Indian, emphatically. "That is too much. The telephone–yes, I understand, for there is a wire, and the man's words go through that wire, inside–I see that. But now you

tell me of a man talking from here to the mesa, twenty miles, without a wire? No—excuse me, but that is too much." (Crane 1925:227)

The 1920s

The 1920s brought Superintendent Robert Daniel's policies of continued forced education, persecution of conservative Hopis, and, as an added dimension, favoritism toward the Navajos. He instigated the infamous delousing incident at Hotevilla where women and children were thrown into sheep dip-vats in 1921. He also waged campaigns against outsiders (artists and writers) who wished to support the Hopis against the oppression of petty officials like him. The Hopis became a symbol for a number of national movements such as the Indian Welfare League, the National Association to Help the Indian, and the General Federation of Women's Clubs. An indicator of the political climate at the time was the proposed Bursum Bill of 1922, which would have deprived the Eastern Pueblo groups of their lands and which led to further opposition by national movements. This opposition sparked an attempt to discredit the religion and morals of the pueblo peoples thereby discrediting the activities of the national movements as well. The Hopis were warned by Daniel that their turn would soon come. All of the debate led to congressional legislation in 1924 which granted citizenship to the Indians, thereby securing them freedom of religion.

By 1927 the Navajos had completely surrounded the 1882 Executive Order Area, and Congress promptly enacted a law curtailing Navajo expansion into areas held by Whites. Navajo expansion had thereafter only one way to go, namely, further into Hopi territory.

The 1930s

In 1930 a proposal was launched to confine the Hopis to a 438,000-acre reservation within the 1882 boundaries and to attach the rest of the land to the Navajo Reservation. A bill was passed in 1934 doing more or less that, allowing, however, a certain degree of joint use.

Four days later, the Indian Reorganization Act was enacted by Congress.[7] Under the act, rules and regulations for the management of Indian lands and resources were to be developed by the Secretary of Interior. By 1936, the Executive Order Area and the 1934 Navajo Reser-

7. A detailed description of this important period in Hopi history is found in Hopi Lands Office 1988. For opposing views, see Kammer 1980:20–48. I extend my gratitude to Patrick Dallas, formerly at the Hopi Lands Office and presently vice-chairman of the Tribal Council, for enlightening conversation and for providing me with various tribal reports.

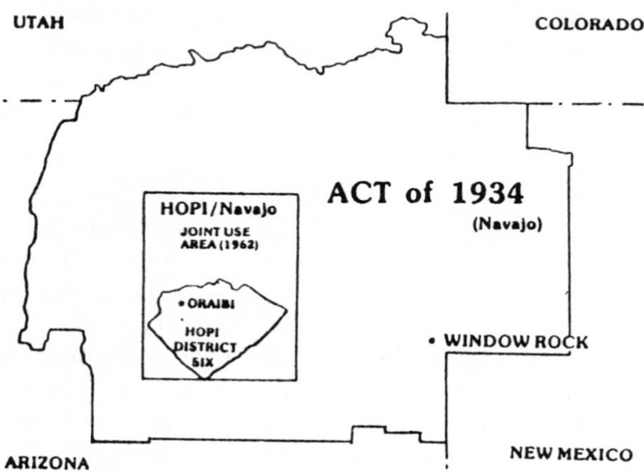

Map 3. The Executive Order Area and the 1934 Navajo Reservation reorganized into land management districts, 1936. Hopi territory was reduced to District Six and the rest of the 1882 Executive Order Area is declared a Joint Use Area by a federal court ruling in 1962 (*Healing vs. Jones*). SOURCE: *Hopi Tutu-veh-ni,* vol. 1, no. 1, Spring 1986. Courtesy of the Hopi Tribe, Office of Public Relations.

vation were reorganized into land-management districts, and District Six became the effective boundaries of the Hopi Reservation; in other words, the 438,000 acres enacted by Congress.

That same year, the Hopi Constitution and Bylaws were adopted under the impression that the constitution would protect the Hopi aboriginal territory. Most of the eligible voters, however, stayed home in protest. Later scrutiny revealed that the constitution bound the Tribal Council to formal agreements with the U.S. government and the Navajo tribe, which restricted Hopi authority to District Six. Realizing this, the villages withdrew their representatives, and the council was disbanded in the early 1940s.

Oliver LaFarge, the anthropologist who wrote the "Constitutions and By-Laws of the Hopi Tribe, Arizona," had pressured the Hopis into accepting it. According to the Hopis, he evidently considered himself to be the long-awaited Pahaana. The following statement given by Dan Qötshongva to the Hopi Hearings Committee in 1955 is a good indication of recasting historical events in prophetic terminology:

> When we began to talk he said that what he brought was all good for the Hopi people; that everything in it is almost like the Hopi beliefs and if you

> are really a person who knows the teachings of the Hopi people you will recognize it and know that it is going to be good for the Hopi people. "I am the one you have been waiting for. I am the one who is going to help you. I have been instructed to do this for you by my mother, so I am here to help you because I am the one you have been waiting for."
>
> I said to him "It is true that these things are known to me. I am well prepared to explain some of my own instructions. I am well settled already and know where I am going in following my own way of life so I will not accept your new plan of life which you have brought with you. I am going to continue to follow my own way of life walking toward the future for my people."
>
> Another warning was given to me by my forefathers that some where we will come to this problem of organizing in another way and this must be what they are talking about that this man is bringing at this time. I was told to never accept it because if we did it would only work to defeat us at the end. (Bureau of Indian Affairs 1955:58)

It is worth remembering that this statement was made twenty years after the event described.

The first prophetic statements we have from the period are from Tawakwaptiwa, who now vented his bitterness towards his earlier opponents. Yukiwma, having died in 1929, was now safely out of the way and unable to defend possible accusations. Tawakwaptiwa's statements also justify his quarrelsome and destructive behavior and are in tone and turns of phrase similar to those of the conservative opposition.[8] Titiev (1944:95) related the following (3.4.1.):

> According to Tawaqwaptiwa, the time is quickly approaching when he will lose his entire following and will remain alone at Oraibi with his ceremony (Soyal). All other rites, dances, and prayers will be given up, and there will come a great famine, after which the full ceremonial calendar will be revived. Such does Tawaqwaptiwa regard Old Oraibi's destiny to be, and complacently he awaits its fulfillment.

The new leader at Hotevilla after Yukiwma's death was Dan Qötshongva (called Katchongva by White people). Qötshongva's prophecies of 1935 were published in a Mormon journal called *The Improvement Era*.[9] The Mormons were still interested in the Indians and in their possible connection to the *Book of Mormon*. When Qötshongva heard about their magazine, which had published an issue on Indians in March 1933, he traveled to Salt Lake City for the specific purpose of telling the Hopi prophecies. He traveled with his spokesman, Ralph Tawangyawma, and

8. 1.19.0., 1.20.0., 3.4.0.–3.5.0.

9. I wish to thank Dr. Peter Whitely for the reference.

interpreter Harry Nasewaytiwa, and related the prophecies to a group headed by President Levi Edgar Young. These were published a year later.

What exactly were Qötshongva's motives? According to the editor, Qötshongva was "seeking his white deliverer and the deliverer of his people" (Kotchongva 1936:82). Already at this point in time we find the germinal idea of the soon-to-be-established Traditionalist Movement that their mission is not concerned with converting new supporters but with the functional goal of precipitating the arrival of the White Brother:

> So I, Dan Kotchongva, Chief of Hotevilla Village, am not looking at the office at Washington for help right now, but we Hopis are looking for the return of our White Brother, who will come to us and bring forth a relief of the suffering of all the people. We have looked toward Washington, Chicago, and Santa Fe, New Mexico, as places for this Word to go out in search of our White Brother, but so far nothing has been done. That is why I am here today talking to you people and if this word goes out from here, maybe He will know of our search for Him and come to us. This is the time to which we have looked for generations. We were told that his time was when a road was made in the sky. The road of the airplane is well made. If we do not find Him through this effort we will keep on searching and shall not stop looking until He returns. (ibid.:119)

Qötshongva's statements reveal an emergent collated recension that became more evident and more refined in the discourses of the Traditionalist Movement by 1961.

Qötshongva's statements neatly summarize earlier expectations and rectify his conservative stance, which must have seemed anachronistic so many years after the split.[10] Further, natural cataclysms have become more evident (1.23.0.) in connection with a purgative destruction brought by the White Brother (1.23.3.–1.24.0.). American technology enters into Hopi prophecy for the first time, i.e., the White Brother will return when "a road is made in the sky" (1.22.0., 1.23.0.). Qötshongva's expectations are more soteriological than earlier prophecies, but he also envisions a universal brotherhood, a common language, as well as intermarriage![11] And even though the land is now an issue (6.0.0., 6.1.0.), as might be expected, Qötshongva actually envisions a mutual sharing of the land[12] by "the faithful Indians and the righteous Whites," which later turned out to be effective in recruiting outside support. Thus, political

10. 1.21.0., 1.21.1., 4.1.0.
11. 1.22.1., 1.22.2., 1.24.0., 1.24.2., 1.24.3.
12. 1.24.1., 4.2.0., 6.2.0.

resistance coupled with a fundamentalistic focus on morality, which became the mark of the later Traditionalist Movement, is present in Qötshongva's statements. His emphasis on behavior and the possibility of averting catastrophe through proper behavior (1.23.1.–1.23.3.) is actually a return to the traditional Hopi assumption that ecological and human events are directly influenced by human action.[13]

Edmund Nequatewa from Shongopovi, who is known for his successful association with Whites, especially at the Museum of Northern Arizona, was more optimistic in the mid-1930s. Speaking of the time immediately after the emergence, he quoted the chief as saying:

> Then the one who has arrived with his people must settle down and look forward to meeting his brother when he comes with wisdom and truth that he may teach the true religion of god. (Nequatewa 1936:29, cf. 1.25.0.)

For Nequatewa, the motive for the clan migrations was to ascertain whether the sun was their god, a motive not without significance for a member of the Sun Forehead clan, as he was. His other statements account for the two types of Whites. The one type will try to steal the land (1.25.1.), and the other will have a messianic role (1.25.2.–1.27.0.).

In 1939 a group of Hopis presented their grievances to Commissioner of Indian Affairs John Collier and demanded the reinstatement of their aboriginal boundaries. Collier was inflexible, and the discussion revealed in the minutes of the meeting is an object lesson in mutual unintelligibility. During the confrontation at this meeting, Peter Nuvamsa from Shongopovi related prophetic statements to Collier concerning Navajo encroachment and the land issue which could hardly be more concurrent with the discovery that the Hopis had, in fact, been tricked into District Six (1.28.0.–1.28.2.). That same year, District Six was expanded to 520,727 acres.

The 1940s

In 1940 Don Talayesva heard Qötshongva give a speech to a crowd of Indians and Whites during the Snake ceremonial at Hotevilla. During that speech, he not only reaffirmed the basic prophecy, but also suggested that the White Brother might be Hitler (1.29.0.–1.29.2.)! This idea is still evident among the Hopis today. Hitler's use of the swastika was the cause of this identification.

13. See pages 49–50; A. W. Geertz 1977, Part III; 1986; 1990*a*; A. W. Geertz and Lomatuway'ma 1987:67 nn. 16, 17, 81 n. 51, 126 n. 38, 140, 171–175, Whiteley 1988:98–99, 266; 1987.

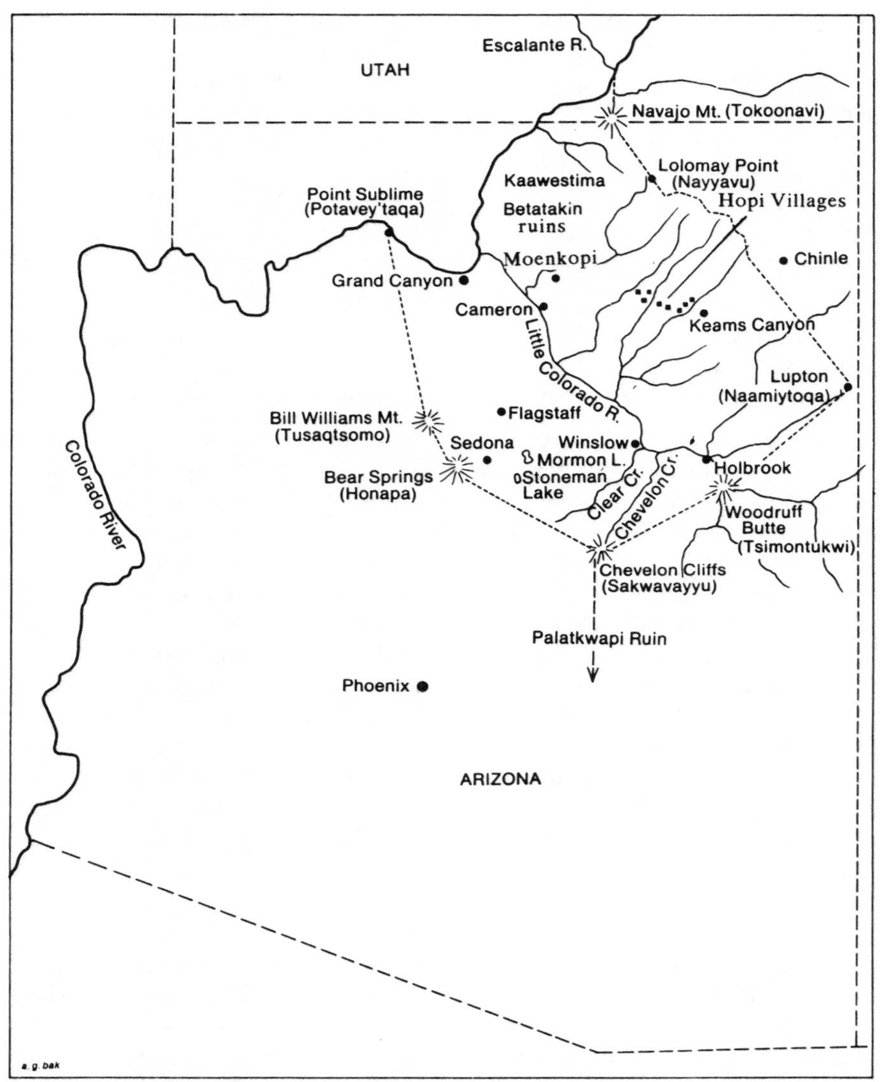

Map 4. Hopi aboriginal territory demanded of the Commissioner of Indian Affairs by a group of Hopi representatives, 1939. The map was presented again as Docket 210 to the Indian Claims Commission in 1951. Courtesy of George Nasoftie, Bear clan, Shongopovi, Second Mesa. Redrawn by A. G. Bak, Gyldendalske Boghandel Nordisk Forlag A.S., Copenhagen, Denmark.

Talayesva's reactions to Qötshongva's speech are particularly enlightening:

> As I sat on the west side of the plaza and listened, I wondered whether the Chosen White Brother would ever come and free us from the curse of the Two-Hearts [i.e., the sorcerers]. I knew this wise old man had been telling the people that Hitler is the Chosen White Brother who will slay all the wicked and deliver the righteous, but I didn't believe it could be true. Misfortunes, strife, sickness, and death—all of which are caused by the underworld people—are our greatest problems. I fear them more than anything else and sometimes I doubt whether anyone will ever be able to destroy these powers of evil, unite us into one race, and restore the good old Hopi life. We might be better off if the Whites had never come to Oraibi, but that was impossible, for the world is full of them, while in numbers we Hopi are as nothing. Now we have learned to get along with them, in a manner, and we would probably live much worse if they left us to ourselves and to the Navahos. We need Uncle Sam to protect us and to feed us in famines, but I wish the United States Government would send us better agent employees, for they are supposed to come out here and help us. (Simmons 1942:379–380)

Talayesva's pragmatic view does not necessarily stand in opposition to the eschatological interpretations of his uncle Qötshongva. On the contrary, even though he disagreed with Qötshongva's identification of Hitler, his pragmatic view complements Qötshongva's and illustrates that ever-present constellation in Hopi cognition of hard-boiled political awareness intercalated with mythical imagery.

World War Two brought more than just speculations about the nature of Adolf Hitler. It also brought the draft system. The two co-chiefs of Hotevilla, James Pongyayawma and Dan Qötshongva, appeared at the Phoenix Federal Court in 1941 to explain the reasoning behind six Hopi youths' failure to register for the selective service, for which they were awaiting sentencing. The two chiefs, together with the young Thomas Banancya, are reported to have explained the Hopi prophecies to the court concerning engagement in World War Two.[14] Their statements reveal that even though they recognized the legitimacy and the need for the American engagement, they felt bound by their traditions not to take sides. This argument did them little good. Conscientious-objector status was first conferred to the Hopis, along narrowly defined lines, only in the 1960s—but the argument signals a series of traditions about great wars which came to dominate later prophecies.

The youths were sentenced to three years' hard labor and were taken

14. 1.30.0., 1.31.0., 4.3.0.–4.4.0.

to a prison camp at Tucson. Waters wrote in more detail about their experiences at the camp, especially concerning their belief that Maasaw was with them there (1963:390–391).

In 1941 District Six was once again expanded and now encompassed 631,194 acres. In 1943, the Hopi Indian Agency took charge of District Six and implemented the BIA livestock-reduction program without compensation. By leaving the administration of the program in the other districts of the Executive Order Area to the Navajos, it became clear to the Hopis that they had lost their aboriginal lands. On the more positive side, it turned out that government officials had been working without the aid of surveys and had computed acreage figures from maps. A survey, first completed in 1965, showed that the final boundaries of District Six, adopted in 1943, included 650,013 acres (Kammer 1980:41). The reduction program hit Third Mesa, the center of resistance, the hardest. This fact could hardly be interpreted other than politically.

Several Hopis attempted to reorganize the Tribal Council in an effort to do something about these rapidly accelerating problems. They were effectively blocked in this by the BIA until the mid-1940s, when it became evident to the BIA that the growing interests in the natural resources on the reservation could not be satisfactorily dealt with without a legal representative body.

The Indian Claims Commission Act was passed in 1946. This commission was authorized to rule on claims for monetary compensation brought against the United States by Indian tribes. As Clemmer noted, "By far the most common proceedings were those over lands taken by the United States without rendering just compensation or without due process of law" (1979:533). The problem with this new organization was that even though Indians could now seek retribution for past wrongs, they were in fact selling all future "rights, claims or demands" to lost lands. At that time, the Hopis also began to hear about another act that was on the way, but which first was enacted in 1950, called the Navajo and Hopi Rehabilitation Act, which authorized the use of $88,570,000 for economic improvement on both reservations.

These significant national events together with the dropping of the atomic bombs in Japan led to a number of reactions from the Hopis. The philosopher Richard Brandt, who visited the Hopis several times during the years 1946–1948, recorded a statement made by Tawakwaptiwa in which he predicted that another war would destroy civilization and mankind would have to start all over again (3.6.0.).

One of the most signal events in modern Hopi history was a meeting held in 1948. Forty years later, one of the witnesses, after describing the significance of a petroglyph near Oraibi, described the meeting in these terms:

> The pictures and symbols in the drawing seemed to match precisely the teachings at a 1948 meeting at Shungopavi attended by a large council of Hopi elders, priests, kikmongwis, katletacas [i.e., *qaleetaqa*, "warrior"] and other respected members of the community. The meeting was held to address the bombing of Hiroshima and Nagasaki, events which many felt fulfilled one crucial prophecy, a prophecy which warned that the Hopi people would receive a sign that the end of the earth as we know it was near. That warning sign, seen in a dream generations ago, was a "gourd full of ashes" which many thought might represent the incinerated earth.
>
> The teachings said that upon receiving this sign it would be the duty of those who kept to the Hopi Way, a path actually illustrated by the petroglyph, to begin seeking out other spiritual beings. And the elders told the story of man's emergence upon the earth and how the Hopis had been given special responsibilities to pray, fast, meditate and hold special ceremonies taught to them by the Masau'u, in preparation for the destruction of the world and for living the righteous life in the world to come.
>
> This historic meeting was said to be the beginning of that preparation. And to pass on this crucial knowledge elders recounted the story of how men became separated into groups which then migrated to different hemispheres. A white brother, the elders said, was among those who left on these migrations, a white brother with a special gift of invention with which it was hoped he would create things to make life better for all people. (Jenkins and Kooyahoema 1984:71)

The results of this meeting reverberate up to this day, not only for Hopis, but also for all people who attach special significance to the Hopi people.

It was during this and other similar meetings that the traditions of various clans were collated into a corpus and that a number of young men who were knowledgeable in the White man's ways and who could speak fluent English were appointed as spokesmen and interpreters. Clemmer formulated this important event in sociological terms:

> Meeting together for several days, the chiefs and religious leaders produced the nascent ideology of the Hopi Resistance Movement. Clan histories, clan functions and duties, religious philosophy, and prophecies were discussed by representatives of all villages. Four interpreters were chosen, one of whom was selected as a special spokesman-interpreter, and other spokesmen were chosen to speak for the various village chiefs. At that meeting, it was determined that younger Hopis were not fulfilling their proper roles in Hopi social and ceremonial activities, and that Hopi cul-

> ture and social cohesion were suffering as a result. The war had indeed forced many young men into the armed forces, leaving performance of traditional religious ceremonies and social functions to older men. At Shungopavi, the famous Snake Dance was being performed by a dozen old men, and the situation at other villages was similar. But it was decided at the meeting that the chiefs and religious leaders would make concerted efforts to fulfill their own roles as social and religious pacesetters and revitalize Hopi culture.
>
> The efforts resulted in an increase in initiates to religious societies; communication of esoteric religious knowledge to younger people; assured perpetuation of religious ceremonies that were about to disappear; and the start of a counter-campaign to the white man's acculturative pressures that would articulate resistance in political language and action which the white man would understand. This counter-campaign of resistance was organized around several key factors which give the resistance its social movement qualities. These factors are: a set of fundamental beliefs, a system of ideological principles, leadership which believes itself to be charged with a special duty by forces other than personal motivation, faith in ultimate attainment of goals, and constant recruitment of new allies. (Clemmer 1978*b*: 70–71)

These various matters may have been true in the beginning of the movement, but it soon developed into a mechanism for the fulfillment of personal motives and also became a vehicle for the destruction of Hopi ceremonial life, the very thing it was sworn to uphold. One need only look at the situation in Hotevilla, the very center of the resistance, to see the truth of the many accusations that have been, and still are, leveled against the leaders of the Traditionalist Movement.

A remarkable document was produced the following year, signed by the "hereditary Hopi Chieftains" of the "Hopi Indian Empire" and addressed to President Truman. The cosigners were, with few exceptions, to become members of the Traditionalist Movement. In this document, which is reproduced in full in Appendix D, the cosigners declared among other things that they did not wish to participate in the North Atlantic Treaty Organization, the Indian Claims Commission Act of 1946, the leasing of land to oil companies, the Navajo and Hopi Rehabilitation Act, or the Hoover Commission's proposal to return Indians to state jurisdiction. They stated that they still held to the traditional path, still had their stone tablets, and were still waiting for the White Brother and the advent of the end of the world.

The specifications in the document were also interspersed with a number of prophetic statements that revolve around the stone tablets, the meeting of the Hopi and the White Brother, and the new idea that a judgment will be initiated by the true White Brother in "the Hopi Empire."[15]

The 1950s

In 1951 the Tribal Council was revived in order to meet the deadlines of the Indian Claims Act. That same year, a statement was presented to the Commissioner of Indian Affairs by leaders from Shongopovi, who had all been cosigners of the 1949 letter to Truman. The statement now clearly brought the Hopi land issue into focus and demanded the reclamation of most of northern Arizona as Hopi territory.[16]

One of the cosigners of the statement was Andrew Hermequaftewa, leader of the Bluebird clan at Shongopovi, who played a significant, supportive role in Traditionalist activities. In 1953 his "statement to Congress and the world" was recorded by Thomas B. Noble, Meredith Guillet, superintendent at Walnut Canyon National Monument, and Platt Cline, secretary of the Arizona Commission of Indian Affairs. The statement, evidently translated by Banancya, was published by the Hopi Friendship Association in Santa Fe. The prophetic statements are similar to Qötshongva's 1935 statements, but with a greater emphasis on Maasaw, on remaining faithful to the Hopi way, and on the land issue.[17]

Two important events occurred in the middle of the decade. Hearings were conducted by the BIA on the reservation in 1955 and, in 1956, the so-called Meeting of Religious People was held in Hotevilla by the Traditionalists. Both meetings gave ample opportunity to air grievances and to discuss Hopi dissension and prophecy. They constitute invaluable documents for the study of Hopi affairs. The very volume of the material and the great number of witness statements invite enriching systematic analyses.

These two sources are significantly different in character. This is so despite the fact that both the hearings and the meeting were brought about by the energetic Qötshongva. The hearings were a result of a meeting in Washington in May, 1955, between commissioner of Indian Affairs Glenn L. Emmons and a party of six led by Qötshongva. Emmons's letter of May 19, 1955, to Qötshongva set the tone for the hearings that were held in July. He wrote:

15. 1.32.0.–1.33.2., 4.5.0.
16. See this statement in James 1974:102–105.
17. 1.34.0., 1.34.1., 4.6.0., 6.3.0.

> As I indicated . . . I am sympathetic about the problems which you face and I am convinced that something constructive can be done about the situation if we can just have the right kind of consultations. This means that we should meet together with full faith in each other's good intentions and with the underlying purpose of eventually reaching an agreement that will be satisfactory to everyone concerned. From what you and the other Hopi members said at our meeting, I feel sure that you are prepared to meet with us in such a spirit. I want to assure you that our Bureau representatives will come to the meeting with the same frame of mind. (Bureau of Indian Affairs 1955:402)

At the 1956 meeting the supporters and participants were outside religious organizations and activists who were attracted to the Traditionalists' "last stand" against the U.S. government. Even though state and federal officials were invited, none showed up. The tone throughout the minutes of the meeting is pious, strident, and posturing. Whereas the hearings were truly representative of all persuasions in all the villages, the 1956 meeting was mostly a stage for Hotevilla Traditionalists.

The statements of both meetings are far too numerous to reproduce in this chapter. They are all found in Appendix C. Only trends and isolated examples will be mentioned here.

Reading the minutes of the hearings, one cannot avoid noticing the obvious disagreement evident in statements from the opposing factions on the reservation. The terminology and details of supposedly age-old prophecies were no exception to this. On the one hand, we read statements describing the coming White Man in messianic terms (1.35.0.) and, on the other hand, statements describing him as the great deceiver (1.40.0.).

Besides all of the traditional elements of Hopi prophecy, we find a whole array of statements that specifically address the problems the Hopis were confronted with: Navajo encroachments;[18] the Indian Reorganization Act;[19] wars;[20] tricky legislation;[21] the Tribal Council;[22] stock-reduction programs;[23] the Oraibi split;[24] land allotments, district programs, and the Indian Claims Commission;[25] and the leasing of mineral rights.[26]

18. 1.36.2., 1.43.0., 6.9.0.
19. 1.38.0., 1.39.0., 1.40.0.
20. 1.45.0., 3.7.0., 4.11.0., 4.12.0., 4.18.0.
21. 1.46.0.
22. 3.8.0., 3.10.0., 3.11.0.
23. 4.19.0.
24. 3.12.0., 3.12.1., 4.20.0.
25. 1.39.0., 6.4.0., 6.6.0., 6.7.0., 6.8.0., 6.10.0.
26. 6.5.0., 6.5.1., 6.5.2.

New elements that had become prominent in Traditionalist statements are details concerning the immanent approach of the day of purification. These details are clearly linked to the modern inventions of the White Man, but also to the coming of a third or fourth world war.[27] Qötshongva's statement is characteristic:

> The Hopi only knows of three great wars to take place. The third war will be the one to take place at purification time upon this land. Therefore, the Hopi, knowing all this, did not consent to any of these wars anywhere. He was especially warned never to allow himself to go to foreign countries to make wars upon other people because this is our home land. Here we must stay and take care of it. Because we are still waiting for someone—a brother of the Hopi—who will come to prove this land for us. So we will continue to follow instructions of Massua and waiting for the time of our brother to come to prove this land. We have our stone tablet with us here today which was given by him when we first came here. Our brother will come and look for this stone tablet when placed side by side which will show whoever comes to this land to purify this land for us and will be recognized as our true brother. (Bureau of Indians Affairs 1955:25)

In the words of Julius Doopkema from Bacavi,

> it is because I have foresight and can see what there is in store for the Hopi people and because we have received much knowledge and wisdom from our forefathers who taught us in the past and prophecized that such conditions would exist, that there would be many conflicts, that there would be great strife between the people and so, therefore, it was a warning from our forefathers that when such times come if we would not be discouraged then many great things would come that we would see. . . . I might say, too, here that it was told to us by our elders in the tribe that there would in time be a road in the sky, and they also had predicted that there would be many types of vehicles travelling these roads and there would be broad roads that would be graded upon the land. (ibid.:222)

Again, we must remember that he is describing events that were decades old.

The White Brother is still identified by many as the one who will initiate the purification day and even bestow eternal life,[28] but the Traditionalists either downplay this role, make no mention of the Pahaana, or refer more often, instead, to Maasaw.[29]

One element of interest is Qötshongva's justification for usurping the chieftainship at Hotevilla:

27. 1.36.0., 4.11.0., 4.12.0., 4.24.0.–4.26.1.
28. 1.35.0., 1.41.0., 1.42.0., 1.50.0., 1.50.1., 1.51.0.
29. 4.7.0., 4.7.1., 4.8.0., 4.9.0., 4.10.0., 4.10.1., 4.14.0., 4.16.0., 4.16.1., 4.17.0.

> It was there that while he [Loololma] was holding fast to this stone tablet and life many of his people began to urge him to change so they could have a new life, and finally the people convinced him that they will support him in everything if he will change the stone tablet, so he did. And it was done so the people will follow the white man's way of life.
>
> Now to the future. My teachings have been handed to me from my forefathers because I belong to that group who belong to the great leaders, leaders who have been the ones who carried this stone tablet, and we are told that some where one of these great leaders will fail their duties and will turn aside. Then it will be up to me, I was told, because I come from the clan who are the keepers of the stone tablets. I will have to take on the great duties that belong to the other leaders ahead of me, but since they have fallen down everything will be left upon me to carry on. (ibid.: 258–259, cf. 3.12.0., 3.12.1.)

Something along these same lines can be found in statements that justify the Traditionalist Movement.[30]

The 1956 meeting introduced new details about the signs of the coming purification day,[31] but, more importantly, there seems to be a disagreement between Qötshongva and the coming new leader of the Traditionalists, David Monongya. These two figures fell out with each other in 1960, so it is not surprising to see ideological differences already at this time. Qötshongva still maintained that the White Brother will initiate the purification day and function as the purifier (1.54.0., 1.59.0.), and his closest adviser, Ralph Tawangyawma, agreed (1.60.0.). Monongya, however, claimed not only that it would instead be Maasaw who would initiate the purification and function as the purifier (4.29.0., 4.29.1.), but also that Whites will have little or no place in the apocalypse at all (1.56.0.):

> When the Purification Day comes the white man will be allowed to live on this land again. Teachings tell us that a few of them will be saved. But perhaps all will be destroyed, we don't know. The white race must think about this because these are the teachings which the Great Spirit has given. (Bentley 1956:10)

Monongya's ambivalence towards Whites is clear. In this, he resembled the American Indian Movement, with which he had a close association. Other examples of this ambivalence are also apparent (1.55.0.). All in all, the tone of the meeting is of missionary vision and zeal, padded with self-righteousness and political ambivalence.

30. 1.36.4., 1.40.0., 1.48.0., 3.8.0., 3.9.0., 3.10.0., 3.11.0., 4.7.1., 4.13.0.

31. 1.53.0., 1.55.0., 4.28.0., 4.30.0., 4.30.1. There is no pagination in Bentley 1956. The numbering system adopted in this book begins with the title page as page 1.

In 1958 H.R.3789 was enacted by the House of Representatives, which provided for the Hopis and "other such Indians as the Secretary may settle thereon [the Executive Order Area]" to resolve title to the Executive Order Area via litigation. The attorney for the Hopis, John S. Boyden, filed the lawsuit known as *Dewey Healing vs. Paul Jones* in Federal District Court in Arizona claiming title to all of the land area.

In a letter sent to a pan-Indian meeting in 1958, Qötshongva indicated that the Traditionalists would present their grievances to the United Nations. In the letter he claimed that it was prophesied that as the day of purification approaches, the chief must knock on the door of the White House, and if the door is not opened, then he must knock on the door of the United Nations and tell about all the problems brought upon the Hopis by the White Man (1.62.0.). A six-man delegation traveled to the U.N. the next year, but were not allowed to address the assembly.

THEMES OF THE 1960s, 1970s, AND 1980s

The typology in Appendix C ends in the beginning of the 1960s. In 1960, Qötshongva and Hermequaftewa sent a letter to the Honorable Frederick Hanley, U.S. Court of Appeals in San Francisco, protesting court action involving the land dispute and a whole series of related actions. In the said letter, they warned the judge about the immanent return of the true White Brother, who will come to judge, punish, and destroy all evil and wicked people on the day of purification (1.63.0.).

A year later, as the Tribal Council concluded its first mineral agreement with Fisher Construction Company to prospect for coal in District Six, Thomas Banancya wrote his famous letter to M. Muller-Fricken, which introduced a coordinated prophetic corpus and thus marked the beginning of a new and important era in the lives of not only the Traditionalists, but also the rest of the Hopi people. Banancya's long letter is reproduced in full in Appendix B.

The letter introduces a series of statements that clearly reflect the disappointing rejection by the U.N. (1.64.0.–1.64.2.). Banancya had the same ambivalence towards Whites that marked Monongya's statements in 1956. Now the categories of persons are clearly delineated: the true/good Hopis, the true White Brother, and good White men (if there are any) stand opposed to evil White men and evil Indians. A new element is introduced, which seems to be the flip side of the same coin, namely, that Indians are the chosen race. Developing this idea further, his statements reveal that he conceived of the Hopis as being guardians of *all* land and life given to them in trust by the great god Maasaw (4.32.0.).

Banancya's statements also reveal important new details concerning the purification, which now had greater significance in Traditionalist prophetic thinking. According to Banancya, purification day will be effectuated by both the Older Brother *and* the Younger Brother (1.65.0.). Not only that, both of the brothers will pass judgment and deliver punishment on that day (1.67.2.). Thus, the fundamentalism noted in 1935 and in 1956 has reached fuller expression in 1961.

Of interest here is the description of the identity of the true White Brother which once and for all removes the possibility that Americans could ever be that brother:

> It is known that our TRUE WHITE BROTHER when he comes will be all powerful and he will wear a RED CAP OR CLOAK. He will be large in population, belongs to no religion but his very own. He will bring with him the Sacred Stone Tablets. Great will be his coming. None will be able to stand against him. All power in this world will be placed in his hand and he will come swiftly and in one day get control of this whole continent. (Banyacya 1-12-1961, Appendix B, cf. 1.69.0.-1.69.1.)

These interesting new details are an integral part of his grandly conceived, four-step purification day which he would come to repeat hundreds of times during the next three decades. Whereas the first step obviously refers to the main characters of the Second World War, the other steps are of a predictive nature (4.33.0.-4.33.4.).

An added feature is his vision of the post-purification world which clearly reflects the traditional attitude of *tiingavi* as well as Qötshongva's 1935 vision of harmony, brotherhood, mutual sharing, common language, intermarriage, and—a new feature—a new religion (4.33.5.-4.33.8.).

Tawakwaptiwa died in 1960. The reigns of leadership in Oraibi were subsequently usurped by a woman of the Parrot clan, Mina Lansa. Her husband, John Lansa, was an active member of the Traditionalist Movement, and Mina Lansa's policies were intimately linked with that movement until her early death in 1979.

The 1960s also brought a wave of hippies. Jerry Kammer's characterization gives a feeling of the times:

> During the years of the Vietnam War, the Hopis began to see a different type of American. Disaffected with the science that they said sapped their spirituality, fearing that technology was about to conjure the Apocalypse, some American young hailed the Hopis and urged them not to be seduced by convenience. They were drawn to a system religiously far more intense and materially far simpler than their own. In the Hopi way they saw an an-

> tidote to their spiritual poverty. "Hopi," they learned, means "People of Peace."
>
> The flow of dissenters from America began shortly after Frank Waters published his *Book of the Hopi* in 1963. Billed by its publishers as "the first revelation of the Hopi historical and religious world view of life," the book became part of the 1960s counter culture, and the Hopis became Native American gurus.
>
> Some Hopis received the new comers hospitably. After decades of misunderstanding from government agents and missionaries, they were pleased to find recognition. A few of the traditionalists accepted invitations to speak at religious conferences in New York, San Francisco, and Stockholm, where they warned that the West had severed heart from head. They became militants in the cause of blocking the entry of the twentieth century into their villages. But back home matters were not so simple. The tribal council . . . petitioned the BIA to remove the "hippies." A decade later, Wayne Sekaquaptewa, publisher of the Hopi newspaper *Qua Toqti* ("The Eagle's Cry"), spoke contemptuously of whites "who want to keep us in our 'primitive' state and display us to the world as some primeval culture out of the past." His brother, Tribal Chairman Abbott Sekaquaptewa, said the outsiders would be less enthusiastic if they knew the discomforts of an outhouse in subzero weather. (Kammer 1980:49–50)

While the hippies were fighting against American involvement in Viet Nam and the growing corruption and ruthlessness of the "establishment," they thought that they had found allies in the Hopis. They considered the Hopis to be a symbol of their own concerns and, by the end of the 1960s, a focal point for the peace movement. But, except for the Traditionalists, who had their own designs, the continual presence of thousands of unwashed and shaggy hippies caused a lot of hostility on the reservation, and still does for that matter. There were many incidents of ridicule heaped on hippies by the Hopis and conflicts of various sorts.

Concerning the land issue, a three-judge tribunal gave its decision on the *Healing vs. Jones* case in 1962. The decision gave exclusive ownership of District Six to the Hopis and divided the rest of the Executive Order Area equally between the two tribes, the so-called Navajo-Hopi Joint Use Area. This decision, however, was neither respected by the Navajos nor enforced by federal officials.

By 1964 the Navajo tribe signed a coal lease in the Executive Order Area without the consent of the Hopi tribe. The terms of the lease agreement stipulated that the Hopi tribe had no choice but to approve the lease as well.

1966 brought a questionable lease and water agreement with the Peabody Coal Company, perpetrated by attorney Boyden and Secretary of Interior Stewart Udall. This began the stripmining controversy and induced the growing involvement of outside interest groups in support of the Traditionalist Movement's battle against the Hopi Tribal Council, which the Traditionalists considered to be an illegal "puppet council."

1966 also brought the granting of conscientious-objector classification to all Hopis who could document their initiation into the Katsina cult, a move that further endeared them to the hippies. In 1967, however, the Tribal Council passed a resolution requesting and authorizing the superintendent of the Hopi Indian Agency to remove the hippies, a resolution that was never enforced, however.[32]

A newspaper article about Thomas Banancya in the *Winslow Mail* of June 5, 1969, aptly rounds out the concerns of the decade and the prophecies that went with it:

> Thomas Banyayca is an unlikely appearing missionary. His home is in the desert; he lacks sophistication in thought and speech; his understanding of world events is simple; he seems hardly the prophet to stand against the flood tide of history which has made North America a white man's land with a white man's religion.
>
> Yet Banyayca, as the religious leader of the Hopi Indians, is sustained by a strong faith in what he believes and by the uncounted centuries of the traditions and teachings of his people.
>
> About the prophecies of his people as he relates them, there is an imagery of words that is poetic. According to Hopi understanding, these are the final days of this world when the purifiers are about to come for an accounting of how well or how poorly man has used the earth entrusted to him by the Great Spirit.
>
> The prophecies tell of these last days as a time when people will talk to each other across distances "through a cobweb" and of "a little gourd of ashes" which, if it falls to the ground, will boil up with fire and burn a large area so nothing will grow for years.
>
> The telephone and the atomic bomb, of course. And how much was prophecy in the sacred stones of the Hopi and how much was simply an accomodation to later events? Banyayca said the Hopi teachings have been recorded on sacred stones which say the instructions were given by the Great Spirit. . . .
>
> That these may be the last days when purification (judgment) is approaching is born out by Hopi teaching that man will be shaken by three great destructions, Banyayca said.
>
> The first would come under the swastika, "a very sacred sign to the Hopi, representative of the very center, the very core of life of everything." Banyayca added: "If we destroy that, there won't be any more of anything."
>
> The second destruction would be under a sun symbol "which also repre-

32. Concerning hippies, see Hieb 1972:184, 187, 196–198; Courlander ed. 1982:138–141; and chapter 10 of this volume.

> sents the power of the sun which gives power and warmth and because of that power things will grow."
>
> The third destruction will come from people "with a red cap or red cloak." Banyayca said: "We don't know who they are."
>
> He warned: "When you see these things, you will know time is short." The prophecies tell of a small fire which will begin and "if mankind does not listen, the fire will get bigger and bigger and we'll be caught in it and not get out."
>
> Banyayca said: "We're in that period now. That fire over there (Vietnam) is getting bigger now. It might come when those doing it might use this ball of ashes and that would bring much destruction, more property and life would be destroyed. . . ."
>
> "If all of us fail what we are supposed to do in this world, then the Great Spirit will have to act and nature will have to act."
>
> "That's when, according to the Hopi, this whole continent will just sink. Not only California, but this whole continent will sink."
>
> "That's what happened to another world, in another land someplace. It happened before. So they know it's going to happen again."
>
> But if man will live in harmony with nature, as the Great Spirit intended, then there will be "enough wind to bring rain to water the fields." (Anonymous 1969)

As Whiteley noted, the 1960s and 1970s brought a remarkable decrease in farming throughout District Six (1988:139). This tendency had already begun after World War Two, as Kennard has noted (1965:25). The significance of this is not simply that the subsistence economy was now peripheral to a cash economy, but that agricultural pursuit, as with corn itself, became a symbol of Hopi identity. As Whiteley put it, "where the symbolic connection between corn and human life was previously founded in the sheer conditions of existence, it has now become a more abstract statement of Hopi ethnicity" (1988:140).

The 1970s witnessed an increase in Tribal Council activities as well as increasing confrontations on the reservation between the Traditionalists and their American Indian Movement and White supporters, on the one hand, and the Progressives and the rest of the Hopi population, on the other.[33]

The focus of Hopi ritualism in the 1970s began moving away from the complex ceremonials towards the Katsina cult. A number of factors seem to be involved, e.g., changes in the economy and in kinship patterns coincided with the consequences of the destructive ritual and political policies, especially on Third Mesa, and a need for a less burdening and less time-consuming expression of religiosity. A Katsina dance could

33. See the incident related in James 1974:219–220.

easily be held during weekends, whereas the ceremonials could require anywhere up to half a month.

The 1970s also saw the emergence of environmental issues centered around the Peabody Coal Mining Company's activities on Black Mesa. Once again prophecy came to the fore (Clemmer 1979:536) and even attracted national news coverage (Clemmer 1978*a*:28–29). During the 1970s the Traditionalists attempted to speak at the United Nations again, but failed to gain official entry. The strong support they experienced from environmental organizations quickly deflated during the first half of the decade and by the end of the 1970s outside support had dwindled to a few spiritual movements. A statement published by Banancya in the December 1975 issue of the underground newspaper *East West Journal* is instructive of the types of prophecies that were then being developed. These prophecies are clearly in tune with the growing ecological and political crises:

> The ninety-year-old man who called the meeting in 1948 was told by his grandfather that he might be able to see some of the inventions the white brother will be bringing: "You will see carriages pulled by animals at first, carrying people across the land. Pretty soon, they are going to run by themselves. They're going to build trails in every direction from their homes upon the land. If you go down one of these trails, you may see water in front of you." We have no word for pavement, but that's the way to describe actually seeing a mirage on a hot summer day. "Pretty soon we'll be talking to each other through cobwebs (telephone lines). We're going to close all windows and doors, but way over the mountain some of us are going to be hearing and talking (radio and TV). There will be another world-shaking event taking place: somebody will invent something. A gourd full of ashes, a small thing that's going to be so powerful, if whoever invents it ever allows it to fall on the earth someplace, it will boil rivers and oceans and burn everything to ashes. Out of it will come sickness that our medicines will not be able to cure."
>
> Then he said, "There will be roads in the sky. If man goes to the moon and brings something back with him, we will not be able to control what will happen, because balance will be disturbed. When man starts messing around with moon and stars, look at your life.[34] It will be similar to the way it was before the destruction of the last world: Men will not listen to each other. Men with the same language will not be able to control themselves; they will desecrate each other and assassinate high leaders. Children will

34. See M. Jane Young's interesting 1987 article on similar Indian reactions to the Apollo program, which clearly illustrate the conflicting understandings of "space," where the Euro-American view is the notion, all too well known to Native Americans, of an expanding "frontier" in "unoccupied" territory. Thus, the title of Young's paper, taken from the transcript of a convocation of Native American scholars in 1970: "Pity the Indians of outer space whose territory is regarded as unoccupied land" (ibid.:272).

> not listen to their parents, and parents will neglect their children. There will be restlessness all over this land. They're going to invent more things and will start interfering with male and female. They can even invent man. If they succeed, then those people will have no mercy for anyone. They will be very cruel and destructive and we cannot control them. Animals will become bigger and stronger, more aggressive, because of all the chemicals we put in them. There will be changes in seasons and destruction by earthquake, fire, and lightning. Mountains will sink. We will know that the time has come that man has to get together when the sun will rise blood-red and will set blood-red." They could not understand this then, but I see now there will be such pollution that the sky will be dark red. We've already seen that. The Six-Nation Iroquois Confederacy prophecy said pollution will get so great that tall trees standing straight will now bend low. When you see this, the dangerous point has been reached. We will be at the end of the path that the Great Spirit has laid down for this world. (Banyacya 1975:37–38)

It is obvious that the story has changed now in order to play to the tunes of another audience. It is equally obvious that prophecy is not a static configuration, but a continual reevaluation.

Throughout the 1970s the Hopis and Navajos were confronting each other in a series of court cases. The Hopis were trying to get the Navajos to comply with the joint-use decision and the Navajos were filing appeals.

In the *Hamilton vs. MacDonald* case, the Court of Appeals for the Ninth Circuit in California rejected an appeal by the Navajos and placed the blame squarely on the Navajos and the government:

> A long history of the dispossession, with its attendant economic retardation, of the Hopi from lands to which they were legally entitled under the United States Treaty obligations; a dispossession resulting from the combined efforts of Navajo intrusions and depredations often in violation of Navajo treaty obligations, expediently sanctioned bureaucratic indifference and furthered by illegal governmental restraints on Hopi use of the reservation. (Office of Hopi Lands 1984:4–5)

In 1974 the Navaho-Hopi Land Settlement Act became law and led to the establishment of a joint-use area which declared 1.8 million acres of the 1882 reservation lands to be jointly owned by the two tribes. But the enactment of the settlement act did not occur until 1979, and the Ninth Circuit Court of Appeals determined in the *Sekaquaptewa v. MacDonald* case that the Navajo tribe was in contempt (Hopi Lands 1984:7).

The end of the 1970s saw continuing dramas on the reservations, in the courts, and in Washington concerning the forced relocation of thousands of Navajos and a small number of Hopis back to their side of the JUA boundaries (A. W. Geertz 1987*c*). As the deadline for the relocation approached, more and more demonstrations and lobbying were being

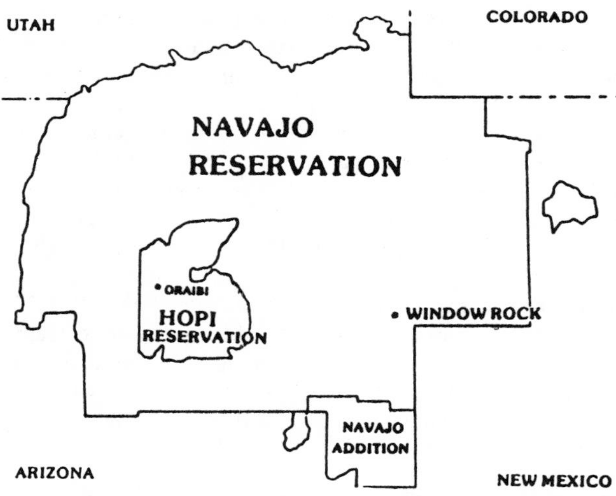

Map 5. Navajo-Hopi Land Settlement Act. In 1974 the act became law, although it was first enacted in 1979. This resulted in a congressional provision of 400,000 more acres to the Navajos in 1980 to handle the relocation of Navajo families residing on Joint Use Area lands belonging to the Hopis. SOURCE: *Hopi Tutu-veh-ni,* vol. 1, no. 1, Spring 1986. Courtesy of the Hopi Tribe, Office of Public Relations.

conducted by both Navajos and the American Indian Movement. But as 1986 came and went without the resolution of the problem, public interest seemed to support the Hopi claims.

The 1980s showed an increasing interest by the tribal government in solving not only the land issue, but also a whole series of internal problems such as alcoholism, suicide, child abuse, drug abuse, and so on. In a document entitled *Hopi-Tunat'ya. Hopi Comprehensive Development Plan. A Summary,* published in July, 1987, by the Tribal Council, one can find among other issues, the following goals and policies concerning cultural resources:

> CULTURAL RESOURCES
> The Hopi way is a living tradition that shapes every aspect of the lives of Hopi people. Religion and culture are evident in many tribal laws, policies, and programs. Hopi Ordinance Number 26 makes it a criminal offense to disturb "places and objects of sacred, historical, and scientific interest." The HPL Land Assignment Guidelines protect religious and subsistence gathering rights.

In 1982, the Tribe initiated a Cultural Preservation Program. Recent activities include protecting religious sites off the reservation and evaluating proposed sites for a new museum and cultural education facility.

GOALS

1. Preserve the Hopi way of life.
2. Protect sacred places and subsistence gathering areas.

POLICIES

1. Develop regulations and a tribal review process to protect culturally sensitive areas from new development and land use changes.
2. Consult traditional leaders before land assignments are granted in culturally sensitive areas.
3. Prepare guidelines to control tourists visiting the reservation and adopt regulations to enforce the guidelines.
4. Select and secure a site for the museum and cultural education facility. (Hopi Tribe 1987:13)

The Tribal Council had now become a more effective organ made more aware of tribal needs due to an overwhelming participation and support by tribal members. An era had come to an end. The main figures of the confrontations of the 1960s and 1970s had either moved on to other things or passed away. The young people were not interested in continuing the self-destructive internal confrontations any more. The Traditionalist leaders thought that the purification day would be coming during their lifetime, and, now, their lives had passed without it. If the genuine intentions of the movement were to have any meaning in modern times, then a change of tactics was required, for life must go on.

Thomas Banancya's participation in the Hopi mental health conferences may be an indication of such a change of tactics. It seems as if he was seeking a dialogue with his own people after concentrating almost forty years of activity and interest in national and international circles. Equally surprising is that the other Hopis were also interested in a dialogue.

A further indication of how things were developing on the reservation was that the once-active interpreter for the Traditionalist Movement, Caleb Johnson, ran for the post of tribal chairman in 1989. Johnson was quoted as saying that the only issue in the election was "for the Hopi people to elect a leader who will not only protect Hopi's resources, but who will also insure that all Hopi's benefit from their natural resources" (Bindell 1989). The latter part of his statement was a pledge to ensure that all the Hopi villages received a greater share of the seven-million-dollar annual royalties from the Peabody Coal Company, the whole idea of which the Traditionalists had fought against for decades. Furthermore, he stated that he was neither against road projects, and economic development, nor increased education, again, all former Traditionalist targets.

MODERN PROPHECY AND COLLECTIVE MENTAL HEALTH

At the First Hopi Mental Health Conference, held by the Hopi Health Department at Kykotsmovi in 1981, the Hopi Prophecy Workshop Committee under the direction of a Hopi artist by the name of Terrance Talaswaima, formulated a number of astute observations about the nature and function of Hopi prophecy:

> The forementioned issues of Hopi prophecy and the Hopi view of mental health hold important lessons for those who wish to assist members of the Hopi population in need. One cannot ignore the legitimacy of prophecy and underlying beliefs in mental health. Prophecy provides one with a strong direction in life. It illustrates definite patterns of evolution in this world, lets individuals know what to expect for the future, and as such prepares them for the inevitable. By taking note of prophecy and recognizing the signs of its fulfillment, people can adjust their lives in accordance with the ways of the universe and, by doing so, prolong the existence of this world. There is a definite strength in prophecy: it provides a clear recognition of present-day realities, it calls for an acceptance of disharmony and corruption in spirit, and it points towards the importance of self-sufficiency, self-discipline, and attentiveness to Hopi teachings and practices in preparation for the next world.
>
> Unfortunately, few Hopis appear to be taking note of prophecy and adjusting their lives for the better. Mental health and social problems are getting worse. Most people express frustration and depression when talking about prophecy; they throw up their hands in a kind of helplessness and declare that there is nothing one can do to improve the present climate and situation. Prophecy has been used as an excuse to avoid personal responsibility in improving the qualities of life and behaving in a way that follows Hopi teachings and beliefs. There runs a tremendous pessimism throughout Hopi that things will only get worse. This has immobilized a great deal of the population to either watch life deteriorate from a distance, or join in on the fun and go downhill as well. People who wish to help others and lead productive lives are frustrated at every turn. As such Hopi prophecy becomes a self-fulfilling prophecy—the people help to make it happen sooner. (Hopi Health Department n.d.:51)

These indigenous interpretations clearly support my comments on Hopi fatalism in chapter 2 and in the songs mentioned in chapter 3. As I wrote elsewhere, "many Hopis are . . . by-standers to their own cultural disintegration" (A. W. Geertz 1990*a*:314).

At the next Mental Health Conference in 1983 the Hopi Prophecy Workshop Committee was expanded to include both progressives such

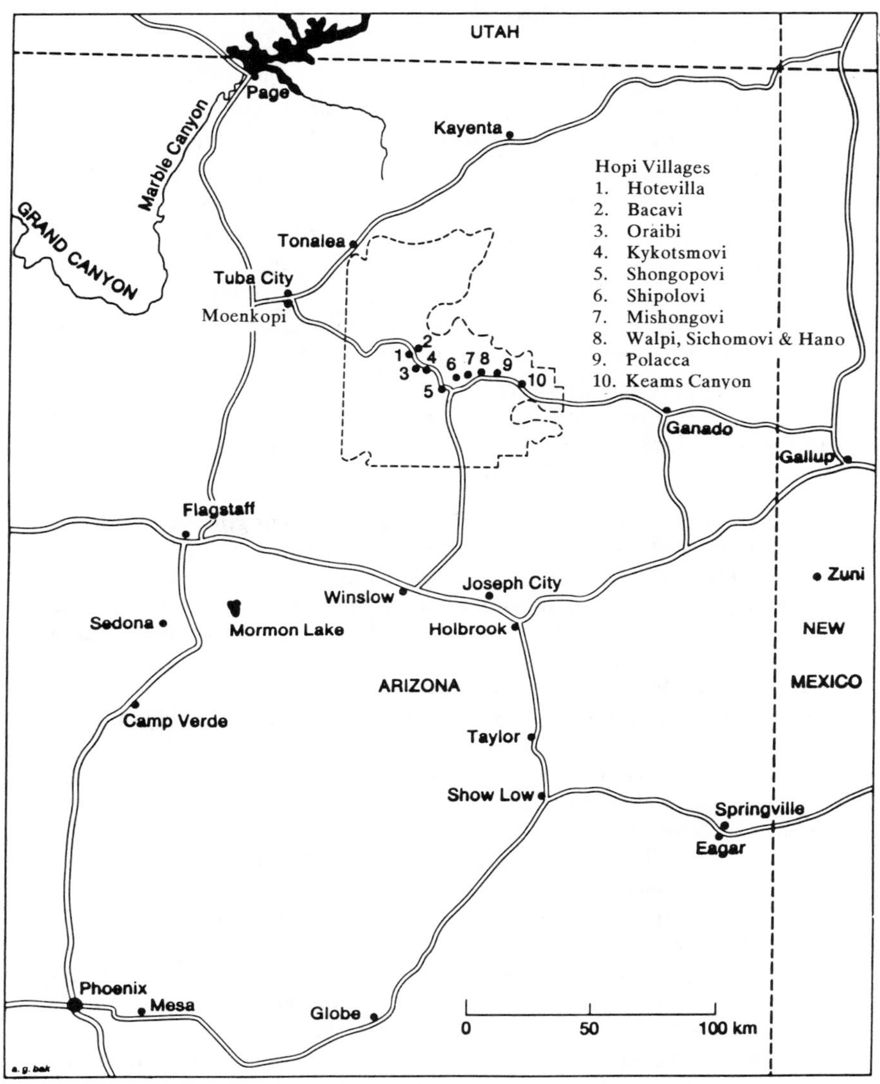

Map 6. Present Hopi territory. Drawn by A. G. Bak, Gyldendalske Boghandel Nordisk Forlag A.S., Copenhagen, Denmark.

as the now-deceased Percy Lomakwahu from Hotevilla and Traditionalists such as Thomas Banancya, who had been concerned with prophecy for many decades. The result was not only admirable, but signal, even though chairperson Leigh Jenkins, then assistant director of the Hopi Health Department, hastened to add that "the following information . . . is not meant to be the authoritative 'word' of the Life Plan, but rather a perspective of various interpretations and viewpoints" (Robin 1983:35).

The report contains nothing less than a chart depicting the *qatsivötavi* ("life path"), or the mythical history of the Hopis, reproduced here as figure 1. This is accompanied by Banancya's interpretation of prophecy rock and concludes with a systematic examination of the major prophetic statements in Hopi tradition (quoted in Hopi) wherein the statements are compared with statistics and other information *as proof of the legitimacy of each statement*. But the catalogue of dire signs is first introduced by positive and soothing words of hope. Once again, Hopi prophecy has been transformed, this time in the face of other needs:

> All Hopi informants say the same thing: That it is *our generation* which is witnessing the fulfillment of the Life Plan made known to us at the time of Emergence. All informants noted that the signs are quite clear as to the current stage of life we have entered into—a perilous period of life preceding an event known in Hopi theology as the punishment, purification and the judgment of all mankind by the Creator.
>
> We have reached a point in life where we must begin to work together so that we reach the right decisions. We have to look at ourselves so that we can again have respect for our fellow man, for the world, for if we don't, then we will all be judged accordingly for our mistakes. [Hopi elder]
>
> So is there hope for mankind? A simple Hopi proverb might kindle a measure of hope: Kaiitsivu, kapustamokca, konakopanvungya hakapii hihita ung kyataimanii! He who is slow to anger, frustration and self-pity *will live* to see and wonder at the many changes.
>
> An elder Hopi man underlines this positive approach towards life: "Pas-us kachi lolmai . . . su-an katuqt! Life is so good . . . if lived right!" The proverbial message to all Hopis then is to search out that kind of life that will truly represent what the name *Hopi* stands for. For the message simply says that if one has a strong, yet humble heart, then one will be able to survive both in the physical and spiritual sense to witness a constantly changing world, be it good or bad: "If you are willing and able to live my way of life. . . ." (Robin 1983:43)

The report then examined "those predictions that are in the process of occurring or those which are yet to occur" (ibid.:44). This section of the report provides a unique insight into the combination of prophetic cognition and Western methods of inquiry that characterize the

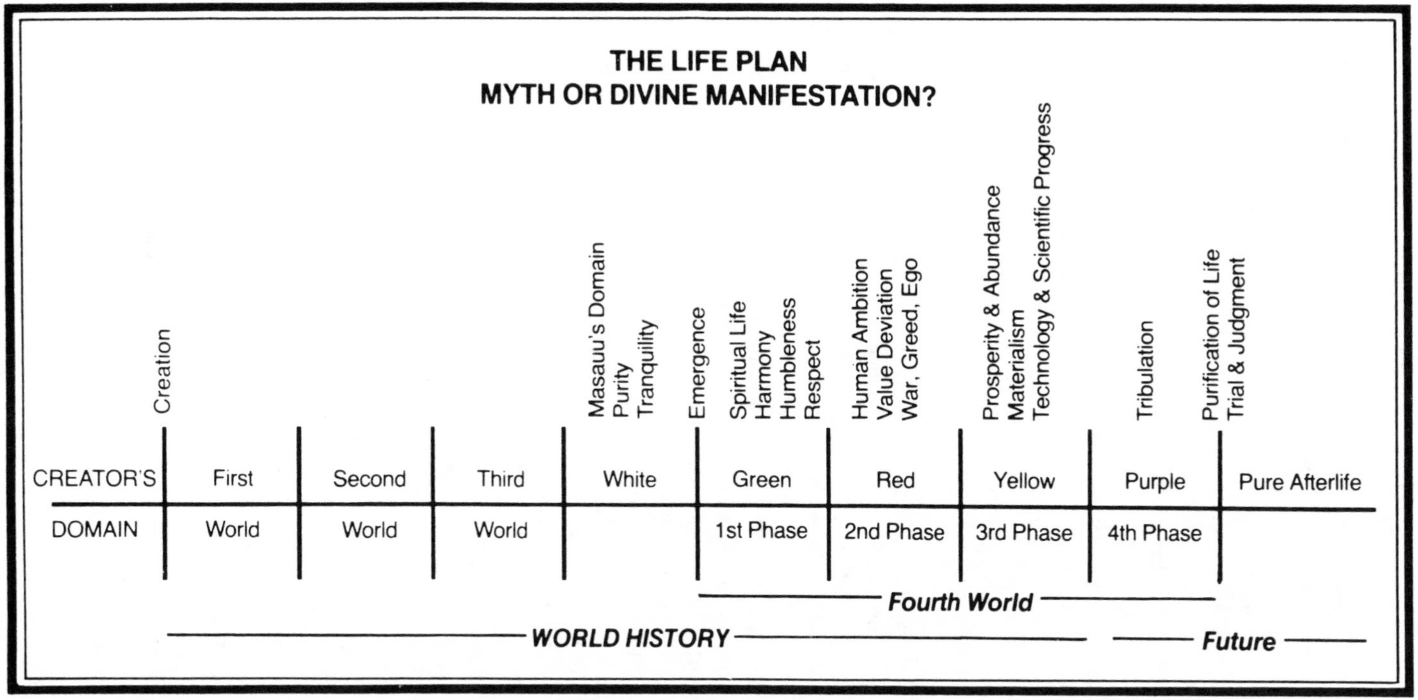

Figure 1. The Hopi Qatsivötavi. SOURCE: Robin 1983. Courtesy of the Hopi Health Department.

Hopi cognitive environment today. The catalogue of prophecies includes global overpopulation, the conquering of the United States by a foreign power, the advent of coastal earthquakes, catastrophic changes in the weather, the rise of starvation and pestilence, the political machinations of the Navajos, the presence of mineral development and exploitation, the discovery of life on another planet, the conquest of death by scientific technology, the dominance of women in political affairs, and other matters.

I will quote the section on the meaning of the prophecy of the ash bomb and the highly illuminating section on Hopi ethnic identity:

> ASH FALLING FROM THE SKY
> Hopi informants hold various interpretations as to the true meaning of this prophecy. Let us examine a few of them.
>
> **Nuclear Fallout: If current world trends continue, the final outcome will most likely be nuclear war and subsequent radioactive fallout. At present, the Soviet Union has 12,000 nuclear warheads aimed at American cities while the United States points 9,000 warheads in their direction. The continuation of current tensions may well lead to a final confrontation between these two global powers.
>
> **A Volcanic Eruption: This refers to our previously discussed prediction of the eruption of the San Francisco Peaks. Ash from the sky?
>
> **Air Pollution: Can one imagine the valley between Ozaivi and Second Mesa being filled with polluted air? It is indeed possible in this day and age! Huge clouds of polluted air now occasionally reach Hopiland. Flagstaff now generates enough industrial smoke and automobile emissions to create a haze known as smog. . . .
>
> JUDGMENT BY THE TWO-HORNS
>
> Our old people talk about the day we will all be judged by the *Ah-alt.* (two-horns). We will all be lined up in a single file. Then we will be pulled one by one to be judged. The head priest will grab a hold of our hair and pull us toward him. Then he will ask us: "Are you a Hopi?" We will nod our heads indicating that we are. Then he will say to us: "If you are a Hopi, then speak to me in Hopi!" If we know how, we will speak to the priest in Hopi. He will lead those who can speak Hopi to one side. Those who cannot speak Hopi he will put on the other side of him. This is how he will judge and divide us. Now those people who can speak Hopi will earn a right to stay here on our land for awhile longer. Those who cannot will be told to seek places to live elsewhere. [A Hopi Elder]
>
> Does the passage above resemble something out of a mythological textbook? A closer look at the symbolic language contained in the prophecy reveals a fulfillment that is happening now—this minute! At present, Tribal Council is attempting to determine exactly WHO and WHAT is a H O P I. This determination of tribal enrollment and membership has important

> implications for the "rights" that go along with belonging to the tribe (for example, health and educational benefits). . . . Lack of eligibility might well mean the absence of tribal rights to land and other resources! This prediction is now–staring Hopis in the face. (Robin 1983:48–49)

These prophecies and interpretations indicate that despite acculturation and borrowed forms of argumentation, there is no indication of secularization or decline in the Hopi traditional way of thinking. The prophecies have placed, and still do place, the Hopis squarely in the center of world events in Hopi thought, and they continue to serve as mechanisms of evaluation and systematization in the computer age.

At the Third Hopi Mental Health Conference in 1984, which had the theme "Prophecy in Motion," Leigh Jenkins emphasized that "the Hopi Life Plan must be presented and taught as a practical and 'livable' answer to today's problems" (Jenkins and Kooyahoema 1984:12). Hopi tribal chairman Ivan Sidney explained the theme's meaning: "Well, it's around us, whatever we do—we're the prophecy in motion. . . . And we must think about what that means, not only for ourselves, but for our kids who are coming and our kids yet to come" (ibid.:14).

Thus we meet once again with the ontological and existential experience of prophecy by religious Hopi individuals. The motto of the conference, published in *Qua' Töqti* and reproduced here as figure 2, illustrates the present concerns of the Hopis, all of which are symbolically placed in the drawing within the viable, living, prophetic contexts of today.

My interpretation of these symbols is as follows. The four corners symbols rest at the four corners of the drawing. Maasaw stands in the very center, at the foot of the District Six boundaries. The parallel verticle lines mark the Hopi half of the Joint Use Area. The stippled boundaries connect the sacred places, which constitute the traditional boundaries of Hopi territory. On Maasaw's life path we see two human figures having emerged by the reed on the left and moving along Maasaw's path that stands at the boundary between the underworld and the world of the living. The cloud and rain symbols represent the central theme of Hopi ceremonialism. Maasaw stands with a corn plant and digging stick in hand—both symbols of his status as the owner of the land and the source of agriculture. They are also symbols of the life of the Hopi people. The symbols to Maasaw's right consist of a spiral ending in a series of "closed path" symbols and the zigzag of lightning that points at the symbol of brotherhood. This complex symbol probably represents the migrations of the clans and the theme of hope imparted by the organizers of the conference.

One by one, the speakers gave words of encouragement. As Ebin Leslie, village chief at First Mesa, said: "So I urge everyone of you: Let us

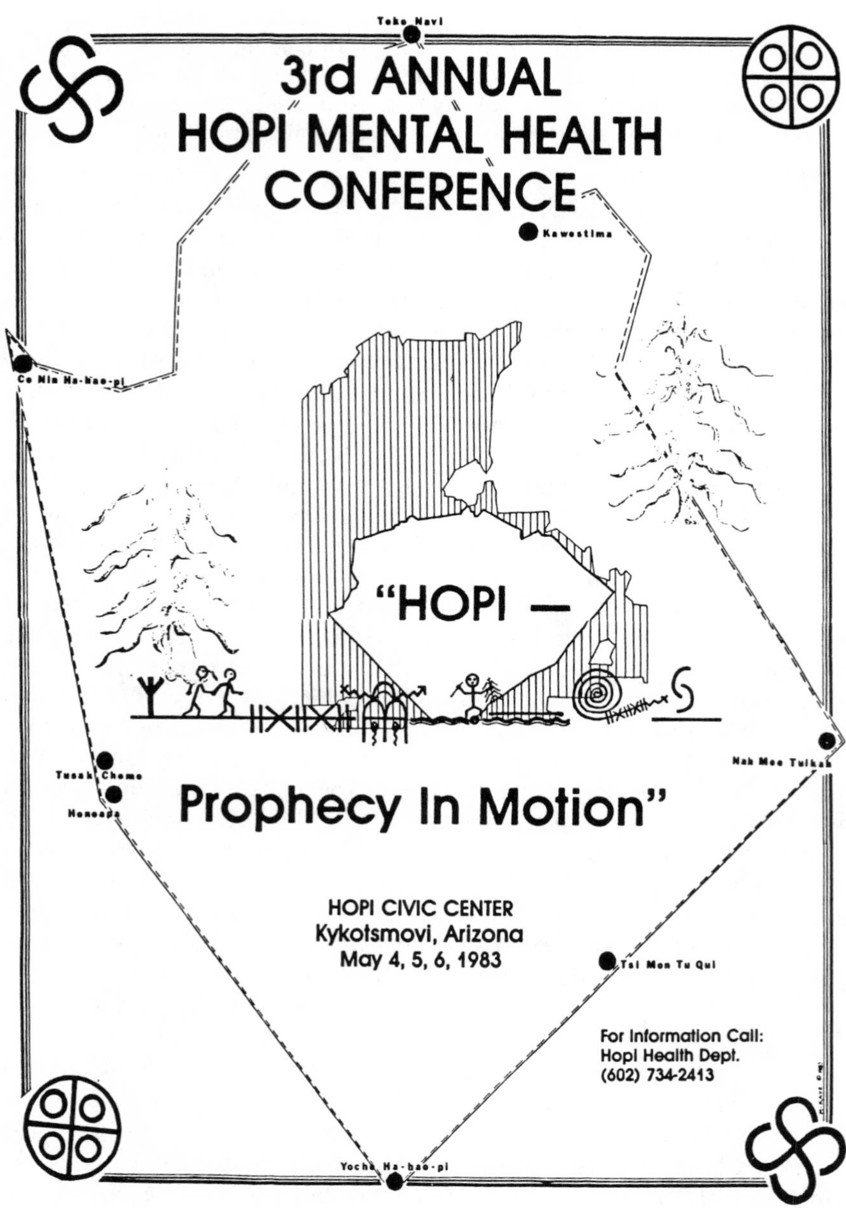

Figure 2. Motto of the Third Hopi Mental Health Conference in 1984.
SOURCE: *Qua' Töqti*, April 21, 1983, page 7.

go forth for one purpose—to help one another for we are one people" (Jenkins and Kooyahoema 1984:35).

In the true spirit of ecumenism, a brief comparison with the prophecies of the Bible were made during that same conference. The a priori position of the workshop was that "serious students of theology do not negate the possibility that men of all races actually may have received their religions from the same God or Creator, each religion designed to speak to a specific culture" (ibid.:64). The results of their comparison were that "both Hopi and Biblical teachings presented surprisingly similar warnings, and that current events seemed to match those warnings almost to the letter" (ibid.:65). The workshop called for mutual understanding between denominations and "helping one another prepare for the Judgement to come" (ibid.:66). In a single, elegant stroke, the Hopi religion has been placed on equal footing with at least Judeo-Christian tradition. This fundamental attitude is aptly illustrated by the drawing provided here as figure 3.

The Fourth Annual Hopi Mental Health Conference, held in 1984, concentrated on a number of central problems in preserving Hopi identity and lifeway. One of the important themes was the preservation of the Hopi language and its use in the schools. Another was the preservation of the clan system and its importance in preserving Hopi identity. The report showed an interesting chart on Hopi education, presented here as figure 4. Today, the balance is on Western concepts and the requirements of the dominant society. But tomorrow, the scales are balanced by Hopi concepts and the requirements of Hopi society. The dominant society focuses on economic survival, and Hopi society focuses on spiritual survival. This chart is, of course, simplistic and ethnocentric, but the point to be noted here is that the Hopis who are in positions of authority, both traditional and contemporary forms of authority, have analyzed their situation and have found and articulated the resolution to their problems. Whether the resolutions can be realized by the populace at large is another question entirely. The Hopis have solved their problems before, and they will do it again. It is important for our study to emphasize that prophecy has been identified by the Hopis as a relevant and viable vehicle of self-help, and that functional solutions are provided along with ideological ones.

The development of ideas exchanged during the four years of mental health conferences seems to indicate that Hopi prophecy and its ideology are major keys to attaining the balance and equal opportunity which are so necessary for cultural survival. The conferences demonstrate the functional category of the use of myth to recreate psychosocial stability and meaning.

Figure 3. Hopi religion and other religions. SOURCE: Jenkins and Kooyahoema, 1984. Courtesy of the Hopi Health Department.

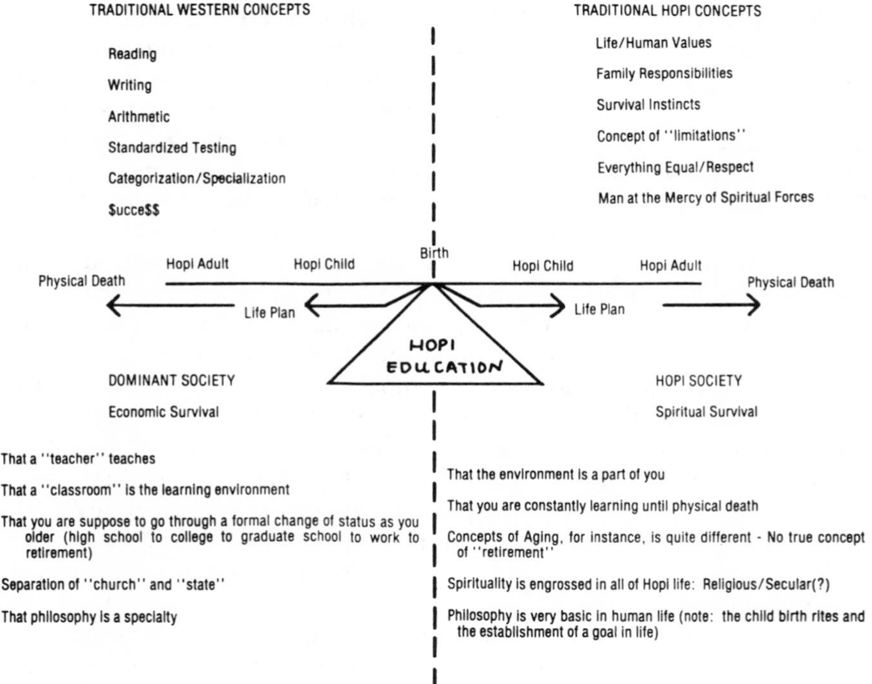

Figure 4. The balance of Hopi identity. SOURCE: Dagnal and Jenkins 1985. Courtesy of the Hopi Health Department.

In conclusion, it can be stated that in Hopi history from 1830 to 1989 no prophetic statements are demonstrably precognitive. On the contrary, many of them first appear a decade or more after the fact, despite ever-present claims of precognition. As this chapter has shown, prophecy incorporates contemporaneous affairs into the interpretive framework of prophetic discourse and subjects those affairs and the forces behind them to evaluation in terms of conceived tradition. This evaluation, or pronouncing of judgment, derives authority from tradition and serves as a mechanism in social and political strategy.

SIX

Interpreting Significant Objects

The Politics of Hopi Apocalypse[1]

The delineation of the meaning of an iconographic object goes hand in hand with an analysis of its use and the place it has in the cultural scheme of things. A topic particularly well-suited to this approach is the analysis of the use and significance of stone tablets in Hopi eschatology. As chapter 5 has demonstrated, Hopi prophecies about the end of the world are intimately tied to an indigenous, hermeneutical process in which contemporary affairs are evaluated in relation to conceived tradition. Contrary to the opinion of most Europeans and Americans who are interested in the Hopis, prophetic statements are neither exact reproductions of tradition nor do they have absolute precognitive value. As with any type of hermeneutic, the end product is precisely a "product"—sometimes spontaneous—of historical factors, contemporary events, and ideological rhetoric.

Although this chapter begins a series of chapters which pay close attention to the Traditionalist Movement, it also indicates further how tradition is used by all leaders, regardless of their political persuasions.

Stone tablets function in Hopi thought as symbols of authority which are owned and used by the village chief. These tablets also function as signs of the immanent apocalypse and play a major role in Hopi prophetic tradition. The mention of the word "prophecy" to a knowledgeable Hopi will inevitably bring the response "stone tablet."

One would think that objects of stone are somehow eternally im-

1. Portions of this chapter were read at the 10th American Indian Workshop, Vienna, Austria, March 30, 1989, in a paper entitled "The Politics of Iconography: Hopi Indian Stone Tablets." I wish to extend my thanks to Clifford Geertz, Alice Schlegel, and Peter Whiteley for comments and criticisms of the paper.

mutable and constant, the mute yet eloquent beacons of tradition standing as irrefutable proof for all ages to come. Indeed, this is how they are conceived and presented by the Hopis, and the more impressionable among us have a similar opinion. A quote from the American editor of the minutes of the "Meeting of Religious People" at Hotevilla in 1956 is instructive:

> The Great Spirit is their King or President or Executive Leader and they follow His laws. He transfered this land to the Hopi when they first came on this world–and they have the unforgeable, un-counterfeitable, stone documents, and Divine Life Plan to prove it. (Bentley 1956:18)

However, an analysis of how the stones are used and of the forms they take in rhetorical contexts clearly indicates that the only perennial aspect about them is their significance. Everything else about them is open to manipulation and speculation and shows every sign of being subordinate to political, social, and religious factors. Warring ideologies produce mutually incompatible interpretations and, therefore, even solid stone becomes as malleable and transformative as other more ephemeral communicative devices.

POLITICS AND POWER IN HOPI ICONOGRAPHY

My approach to politics follows that of recent political anthropology. I define politics in the Hopi context as "the striving for or exercise of power over things which concern the interests of a group of people" and power as "the capacity to limit the behavioral alternatives of other people" (Claessen 1979:8). Power in this sense is a "symbolic medium whose functioning does not depend primarily upon its intrinsic effectiveness but upon the expectations that its employment arouses in those who comply with it" (Swartz, Turner, and Tuden 1966:14). Authority is "the right to use and acquire power vested in a status by a procedure based on the 'authority code'" (ibid.:18). Central to the exercise of power in Hopi culture are claims to authority coupled with mechanisms of reciprocity.

What makes the study of Hopi politics so fascinating is that it is a gratifying example of processual activity.[2] By observing the actors, their purposes, their methods of utilizing power, and their development of power (Gross 1968:266ff), insight may be gained on a whole array of

2. Michael G. Smith was the first to develop an analytical distinction between government and politics in his study *Government in Zazzau* (1960). This distinction represented a breakaway from the earlier focus on political institutions and became important to studies of competition for political power, political change, and the processual approach to politics.

otherwise-opaque matters in Hopi affairs. Seen in terms of processual anthropology, the next few chapters will demonstrate the historical texture of Hopi political fields (i.e., "the totality of actors involved in one specific political event")[3] and arenas (i.e., "the social and cultural space in which the field is located") (Claessen 1979:12).[4]

The discussions will show how Hopi political strife is primarily a question of the partners in acculturation (i.e., the Friendlies/Hostiles and, later, the Progressives/Traditionalists) being engaged in striving for and/or establishing legitimation. In this sense, I agree with Myron Aronoff that legitimation "is a form of meaning which ideally integrates disparate institutional processes and subuniverses of meaning, thereby making sense of the entire social order. . . . Legitimation provides information, explanation, rationalization, and justification" (Aronoff 1983:3). Thus, legitimation in this case is a question of the competitive construction of meaning or, perhaps better, a battle of meanings staged by the rules of a "meaning hegemony." Ritual objects and ritual behavior are central to Hopi hegemony (cf. Kertzer 1983), and, therefore, the analysis of the stone tablets is the thread that will illuminate the whole web of meaningful interrelationships.

As I mentioned in *Children of Cottonwood* (A. W. Geertz and Lomatuway'ma 1987:143 n. 94; cf. A. W. Geertz 1987*c*:38), Hopi society is hierarchical, being composed of the *kiikyam*, "the elite," *pavansinom*, "the strong people," and the *söqavungsinom*, "people with no status." Drawing on the results of Steadman Upham, I noted that one of the most important factors in this system is not the distribution of wealth but, in Upham's words, "access to, and possession of, ritual and ceremonial knowledge" (1982:19–20).

Peter Whiteley has argued along similar lines in his highly important paper on Hopi politics (1987). In that article he was concerned with the structures, concepts, and practices of "power" within the Hopi cultural context. One of his main points was that the primary source of power

3. Thus:

> A political field does not operate like clockwork, with all the pieces meshed together with finely tooled precision. It is, rather, a field of tension, full of intelligent and determined antagonists, sole and corporate, who are motivated by ambition, altruism, self-interest, and by desire for the public good, and who in successive situations are bound to one another through self-interest, or idealism—and separated or opposed through the same motives. At every point in this process we have to consider each unit in terms of its independent objectives, and we also have to consider the entire situation in which their *inter*dependent actions occur. (Swartz, Turner, and Tuden 1966:8)

4. See the excellent discussion on this approach and the holistic "paradigm for political anthropology" in Kurtz (1979).

in Hopi society lies in esoteric ritual knowledge. Drawing on recent anthropological discussions of the political effects of secret knowledge,[5] Whiteley indicated that "through secrecy, knowledge takes on the character of property" (ibid.:703). Seen in this perspective, "secret knowledge can be used . . . as a medium of social value and a calculus of social differentiation" (ibid.:704). This knowledge is gained through gradual initiation throughout the life of an individual, but even in the upper echelons of knowledge, the hierarchy pervades so that the most knowledgeable are the oldest kiikyam and/or pavansinom.

I have argued that "religious as well as secular power resides almost completely in the possession and use of important ritual objects" (1987*a*:vii; cf. A. W. Geertz 1986). Seen in the context of the politics of secret knowledge, I wish to add the following: Hopi ritual objects materialize the power of secret knowledge, providing it with an iconographic medium that expresses the ineffable in the world of objects, but which, even more importantly, gives actual physical substance to the "property" aspect of secret knowledge. Thus, the possession of these objects is, in actual fact, the possession of social, political, and religious power. The only ones who ideally possess the "meaning" of any particular ritual object are its legitimate owners.

This is an important point to remember when analyzing the rhetoric of Hopi prophecy. The many contradictory interpretations of religious matters among the Hopis are due not only to conflicting clan traditions, but also to the varying degrees of insight held by the consultants in question. Since the only legitimate meanings or interpretations are those which stem from the legitimate ownership of ritual objects, and since ritual objects are precious social currency that is hard to come by, then Hopi political rhetoric and bluster are very sensitive to the language and the symbols of legitimate authority. Those who do not have it can either persuade others to think they have, or they can make or steal their own objects. Thus, ritual objects and ritual knowledge are strategic resources in the struggle for prestige and power (cf. Rubinstein 1981:161ff).

STONE TABLETS IN HOPI PROPHECY AND HISTORY

As noted in earlier chapters, Hopi prophecy can be formally defined as statements about the future which were reportedly pronounced by the Hopi tutelary deity, Maasaw, and by the first people who appeared at

5. Barth 1975; G. Lewis 1980; Murphy 1980; Rubinstein 1981; Bellman 1984; Lindstrom 1984; and Fardon 1985. Elizabeth Brandt seems to have found a similar situation at Taos Pueblo. She considers what she calls "internal secrecy" a prime factor in Pueblo factionalism (1980:126 n.3).

Sipaapuni, the place of the emergence of mankind. Two brothers were at this meeting, the elder one being White and the younger one being Hopi, and each received a stone tablet called *owatutuveni.* The White Brother was commissioned to keep an eye on the Hopi Brother and to succour him in the hour of his need, which will be the prelude to the end of this fourth world. The return of the White Brother will be signaled and his identity will be proven when he produces his stone tablet.

Now, matters of great dispute among the Hopis are the number of stone tablets, who owns them, who gave them to the Hopis, what is incised on them, what they signify, and their import and use during the apocalypse. All of these are inextricably bound up with the genealogy of power and the people who wield it in Oraibi and Hotevilla. Therefore, any study of Hopi tablets and prophecy which does not take the politics of power into consideration will be a curious study at best.[6]

Of the thirty-five reports of stone tablets listed on the accompanying chart B, fifteen are based on eyewitness accounts (type A), seven are based on accounts we can reasonably assume are based on eyewitness knowledge (type B), and thirteen are most likely based on hearsay (type C). The twenty-two accounts found in the first two categories deal with three tablets that are owned by the Bear and Kookop clans respectively. But others probably do exist. If we believe all the accounts, we have at least five stones in all, not counting the tablet purported to be in the hands of the legendary White Brother.

It seems that most consultants believe that there are only two tablets, one owned by the Bear clan and one owned by the Kookop (incorrectly translated as "Fire") clan. The Bear clan tablet is concerned with authority and land, and the Kookop clan tablet is concerned with beheading and dire warning. This fits well with the history of the conflict between the two clans on Third Mesa where the hereditary chiefs of the Bear clan wished to demonstrate proof of authority and the usurpers wished to demonstrate the incompetence of those in authority as well as their own right to usurpation by eschatological proxy.[7]

The fact of the existence of at least two tablets was already brought to light in 1882 when the rebel leader at Oraibi, Talay'ima, told Cushing: "We, too, have records in marks on magic stones. One is the Rock of Death given to us by the corpse demon after we came from the cave

6. Kaiser's recent book (1989, 1991) is neither definitive nor critical. Even though the book does not address the academic community, it nonetheless shows no real insight into Hopi ethnography, language, sociology, or religion. See my paper on Kaiser in A. W. Geertz 1991.

7. Titiev (1944:73–75, 98–99) and Krutz (1973) allow this sociological theory, whereas Clemmer (1978*b*:58) wishes to somehow separate ideology from its social context.

Informant	Date	Owner	Bear	Kookop	Unspec.	Symbols
Young	1871	Oraibi			1 stone	Clan syms., other syms., human figs.
Talay'ima	1882				2 stones	Marks
Fewkes	1890				1 stone	Marks
Qöyawayma	1903				4 tablets	Characters
Yukiwma	1903				2 stones	Marks/figs.
Yukiwma	1911				2 rocks	Headless humans/ unspecified
Yukiwma	1911	Yukiwma		2 tablets		
Waters	1911	Yukiwma		1 tablet		
Yukiwma	1911	Tawa-kwaptiwa	1 stone			Serpent /man
Yukiwma	1911	Yukiwma		2 rocks		
Yava	1911	Yukiwma		1 tablet		Headless man
Tawakwap-tiwa	1911	Yukiwma		1 stone		Headless man
Talayesva	1911	Yukiwma		1 stone		
Wallis	1912	Kiy'oma	1 tablet			Engraved & broken
Tawakwap-tiwa	1933	Tawa-kwaptiwa	1 tablet			Clan/other symbols, human figs.
Tawakwap-tiwa	1933	Loololma's grandsons			1 tablet	
Qötshongva	1935			1 tablet		
Pongyayaw-ma/Qöts-hongva	1941	Pongya-yawma		2 tablets		

Chart B. Tablets of stone in Hopi history (part 1).

Giver	Significance	Eschatological Drama	Type
		Shown to Mormons	A
Maasaw/Ancients	1. Rock of Death 2. Remembrance of words	Told to Cushing	B
Gods	Testament, control of clan lands	Shown to soldiers	A
Huru'ingwwuuti/ Spider Woman	1. Knowledge to Brothers 2. Knowledge to Spaniards	Told to Voth	C
	Fit together: White Brother returns/decapitates witches		B
Maasaw	1. Hostile people beheaded 2. Proof of land claim	Told to BIA Commissioner	B
Maasaw		Given to BIA Commissioner	A
		Taken from him/ Carlisle	C
Underworld	Serpent = ocean; man = White Brother; ocean flood & decapitation	Told to Col. Scott	B
Maasaw		Given to Col. Scott	A
	Other half White Brother will bring: fits with Hopi half	Shown at Keams Canyon	A
	Tawakwaptiwa to be beheaded	Shown to President Taft	B
	Two paths for Hopis; decapitate witches/become Christian	Shown to President Taft	C
Maasaw	Emergence Myth; land kept as long as tablet kept, but disaster if forgotten		C
Matsito	Matsito's intentions with land; Hopi path; fit with brother's, will become brothers again	Shown at Soyalangw Shown to Titiev as ally	A
			C
Maasaw	Map of land; White Brother will return to translate	Told to Mormons	A
	1. Hopi Land and Prophecy; 2. The home; will be read by White Brother who will bring equality	Shown at draft resistance trial	A

Chart B. Tablets of stone in Hopi history (part 1, cont'd).

Informant	Date	Owner	Bear	Kookop	Unspec.	Symbols
Hopi Empire	1949				2 tablets	Writing
Qötshongva	1955	Qötshongva Loololma	1 false	1 true		
Monongya	1955	Qötshongva		1 tablet		
Secquaptewa	1955	Qötshongva			1 tablet	
Hermequaf-tewa	1955	Shongo-pavi	1 stone			
Banancya	1956				1 tablet	
Simon Scott	1956				2? tablets	
Banancya	1960	Qötshongva		1 tablet		
Mina Lansa	1960	Mina Lansa	1 tablet			Clan & other sym-bols/hu-man figs.
Frank Waters	1960	Yukiwma		1 tablet		Headless man, sym-bols; broken
Frank Waters	1960		2 tablets			Symbols & figs.
Yava	1969	Shongopavi			1 tablet	
Qötshongva	1970	Qötshongva		1 tablet		
3rd Mesa elder	1981				2? tablets	Headless man & coyote
Pongyayaw-ma	1988			2 tablets		Headless man/two men reach-ing out
Pongyayaw-ma	1988	Oraibi	1 tablet			
Sekenaayoma	1988	Pongyayaw-ma		2 tablets		

Chart B. Tablets of stone in Hopi history (part 2).

Giver	Significance	Eschatological Drama	Type
	Boundaries of Hopi Empire; fit with brother's, prove land claim, bring order & judgment	Written to Pres. Truman	B
	1. Instructions/life plan, 2. forgery; proof in the end	Told at BIA hearings	A
	Convenant concerning land	Told at BIA hearings	B
	Hopi life, crops; map; guardian of land; maybe beheading; lose it, serpent destroys earth	Told at BIA hearings	C
Maasaw	His teachings, life plan; two brothers; destruction if lost	Told at BIA hearings	C
Maasaw	Proof of land claim	Meeting of Religious people	C
Great Spirit	To be used in future	Meeting of Religious people	C
Bow Clan father	White Brother reads it, matches with Hopi tablet, show true brotherhood	Written to German supporter	C
Söqömhonaw			A
Maasaw	Leader beheaded if choose another religion; White Brother matches missing piece; identity of Hopi revealed; universal brotherhood		C
Söqömhonaw	Land claims; maybe decapitation	1. Stolen; 2. disappeared, but will be revealed	C
			C
Great Spirit	Laws, instructions; White Brother matches, shows true identity		A
	White Brother will punish in the end		A
Younger Brother	1. Decapitation when White Brother comes, match with Hopi stone; 2. the two brothers will unite		A
	Represents the land		A
	White Brother has other piece		A

Chart B. Tablets of stone in Hopi history (part 2, cont'd).

worlds. The other is the stone which our ancients made that we might not forget their words" (Cushing 1922:266). He was, in other words, referring to the Kookop stone and the Bear stone. Being the main critic of and rebel against the Bear clan, he did not in his statement shy away from the politically significant insinuation that the Bear clan stone was only man-made whereas the Kookop clan stone was divinely made.

I will concentrate in this chapter on the stones of the Bear and the Kookop clans.

STONE TABLETS IN BEAR CLAN HISTORY

During the 1870s the Hopis had contact with Mormon missionaries and even visited Mormon settlements in Utah.[8] The Mormons Andrew S. Gibbons, his two sons William and Richard, and John W. Young were shown a "sacred stone" by Tuuvi in Oraibi in 1871. He is called "chief," which he was not, nor is it clear why he was allowed to show the stone to the Mormons. This meeting was described in a 1921 publication by James H. McClintock from the State Historian's office in Phoenix, which he claimed to be based on Mormon manuscripts. However, his description of the stone seems to be taken from a later source, to which I will return. He quoted Tuuvi as saying that "at one time, the stone incautiously was exhibited to an army officer, who attempted to seize it, but the Indians saved the relic and hid it more securely" (McClintock 1921:82). But I wonder if he again has based his commentary on an incident that took place at a later time, for example, the Cushing incident in 1882 or even the confrontation in 1890.

McClintock then made superficial reference to a report in the *Fourth Annual Report of the Bureau of Ethnology* which, on closer examination, proved to be his source. The report contains Garrick Mallery's study of Indian pictographs wherein he cited the notes of G. K. Gilbert, which were based on notes and drawings made by John W. Young. In January 1990 I located Gilbert's notes and drawings, done in pencil on file cards, at the Smithsonian Institution, National Anthropological Archives in Washington D.C.[9] The drawings are reproduced here as figure 5. Garrick Mallery's account sums up what is found in Gilbert's notes:

> Mr. Gilbert furnishes some data relating to the sacred stone kept by the Indians of the village of Oraibi, on the Moki mesas. This stone was seen by Messrs. John W. Young and Andrew S. Gibbon, and the notes were made by Mr. Gilbert from those furnished to him by Mr. Young. Few white men

8. Cf. Peterson 1971; James 1974, 85–99; Whiteley 1988, 33–37.

9. I wish to extend my thanks to acting director Dr. William Merrill and his staff for their helpful assistance.

Figure 5. Drawings of the Bear clan stone copied from the notebooks of John W. Young (1871) by G. K. Gilbert. SOURCE: Smithsonian Institution, National Anthropological Archives, Washington, D.C. Courtesy of the Smithsonian Institution. Drawn by Poul Nørbo, Aarhus, Denmark.

have had access to this sacred record, and but few Indians have enjoyed the privilege.

Mr. Gilbert remarks that "the stone was evidently squared by the eye and not by any instrument. The engraving seems to have been done with some rude instrument, but executed with some degree of skill, like an ancient art faded into dim remembrance of the artist or writer of the characters. The stone is a red clouded marble, entirely different from anything found in the region, so I learn by the Indians. The stone is badly worn, and some of the characters are difficult to determine."

According to the notes accompanying the rude drawings of this stone, it is an oblong rectangle, measuring 11 3/4 inches long, 7 1/4 inches wide, and 1 1/2 inches thick. On one side there is an interior space, also an oblong rectangle measuring about three-fourths of the size of the whole tablet, between which and the outer margin are six nude human figures resembling one another, one at either end and two on each of the two sides. The interior space may have contained characters, though no traces are now visible.

> On the other side are drawings of the sun, clouds with rain descending therefrom, lightning, stars, arrows, foot-prints of the bear, and several other undeterminable characters.
>
> No history of the origin and import of this tablet has been obtained. (Mallery 1886:58)

The description matches exactly with later reports and with the illustrations, figures 6 and 7 below. As will become evident, there is no doubt that this tablet is the legitimate Bear clan tablet.

The archaeologist Jesse Walter Fewkes was present at the armed confrontation between American soldiers and the hostiles at Oraibi in 1890. Fewkes saw one of the leaders hand a flat stone with marks on it to Major Corbin. When asked for an explanation, the Hopi replied that "it was the testament given to his ancestors by the gods securing to the clans of Oraibi control of all the country about their town" (Fewkes 1922:277).

As was mentioned in chapter 6, the Hopis were convinced that this armed confrontation was the beginning of the apocalypse, and therefore it was an appropriate occasion to test whether the soldiers were the long-awaited Pahaana. The Hopis found out, evidently, that they were not, since, in Fewkes' words, "This stone was later passed to other officers and then returned to the Indians. A search was made for it subsequently, but it was impossible to find it or to gain any further information regarding its whereabouts" (ibid.).

Since this stone was evidently in the hands of the rebel leaders, I am not quite convinced that it was the Bear Clan stone. The interpretation given indicates that it was, but the circumstances seem to indicate that it was not.

Yukiwma, the Kookop leader who was forced out of Oraibi in 1906 and who founded Hotevilla that same year, mentioned the existence of two tablets on several occasions.

During March 1911, Yukiwma visited President William Howard Taft and Commissioner of Indian Affairs Robert Grosvenor Valentine in Washington. In a report on a conference between Yukiwma and Valentine, we find that Yukiwma related the emergence myth and not only provided detail on the tablets, but actually presented them to the commissioner. Yukiwma claimed that two stones were brought up from the underworld. The one belonged to the Younger Brother and the other to the Older Brother. A few lines later, he reportedly claimed that Maasaw, having stolen two stones, gave them to the brothers after the emergence:

> And on the other one, one Oraibi's got, it is almost like a paper, it is a piece of rock which is like granite, and it has got human figures on with no heads on. He said that describes what is going to be done with these hostile people, lose their heads. . . . He said this other chief at Oraibi, he had

> this stone, and these people from the East were coming to take that land away from them, and if they tried to do it, he was to show them this stone, and they would leave him alone. (Valentine 1911:2)

This peculiar description does not match Young's drawings. And, although it seems to describe the symbols and meanings of one stone, later sources indicate that this description is actually a description of two separate tablets, i.e., the one owned by the Bear clan, which gives them legitimate authority over the land, and the one owned by the Kookop clan, which represents the prophecy of the return of the apocalyptic punisher. The fact that Yukiwma chose to use the startling phrase that Maasaw "stole" the tablets has interesting relevance to the theme of this section.

Yukiwma then produced two tablets and handed them over to the commissioner. Even though his narrative clearly refers to only two primordial tablets–the one kept by the Hopi Brother and the other by the White Brother–Yukiwma inexplicably produced one more stone. He then said,

> the Red Headed Spirit made those stones and put those inscriptions on it, that the land belongs to him. Those stones show that he has a right to that land, and that is why he don't want the civilized way, he wants to live the Indian way. (ibid.:6)

This was no explanation at all for the obvious inconsistency. It seems that there are also inconsistencies concerning the origins of the tablets in Yukiwma's account: they were either brought from the underworld by the brothers, stolen by Maasaw and given to the brothers after the emergence, or created by Maasaw himself at some unspecified point in time. These inconsistencies could have been due to misunderstandings and poor translations between narrator, intrepreter, and receiver, or they may simply reflect the fact that there are more than two stones and the Hopis had not resolved the fact in their explanations. It seems equally striking to me that Yukiwma was somehow in possession of both his own and Tawakwaptiwa's Bear clan tablet. There are two possible solutions to this problem: either one of the tablets was loaned to him by his enemy, Chief Tawakwaptiwa, or Yukiwma's clan was in possession of two tablets. The former would confirm Whiteley's thesis that rather than being bitter enemies, Yukiwma and Tawakwaptiwa were, in fact, fellow conspirators (1988). But, as Whiteley also noted, things had changed by 1911. There were evidently some secret agreements that were not being honored, and matters became even more complicated when the people of Hotevilla evidently found out about the conspiracy. They were not interested in ending the ceremonial cycle, and they forced Yukiwma against his will to reinstate it (Whiteley 1988:274, 279–283). Meanwhile, Tawakwaptiwa had recently returned from his forced residence at Riverside, California (1906–1909) and was frustrated by the political machinations of his opponents during his absence. He brought another "split" into effect in Oraibi in 1909 and forced the returned Hotevillians, who were under Kewanimptewa's leadership, out of Oraibi, an event that led to the founding of Bacavi. The presence of Bacavi placed a strain on the agripolitical balance in the area, and Yukiwma was not very pleased with the competition Kewanimptewa offered in their relationships with the Whites (cf. Whiteley 1988). This state of affairs must have had profound affects on the relationship between Yukiwma and Tawakwaptiwa.

The above-mentioned second solution would confirm later reports of the existence of more than two tablets. One of these reports was a conversation with Tawakwaptiwa reported in Mischa Titiev's diary entry for September 30, 1933:

> He also said that Yokioma had had a stone picturing a decapitated man, which he is alleged to have shown to Theodore Roosevelt. Tawaqwaptiwa claimed that this meant Yokioma wanted to cut his (Tawaqwaptiwa's) head off, but the chief said Yokioma "wasn't man enough to do it." (Titiev 1972:65)

I am certain that Tawakwaptiwa was referring to the meeting with Taft in 1911 and not to an alleged meeting with Roosevelt, which would have been several years prior to 1911. The chief mentioned only one tablet, namely, Yukiwma's. Either Tawakwaptiwa did not know about the other tablet or he neglected to mention that Yukiwma had also shown Tawakwaptiwa's tablet to the president.

A third possibility is that the two tablets presented by Yukiwma to the commissioner were both Kookop tablets. A fourth logical possibility is that Yukiwma owned one Kookop tablet and was in illicit possession of a Bear clan tablet. Tawakwaptiwa's reference to the beheading legend can be interpreted as indicating that Yukiwma did not have Tawakwaptiwa's stone with him, but that he was actually trying to secure his own political position. In other words, he was indeed showing the Kookop stone in order to convince the commissioner to behead Tawakwaptiwa. The fact that he was also trying to prove a legitimate claim to the land seems to indicate that he also had a Bear clan tablet in his possession (i.e., a second Bear clan tablet).

The report of the conference proves both of these intentions beyond a shadow of a doubt: Yukiwma explicitly named Tawakwaptiwa as the one who was to be beheaded (Valentine 1911:5) and, as the quoted explanation given by Yukiwma after handing over the tablets indicates, he also laid claim to the land.

Further confirmation of the existence of a third tablet was given to Titiev by his friend and informant Don Talayesva, called "Ned" in Titiev's diary.[10] On January 30, 1934, Talayesva told him:

> When asked if the sacred stone . . . was connected with the Schism of 1906, Ned replied that there was no direct connection. He did know, however, of another "wonderful" stone that was supposed to have been in Yokioma's possession. This stone Yokioma is said to have shown in Washington to the president of the United States. . . . It is reputed to have symbolic meaning and to depict the two paths lying before the Hopi. Either they could take the right path by decapitating witches or else they could travel along the road of the "Whites" that leads to Christianity. (1972:215)

This third stone does not match the Young report.

There were quite a number of rumors about beheadings and prophecies of beheadings. Most consultants were in doubt, though, as to whether it was to be the Bear clan leader or the Kookop clan leader. It seems that the leaders of the two clans had been challenging each other since the time of Loololma to submit themselves to the apocryphal sacrifice in order to save the Hopi people from destruction and to secure their safe emergence into a new world of peace (Waters 1963:363–365; Nequatewa 1936:70–71).

At any rate, Valentine expressed his satisfaction both during the conference and two weeks later in a letter to Yukiwma (Valentine 3-30-1911) that the tablets were evidence enough of the Hopis' title to the land. But, the land was not an issue with the Office of Indian Affairs at that time. The issue was education. So when it became clear that Yukiwma still refused to send the Hotevilla children to school, Colonel Hugh L. Scott was sent to the area to remove the children to the school at Keams Canyon. But before fulfilling that order, Colonel Scott went to Hotevilla together with an interpreter and a servant in order to find out why Yukiwma would not comply. On December 15th, Yukiwma satisfied Scott's curiosity by relating the emergence myth. The narrative also contained references to two stone tablets. Yukiwma reportedly stated:

10. Edward A. Kennard wrote in his review of the book:

> In keeping with the custom of protecting one's informants, all of the individuals are given pseudonyms in this account. However, Don Talayesva (Ned) shown in two pictures (Figs. 4, 5) and in note 19 (p. 358) referring to his autobiography, *Sun Chief* (1942), is clearly identified, particularly to any Hopi who happens to pick up this book. Nevertheless, Fred Eggan told me in October 1973 that Don was angry with the author because the use of the pseudonym deprived him of recognition for his contribution to the ethnography of the Hopi, if not to American anthropology. What price ethics? (1975)

> At Oraiba, the chief has a square stone plate representing the earth. A serpent is carved on one side and a man's figure on the other. The serpent represents the ocean which is [to] swallow up the land. The other figure [is] the white brother who is to come and cut off the heads of the bad people. . . . Oraiba holds a stone plate brought from the underworld and it gives him the right to the country. (Scott 12-5-1911:17, cf. Appendix B)

This description, again, does not seem to match with the stone described and drawn by John W. Young. It should also be noted that the headless figure of his earlier narrative is no longer explicitly headless. Yukiwma's narrative ended with a parenthesis, added by the author of the report, which indicates that he indeed possessed two other tablets:

> Ukeoma here presented two slabs of rock on which he said was inscribed the tradition. The red-headed ghost gave them to his people upon their arrival at Oraiba. (ibid.:18)

The same problems arise with this narrative as with the March narrative. But my arguments in favor of the existence of either two Kookop tablets or a Kookop tablet and the illicit possession of a Bear clan tablet seems to be further supported. If Yukiwma had shown both the Bear clan stone and the Kookop stone to officials in Washington, why would he still be in possession of them nine months later when the rightful owner of the Bear clan tablet was only a half-hour pony ride away in Oraibi? One could accept the possibility of an extraordinary gesture on the part of Tawakwaptiwa in March 1911 when he might have found it useful to loan the tablet to Yukiwma, since he was on his way to Washington. Even though this possibility seems unlikely, it was most certainly unlikely that Yukiwma would be allowed to keep the stone in his possession upon his return to Hotevilla. By all the evidence, it seems as if Tawakwaptiwa did not know about Yukiwma's possession of a second tablet.

Further confirmation of the existence of two tablets other than the primordial ones came to light when the Bear clan tablet was shown to Mischa Titiev by Tawakwaptiwa. Under his diary entry for October 2, 1933, Titiev wrote:

> Ned accompanied me to the house of Tawaqwaptiwa, who showed me a sacred stone that he claims to have inherited from Matcito, legendary founder of Oraibi. The chief says that when the Hopi originally emerged from underground, there were two such stones. One was kept by the ancestral Hopi and the other by the "White" man Bahana, who is supposed to have come out of the underworld together with the Hopi. According to legend, says the chief, if ever the two should meet and show their respective stones, they would treat each other as brothers rather than mere friends. The chief says that he was instructed never to disclose his stone to

> outsiders unless he was in a tight spot and thought he had "White" friends who might help him. He speaks of another Hopi stone, smaller in size, that was held by Yokioma; and he refers to a third that was held by Lololoma's grandsons who had turned against him because they were partly Navaho. (1972:68–69)

Titiev concluded that part of the entry with a note: "I could never get confirmatory information about the other stones, or about the identity of Lololoma's grandsons." The question of other Bear Clan stones received unexpected confirmation from Frank Waters, to which I will return shortly.

Titiev published a sketch in 1944 of one side of Tawakwaptiwa's stone, which is reproduced here as figure 6. He wrote that Matsito reportedly brought the stone with him from the underworld and that it was kept in the custody of the Bear clan. The markings were believed to convey Matsito's "intentions regarding the control of Oraibi's lands" (1944:60). Titiev warned that his description of the stone is tentative because he only saw it once:

> In a most unusual burst of confidence, Chief Tawaqwaptiwa once allowed me to examine this important relic. It is a rectangular block of greyish-white, smooth-grained stone, about 16 inches long, 8 inches wide, and one and a half inches thick, splotched here and there with irregular red dots which the chief interprets as points of land. On both sides there are lightly incised markings which are explained in the following way.
>
> One surface is covered with miscellaneous symbols, including a row of eight little scratches, said to stand for the eight-day period during which the Soyal is observed; cloud and lightning emblems in a random arrangement; an unidentified Katcina figure; two or three sets of bear claws; an old age crook; a poorly executed serpent, said to represent the Little Colorado river; and eight circles, arranged in two parallel rows, which the chief explains as thunder (?) because the sound of a thunder clap is like that of a number of objects being struck in succession. Along the edge of one of the long sides of the relic there runs a series of little lines which were not interpreted; and along the other edge there is a succession of conventional cloud and rain symbols to indicate that in Matcito's lifetime there was always plenty of rain. The pictures on the other surface of the stone tell a connected story. . . . A double rectangle in the center is supposed to represent the Oraibi domain. About this are grouped six figures which depict the Soyal officers. Reading from the bottom in a counterclockwise circuit, they refer to the Village, Pikyas, Parrot, Tobacco, Crier, and War chiefs. Each figure stands with the left hand across the chest and the right extended downwards to cover the genitalia. This posture is said to indicate that the chiefs are claiming the land enclosed within the central rectangles. Along the edge representing the east, there is a line of small scratches, interspersed with occasional circles or crosses, which depicts the proper

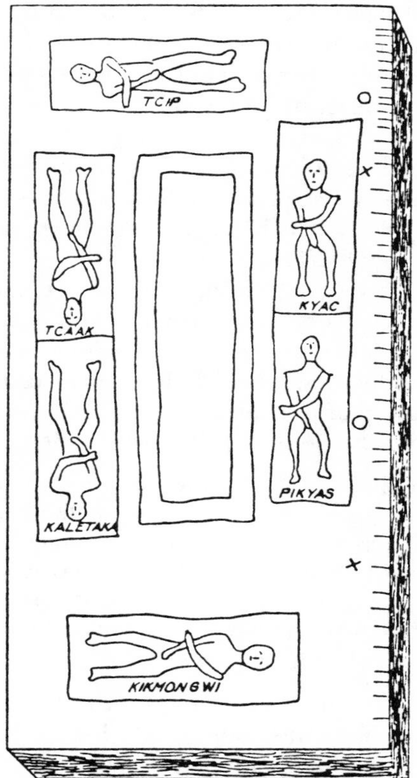

Figure 6. Drawing of the Bear clan stone by Mischa Titiev.
SOURCE: Titiev 1944, 60.

> Hopi path that the chiefs are supposed to travel. The War chief brings up the rear to make sure that no one turns aside from the correct road. (ibid.:60–61)

This description and the drawing match Young's drawings to the smallest detail. We can draw no other conclusion than that it is the same stone that was shown to Gibbons and Young in 1871. The description also gives us additional details on the meaning of the symbols on the reverse side of the tablet. The only discrepancies between Young and Titiev are that Young found thirty notches on each end and sixty along each side of the obverse face. Furthermore, Young's drawing seems to indicate a raincloud series rather than Titiev's circles-and-crosses series.

Concerning the obverse face, a curious point noted by Peter Whiteley is that the list of "officers" provided by Tawakwaptiwa does not coincide with other reports and is probably a distortion introduced by Tawakwaptiwa which downplays the offices owned and controlled by the rival hostile faction which he ousted in 1906. It is more than likely that the figures represent the *wimmomngwit* ("heads of the ritual sodalities"), *kikmongwi* ("village chief"), *kwanmongwi* ("Agave Society chief"), *almongwi* ("Horn Society chief"), *tawmongwi* ("Singer Society chief"), *wuwtsimmongwi* ("Wuwtsim Society chief"), and *qaleetaqmongwi* ("Warrior Society chief") (Whiteley 1987:701ff).

Jumping some thirty years ahead, to 1960, we find the same tablet with both obverse and reverse sides sketched (reproduced here as figure 7) in Frank Waters' *Book of the Hopi*. The tablet was shown to Waters by the usurper chieftainness and Traditionalist leader, Mina Lansa of Oraibi. The description of the color, size, and weight of the stone agrees with the Mormon observations as well as with Titiev's:

> This . . . Bear Clan tablet was shown to the writer in December 1960 by John Lansa's wife, Myna, of the Parrot Clan, in Oraibi, who now has it in custody. The tablet was approximately 10 inches long, 8 inches wide, and 1 ½ inches thick. The stone resembled a dull gray marble with intrusive blotches of rose. It was very heavy, weighing about 8 pounds. The markings on it were as described. There was no means of estimating how old it or the markings were. (Waters 1963:39, note)

According to Waters, this tablet was given to the Bear clan by a deity named Söqömhonaw, who was supposed to have led the Bear clan onto this fourth world. This explanation is clearly an alternative to the explanations of both Yukiwma and Tawakwaptiwa. Comparing figures 5, 6, and 7, we find them in basic agreement concerning the obverse side, except for the fact that figure 7 is in an inverse relation to the others. Concerning the symbols on the tablet, Waters wrote:

> On the front . . . six men, arms folded across belly and crotch, were enclosed within the borders of two rectangles. The double-lined borders of the rectangles again symbolized the rivers enclosing the land; and the six men represented the leaders of the most important clans. Along the left side, whose edge was notched with tiny cuts, were marked sun, moon, stars, and the *nakwách* symbol of brotherhood. The back . . . was covered with a maze of symbols: corn, cloud, sun, moon, star, water, snake, *nakwách*, spirit of the Creator, and bear tracks. (ibid.:39)

Waters refrained from conjectures about the meaning of the symbols. There are obvious discrepancies between Waters' and Young's sketches of the reverse face. The striking thing about the two sketches is that they share many of the same symbols, but they are situated differently. The bottom quarter of each drawing has bear tracks, notches, and a large ser-

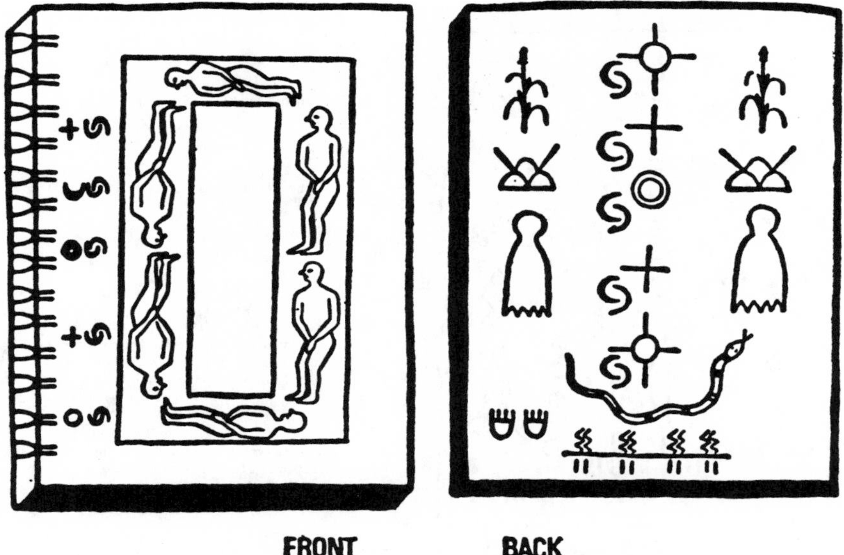

Figure 7. Drawing of the Bear clan stone. SOURCE: Frank Waters, *Book of the Hopi,* New York (copyright 1963). Courtesy of Viking Penguin, a division of Penguin Books USA, Inc., New York.

pent. The middle sections are dominated by circles, crosses, rain clouds, and a ghost-like figure.

The arrangements are somewhat different, however, and each contains symbols not found in the other. Thus, Young's drawing shows notches, crooks, arrows, lightening, and four corners symbols, whereas Waters' drawing shows friendship symbols and corn plants. The small symbols in the upper third of Young's drawing can be construed to be corn plants. Waters' drawing has also combined the circles and crosses and doubled the ghost-like figure, whereas Young's holds the circles and crosses separate and shows only one ghost-like figure. I would suggest that Waters' sketch is the inaccurate one. It strikes me as being a stylized reconstruction from memory. Young's is too detailed to be a reconstruction.

I think that Tawakwaptiwa's interpretation is correct. Turning to figure 8, I suggest that the bottom quarter consists of symbols of bear tracks, the world quarters, and the Soyalangw, which conceivably would refer to the dominance of the Bear clan in terms of land ownership and authority. The quarter symbols are the same as those painted on the shield of the warrior priest during the Soyalangw, pictured in Dorsey and Voth (1901, pl. X). Then follows the serpent which in Young's draw-

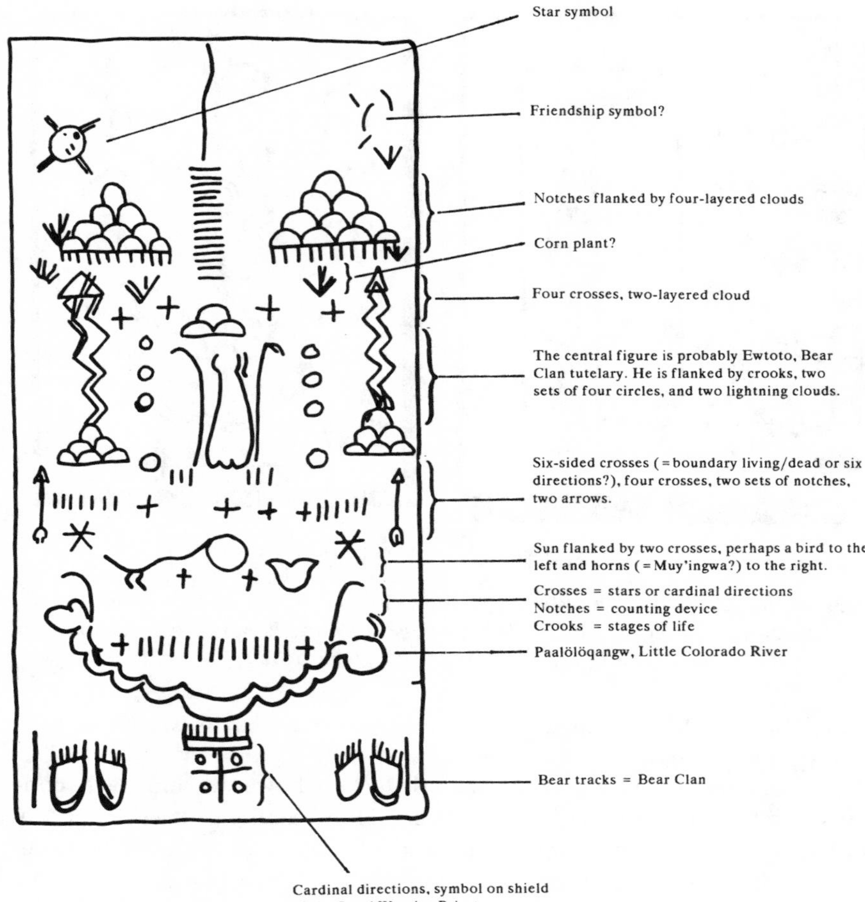

Figure 8. An interpretation of the reverse side of the Bear clan stone by John W. Young. SOURCE: Smithsonian Institution, National Anthropological Archives, Washington, D.C. Courtesy of the Smithsonian Institution. Drawn by Poul Nørbo, Aarhus, Denmark.

ing is clearly Paalölöqangw (because of the horns on its head). This may represent the Little Colorado River, which roughly follows the southern and western boundaries of the aboriginal territory. It could also refer to Paalölöqangw, whose presence would indicate its role in the apocalypse or, perhaps, to some event at Palatkwapi where Paalölöqangw played a cataclysmic role. Directly above the serpent are fourteen notches flanked by two crosses and crooks. The crosses might be stars or the four directions again, the notches are a counting device, and the crooks are symbols of the stages of life. Directly above these are the sun flanked by two crosses and two unidentifiable symbols. The one on the left may be a bird, the one on the right may be a set of horns (symbolizing Muy'ingwa?). The middle band consists of four crosses flanked by two sets of notches (7 and 6 respectively), six-sided crosses, and arrows. The six-sided crosses may refer to the boundary between the living and the dead or to the six directions. The central figure is an "unidentified Katsina" according to Titiev (1944:60). This is strange since the rounded shapes bring immediately to mind Ewtoto, the Bear clan tutelary. He is flanked by crooks, two sets of four circles, and the lightning clouds. Above him are four crosses and a two-layered cloud symbol. The top third of the drawing consists of fifteen horizontal notches flanked by four-layered rain clouds and, presumably, corn-plant symbols. These are topped by a line reaching to the top edge flanked by a star symbol to the left and either corn-plant symbols or friendship symbols to the right.

The overall meaning of the reverse side is difficult to determine. Titiev seems to suggest that it does not tell a connected story like the obverse side, but I think that it does. It most likely relates the Bear clan migration story and refers to its paramount ceremonial, the Soyalangw. There are many symbols in that ceremonial which seem to appear on the stone. The crooks are the Soyal prayersticks, the star/stars the star priest, the center figure Ewtoto, the arrows the warrior priest, and so on. The sun is present because it is a solstitial ritual.

A further point of importance is how the stones were used. Titiev wrote that "at each Soyal celebration the sacred stone is brought from its repository, the officers examine it closely and then reaffirm their rights to hold office and their claims to the land" (1944:61). This fact is proof enough that Tawakwaptiwa would never loan his tablet to Yukiwma, no matter how conspiratorial they may have been.

Seen from a sociological point of view, the Soyalangw is probably the most important Hopi ceremonial. The Wuwtsim would then qualify as the most important from a theological point of view.[11] On the Soyalangw, Titiev proposed a series of important characteristics for consideration:

> From many points of view the Soyal is the keystone of Hopi ceremonialism on Third Mesa. Its control lies in the hands of the ruling (Bear) clan, its leader is either the Village chief or a proxy appointed by him, the kiva in which its observances are held is known as the Chief kiva, and its supporting officers comprise the most important men in the pueblo. These in-

11. See my 1987*a* for a description of the place of these two ceremonials in the ceremonial cycle and for references to the literature.

clude the Parrot chief, who heads the Singers' society; the Pikyas chief, who impersonates the Aholi Katcina . . . and who is in charge of the Moenkopi colony; the Tobacco chief, whose duties in connection with ritual smoking are indispensable in the performance of all important ceremonies; the Crier chief, who is the highest spiritual officer in the pueblo since he serves as the Village chief's mouthpiece in addressing the Cloud people; and the War chief, whose office embodies both religious and executive functions. These are the officials who hold the Chiefs' Talk (Monglavaiyi) at the close of the Soyal, and they are the ones who supervise the sponsorship of a number of activities that may be in prospect during the coming year. (ibid.:142)

The Hopi practice of examining the tablet and holding ritual speeches over it during a ceremonial of such significance clearly supports my arguments in the beginning of this chapter about the significance of the tablets in relation to the politics of power. And Yukiwma's explanations seem to justify the conclusion that he was simply exporting the "social drama" of Hopi politics to Washington—expanding the arena—in an attempt to outmaneuver his political opponent in a final "checkmate" gesture.

Whereas the performance of the Soyalangw ceremonial by its legitimate owners replicates, dismembers, remembers, refashions, and vocally and mutely reproduces meaning—to borrow Victor Turner's turns of phrase (1986:43)—Yukiwma was attempting to "put into circulation," or dramatize the "hard-won meanings" (ibid.:37) of Hopi resistance. In this manner Yukiwma was authoring his own social drama in order to activate public reflexivity (both at home and in Washington) and draw new meaning out of the clash between present and past experience. Yukiwma's action is the "authoring of self" writ large (C. Geertz 1986), a social construction of units of meaning (Bruner 1986*a*:7).

Frank Waters claimed that the Bear clan owned two more tablets (making three in all), which are reproduced here as figures 9 and 10. These were given by the same Söqömhonaw. Figure 9 concerns the land holdings to be appointed to all the clans:

[It] was small, with a strange pattern scratched on one side. This, he [Söqömhonaw] said, was the land pattern around the permanent village where they would settle, showing the land holdings to be apportioned to all clans supporting the religious ceremonies. On the other side of the tablet were marked two bear tracks, indicating that all the land beyond these religious land holdings was to be held in the custody of the Bear Clan, which was to reserve it for the animal kingdom upon which the people depended for food. (1963:38)

The tablet was reportedly stolen by a Spider clan woman who had married into the Bear clan. This was evidently because the Kookop,

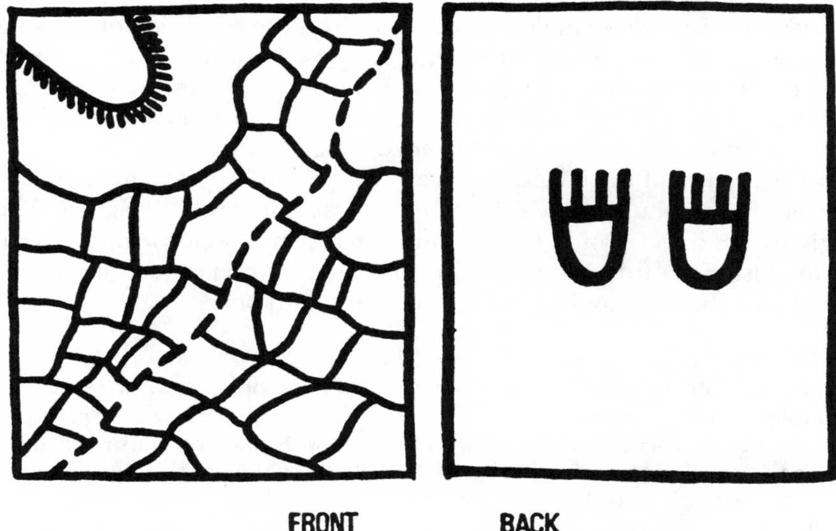

Figure 9. Drawing of a second stone owned by the Bear clan. SOURCE: Frank Waters, *Book of the Hopi,* New York (copyright 1963). Courtesy of Viking Penguin, a division of Penguin Books USA, Inc., New York.

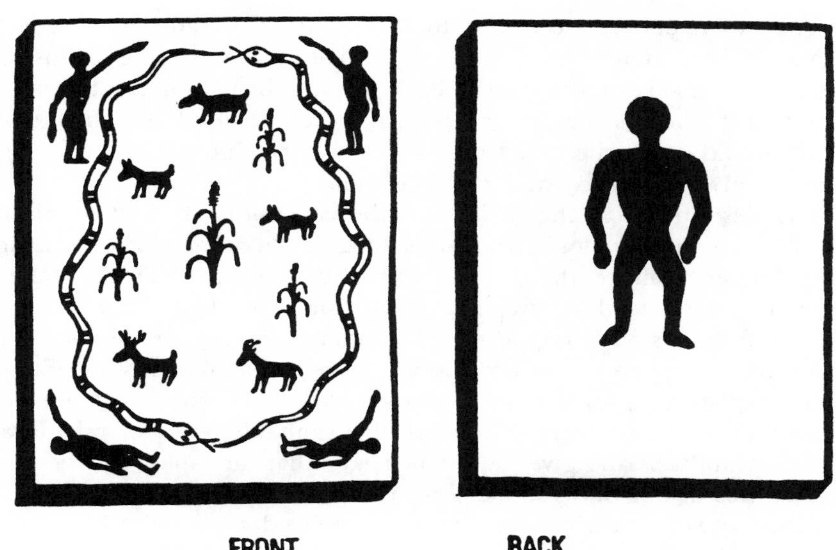

Figure 10. Drawing of a third stone owned by the Bear clan. SOURCE: Frank Waters, *Book of the Hopi,* New York (copyright 1963). Courtesy of Viking Penguin, a division of Penguin Books USA, Inc., New York.

Spider, and Sun clans (the clans which were on the rebel side of the split of Oraibi) felt humiliated for several reasons: because of a purported crime they had committed against the Bear clan at the legendary village of Palatkwapi; because they had no ceremonials of their own; and because they were consequently denied the right to land holdings (ibid.: 365). The theft of the tablet was an attempt to remove the damaging evidence of their situation, which the tablet was purported to signify. The logic of this action would be that since each clan is supposedly ignorant of the histories of the other clans, sooner or later everyone would forget the shame that the Kookop, Spider, and Sun clans bore.

> The third table (figure 10) is described as follows: The front of the larger . . . Bear Clan tablet . . . was marked with a cornstalk in the center, around which were grouped several animals, all surrounded by two snakes; and in each corner was the figure of a man with one arm outstretched. The two snakes symbolized the two rivers that would mark the boundaries of the people's land. The out-stretched arms of the four men signified that they were religious leaders holding and claiming the land for their people; no one should cross the boundary rivers without permission, or destruction would come upon them. The back of the tablet . . . showed a man who represented the leader or village chief, who was always to be of the Bear Clan. (ibid.:38)

The two rivers are, according to Waters, the Colorado and the Rio Grande. Waters noted the interesting fact that there was some confusion about the man-like figure on the back of the tablet: "Some informants state that the man is headless, prophesying, like the Fire Clan tablet, that a time would come when the leader would sacrifice himself by having his head cut off in order to save his people" (ibid.).

The description of the tablet and the confusion of interpretations seem to match very closely the two tablets in Yukiwma's possession in 1911. Waters claimed that this as well as the second Bear clan tablet were passed on to Tawakwaptiwa when Loololma died. Shortly afterward, the third stone disappeared. This would account for the fact that Yukiwma was apparently in possession of one of Tawakwaptiwa's stones. Three explanations suggest themselves: That Tawakwaptiwa loaned the tablet to Yukiwma, evidently in secret; that the tablet was stolen by Loololma's grandsons and given to Yukiwma; or that the tablet was secured by Yukiwma or one of his supporters in some other way.

It seems as if the Hopis themselves suspected one of the latter two possibilities. Waters claimed that on his way back from Washington in 1911 Yukiwma stopped at the Carlisle Indian School in Pennsylvania, where several Bear clan members had been sent as students:

> These young Hopis, thinking that Yukioma might have the missing Bear Clan tablet, grabbed Yukioma and searched him. They found the small Fire Clan tablet tied to his loincloth and took it from him. So for a time this tablet too disappeared. (ibid.:366)

We now know that Yukiwma had both stones in his possession during his confrontation with Colonel Scott nine months later. Waters is in many instances an inaccurate source, but in this case and on this particular topic we have independent evidence in both time and space that supports at least an important part of his statements. Having said this, it must also be noted that Waters only claimed to have been shown the stone pictured as figure 7 (ibid.:366, note). This means that figures 9, 10, and 12 (below) were evidently sketched on the basis of oral descriptions (ibid.:365, note).

Albert Yava, the Tewa mentioned earlier who was initiated into the Hopi Kwan brotherhood, claimed that he did not believe in Waters' three Bear clan tablets. He wrote:

> And I believe that if genuine Bear Clan tablets really exist, our Bear Clan people on First Mesa would have wanted to give that information to members of the kiva societies. Of course, there are plenty of contradictions in Hopi traditions. There have been many discussions and arguments in the kivas about them. Nevertheless, quite a few things in the Waters-White Bear book are so ridiculous that no knowledgeable person can accept them. (1978:80–81)

I cannot believe that he actually doubted the existence of other Bear clan tablets, since Yava's half-brother was Yukiwma's interpreter in Washington in 1911 (Courlander 1971:273), and he was probably the same interpreter in Hotevilla in December of that year. Yava's statement may have political motivations unknown to me.

He mentioned another tablet at Shongopovi, without mentioning any details, which may well be an expression of the ongoing competition between Shongopovi and Oraibi concerning which of the two is the oldest and (consequently) most important town in North America. It is only the Oraibians who believe that the center of the world is at their own doorstep. In fact, Wilson D. Wallis' Second Mesa consultant told him another story in 1912. According to him, Maasaw gave a tablet to the Hopis with the story of the emergence engraved on it. Maasaw then said to the Hopis: "The whole earth is mine. As long as you keep this, it all belongs to you." One piece of the tablet was broken off and the chief of Shongopovi, Kiy'oma, supposedly possessed the stone (Wallis 1936:16).

I am convinced that the two stones Yukiwma produced in Washington and at Hotevilla in 1911 consisted of the Kookop tablet (described in the next section) and the missing third Bear clan tablet described by Waters.

This would bring the total to five tablets on Third Mesa: the two primordial tablets (one of which is said to be held by the legendary White Brother), two other Bear Clan tablets, and the Kookop tablet.

According to Waters' informants, the missing Bear clan tablet (the third one) is still in Oraibi, "but . . . it is not yet time to reveal who took it and who now keeps it in custody" (1963:366). In this case, I think that Waters' informants were laying a smoke screen. One might counter that perhaps they really did not know. But the turns of phrase seem to indicate that his informants were knowledgeable–and we know for sure that Mina Lansa was one of them. I have circumstantial evidence that suggests that the stone is not in Oraibi, but in Hotevilla where it has always been since it first passed into Yukiwma's hands. I will return to this in the next section.

STONE TABLETS IN KOOKOP CLAN HISTORY

The Kookop stone appears in our sources in the most unexpected contexts, but we unfortunately have no independent confirmation that the drawing in Waters' book (figure 12) is that tablet.

The role and meaning of the Kookop tablet closely follows the political strife between the Bear and Kookop clans. As Whiteley cogently noted, the relationship between the kikmongwi and the qaleetaqmongwi in the structure of political power in Oraibi was one of complementarity: The village chief was responsible for internal affairs and the warrior chief was responsible for the protection of the village from external forces; thus, an "inside chief" as opposed to an "outside chief" (1987: 702–703). The split of Oraibi and the subsequent founding of Hotevilla in 1906 followed this line of division, which I would characterize as a transformation of their complementarity in times of peace to a dichotomy in times of stress. Despite the complementarity, the problem of legitimacy nontheless rested heavily on Kookop shoulders.

To recapitulate what we know so far about the Kookop tablet: Talay'ima claimed in 1883 that one of the stones was the "Rock of Death" given to the Hopis by the "corpse demon," or Maasaw. In 1911, we find Yukiwma showing two tablets to authorities in Washington and on the reservation. Either the Kookop stone or both of the tablets were interpreted as representing a coming death by decapitation.

Yava claimed to have seen the Kookop stone at Keams Canyon, probably sometime around 1911, and described it as follows: "It had a design there with a body, the lower part, but the head was off. And then there was a line along the edge. I don't know what it signified, but this other half, the head part, was gone" (Courlander 1971:273–274). In 1933 Tawakwaptiwa also confirmed the fact that Yukiwma had a stone of his own which pictured a decapitated man.

Yukiwma's tablet was evidently brought to light in Phoenix in 1941 at the trial of the draft resisters mentioned in chapter 5. On page 10 of the May 23, 1941, afternoon edition of the *Arizona Republic*, a photograph was published picturing the corulers Pongyayawma and Qötshongva examining two stone tablets.[12] It was not possible for me to trace the original photograph, but since it has such historical value, I reproduce my photocopy here as figure 11. Even though the quality prevents us from noting details, the picture at least indicates the size and shape of the larger of the two stones. The caption reads:

> TURMOIL PROPHESIED: Chief James Pongonyuma (holding two stones) and Chief Dan Katchgonva, corulers of Hotevilla Hopi clans, yesterday were in Phoenix to interpret their religion to the white man in an effort to aid tribal youths under sentence for evading selective service registration. The larger stone is sacred, and represents the Hopi land and its religion. Legends carved on it prophesied the present war of the nations and a great, equal peace which someday will be brought by a white man who can read the stone, the chief said. The smaller stone represents the home, but is of lesser importance, the chiefs explained, because without the land there is no place to put the home. (Anonymous 1941:10)

It seems clear enough that these are the same two stones that Yukiwma had in his possession in 1911. The larger stone is the Bear clan stone and the smaller is the Kookop stone. The chiefs had evidently chosen to withhold the "true" meaning of the smaller stone either because the decapitation myth would have been inappropriate in the defense of draft resisters or because they did not want Tawakwaptiwa to find out that they had one of his stones. Reference is consistently restricted to one stone throughout the article even though the photograph shows two.

Present at this meeting were Thomas Banancya (called Jenkins), Chester Mota, and Waters' main informant Oswald Fredericks. They came as interpreters, but Banancya was one of the draft resisters as well.

The accompanying article clearly shows Qötshongva using the stones to secure his political position, just as his father Yukiwma had done:

> Rule By Tradition
>
> They said that they rule according to tradition and prophecy. Chief Dan, speaking for himself and Chief James, said—with Thomas Jenkins, a Hopi youth who has been to the white man's colleges, interpreting:

12. The story was evidently carried forward into the morning issues of May 24th on page 10 in the "Bulldog," "Mail," and "City" editions. I am grateful to Dr. Louis Hieb for this information.

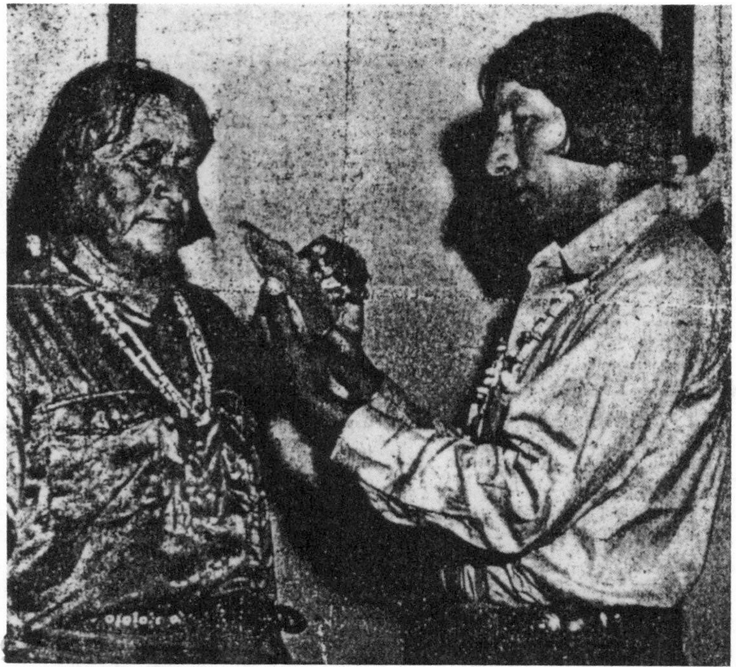

Figure 11. Qötshongva and Pongyayawma examining two stone tablets. SOURCE: *Arizona Republic* May 23, 1941, p. 10.

"All these things, including the strife in the world, have been predicted in the religion of the Hopi. It was predicted, for instance, that when the main chief fell away from the old tradition, new rulers would arise. We two have come to rule after the main chief, as prophesied, failed to live up to everything in our religion.

"For the tribe to go forward, it must stick to the religion. We Hopi want to stand where we are, which is simply that we want no part in the white man's quarrel. . . .

"We have a stone tablet on which is carved a legend. That tablet has been handed down from generation to generation. It says that there will come a time when there will be great trouble involving many nations. The Hopi are to show their bows and arrows to no one at that time.

White Brother Awaited

"The legend says that someday a white brother will come who will be able to read the things on the stone. When he comes we will know him and he will enable the Hopi and all the other people of the world to share equally in the wealth that is given to us who are living.

> "Prior to that time, all people will fight. We Hopi are warned to stay out of that fight. The fight, though, will put all the people of the world in the same position. This white brother will be the only person who will be able to tell the entire and true meaning of the stone." (Anonymous 1941:10)

The article ends with the statement that "the stone" is in Pongyayawma's keeping. Are there or are there not two tablets? I will present evidence below that suggests there were two tablets and that they were identical to Yukiwma's two.

The next mention of the tablets is found in the letter sent to President Harry Truman on March 28, 1949, by the newly established Traditionalist Movement:

> The boundaries of our Empire were established permanently and were written upon Stone Tablets which are still with us. Another was given to his white brother who after the emerging of the first people to this new land went east with the understanding that he will return with his Stone Tablet to the Hopis. These Stone Tablets when put together and if they agree will prove to the whole world that this land truly belongs to the Hopi people and that they are true brothers. Then the white brother will restore order and judge all the people here who have been unfaithful to their traditional and religious principles and who have mistreated his people. (Hopi Empire 3–28–1949)

From this time forward, the Traditionalists mention only two primordial tablets. Any extraneous tablets seem to have been deliberately ignored. Furthermore, Qötshongva had evidently chosen to emphasize the stolen Bear clan tablet rather than the Kookop tablet. What happened here?

The political status of the Bear clan tablet had much greater significance for the Traditionalists than the Kookop tablet did. The dire prophecies about beheadings were too specific and too obviously manipulatory. No one in his right mind was willing to lose his head. That particular "prophecy" probably led to too many humiliating confrontations and reports of confrontations, thus casting a pallor of incompetence on both sides. It seems that the impetus given to the Traditionalist Movement during the 1950s, when the movement was establishing itself as the voice and guardian of traditional ways, caused them to emphasize the Bear clan tablet, which allowed a broader rhetorical base: The tablet now contained "instructions," "life plans," "warnings," and so on, of an unspecified nature, and was easily incorporated into the contexts of a growing dialogue with non-Hopis.

But Yukiwma had left his successors with an unfinished job, namely, how to justify the possession of a Bear clan tablet. Possession of the tablet does in fact mean possession of the office of village chief. As will become evident in the next chapters, Yukiwma expected the resistance and the prophecies to end with his death. But his son had other plans, and it was Qötshongva who performed the sleight of hand necessary to make the Bear clan tablet the symbol of the Traditionalist Movement.

The trick was very simple: A combination of accusations of incompetence and of corruption were aimed at the legitimate owner of the stone. Qötshongva began the tactic in the *Arizona Republic* in 1941 by claiming that the chief, as prophesied, failed to live up to the Hopi religion and finished the job in 1955 during the BIA hearings when he spoke about the tablets on several occasions (Bureau of Indian Affairs 1955:6, 24, 25, 258). The single stone tablet he emphasized contained "the instructions and . . . all the life plan of the Hopi people" and will serve as proof at the time of reckoning. (ibid.:24). In an obvious attempt to villify the Bear clan leadership, he accused the long-dead Loololma of changing his stone tablet at the urging of his people in order to justify their desire to follow the White man's ways:

> We have our own leaders who are looked up to as the proper leaders to carry on this life for us. They were provided with these stone tablets which tell all the life of the Hopi, and during this time, Sakhoneoma's time, there seems to be a talk among the people that things were about to be changed, and finally it came, when Loloma was the leader there. That is when they changed the life pattern of the Hopi. It was there that while he was holding fast to this stone tablet and life many of his people began to urge him to change so they could have a new life, and finally the people convinced him that they will support him in everything if he will change the stone tablet, so he did. And it was done so the people will follow the white man's way of life. This was done, fully realizing that he should have never changed this stone tablet because that was the instructions, but since the people have urged him and influenced him he did change it. (ibid.:258)

Qötshongva even added a prophecy to his claim:

> It has been told in their tradition that when one of these great leaders who are vested with all power and authority turn these stone tablets, once they have been dropped or their duties have been neglected, he was finished. He cannot get back in his old place again. No one can put him back in his place. (ibid.:258)

Qötshongva then insinuated that Tawakwaptiwa was great only because the Whites recognized his authority. But the true leaders do not turn away from the life pattern of the forefathers. At this point he stated that he belonged to this line of "great leaders" and, as one of the keepers of the stone tablet, he must carry the burden of leadership onward (ibid.:258–259). The logic is evident: Only Qötshongva owns the "true" tablet.

Qötshongva used the following fifteen years until his death in 1972 to legitimize his takeover and to develop the story of the tablets (cf. Skidmore 1970 and Tarbet 1972). Not only do the tablets contain the life plan, but also a warning about wicked people who will try to influence them to forsake their way of life and instructions "to be followed in such a case" (Tarbet 1972:10–11). The two primordial brothers will unite their tablets in the end and, as it turns out in Qötshongva's version, they are both from Qötshongva's own clan, the Sun clan: "The stone tablets will be the final acknowledgement of their true identity and brotherhood. Their mother is Sun Clan. They are the children of the Sun" (Tarbet 1972:11; cf. Appendix B; Katchongva 1973). Thus we see that Qötshongva not only threw mud at his political opponent, Tawakwaptiwa, he also described his own role in glowingly apocryphal terms.

Other Traditionalists mentioned the tablets at the 1955 hearings as well. David Monongya from Hotevilla said that they were a covenant concerning land ownership (Bureau of Indian Affairs 1955:21). Secquaptewa from Hotevilla said that the stone represented Hopi life and that the snake on the tablet is the guardian of the land and life who "will hold back the punishment that will take place in case we let go of this stone map and this life pattern" (ibid.:55). Secquaptewa's further description and statement clearly indicates that he is talking about the missing Bear clan tablet:

> They have accepted many things and later on because the people in Oraibi would not accept anything and Loloma, the keeper of the stone tablet, would not turn away from it these people from other villages came to him during the night and tried everything to make him break away from the stone tablet. When they saw the tablet they saw that there were picture writings on both sides of the stone tablet. One side represents crops as earthly things which grow on this earth and the material life of this land, and once they saw this they worked harder to get Loloma to turn it over. If he was going to lead this life it is good and he would continue to hold it. So when we reach there this land will be purified as it shows on the stone tablet. A beheading might have to take place, because it is the evil man who must choose. They made him turn this stone map over and caused him to break away from this duty that was placed upon him. (ibid.:55)

It is also clear that Secquaptewa did not conceive of the theft as a theft at all. Loololma was portrayed as willfully giving up the tablet in order to forsake the Hopi life pattern. This argument is different than Qötshongva's, but it is probably more accurate. Loololma's grandchildren probably did convince him for one reason or another to give up the tablet to them. Or perhaps Loololma tricked them by giving up one stone—perhaps a recent forgery—and retaining the true stone, which is examined annually during the Soyalangw.

The various accounts seem to indicate that, contrary to Waters' statement, Tawakwaptiwa had never received that particular tablet from Loololma. In other words, it had changed hands before Tawakwaptiwa became chief around 1904. This could explain why he was seemingly ignorant of Yukiwma's ownership of two tablets.

Secquaptewa's explanation received confirmation from Andrew Hermequaftewa from Shongopovi. Hermequaftewa's Second Mesa variant was further supported by George Nasoftie, who later became a Progressive:

> Then Massua realized that he did not make any provisions for himself because he had given land and life to these people, so he asked the women to grind some corn so that he could make a stone tablet, and when that was made out of cornmeal, our life plan and the things that they were told were put in on the stone tablet. Two were made of the same thing and each brother received one of them to carry in this life, and they were instructed to never let go of it because it will be upon these stone tablets that this Hopi life will be based. . . . Massua said they must never forsake, never doubt his teachings and instructions, for if they ever doubted it and forsaked this stone tablet and all its teachings, they will cause a destruction of all life in this land, so they were warned to always remember and carry on these instructions for all his people. (ibid.:81)

Other references to the tablets made by Traditionalist spokesman Thomas Banancya through the years mesh closely with Qötshongva's accounts.[13]

A drawing of the original Kookop tablet was reproduced in Waters' publication. It is reproduced here as figure 12. Its description answers to the early evidence about the stone:

> One of the tablets Másaw gave to the Fire Clan. . . . [It] was very small, about four inches square, made of dark-colored stone, and with a piece broken off from one corner. On one side were marked several symbols, and

13. Banyacya 1-12-1961 in Appendix B; Hodge 1980, 44; Dagnal and Jenkins 1985, 60. An interesting variant was related by an unidentified Third Mesa elder at the First Hopi Mental Health Conference:

> The Oraibi stone tablets—and I have seen them—show a figure with a long robe and a coyote . . . both have no heads. Hopi predictions say that this is how it will end. Now when you are judged unworthy to live, your head will be cut off. These whitemen who come will be merciless and will have no regard for life. Only those they think are worthy to live with them will survive. (Hopi Health Department n.d.:54)

This somewhat confused description may very well be a poor description of the stolen Bear clan tablet.

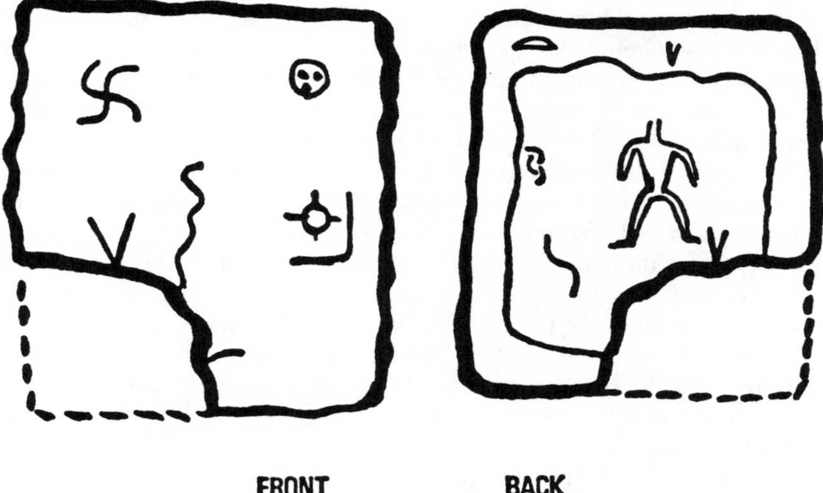

Figure 12. Drawing of the Kookop clan stone. SOURCE: Frank Waters, *Book of the Hopi*, New York (copyright 1963). Courtesy of Viking Penguin, a division of Penguin Books USA, Inc., New York.

> on the other the figure of a man without a head. Másaw was the deity of the Fire Clan; and he gave them this tablet just before he turned his face from them, becoming invisible, so that they would have a record of his words.
>
> This is what he said, as marked on the tablet: After the Fire Clan had migrated to their permanent home, the time would come when they would be overcome by a strange people. They would be forced to develop their land and lives according to the dictates of a new ruler, or else they would be treated as criminals and punished. But they were not to resist. They were to wait for the person who would deliver them.
>
> This person was their lost white brother, Pahána, who would return to them with the missing corner piece of the tablet, deliver them from their persecutors, and work out with them a new and universal brotherhood of man. But, warned Másaw, if their leader accepted any other religion, he must assent to having his head cut off. This would dispel the evil and save his people. (Waters 1963:37–38)

According to Waters, it was said that "at the proper time the tablet will be split open to reveal other markings on the inside which will reveal the identity of the Hopi people" (ibid.:366, note).

During the spring of 1988, I presented Waters' sketches to Chief James Pongyayawma, the maternal nephew of Yukiwma. He claimed at first that the drawings resembled neither the stone in his possession nor any stone he had ever seen. This claim was puzzling, but I began to suspect political overtones when brief glimpses into the nature of Pongyayawma's tablets came out during the interview. On the face of it, Pongyayawma's interpretation should have coincided with Qötshongva's and that of the Traditionalists, but that is not the case. A falling out had occurred between the two of them during a power struggle sometime during the 1950s which sent them each their own way. Pongyayawma dropped out of sight until the latter half of the 1960s when it became evident that Monongya was outmaneuvering Qötshongva in yet another power struggle.[14] Whereas Pongyayawma and Qötshongva were both pavansinom, Monongya was only söqavungsinom, which gave Pongyayawma sufficient incentive (and the right) to heap scorn on Monongya and his supporters—scorn that clearly came out during my interview with him in 1988.

Pongyayawma told me, finally, that he had seen the Bear clan tablet and that it resembled the Titiev's and Waters' sketches. He said that it represented the land. He admitted too that his own tablet depicts a headless person, which represents the decapitation of the evil ones who will be living when the White Brother returns. The day of decapitation is inexorably linked in Pongyayawma's mind with the day of purification.

Thus, in tune with changing political affairs, the headless one on the Kookop stone is no longer the Bear clan chief. It is, instead, all ambitious and wicked people, including the Traditionalists (particularly Monongya and Banancya), who are concerned with their own material and political gains. Pongyayawma told me: "They made up their own version. This is not how it was at the beginning of life. This is their own fantasy. They have done this and, therefore, they are the evil ones."

One more interesting twist: Pongyayawma spoke of how the stone held by the White Brother will match the stone held by the Hopi chief. It was obvious that the existence of several stones had no apparent effect on this particular belief. In fact, Pongyayawma claimed that his stone also has two figures resembling the third Bear clan tablet (figure 10) in which the figures reach out to each other from their respective corners of the tablet. According to Pongyayawma, this represents the two brothers waiting to be united on the last day:

> We are all living on land owned by the Being who was here first. And, see, you [Pongyayawma's counselor Charley Sekenooyoma] have seen the stone tablet, and the hand of the figure is stretched out along the top like that (picture) towards the other side. It has got its hands down along there on the top. You probably haven't thought much about its significance. It is the Older Brother reaching out to his Younger Brother.

14. Whiteley stated that Pongyayawma left Hotevilla in 1967 (1988:229), but this must refer to something else, perhaps a second exodus.

This last statement is the circumstantial evidence I was alluding to earlier. I do not think that the figures he was refering to are on the Kookop tablet. I think, instead, that he was obliquely referring to the missing Bear clan tablet he had in his possession at the time. During the interview, his aide Sekenooyoma told me that Pongyayawma had two tablets. One was broken, and the other was not. The awaited Pahaana has a tablet that is identical to one of them. He confided, "I don't know if the White Brother has two of them [too], but that's what he [Pongyayawma] is talking about."

Pongyayawma was evidently not very interested in the Bear clan stone except for the fact that the two stones were to be matched at the end of the world. He was mostly concerned with the decapitation theme. Asked about the identity of the victim of the decapitation, he answered:

> We are going to be purified; we are not purified as yet. Life is still crazy. The witches are still around trying to increase the length of their lives (through sorcerous activity). They came here with intentions and plans. They want to destroy the earth, to ruin it and make it unclean. . . . And so we are to be purified, and then our life will change. And these evil ones will be beheaded and will be destroyed.

I then asked him who would decapitate them, and he answered:

> Our White Brother from the east, from ancient times. His Younger Brother had two stone tablets made, and he gave the one to him. And as time went by, the Younger Brother's lifeway became weak. And our White Brother, who has the other half somewhere, will come. And when he does, he will chop the heads off and purify us. And after that, we will not live wickedly anymore. That's how it is.

Further confirmation of the existence of the two tablets in Hotevilla occurred in 1990. Pongyayawma's successor, Kyarwisiwma, was evidently persuaded by Banancya to meet with the governor-elect of New Mexico in order to give America "one last chance" before the day of purification. Both global warming and the Persian Gulf War were claimed at the meeting to have been prophesied by the Hopis, and after a twenty-minute speech, Kyarwisiwma "untied a red and white scarf that circled his waist and produced two small pieces of sacred stone tablets" (*Gallup Independent* December 14, 1990).

THE SIGNIFICANCE OF THE STONE TABLETS

It is hopefully evident by now that the nature of the tablets and the hermeneutics associated with them are both volatile and mutable. They are intrinsically connected to the collective apocryphal concerns of the

Hopi people, and they clearly reflect the dynamics of changing political and social situations.

The Bear clan stone has been positively identified by different informants and shown to outsiders at different times. The Kookop clan stone has been identified by different informants, but we have no proof that figure 12 is that stone.

As to which stone has its counterpart in the east, I cannot say. But whether the one or the other, the evidence indicates that the Hopis believe that a White Brother will return from the east with his tablet, or his piece of tablet; and when he fits his part with the Hopi part, whichever one that may be, then one of two things should happen: The Hopis will then know the owner of the tablet to be the long-awaited Pahaana, or the Hopis will be acknowledged by the world as the true owners of the land. Then the Pahaana, or perhaps Maasaw, will judge the people and establish universal brotherhood. Thus, we see that ownership of the tablets is of the utmost importance.

The Hopi example provides us with an excellent opportunity to briefly reflect on the nature of significance and meaning. Even though the history of the use and interpretation of the tablets exemplifies the reflective and processual nature of Hopi prophecy, they nevertheless embody denotative and connotative dimensions as well (cf. Foster & Brandes 1980:xv). Thus, if we try to develop a neat formula to capture *the* meaning of the stone tablets in Hopi thought, we are confronted with just about every conceivable definition of "meaning," each further complicated by interaction with fluid social reality.

The stone tablets in Hopi history teach us something about meaning in its changing contexts. They show us how the participants have been engaged in defining and interpreting themselves and the tablets to themselves, which again shows us how meaning is negotiated (Almagor 1987: 13), manipulated, deconstructed, and reconstructed.

My concern with the meanings of a set of symbols can be understood as a semiotic concern (Pelc 1982), although the exigencies of my case study demonstrate affinities to the ontological flexibility of structuration theory. The latter is characterized by Ira Cohen as

> addressed exclusively to the constitutive potentials of social life: the generic human capacities and fundamental conditions through which the course and outcomes of social processes and events are generated and shaped in a manifold of empirically distinguishable ways. (1987:279)

I will conclude this chapter on an explicitly semiotic note, although heavily saturated with interactionistic significance, by considering the stone tablets as objects "bathed in pure significance" (C. Geertz 1976: 95).[15]

I think he is correct in stating that no object or experience in human intercourse is ever allowed for long to remain in the somewhat static state of pure significance. Such states invite description, analysis, comparison, classification, interpretation, and evaluation. It is the job of the believer to construct the meaning or meanings of the object or experience. Our job is to relate this hermeneutical process to its particular cultural context in its particular historical development. This combination of exegesis and comparison produces results and points out factors which the people under study are not aware of and which are highly important in helping us to find and define human universals.

My first example of a conscious observer faced with an object of pure significance is a fifty year-old Hopi consultant working for the tribal office, who was kind enough to show me in 1988 some of the sites in Hopi country that have been used by the Traditionalists and others in their apocryphal rhetoric. I showed this man Titiev's and Waters' drawings of the Bear clan tablet (figures 6 and 7). He readily admitted that he had no idea what it meant, and he asked me to tell him what I knew about it. So I repeated Titiev's explanation. After studying the drawings for perhaps ten minutes, he told me that the more he looked at it, the more he understood it, even though he had never seen it before.

He noted that it was the proper seating arrangement for the chiefs on the obverse side and their clan symbols were pictured on the reverse side (figure 7). Then he said that the symbols on the reverse side are to be read starting in the lower left-hand corner with the Bear clan marks up along the left margin over to the right and down, and then up the middle. After telling me this, he became excited, as if he had discovered some insight, and said, "If this shows the inheritance route of the village chieftainship, then the end of the world will occur when all the clans have become chief."

The fact that the picture is most certainly incorrect is unimportant here. It seems clear enough that during the intervening ten minutes, and even while speaking, my consultant was able to draw on a number of elements in order to construct an on-the-spot interpretation of this object of pure significance as an exercise of indigenous hermeneutics. I am sure that we all can recognize this process. We sometimes forget this, however, and conceive of "tradition" as consisting of a rigidly restricted set

15. See Wim Staat's arguments, which advocate a convergence between Peirce's theory of meaning and interaction metaphor (1990).

of possibilities. And, of course, relatively speaking, this is true. We are not talking about a universe of possibilities, but we can imagine that within the boundaries of a particular culture, there exists a repertoire of possibilities which can be applied in various combinations as suggested solutions to hermeneutical problems in much the same way that good storytellers draw on various motifs and episodes in order to create a tale suited to their audience.

Whereas my first example shows how in drawing creatively on a conceived cultural context, an object of pure significance is given meaning, my second example will indicate how this object is given meaning in the face of conceived cultural disintegration.

As mentioned above, Chief Pongyayawma was waiting for the White Brother to come and match stones with him whereby the day of purification will be signaled. The evil ones will then be beheaded and a new life of goodness and peace will be established.

But the chief found himself to be the questionable head of a village in which cultural disintegration was rampant. It was his conviction, in total agreement with Peter Whiteley's main point in his book *Deliberate Acts* (1988), that the split of Oraibi in 1906 was planned and that the ceremonial structure was to be deliberately ended. Pongyayawma was against the reestablishment of the ceremonials in Hotevilla because of this plan, and he considered the attempts made in reestablishing the ceremonials to be excuses for ambitious men who were trying to secure political power to which they had no right. In other words, hearkening back to my comments on power, legitimacy, and authority, since the true owners of this power had decided to end it all, others were ready to fill the void by proxy, swindle, or any other technique available to them.

On being asked whether he thought that the ceremonials will be reestablished after the purification, he answered doubtfully that he did not think so. His skepticism seemed to rest on a number of conditions that still needed to be fulfilled, such as whether there would be enough good people left in the world to carry on. Another condition seemed to imply the full disintegration of Hopi ceremonial life:

> Whoever was living here first, the one called Maasaw, he does not own the ceremonials (wiimi). They belong to those clans from the south. Maasaw has of course his own wiimi, but they are for the future! As I told you, those people from the south carry it (their ritual objects), and they are the good ones. And so, when the purification day arrives, they will survive; but if they do not stick to it, and only evil ones are left, then all is lost.

He was convinced that the end would come during his lifetime, but, being at an advanced age, he expressed doubt as to whether this would be. All he had left was his tablet and to live a life of humility and expectation. He told me: *Itaaqatsi sakwiwta,* "Our life is ruined."

Asked whether his successor would be installed as chief in the traditional ritual manner, he replied: "No, that is finished. He will carry on with the instruction and the tablet, and, like me, he will await the coming of the White Brother."

It is impossible for me to convey the full ramifications of this tragic situation, but I think that it is clear now that the object of pure significance retains meaning in the face of the disintegration of its context. One might say that its symbolic meaning is precisely the disintegration of its context. Seen in human terms, the tablet becomes an object of significance on which to cling. It gives meaning by its mere presence even where meaning is difficult to find.

Thus, these two examples give the hermeneutic process particular visibility because they are each at their own end of an otherwise impenetrable web of conceptualization and process. By paying heed to changing interpretations within changing social and political contexts, it is possible for the student of Hopi prophecy to gain insight into the nature of significant objects and the evidently universal activity of bathing objects of pure significance with meaning (cf. Foster and Brandes 1980:3–7).

SEVEN

From Resistance to Messianism

The Politics of Analysis and the Realities of History[1]

THEORIES OF FACTIONALISM

The Hopi terms for the progressive and traditionalist factions are *pahannanawaknaqam*, "those who want the White way (of life)," i.e., the Progressives, and *qa pahannanawaknaqam*, "those who do not want the White way (of life)," i.e., the Traditionalists. As it turns out, these fairly straightforward epithets have very little to do with what the two factions stand for. In fact, we are confronted with the very serious problem of deciding whether they are factions at all. As figure 13 indicates, even the Hopis have trouble figuring out who is who! Our problem is, if we can not call it factionalism, what can we call it?

Nagata grappled with the problem of factionalism and how the term is to be understood in relation to the Hopi situation. He identified three main views of factionalism in the theoretical literature: 1) that it is often a highly negative characteristic of small communities undergoing change;[2] 2) that it may sometimes provide the most efficient channel of political participation in communities of limited resources (Nicholas 1965:26f); and 3) that it results from the breakdown of legitimacy in the traditional political order and is therefore processual and a means of socialization through conflict (Firth 1957). He attempted to provide empirical support for the latter by assessing the positive role of factionalism (Nagata 1968:3).

Nagata argued that there are three arenas of Hopi factionalism: the

1. Portions of this and the next chapter have appeared in Danish in A. W. Geertz 1989*c*.

2. French 1962:242; Nicholas 1965:46; Siegel and Beals 1960*a*:399; 1966:158ff.

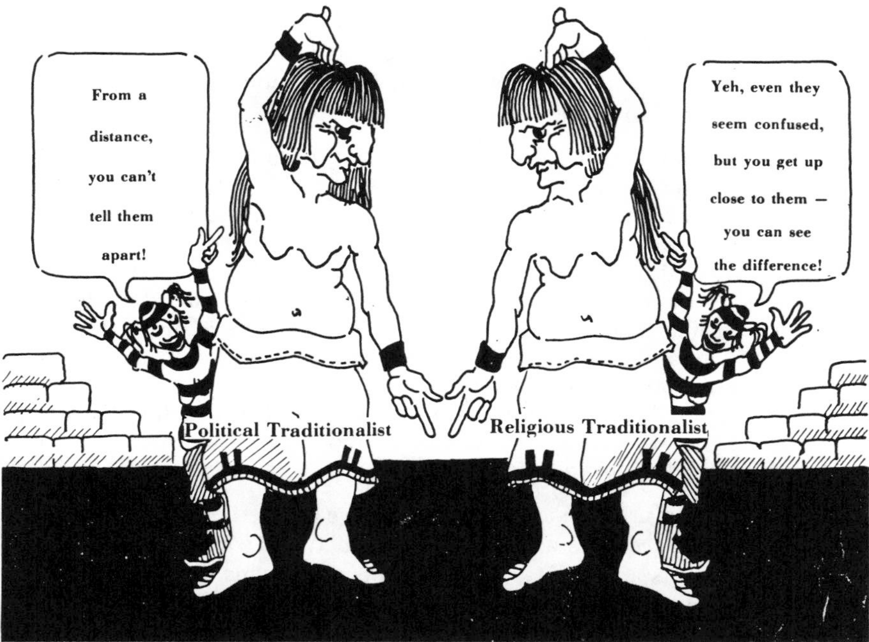

Figure 13. "Look-Alikes." SOURCE: *Qua' Töqti* December 16, 1976.

village, the reservation, and the nation. Villages were labeled either "Council" or "Traditional," depending on the preferences of the village leadership. At this level, both factions were on equal terms concerning political activity. In the reservation arena it is obvious that the Council had the advantage. Whereas Traditional villages have had great difficulties in mobilizing support from other villages because of the principle of village autonomy, the Council villages have had a central forum in the Tribal Council. The third arena concerns the expansion of Hopi factionalism onto the national level, where each faction mobilized non-Hopi groups and institutions in order to bring pressure to bear on the other. The Council reinforced its ties to the BIA, and the Traditionalists sought support among antigovernment factions on other reservations and among the non-Indian public. In some instances, support was sought at the international level through visits to the United Nations and lecture tours in Europe and Canada. A third group of supporters is found among non-Hopi activists and sympathizers who have made their presence felt on the reservation.

In Nagata's opinion, it is in the reservation and the national arenas where susceptibility to innovation and potent socializing effects are to be found in both factions (ibid.:10). Nagata summarized the evidence that suggests that the Traditionalists in competition with the Council have modernized their conduct so much that it clearly demonstrates how factionalism became an agent of innovation:

> The Traditional faction has come to employ increasingly many kinds of "weapons" which have already been in use in the Tribal Council. In the practice of public meetings, relaxation of criteria in political participation, concern with the size of following, awareness of the need and increasing use of the English language, use of newspaper media, coordination of intervillage relationships in public meetings and in raising political funds, attempt to maintain the record of their activities by tape recorders and in written form, and finally, in an emergent quality of secular leadership it seems possible to see a convergent pattern of factional conducts between the two factions. . . . By approximating the norms of their political action to those of the Council, therefore, the Traditionals are learning the art of American politics. (ibid.:26–27)

Nagata quoted a Moenkopi woman who realized the same thing: *Itam hapi palöngawhoyam,* "We are really the little War Twins,"[3] meaning that the Traditionalists and the Council members are twins in nature. This insight raises the question of whether we are indeed confronted with factionalism at all. If factionalism is to be defined as "a disagreement over the means . . . [and] not over the goal" (Siegel and Beals 1960*b*:109), then increasing similarities in means negates the term. Since they cannot be called political parties because there is no consensus of representation, Nagata retained the term factionalism. In his other work, Nagata seems to vacillate with regards to the problem. Whereas in his monograph he argued persuasively against using the term factionalism (1970: 92, 96), he reintroduced the term "schismatic factionalism" from Siegel and Beals in his 1977 paper.

James A. Clifton was confronted with the same problem in his work on the Prairie Potawatomi. He suggested that in cases where prolonged factional conflict slurs the boundaries between conflicting groups, factionalism should be understood as a condition of a sociocultural system rather than of special interest groups:

> Factionalism thus is characterized as a type of overt conflict within a given social system, a type of conflict which persists long enough so that traditional control mechanisms can be brought to bear. Factionalism differs from other types of conflict in that these control mechanisms fail, so that the dispute continues unresolved and unregulated. . . . [As] they persist

3. I have adjusted the orthography and the translation.

> their effects may be diffused, felt and acted out on other levels or in other parts of the total social system. (Clifton 1968:185)[4]

Turning now to his paper on Qötshongva, Nagata focused more on Traditionalist ideology. Borrowing the terminology of L. A. Fallers (1961), he viewed the Pahaana prophecy as a mechanism of "cultural management" (1978:74), and, drawing on Weber he posited the psychological need for the search for Pahaana as functionally equivalent to "the early Calvinist pursuit of this worldly signs of *certitudo salutis*, which according to Max Weber, is 'the origin of all psychological drives of a purely religious character'" (ibid.:81).

Nagata consigned the failure of the Traditionalist Movement to two factors. In the first place, the Traditionalists had no control over the resources that attracted many Hopis (ibid.:75). Only a modicum of ideological discipline concerning a denial of American goods could be maintained in the ranks of professed members (ibid.:83). I would add as well that ideological discipline was wanting among the leaders themselves, as any Hopi, Traditionalist or otherwise, is quick to point out. Many discussions with a variety of informants have confirmed this point (cf. A. W. Geertz 1987*c* for some examples). A typical example of the ever-present suspicion of the behavior of the Traditionalist leaders was evident in the gossip in Hotevilla the day after David Monongya died in 1988. The village was rife with rumors of the discovery of hidden caches of foreign currency in Monongya's home, the possession of which would contradict everything Monongya had stood for. The truth of the gossip is unimportant here; it is the symptomatics of the suspicion that are more significant.

In the second place the Progressive and Traditionalist factions were unable to establish clear-cut boundaries because of the "considerable degree of side switching on the part of the followers" (ibid.:75), a fact Nagata attributed to the web of cross-cutting ties in Hopi social reality and to the similar political analyses, goals, and methods of the two factions (see Nagata 1970, 92–96).

Applying the terminology of millenarian studies, Nagata labeled the ideology of the Traditionalist Movement as "nativistic," whereas the Tribal Council preempted the ideology of modernization (1978:75–76, 81). Although he did not define what he meant by "nativistic," it is apparent that he was referring to Linton's definition: "Any conscious, organized attempt on the part of a society's members to revive or perpetuate selected aspects of its culture" (Linton 1943:230).

4. In this latter point, he followed French's emphasis on the persistent lack of regulation as a defining criterion.

I find Nagata's analysis to be essentially correct and still useful. Even though many things have changed since the 1960s when he conducted his fieldwork, his basic analysis of the Traditionalist Movement and its activities and problems are still valid. A weakness that is clearly present in his article on Qötshongva is that he does not clearly distinguish between Hopi traditional thought and Traditionalist ideology. The absence of a distinction invites the assumption that Hopi prophetic thought is restricted to and identical with the Traditionalist Movement. But this is hardly the case, as this book shows.

GOSSIP AND INFORMATION MANAGEMENT

Nagata paid attention to the methods of persuasion that distinguish the two factions, but he also noted in passing that gossip and rumors are two methods used by both groups (1968:11). Anthropologist Bruce Cox took a brief but closer look at the role of gossip in information management[5] on the reservation in his article "What Is Hopi Gossip About?" (1970). The term "information management" is evidently derived from Erving Goffman's concept of "impression management" (Goffman 1959:6). These terms refer to how individuals communicate their social identities and roles to each other. In most cases the individual makes use of selective communication where we find "overcommunicating that which confirms the relevant (social identities) and relationships, and undercommunicating that which is discrepant" (Barth 1966:3). Cox defined gossip as a process in which "a person directly interferes in another's impression-management, hence forcing the audience to redefine his victim's role" (1970:88). Further, Cox noted that political gossip, that is, "gossip concerning others' fitness to have access to power . . . has the particularly salient point of permitting an increase in one's own party's access to power" (ibid.:89).

Based on fieldwork at First Mesa during 1965–1966, Cox applied his ideas to gossip between the two Hopi factions. Cox considered Hopi factionalism as approximating Siegel and Beals' ideal type of "pervasive factionalism," which is defined as "conflict between unorganised and transient groups" (Siegel and Beals 1960*a*:399). The two groups are, as with Nagata, pro-Council and Traditionalist, but, again, as with anyone who has done serious research on the topic, Cox is aware that these are merely labels which can and do veil a much more fluid situation (cf. A. W. Geertz 1987*c*). Instead of viewing factions in terms of their social relations, as Nicholas and Nagata did, Cox viewed them in terms of what

5. Cf. Paine 1967, 1968.

they were striving for (1970:97). The latter point of view is for Cox what information management is all about. Such a point of view, furthermore, cannot accept Siegel and Beals' (1960*b*:108) and Nicholas' (1966:53) opinion that factional rivalry is a pseudo-conflict, nor Firth's (1957:293–294) that it is a kind of "war game." The issues are real enough to the Hopis (Cox 1970:96).

The game metaphor, however, may be an expression of the growing discontent at the time with the view that the rules of a culture are internalized and mechanically guide people's real behavior. Anthropologists,[6] sociologists,[7] and philosophers such as Alfred Schutz (1967) and Ludwig Wittgenstein (1953) were beginning to realize that humans are actors who skillfully manipulate rules in order to achieve personal advantage, a ploy which Edgerton (1985:9ff) called the "strategic manipulation of rules".[8] It was even suggested that "endemic conflict" (including "exceptions" to the "rules") is neither an exception nor a defect. It is, in fact, the system itself (Stanner 1959:216). Holy (1986:198ff) called it "norms as a strategic resource".[9] As Giddens noted:

> While not made by any single person, society is created and recreated afresh . . . by the participants in every social encounter. The production of society is a skilled performance, sustained and "made to happen" by human beings. (Giddens 1976:15)

Edgerton called for a balance of opinion in his 1985 publication on rules and exceptions to rules. He argued that there are different types of rules which may or may not have exceptions depending on various factors. But since all societies do have rules for which there are no exceptions, there is a need to reappraise current social theories "that conceive of social systems as being made up of rules that are flexible, negotiable, and subject to exceptions" (1985:3). He wrote that it is essential to recognize that rules for which there are no exceptions are also universal: "An important corrective to the strategic interaction perspective is the recognition that rules sometimes have great power to constrain behavior and sometimes are enforced without exceptions" (ibid.:16).

I agree with Edgerton, and therefore I prefer to evaluate gossip in terms of cultural values rather than in the organizational metaphors of sociology. Gossip is, in my opinion, one of the major expressions of social identity in traditional Hopi contexts. Gossip not only redefines the roles and identities of others, it also defines the social identity of self. It

6. V. W. Turner 1957; Stanner 1959; Leach 1961; Barth 1966.
7. Mills 1959; Goffman 1959, 1969.
8. Cf. Evens 1977, Nader and Todd 1978, Gulliver 1979, Comaroff and Roberts 1981.
9. Cf. Holy and Stuchlik 1983:107ff.

is the ongoing dialogue about oneself and others, both implicitly and explicitly, which characterizes gossip. As a subject of analysis, it is perhaps one of the best-suited to bridge the weaknesses of the ethnomethodologists' attempt to map out "cultural competence." One of the main problems with the latter approach is a question of which parameters we should choose to set when confronted with a basically infinite variety of contingencies and exceptions to the rules:

> Such questions arise directly when anthropologists try to catalog favorite facts. What, for example, is an appropriate residence choice? The answer is muddled by a seemingly endless string of contingencies. I live with my father after marriage; except that, if he is dead, I may live with my father's brother; except that, if he is too young, I may live with my mother; except that, if she has moved back to her father's house, I may move in with my wife's family; and so on. (Haviland 1977:174)

Peter Whiteley (1985, 1986) has convincingly demonstrated that even in the case of the seemingly impregnable bulwark of Hopi inheritance and kinship rules, contingencies are quite often the rule rather than the exception.

Haviland's point is that cultural competence is a way of "figuring out" solutions to baffling problems and figuring out "how to interpret what has happened, how to understand or justify it, and usually how to feel about it" (1977:175).[10] Understanding gossip is one of the few mechanisms that allows us to capture a picture of this wider cultural competence. In Haviland's opinion, it is in the capacity to assess others' actions, to pronounce on the rules involved, and to distinguish the exceptional from the ordinary that the capacity to participate in gossip is constituted.

The idea that the contingencies of life restructure and change ideal rules stands in opposition to the orthodox idea in anthropology that culture provides the sets of ideal rules (ibid.:182). In gossip, the rules are directly confronted not as independent but as contextually bound entities in particular settings. Thus the end result can be any number of mutually contradictory native interpretations:

> In gossip the nonparticular is irrelevant before the actual; the contingencies determine the general principles—for they are all there is. In gossip, the world becomes more than ideal schemata and codes; it rests on the Who's Who, much expanded, on history, on reputations, on idiosyncracies, on exceptions and accidents. Gossip exalts the particular. Much of an actor's cultural competence rests on a vast knowledge of contingent fact,

10. See Howard Gardner's interesting model of the development of cultural competence (1984).

> raw unconnected trivia—in addition to the understanding of taxonomies and lexical subsystems which we have always suspected to be there. (ibid.: 181)

Taking a discourse-centered approach, similar to Sherzer (1987), I consider Hopi gossip to be a type of "narrated ethics" that mobilizes Hopi ethical ideals in the face of Hopi practice, which ideally is the pursuit of ethical behavior (cf. A. W. Geertz 1986, 1990*a*). I distinguish therefore, as Roger Keesing does (1974:90), between the ideational system and behavior, but hold with Sherzer that "language, culture, society, and the individual . . . [provide] resources in a creative process which is actualized in discourse" (1987:305).

Peter Whiteley countered that if discourse is opposed to practice, where is the line of demarcation? He also suggested that the exchange of words itself is a form of practice. Furthermore, he suggested that narrated ethics are found in areas other than gossip. They are found, for example, in ritual discourse (personal communication 1987). These are points well taken. I propose, therefore, a model in which ideal discourse and behavior—which in the Hopi context is ritual discourse and behavior (cf. A. W. Geertz 1986, 1990*a*)—are separate from everyday discourse and behavior. Gossip is a bridge between the two, and it serves as a social conscience (e.g., the social Other) judging everyday behavior in relationship to cultural and ethical ideals. The model, then, is in accordance with my definition of religion in the Introduction.[11] But gossip can be used to undermine those ideals as in malicious or false gossip, and thus the causeways in the model go both ways.

Seen in this wider perspective, I think that Cox's definition of gossip as interference with another's impression management is too vague. This vagueness is obvious in his choice of examples. He did not present his case at all in the context of actual down-to-earth gossip. Instead, he mentioned clown skits, letters to the editor, editorials, and name calling. The latter three can equally be defined in terms of a variety of other social activities, such as normal political debate, and the former is a ritual activity that is part of an "information-management" process of greater dimensions than gossip. Clowning is, in fact, an intimate part of what I call "ritual or ideal behavior and discourse" (cf. Hieb 1972). Cox's arguments would have had greater impact if he had presented and analyzed examples of real gossip, especially if presented in the vernacular (cf. A. W. Geertz 1990*a*).

11. Herskovits (1937*a*, 1937*b*), Herskovits and Herskovits (1947), West (1945), Colson (1953), and Gluckman (1963) have all argued along similar lines.

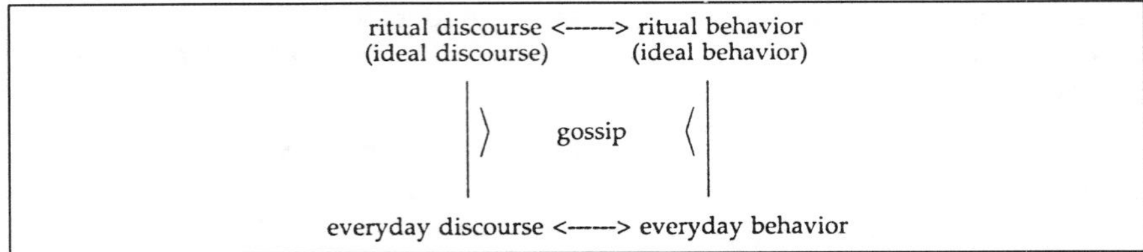

Figure 14. A model of gossip and religion.

THE POLITICS OF ANALYSIS

Cultural anthropologist Richard A. Clemmer is the only scholar who has worked extensively on the Traditionalist Movement. Not only that, he has participated as an activist in the movement itself and has consequently been accused of unethical conduct and of producing biased reports (cf. Washburn 1979, 1985, 1989). This criticism has been met head on with the reply that anthropology can make no claims to objectivity (cf. Clemmer 1969, 1972). Anthropology is, in his words, the "Euro-American culture's intellectual mechanism for self-scrutiny through cross-cultural comparison" (1978*b*:1).[12] This realization is in full agreement with the latest reflections by social anthropologists. As James Clifford wrote concerning an important collection of essays on writing culture:

> [These essays] see culture as composed of seriously contested codes and representations; they assume that the poetic and the political are inseparable, that science is in, not above, historical and linguistic processes. They assume that academic and literary genres interpenetrate and that the writing of cultural descriptions is properly experimental and ethical. Their focus on text making and rhetoric serves to highlight the constructed, artificial nature of cultural accounts. It undermines overly transparent modes of authority, and it draws attention to the historical predicament of ethnography, the fact that it is always caught up in the invention, not the representation, of cultures. (Clifford 1986:2)

True as this may be, instead of following the premises of anthropology, Clemmer pursued an existential "search for community in a complex universe, and for the integral concept of self which I think a successful community should produce in its individuals" (1978*b*:1). In other words, his objectives were soteriological and were, in fact, part of a larger pattern of utopian ideals which were much in evidence in the U.S. during the 1970s. But I find it difficult to see what relevance these ideals

12. Clemmer's earlier honesty in admitting his partisanship is camouflaged in the corporate "objective" response to Washburn's criticisms in Clemmer et al. 1989.

have to the study of historical and contemporary affairs on the Hopi Reservation. In my opinion, academic discourse has its own objectives, which are better suited than activism to the global study of human culture.

Clemmer's only major work (1978*b*) is basically a repetition and summary of his earlier papers in which he reveals a penchant for biased reporting (cf. 73–74) and a "New Age" type of argumentation in support of religious opinion (cf. his theories on myth, 41, 51). His book ends on an apocryphal note that clearly reveals his ideological and theological commitment, and consequently any criticism of his work will inevitably carry at least a political implication if not a political response. But since his point of view closely corresponds with that of the Traditionalists and of their many non-Hopi supporters, it is essential to summarize his arguments fairly and to deal with them directly.

Despite the weaknesses of his approach, his book contains useful reviews of the history of the Hopis and of the Traditionalist Movement as well as an important chapter on the political use of myth (ibid.:44–50). Clemmer notes that it is the "strongly mythic, nationalistic, and visionary character" of the Traditionalist Movement that gives it a "revivalistic quality" (ibid.:70). But, in reviewing Wallace's understanding of revitalization movements (1956) and Linton's understanding of nativistic movements (1943), Clemmer rejects the former for being psychologistic and the latter for ignoring political factors (ibid.:75–76). He rightly points to the main issue in the Hopi context as being "the definition and exercise of political authority" (ibid.:77). He maintains, therefore, that the Traditionalist Movement is a "resistance movement" which has at its base "a psychological commitment . . . to resist forced acculturation and assimilation" (ibid.:70; cf. Clemmer 1972).

Clemmer noted that both the Tribal Council and their bitter opponents, the Traditionalists, have demonstrated political acumen in pursuit of the same goals, namely, increasing self-determination. The difference between them lies in their chosen strategies: The Tribal Council chose to attain its goals through its position as an institution of the U.S. government, whereas the Traditionalists have chosen traditional social and political organization and "the appeal of Hopi culture as an adaptive strategy unto itself" (ibid.:70).

An important point, to Clemmer's credit, is that he noted that the aforementioned "appeal" of Hopi culture "is directed at non-Indian people, and rests on the incorporation of non-Indians into the Hopi mythic process" (ibid.). But Clemmer did not explain why this must be so, nor did he clarify the obvious contradiction in terms: How could the Traditionalists build a viable platform on the dichotomy of maintaining traditionalism and incorporating foreigners? Clemmer seems to imply that the answer lies in the Pahaana myth. But this is no answer since the Pahaana myth is a pan-Hopi myth completely independent of political stances.

The answer is to be found in the fact that the Traditionalist Movement is not what it purports to be. This is the position I took in my article "Prophets and Fools" (1987*c*), but more on this problem below. Clemmer's summary of Hopi "resistance ideology" can be paraphrased thusly:

1. The U.S. government has no legal right of authority over the Hopis. They constitute a sovereign nation which has never bound itself by any treaty.
2. The U.S. government has no moral right to force acculturation on the Hopis.
3. The Tribal Council cannot represent or act on the behalf of the "traditional villages." It does not fit the "Traditional Hopi Life Plan."
4. Neither the U.S. government nor the Tribal Council has the right to lease or sell Hopi land, nor has the Indian Claims Commission, the federal court, or anyone else the right to establish its boundaries.
5. Only the "Hopi Traditional Chiefs" are the rightful leaders–a right which was given to them "in accordance with the Great Spirit's Hopi Life Plan."
6. They will resist anything that increases Hopi dependence on the U.S., and "material comfort is an illusion that must not be indulged until certain worldwide behavior patterns, fundamental beliefs, and ideologies are changed."
7. "Hopi tradition and prophecies by many elders set out a practical interpretation of the Hopi Life Plan which obligates Hopi Traditional Leaders to disseminate information and knowledge, search for allies among non-Hopis, and work for the awakening in as many people as possible of an ethic that once bound all mankind together and must bind them once again if mankind is to survive." (ibid.:75; cf. Clemmer 1969, 1972)

These seven points clearly summarize what Traditionalist ideology and rhetoric is all about. My main criticisms of Clemmer are that he accepts Traditionalist ideology at face value, that he unquestioningly accepts their stance and claims to power, that he views tradition and its rhetoric as static truth untainted by historical and idiosyncratic factors, and that he relies too heavily on a caricature of the differences between the Hopi worldview and the "U.S." worldview.[13] It is especially the latter

13. On the latter, see especially Clemmer 1969, 1972. For a more balanced interpretation of the diverse American creeds, values, attitudes, and institutions that have made themselves felt on the reservation, see Thompson 1950:136–151, Spicer 1962, and Whiteley 1988. Seen from another (i.e., European) point of view, one could equally criticize

point which has moved him to consistently misrepresent the data concerning the rise and legitimacy of the Tribal Council and which has moved him to actively join forces with the Traditionalists in their attempts to remove the Tribal Council, an activity Washburn rightly denounces as unethical (1989:738).

Following up on Nagata, one of the main points of this book is that the Traditionalist Movement, its rhetoric and ideology notwithstanding, has been just as much an instrument of change as the Tribal Council. Whereas the Tribal Council has introduced deliberate economic change, the Traditionalists, in changing their "traditions" more radically than any other Hopis, have introduced deliberate ideological change. Both opponents have contributed to a modification in the Hopi worldview.

I hope that this book demonstrates that a crucial number of Traditionalist postulates are false. By false, I am referring primarily to indigenous and secondarily to historiographical norms, both of which in this case are unambiguously in agreement:

1. Hopi prophecies are not static bastions of absolute truth, but rhetorical devices for communicating meaning to changing audiences through conceived truths.
2. The Traditionalist claim that only chiefs are the rightful wielders of power in no way legitimizes their own claims to power—on the contrary.
3. Instead of providing resistance to change, the Traditionalists have, in fact, been used and influenced by larger social and cultural factors originating in exactly the society they have been resisting.
4. The Tribal Council is a legitimate representative body and it has not destroyed Hopi lifeways, although earlier, short-sighted (and sometimes desperate) policies were leading them to it.

History has overtaken both Clemmer and the Traditionalists. Whereas the Traditionalists have failed, the Tribal Council has not. The Traditionalist Movement was influential in changing the material determinism of earlier Council policies, but the movement was not able to improve its own image for the majority of the Hopis, i.e., that Traditionalist leaders are power-hungry authoritarians whose obstructionism and inflexible policies literally drove the voters to the booths. It became clear especially to the young and the middle-aged that thirty years of anachronistic squabbling were enough. By 1985 the elections brought out about 60 percent

---

Clemmer for his distinctively American assumption of the individual as a self-motivated agent. This point of view motivates and informs Clemmer's moral indignation, and yet it is perhaps *the* paradigmatic assumption in the United States (cf. Varenne 1984).

of the registered voters (A. W. Geertz 1987*c*:41). And, as we saw in chapter 5, a former Traditionalist was actually running for the chairman's post in the 1989 elections.

The Tribal Council presently serves as the only platform for survival, both political and cultural, in contemporary affairs. Instead of being a "puppet," it secures Hopi sovereignty. As Wilcomb Washburn of the Smithsonian Institution recently wrote:

> Like the states, Indian tribes have limited powers, and their sovereignty is restricted in various ways, but again like the states their sovereign power is acknowledged and recognized and upheld by the Supreme Court in numerous cases (Washburn 1971, 1976). Indian tribes exist on a government-to-government relationship with the surrounding states and with the federal government. (1989:738)[14]

The accusation by non-Hopis that the Tribal Council is run by mormonized Hopi puppets is, even in historical perspective, a gross misrepresentation.[15]

At any rate, the Council of the 1980s pursued a clear policy of cultural preservation in all of its aspects. Not only are there cultural programs as such, but there are also programs dealing with the causes of cultural dissonance such as alcoholism, educational policies, and the theft and sale of religious objects. The Council does not interfere with value-preserving ceremonialism nor with any other aspect of Hopi religion. Its members act just like any other Hopis, living and taking part in the "traditional" way of life whenever and wherever possible. This is true of all of the tribal officials with whom I have dealt.

The whole tribe is admittedly changing, but this is not equivalent to cultural disintegration. Action anthropology has perhaps helped to avert conspiracies of one kind or another in an apparent "age of conspiracies" in the U.S. of the 1960s and the 1970s (cf. Clemmer 1977, 1978*a*), but it has pursued its own form of puritanism by "fast-freezing" a particular moment in the fluidity of social reality, elevating that moment in absolute terms, and reducing all other factors as dependent variables.

14. See the well-argued response to the issue of sovereignty in Clemmer et al. (1989:747–748).

15. Jorgensen's sweeping statement about Mormon Hopis becoming active in tribal government (1985:120) is as characteristic for activist polemics as it is ridiculous. Abbott Sekaquaptewa, council chairman for many years, is usually pointed out as an example of a Mormon Hopi. The problem is that he is *not* a Mormon. His late father, mother, and brother, Wayne Sekaquaptewa, the founding editor of *Qua' Töqti*, are Mormon, but neither Abbott nor his other brother Emory are. One or two Mormons have indeed been members of the council, but this is neither a disqualification nor reason to label the council as a mormonized institution, nor even to claim that the council was under the sway of Mormon Hopis.

Edward Bruner noted in his essay on the role of the implicit narrative structures in our study of foreign peoples (in other words, the "story" we tell about the peoples we study), that informants and field workers share in the same implicit narratives, and sometimes even select each other on the basis of this compatibility:

> I see both anthropologist and Indian as being caught in the same web, influenced by the same historical forces, and shaped by the dominant narrative structures of our times. . . . My point is that both anthropologist and native informant participate in the same symbolic system. Not that our cultures are identical; rather, we share, at least partially, those narratives dealing with intercultural relations and cultural change. (1986*b*:149–150)

Even though economic and political realities may have created action anthropology, it is important for the humanistic study of religion and culture to perceive our activities within wider metahistorical perspectives, such as Hayden White has done in his typology of the historiographical styles of historians and philosophers of history (1973) or as the participants of the 1984 symposium on the social contexts of American ethnology have done (Helm 1985).

THE TRADITIONALIST MOVEMENT IN ANALYTICAL TERMS

There is an ever-growing literature on and a considerable number of typologies of millenarian movements. It is not my intention to go through them all nor to provide an alternative typology,[16] but to relate, or at least to make available, the Hopi example to the comparative and theoretical discussion. Therefore, I will try to illustrate the peculiarities of the Traditionalist Movement against the backdrop of a number of existent analytical categories.

Until recently, the two main explanations for the birth of millenarian movements, according to Hillel Schwartz (1987), have been feelings of relative deprivation and contact with a technologically superior culture. The former is a psychological theory and the latter a sociological one. Both explanations have been persistently criticized, most recently by Burridge (1987) and H. Schwartz (1987) in their articles in *The Encyclopedia of Religion*, for a variety of reasons ever since the theories were first ventured.[17]

16. For useful typologies and discussions of prior research I would recommend the following: Stanner 1958, M. Smith 1959, Voget 1959, Jarvie 1963, Fernandez 1964, Clemhout 1964, 1966, Burridge 1969, La Barre 1971, H. Schwartz 1976, H. W. Turner 1979, and Siikala 1982. The standard reference work is Harold W. Turner's *Bibliography of New Religious Movements* (1977, 1978).

17. See Burridge 1969:117–164, 1985, and Siikala 1982:15–54 for more detailed evaluations of types of theoretical explanations.

It should be noted that the sociology of religion and the psychology of religion have encountered similar problems with typologies of new religious (Euro-American) movements.[18] As both Thomas Robbins and a number of other scholars have noted, typologies of both new religious movements and millenarian movements have specifically been linked to theological or other normative objectives that have served ecclesiastical and/or colonial policy tactics. Accordingly, the value of a typology must lie in its relationship to theoretical constructions which suggest criteria for evaluation (Robbins 1988:135).

Hillel Schwartz noted that there are a number of factors other than "contact" which predispose to millenarian movements and which combine with any one of four precipitant factors other than "relative deprivation." The six factors which predispose are:

> 1. permeable monastic communities and lay sodalities that extend loyalties beyond the family;
> 2. itinerant homeopathic healers who carry ritual and rumor across regional borders;
> 3. a mythopoetic tradition in popular drama and folktale, which makes history prophetic and the people the bearers of prophecy;
> 4. numerology and astrology, which encourage people habitually to search out relationships between number, event, and time;
> 5. rituals of inversion, such as carnival or exhaustive mourning, in which endings and beginnings are willfully confused;
> 6. migration myths that call for the return to an ancestral land or for the return of the dead to a renewed land. (1987:528–529)

Of these six predispositional factors, numbers 1, 3, and 6 are directly applicable to Hopi reality whereas 2, 4, and 5 can be applied in modified form.

The four factors that precipitate millenarian movements are:

> 1. the evangelism of foreign missionaries whose success requires the reordering of native patterns of marriage, family, diet, and calendar;
> 2. displacement by refugees or invaders, or as a result of persecution, economic decline, or natural calamity;
> 3. confusion about landholdings due to shifting settlement, the superposition of a new legal grid, or the advent of new technologies, as foreshadowed most particularly by census taking, geological surveys, rail laying, and road building;
> 4. generational distortion, where the traditional transfer of loyalities and moral authority is profoundly disturbed by war deaths, schooling, long-distance migrations, or urbanization. (ibid.:529)

18. See Robbins' splendid summaries in his *Cults, Converts and Charisma* 1988: 134–160.

The above-mentioned predispositional factors enter into a mixture with precipitative factors numbers 1, 3, and 4 and to a limited extent number 2 (i.e., the displacement of Oraibi refugees after the 1906 split).

The Hopi example raises the question of whether we are confronted with traditional-style religious experimentation, nativism, revitalization, pietism, or millenarianism. The answer is "yes" to all five terms depending on how one looks at it. The widespread dominance of prophetic thought in contemporary Hopi religion can be called both traditional-style religious experimentation and pietism, whereas the Traditionalist Movement's activities function as a distinctly political type of nativism on the reservation and a deeply millenarian revitalization outside of it. I follow Beckford's definition of revitalization as "attempts to invigorate a declining primal or traditional culture in response to perceived threats to that culture's integrity or survival" (Beckford 1987:390).

It is important to realize that traditional Hopi religious thought has the very same characteristics as those applied to what is labeled "millenarianism." H. Schwartz defined it as follows:

> Millenarianism, known also as millennialism, is the belief that the end of this world is at hand and that in its wake will appear a New World, inexhaustibly fertile, harmonious, sanctified, and just. (1987:521)

Millenarianism is, in theory, properly "an adjunct of eschatology" and, in practice, a "close scrutiny of the present from which arise urgent issues of human agency" (ibid.:522). For millenarianism is also a movement that provides more than a diagnosis of a culture in metastasis (ibid.:524) or predictions of a catastrophic future. Millenarianism provides answers to contemporary dissonance and, especially, a plan of action.

As Burridge noted, the morphology of such movements is generally: 1) A leader or prophet receives a revelation, 2) While disclaiming personal authority on the grounds that he or she is an agent of some transcendent source, 3) the prophet "articulates to a given community a seemingly imperative program of action," which 4) is usually sanctioned by threats of imminent disaster and from which 5) believers will be saved and unbelievers not (1987:369).

The participants in such movements usually excite notice by their own mimetic acts, which not only serve as public commitments to the prophecies, but also serve as activity harmonious with and precipitative of conceived historical forces (H. Schwartz 1987:525).

All of these characteristics are present in traditional Hopi thought. And although the Traditionalist Movement has emphasized certain of the more dynamic characteristics, it is also important to note that traditional thought does not mean static or torpid thought. On the contrary, just as in millenarian contexts, I have shown here that reinterpretation and new meanings are drawn from old myths in an attempt to get at the truth of things in changing circumstances; what Fernandez called "world reconstruction" (1982:ix).

Traditional Hopi thought maintains a "keen sense of historical and cultural threads linking past, present, and future" (Beckford 1987:392), which at the same time allows the "meaning and periodization" of historical change to be reinterpreted from time to time. Thus, we can view the more dynamic events in Hopi history, such as the burning of Awat'ovi in 1700 or the split of Oraibi in 1906, as extreme examples of this ongoing process of reinterpretation, where not only the conflict of foreign and indigenous worldviews is evident, but perhaps even more so the conflict of disparate indigenous interpretive models is evident as well.

Thus, seen from within, the Traditionalist Movement is neither a movement nor does it tender anything new to the Hopis. Its leaders have simply attempted to usurp political power and have led a Quixotic battle against the Tribal Council. Seen from without, the Traditionalist Movement is a movement that demonstrates all of the characteristics of millenarianism, but it is neither a new faith in a new god nor a new communal ritual. It is neither vision nor healing nor a new social community ideal.

The Traditionalist Movement is simply the politicization of an already existing "reforming ethic" and a reaffirmation of traditional Hopi values which have been exported to impressionable Euro-American youth and new religious-movement support groups. In the latter capacity, the Traditionalist Movement has satisfied a response category called "appropriation" by Andrew Walls "whereby primal religions are being adopted or recommended by those who historically belong to quite another tradition" (1987:276)—as in my strategic categories 4 and 5 (cf. chapter 2).

FROM RESISTANCE TO UNIVERSALISM

Clemmer's seventh summary point of the "resistance ideology" by its very wording clearly demonstrates that Traditionalist ideology is not what it purports to be. The missionary endeavor of a universal awakening is utterly alien to Hopi "tradition."

The Traditionalists have attempted to reformulate their religion, including its prophecies, so that the thrust of Hopi religion is moved from local, agricultural concerns to universalistic and missionary ones. The attempt failed, not because Judgment Day failed to arrive, but because the Traditionalists failed to mobilize their own people and have instead recruited White Euro-Americans. This development needs explaining, and the explanation is not without interest. In the process of our explanation, we will see how resistance (strategic category 2) developed into the wooing of subversive groups (category 3) and the subsequent attempts at messianism, which may be the extreme expression of category 3.

The best examples of the use of myth in resistance to the dominant Anglo culture do not need to be repeated here. I am referring to the strident tones of Talay'ima's emergence myth, told to Cushing in 1882, and Yukiwma's version after the split of Oraibi, told to Colonel Scott in 1911.

What is of special interest to the theme of this chapter is the statement by Yukiwma to Crane during one of Yukiwma's many prison terms: "I am doing this as much for you as for my own people" (Crane 1925:188). This statement contains the germ of an idea growing among Hopi prophecy tellers, namely, that the Hopis will somehow save the world from destruction.

Most prophetic accounts were, however, concerned with clan-specific interests, as we have seen. It took two world wars and especially the atomic bombs to move the so-called Hostiles to establish themselves shortly thereafter as the Traditionalists. In 1948 a number of men met to discuss the prophecies concerning the ash gourd. During this meeting they reached a concensus and agreed that the old ash-gourd stories were actually prophecies about the atomic bomb. Once this premise was accepted, they were in no doubt that the "last day" was imminent. A series of meetings during that same year resulted in a loose collation of disparate clan traditions which were developed into a seemingly coherent prophetic corpus.

In 1949, they wrote a letter to President Truman in which they rejected the North Atlantic Alliance and a whole series of laws and resolutions (cf. Appendix D). The letter demonstrated a carefully plotted and solid platform for the emerging Traditionalist Movement. As mentioned in chapter 5, almost all of the cosigners became leaders of the movement. An important point to note is that the letter laid claim to power, authority, and spokesmanship, and yet only two of the twenty-six cosigners were actually village chiefs; and, as noted, Qötshongva took over after Pongyayawma, one of the cosigners, left. A number of cosigners did possess priestly positions, but their presence can only rightfully support the letter's claims to *cultural* competence. Besides cogent arguments against the imperialistic assumptions of the policies of the U.S. government, the letter cast the Traditionalist stance in clearly millenarian terms. Seen in apocryphal terms, the inviolability of tradition was reaffirmed and served as a point of departure for their analysis of past, present, and future events. Hopi rights were god-given and would be proven so at the end of the world.

Even though the theme of resistance is present, the tone is clearly universalistic, where Hopis have received responsibility for the whole world. Those responsible for the letter conceived their eschatology in universal terms in which the end of the world is global and where the Hopis play a pivotal role in the world theatre:

> Today we, Hopi and white man, come face to face at the crossroad of our respective life. At last our paths have crossed and it was foretold it would be at the most critical time in the history of mankind. Everywhere people are confused. What we decide now and do hereafter will be the fate of our respective people. . . . The time has now come for all of us as leaders of our people to reexamine ourselves, our past deeds, and our future plans. The judgment day will soon be upon us. Let us make haste and set our house in order before it is too late. (Hopi Empire 3-28-1949, cf. Appendix D)

This letter marked the beginning of a veritable trafficking in prophecies, which began to attract many young Americans who searched out Qötshongva as a messianic figure.

The growing presence of young people attracted to the Hopi stand during the 1950s provoked instances of hostility and irritation from some of the speakers at the BIA hearings in 1955.[19] The grandson of Loololma, Willard Sakiestewa, Sr., from Kykotsmovi, even called for federal legislation against outsiders coming in to talk with other leaders (Bureau of Indian Affairs 1955:184).

The following year, the true nature of the Traditionalist prophecies and the interest groups that supported them became evident. The advertisement for the "Meeting of Religious People," as it was called, at Hotevilla in 1956 eloquently illustrates strategic categories 3 and 5:

> I strongly urge you to attend this gathering of chosen ones selected from his [the Great Spirit] wide variety of religions on this land. The roots of the Hopi stand reach, as time will show, to every man on earth, and contain the cause and cure of our global crisis. A supreme tragedy of our age is that most men are being hoodwinked into choosing between "communism" or "capitalism"—both mammon—never even realizing there is a third way beckoning unto them; for of a truth the Father's kingdom is now on earth. The concensus reached as a result of the meeting will rapidly reverberate around the world. (Bentley 1956:4)

The editor, Wilder Bentley, filled the minutes of the three-day meeting with pompous and moralistic tirades against the U.S. government and the Tribal Council in editorial parentheses.

19. See Bureau of Indian Affairs 1955:116, 157, 174, 184, 308, 319, 321, 362.

What is important to note is the growing universalistic thrust of Hopi prophecy. As Dan Qötshongva stated in his opening speech:

> Let us remember that we are gathered here not only for the Hopi people, but we are seriously thinking of the future and benefit of ALL other Indian people on this continent, and we include the white people who have come upon our land and settled with us. (ibid.:2)

Even though Qötshongva stated that all people will be involved, purification day will nonetheless take place in Oraibi, as the old traditions state.

In the process of universalizing Hopi prophecy, the concerns of the end of the last century about a returning White Brother who will punish the bad Hopis and begin purification day have now been replaced with the return of Maasaw—now called by the pan-Indian term "Great Spirit"—who will punish all bad people, especially the Whites! As Monongya said in his speech,

> when the Purification Day comes the white man will be allowed to live on this land again. Teachings tell us that a few of them will be saved. But perhaps all will be destroyed, we don't know. (ibid.:10)

The transformation of Maasaw from a local tutelary deity to a universal supreme being is one of the clearest examples of the universalization tendencies. Hamilton A. Tyler was the first to note Maasaw's transformation (cf. Tyler 1964:36–40 and A. W. Geertz 1987*c*:41). He credited this transformation to Qötshongva and Simon Scott, an assumption he based on the speeches they gave during the 1955 hearings. Even though he was mistaken about the age and themes of the stone tablet, I believe that he was correct in identifying these two men as the promulgators of the new Maasaw.

It seems as if Simon Scott was the more agile theologian of the two. And it seems that he was steeped in apocryphal imagery. He proclaimed at the hearings in 1955 that "this supreme being who is over all of us is here with us and listening to all of us in this meeting and will be with us until this meeting is adjourned" (Bureau of Indian Affairs 1955:31). Later, he emphasized again that this supreme being, who created both Indian and White, had instructed both races to live peacefully (ibid.:24). Through the use of biblical language and turns of phrase, he identified the Hopi tutelary as the supreme god who created and rules over all humanity. During the meeting of religious people in 1956, he went much further than transposing and identifying deities, and declared that the content of all religions—especially the eschatological content—is basically the same:

> We are gathered here today, many religions with many different beliefs, and yet each and every one of them has basically the same teaching, with the same beginning and the same end. Each one of us knows these basic religious instructions which are common to all religious people and we also know that these teachings seem to have been forgotten.
>
> We know that The Creator has given each of his various peoples various religions. The white man was given the Bible and several other books. . . . The Great Spirit also gave another book and it is of stone tablets. The Hopi have them in their possession even today and they are to be used also in the future.
>
> Each of us are from a different race, speaking different languages and having different religions. Yet these things we have spoken of today are common values which bind us together as one people. I know that because of your strong beliefs and because of your sincere desire to serve your people and your children, you have come here to listen to us. . . . All of us here will continue to work and worship in our own respective ways and therefore be united in our reverent service to our One Great Spirit, continuing to uphold His various Life Patterns so that He will not destroy us. (Bentley 1956:14–15)

Thus, Hopi religion is considered to be of the same nature as Christianity and Judaism, and is equally legitimate. Simon sets the Traditionalist's political battle in universal religious terms so that it becomes a common battle for all religious people who are consequently portrayed as simply trying to obey the supreme god. During the next forty years the Traditionalists continued to refer to Maasaw as the Great Spirit, even though there is no basis for this term in Hopi tradition. Even today the term is still peculiar to Traditionalist terminology.

In his monograph on Maasaw, Malotki recorded contemporary statements by Hopis concerning the nature of that deity which concur with Tyler's observations (Malotki and Lomatuway'ma 1987*b*:247–262). The older associations with the land and the world of the dead are often underplayed, whereas his invisible and omniscient character is emphasized. Malotki presented a number of commonly used periphrastic locutions that emphasize Maasaw's "divine aspects": *i' hikwsit himuy'taqa* ("the one who has the breath"), *i' hak tuuwaqatsit himuy'taqa* ("this unknown one who owns the earth"), *i' hak itamuy tumalay'maqa* ("this unknown one who goes along taking care of us"), *pam hak itamumi tunatyawtaqa* ("the one that devotes his attention to us"), and *i' hak itamuy it hikwsit maqaaqa* ("the unknown being who gave us breath") (ibid.:248). But even though periphrastic locutions exist, there is no term for "the Great Spirit" in the Hopi language.

The image of Maasaw as the creator is not backed up by any earlier myth. Hopi mythology never really considered the creation of the world as being important, the *Book of the Hopi* notwithstanding.[20] In fact, one of Malotki's informants, who considered Maasaw to be the creator, had no idea about how such a creation should have taken place:

> Maasaw created this world, but it is not known what he made it with. *Pam maasaw yep it tuuwaqatsit yukukyangw pu' hiita pi akw yuku.* (ibid.)

If anything, the folklore and mythology overwhelmingly emphasize Maasaw's original characteristics.[21]

Various explanations for the change in conceptions about Maasaw have been offered. Tyler's theory that the Maasaw impersonator's humiliation during the 1891 confrontation at Oraibi required a change in the nature of the god is only one of many factors, as Malotki pointed out. A whole host of cultural, religious, and political events must have contributed to the changing perceptions of the god. Malotki also drew attention to the changing roles assumed by Maasaw, particularly in reference to the prophecies, where the god replaces the Pahaana as the apocryphal punisher, *powataniqa* ("the one who will purify"). This purification will occur when Maasaw uses his *qöötsaptanga*, ("jar of ashes"). Maasaw has become the beginning and the end of Hopi life: "I'm the first but I'm also going to be the last," *Pay pi as nu' mootiy'makyangw pay nu' piw naat nuutungktato* (Malotki and Lomatuway'ma 1987*b*:261).

It is precisely in the area of prophecy that Maasaw's change of nature is most noticeable, and since prophecy was mostly developed by the Traditionalists during the 1950s to the 1970s, I am convinced that Tyler's theory about the influence of Dan Qötshongva and Simon Scott in the changing perceptions of Maasaw is still viable. I would like to add the observation, however, that it seems as if this "Great Spirit" was developed in direct relation to the religious and apocryphal language of non-Hopi interest groups and not so much as part of an indigenous need to reformulate the nature of Maasaw. The term has indeed become more common in contemporary Hopi English, but even in situations where one would expect it to be used quite often (for example in the Mental Health Conference reports), it occurs hardly at all. I am therefore led to believe that it is more a rhetorical phrase than an ontological characterization.

Keeping these observations on Maasaw in mind, we must look at an-

20. The first thirty-two pages of Waters' book are too peculiar to be taken seriously. See A. W. Geertz 1983, 1987*b*, 1990*b* for my reasons.

21. See, for example, Malotki and Lomatuway'ma 1987*a*, as well as the older sources of Hopi mythology, such as Voth 1905, tales 3, 12, 17, 31, 32, 34, Curtis 1922:78, 102–103, 190–195, Stephen 1929, tales 3, 18, 20, 21, 22, 27, Wallis 1936, tales 1, 6, and Nequatewa 1936, tale 2, and pages 91, 121–123.

other important facet of the universalization of Hopi religion, i.e., that it became a missionary endeavor. Hopi religion, as Traditionalists spoke of it, now began to look like a new religion, partly because of the dialogue with non-Hopis and partly because personal piety and participation in agricultural ceremonies were replaced by personal piety and participation in the apocryphal mission.

At the same meeting of religious people in 1956, and with a strong belief in the fact that the creator was listening in on the meeting, Qötshongva's spokesman Ralph Tawangyawma stated:

> I believe that our main purpose here today is to bring forth these true messages from our Hopi people as it is now time that these truths and facts be known throughout the world. We want all of you to take our message and spread it throughout this land and into other countries. It is our desire that this should be done. We are waiting for our True White Brother. . . . We want Him to hear about this message so that He will come as soon as possible. (Bentley 1956:23)

This echoes Qötshongva's 1935 statement quoted in chapter 6. But the type of missionizing the Traditionalists had in mind was of a more instrumental nature. The goal was not to convert Whites to the Hopi religion, but to make use of a growing network of communication in order to catch the attention of the apocryphal Pahaana and speed him along on his predestined soteriological task. In other contexts, the missionizing took on a political nature where the tactic was the larger the following, the more effective the lobbying. In other words, Traditionalist rhetoric attempted to deal with the log-rolling mentality in Washington. Witness Qötshongva's closing speech in 1956:

> Then it has been told in the prophesies that the next step would be, once the people are informed, all will start to undermine the White House for a great wrong is being done by it to the Hopi (as a religious people we would not do such things to other tribes or nations or religions). Therefore, once religious people know these facts they will send letters, or anything, to the leaders in Washington, D.C., telling them to change their ways. We were told that under the whole stack of laws, perhaps at the very bottom, there are well-understood policies or plans, which, if once uncovered and taken out, would settle all this dictatorship for us without much trouble.[22] Who is going to be the person that will pull out the right paper? That person we will all start to look for. We know from our teachings that someone will go to the White House and sincerely look and turn the thing upside down in order to find it. That then we will move us on toward the Purification Day.

22. This prophecy was still alive in 1988 and was one of the hopes of the Office of Hopi Lands.

> That is how this Life Plan has been set out for us and that is what you wanted to find out. (ibid.:35)

It is first during the messianic stage of development, discussed in the following section, that the mission took on the full sense of the term, i.e., converting the world to the Hopi view of things.

Hopi prophecy did not grow in a vacuum, as chapter 5 has shown. By 1956 it became evident that the idea of Hopi land as the "sacred center" of the whole North American continent began finding its way into the rhetoric of non-Hopi supporters. One non-Hopi, Indian representative, who attended the 1956 meeting, expressed a view that has remained in pan-Indian thought ever since:

> I represent the League of North American Indians. It is an organization of Indians from all over the United States, Alaska and Canada. We stand up for Indians in trouble, whatever they are, or wherever they are. We are particularly interested in this area and some Indians as far as Indiana still consider this Hopi Land as the sacred center of this continent. We are looking to you and depending on you. Do not give up. You Hopi are one of the tribes that are the least touched by the white man, and the tribe that has lived here the longest. The welfare of the Hopis affects all the Indians on the continent and they are all interested to see that the Hopi Way is not changed. (ibid.:29–30)

Another example of this idea was reported to have been expressed by Mrs. Janet McCloud of Yelm, leader of an Indian movement in the Pacific northwest during the late 1960s, during a visit by Thomas Banancya: "Mrs. McCloud said that for her and for other Indians the Hopi homeland 'is the heart of our people' where they go 'just like a pilgrimage'" (Ruppert 1969:10).

Seen within the Hopi indigenous context, the idea of a sacred center is clearly an outgrowth of the original idea of Hopi land (especially Oraibi) as being the center of the world, an idea implicit to the six-directional system.[23] This idea is not unique to the Hopis, but is, on the contrary, commonly found throughout the world.

The idea became transformed into a literal geo/psychophysiology during the 1960s and the 1970s when "New Age" rhetoric was still in its infancy. Other centers of the world were replaced by this particular center near the Four Corner states.

As discussed in chapter 4, the Traditionalists produced a news bulletin called *Techqua Ikachi. Land and Life–The Traditional Viewpoint from the Hopi Nation* during the 1970s. It is evident that the language of the

23. See A. W. Geertz 1984, A. W. Geertz and Lomatuway'ma 1987:100 n. 11, Hieb 1979.

news bulletin was closely aligned to Californian New Age terminology and issues. Within this context, we find the sacred center idea fully developed, as the following quote from a speech given by David Monongya during the 70th anniversary of the village of Hotevilla illustrates:

> Hopiland we hold to be the center of the earth's body. It is the spot of power, with the duty to foretell the future by comparing the actions of mankind with the prophecy told to us. (Monongye 1976:3)

Shortly after the death of Mina Lansa, an anonymous article was published in *Techqua Ikachi* in 1978 which further illustrates my point:

> We are all aware that here as well as in other places certain mystical changes are occurring in society causing us to question our very basis of existence. Some of us know the sacred purposes and designs given to us by our creator and realize that the spirit dwells within all of us. But unfortunately, some other people, giving way to great ambitions, are trying to control others. Instead of correcting certain imbalances found in today's world, they are busy trading blame which further drains our planet of spiritual energy. These people are weaving self-destructive circles causing great harm to all land and life. (Anonymous 1978: 1)

It is equally significant to note that these words were a preamble to a political tirade against the five-million-dollar settlement with the Indian Claims Commission mentioned in chapter 5.

The Traditionalist Movement was at its height during this time. A whole series of non-Hopi movements and subcultures in the U.S. and Europe were using the Traditionalists as a symbol and focus for their own identity and their own battle against the technocratic worldview (strategic categories 4 and 5). I will return to these movements in chapter 10.

FROM UNIVERSALISM TO MESSIANISM

The 1960s saw the rise of a tremendous extrovertive activity on the part of the Traditionalists and a great influx of adorants. By this time Traditionalist activity was outright proselytical. Thus we find in the May 10, 1969, edition of the *Seattle Times*, Thomas Banancya hailed as "an unlikely appearing missionary":

> As a missionary sent by the Hopis to warn other Indians and all people, Banyayca has found a similarity of belief running like a thread through the religious thought of many Indian tribes. (Ruppert 1969)

By 1969 we find that it has all gone to Qötshongva's head. After Qötshongva's death the movement itself continued going strong throughout the 1970s and continually adjusted its image and language in order to remain the focal point and symbol for subversive groups (categories 3, 4, and 5).

Going back to what appears to be the beginning of Qötshongva's political downfall, we find the following statement in the minutes of a multicultural meeting held at Shongopovi on May 6–7, 1961, shortly after the death of Andrew Hermequaftewa:

> In a deeply moving, powerful declaration, Katchongva called upon the Sun as his witness, that he would not under any circumstances desert the Hopi way of life, and that from this moment forward he would give all of his energy to notify people throughout the land of the sacred teachings of the Hopi. In August, following his setting out of his crops and securing some food, he would convene another meeting, which would mark the first preparations for the Day of Purification. (Anonymous 1961:12–13)

In a talk recorded on January 29, 1970, Qötshongva told his account of the emergence myth and its prophecies. The account was published posthumously in several editions beginning the year of his death in 1972 (Tarbet 1972; Katchongva 1973; cf. Appendix B). In this message he successfully appropriated the many clan prophecies and collated them as if they were the prophecies of his own Sun clan. In one stroke he made both his clan and himself the saviors of humanity. Having claimed to have received the instructions and prophecies directly from the Great Spirit in primordial times, Qötshongva stated: "Since I am Sun Clan, and the Sun is the father of all living things, I love my children. If they realize what I am talking about *they must help me save this world*" (Tarbet 1972:20, emphasis mine). He continued:

> The Hopi have been placed on this side of the Earth to take care of the land through their ceremonial duties, just as other races of people have been placed elsewhere around the Earth to take care of her in their own ways. Together we hold the world in balance, revolving properly. If the Hopi nation vanishes the motion of the Earth will become eccentric, the water will swallow the land, and the people will perish. (ibid.)

In his final statement, Qötshongva himself approaches divine status:

> I am forever looking and praying eastward to the rising sun for my true white brother to come and purify the Hopi. My father, Yukiuma, used to tell me that I would be the one to take over as leader at this time, because I belong to the Sun Clan, the father of all the people on the Earth. I was told that I must not give in, because I am the first. The Sun is the father of all living things from the first creation. And if I am done, the Sun Clan, then there will be no living thing left on the earth. So I have stood fast.
>
> *I am the Sun, the father. With my warmth all things are created.* You are my children, and I am very concerned about you. *I hold you to protect you from harm,* but my heart is sad to see you leaving my protecting arms and de-

> stroying yourselves. From the breast of your mother, the Earth, you receive your nourishment, but she is too dangerously ill to give you pure food. What will it be? Will you lift your father's heart? Will you cure your mother's ills? Or will you forsake us and leave us with sadness, to be weathered away? *I don't want this world to be destroyed.*
>
> I have spoken through the mouth of the Creator. May the Great Spirit guide you on the right path. (ibid.:32–33, emphasis mine)

Thus, we see the gradual development of Hopi prophecy from local, apocryphal, clan traditions to universalism and, again, through occultism and nature mysticism to a final messianism.

EIGHT

On Charisma and the Downfall of a Prophet[1]

POWER STRUGGLES IN THE MOVEMENT

Whether Yukiwma foresaw the apotheoetic propensities in his son Dan is difficult to say. Our mysterious Mr. Johnson stated as much in 1955. He claimed that he had visited Yukiwma shortly before he died, and Yukiwma reportedly said the following to him:

> You have finally caught up with me so I might as well give in and tell you I had been willing to sacrifice my head but my plan did not materialize. The white man is not willing to cut off my head. One of these days I am going to die and when I die I want you to go to my son and tell him definitely not to follow in my footsteps. Knowing his nature, he is a proud man, and no doubt he will want to grab and usurp the powers that were vested upon me. Tell him that when I go to my grave that my knowledge goes with me; that I pass my knowledge on to no one else. (Bureau of Indian Affairs 1955:170)

This speech may be more a contemporary criticism of Qötshongva's struggle with Pongyayawma over the office of village chief during the late 1940s than a true quote of Yukiwma's words. At any rate, Qötshongva lost his following primarily due to two things: the political machinations of David Monongya and his own participation in Paul Solem's flying-saucer cult.

At the 1955 hearings Qötshongva explained how he had organized the trip to Washington which eventually led to the hearings. This de-

1. Portions of this chapter were published in Danish in A. W. Geertz 1989*c*. I wish to extend my thanks to Professor Tove Tybjerg at the University of Copenhagen for helpful comments and criticisms.

scription indicates the type of relationship he had with his advisors. After finding a supporter from the Kookop clan, "the keepers of the stone tablet," and from the Spider clan, he found Monongya, who belonged to the clan that "deals with the earth"—some sources say the Sand clan and others the Pumpkin clan[2]—and Ralph Tawangyawma, who belonged to the clan that "deals with the food of the people," which refers to the Piikyas clan (ibid.:259).

By 1960 Monongya and Banancya had taken on the roles of Qötshongva's interpreters and spokesmen—roles that were the prerogative of Ralph and Carolyne Tawangyawma, Ralph being one of the contenders to the chieftainship after Qötshongva.

After meeting the Chinese Buddhist priest (mentioned in chapter 2) in 1962, Qötshongva was convinced that the priest was the Pahaana. Now that he had met the real White Brother, "he was handing over the job of protecting the Hopi to Thomas and others, while Dan himself retired" (Nagata 1978:78). During that episode, Nagata quoted Banancya as directly countermanding a request from Qötshongva to Nagata (ibid.: 81). This probably indicated that conflicts of interest were at stake at this time.

In an interview with Qötshongva at Hotevilla on May 8, 1963, the leader said that Banancya and Monongya were his "ear and tongue":

> They have my authority to listen and speak for me and they will convey all messages to me in turn. They have my authority to represent me and those who wish to [talk] with me can talk with them to inform or get information. It would be ill for anyone for whatever motive to try to deceive these two men. They have my authority to serve and represent me. (Anonymous 1963:3)

But things were evidently not what they seemed to be. In *Pumpkin Seed Point* Waters described how Monongya, whom he called "Mr. Hopi," used Waters' presence and his project as a political wedge against Qötshongva.[3] Speaking about Qötshongva's career, Waters wrote:

> Now that he was getting old and his power was waning, Mister Hopi emerged as a would-be contender for leadership. Mister Hopi, however, belonged to a minor clan without a ceremony or any standing whatever. He

2. This is an excellent example of the notion of "negotiable clan identity" noted by Whiteley (1988:180). See chapter 1.

3. Although Frank Waters does not provide dates in his book, *Pumpkin Seed Point* (1969), he describes events that occurred during the research phase of his *Book of the Hopi*. The latter contains no dates in the introduction; however, comparing the footnote commentary with the anterior date of publication, the research phase was a three-year period, 1959–1962. See Waters 1963:39, 69, 189, 209, 214, 219.

> needed something with which he could nudge tottering Old Dan off his insecure throne. That, I saw now, was Old Dan's disgraceful sponsorship of us two spies under the bountiful pay of the government or a white church. It had worked. We were out, and it looked as if Old Dan were out too. Still, one never knew. Old Dan was not the son of the indomitable and irascible Yukioma for nothing. In the intricate game of Hopi politics he might merely have sacrificed White Bear and me to gain more worthy ends. The incident, tragic-comic as it was, turned out to our advantage. But I missed Old Dan. It was months before I saw him again. A public meeting was called in the abandoned schoolhouse near Shongopovi on Second Mesa. Mister Hopi and his cohorts were there in a vociferous body to protest the acceptance of state welfare benefits by any impoverished Hopis because such dependence would destroy their faith in the Creator. After the meeting was over, I happened to see Old Dan come limping up the road in his ragged red sweater. Mister Hopi and his other former leaders had not offered to bring him. So Old Dan had walked and hitchhiked the twenty miles. He did not speak, but I saw in his sweat-filled eyes a look of warm recognition and ironic amusement.
>
> What an admirable old rascal he was! Dispossessed in the field of secular affairs, like Yukioma, he functioned only in the mystic realm of rituals, dreams, and visions—a true Hopi. (1969:38)

So, evidently a power struggle occurred between Qötshongva and Monongya, which left the latter as victor. This may account for why we do not find any close association between them after that. By 1970, at least, the Tawangyawmas were once again Qötshongva's interpreters and spokesmen.

It is difficult to reconcile the forceful messiah described in the last chapter with this seemingly pitiable predecessor ten years earlier. Monongya and Banancya dominated the activities of the 1960s, and Qötshongva became a messiah without a following by 1970.

THE FLYING SAUCER CULT

Evidently, one of the final blows to Qötshongva's position among the Traditionalists was his involvement with the "Flying Saucer Prophet," Paul Solem. During the period of approximately August 5th to August 21st, 1970, numerous nighttime sightings of unidentified flying objects were reported by hundreds of witnesses in Prescott, Arizona. One of the most memorable sightings occurred on Friday, August 7th, described here by a reporter from the *Prescott Courier* and accompanied by a photograph taken by a staff photographer at Highland Pine lookout:

> I stood in a backyard in Prescott with several neighbors and watched spellbound for almost a half hour Friday. It looked like a star—almost. It rose in

> the sky, stopped, hovered, wavered to one side and then continued across the sky repeating the maneuvers. It was a long ways away, but we thought it changed colors from a white to a reddish orange and then to a purplish blue and then a reddish white. And then it was gone. A flying saucer? Yes, if we could believe our eyes (Kraus 1970:1).

A man from Idaho by the name of Paul Solem explained that the flying saucers were appearing because he was calling them there. They had first revealed themselves to him in 1948 and had followed him all over the country ever since, where he would provide opportunities for a series of sightings. According to Solem, "the sightings will continue [in the Prescott area] until the message of why they came is given."

The following description, provided by Joe Kraus, managing editor of the *Prescott Courier*, describes the August 7th sighting in another way:

> He stood off by himself, alone Friday, gazing into the sky while the rest of us watched only a few feet away. He was calling–mentally, he said. And then after about 15 minutes he yelled–"They are here. I can't see them yet, but I know they are here. One just said, 'We're here, Paul!' There are several people in the saucer. I can hear them talking."
>
> After a couple of minutes a star appeared in the sky that wasn't there before. It looked at a dead stop. And then it started to move, first to one direction and then the other.
>
> As the saucer hovered overhead, Solem repeated to us the words he said he heard through mental telepathy from the space craft.
>
> "My name is Paul, the second, fourth in command of all ships that enter the atmosphere of the planet called Earth. We come to lend credence and as a sign or token that the Hopi prophecy was of a divine [sic] nature. Great sorrow and fear will be coming to this planet very soon and few will escape it. Our leader as spoken of in Hopi prophecy is already here (on Earth) in mortality and is known as the Apostle John (the same as in the New Testament). The white brother shall be introduced by a huge fire and the Earth shall quake at his arrival. We are of the 10 lost tribes and we will return several nights unless there is contempt for us."
>
> The remarks then ended, the saucer disappeared. (1970:1–2)

This highly syncretistic/eclectic statement raises the question of the sources of Solem's information and/or inspiration. Kraus wrote further:

> Since his first saucer contacts in 1948 in Idaho he has become an expert in Mormon doctrine and the Hopi prophecy. According to Solem, Mormon scripture teaches that the keys which the Latter-Day Saints Church holds will in the last days be turned over to the American Indians.
>
> Not a Mormon or a Hopi, Solem says for the most part members of both religious and Indian groups have fallen away from their original teachings. He added this has happened today, just as the original church had fallen away following the death of the apostles. But Solem said both

> groups do have the doctrine, the same as in the beginning, for those who will believe.
>
> "There is no reason to fear these people," Solem said later in a personal interview. "They are like Angels. They come from the planet Venus and they are here only to lend credence to prophecy, not to harm anyone."
>
> Solem said they look just like humans, but of almost a divine [sic] quality. They have hair cut neatly to their shoulders and due to their fine qualities and almost musical tone to their voices it is difficult to tell male from female.[4]
>
> He said the saucer people contacted him in Idaho, called him by name and told him that in a previous life before living on this planet, he had lived with them on Venus. He said they told him he is among many people on earth with a similar background many of whom will accept the call to work with them in fulfilling prophecy.
>
> Since that first saucer contact Solem said he has been directed to several areas where he would speak to people about the prophecy and they in turn would come as a sign that it is true. This, he says, is why he is now in the Prescott area working not only with several Indian tribes, but with others as well. (ibid.:2)

This event did not escape Qötshongva's attention. He had been waiting for something like this ever since the beginning of the 1960s, and had met with Solem in 1969. The day after the front-page story on the August 7th sightings, the headlines of Monday the 10th read "Hopi Chief Arrives for Saucer Contact," accompanied by a photograph of Paul Solem, Dan Qötshongva, Ralph Tawangyawma, and Carolyne Tawangyawma. They had come in order to witness the sighting that was to occur on the evening of August 10th:

> Chief Katchongva said he desires to make contact, ask for direction and to learn when the great migration of Indians in Hopi prophecy is to occur. According to the chief, flying saucers are not new to the Hopi. They play a big part in Indian history, he said, and are drawn on petrograph rocks near the Hopi mesas in Northern Arizona. (Anonymous 1970*a*:1)

Cloudy conditions had evidently prevented the sighting, however. Solem was later quoted as saying, "The last day Chief Dan Katchongua of the Hopi Nation was here the ship came in real low, about 800 feet" (Anonymous 1970*b*:1).

During that eventful week a poster[5] appeared on the door of Se-

4. See the recent article by Bullard (1989) on the stereotypical characteristics of flying-saucer accounts and their relation to legends of supernatural encounters and otherworldly journeys. Of particular interest are themes concerning prophecies and warnings and encounters with divine beings. See also Drees (1990).

5. Thanks to Louis A. Hieb for the information on the poster. His notes are housed at Cline Library, Special Collections Department, Northern Arizona University, Flagstaff.

hongva's store in Hotevilla, which proclaimed that the Hopis were to listen to an important message, "Hopi Prophecy and Flying Saucers," on radio station KCLS at 9:30 A.M. on Wednesday and station KINO at 9:00 A.M. on Thursday, "by order of Chief Dan Katchongva and Ralph Tawangyawma." The poster was illustrated with drawings of a flying saucer and a supposed petroglyph from Second Mesa accompanied by the text "Second Mesa petroglyph shows flying-saucer; Hopi woman–purity; dome shape–flying saucer; arrow–travel through space to other planets." The fact that the poster was also filled with graffitti written by villagers, such as "Chief is crazy," did not prevent Qötshongva from issuing a warning in October to "the Pueblo Indians and to all people everywhere" that the day of purification was close at hand:

> We come to warn all people of what is going to take place soon. Great judgements and punishments to those who do not turn to the Great Spirit for guidance . . . and to those who have forgotten the teachings of Maasau, the Great Spirit.
>
> We, the traditional Hopi, know that our true white brother is coming with great power to cleanse this land. He will bring with him the sacred stone tablets matching the ones we now have. None will stand against him. All power will be placed in his hands.
>
> We know the faithful are to be gathered to escape purification day. Therefore when the great fire and explosion takes place, it will be seen all over North and South America and the earth will shake. Therefore, when the true white brother comes, listen to him and gather when the power comes from the south.
>
> We give you our testimony and all that we tell you is true. So you have no excuse that you were not told. (Rushton 1970)

It is clear from the above quote that Qötshongva had incorporated new elements from Solem's interpretations into Hopi prophecy. Our documents indicate that Qötshongva considered the Mormons to be his allies, if not politically then at least in spirit (cf. Kotchongva 1936, mentioned in chapter 5). During the meeting in Hotevilla in 1956 he explained some of his thoughts on the Mormons:

> I know the Mormons have their own beliefs and that they too have suffered great persecutions because of them, just as has Hotevilla Village. As I understand their teachings and beliefs, they know that this land does belong to the Indian people and that the present persecuted life of the Indian must be raised. They will keep their eyes on the Future Day and help to keep the Indian culture from destruction. They will look for someone who has held fast to the Great Spirit's Indian teachings, someone who will be preserved and not destroyed. It was then that the Mormon people were to help uplift him and in that way he would have a part in helping to preserve the Righteous (Hopi) way of life. (Bentley 1956:20)

It is equally clear that Qötshongva had his own peculiar ideas about the Mormons, and, so, instead of wholesale borrowing from the Mormons, we find one small item and a niche for the Mormons in the Hopi worldview.

Sightings had also occurred at Hotevilla when Solem visited that village. Independent witnesses told me eight years later in 1978 that saucers were sighted in Hotevilla. Even Pongyayawma admitted to me during an interview in 1988 that Qötshongva and Solem, together with a group of hippies and other supporters, had waited for sightings that were reported to have occurred near Apoonivi (the place of judgment for individual souls on their way to afterlife in the underworld—a truly fitting stage for apocryphal drama) and also at Suwuminewa's field in 1970.[6] But he was convinced that this was just one more attempt by Qötshongva to promote himself as a great prophet and magician who could invoke the presence of flying saucers and do other wonderful things. In Pongyayawma's opinion, Qötshongva was under the sway of his White supporters and had fallen from the Hopi way. Pongyayawma's conclusion was based on the fact that the prophecies as he knew them did not support Qötshongva's saucer-inspired interpretations.

Let us briefly raise the question of the reliability of Pongyayawma as a witness. As chart C indicates, the line of chiefs and/or political leaders in Oraibi and Hotevilla is a colorful and highly inconsequent series of inheritance practices.[7] When Yukiwma, the founder of Hotevilla, died in 1929, there were three contenders to his office: 1) Poliwuhiwma of the Spider clan, who was the nephew of the Oraibian rebel leader, Lomahongyiwma; 2) Pongyayawma of the Kookop clan, who was Yukiwma's nephew and therefore the legitimate heir according to traditional heritage practice; and 3) Qötshongva of the Sun clan, who was Yukiwma's son. Poliwuhiwma evidently had the required prestige, being the chief of the Soyalangw—an office usually owned by the village chief—and so he became village chief. But he died shortly thereafter and the chieftainship passed on to Pongyayawma.

Pongyayawma was too young to assume the duties of village chief, and so Qötshongva functioned in his stead during the 1930s. According to Clemmer, a meeting was held around 1943 during which Qötshongva formally invested Pongyayawma with his office (1978*b*:36). The event was described by Lewis Numkena at Moenkopi during the 1955 hearings:

> I learned that during Commissioner Collier's time there was a meeting at Kyakotsmovi where Dan acted as spokesman and told the committee there

6. Qötshongva's "Hopi Prophecy" text quoted below confirms this part of the story by naming Suwuminewa (Paul Sewaemanewa) as one of the faithful.

7. See Titiev 1944:207, 211, A. W. Geertz and Lomatuway'ma 1987:123, n. 31.

ORAIBI CHIEFS	HOTEVILLA CHIEFS	HOSTILES & TRADITIONALISTS
Talayyawma chief 1825?-1850? (Squash Clan)		
Nakwayyamptiwa chief 1850?-d.1865? (Bear Clan, an albino)		HOSTILES (Oraibi) 1880
Kuyingwu 1865?-1880 (regent, Water Coyote Clan) [Moenkopi established as colony ca. 1870]		The core Hostile leadership in Oraibi around 1880 were: Patupha (Kookop Clan); Tuvewuhiwma (Spider Clan); Heevi'ima (Kookop Clan); Talay'ima (or: Kuyangayniwa, Spider Clan)
Sakwhongiwma & Loololma (co-rulers during the last years of Kuyingwu's regency, Bear Clan, sons of Kuyingwu)		
Loololma 1880-d.1904 (the youngest of the sons becomes chief of Oraibi) [Sakwhongiwma performs the Soyalangw on Loololma's behalf; Loololma becomes pro-American not long after 1880]		Lomahongyiwma 1894-1904 (Talay'ima's nephew, Spider Clan) [Becomes rival to Loololma for chieftainship]
Tawakwaptiwa chief 1904-1906 (Bear Clan, Loololma's nephew)		Yukiwma 1904-1906 (Kookop Clan) [Becomes rival to Tawakwaptiwa for chieftainship]
ORAIBI SPLIT IN 1906	HOTEVILLA ESTABLISHED IN 1906	
[Tawakwaptiwa forced residence in Riverside, CA, 1906-1909]	Yukiwma chief 1906-1929 (Kookop Clan)	Yukiwma (now in Hotevilla, continues resistance, dies 1929)
Interim Ruling Commission: Principal of Oraibi Day School, Kuyangayniwa & Kewanimptewa		
SECOND SPLIT IN 1909		
Tawakwaptiwa chief 1909-d.1960		
[Bacavi establ. in 1909 by Kewanimptewa, Sand Clan]		
[Kykotsmovi establ. ca. 1920]	Poliwuhiwma chief 1929 (Spider Clan, Lomahongyiwma's nephew)	
	Qötshongva (Sun Clan, Yukiwma's son) & Pongyayawma (Kookop Clan, Yukiwma's nephew) co-rulers 1930-1943	
	Pongyayawma chief 1943-1950 (leaves Hotevilla around 1950)	TRADITIONALISTS (Hotevilla) 1948
	Qötshongva chief 1950-d.1972	Qötshongva 1948-d.1972, nominal leader 1960ff.
	Tawangyawma 1972 (dies before taking office)	Monongya 1948-d.1988, real leader 1960ff.
Mina Lansa chief 1960-d.1978 (Parrot Clan, adopted child of Tawakwaptiwa, only female chief in recent Hopi history)	Pongyayawma chief 1972-d.1989 (comes back around 1967, assumes rule after Qötshongva's death)	Mina Lansa (Oraibi, leader 1970-1978, for a brief period has greater political base than Monongya)
Bahnimptewa chief 1978- (Parrot Clan, adopted child of Tawakwaptiwa)	Kyarwisiwma chief 1989- (Kookop Clan, Pongyayawma's nephew)	Banancya (Kykotsmovi, Water Coyote Clan, spokesman 1960ff.)

Chart C. The line of chiefs in Oraibi and Hotevilla and the leaders of the Hostiles/Traditionalists on Third Mesa.

> that he was not a recognized Kikmongwi [i.e., village chief], but his purpose was only to be an advisor to James, and that he was instructed by his father to teach James of these things because James Ponyoinyowma was still a young man. He told that these things were instructed to him by his father, and after talking there for quite a length of time Dan made the statement that the time had now come that James was of mature age where he, himself, would take upon himself this responsibility. After explaining these things, Dan brought out a stone tablet, and he passed this tablet out among the members of the committee, and the Commissioner after studying this stone tablet, Mr. Collier said he did not know what the tablet speaks of. Dan asked him if he could analyze the writings thereon, but Mr. Collier said he could not, but the only thing Mr. Collier told him was that his guess was that the stone tablet was to be used in the next world to come. After these things were explained to the committee there, Dan gave the stone to James Ponyoinyowma, declaring that he was now in full authority to stand as the leader for Hotevilla Village. These things were brought to light at that meeting, but as time went on and later in the years, Dan began to present himself as being the leader of that village, and the trouble began between these two men. Dan Katchongva committed a crime against James by commiting adultery upon his household, so then in a year that went on and the woman passed away. This left James without anything to look forward to, so therefore, James, who is the proper Kikmongwi of Hotevilla, left the reservation and is now living in Albuquerque, and according to his testimony he will return in time, but not yet because he is watching the movements of Dan to see what he would carry out here among the Hopi people. (Bureau of Indian Affairs 1955:285–286; cf. Waters 1963:383–384)

Clemmer wrote that the cause of the conflict was political (1978*b*:36), but it seems more likely that a combination of factors is the root here. Exactly when this falling out occurred is difficult to confirm. Wayne Sekaquaptewa (1976) wrote that this had already happened by 1940, but this may be an oversight. At any rate, Qötshongva consolidated his position with the help of a "power bloc which consisted of many of the high priests of the reconstituted orders," according to Wayne Sekaquaptewa (1976). Pongyayawma returned again—Clemmer wrote that this happened in 1967—but remained in a political vacuum until the 1970s.

As noted above, in the 1960s when Qötshongva became older and more involved in preparing for the coming day of purification, Monongya of the Pumpkin clan rose to prominence. His supporters were political activists and not priestly leaders.

Whiteley has argued convincingly that the split of Oraibi in 1906 was a conscious attempt to end the ritual order, with all that it implied; in other words, a veritable democratization of the ecclesiastical hegemony. As one of his Hotevilla consultants claimed, the old division of pavansinom/söqavungsinom was to be suspended and the basis for chiefly and priestly office was to be destroyed. This meant, in the words of a Hotevilla consultant, that "those claiming authority in Hotevilla, or anywhere else on Third Mesa, by their religious offices, don't really have it" (1988: 258).

Whereas Hotevillian attempts to recreate the ritual order succeeded for a while, the attempts ultimately failed because of the problem of legitimacy. So we find a contradiction in Hotevilla history consisting of the democratization of Hopi society, on the one hand, and the semblance of a ritual-knowledge-based, hierarchical society, on the other. Qötshongva could maintain a seat of power, even though his father forbade it, because he was the son of a powerful man and a member of an important clan and because his major opponent, Pongyayawma, had left the village in his hands. His political verve and strong personality secured his position as well in the face of democratization mechanisms. However, as we have seen, as soon as people began to suspect his sanity, his support quickly dwindled to virtually nothing.

Monongya had other problems to cope with. He was politically agile and subtle and had little trouble out-maneuvering Qötshongva, but he was from a lower-class clan and did not participate in religious activities even though he purportedly held religious office. His power base was gained through an uncompromising stance against the Tribal Council, which attracted some support at home and the untiring support of non-Hopis for reasons of their own.

Qötshongva died in February 1972 and was succeeded by his former spokesman, Ralph Tawangyawma of the Piikyas clan, who died before he even took office. Monongya thus took over the leadership, but, of course, not the office. James Pongyayawma once again asserted himself during the 1970s as the Traditionalist star waxed and waned. Progressively minded people at Hotevilla and the Hotevilla Village Committee became aggressively anti-Traditionalist, and especially anti-Monongya, and they considered Pongyayawma to be the lawful village chief. While thousands of White Monongya adorants besieged Hotevilla year in and year out, the villagers became more and more angry, and Monongya began losing his Hopi supporters (cf. A. W. Geertz 1987*c*). As Sekaquaptewa wrote: "Many villagers said that this man and his supporters have created more turmoil than anyone else since the Hotevilla people left Old Oraibi" (1978). Sekaquaptewa was strongly anti-Traditionalist, but this statement is mild compared to the widespread vehemence I experienced in Hotevilla during my first stay in 1978–1979. A common experience for White visitors to Hotevilla was to be questioned, sometimes outright, sometimes more subtly, until it became clear to the inquisitive whether the visitor was one of Monongya's followers. I have also witnessed how inquiring visitors were told, with the typical Hopi sense of humor, that Monongya had passed away. Unfortunately, most reactions were of disgust, irritation, and anger.

Already during the late 1970s, Thomas Banancya of the Water Coyote clan from Kykotsmovi began vying for the leadership post. Carolyne Tawangyawma, however, was also a contender. Monongya died in Hotevilla on April 9, 1988, and no successor was apparent when I was there. Banancya is the most influential of the two contenders and will probably become the last leader of a dying movement, but he was not able to contend with Pongyayawma, who had already named his successor before he died. Pongyayawma died in 1989 and the village chieftainship was passed on to his nephew Martin Kyarwisiwma of the Kookop clan. Time will tell whether he will succeed in reifying the chieftainship in Hotevilla affairs. It seems as if Kyarwisiwma's political career was over even before it began. As mentioned in chapter 6, Kyarwisiwma was evidently persuaded by Banancya to present the Kookop tablets to the governor-elect of New Mexico in 1990 and to issue the "fourth and final warning" about the immanent destruction of the world. My consultants claimed in 1992 that he left the tablets with Governor-elect Bruce King and when he returned to Hotevilla he was forced to go back and get them again, whereupon he was promptly dethroned and the village leadership was taken over by the chief of the Kwan Kiva. Banancya was reportedly physically removed from a public meeting that was being held on the issue. Even though he was a major actor in the affair, he was nevertheless an unwanted outsider. A movie is being produced about the event and, characteristically enough, the transcripts of Kyarwisiwma's speech and Banancya's translation show little resemblance to one another.

It should be clear now why Pongyayawma had a vested interest in presenting Qötshongva's activities in a negative light. But the external evidence supports the substance of his commentary.

Qötshongva's saucer cult evidently meshed well with the prophetic framework. By October 1970 Qötshongva was characteristically pronouncing profoundly moralistic commands to his supporters. As Carolyne Tawangyawma told reporters,

> These are the last warnings, these flying saucers coming over. . . . The Day of Purification will come within this generation. . . . Only through their original teachings will they [Hopis and non-Indians] receive salvation." (Rushton 1970:12)

Qötshongva's statement to those same reporters was:

Do not drink strong drink. Stop all light mindedness. Live sober so that the Great Spirit may guide you through what is coming. Do not listen to rock and roll music, it will cast a spell on you. Young women dress so that your appeal is not to the body. Let our Indian people be an example to all people. (ibid.)

By the end of the year an official pamphlet from the "Hopi Independent Nation, Hotevilla, Arizona U.S.A." printed "Chief Dan Katchongva's Message." The pamphlet was illustrated with the above-mentioned Second Mesa petroglyph and a flying saucer (see illustrations in figure 15). Under the heading "Hopi Prophecy," Qötshongva opened with an abbreviated summary of the emergence and migration themes followed by specific references to the saucer cult:

Our petroglyph near Mishongnovi on second mesa placed upon the rocks in the beginning describes "flying saucers" and travel through space. The arrow on which the dome shaped object rests, stands for travel through space. The Hopi maiden on the dome shape represents PURITY. Those HOPI who survive Purification Day will travel to other planets. We, the faithful HOPI, have seen the ships and know they are true. We believe other Planets are inhabited and that our prayers are heard there. We have watched nearly all of our brethren lose faith in the original Teachings and go off on their own course. Near Oraibi was clearly shown the Plan of Life and we know that those who have forsaken the original teachings will pay with their lives when the True White Brother comes.

We Hopi Traditionalists were divided in 1906 when my father Chief You-kew-ma and those who would not adopt white man's way were beaten and driven out by our own people. We took the trail to the land which is now known as Hotevilla. It was prophesied in the beginning that we would divide three times. The second division took place in 1969 when Paul Solem came and contacted the "flying saucers" and they flew over and whispered their message. Shortly before Mr. Solem came, Titus Quomayumtewa saw a "flying saucer" and the Kachina that piloted it. Paul Sewaemanewa saw the saucer years before when he had made his prayer rites. These two men are of the faithful. We know we are to be divided once more and few will be left just before our True White Brother arrives with the matching pieces of stone tablet. Many Hopi men wear bang hair cut that represents a window from which they continue to look for the True White Brother. Our land was also prophesied to be divided four times each cut smaller than the other. This was fulfilled by three highways. Our prophecy states that a "Power from the south" will come to help when the time comes and we know this will be fulfilled soon. We know the faithful are to be gathered near Old Oraibi when our True White Brother comes—and we are waiting.

I, Chief Dan Katchongva, my counselor, Ralph Tawangyawma and the faithful, wish to tell you all that the time is close and advise you all to return to your original teachings. (Skidmore 1970:1)

Figure 15. Symbols drawn on Qötshongva's flying-saucer statement.
SOURCE: Skidmore 1970.

The paper is signed by Carolyn Tawangyawma, interpreter, Nonnie S. Skidmore, corresponding secretary in Prescott, and Chief Dan Katchongva.

Qötshongva evidently admitted in this text that a fall-out had occurred among the Traditionalists in 1969 due to the presence of Paul Solem. It is significant that neither Monongya nor Banancya is mentioned in this text and that neither of the two ever mentioned the event in his letters and articles thereafter. Still, the rest of the pamphlet, which contains "Briefly Hopi Ancient Teachings and Prophecy," is an exact replica of the letter written by Banancya to M. Muller-Fricken in 1961. Thus, we have a documentary demonstration of three layers of lore: the Traditionalist prophetic corpus of 1961, Paul Solem's eclectic mormonized ideas, and Qötshongva's own prophecies in connection with the flying saucers. It is noticeable that Solem's Mormon idea about the Indian migrations from the south has been incorporated by Qötshongva, but it is not mentioned at all in the rest of the pamphlet. Thus, it is reasonable to assume that the idea does not belong to the Traditionalist prophetic corpus.

Comparing the "Briefly Hopi Ancient Teachings and Prophecy" text with Qötshongva's father's (Yukiwma's) text (see Appendix B), one is struck by the undeniable distance between the two accounts. Qötshongva's last text of 1970 resembles more his father's tale and tones down the apocalyptic detail of the Banancya text, but emphasizes Qötshongva's divine nature–an idea equally foreign to indigenous thought.

The flying-saucer cult evidently played a major role in Qötshongva's political downfall. As Clemmer wrote:

> In 1971, however, Katchongva seemed to be slipping in matters of judgment, perhaps because of his advanced age. He became vulnerable to one of the many unbalanced and unscrupulous non-Indians who wandered through the Indian reservations in the late 1960s and early 1970s looking for a free lunch and a free ride (this particular individual tried to convince

> people he could communicate with flying saucers), and the heads of the other religious societies in Hotevilla decided to collectively remove Katchongva from the responsibilities of Kikmongwi. A year later, Katchongva died. (1978*b*:36)

A modification is in place here: Qötshongva's downfall had already begun in the early 1960s. His evident removal in 1971 was just the final blow.[8]

THE QUESTION OF CHARISMA

Whether Qötshongva's story is that of a man never having experienced prophetic revelation yet being driven by hybrid-clan "tradition" is not really relevant in a context that denies per se the concept of prophetic "revelation." The fact of the matter is that during his early years he had marked support from outsiders, nominal support at home, and during his later years hardly any support at all. I have explained the political and cultural factors that were behind Qötshongva's career. Turning now to a discussion of the role of charisma in Qötshongva's career and to the complexities of charisma in Traditionalist history, we may discover some insights relevant to sociological theory.

The problem in applying Max Weber's concept of the ideal types of domination, of which charisma is the third type, is twofold. First of all, as Weber pointed out himself, these ideal types do not exist in historical and social reality (1911–1913:124). Furthermore, his ideas about charisma are clearly a product of his reaction against the philosophical, ideological, and political climate of his time, which were not necessarily universally binding.[9] And, as Talcott Parsons noted in the Introduction to Weber's *Sociology of Religion*, many of his detailed facts and interpretations cannot be considered reliable today (Parsons 1963:xxvi). Secondly, the actual historical and social example presented by Qötshongva and the rise of the Traditionalist Movement is of such complexity that Weber's ideal types are of little use. As I will show, the Hopi example is an equal blend of Weber's second and third types, traditional domination and charismatic domination.

I will concentrate on two aspects of charisma in this section, namely, the semiotic and the psychological. By charisma and charismatic persons, I follow the definition by Shils:

8. See Festinger, Riecken, and Schachter 1956 for an in-depth study of a flying-saucer cult.

9. Bendix 1968:499–500; Bendix and Roth 1971:72–94; C. Geertz 1977; Brian Turner 1981:142–176.

> Charisma . . . is the quality which is imputed to persons, actions, roles, institutions, symbols, and material objects because of their presumed connection with "ultimate," "fundamental," "vital," order-determining powers.
> Those persons who possess an intense subjective feeling of their own charismatic quality, and who have it imputed to them by others, we will call charismatic persons. (1968:386)

Clifford Geertz, in his 1977 contribution to a volume dedicated to Shils, approached the subject from a semiotic point of view. He resisted the overwhelming emphasis on a psychological interpretation of Weber's thoughts on charisma by following Edward Shils' work (1958, 1961, 1965), which can best be formulated in Shils' own words:

> The charismatic quality of an individual as perceived by others, or himself, lies in what is thought to be his connection with (including possession by or embodiment of) some *very central* feature of man's existence and the cosmos in which he lives. The centrality, coupled with intensity, makes it extraordinary. (1965:201)

Geertz emphasized the connection between "the symbolic value individuals possess and their relation to the active centers of the social order." (1977:122) He concluded that

> no matter how peripheral, ephemeral, or free-floating the charismatic figure we may be concerned with--the wildest prophet, the most deviant revolutionary—we must begin with the center and with the symbols and conceptions that prevail there if we are to understand him and what he means. (ibid.:143)

We have seen the symbols, conceptions, and cultural institutions that made Qötshongva what he was. Taking up on the implications of Shils' use of the idea of a sacred center, there are a number of matters that require our attention.[10]

As I noted elsewhere (1984:230–231), the idea of the center is a significant factor not only in Hopi cosmology, but also in Hopi political ideology. The idea of the center runs through Hopi culture as an ever-present sign at every location where one finds significance and meaning.

10. It is no coincidence that Shils' theory has a certain appeal to this study. In his autobiographical introduction to his collection of selected papers on the subject—actually, a biography of the history of his ideas—Shils wrote:

> I read Professor Mircea Eliade's *The Myth of the Eternal Return* (London: Kegan Paul, 1955), which interpreted rituals as reconstitutions of the moment of origin, only on the occasion of its appearance in English translation. This was about the time when I first began to think about center and periphery and about the sacred overtones of centrality. It made my way somewhat easier. (1975:xxxvii, n. 17)

Thus, we find a series of center/periphery relationships along every major dimension in Hopi culture: cosmology, politics, social space, social relations, ritual, gender relations, and even national relations.

Concerning cosmology, according to the emergence myth, humanity emerged from the huge birth canal of the primordial center of the world, the sipaapuni. Clan migration myths then relate how separate groups of people explored the new world and developed their own historical identities. Even though these narratives are widely divergent, they all nevertheless have one overriding theme, namely, that the travelling clans were irresistibly drawn towards Tuuwanasavi, the historical and present center of the world.

Concerning politics, the cultural construction of political power is based on the same "world center" model. As we have seen in chapters 1 and 6, Hopi society is based on a hierarchy of clans which draw their power from esoteric knowledge and invested ritual objects. Even though the ecclesiastical hegemony is hierarchical, it is not vertical, as we would conceive of it, but centripetal, as Hopis conceive of all ritual and cosmological matters.[11] The migrations and arrivals of the various clans in clan mythology constituted a process of gradual accretion, where the Bear clan, which allegedly arrived first, became the epicenter of power and was instrumental in the distribution of the power of others.

Concerning social space, the most centrally placed houses (residing at the heart of the village, or the *kiisonvi*, the plaza) were in principle owned by the most powerful clans. And the best-placed lands, situated closest to the village, were owned by centrally placed clans (in the migration narrative "historical" sense).

Concerning social relations, Whiteley has shown that the class division between pavansinom and söqavungsinom also applies within the clans. Thus, using the Bear clan as an example, the *kiikyam* was that group of centrally placed lineages within the Bear clan that provided the kikmongwi, "village chief" (1988:66). Again, the idea of a center is implied.

Concerning ritual, at the heart of every clan, which carries with it the memory and power of primordial events, is the *tiiponi.* The tiiponi is the "mother" of the clan, its "source," and is placed in the center of clan ritual paraphernalia and/or altars during ceremonial events where it constitutes a central focus of power. The tiiponi is itself an object with a central core consisting of a corncob that is packed in cotton string and other objects of cultural significance. Furthermore, the whole structure of the kiva, its altars, the ritual songs, and the ritual movements are based on

11. A. W. Geertz 1984:232; A. W. Geertz and Lomatuway'ma 1987:100 n. 11.

centripetal action and symbology (cf. A. W. Geertz 1984).[12] The same holds true for the ritual sodalities as well as for their cult houses. The kivas represent a chain of centers of ritual power, all of which contain replicas of the symbol of the center par excellence, i.e., the sipaapuni (cf. A. W. Geertz and Lomatuway'ma 1987:91).

Concerning gender relations, Whiteley's structural argument on the division of gender in economic, ritual, and political affairs is useful here (1988:164). In economic matters, the women and their households stand at the center in relation to the men and their fields at the periphery. In ritual and political matters, the men and their kivas stand at the center in relation to the women and their houses at the periphery.

How did this evidently fundamental idea of the center and periphery affect Qötshongva's political career? The trappings of power associated with the center were in his possession: He had the stone tablet and the ritual knowledge not only of a chief (he was, after all, regent for Pongyayawma until he came of age), but also of a leader of the important Sun clan. Like mass and energy, to borrow Clifford Geertz's metaphor, the trappings and the power are transformed into each other (1977:124).

Secondly, he was the son of the founder of Hotevilla. This argument would not have counted for much in matrilineal logic, had the legitimate heir not left his center of power.[13]

Concerning national relations, the idea of the center also played an important role here. The "glowing center" thesis is highly relevant in relation to the non-Hopi concept of Hopi land being the sacred center of the North American continent. The very idea implied charismatic expectations even before the Traditionalists made use of it. And those who did, quickly found out which trappings and which ideas were accepted by Whites as the marks of persons in power at the center. One of the most important marks was the possession of prophetic knowledge.

I have indicated briefly in the previous chapter that the Traditionalists had learned the language of their audience. They were, in effect, sharing in the same "orectic ethnography" (such as that of the works of Carlos Castaneda) which, according to Needham and others, provided vehicles for an alternative worldview (Noel 1976, Needham 1985). This worldview consisted of eclecticism, "pseudo-holism," esoteric knowledge, respect for an authoritarian master, and the idea of achievement through hazardous or strenuous training (Needham 1985:190, 217). The Hopi

12. A. W. Geertz 1986:44; 1987*a*:17–18; A. W. Geertz and Lomatuway'ma 1987:54 n. 36.

13. Cf. Clifford Geertz: "A woman is not a duchess a hundred yards from a carriage," 1977:124–125.

Traditionalist Movement was in the position to contribute a highly articulated apocalypse which received further significance in the face of the violence, social uproar, and environmental scares of the 1960s and 1970s.

Thus, even in their commerce with White supporters, the traditional role of the political power of esoteric knowledge was essential to the Traditionalists' success outside the reservation. What their supporters did not suspect was that most of the Traditionalists had no legitimate power base in their own culture. Such matters were entirely unknown to outside Whites (cf. A. W. Geertz 1987*c*:38). For those who do not know better, a chief is a chief because he says so. That is why every prominent Traditionalist leader has been labeled a "chief" or a "spokesman for the Hopi people" (as opposed to the "puppet Hopis" of the Tribal Council) by White supporters and the press.

Essentially, there was no actual change of power between Qötshongva and Monongya seen from the perspective of outsiders. They were undifferentiated within the same aura of sacredness as far as White supporters were concerned. Qötshongva's messianic statements and advanced age gave him a relative edge over Monongya. At home, though, Monongya never succeeded in gaining the traditional power base Qötshongva had possessed.

The question of the possible psychological dimension of charisma brings us to a possibly major reason for Qötshongva's nominal support at home. The Hopis have a notoriously ambivalent attitude towards what we would call the psychological side of charisma; in other words, a personality that exudes power and/or unusual ability. According to Hopi ethics, those who have these traits are highly suspect.[14] People with special abilities have what is called *tuhisa*, "power, skill" (A. W. Geertz 1982*a*:184), and those who have such power are chiefs (or leaders) and priests, medicine men/women, and sorcerers/witches. The chiefs and priests have power over nature and the major events of the community. The medicine men/women and sorcerers/witches are two sides of the same coin. They are able to transform themselves into spirit helpers and they can affect the health and well-being of the individual. The fine dividing line between these three groups often disappears in popular thought and, consequently, they are all automatically suspected of misusing their occult power for personal and antisocial ends.

An unfortunate lacuna in our understanding of Hopi thought and religion is that we know very little about Hopi witchcraft. Loose conversations, bits and pieces in texts and in the literature, and field experiences indicate that Hopi conceptions of evil and of those who wield it are co-

14. A. W. Geertz 1986:46–49; 1990*a*; Voegelin and Voegelin 1960.

herent and richly imaginative. And, of greater importance, it is an essential mechanism in the maintainance of Hopi ideals. These factors alone require a full-scale analysis. A quote from Titiev's seminal article will impart the flavor of Hopi witchcraft:

> Another reason why the Hopi suspect their shamans is based on their tendency to regard with distrust any person who shows exceptional power, or whose behavior is marked by individuality, eccentricity, recklessness, aggressiveness, daring, or bragging. This concept may be carried to extremes, as in the case of a woman who aroused suspicion merely because she broke her leg as a result of what looked like an easy fall. Similarly, even the highest officers in a pueblo may be accused of witchcraft, sometimes for no better reason than that they hold positions of such extraordinary importance. In other cases village chiefs may be accused of being two-hearted whenever anything goes wrong, or whenever they behave in unconventional ways. Thus, for example, Chief Tawaqwaptiwa of Oraibi was denounced to me as a witch by one of his subjects because he had recently been earning his living by the manufacture and sale of *katcina* dolls, instead of by farming in the usual Hopi manner. Since this was a very uncommon practice, and meant that the chief no longer had any personal need for rain, it was argued that he had taken to using his great power for the evil purpose of driving off the clouds. In a comparable vein charges of witchcraft were leveled against Yokioma, leader of a rebellious faction that had seceded from Oraibi in 1906, simply because he had been sufficiently daring to challenge the authority of the traditional ruler and had been enterprising enough to rally a large following to his cause. Apparently, Yokioma was not averse to impressing the populace with his supposed magical power, for when his enemies accused him of having caused the great influenza epidemic of 1918 he boldly accepted the guilt. (1943:553)[15]

This description, which mentions the main antagonists of the Oraibi split, fits well with some of the factors Qötshongva had at his disposal.

The word *hopi* means "well behaved/well mannered" and implies that the well-mannered person (*hopivewa*) is one who keeps heart, speech, and action pure; one who is diligent, merciful, hospitable, peaceful, and humble.[16] Ill-behaved and bold people are *qahopi*, "not hopi." They are capable of awakening disgust and/or fear if they are bossy (*tota'tsi*), braggarts (*tsomo*), or if they act as if they are chief (*mongwiwuwanta*). The last is especially the complaint against the Traditionalists.

Whiteley maintained a similar argument in his description of the great influence that Kewanimptewa, the founder of Bacavi, had not only

15. Yukiwma's reported bravado receives independent confirmation in two of my texts published in A. W. Geertz and Lomatuway'ma 1987:138, 141.

16. A. W. Geertz 1986:47–48; 1990*a*.

at the other Third Mesa villages, but also at the other mesas. Whiteley characterized Kewanimptewa as a clairvoyant and a prophet with a "fearsome supernatural reputation" (1988:214–215). He argued that Kewanimptewa was a *powaqa*, "sorcerer/witch," in a positive sense. We are in agreement concerning the ambivalence such power holds in Hopi minds, but I do not think that powaqa has any positive nuance at all. I have only encountered this interpretation with one consultant, whereas several medicine men and a medicine woman as well as priests and a large number of ordinary people have expressed to me their unconditional horror and disgust for sorcerers and witches.[17]

It is possible that Qötshongva maintained his position as a real leader in Hotevilla for almost thirty years because of the doubt and fear that lies at the base of Hopi ambivalence towards persons in authority. But when it became evident during the 1960s that he was using his power in a destructive and irresponsible manner, it is quite possible that suspicions of witchcraft weakened his position. Together with the secondary political role he was left with and the fact that Pongyayawma had returned to the village, Qötshongva faced certain defeat.

It can be argued that the Hopi example contrasts Weber's categories as well as the various typologies developed by sociologists inspired by Weber. Whether the Hopi example can serve as a corrective or may be considered an empirical fluke, an evaluation in terms of these types and categories nevertheless sets a number of matters in Hopi affairs in a new light.[18] The Hopi example can, on the one hand, be classified as the "traditional domination" type—I use Mommsen's translation of the term *Herrschaft* (1974:72, n. 1)—and, on the other hand, the "charismatic domination" type, but which combines charismatic authority in both the sense of personal leadership and routinized charisma (cf. Bendix and Roth 1971:173). At the same time, the Hopi example follows Shils' emphasis on the protean character of charisma (1965), Weber's emphasis on the disruptive effects of charisma, but combines the two opposite categories of Loewenstein concerning the magico-religious contexts that encourage charisma and the secular contexts that discourage it (Loewenstein 1966:74–87). The split of Oraibi exemplifies the disruptive and

17. In response to this argument, Whiteley related to me that a public meeting was held in Bacavi in 1989 during which this issue was debated. He wrote, "some people felt that *popwaqt* carried no positive connotations; but over the course of two hours these were persuaded, by numerous examples from others brought forth, that there were indeed such usages and meanings" (personal communication). There can be no doubt that the topic warrants an in-depth analysis.

18. See Theodore Long's balanced argument for a re-reading of Weber on the topic of prophecy and charisma (1986). See also Fabian 1969.

revolutionary effects of charisma. The ambivalence towards persons in power reflects the basic framework of magico-religious contexts *and* ecclesiastical tradition. And, the charismatic role played out for White supporters reflects a framework shared by two different cultures based, on the one hand, on a moral and prophetic resistance to the secularization of the sacred for the Hopis and, on the other hand, a rationalization of prophecy and/or a sacralization of the secular for the Whites.[19]

In other words, Qötshongva had both tradition and charisma (in its various meanings) going for him, depending on which audience he addressed. This combination parallels Eisenstadt's argument (1973:119–149) that charisma and tradition are both rooted in the same processes of extending meaning to human existence, and, therefore, they both inform and reinforce each other in otherwise-normal circumstances.

This blend of traditional and charismatic domination has structural affinity to Weber's thoughts on the routinization of charismatic domination, but the latter implies the idea of a "first bearer" of charisma whose authority and charisma are passed on to others in five different ways. This postulated "first bearer" is nowhere evident in either Hopi oral tradition or in the documents at our disposal.

Two problems arose for Qötshongva which usually arise in Weberian thought: the problem of a successor, and the problem of the disappearance of charisma. These problems are often related and mutually opposed (cf. Bendix and Roth 1971:184).

Concerning the first problem, Qötshongva chose what Weber designated as the third of six alternatives (1911–1913:143–144), i.e, the charismatic leader designates his own successor. But the Hopi system, built as it is along the lines of traditional domination, is a combination of alternatives. It is true that a leader can break the normal line of lineage succession (as was the case, relatively speaking, with the appointment of Tawakwaptiwa as chief of Oraibi—the next in line was passed over in favor of the younger Tawakwaptiwa). A combination of Weberian alternatives, however, are essential to Hopi succession: kinship claims (alternative 5), the authority of the ritual sodalities (alternative 4), and the transference of the charisma of office by sacerdotal means (the initiation of the chief by the Kwan brotherhood, which has access to the frightening power of the Hopi tutelary deity, Maasaw [alternative 6]). Monongya was a poor choice, seen from virtually every angle of the Hopi perspective, and it is evident that Qötshongva realized his mistake too late.

19. By this, I am referring to the attempt to "explain" religious beliefs in terms of modern Western science, for example, sacred centers as the interstices of the earth's electromagnetic "grid system" or magic and the occult seen as psychic "science," and so on.

The second problem became a pressing matter as Qötshongva grew older. Only the end of the world could prove him right, and when Paul Solem showed up Qötshongva finally found the means by which to give a "sign" to his doubting disciples. But, as Pongyayawma noted, the only disciples left by that time were Whites and a handful of old friends and advisors.

The Traditionalist Movement moved on to greater heights, not necessarily reflecting what Festinger, Riecken, and Schachter formulated as the need of believers to proselytize their expectations even more in the face of undeniable disconfirmatory evidence (1956:4, 216), but because the movement had already adjusted course, changed leadership, widened its corpus of prophecies to appeal to the wider ecology-conscious audience, and especially because no precise date for the end of the world was attempted. Qötshongva's failure was his own personal failure. The movement as well as the general Hopi populace (which had very little to do with one another) still believed in the immanent "last day," but in each its own way and for each its own purpose. Qötshongva died a marginalized Hopi, but he at least became a venerable symbol in the eyes of the White supporters of the Traditionalist Movement.

PART III

Prophecy and Meaning

NINE

The Legacy of Prophecy Rock

On the Mutability of Petroglyphs[1]

This chapter deals with an intriguing petroglyph etched into a large boulder just east of Oraibi, on a cliff called Wutatakyawvi. An account of the interpretation of the petroglyph and its use will address several objectives: to give an indication of the style and methods of "second generation" Traditionalists, especially the main spokesman of the movement, Thomas Banancya; to give an indication of the kinds of interrelationships that exist between the Traditionalists and their White supporters; and to show that objects of significance, even though of stone, are highly mutable. This chapter will, therefore, address the issue of changing meanings.

THE HISTORY OF PROPHECY ROCK

The earliest mention of the petroglyph I could find is in John Wesley Powell's 1875 report of his visit to the Hopi villages in 1872. His description, like all the other descriptions prior to 1970, is not illustrated. Therefore, we can only surmise that these earlier reports refer to the same petroglyph. It is easier to follow along the descriptions looking at the drawing of the petroglyph and its surroundings which my colleague Poul Nørbo reproduced from photographs taken by me (figure 16). Powell wrote the following in his report:

1. Portions of this chapter were read at the "Conference on Amerindian Cosmology" held by the Traditional Cosmology Society at St. Andrews, Scotland, 30th August–6th September 1987, entitled "Traditional Hopi Indian Cosmology: the Evolution of an Idea, Its Use and Misuse."

Figure 16. Prophecy Rock (Wutatakyawvi) near Oraibi.
Drawn by Poul Nørbo, University of Aarhus, Denmark, 1989.

> On the cliff near Oraibi, I found a record like this etched on a stone. Below and to the left were three Spaniards, the leader with a sword, the two followers carrying spears. Above and to the right were three natives in an attitude of rolling rocks. Near by was a Spaniard prone on the ground, with a native pouring water on his head. Tal-ti, whose name means "peep of day," because he was born at dawn, explained to me that the record was made by their ancestors a very long time ago, and that the explanation had been handed down as follows: Their town was attacked by the Spaniards; the commander was a gallant fellow, who attempted to lead his men up the stone stairway to the town, but the besieged drove them back with rolling stones, and the Spanish captain was wounded and left by his followers. The people, in admiration of his valor, took him to a spring near by, poured water on him, dressed his wounds, and, when they were healed, permitted him to return. Tal-ti's description of the scene was quite vivid, and even dramatic, especially when he described the charge of the Spaniards rushing forward and shouting their war cries, "*Santiago! Santiago! Santiago!*" (1875:32)

The only detail that does not fit the petroglyph as it is today is the absence of the three Spaniards in the lower left-hand corner. The solitary figure does look like a captain of sorts. There is a break in the rock at the lower left-hand corner which might indicate that there could have been more rock and subsequently more figures. But the rest of the description fits the petroglyph so closely that I am convinced that Powell is referring to the same rock.

I am also convinced that the explanation given to Powell was the Hopi consensus at that time. As indicated in chapter 1, the confrontation with the Spaniards was painful, and it would have been natural to mark the event. We have no way of knowing the provenience or age of the petroglyph, however. Hopi oral tradition seems to date it to the end of the last century, but no definitive evaluation can be made, nor is the age of the petroglyph significant here.

Divergencies in Powell's description with figure 16 do not raise doubts in my mind about its validity. The petroglyph is difficult to examine in detail, since the lighting plays tricks on the observer. I photographed the rock at three different times of the day, and although the major features are easily distinguishable, some of the detail is not. In some instances it is difficult to determine where the line of demarcation lies between natural deformities in the rock and man-made etchings. The changes in coloration help, of course, but not concerning all the details. This applies especially to the type of instruments held by the figure in the lower left-hand corner, to the shape and detail of the figure treading on the zigzag line, and to the detail of the figure with the crook in his hand in the upper right-hand corner. Later reports have also been unable to resolve this problem.

New times brought new interpretations of the petroglyph. Some informants told me that it depicts a wagon, others said a railroad engine. Either could be the case since the railroad lines were already in California during the middle of the 19th century, and the joining of the Atchison, Topeka, and Santa Fe with the Southern Pacific in Needles, California, occurred in August, 1883, having first passed through Albuquerque in April, 1880, Fort Wingate in February, 1881, and Holbrook in September, 1881 (Weigle 1989:116). It is therefore reasonable to assume that the petroglyph in question has been interpreted as a horse-drawn wagon—which was an essential part of Hopi economy during the 1880s and 1890s—and/or as a locomotive. We have only contemporary oral commentary on this topic, however, and so it must remain speculative until further evidence arises.

The first of a series of documents relating to the rock and the iconography of its petroglyph began in 1955 at the BIA hearings. This and all subsequent reports stem from the Traditionalist Movement, either from Thomas Banancya or Whites who got it from him. Most surprising is the high degree of variation not only in his accounts, but also in the illustrations he used.

During the 1955 hearings, David Monongya, who was on the rise at the time, brought out a "map or drawing" copied from a rock near Oraibi" which he claimed to be one of the life patterns of the Hopis. Since the drawing was not reproduced, it is difficult to follow what he is referring to in his long and eloquent speech. All of the elements we know of from accounts twenty years later are present in his speech, but we do not know how these elements were applied in relation to the drawing. In his speech he referred to the emergence and to the meeting with Maasaw, followed by the clan migrations and the selection of one of the two roads or ways of life. He set this choice within a loosely historical context by referring to the Spaniards and to the present use of the minerals in the earth. He mentioned a prophecy about three great wars to take place and about a coming purification. In other words, with the addition of a few new details, Monongya related the basic story of the emergence, added Traditionalist prophecy, and placed it in relation to the drawing. One of the roads in the drawing is, according to Monongya, the Hopi path, the life of poverty that leads to old age—in reference to a figure bent over a cane. I surmise that he was referring to the first diagonal line with the circles and the human figure in the upper right-hand corner. Those who maintain that path will gain everlasting life. The other road represents the road of evil, and even though it may bring wealth and power, the life it represents will but end in a fall:

These figures up here represent a man without a head. These are wicked people because wicked people cause other people hardship and do all manner of wickedness in this life, and if we follow them up to purification time which we all know from our tradition, all wicked people will be beheaded. (Bureau of Indian Affairs 1955:46)

The headless figures are the group of four figures treading on the second diagonal line that ends in a zigzag. The Traditionalists more or less consistently presented these figures either as headless or as having no connection between head and body. This interpretation is clearly inspired by the Kookop decapitation tradition discussed in chapter 6.

THOMAS BANANCYA, TRADITIONALIST SPOKESMAN

The next reference to the petroglyph came in 1968, but was first published in 1978. This time the speaker was Thomas Banancya. Banancya plays such a dominant role in this chapter that it would do well to reflect on his personal history and on his distinctive status in the Traditionalist Movement. Shuichi Nagata described Banancya in his 1978 publication on Qötshongva. Since his comments are succinct, I will quote the four paragraphs in their entirety:

Dan's [Qötshongva's] "lieutenant" is Thomas Banyacya. Born in 1902, he comes from a highly acculturated family in Moenkopi, a colony village of Oraibi. His brother has been quite successful in business in Moenkopi and one of his paternal sisters belongs to a group of the earliest Christian converts; Thomas himself is one of the first Hopi to receive college education, though he did not complete it. On the other hand, his roots in traditional Hopi society are not very significant. A member of the Coyote clan, which is not very important in the assumption of ceremonial roles, he is also a member of the Kachina society, which is a minimal requirement for entry to more esoteric ones. He has been residing in New Oraibi, a Council village of Third Mesa, where his wife was born.

Thomas's background thus tends to indicate his 'marginal' locus among the Traditionals. In fact, his early political career was oriented somewhat against the traditional authority and his initiative in establishing a self-governing organisation in separation from the Moenkopi chieftainship in the late 1920s is still regarded by many as a challenge to the traditional order. During the implementation period of the Indian Reorganization Act and the Second World War, he grew disillusioned by the Indian policy of the American government and was imprisoned for his campaign against compulsory military service. Soon he changed his English surname to one of the initiation names of the Kachina society. Through these experiences, Thomas emerged as a firm right-hand man to Dan and became the most articulate of the Traditional leaders. In acting as a Traditional leader,

> Thomas so far has refused to assume government employment[2] and, like Dan, been engaged in farming and weaving, only occasionally working for wages in his village.
>
> In contrast to Dan, Thomas's leadership lies in his ability to provide contacts with the outside world for the Traditional cause. Unlike Dan, he does not possess as strong a village identity and hence can manage to create supra-village consensus without much suspicion of domination by a particular village. On the other hand, the legitimacy of his Traditional leadership is supported by Dan, who provides Thomas's ideological basis and on whose behalf Thomas is said to be working. This mutual role articulation has been important for the Traditionals, who often splinter without ever achieving unity in opposition to the Council. I am almost tempted to characterise Dan as an expressive leader and Thomas as an instrumental one.
>
> But Thomas's role has not been limited only to politics in Hopiland. He was able to establish contacts even outside Hopiland for the Traditional cause. The two most important contacts during the 1950s were one Mohawk Indian, who organised *American Indian Restoration Enterprises*, a retired Army general, who organised *Constitutional Provisional Government of America* [mentioned in chapter 2]. Both men have been active in promoting the Indian cause in America and aired their views through numerous mimeographed pamphlets. They have all visited Hopiland in the past and came to know both Dan and Thomas intimately. The latter were in turn invited by them to attend meetings outside Hopiland. The linkage thus established resulted in Dan's visits, with Thomas accompanying him, to the United Nations in New York, Washington, D.C., Chicago, Six Nations Reserve at Brantford, Ontario, Canada, and numerous other places in North America as well as the publication of many obscure pamphlets, in which Dan's messages were propagated. (1978:76–77)

Nagata had already emphasized Banancya's marginal status in the "traditional" scheme of things in his 1968 paper on the Traditionalists. Two important factors were raised in that paper: 1) that his marginality "has been a helpful factor for his instrumental leadership as it extricates him from strong identification with any particular village and thus enables him to coordinate the different Traditional villages"; and 2) "to a certain extent, therefore, he appears to represent the first leader with secular political qualifications in the Traditional faction" (1968:21). These two points are an example of the acculturative mechanisms of Traditionalist activities discussed in chapter 7.

Richard Clemmer noted Banancya's marginality, but glossed it over with an inventive explanation tendered by his informants:

2. According to Fred Eggan, Peter Whiteley, and several of my Hopi consultants, Banancya was in fact an employee of the Bureau of Indian Affairs during the late 1920s and early 1930s. Several sources claim that he was dismissed from the BIA.

> The new interpreter's secular qualifications were enhanced by his clan affiliation. Being of the Water Coyote clan, he was automatically charged with a duty to act in a "coyote" manner: keep eyes and ears open, know what is going on, learn to operate on the periphery of the white man's world, interpret Hopi custom and belief in the light of changing events, warn of danger. As interpreter-spokesman for the traditional chiefs, Banyacya was thus considered as fulfilling his clan duties in the most proper way possible. (1978*b*:71)

Ekkehart Malotki's illuminating information on the Coyote clans (Malotki and Lomatuway'ma 1985:1–22) indicates that Clemmer's information is most likely a rationalization by his consultants. The Coyote clan (Isngyam) as well as their relatives the Water Coyote clan (Paa'isngyam) represent a uniformly negative impression in Hopi totemistic thought, and, having no useful function in the Hopi social scheme, they have a correspondingly low status. The Water Coyote clan is especially despised for a variety of reasons even by their relatives the Isngyam. Waters' claim (1963:85) that the Coyote clan owned the Qaleetaqa, "Warrior/Guardian," office is clearly an exaggeration since the office traditionally belonged to the Momtsit, "Warrior Fraternity," which was owned by the Reed clan on First Mesa and by the Spider and Kookop clans on Third Mesa. This fraternity evidently died out on Third Mesa during the 1930s[3] and, therefore, any Isngyam claims are met with an accusation of theft (Malotki and Lomatuway'ma 1985:13–15).

Thus, Banancya's marginality is a fact and not an issue. The issue lies in evaluating the depth of his insight and the authenticity of his interpretations. Banancya has spent thirty years on the lecture circuit, and even though his interpretations have changed, he has had a tremendous impact on his non-Hopi public and is probably responsible for the fact that the Traditionalist Movement did not die out sooner than it did. The frontispiece photograph of Banancya and Elizabeth Taylor is characteristic of Banancya's talents.[4]

Richard Clemmer wrote that the etching on the rock was placed there by the grandfather of John Lansa, Mina Lansa's husband. This would either mean that the petroglyph had been carved shortly before Powell saw it in 1872 or that Lansa's information was wrong. Pongyayawma told me in 1988 that he thought the petroglyph had been made by the Bad-

3. Titiev 1944:156 n. 12. Cf. references in A. W. Geertz 1987*a*:2.

4. The accompanying article by Steven Edwards (1986) explained that the photo was taken at a star-studded Hollywood press conference where actor Jon Voight revealed that he would announce "an earth-shattering prophecy . . . the holy prophecy of holy elders" that "spiritualist" Banancya would convey to him "when the time is right." Thanks to Professor Alfred YoungMan, University of Lethbridge, Alberta, Canada, for the reference.

ger clan, which would confirm Lansa's claims, since Lansa was of the Badger clan.

Banancya related his interpretation to Clemmer in 1968, but no illustration was provided in Clemmer's monograph. But, familiarity with figure 16 and with Monongya's account make Banancya's statements understandable:

> This figure is the Great Spirit. He gave us this land and this path to follow. This path leads up to two horizontal roads, connected by this vertical line here. Hopis have a choice—they can take either road. This one above is the white man's road. It gets rocky and is no good; we don't know where it leads. But this line below, it is the Hopi road. It's real narrow. You can't go much one side or the other. But there's a line leading back down to the Hopi road before it's too late; before the white man's road gets rocky.
>
> On this white man's road, there's three men. They'll be destroyed in the purification. They're supposed to have their heads chopped off, but somebody put heads on them (unlike the figures of the Great Spirit, however, these figures have no facial features). These two circles on the Hopi road are great destructions or catastrophies. On the other side of the vertical line leading down from the white man's road, there's another circle. This also represents a catastrophe—the Purification Day.
>
> But after that there's corn stalks, shaped like canes, and also the Great Spirit again. This means if Hopis stick to the right road and undergo all these things, the Great Spirit will be waiting for them. There will be plenty of corn and the good life. The canes mean Hopis will live to old age. Down here, halfway up the road leading to the split between the white man's road and the Hopi road, there's a circle and a cross. This represents a white man coming in bringing us Christianity. That's the Catholic. But we shouldn't accept all these other religions. We know if we ever let the Catholic back in, only a few men will accept him.
>
> That's what our Life Plan says. (1978*b*:49)

Thus, we find that Banancya has developed Monongya's interpretation, but in full accordance with his standardized version of the prophecies he wrote to Muller-Fricken in 1961.

Anthropologist Louis Hieb attended a meeting held by the Traditionalists on September 12, 1970. During the meeting, Banancya brought out a folder board with a drawing of the petroglyph. Hieb provided me with a copy of the illustration, and I reproduce both the illustration (figure 17) and summarize his diary commentary in the following.

While holding up a large sheet of yellow poster board with the help of another man, Banancya explained that a full interpretation of the drawing would take four days to relate and therefore his comments would necessarily be only a brief report. The figure in the left-hand corner is the Great Spirit who gave permission to the emerging peoples to enter his world. At the time of the emergence, the people agreed to follow the

Figure 17. Drawing of Prophecy Rock by Thomas Banancya. SOURCE: Louis Hieb, field notes, September 12, 1970. Courtesy Louis Hieb and Northern Arizona University Archives at Flagstaff.

path of the Great Spirit, which is represented by the lower horizontal line, "all the way through," and were given care of the land and of life. They went off in the four directions and held the land, as the quadripartite shield design in the lower right-hand corner symbolizes. This represents the Four Corners states. The empty circle was also a symbol that both the Indian and the White Brother had, but, when the White Brother went away he changed it and created something else. So by the time he came back with the new symbol of the cross, the Hopis had been warned not to follow him. The three figures on the upper horizontal line are the tempters who tempt the Hopis with sweet words, inventions, and clothes, and who try to coax the Hopis into abandoning their religion.

The three circles on the spiritual path represent the destruction of life and property which are meant to warn the people that they are straying from the right path. And if they do not stop, they will blow themselves up or destroy all of nature. The third circle represents the purification day through which everyone must pass. And the Great Spirit will be waiting on the other side to see whether each people has retained its original identity, language, and religion. Those who have not, such as the young people who wear White clothes and get their hair cut, will not be recognized by the Great Spirit.

And those whose job it was to shake the people up were symbolized by the designs on the Powamuy rattle, pictured in the upper left-hand corner, i.e., the swastika and the sun. Their job was to warn the world about the coming third event which will be inaugurated by a "man with a red cap or a red cloak." He will be joined by the first two and together they will purify the whole Western hemisphere.

Banancya ended his interpretation by repeating his basic catalogue of prophecies from 1961.

ECOLOGY AND MYSTICISM

The first published drawing of the petroglyph I could find appeared in 1972 in a monthly environmental publication based in San Francisco. In a special issue, "Black Mesa: Cultures in Collision," guest edited by Jack Loeffler, a photograph of the rock was published accompanied by a rambling account of Hopi philosophy by an unidentified Hopi and a fanciful line drawing with an interpretation. Anyone comparing the two illustrations would have noticed obvious divergences (see figure 18 here). The narrator is quoted as having said the following:

> Carved on a rock not too far from Oraibi village is a petroglyph that conveys the prophecy of the Great Spirit. This prophecy concerns the coming purification which will mark the end of the third age. The Hopi have been preparing for this time of purification in their ceremonies. Before they perform the ceremonies, they fast for three days to prepare for the fourth day. "Interference has gradually caused Nature to turn her face. When the Sun rises and sets blood red, the people know that Nature is out of balance.
>
> "Each morning, we bathe in cold water so that our hearts will be strong enough to face the purifier.
>
> "Only people with strong hearts will be able to face the purification. Eventually, the purifier will come. He will be able to see who is good and who is bad."
>
> The Hopi prophecy speaks of the gradual devastation of the Earth processes because of mankind's interference. The symbols carved on the rock represent events, many of which have already occurred, that allow the Hopi to understand how Nature is being thrown completely out of balance.
>
> They are fearful for the whole land and that every living thing might be destroyed. They are desperately concerned for the spiritual center, that all people must adhere to the spiritual instructions of the Great Spirit—"otherwise everything will go down." (Anonymous 1972:34)

This statement is clearly what the ecologists were looking for. Loeffler's introductory article indicates which ideas the ecologists needed from Indian thought:

> The Southwest is a song sung by the afternoon wind passing through deep canyons and the night gatherings of coyotes. It is a place of wildcats and

Figure 18. Drawing of Prophecy Rock. SOURCE: *Clear Creek: The Environmental Viewpoint* 13, 1972. Courtesy of Special Collections, The University of Arizona, Tucson.

eagles, of buzzards and deer, of seven wild mustangs running side by side. In the American Southwest, the emptiness of space touches a vast diversity of land and life forms and frees the human mind to reflect on the nature of reality beyond the objectivist restrictions of western culture. The horizon is determined by distant mountain ranges, and the dry landscape, broken by mesas and monoliths, is mottled with patches of cedar and piñon, crested wheat grass and cactus. It smells good and clean and fresh. Springs mark the sides of barren cliffs with small patches of vegetation that show the water is there—sometimes sweet, sometimes brackish and salty. And everywhere is the sense of space and time out of mind. . . .

Before the Europeans arrived, the Indian cultures functioned within a system of recognized balance. Though the process of recognition was very different from the white man's scientific approach, we would say the Indians comprehended inter-relationships within a balanced eco-system. A steady state evolved, and the environment remained relatively stable.

For those early people, who are still reflected in the traditional Indians of today, the Southwest was the spiritual center of the land mass we know as the North American continent. Life in this sacred place required a synthesis of intuitive awareness of the flow of nature and a basic minimum technology born of common sense. To grow crops of corn, beans and squash in Hopi country, one must plant, pray—and haul water. . . .

What is it about western man that can see a landscape as lovely as the Southwest simply as a reservoir of natural resources to be extracted with little or no regard for the environment? Has something in our civilization's consciousness focused so exclusively on the intellectual processes that we have submerged all other aspects of human existence and rendered them garbled and inaccurate?

If so, we reside in the very heart of total jeopardy. Western thought has produced such technologic prowess that today we appear little more than super-technicians. Our techniques have so fascinated and allured us that we feed our technology far more than ourselves. Our techno-fantasy has become, among other things, the perfect vehicle for self-fulfilling prophecy. And it has gotten away from us—the steering mechanism is broken and the brakes are fading. (1972:11)

Genuine ecological concern blended with nature mysticism, antitechnological philosophy, and the romanticism of "primordial" peoples are all vital components of the emerging New Age rhetoric. Loeffler's article is filled with rhetorical terms that are standard New Age terminology today: balanced eco-systems, biospheric continuum, sacred centers, intuitive awareness, flow of nature, the juggernaut quest, the "rape" of the "Earth mother," psychic gene pool, techno-fantasy, life-dance, primordial womb, bio-ethic, and so on.

It should be noted that the Traditionalists were very much aware of ecological issues and specifically addressed not only the ecology movement, but also the officials of government policy. In an interesting letter to President Nixon in 1970, Banancya formulated a statement that encapsulated the concerns of the ecology movement within the context of Hopi prophecy:

The whiteman, through his insensitivity to the way of Nature, has desecrated the face of Mother Earth. The white man's advanced technological capacity has occurred as a result of his lack of regard for the spiritual path and for the way of all living things. The white man's desire for material possessions and power has blinded him to the pain he has caused Mother Earth by his quest for what he calls natural resources. All over the country, the waters have been tainted, the soil broken and defiled, the air polluted. Living creatures die from poisons left because of industry. And the path of the Great Spirit has become difficult to see by almost all men, even by many Indians who have chosen instead to follow the path of the white man.

We have accepted the responsibility designated by our prophecy to tell you that almost all life will stop unless men come to know that everyone must live in Peace and in Harmony with Nature. Only those people who know the secrets of Nature, the Mother of us all, can overcome this. (Banyacya 8-4-1970)[5]

5. Special Collections at the University of Arizona, Tucson, dated this undated letter to 9-3-1970, but with a question mark. Both Garment's and Brice's responses refer to Banancya's letter as 8-4-1970.

The one-and-a-half-page letter was not only reprinted in *Akwesasne Notes* (2 no. 6, October 1970:3), but it also elicited two responses from Washington. Leonard Garment responded on President Nixon's behalf that he sympathized with Banancya's concern with the strip-mining activities on Black Mesa, but that the only way to solve the conflicts on the reservation over this and other issues was to resort to the democratic system: "The place for the resolution of issues between majorities and minorities is first of all the ballot box" (Garment 9–22–1970). The second response was much more encouraging. Deputy Associate Commissioner of the Bureau of Indian Affairs Calvin N. Brice wrote on behalf of the president:

> It is very gratifying to see the unified response which the American people are giving the President in support of [his] control and corrective programs. . . .
>
> The Hopi Traditional Village Leaders are to be congratulated for their awareness of the environmental pollution problems. We are certain your contribution and active participation with ongoing programs will be welcomed. (Brice 11–5–1970)

Even though Brice cleverly steered Traditionalist protest into support for government policy, these responses helped strengthen the Traditionalist position during its greatest period of success.

Coming back to the drawing in question (figure 18), it is accompanied by the following anonymous interpretation:

> Starting in the lower left hand corner and moving to the right; the petroglyph means roughly the following: The Bow and Arrow are the tools which the Great Spirit (to the right) gave to the Hopi. He is pointing to the spiritual path of the Great Spirit. The upper path is the White Man's path, with two white men and one Hopi to represent the Hopi who adopted white man's ways. The verticle line joining the two paths (just to the left of the first man and circle) represents the first contact between the Hopi and the White Man since the emergence from the lower world. The lower path is the spiritual path of the Hopi. The first circle is World War I, the second World War II—and the third is the Great Purification, which the Hopi feel we are now approaching, after which corn and water will be abundant, the Great Spirit will return, and all will be well. Notice how the White Man's path eventually becomes very erratic and finally just fades away. The quartered circle in the lower right corner is the symbol for the Spiritual Center of the Continent, which for the Hopi is the Southwest. (Anonymous 1972, 35)

As the ecological movements lost interest in the Hopis by the mid-1970s, the more religious elements of the growing New Age movement began to take notice. A drawing of the petroglyph appeared in 1975 in the underground New Age newspaper called *East West Journal.* The drawing and its interpretation appeared in a special issue on American Indians in July. In an article by Tom Tarbet we find the Hopis being placed squarely within the eclecticism and romanticism of the times:

> How gladly I would have traded my college education to be born and raised a Hopi, and taught the higher truths in an ancient religious society! A whole science is there, practical, timeless, out of which grow the prophecies that explain the modern world in perfect clarity. The truth that was the religion of Lao-Tsu, Buddha, Moses, and Pythagoras, the order of the universe.
>
> I had been taught these people were savages who someday might become sufficiently educated to merit adult participation in the miracle of modern progress. Instead, I found brilliant people, with an amazing sense of humor, whose teachings more than encompass the modern world and warn against the folly of blindly believing in that miracle of modern institutions and technology. I had been told that they needed Christ's teachings so that they could be saved, but I discovered that their religion was in far better shape than that of the missionaries who instituted what the Hopi call the slave-church.
>
> At Oraibi, the oldest continuously inhabited village site in the western hemisphere, even nature seemed to conspire against religious colonialism. The only church was destroyed by lightening and never rebuilt. Its stone shell sets Oraibi apart from the mission-dominated pueblos of the southwest, yet a more sacred place is not to be found. At night under a winter snow, one might mistake it for the mind's image of Bethlehem. . . .
>
> If we only look, we can see the character of ancient world government, the forces involved in the present world revolution, and the possible birth of a new, peaceful world order. If we can't and our stubborness runs its course, bringing death to this remaining vestige of fully enlightened government, the chances for a peaceful world will fade away, and what ensues will be more than most of us can bear. . . .
>
> I know of no books on "Indians" that adequately explain the Hopi way of life. Perhaps the best clues available are in the *Tao Teh Ching*, and the *I-Ching*, from ancient China.
>
> Since the Hopi way is rooted in the ancient world, it definitely is not a mere coincidence that Hopi ceremonies are structured by the same mathematical system as the *I-Ching*, nor that the *I-Ching* offers the same theory of life as that which appears in the basic Hopi symbols. The sign for "Inner Truth" in the *I-Ching*, for example, describes seed-force in the same terms as the design on Hopi gourd rattles. (1975:13)

This list of claims which were and are standard stock in New Age myths about the Hopis was then followed by a comparison of the petroglyph with a supposed Chinese character reproduced here as figure 19 in "proof" of his imaginative apocryphal statements:

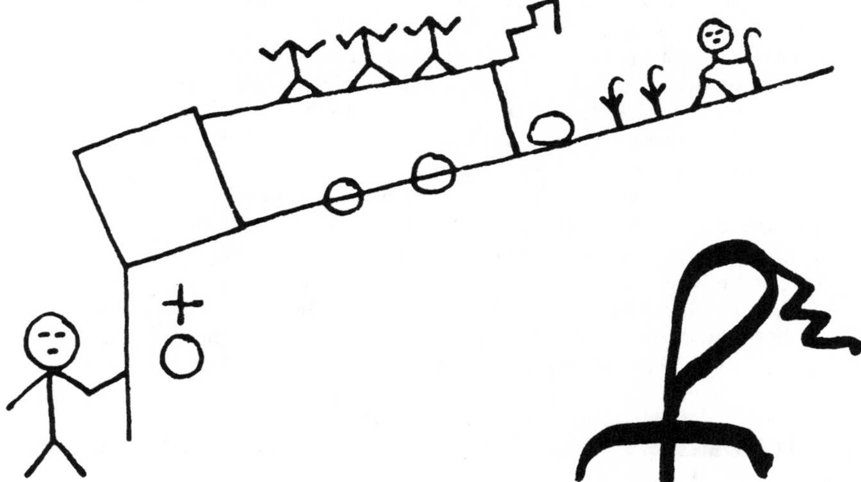

Figure 19. Drawing of Prophecy Rock by Thomas Tarbet. SOURCE: *East West Journal* 5 (7), July 15, 1975. Courtesy of *East-West Natural Health: The Guide to Wellbeing,* Brookline Village, Massachusetts.

> The vertical (yin) line is the path of life emerging from the underworld. The loop is its return, a complete cycle. The zig-zag line shows the path of life gone astray from the spirallic cycle. The angles signify ignorant attempts to return, which only stray further and end in annihilation. (ibid.:14)

He then claimed that the Hopis knew all about the hemispheres of the brain and that man's dependance on the right hemisphere, which is the clever and powerful side of man, brought nature out of balance and led to the present ecological crisis as it did in earlier catastrophes in the history of humanity. Throughout the article Tarbet demonstrated a naivety and ignorance concerning the specific nature of the religions which he poured into his own personal mould. And he also completely accepted as his own the particular version of the Hopi prophecies and worldview presented in the article.

Then follows an interpretation of figure 19, which, by the way, was laid out opposite a photograph of Dan Qötshongva:

> The figure [in the left-hand corner] . . . represents *Maasauu,* the Great Spirit. In his left hand he holds the path of life, the reed through which we emerged into this world. The circle and cross symbolize the sun and the four directions, or forces. Between the emergence into this world and the founding of Oraibi, the legends tell of a long migration, during which

> the Sun Clan twins provided a plan to avoid a future repetition of the catastrophe. One of them was to continue toward Oraibi to meet the Great Spirit and establish the way of life according to His instructions. The other, the White Brother, was to travel toward the rising sun, later to return. Were the one returning only to show the cross, this would signify that he had left the spiritual path for an arrogant and materialistic way of his own invention, which they must not accept.
>
> The square on the reed in the diagram is the land. Having reached the land, there are two possible paths. The upper one is the short, materialistic path, ending in the zig-zag line, annihilation. The zig-zag also represents the steps to the comfort of riches, which one may climb, but which drops off catastrophically and inevitably in the end. The lower path is the spiritual one. It continues indefinitely, for as long as it is followed. At the end, we meet the Great Spirit again, an old man who establishes the way of life with his planting stick and corn. "I am the first, and I shall be the last," he told the Hopi, "All I have is my planting stick and my corn. . . ."
>
> The figures on the upper path are often shown with heads disconnected or missing. This means that the followers of this path lose their unifying judgment. We may thus appreciate the prophecy of the "beheading of the wicked ones" as a representation of Western man's inner state. It can also mean that the heads of the power structure become mysteriously invisible, cut off from the people and nature, with even the elected heads being mere pawns of invisible interests.
>
> The injustice that engulfs the world as a result of man's powerful, clever, and analytical, fear-driven side is resolved in three world-shaking events, shown as three circles on the lower path. The first two are split by the line, signifying a dualistic principle at work. The third is whole, signifying unification. The first two are governed by the *swastika* and the *sun* [for which he provides no explanation]. Since these signs appeared in Germany and Japan, the Hopi regard the two World Wars as the fulfillment of this part of the prophecy. Like the two corn stalks, they grew quickly, then died out to sprout again.
>
> The third and final event is the Great Day of Purification which, like the old man, works through "The Power of Weakness" and persists endlessly. The line connecting the two paths at the end shows the course which must be taken to avoid annihilation. Dan Katchongva, the Sun Clan leader in Hotevilla village, was told by his father, Yukiuma, that he would live to see the beginning of Purification Day. Dan died in 1972. (ibid.:14–15)

Tarbet evidently adapted both the interpretation and the drawing to his own particular rhetorical goals. The basic narrative is clearly that of Qötshongva and Banancya, but the interpretation as well as the drawing of the three figures on the upper diagonal line are Tarbet's own invention. They are entirely consistent with the tone of cultural self-disgust in his article.

The article ends with a description of the "insidious" policies of the government, such as the "forcing" of power lines, water pipes, and housing on the reservation. "The final degree of degradation is reached with the gradual replacement of the Hopi diet with imported packaged foods, sugar, white flour and lard. Their original food was not merely natural, but, in the larger sense, macrobiotic, since it was part of a unifying cosmology" (ibid.:15).

Tarbet evidently fancied himself a sort of self-appointed, White "spokesman" for the Traditionalists. The *East West Journal* article and a number of other similar essays by Tarbet were distributed in pamphlet form to many organizations that supported the Traditionalist Hopis and other related issues. And it was Tarbet who secured Qötshongva's final narrative in 1970, which was published by one of his organizations, the Committee for Traditional Indian Land and Life, based in Los Angeles.

Half a year later, Banancya's drawing and interpretation appeared in a December issue of the *East West Journal.* The article was buried in a collage of advertisements for samadhi cushions and Sufi wings, the views of Michio Kushi and Bubba Free John, the programs of the Transpersonal Education Conference and the Christananda Hesychast Ashram, and perhaps the best indicator of the times, the "Communities and Personals" ads:

> UTOPIAN COMMUNAL FAMILY seeks more adventurous partners. We're into art, writing, utopian psychology, lifelong learning. Our life-style is polyfidelitous (non-monogamous); we have no guru/leader and are rational pan-theists (we see reality itself as divine). Want to meet people at a turning point in life, and seasoned enough to make lasting commitments if they find the right trip. (*East West Journal* 5 [12]:53)

Thomas Banancya's drawing, reproduced here as figure 20, is more detailed than Tarbet's, and is evidently the drawing he used on his lecture circuit. The drawing he used was always reproduced on a large poster board with an old map of Hopi territory as its backdrop. Only the drawing of the petroglyph, however, was published in this issue of *East West Journal.*

Banancya's sudden appearance in *East West Journal* only five issues after the Tarbet article was not explained. But now we find a Hopi entering the New Age market. He was quoted by the associate editor Meredith James in terms that clearly reformulate the Traditionalist program into New Age sales jargon:

> "Meditate, fast, pray, walk through the earth, look at animals, look at the sky, think about these things, nature, and you're going to be filling yourself with spiritual power and you will have better respect for one another."
>
> Thomas Banyacya is an interpreter for the spiritual leaders of the Hopi Nation. Their whole spiritual life is based on seeing to it that living things

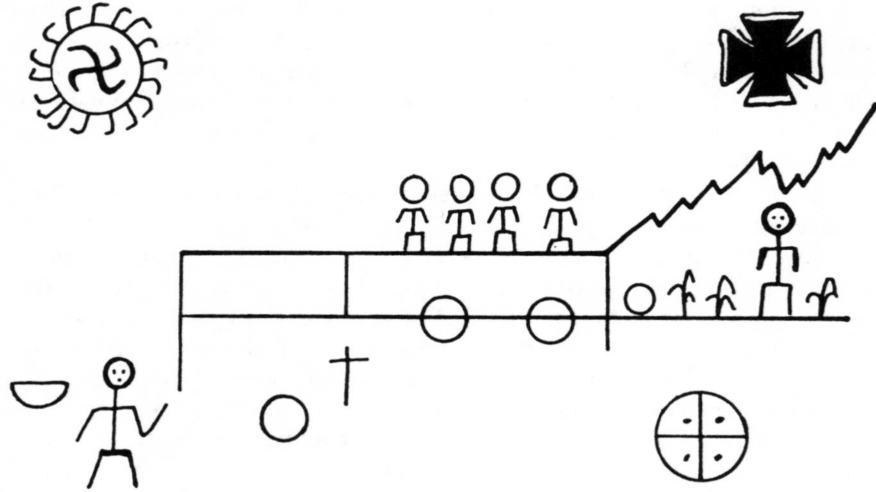

Figure 20. Drawing of Prophecy Rock by Thomas Banancya. SOURCE: *East West Journal* 5 (12), December 15, 1975. Courtesy of *East-West Natural Health: The Guide to Wellbeing,* Brookline Village, Massachusetts.

> are not interfered with: "We are all related; we are all one with nature. At this very moment we are all linked together by the air that we breathe. Hopi believe that everything is alive. Hopi believe that we must, from our heart, give that spiritual feeling to others so that nature will continue on its natural course." (Banyacya 1975:36)

James wrote further concerning Banancya's activities:

> The Hopi religious leaders also instructed their people to search for their native American brothers, so Thomas Banyacya met with Mad Bear and Beeman Logan, a chief from the Seneca Tonawanda reservation. They were surprised to find that the ancient knowledge and drawings of the Hopi and the Iroquois were very similar even though they had never had contact before. They traveled around the country, holding spiritual meetings to help reestablish the traditional religious principles that "are now being broken down by pressure from the Bureau of Indian Affairs' programs across the land." (ibid.:36)

Banancya's interpretation was evidently presented at the Temple of Understanding's Spiritual Summit Conference V at the Cathedral of St. John in New York City in October of that year. It is interspersed with a whole series of sensational prophecies. Maasaw, who is now equated with the messiah in the Bible, met the Hopis in the lower left-hand corner and presented them with the spiritual path and told them what to expect in the future. The Hopis were then given the duty to take care of the North American continent. Then followed the story of the stone tablets and the two brothers: If the White Brother leaves the true path he will change the circle to the cross and will try to tempt his Hopi brother from the true path with the promise of ever new inventions. Then he listed the issues involved: the destructive mining on Black Mesa, the use of chemical fertilizers, housing programs, water and sewage lines, smog; all of which are signs that the true Hopis should go to the United Nations and find support there. Then follows a listing of all the inventions Hopi prophecy purportedly knew about—couched in crypto-primitive terminology: carriages pulled by animals (buckboard wagons), carriages running by themselves (automobiles), trails in all directions (highways), cobwebs in the sky (telephone lines), closing the windows and doors but hearing and talking over the mountains (radio and television), the invention of a gourd full of ashes (atomic bombs), roads in the sky (air travel), man messing around with the moon and the stars (space travel), wars, violence, natural catastrophes, interfering with male and female (feminism), inventing human beings (genetic technology), and so on. Then he said:

> We are in the third world now,[6] and if we straighten ourselves out, we are ready to go into the fourth world. When it looks as though everything we have invented is going to go on forever, that things are perfect, some of our own people will join the others. The figure on the top line separated from the other three represents one of our own people leaving the Hopis; the zigzag line represents man's advancement in technical, scientific knowledge.
>
> We let the white brother go on his own path to see which one would bring a good life. We have seen mineral resources running out: oil, gas, iron. Man invented so many chemical things: highly developed nuclear power, atom bombs—we have those planted all over this land. (ibid.:38)

He referred to the symbol in the lower right-hand corner as the symbol for the four-corner area, which is considered to be the spiritual center of North America by New Age groups and by other Indian peoples as well. The upper left-hand corner is taken from a Powamuy rattle and signifies, according to Banancya, two powerful nations—one with the swastika, the other with the sun symbol—who were given the sacred mission of purifying themselves and thereby warning others. A third nation will arise wearing the red paint on the rattle, and will come by flying saucers. If the third nation does not bring on the purification, a fourth

6. This is in disagreement with every other known version of the emergence myth, all of which assume that the present world is the fourth world.

nation from the west will destroy everything. If they fail, then the Hopis must ask the Great Spirit for the complete destruction of the world. But if all goes well, Maasaw will lead humanity into a paradisic life-everlasting, where the earth will be renewed and all people will speak one tongue and believe in one religion.

TRADITIONALISTS BECOME TRADITIONAL

By the end of the 1970s things were changing in the United States, and the religious scene was quickly becoming occupied with other topics such as the cult scare, the accusations of brainwashing in Asian cults, and the drastic measures employed by concerned parents.[7] The Hopis were left to themselves.

Of signal importance, noted in chapter 5, is the fact that Banancya appeared again eight years later, only this time the audience was quite different: It consisted of other Hopis! Banancya attended the Second Hopi Mental Health Conference in 1983 and showed an illustration of the petroglyph, but the illustration (figure 21) had now changed again. It was a combination of figures 18 and 19.

He related that the interpretation was given to him by John Lansa of Oraibi in 1951, but a few details had changed in relation to his earlier interpretation. The circle to the right of Maasaw now symbolized the physical world and creation:

> So the first three figures shown on the top line symbolize the stages of the whiteman, his scientific advancements, from the carriage to the automobile to the airplane. The circles right underneath the figures prophesize the three gourds of ashes that would fall on earth. The first and second circles are interpreted to mean the bombs that fell on Hiroshima, Japan in World War II. The four headless figures on top show our Hopis who have become like the whiteman. These are Hopis who have forsaken their Life Plan and who have become like the *bahana*. They have fallen for their way of life—the easy life, the modern conveniences—and do not care for Hopi life anymore. These Hopis will say to other Hopis to follow their ways. Now if all Hopis fall for this trap, then life will be like the line going up. It will be up and down, turmoil, earthquakes, floods, drought. The old people say we are at this stage of life now. But it is prophecized that a phase of life will come when those Hopis who have become like the whiteman will realize their wrong-doings and attempt to join again the Hopis who are holding on. This is symbolized by the line going down back to the Life Plan of the Hopis. Now if this happens, then there will be times of unity, of all Hopis,

7. See Bromley and Richardson 1983, Shupe, Bromley, and Oliver 1984, Beckford 1985, Robbins, Shepherd, and McBride 1985.

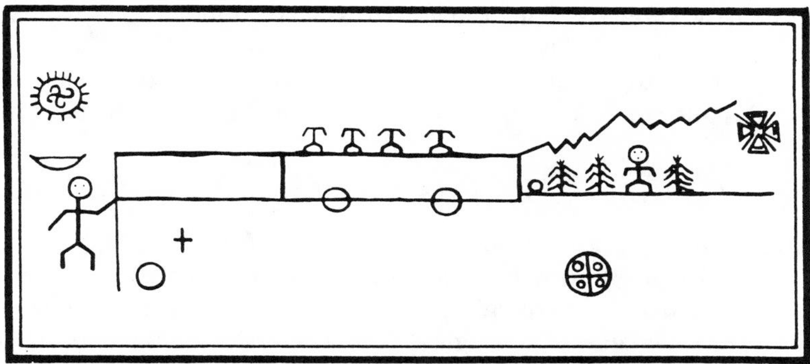

Figure 21. Drawing of Prophecy Rock by Thomas Banancya. SOURCE: Robin 1983. Courtesy of the Hopi Health Department.

> working together. We would have then come back on this Life Plan set out by the Great Spirit for us. This is symbolized by the circle (life) and the corn.
>
> Now it is foretold that we would meet up with Masauu one more time (purification?) as symbolized by the figure. He will judge us and if we are deserving to go on with him, he will accept to be the leader of the Hopis. And thereafter we will have a happy life.
>
> I want to give my appreciation for your interest in your own culture. I am happy that you are beginning to show this interest.
>
> We are fortunate. We still have our Hopi things. Let us keep it. Let us show dedication to our way of life so that we (the world) may benefit from it. Learn your language and use it. It is yours. I want to encourage each of you to learn, to benefit yourself. This is what I want to leave you with. (Robin 1983:41)

Despite the jibes to the Tribal Council, this quote clearly demonstrated a changing interpretation of details and a change of policy for the Traditionalist Movement: Where doom and alienation from the mainstream of the Hopi people had been the theme of so many decades, the hope of reconciliation during the 1980s brought other prophecies with it. The story is more in line with the "traditional" (not "Traditionalist") story again. As the dwindling support by Whites faded with the turn of the decade, the only possible choice available was reconciliation with the rest of the Hopi people.

At the Third Annual Hopi Mental Health Conference, which had the theme "Prophecy in Motion," in 1984, Banancya once again came as a key speaker for the "Land and Hopi Teachings Workshop." This time he used the reproduction of the petroglyph he had been using during the 1970s, namely figure 19. No explanation was offered in the published report, but it was stated that "the pictures and symbols in the drawing seemed to match precisely the teachings revealed" by the activist group that met in 1948 to discuss Hopi prophecies. At the Fourth Annual Conference, Banancya retold his prophecies without the use of the drawing.

CHANGING AUDIENCES, CHANGING MEANINGS

Meaning is in the mind and not in the object: In other words, both interpretation and iconography have changed over the years in keeping with changing audiences and changing times. It is also evident that changing messages reflect changing strategies. Tarbet's version represents strategical categories 4 and 5. Banancya's 1975 version represents category 3, whereas his 1983 and 1984 versions represent category 6.

The kaleidescope of change the accompanying chart of comparisons (Chart D) illustrates may seem to be sensational. What may have been a record of a Spanish military campaign became a record of White American inventions and ended up being a record of mysticism and prophecy. Such an odyssey stretches the imagination. With what might politely be called "poetic license" we find that the attacking Spaniard became the Great Spirit and that the Hopis defending their mesa crag became Americanized Hopis on their way to destruction. The rolling rocks became wheels and ended up as wars.

Besides the incongruency of various interpretations, we are confronted with the incongruency of divergent drawings. Compared with the drawing reproduced as figure 16 (compare with plate I), there are many details that do not mesh with the published drawings used by the Traditionalists. Although I cannot conclusively interpret the picture, the divergencies are instructive. First of all, the figure in the lower left-hand corner, who has been consistently interpreted as Maasaw (called by the pan-Indian term "the Great Spirit"), does not have the characteristics common to symbols and drawings of Maasaw.[8] The figure I photographed seems to be a weapon-carrying figure with a feather on his head. He may be carrying a staff and/or bow and arrow. He is in movement and is holding on to the vertical line. If he is not a Spanish captain, then he may perhaps be one of the superhuman guides of the emergence from the underworld, such as one of the warrior Twins. Maasaw is normally called *qataymataq qatuuqa*, "one who lives without being seen," because he allegedly disappeared after granting the Hopis their rights to the land, and therefore we should not expect to see him depicted at all. It is dangerous to picture Maasaw, or even talk about him,

8. See illustrations in Malotki and Lomatuway'ma 1987*b* and in Colton 1949.

A Spanish captain leading an attack on Oraibi

Stone stairway to the mesa crag

The Great Spirit is granting access at the time of the Emergence

Lower horizontal line is the path of the Great Spirit

Symbol belonging to both the Indian and the White, but the Whites change it to the symbol of the cross.

The bow and arrow are tools given to the Hopis by the Great Spirit. The Great Spirit points to the spiritual path. The upper path is the White man's, the lower path is the spiritual path of the Hopis. The vertical line connecting the two paths represents the first contact between the Hopis and the Whites since the Emergence.

Maasaw, the Great Spirit, holds the path of life and the Emergence reed.

Sun and the four directions

Symbols to be held by the White man.

The land

Maasaw, "Messiah" meets the Hopis, presents the spiritual path.

The White Brother changes the circle to the cross.

The figure is Maasaw.

The circle is the physical world and creation.

My interpretation of figure 16 based on the earliest interpretation and reasonable metaphorical possibilities.

Either a Spanish captain or one of the Warrior Twins during the Emergence

The valley floor or a metaphor of the Hopi way.

Chart D. Comparisons of drawings and interpretations of Prophecy Rock.

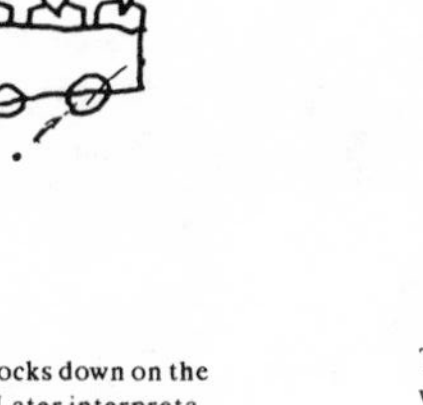

Three Hopis rolling rocks down on the attacking Spaniards. Later interpretations say it is a wagon, and others that it is a locomotive.

The "tempters" who tempt the Hopis with sweet words, inventions, and clothes, and try to coax them to abandon their religion.

The destruction of life and property.

Two White men and one Hopi representing the Hopis who have adopted the White man's ways.

World War I and World War II.

Loss of unifying judgment, beheading of wicked ones (= Western man's inner state), heads of power structure who are invisible and cut off from the people and nature.

World War I and World War II

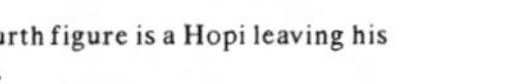

The fourth figure is a Hopi leaving his people.

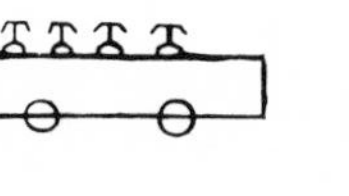

The first three symbolize scientific achievements: carriage ---> automobile ---> airplane

The ash gourds (=atomic bombs) dropped on Hiroshima, etc.

All four are Hopis who have become like Whites.

The group on the mesa top do not seem to be throwing rocks. Heads with faces, firmly on shoulders, holding hands.

The wounded captain is taken by the Hopis to a spring where water is poured on him and his wounds are healed.

The Purification Day.

The Great Spirit waits on the other side of Purification Day to see whether people have retained identity, language, and religion. Those who do not are lost.

The Great Purification, after which there will be abundant corn and water. The Great Spirit will return and all will be well.

White man's path becomes erratic and finally just fades away.

The short, materialistic path, ending in annihilation; steps to riches drops in catastrophe.

The spiritual path which is indefinite

The Great Spirit with planting stick and corn establishes his way of life.

World shaking event which will unify and make whole, the Great Day of Purification

Path back to the proper way in order to avoid annihilation.

Man's advancement in technical knowledge, the White man's path.

Maasaw leads humanity into paradisic eternal life.

A life of turmoil, earthquakes, floods, drought, if people choose the easy White man's life.

Those Hopis who have realized their wrong-doings will try to join the right path again.

The life plan, times of unity.

Life and corn

Maasaw will judge and will become leader and humans will have a happy life.

A double person or someone pouring water on the wounded Spaniard.

A wounded Spaniard at a water hole near the fields or a metaphor of the Hopi ethical path of life.

Chart D. (continued)

Plate I. Photos of Prophecy Rock by Armin W. Geertz, 1988.

Plate I. (continued)

Plate I. (continued)

Plate I. (continued)

because he may suddenly appear and scare a person stiff. The bottommost horizontal line could be the valley floor where the crops are raised, or it could also serve as a metaphor of the Hopi path of life. The old and bent figure who moves among the corn with his corn plant crook could be interpreted as the stages of human life, the result of which is to become so old that one is bent over and needs the use of a cane. But, it could also represent a dying Spaniard at a spring.

The uppermost horizontal line that ends in zigzag is intriguing and mystifying. Not only do the figures have heads and faces, but their heads also sit firmly on their necks. So they can hardly be Banancya's headless Hopis nor Tarbet's headless Whites. Not only that, but they are also holding hands! Perhaps the first three figures belong to an iconographic unit consisting of the square on which they stand and which is crosscut by two circles. In that case this unit might indicate a group on top of the mesa, but they do not seem to be throwing stones. The most intriguing figure is the one walking the zigzag path. Instead of representing a double person or a siamese twin, one with a headband and one without—which is unheard of in Hopi mythology—it could also represent someone pouring something on the figure with the crook.

Pongyayawma claimed that the petroglyph is a fraud. He related that Monongya was speaking about the rock one time during wedding preparations at Naasavi kiva. Pongyayawma's successor, Kyarwisiwma, challenged Monongya to bring out his drawing of the petroglyph, to which he acquiesced. As it turned out, Kyarwisiwma had visited the rock on an earlier occasion and had made his own drawing. Upon comparing the two, Monongya was promptly accused of fraud.

One might counter that both Pongyayawma and Kyarwisiwma had their own reasons for discrediting their political rival; undoubtedly, but no ulterior motives are needed in this instance. Monongya and Banancya had changed their story and their drawings. How do we explain this? Are accusations of charlatanry sufficient for our academic purposes?

I think not. The question might better be reformulated in this manner: Do our (and the Hopi) conceptions of truth have anything to do with meaning? To answer this question, we need to look once again at the mechanisms of meaning.

Roy D'Andrade's view of cultural meaning systems is useful in articulating the analytical dimensions of this case study. He conceived of the relationship between culture and meaning systems in the following terms:

> The position taken . . . treats culture as consisting of learned systems of meaning, communicated by means of natural language and other symbol systems, having representational, directive, and affective functions, and capable of creating cultural entities and particular senses of reality. Through

> these systems of meaning, groups of people adapt to their environment and structure interpersonal activities. Cultural meaning systems affect and are affected by the various systems of material flow, such as the flow of goods and services, and an interpersonal network of commands and requests. Cultural meaning systems are linked to personality systems through the sharing of specific items that function in both systems for particular individuals. Various aspects of cultural meaning systems are differentially distributed across persons and statuses, creating institutions such as family, market, nation, and so on, which constitute social structure. Analytically, cultural meaning systems can be treated as a very large diversified pool of knowledge, or partially shared clusters of norms, or as intersubjectively shared, symbolically created realities. On the individual level, however, actual meanings and messages that people learn, encounter, and produce are typically not divided into separate classes of items that can be labeled knowledge, norm, or reality, but rather form multifunctional complexes of constructs, organized in interlocking hierarchical structures, which are simultaneously constructive, representive, evocative, and directive. (1984: 116)

D'Andrade noted four important properties of meaning systems: 1) modifiability, 2) reflexiveness, 3) interdependence, and 4) redundancy (ibid.:104–105). These four properties account for the fact that people change their own meaning systems, that they think things through "and get things straight (or get themselves into a terrible muddle)," that they "construct messages about messages and meanings about meanings," (ibid.:104) and that they repeat messages in order to keep specific meaning systems alive.

D'Andrade's insights provide a theoretical basis for understanding Banancya's talent for changing meaning systems. The Traditionalists found themselves in 1948 on the threshold of an accelerating process of change. Faced with a perceived threat of political, social, and existential disintegration in a greater sea of change (postwar U.S. society), the Traditionalists joined and helped develop complex networks of information flow. These networks linked groups as disparate as Indian organizations, ecology movements, hippies, and New Age proponents. Each group addressed the others in terms common to displaced or minority groups in reference to common meaning systems or sets of meaning systems. But each group has also used the others for its own particular needs and goals and in reference to its own particular meaning systems. Therefore, a type of mutual misrepresentation is unavoidable.

The Traditionalists have changed their story, but their basic message resistance to acculturation, has remained constant. Thus, students of the Hopis should not look for meaning in curious details about rocks and stones, ash gourds and prophecies, but in historical processes, cultural systems, and the Hopi mind.

TEN

Hippie-Sinom (Hippie People) and the Crisis of Meaning

MUTUAL MISREPRESENTATION

In 1967, the Hopi Tribal Council enacted the following resolution:

> WHEREAS, the Hopi Tribal Council has been informed that a group of California people known as "Hippies" is likely to visit the Hopi Reservation in the near future; and
> WHEREAS, this group is known to have radical ideas and practices which are incompatible with the Hopi Culture;
> NOW, THEREFORE, BE IT RESOLVED by the Hopi Tribal Council that this group is declared undesirable and all members of this "hippie" group shall not be allowed on the reservation.
> BE IT FURTHER RESOLVED that the Superintendent is hereby requested and authorized to employ whatever means are necessary to remove individuals or groups of "hippies" from the Reservation at his own discretion.
>
> CERTIFICATION
>
> I hereby certify that the foregoing Resolution was regularly adopted by the Hopi Tribal Council on the 1 day of June, 1967, by a vote of 9 in favor and 0 opposed, the Chairman not voting after full and free discussion on the merits.
>
> Logan Koopee, Chairman
> Hopi Tribal Council
>
> ATTEST:
> Kedric Outah, Acting Secretary
> Hopi Tribal Council
> (SOURCE: The Hopi Tribe 1967)

This resolution was evidently passed because word was out that a horde of 2500 hippies were on their way to stage a "love-in" near the

Grand Canyon and would then move on toward the reservation. As the *Hopi Action News* (16 June 1967) commented:

> It was reported that Hippies are devout readers of Frank Waters's book, "The Book of The Hopi" and are getting a wrong impression of the Hopi religion and the Hopi way of life.
>
> It should be said at this point that the Hippies can or have nothing to contribute to the Hopi people. They do no constructive work and yet expect other people to supply them with food and other necessities of living, and they take drugs of various kinds. Hippies are apparently declared persona non grata on Hopi land.

The resolution was never put into effect, but the Traditionalists opposed it anyway. The resolution was answered a year later by Qötshongva in a letter addressed to the superintendent:

> Dear Sirs,
> I have just been informed about the resolution Hopi Tribe NO-H-9-67. Adopted by the Tribal (Hopi) Council on June 1, 1967, authorized by you.
>
> That you have requested and authorized to employ what ever means necessary to remove any individuals or group of "Hippies" from the reservation at your own discretion.
>
> Your attitude toward people is wrong and wicked, removing people from my village by police force is very wrong for the Hopi. I hereby reject the above RESOLUTION NO-H-9-67.
>
> On the ground that this resolution was acted upon without my approval, nor none of the information concerned this resolution ever come to my attention, that the village of Hotevilla will be subject to it.
>
> Now for years I have retold my reasons to the people at the Agency as to why the village of Hotevilla refuses to accept all your programs. That is by high reasons, the Hotevilla Village was settled by traditional way from the beginning, and will continue to be. All your law enforcements must discontinuing within the Village, during the ceremonials and at all times.
>
> The village will govern itself, as it has been doing for years, I hope you comply according to my wishes, otherwise your removal will be considered in very near future. Our independency will continue on.
>
> Let this be heard throughout the world, that all the laws and regulation you put before us will not solve the Hopi problem, only solution is INDEPENDENCE yours and ours, as "Hopi Independent Nation."
> Sincerely,
> Chief *Katchongva
> (SOURCE: Katchongva 7-15-1968)

Both the resolution and Qötshongva's reaction present a clear idea of the conflict the hippie presence caused among the Hopis. Both documents are obviously political, but serve to warn the reader that even though this chapter may seem to be a documentation of cultural madness, the topic is serious enough and raises questions about American and European values, conceptions, and stereotypes.

Robert F. Berkhofer, Jr., explained it in this way:

> In the end, to understand the White image of the Indian is to understand White societies and intellectual premises over time more than the diversity of Native Americans. Although the social and cultural attributes of Native Americans influenced the conception of them by Whites, it is ultimately to the history of White values and ideas that we must turn for the basic conceptual categories, classificatory schema, explanatory frameworks, and moral criteria by which past and present Whites perceived, observed, evaluated, and interpreted Native Americans, whether as literary and artistic images, as subjects of scientific curiosity, or as objects of philanthropy and policy. As fundamental White ways of looking at themselves changed, so too did their ways of conceiving of Indians. Since the description, interpretation, explanation, and manipulation of the Indian as image and person were and are inextricably combined in White minds, the scholarly understanding of past and present White images becomes but the latest phase of a centuries-old White effort to understand themselves through understanding Native Americans and vice versa. (1978:xvi)

In this chapter we will examine a particular kind of conception of the Indian, which Whiteley characterized as "white, post-hippie hippies who, having read *Book of the Hopi* . . . attempt to enact quasi-Hopi identities." (1988:2). In other words, this chapter will deal with Euro-Americans who more or less adopt Hopi ideology as their own, enacting, as it were, their own fantasies about the long-lost White Brother. It resembles the "Pocahontas perplex," formulated by Rayna Green (1976), but differs because the White man's self-image is created within the framework of the Hopi (and therefore a foreign) cosmology. Furthermore, it involves the question of mutual reinforcement, noted by Stewart Brand (1988:572), in which American Indians have provided the counterculture with a living identity base. The consequent role which the hippies and those like them came to play are what I will call the "apocryphal White Brother conceit," or the "Pahaana syndrome" for short, a (perhaps tongue-in-cheek) syncretism of Hopi and psychological terminology.

This chapter is more a catalogue than an analysis since it is well-nigh impossible to document each and every idiosyncratic group that has made its presence felt on the reservation. I present a typology here, but this must not be construed as a statistically secure typology, nor can it be assumed that the categories are exclusive. This chapter complements chapter 9 by illustrating what White supporters have looked for and gained by their activities on the reservation. Whereas I have paid attention to Traditionalist rhetoric and activities in chapters 6 through 9, this chapter serves to show that there was indeed an audience for which the

Traditionalists adapted their language and style. After presenting an array of documents concerning exotic Euro-American interest groups, I will once again return to the question of meaning.

THE *PAHAANA* SYNDROME

We have seen, especially in chapters 2 and 6, that an important part of the Hopi apocalypse is the return of the mythological White Brother, Pahaana, who will identify himself by returning a piece of stone tablet that will match the stone tablet in the village chief's possession. This figure, although long known to scholars, became popularly known only after the publication of Frank Waters' *Book of the Hopi*. That book signaled a veritable invasion of the reservation by hippies and other Euro-Americans driven by curiosity and not a few exotic delusions. Most of these delusions fall under what I labeled the Pahaana syndrome.

All too common are incidents such as the following described in *Qua' Töqti*:

> Yesterday . . . a Bahana man appeared at Hotevilla and inquired after spiritual leaders of certain villagers. Somehow he found his way to the home of James Pongyayouma, the recognized chief of the village and offered him a piece of stone.
>
> Pongyayouma inquired as to the purpose of the stone and the visitor told him that the stone had certain spiritual powers, and that it was meant for him, the chief.
>
> The chief replied, he said, that he had a stone (tablet) of his own, and that he saw no necessity of having another which he did not understand or desired. The man insisted that he was giving the stone to the chief, who refused to accept it.
>
> Pongyayouma stated that he told the visitor that the Bahana was just using the Hopi people for his own purposes, and that many come for information and then turn the information around to use it for personal gain and against the Hopis. For this reason he said that he does not talk with Bahanas anymore, and that he was not going to, in the future.
>
> He said he walked away from the visitor who still insisted on talking to him.
>
> Earlier that same day, this man had shown the stone, of which he had two, to other villagers and told them to hold the stone in the hand to get a spiritual message. They said they tried the stone but received no response. They then directed him to the house of "Granpa" David Monongye, factional leader in the village, telling him that the man could speak fluent English and that he claims to know all about these things, and has told the outside world that he is chief of the village.
>
> The visitor replied that he was not interested in a "political" Hopi, that he did not come to see them, although he had heard of Monongye. The visitor stated that he was not going to David's house, and left. The man

> was never identified nor did he explain himself, only that he came from New Mexico, or Old Mexico. (June 15, 1978)

One could easily imagine the villagers humoring this man, but firmly telling him in their own way that his world was as foreign to them as that of the soldiers, missionaries, superintendents, and oilmen. This message has never really had the impact that it should, however, because it has fallen on deaf ears, and this is not because the Hopis have not tried.

One indication of the social effect the hippies have had on the Hopis is the place accorded to them in Hopi ritual clowning. Ritual clowning is a complex activity that draws on and operates in at least three major domains of Hopi reality at once: the mythical, the ritual, and the social.

Louis Hieb's unpublished dissertation is the best study to date on Hopi clowning (1972). According to Hieb, the ritual clown is a "practical ethicist" who uses humor as a strategy for dealing with problematic situations (ibid.:iii). He characterized humor and ritual clowns from a structural perspective:

> Humor consists in the perception of a multiplicity of meanings in one or more terms, the existence of correspondences permitting passage from one group (or domain) of meanings to another, and a quantitative or qualitative reversal or inversion of one pattern of meaning against another consciously or unconsciously accepted pattern of meaning with an element of incongruity in the juxtaposition of the two patterns. The ritual clown brings problematic patterns into juxtaposition with accepted patterns by focusing attention on the semantic plurality of the pivotal term(s) which relate the two patterns, levels of meaning, systems of classification, conventions and practical behavior, structures of perception, and so on. (ibid.:iv)

Thus, the ritual clown is a specialist in dealing paradoxically with meaning systems in order to clarify, justify, and realize these systems. The ritual clown is a social commentator who, in orchestrating a social drama, excels in transforming local gossip into categories of ultimate significance. The fact that hippies have appeared in clown skits throughout the 1960s and 1970s is actually no laughing matter at all.

A few examples from Hieb's work will suffice. In a skit where the clowns were dealing with Black Americans as a category of the "Other," a hippie was more or less involuntarily drawn into the act. The clowns were about to eat together with four black-colored clowns, when they remembered to say their prayers:

> But, first, they must pray and so they look around for a "hippie" saying, "Where's a Jesus?" With little effort, they find a "volunteer" whom they march into the plaza. He is stood on a chair, prayers of a Christian character are offered to him, and then he, too, is invited to eat with them. (ibid.:184)

Hieb wrote that there is no readily available evidence to clarify the degree of "otherness" that Black Americans have in relation to Whites, Navajos, or Mexicans in Hopi thought. But one thing is clear: Hippies are at the bottom of the social scale in the above skit. He wrote elsewhere:

> If any one subject seemed to have consistent attention from the clowns, it was the long-haired, bearded Anglos who frequently attend the summer kachina dances. In nearly every kachina ceremony, the clowns would notice a "hippie" entering the plaza and say, "There's Jesus." More recently the "Jesus movement" has begun, but the Hopis sense of humor involves—in this instance—a perception of a visual correspondence between the appearance of these visitors and the Heinrich Hofmann portraits of Christ, which are commonly used in popular Christian religious materials—calendars, paintings, etc., which Hopis see in off-reservation towns. Attitudes towards "hippies" vary. . . . Nevertheless, there are many aspects of "hippie" behavior which Hopis do not like:
>
> > They lack respect. At Bacabi one girl imitated the Butterfly dancers with arms upraised. She really put on a show. . . . They wear bells. . . . They sometimes walk right in and use the toilet without even asking. They're dirty. . . . They don't wear shoes. They have intercourse like animals [i.e., they make love in public]. . . . They wear beards.
>
> At the same time both "progressive" and "traditionalist" Hopis are aware that many of the medical and other professional services they benefit from are performed by bearded Anglos. The following humor, however, is motivated in part by these attitudes and experiences:
>
> > Clown: Are you Jesus?
> > Hippie: No.
> > Clown: Are you Moses?
> > Hippie: No.
> > Clown: Are you his brother?
> > Hippie: Yes.
> > Clown: Well, we don't believe in you!
>
> Frequently "hippies" are invited to come and eat in the plaza—in the manner one is informed he is to be a clown! The following comments were made while one vistor tried some Hopi food. . . . :
>
> > Clown: Go ahead, help yourself. Drink my coffee. Eat my food. This is the last supper.
>
> When the clowns' aunts began bringing in food at another dance, one clown announced: "I shall never be hungry. Only hippies are hungry." On still another occasion, three "hippies" were lined up next to the *kachinum* and told to dance. Their awkward efforts to follow the complex dance steps and movement was accorded much laughter. Outside the ritual context, Hopis look on these activities of the clowns as being impolite, indeed *kahopi*. (1972:196–198)

Part of the conflict between the hippies and the Hopis was due to the fact that the hippies never tried, and were incapable of, perceiving Hopi reality. Another part was due to the fact that the Traditionalists needed their support in their battle against the Tribal Council and therefore played along with them.

As will be seen below, New Age groups have consistently misinterpreted, misrepresented, and exaggerated Hopi reality. My explanation for this is that even though they shared the same network of meaning systems with the Traditionalists, hippies and New Age practitioners have simply been using the Hopis "as an excuse for something else, as a focus for a movement bound up in its own voraciously apocalyptic vanities" (A. W. Geertz 1987*c*:40). As I wrote in the article just cited: "To me the Peabody Coal Company and the Friends of the Hopi [a New Age organization] are one and the same: each has a vision all their own which is only obliquely relevant to the Hopi vision" (ibid.:44). I will return to this problem below.

A TYPOLOGY OF EURO-AMERICAN INTEREST GROUPS

All the examples chosen here have one thing in common, i.e., some extent of identification, subtle or otherwise, with the Pahaana in Hopi prophecy. The various categories I have found are explicit identification, symbolization, eclecticism/syncretism, activism, and tourism/hobbyism.

Explicit Identification

This category involves individuals and groups who explicitly believe that they incarnate one or another aspect of the Hopi prophecy. It is most often the belief that they are the long-awaited White Brother. The newspaper story of the man with the two stones is an example of this category. The Buddhist priest mentioned in chapter 2 is another example. The flying-saucer prophet of chapter 8 is a third. A doctoral student at the Carl G. Jung Institute in Zürich concluded her dissertation with the statement that she considered Jung to be the long-awaited Pahaana (Wallgren 1973).

In the January 1975 issue of the *East West Journal*, Karmapa is equated with the "Man in the Red Hat" in Traditionalist prophecies:

> When Karmapa visited the Hopis recently in the Southwest and put on his red ceremonial hat in order to give them Tantric initiations, the chiefs recognized him as the "Man in the Red Hat" whose arrival their own legends predict.

A more recent example is Robert Boissiere, who has visited the Hopis ever since 1948. He recently published a book for a New Age press, *Meditations with the Hopi*, in which he describes a vision he received near Shipolovi in 1951:

> On a hot summer day, around noon, thirty-five years ago, I was lying on a slab of stone, exhausted from working in the fields with my long-time friend and Hopi brother, Leslie Koyawena. The burning sun of mid-day was penetrating my whole body as I lay flat. Some Hopi fields are several miles from the villages, and it was a relief to be napping on this rocky ledge called Soyok Mesa, only a few hundred yards from the village of Shipaulovi, my temporary home. Lying there, I saw a vision, and recounting it thirty-five years later, it still fills me with wonderment.
>
> In the hypnotic twilight that precedes sleep, I distinctly saw the form of a man-like figure. He was incredibly tall, and he did not appear to have any Indian-like features. He had long blond shoulder-length hair.
>
> I said, "Who are you?"
>
> "Somiviki," he replied. And then he said, "You shall have your own clan, which will be named 'The Banana Clan.'" This was thirty-five years ago, and the Banana Clan is a reality today.
>
> Stunned as I was, of course, I reported the incident to the family I was living with at the time. They seemed to grasp what had happened much better than I did, because after a pause, they all burst into loud laughter that still echoes in the village today. The Hopi name for white man is "Pahana," or rather sounds like it, since Hopi is not a written language. This leads to a pun, of course, which is still in the people's minds to this day. A clownish situation, as they saw it, this freshly imported Frenchman telling them of a clan of outsiders wanting to learn to be Hopi.
>
> Hopi clowns drum up incredible situations in order to teach Hopi truths to the people, which made my friends much more prepared to understand this than I was. Looking back, now I know that Hopi prophecies tell of the white brother, the Pahana, who would, one day, come back to the Hopi from the east, bringing with him the brotherly love of the early beginnings. I did not know it then.
>
> The Banana Clan has established itself through the years, and it has entered the fabric of village folklore. Throughout those years, the clan has developed an understanding of the Hopi Way, and it has enriched our lives with a system of values, and a unique philosophy of life.
>
> *Meditations With the Hopi* is an attempt to make the Hopi Way available on a soul level to non-Hopis. The secret knowledge of the Hopi is protected, as it should be. There is no need to divulge any of it in order to bring this message. Let us remember that all of us, whites, blacks, reds, or yellows come from the same source and will return to it in the end.
>
> No ritual is really the exclusive property of one particular group as long as it can be integrated at the soul or spiritual level. There is a human group consciousness which disperses the knowledge as perceived by individuals

> or groups as a channel to reach the divine. The Hopi Way is one of these ways, and like the Christian, Moslem or Buddhist ways, it will lead the seeker to an understanding of the Creator. (1986:121–123)

It seems clear enough that despite all of the pretence, Boissiere felt that he was the Pahaana bringing to the Hopis his particular brand of universalism, and that his book provided access to the Hopis on a "soul level."

Similar to this type are people who simply "go native." This type of behavior has long been termed the Americanism "Indianization." Anthropologist A. Irving Hallowell generalized the phenomenon by calling it "transculturalization," a term signifying "the process whereby *individuals* under a variety of circumstances are temporarily or permanently detached from one group, enter the web of social relations that constitute another society, and come under the influence of its customs, ideas, and values to a greater or lesser degree" (1963:523).

One of the best-known figures in the Hopi area was a Mrs. P. G. Gates, from Pasadena, who was a member of the Sequoia Club. She wanted to live on the reservation in order to escape the "cares of the fashionable world." She pitched a tent near Oraibi in 1902 and built a house there in 1904, but left shortly after the split in 1906. Superintendent Burton claims to have seen her "dancing in a heathen ceremony with Indians" (Hieb 1972:59). She and the missionary J. B. Epp were evidently deeply involved in supporting the Hostile cause, and the archival evidence seems to indicate that their involvement was more than either they or the Hopis could handle. It was Gates, by the way, who became Burton's bane, since she was one of the main witnesses whose evidence secured a successful conclusion to Charles F. Lummis's campaign for the removal of Burton and several teachers at the Oraibi day school from the reservation (cf. Lummis 1903 and chapter 5 above).

Other examples abound. Hippies have constantly showed up at Hopi ceremonial dances dressed in "Indian" costumes and dancing on the roofs or even in the plaza.

Symbolization

This category involves individuals and groups who use the Hopis as a symbol of or focus for their own particular ideology. One example involves the various ecology movements mentioned in chapter 8. Another example was treated in my 1987 article "Prophets and Fools," in which I described my experiences with the Flagstaff-based umbrella organization, Friends of the Hopi, founded by Richard Kastl. This organization attempted to coordinate fundraising and other activities which various support groups of the Traditionalist Movement were involved in. As they wrote in their second newsletter:

> Friends of the Hopi is not an organization with a membership. It is, rather, a coordinating center whose work is facilitated by a coordinating "consensus group" which meets every three months, and by a Board of Trustees who are presently establishing a non-profit, and hopefully tax-exempt, receptacle for all monies collected in the name of Friends of the Hopi. (*Friends of the Hopi Newsletter* 2, October/November 1977)

The organization acted as a channel of information about the Hopis, held lectures, meetings, and benefits, sold video programs about the Hopis, and coordinated large mail and telegram campaigns aimed at President Jimmy Carter. Concerning the funds, the newsletter editor wrote:

> Money is desperately needed for the purpose of maintaining a resource for the use of the Hopi traditionals in any way they request. Thus far we have been able to provide transportation money for travel to meetings, purchase local T.V. time for showing an excellent short documentary on the intra-Hopi conflict, recently produced by KCET, and the promise of medical care for three Hopis whose present medical care is questionable. It has been suggested that we set a fund-raising goal of say $30,000 to be a reserve fund for all Hopi needs; legal, travel, medical, food, whatever. (ibid.)

By 1978 it became clear that the funds were being used by the Traditionalist leaders to purchase exactly the commodities and luxuries which the Traditionalist Movement was purportedly fighting against—a criticism that other Hopis, even followers of the Traditionalists, have raised against them. I persuaded the information secretary to find a solution to this problem if they were truly interested in the welfare of the Hopis in general. This led to a meeting between representatives of the Friends of the Hopi and the Hotevilla Village Committee in March 1979, but no concrete results came of it.

What is of interest here are the terms in which the Hopis are described in the Friends of the Hopi Statement:

> FRIENDS OF THE HOPI is the name now used to refer to sincere people who are actively involved in a co-ordinating effort to help preserve the traditional Hopi way of life. We cherish the traditional Hopi religious elders as spiritual guardians of the land who, through their prayers and a yearly ritual cycle, help to maintain the balance of Nature and hold land and life for all people and all future generations. The Kikmongwis and Mongwis, traditional Hopi leaders, are the true authority for their nation. Their leadership of the clans, societies, and villages is deeply rooted in Hopi culture and traditions, and in the Creator's law, an everlasting sacred trust. The sovereignty and independence of this ancient nation should ensure the Hopi the right to use what is theirs in any manner they see fit, free from encroachment by vested interests who have no understanding of the religious significance of their land. As part of a growing movement for dy-

namic and peaceful change, we affirm the value inherent in the traditional Hopi culture, the spiritual base of which is grounded in their common land. They protect and embody in every aspect of their way of life profound spiritual truths. (ibid.)

This partly religious and partly political prelude is followed by a paragraph on governmental and corporate injustices and then ends with what seems to be their ultimate goals:

> It is important for our culture to learn to accommodate and uphold other cultures and points of view, especially those older cultures native to this land whose wisdom is rooted in the land itself and goes back many thousands of years. We don't wish to prevent the decay of outmoded customs, but believe it is essential to respect and protect vital cultural diversity. As our ecologically unbalanced techno-culture is heading for disaster, we must open our eyes and hearts to the Hopi message—an ancient message that contains an essential ingredient for our own survival—which is that we must live in harmony with each other and with our Earth. (ibid.)

This statement reveals concern with the symbolic value of the Hopi Traditionalists in terms of the Friends of the Hopi's own concerns (strategical category 5). In the newsletter, the editor is openly self-concerned:

> One reaction to the last newsletter was that the stated assumption that Hopi is a focus for people within the "new age" movement is not applicable to everyone, much as we might wish it to be. Speaking for those of us for whom Hopi is a focus, then, we see the Hopi stand against U.S. power as an archetypal stance. We can almost feel the converging threads of Karma that have led us all as humans to this point in time: a people instructed to maintain their simple lives while also entrusted with the responsibility to guard all land and the dread power of the natural resources beneath their land for the cooperative use of future generations. (ibid.)

Evidently the archetypal and apocryphal sentiments rest on the need to keep the Hopis in a state of primitiveness. This reflects a common tendency in American history. Robert Berkhofer, Jr., noted that Euro-American views of Indians are "inextricably bound up with the evaluation of their own society and culture." He noted that appraisals of Indian life by Whites are based on a comparison with Euro-American culture. Accordingly, the fact that "Indians lacked certain or all aspects of White civilization could be viewed as bad or good depending upon the observer's feelings about his own society and the use to which he wanted to put the image" (1978:27–28). Thus, the interest described in this chapter is simply the other side of ethnocentrism.

Henri Baudet saw the problem as the European development of an image that clothed first the Black African, then the American Indian, then the Oriental and finally the Muslim, with all the attributes man supposedly possessed in Paradise before the fall (1959).

Berkhofer wrote concerning another curious problem:

> Along with the persistence of the dual image of good and bad but general deficiency overall went a curious timelessness in defining the Indian proper. In spite of centuries of contact and the changed conditions of Native American lives, Whites picture the "real" Indian as the one before contact or during the early period of that contact. That Whites of earlier centuries should see the Indian as without history makes sense given their lack of knowledge about the past of Native American peoples and the shortness of their encounter. That later Whites should harbor the same assumption seems surprising given the discoveries of archeology and the changed condition of the tribes as the result of White contact and policy. Yet most Whites still conceive of the "real" Indian as the aborigine he once was, or as they imagine he once was, rather than as he is now. (1978:28–29)

These types of assumptions are clearly the motivations of groups such as Friends of the Hopi.

For Gerald Sider the history of White attitudes towards Indians already began with Columbus, whose diary clearly shows attitudes of domination, deception, and self-deception. These attitudes have a marked continuity throughout postcontact history and can be aptly summed up as "the Europeans wind up parroting their own fantasies of the other" (1987:7). This parroting is, in Sider's opinion, simply the doorway into a more fundamental contradiction, namely, "between the impossibility and the necessity of creating the other as the other—the different, the alien—and incorporating the other within a single social and cultural system of domination" (ibid.).

Eclecticism/Syncretism

This category involves individuals and groups who construct worldviews consisting of bits and pieces of knowledge and dogma from various religions. It reflects what Bharati called the "Aloha-Amigo Syndrome," which he considered to be a peculiarly American phenomenon. Bharati described it as "the all-American mental retardation" of "pathological eclecticism," (1976:11) and which he explained in the following manner:

> My own experience has convinced me that the eclecticism by which the would-be mystics live—hippies young and old, middle-class Euro-Americans—is dysfunctional: it does not permit the individual to enter into the context of genuine mysticism; it remains pretext. Why so? Because in order to achieve the state of the mystic, a person has to follow a genuine

> tradition, whichever he chooses. He cannot do it by picking from what is popularly available here and there—some bad translations from one mystical tradition, some leader who has read and been impressed by similar eclectic readings and feelings. (ibid.:37; cf. A. W. Geertz 1990*b*)

There were several stories circulating in 1988 about visiting cultists on the reservation. One was an oriental fellow who comes once a year to the Tribal Office buildings, beats his drum for two days, and disappears until the next year again. Another story concerned a group of twenty ISKCON people marching from Second Mesa down to Kykotsmovi looking for Banancya. A third story concerned an incident that occurred "about three years back" (prior to 1988). The people of Kykotsmovi were mystified by what they identified as Katsina calls which they heard a number of nights in a row. Their speculations ceased when one early morning a White man came down the path to Kykotsmovi wearing a robe and a special headdress. He was the source of the calls, and he claimed to be Jesus.

This person may very well have been an extraordinary German occultist by the name of Eberhard Kohler who claimed to have spoken to Christ in 1978. He became a missionary for an esoteric kind of universal Christianity. In 1984 he came into contact with Banancya through the assistance of the Austrian support group "Aktionskreis Hopi/Österreich." That same year he flew to Hopi land together with his closest followers, but was ignored by the Traditionalists. His reaction was that they were naive, ignorant, and degraded, and due to their karma, it was right and proper that they follow the path of Christ and make the grand sacrifice of life and land in order to become fellow citizens in the New Age. He then made a pilgrimmage to San Francisco Peaks where he allegedly met the Katsinas and celebrated the Christian sacrament with them. The Katsinas then invested him with the status of "Hopi Mystic in the German-speaking countries" and he became their distinctive missionary (Schweidlenka 1987).

Activism

This category involves individuals and groups who for one reason or another (most often falling into one of the preceding three categories) have actively supported the Hostile or Traditionalist political campaigns. Each decade has seen its particular activist. I have mentioned some of them already: Mrs. Gates of the first decade, Wilder Bentley of the 1950s, Richard Clemmer of the late 1960s and 1970s, and the Friends of the Hopi of the 1970s. Another example is "The Hopi House" in Washington, D.C., which warned the Traditionalists in 1967 about the Harkness Ballet performance at Lisner Auditorium which was an adaptation of a Hopi Katsina dance, and directed their protest to President Lyndon B. Johnson (Hopi House 3-4-1967, Hopi Independent Nation 3-2-1967). A further example is Craig Carpenter, son of Iroquois-White parents from Michigan, California, who played an important role for the Traditionalists during the 1950s and was coordinator between General Holdridge and Banancya in 1961, as mentioned in chapter 2.

Many Hopis have felt disgust for and enmity against the activists, not only because of their influence on the reservation, but also because of their naivety. Former Indian Agent Leo Crane quoted a letter he found addressed to Yukiwma from a woman in Indiana:

> Chief Youkeoma: you are a noble man. Do not let the Government have your children. Their schools are not the place for your Indian lads who know only the hunt and the open spaces. Resist to the last gasp. Die rather than submit. (Crane 1925:174)

Not only does the letter reveal an incredible naivety about the Hopis, but it also reveals a thoughtless death-wish on their behalf.

In my article "Prophets and Fools" I quoted extensively from a long letter written by the secretary of the Hotevilla Village Committee to Walter Manser in Switzerland. Manser had sent a letter to a whole series of organizations in the United States as well as to the Bureau of Indian Affairs protesting against the laying of waterlines in Hotevilla as a moral and ecological sin (Manser 4-8-1981). Secretary of the Village Committee Sally Yaiva-BigPond answered him in no uncertain terms. Her main point was that Manser had absolutely no insight into the blatant contradictions between Traditionalist rhetoric and Traditionalist practices, nor into the harm that meddling Whites create with their misplaced sympathy. Sally Yaiva-BigPond made clear what she considered the issue to be about:

> Apparently, Mr. Manser, all of you foreign interfering bleeding hearts and these self-proclaimed religious leaders here in Hotevilla must certainly have a grand idea of yourselves to feel that the majority of our people don't have enough common sense to know what is best for themselves. Instead, you and these fake "traditionals" take it upon yourselves to interfere in and attempt to obstruct the democratic process in which this village engages to make their decisions. As Swiss people, you should appreciate the blessings of democracy and popular opinion. . . .
>
> In truth, this entire controversy is not about religion or tradition at all but simply one which is as old as the cave man himself—power. The traditionals think the people of Hotevilla are too stupid to go to the outhouse by themselves without the say-so of the wise ones. But the history of man has proven that the most clever tricksters on earth are those who put "religion" before themselves to keep the poor, ignorant flock under domina-

tion and then they proceed to enjoy the better of two worlds. (Yaiva-BigPond 4-24-1981, 1, 9; A. W. Geertz 1982*b*:8, 16)

In my opinion, Ms. Yaiva-BigPond's blunt but astute observations are correct. The issues are neither religion nor tradition. The issues are the politics of meaning and of power. They are about social strategy more than prophecy.[1]

Tourism/Hobbyism

This category involves individuals and groups who come to the reservation as tourists or who imitate Indian life and customs in their free time as a hobby.

Tourism has been a problem ever since the railroad lines began bringing them in the 1880s. Leo Crane, in writing about conditions during the 1910s, complained:

> Probably no other section of Indian country is more visited than is the Painted Desert, where the Snake gods have such influence. From June to October comes a host, packing cameras and notebooks and sketching-blocks, attired in weird garments, big with questions, and expecting to find hotels. Most of them wish to rough it smoothly, and are easily annoyed. They seek the natural wonders of the Empire, and especially the religious "dances" of the Indian people, chief of which is the annual Hopi Snake Dance. A strange crowd, having more enthusiasm than sense, staggering under theories, swelled with importance and criticism, generously stuffed by guides. . . .
>
> The rites are conducted by the Indians with solemnity and reverence. It is not a show in a juggler's booth, to be guyed and ridiculed. But when one of the poisonous snakes has coiled, and is hissing and rattling and striking, just the time when one would think spectators would become more tense, that is when taunts are flung and a perfect bedlam of thoughtless merriment arises. Were there fewer visitors, as at minor ceremonies, they would be reproved; but the Hopi are a patient people, and they never insisted that these strangers behave themselves; they only expected that the visitor would keep his place, and not attempt to join the dance, a thing that some wild whites–including a few wild women–are only too ready to do. You now see all the standpoint of the old priest [referring to Yukiwma's hostility to Whites]. (1925:17, 250–251)

1. Evidently the unusual bluntness of Ms. BigPond's letter led to her resignation, if one can depend on the following quote from the Traditionalist newsletter:

> At least Sally BigPond was forced to resign, or was fired, for being careless in her habit of writing nasty letters to Hopi leaders and to total strangers in Europe who support the Traditionals. She created a situation so unique that it became an international issue which tarnished the Water Committee and most likely the Government whom she follows. Her co-worker M. Lomahaftewa C.D.S. resigned in shame. (*Techqua Ikachi* 19, n.d. [1982?])

Figure 22. Hopi caricature of White misconceptions. SOURCE: *Qua' Töqti*, February 22, 1979.

The problem has continued unabated, and even though the Tribal Council has tried to control the situation by providing a neutral meeting place for tourists and Hopis at the Cultural Center on Second Mesa and by issuing rules of conduct, some villages have had to close their limits to White tourists during the Snake ceremonial.[2] Mina Lansa even went so far as to close Oraibi to Whites (except for those who supported the Traditionalists) for several years.

2. See, for instance, the following articles in *Qua' Töqti*: "Villages to Develop Own Control Policies" (7-15-1982); "Visitor Control at Dance Successful" (8-26-1982); and "Snake Dance Closed to Non-Indians (8-4-1983). The problem is still relevant. During my recent stay in March 1992 most of the villages excluded Whites from the Powamuya. I heard as well that a widespread prohibition continued through the spring Katsina dances.

William Powers believed that hobbyism began in the United States around the beginning of this century with the establishment of youth organizations such as the Boy Scouts of America (1988:557). Although this may be true for its organizational impetus, I think that its roots go further back into the latter half of the 19th century in, for example, the wild-west shows and in spiritualism (Green 1988). Colin F. Taylor (1988) noted similar interests in Europe during the latter half of the 19th century. Hobbyism is described by Powers in the following way:

> A hobbyist may be defined as a non-Indian who has a wide range of interests in American Indian subjects, but mainly in arts and crafts, Indian dancing, and singing. Although here regarded as a movement, hobbyism has no national organization but rather comprises independent groups organized at the local, state, and regional levels. No statistical studies have been made of hobbyism and no population figures are available, but based on the distribution of various hobbyist publications it can be determined that: one or more hobbyist groups are located in every major city; the greatest clustering of groups is in the Midwest, especially Wisconsin, Illinois, Indiana, Ohio, and Michigan; and the average group is composed of approximately twenty members.
>
> The primary activity of hobbyist groups is the sponsorship of powwows, indoor and outdoor activities in which hobbyists dress in Indian costumes and participate in Indian dances modeled after what anthropologists call pan-Indian celebrations (Howard 1955). Indian singing is usually provided by American Indians, and dancing is accompanied by trading, feasting, and other kinds of social activities. Outdoor powwows are usually conducted over a weekend, and participants camp out in tents, campers, and tepees. (1988:557)

The publication of *The American Indian Hobbyist* in September 1954 marked a substantial interest in hobbyism. In January 1960, the magazine took on the new title *American Indian Tradition* in order to promote a wider readership, but it also marked a change of style: Hobbyists were making field trips to Indian communities, and American Indians as well as Blacks and Puerto Ricans were becoming members of hobbyist groups. Throughout its history the goals of hobbyism have been to promote "authenticity" and "Indianness," and measures of status were proficiency in dancing, ownership of one or more costumes, and the ability to "sing Indian" (Powers 1988:560–561).

The Hopis have had their hobbyists too. The worst example is an organization of Prescott businessmen known as the Smoki (pronounced "smoke-eye"), which was founded in 1921. Presently numbering about 300 active members (President Calvin Coolidge was and Senator Barry Goldwater is among them), the Smokis put on annual programs with the aim to "preserve, perpetuate and interpret ancient Indian folklore"

(Keith 1984:4). Smokis imitate Hopi Snake and Katsina dances, use Hopi personal and clan names and symbols, and even imitate Hopi myths.

In one of their official programs from 1937, they related the "legendary history" of the Smokis. The modern Smokis are allegedly descended from a splinter group of the Indian migrants over the Bering Strait:

> Learned students say that the story of the Smoki People is a symbol. That it is an allegory, wherein the spirit of the Smoki People is personified in those actual beings who lived in caves and hid from their elders, to preserve an idea and to labor to attain an ideal.
>
> If this is true, then the men and women of the Smoki of today are idealists. Indeed, they have been called so by wise people who have watched their faithful performances of the dances of the ancient Southwest. They have been compared with those devotees of Ancient Greece, who danced for the honor of their gods and for the love of dancing. (Smoki People 1937, 11, 28)

The organization described itself in the following way:

> UNIQUE ORGANIZATION
>
> With a dual purpose, that of preserving and presenting the ancient ceremonial rites of a vanishing race, and the collection and housing of archaeological treasures found in the vicinity of Prescott, the Smoki People have come to be a unique organization of studious and hard working business and professional men of Prescott like none other in the world. It is believed that no other group has devoted itself to studying, interpreting and dramatizing primitive mystic rites as have the Smoki People and their success is attested by the increasingly large audiences which witness them each year. (ibid.:27)

While the Smokis believe that they are demonstrating absolute empathy and reverence,[3] the Hopis consider it to be mockery and sacrilege. Tribal Chairman Abbott Sekaquaptewa repeatedly attempted throughout the 1970s to get the organization to stop its imitations of Hopi dances, but the Smoki's denied any wrongdoing. Their excuse was that it is entertainment, but, in other circumstances, they admit that there is more to it than that. This is precisely what the Hopis find repulsive (Keith 1984, Anonymous 1980).

Hobbyism demonstrates more than any other category of White interest groups what Euro-American interest is all about: the fulfillment and actualization of stereotypes. Rayna Green sees hobbyism as one of the oldest and most persuasive forms of cultural expression in the U.S.:

3. Parker and Nelson 1964, 37; Kraus 1974, 35.

> Almost from their very arrival in the Americas, Europeans found it useful, perhaps essential, to 'play Indian' in America, to demand that tribal peoples 'play Indian,' and to export the performances back to Europe, where they thrive to date. (1988:30)

In her opinion, the mechanisms behind hobbyism are not only serious, they are also tragic:

> For, I would insist now, the living performance of "playing Indian" by non-Indian peoples depends upon the physical and psychological removal, even the death, of real Indians. In that sense, the performance, purportedly often done out of a stated and implicit love for Indians, is really the obverse of another well-known cultural phenomenon, "Indian hating," as most often expressed in another, deadly performance genre called "genocide." (ibid.:31)

Sider sees it as a form of "incorporation" enacted in the process of domination:

> The process of domination imposes a dialogue between dominators and dominated. Each must speak to the other for the political and economic transactions to occur. In speaking to each other, they seem often to seek to incorporate one another: Western Indians wearing cowboy hats and boots, and army-style sunglasses; whites forming "Red Men's" lodges, dressing like Indians on certain occasions, and often invoking a fraudulent Indian ancestry. This attempted incorporation both defines and denies the dialogue, returning to the basic contradiction of this form of domination—*that it cannot both create and incorporate the other as an other*—thus opening a space for continuing resistance and distancing. (1987:22)

Whether seen as European impressions of the Native Americans,[4] later Euro-American images,[5] conceptions,[6] stereotypes,[7] beliefs,[8] or psychologizing,[9] academics would do well to heed Berkhofer's sobering conclusion concerning the "scientific" image of the Indian. His analysis led him to conclude that images produced by academics are just as stereotypical as those by popularists and hobbyists (Berkhofer 1978:69).

As mentioned in chapter 7, I think this is a general problem for all of human and natural sciences, and is a question of degree and method. Despite Vine Deloria's humorous caricature of anthropologists (1969: 78–100; cf. Lurie 1988), it can be argued that the descriptive, historical, linguistic, and comparative methods, though admittedly bound to larger

4. Chiapelli, Allen and Benson 1976.
5. Baudet 1959; Saum 1965; J. M. Powell 1977; Billington 1981.
6. Fairchild 1928.
7. Berkhofer 1978; Stedman 1982.
8. Pearce 1953.
9. Pagden 1982; Fogelson 1985.

paradigms, when applied with integrity nevertheless create products that approximate our and others' perceptions of reality to a high degree (cf. the Introduction).

THE NEW AGE

The term "New Age" covers an incredible variety of groups, attitudes, and philosophies.[10] The New Age is many different things and yet it is perceived by its exponents as containing one holistic worldview which is characterized by its exponents as an "amorphous cultural transition" without creed, dogma, or leaders, but which integrates such concerns as "environmentalism, holistic health, women's rights, social responsibility, and personal spirituality" (Graves 1988; cf. Adolph 1988). J. Gordon Melton wrote that "the New Age Movement was and is the attempt to find the social, religious, political, and cultural convergence between the new Eastern and mystical religions and the religious disenchantment of many Westerners" (1986:107). Of special interest to this study is that one of its main characteristics is "a transformative vision of a new world which transcended the limitations of any particular culture or religion or political system and surpassed the outmoded thought forms of old world theologies and beliefs" (ibid.:107–108).

The New Age is openly eclectic and apocryphal. It is a search for universal meaning, but it should be noted that it is essentially an *American* perception of what is "universal" and what is to be "transcended." It is this disregard of cultural uniqueness that turns what seems like universal liberation into a new form of imperialism, especially in relation to minority, ethnic, and tribal groups. It is what I have called a self-righteous "spiritual imperialism" (1987*c*:38, 44), a meaning hegemony.

New Age grew out of a long tradition of occult, oriental, and spiritualist movements in interaction with recurrent revivalisms in the United States.[11] As Donald Stone noted, "the excitement about the immanence of a divine force," which New Age offers, "has much in common with the revivalism of the Great Awakenings" (1976:113). But, there are a number of differences in terms of style, worldview, and clientele.

New Age style is highly adapted to the modern media. The various groups package their message in videotapes, audiotapes, magazines, and music; and they clearly compete with each other through advertising. In other words, the growth of these groups and their ability to reach their audience are closely related to the rules and conditions of marketing.

10. Cf. Albrecht 1981, Noonan 1981, Popenoe and Popenoe 1984, Robbins 1988.

11. Cf. Pritchard 1976, McLoughlin 1978, Ellwood, Jr. 1979, Kerr and Crow 1983, and Campbell and McIver 1987.

The worldview New Age offers is a world filled with meaning and purpose, a world on the verge of transition, ready for humanity's great leap into the holistic world of the 21st century. The New Age, which will follow, will be driven by transcendent values in which the Old Age traditions, rationality, and beliefs will be superceded by a new type of human ideal. As McLoughlin put it, "man's duty is not to get from this world into the next; life is not a perpetual battle against internal sin and external evil but a search for the unity between man and nature" (1978:200).

Human beings will no longer be helpless in the face of cosmic exigencies: Each person will through personal enlightenment become united with the god within and will gain control over his or her own destiny, perhaps even over ultimate reality. This new type of person is not bound by morals. He or she need only plug into the divine universal energy or light—*prana*, *mana*, odic force, holy spirit, call it what you will—through meditation, shamanism, "channeling" (functioning as a medium for "ancient entities"), group therapy, dance, hypnosis, and so on (cf. Hurst and Murphy 1987:231–236). It is a question of gnostic insight and not divine revelation. And it is a question of humanity rediscovering itself as embedded in nature (Spangler 1980:87). This realization is what spokeswoman Marilyn Ferguson called the "Aquarian Conspiracy" (1980:29).

New Age has not restricted its clientele to long-haired backwoodsmen. On the contrary, one of its claims to success is that it has found a market in the business world, especially through the management-training courses provided by human-potential groups such as Erhard Seminar Training and Lifespring (Stone 1976). Thus, New Age has made inroads into companies such as International Telephone and Telegraph, Firestone Rubber, and even the U.S. Army (Robbins 1988:11)!

But if New Age does not claim to be bound by any dogma, its political proponents do. Mark Satin described what he called the four New Age ethics in his book *New Age Politics*: self-development, ecology, self reliance-cooperation, and non-violence (1978:83–85). These four ethics are then conceived of "translating themselves" into six basic political values: There are the five "maximizations" of 1) social and economic well-being, 2) social and political justice, 3) cultural, intellectual, and spiritual freedom, 4) environmental quality, 5a) self-reliance of communities, regions, and nation-states, and 5b) the cooperative potential of communities, regions, and states; and the one minimization of 6) violence among individuals, groups, and governments (ibid.:85–86).

Satin's ethics are topped off with a series of social values: enoughness, stewardship, autonomy and community, diversity, many-sidedness, desireless love, reverence for life, species modesty, quality, and being kind to oneself (ibid.:86–89). These ethics and values seem to be a fine blend of Protestant ethics, liberal depth-psychology, and counterculture socialism.

Indians in the New Age

How do the American Indians fit into this "Fourth Great Awakening" (McLoughlin 1978:207)? One could cite hundreds of examples—many of which could be found in New Age advertising—of how Euro-Americans think the Indian should fit in, but Satin stated it simply enough:

> Over the last 10 years or so, many of us have begun to discover whole cultures that share in an alternate way of seeing the world. Zen, Vedanta, Sufism, North American Indian culture—whatever their differences, each of them seems, in its way of seeing, to be the polar opposite of the scientific outlook: sensuous rather than intellectual, receptive rather than active, intuitive rather than analytic. (1978:26)

These are just a few of the stereotypes that New Age exponents have about the American Indians. An important connection was noted by Theodore Roszak in his book on the counterculture. It is interesting that he devoted a whole chapter to the topic of shamanism. The reason shamanism was singled out was because, for him, the essence of the magic in shamanism is the sense "that man and not-man can stand on communicable terms with one another" (1969:245–246). This statement reflects one of the core paradigms of New Age thought and, with it, the American Indian who has become its symbol.

If any one author has been an accessory to the convergence of New Age expectations with its non-culture-specific stereotypes of the American Indian, it is Carlos Castaneda. Starting out at the University of California at Los Angeles as a doctoral candidate in anthropology who was to specialize in Yaqui ethnomedicine, he at first enthralled his readers with the magic of psychotropic experiences under the expert and mysterious guidance of his Yaqui teacher Don Juan Matus. Through each subsequent volume of his work, one detects a keen atunement to the expectations of his American audience: From the use of *datura* and peyote the reader follows Castaneda's growing maturity and his realization that Don Juan's teachings have nothing to do with drugs and everything to do with New Age ideals, i.e., a holistic worldview, strict attendance to the miraculous in nature, concerted efforts at self-development which ultimately lead to liberation even from death, and—especially in his most recent volumes—the creative manipulation of energy fields and cosmic light rays. Even though many critics have doubted the existence of Don Juan and his team of "impeccable warriors," he has nevertheless had an undeniable impact on the New Age public through eight volumes of powerful narrative (cf. Castaneda 1968, 1971, 1972, 1974, 1977, 1981, 1984, 1988; Noel 1976; and de Mille 1976, 1990).

Castaneda became a cult figure himself and many have also tried to emulate his publication success. Lynn V. Andrews (1981) and Florinda

Donner (1985)[12] found a niche in the market through a combination of feminism and Castaneda lore. One of Castaneda's friends, Michael Harner, also moved from ethnography to "going native" by establishing the Center for Shamanic Studies in Connecticut. Indians were becoming highly marketable in New Age circles, and White shamanism became a standard feature in New Age U.S.A.

But what about Indian reactions? The Indian author Wendy Rose wrote that it is just another type of cultural imperialism (1984:13), only this time the imperialists are rootless Whites who have suddenly become "experts" based on an eclectic misunderstanding of Indian thought. Not only that, they are just as arrogant, ignorant, and presumptuous as the pioneers were. She considered White shamanism to be just another type of hobbyism, and she claimed that its main problem lies in its lack of integrity and clear intentions (ibid.:17, 21).

Not all Indians felt that way, however. An interesting modern phenomenon is the appearance of well-educated, younger, Indian shamans, "the new Native shamans" as they are called. Dr. Leslie Gray from the California Institute of Integral Studies in San Francisco and Native American Studies Department at the University of California in Berkeley combines many professions and ideals: university professor, shamanistic consultant, healer, shaman, sophisticated, attractive, young, and Indian! Dr. Gray represents a new generation of Indians who have lost their traditional roots and yet who function as bridge makers between two worlds. As Carolyn Shaffer wrote:

> Those who come to Gray do not have to travel hundreds of miles to a tribal community in jungle or forest, worry about making the right kinds of tobacco offerings, and camp under a tree for days waiting to learn whether the shaman will see them. Instead, they can call her on the telephone and make an appointment just as they would with any professional counselor. (1987:22)

Dr. Gray's therapy is called "self-help shamanism" in which she teaches her patients how to enter altered states of consciousness and to travel to the upper and/or lower worlds in order to get information, health, or personal empowerment.

12. As Carlos Castaneda wrote in his foreword to Donner's book:

> I can't help having a warrior's sense of admiration and respect for Florinda Donner, who in solitude and against terrifying odds has maintained her equanimity, has remained faithful to the warrior's path, and has followed don Juan's teachings to the letter. (1985:viii)

Even though her book is purportedly an accurate rendering of field notes written while studying healers in a town in the state of Miranda, Venezuela, the teachings and the style are that of Don Juan and Carlos Castaneda.

Other Indians have found that there was a market to be made in the "medicine man circuit." These individuals quickly learned the rhetoric of the New Age and addressed themselves to their spiritually ravenous audiences, sometimes offering courses in "shamanism" and herbal medicine, sometimes just lecturing. Of particular interest to this study is the fact that a disproportionately large percentage of these "medicine men" were Hopis, and, equally significant, they were all leaders of the Traditionalist Movement: Banancya, Monongya, John Lansa, and Mina Lansa (Brand 1988:571).

Finally, it should be mentioned once again that Frank Waters' books have served to maintain the bonds between New Age interest groups and the Traditionalists, not only through the *Book of the Hopi*, but also through later works such as *Mexico Mystique* (1975) and articles in New Age magazines (cf. Waters 1987).[13]

Hopi Indians and the Harmonic Convergence

Traditionalist prophecy and prophecy rock have played integral roles in one of the most dramatic and successful New Age events of the 1980s, namely, the "Harmonic Convergence" that occurred on August 16–17, 1987.

It all began with a new ethnic hero of the New Age, a Mexican-American by the name of José Argüelles, who earned his Ph.D. at the University of Chicago in art history. He is an artist, a student of the Tibetan master Chögyam Trungpa Rinpoche, and a professor at Union Graduate School. Today he is acclaimed as a prophet and visionary. His story is like so many others: He has a fabulous talent for finding and producing significance and meaning even (or, perhaps, especially) in the most bizarre coincidences. His narratives reflect a disturbing blend of wisdom, inspiration, simple-minded arguments, pomposity, moral laxity, and frequent use of New Age jargon. Even some New Age critics found him unacceptable (cf. Dunn 1987). He bills himself as the "leading spokesperson for the principles of art as awakened warriorship and the role of art as a dynamic agent of planetary transformation" (Argüelles 1987:219).

A paraphrase of Argüelles' story will give an indication of the subject matter and of his style. Once again, the subject is American Indians, but this time it is the ancient Mayans. Born on January 24, 1939, he spent the first five years of his life on the street called Calle Tula in Mexico City. The purported significance of this is that Tula is a Toltec form of Tulan or Tollan, the name of the Mayan center of origins.

13. Among other things Waters is on the editorial advisory board of *Shaman's Drum. A Journal of Experiential Shamanism.*

He first learned about Mayan culture in 1953—the same year, as he pointed out, that the genetic code and the Van Allen radiation belts were discovered. Having experienced profound sentiments on top of the Pyramid of the Sun in Teotihuacan, he vowed to find out, not as an archaeologist, but as a "true knower, a seer" what exactly happened to the Mayans. After several years of reading Ouspensky, Morley, Eliade, and others, and visiting Mayan ruins, he began to "recollect" what happened. This nourished his growing sense of personal mission during the mid-1960s. He began to develop an "intuitive frame of mind" by painting Mayan symbols and "archetypes," and finally he began receiving intimations of "presences—star-beings, guardians."

Back in California he met two Indians: Tony Shearer, who had developed a theory concerning the prophecies about Quetzalcoatl, and Sun Bear, who was trying to establish an ecology movement. From Tony Shearer, Argüelles learned that 1987 would be a significant year.

In 1972 Argüelles met Thomas Banancya, "who shared the Hopi prophecies":

> I shall always remember Thomas saying, "only those who are spiritually strong will survive the passing of the Fourth World and the coming of the Fifth." I understand that time to be closely related to the 1987 date which Tony shared with me. (ibid.:33)

In an interview in *Newsweek* Argüelles cited a "Hopi Indian legend" which states that on August 16, 1987, "144,000 Sun Dance enlightened teachers will help awaken the rest of humanity" (Barol and Abramson 1987:50). No legend of this sort exists, especially since the Hopis have never had the Sun Dance nor do they have any tradition of "enlightened teachers."

At any rate, having read Waters's *Mexico Mystique*, and after, in his own words, "an amazing series of explorations, meetings and coincidences" (Argüelles 1987:37), he suddenly realized it all: The Mayan great cycle of 5,125 years, that began in 3113 B.C. will end in A.D. 2012. In that year the earth will pass out of a galactic ray 5,125 years in diameter and will enter a "galactic synchronization phase," a "harmonic convergence." The Mayans knew about this because they were galactic pilots who had steered spaceship Earth on its journey through the stars. The Earth is constructed with a Hopi-like central "Sipaapuni"-axis, among other things, which allows a "radiogenesis" or the universal transmission of information in the form of light or radiant energy. This is how the Mayans, who live on another plane in angelic majesty, could come into contact with Argüelles.

The days of August 16–17, 1987, exactly twenty-five years before the critical year of 2012, are a "cosmic trigger point when we shift gears, or miss the opportunity" (Barol and Abramson 1987:50). If 144,000 people can get together, "hold hands and hum" on those two days in August, then the earth will have an easy transition to the harmonic convergence.

Argüelles's book, *The Mayan Factor*, which the publisher claimed has sold 50,000 copies, ended with the following appeal:

> CELEBRATE HARMONIC CONVERGENCE!
>
> Harmonic Convergence, August 16 and 17, 1987, depends upon self-empowered individuals creating rituals, celebrations, and joyful events expressing their feelings of peace and harmony with the Earth and with each other. Take the initiative! Let us know of your plans. Call or write: Healing Our World (H.O.W.), P.O. Box 6111, Boulder, CO 80306, (303) 443-4328. (1987:221)

This appeal brought thousands of people to "sacred centers" all over the world: Mount Shasta, the Pyramid of the Sun, the Great Pyramids of Egypt, Delphi, Mount Fuji, Haleakala, King Arthur's Castle, Machu Pichu, Central Park, and so on (cf. Swan 1987). The event caught the attention of the national media and hundreds of newspapers across the U.S. In a "postconvergence" interview Argüelles claimed that at least one-hundred million people joined this "grassroots" event the world over (Alli 1988).

On August 16–17, 1987, about fifty people met with Banancya and others at prophecy rock where they constructed a New Age altar at the foot of the rock consisting of a central circle of broken pottery with animal bones and seashells and feathers on either side.[14] When I visited the site a year later, I found a crystal sitting in a niche in the rock (cf. plate II).

The visitors danced and performed rituals and slept out near the rock for about two weeks. Finally, the Hopi Police Department was sent out to disperse the group. The Hopis have seen all of this before: the hippie craze of the 1960s, the flying-saucer cult at the end of the 1960s, the ecology freaks of the mid-1970s, and the new religionists of the 1980s. For the Hopis, they were all just crazy Whites (cf. fig. 23).

What's the Meaning of All This?

Meaning is exactly what it is all about. Perhaps it is meaningless to the Hopis and to non-believers, but it is oversaturated with meaning for New Age believers. And so it should be! However, the pursuit of meaning can

14. Peter Whiteley mentioned that Banancya had signed circulars claiming that the harmonic convergence was not a Hopi idea and that the "religious leaders" had disassociated themselves from it (private communication). My sources claim otherwise, so those circulars may have been a postfactum strategy.

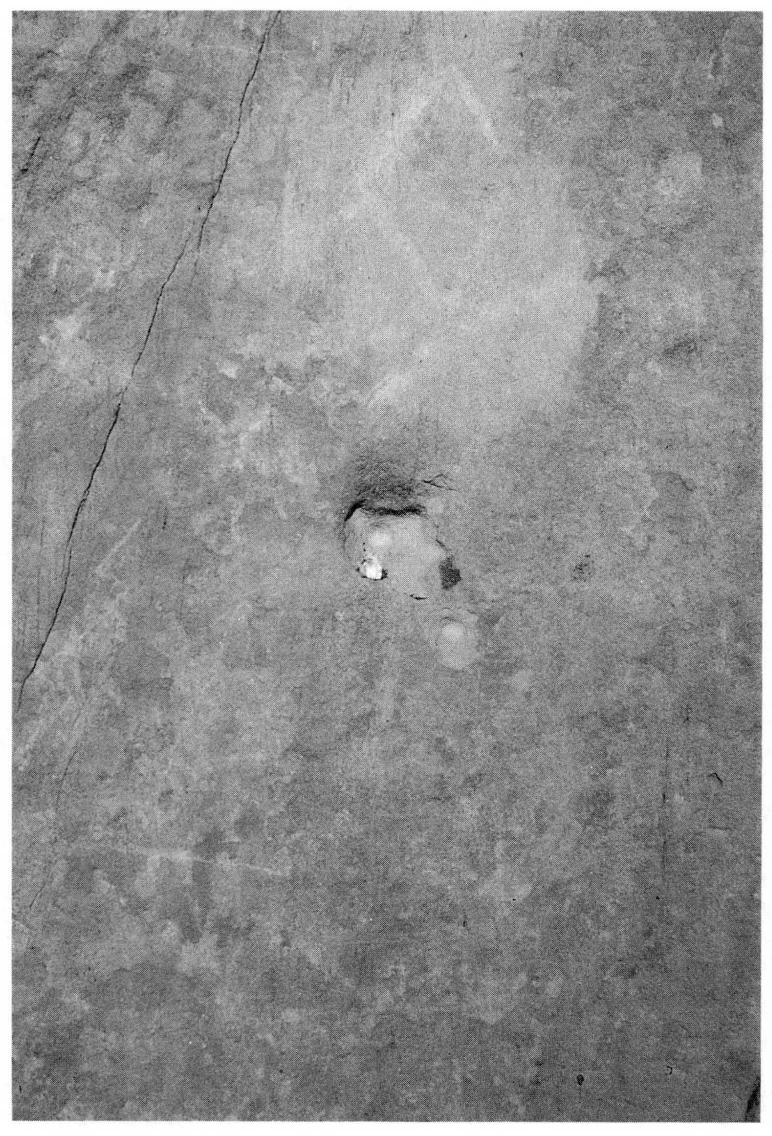

Plate II. New Age crystal offering at Prophecy Rock one year after the harmonic convergence. Photo by Armin W. Geertz, 1988.

Figure 23. Whites fighting over the Hopis. SOURCE: Jenkins and Kooyahoema 1984. Courtesy of the Hopi Health Department.

and does lead to the distorted representation of other peoples' worldviews and sometimes to the presumptuous misuse of their meaning sets and their hospitality.

New Age rhetoric pays just as much lip service to "authenticity" as hobbyism does. Each and every New Age course or event features a doctor this or that, a professor someone or other, an "elder," a "shaman," or a "pipe bearer." But beneath the surface, the professors are from New Age colleges such as the California Institute of Integral Studies and the "elders" are entrepreneurs in one guise or another. In other cases New Age offers simply another new advertising market. For instance, a Southwest jewelry and Indian articles shop now "offers unique objects empowered by the mystic Southwest." And what was once a carved Katsina doll for Hopi children and visiting tourists now becomes an Eagle Katsina which "will allow you to see visions of your future in dream time" (*The*

1988 Guide to New Age Living, 108; cf. figure 24). But, fraud aside, we are nevertheless also confronted with sincere quests for meaning.

Sociologist Robert Bellah suggested what seems to me to be a plausible explanation for religious developments in the 1960s and early 1970s. In his 1976 article "New Religious Consciousness and the Crisis in Modernity" he claimed that the massive erosion of the legitimacy of American institutions that began in the 1960s was the result of a definitive rejection of the two areas that had previously provided meaning and generated loyalty in the U.S., namely, biblical religion and utilitarian individualism. These two interpretations of reality have had complex relations of attraction and repulsion; the fundamentalist and the hedonist uncomfortably combined into one national psyche.

By the 1960s two things had become evident: 1) both interpretations began to resemble each other, and 2) neither could fulfill the ideals it represented. The pursuit of wealth and power and the concern for pure instrumentalism were no longer self-evidently meaningful. On the contrary, that pursuit was destroying the quality and meaning of life. Thus:

> Those things that had been subordinated, dominated, and exploited for the sake of rationalizing means took on a new significance. Nature, social relations, and personal feelings could now be treated as ends rather than means, could be liberated from the repressive control of technical reason. (ibid.:338)[15]

The churches were unable to cope with the new spirituality of the sixties. The Protestants could only offer moralism and verbalism, the intense religiosity of the Black churches remained unavailable for the White counterculture, and the Catholic churches defended themselves with scholastic intellectualism and legalistic moralism:

> The biblical arrogance toward nature and the Christian hostility toward the impulse [of] life were both alien to the new spiritual mood. Thus the religion of the counterculture was by and large not biblical. It drew from many sources including the American Indian. But its deepest influences came from Asia. (ibid.:340–341)

Eliade disagreed with this explanation. He argued in his essay "The Occult and the Modern World" that dissatisfaction with the Christian tradition alone does not explain the occult explosion of the 1970s. The occult offered a purported alternative to the Christian tradition in achieving a personal and a collective *renovatio* (1976:64).

15. For comparative purposes, see Eisenstadt's enlightening explanation of the protest movements in terms of the major premises of European modernity (1966; 1973:244–252). Another approach is Victor Turner's application of his ideas about communitas to hippies, millenarians, and the weak (1969:97–100).

SACRED EARTH TOURS
In magnificent Sedona, Arizona
Experience the spiritual heritage of the Southwest through your choice of tours.

VORTEX TOURS - These tours will take you to the sacred energy vortices where you will encounter powerful planetary forces. Experienced guides will assist you in attuning to the energies, participating in Earth-healing ceremonies, and learning how to find the power spots where you live.
HOPI TOURS - In touring the ancient world of the Sacred Hopi Mesas, you will encounter the oldest, continuously inhabited settlement in the Americas. You will see ceremonies and working craftsmens of a culture virtually unchanged since the beginning of recorded time.

For brochures & information, call
(602) 282-6826 or write to:
RED ROCK JEEP TOURS
P.O. Box 10305, Sedona, AZ 86336

California Institute of Integral Studies
765 Ashbury St.
San Francisco CA 94117
(415) 753-6100
Independent, nonprofit, nonsectarian accredited graduate school offers M.A. program in integral counseling psychology and M.A. and Ph.D. programs in East-West psychology, and philosophy and religion. Also grants a certificate in organizational development and transformation. School emphasizes transpersonal and spiritual dimensions of life with the goal of bridging Eastern and Western traditions of knowledge.

The Four Winds Foundation
PO Box 948
Sausalito CA 94966
(415) 332-1306
Psychologist, author, and holistic healing researcher Dr. Alberto Villoldo leads study retreats to Peru, Mexico, and Brazil. Healing and transformational techniques of shamanism are studied and observed.

The Great Round Vision Quests
PO Box 201
Bodega CA 94922
(707) 874-2736
Ten-day spiritual vision quest into Death Valley and the Inyo Mountains of California for women. Several trips offered for groups of men and women. Trips are based on the traditional quests of Native Americans but are tailored to contemporary needs and involve goals clarification, dream work, and three days of solitary time.

Indian Arts created in the "Heart of the Earth," **The Four Corners Collection** offers unique objects empowered by the mystic Southwest. Above is an authentic Hopi Eagle Kachina, exquisitely carved, 9"-20", from $180. **"This Eagle Kachina will allow you to see visions of your future in dream time..."*** Catalog features Zuni fetishes, Mettje Swift Banners, medicine bags, smudge sticks, distinctive collectors items and *channeled information. **$1.** 303-259-6508. **35**

Institute for Shamanistic Studies
Kathmandu, Nepal
Study trance, healing, and the Shamanistic way of life with practicing shamans of the Himalayas.
Housing, meals, land travel provided.
Dr. Peter Skafte
P.O. Box 1798
Boulder, CO 80306
(303) 444-1588

Southwestern College of Life Sciences
PO Box 4711
Santa Fe NM 87502
(505) 471-5756
Offers transformational education with a holistic perspective. Programs include M.A. degrees in transformational counseling and creative expressive therapy. Also hosts summer institute with workshops in such topics as hypnosis, higher consciousness, and wilderness therapy.

Figure 24. Selected advertisements from *The 1988 Guide to New Age Living.* Courtesy of Rising Star Associates, Ltd. Partnership, Brighton, Mass.

Another critic, R. Lawrence Moore, has offered a completely different line of reasoning. In his book *Religious Outsiders and the Making of Americans* (1986), he argued that Protestantism and other "mainstream" denominations have been overly emphasized in the history books. Sects have consistently been portrayed as weird, curious, or un-American historical deviations which will die out by themselves. But, as Moore pointed out, they have not. In fact, the history of American religiosity *is* the history of "sectarianism." This insight should warn scholars to take another look at new religions, not as social cancers, but as normal, viable expressions of American religiosity.

At any rate, I agree with Bellah that the crisis of the sixties was above all else a "crisis of meaning" (cf. Robbins 1988:1–13). What we are witnessing today in the emergence of the New Age is what I would call a "reconstruction of meaning," a persistent and inspired attempt to reconstruct a cohesive and viable worldview. This worldview is a deliberate eclecticism and syncretism precisely because it denies some of the most fundamental precepts of presixties American values. In Aidala's terms, new meaning systems begin as ideologies developed in opposition to other perspectives and operated as "explicitly articulated, consciously-brought-to-bear interpretations and justifications" (1984:48).

Clifford Geertz was the first comparativist to use the term worldview. His main interest was to explain the role of symbols in coordinating or at least serving as a referent for the "approved style of life," on the one hand, and "the assumed structure of reality," on the other (1957:129). Thus, Geertz distinguished between *ethos* as "the tone, character, and quality of [a people's] life, its moral and aesthetic style and mood; it is the underlying attitude toward themselves and their world that life reflects," and *worldview* as "their picture of the way things in sheer actuality are, their concept of nature, of self, of society. It contains their most comprehensive ideas of order" (ibid.:127). Ethos and worldview reinforce one another:

> Religious belief and ritual confront and mutually confirm one another; the ethos is made intellectually reasonable by being shown to represent a way of life implied by the actual state of affairs which the world view describes, and the world view is made emotionally acceptable by being presented as an image of an actual state of affairs of which such a way of life is an authentic expression. This demonstration of meaningful relation between the values a people holds and the general order of existence within which it finds itself is an essential element in all religions, however those values or that order be conceived. Whatever else religion may be, it is in part an attempt . . . to conserve the fund of general meanings in terms of which each individual interprets his experience and organizes his conduct. (ibid.)

And the meanings he referred to are "stored" in symbols.

Robert Wuthnow has recently argued for a further distinction to be made between meaning systems and worldviews. Meaning systems refer to "the dominant meanings in a culture that are associated with a particular symbol or set of symbols . . . with which interpretations, feelings, and activities can be associated." A worldview, which Wuthnow also calls a "belief system," "consists of all the beliefs that an individual holds about the nature of reality" (1987:45). Meaning systems can be inconsistent with each other, but worldviews are by definition holistically coherent.

Seen in these terms, meaning consists of a series of "nested categories that encompass the individual ever more comprehensively" and religion becomes "a type of symbolic universe that transcends and orders reality wholistically, giving it a sense of sacredness"[16] (ibid.:39).

My explanation of the role of the Hopis in the New Age and of New Age (mis)representation, for analytical purposes, consists of three basic worldviews:

1. The worldview of traditional Hopis in the twentieth century;
2. The worldview of the Traditionalist Hopis in the New Age; and
3. The worldview of the New Age in "dialogue" with Native Americans.

This is admittedly a simplification, but it reflects and explains the jumble of data at hand.

The above-mentioned three worldviews may share meaning systems in part or in whole, but they do not share the same worldview. They are all interconnected in a vast network of meaning systems, but each has its own goals and its own mission: Traditional Hopis are just trying to adapt to the conditions of the 20th century, the Traditionalists are trying to outlive their opponents the Tribal Council, and the proponents of the New Age are trying to revolutionize the whole world. Each combines what Berger and Luckmann called "sub-universes of meaning": the traditional Hopis combine traditional Hopi premises with American premises, the Traditionalists combine politicized Hopi premises with New Age premises, and New Age combines politicized American premises with oriental and Native American premises. Each group has its own millenial expectations, and never the three shall meet!

16. Also see Wuthnow 1986 and Berger and Luckmann 1966:103. Ninian Smart has recently attempted to introduce "worldview analysis" as the major activity of modern religious studies. I would agree to a point, but nowhere in his 1983 work does he define the term in any analytically useful manner. For Smart, worldviews are "both religion and ideologies" (ibid.:2). Neither does he attempt to relate his understanding of the term to those of other scholars who have been working along similar lines.

PART IV

Prophecy and Change

ELEVEN

A Model of Narrative Tradition and Change

The last five chapters have demonstrated some of the problems with trying to analytically capture meaning in a living social process. I have attempted to specify the dynamics of what Jonathan Turner called the three classes of variables in microanalysis: the motivational, interactional, and structuring processes (1987:170–183). In this chapter I present a hypothetical model of narrative tradition and change.

FACTORS OF CHANGE

At this point in our long and arduous journey through the jungle of signs, meanings, and happenstance, it would do well for us to summarize what we have learned so far about tradition and change in Hopi prophecy. Most of this book has presented evidence and introduced arguments that specifically address factors of change.

In chapter 2 I described some of the mythological, rhetorical, cognitive, and sociological aspects of Hopi prophecy. I argued that Hopi prophecy is couched in the framework of the emergence myth and that it is a subcategory of clan tradition, *navoti. Navoti* is not only clan tradition, but it is also an indigenous interpretive framework that is part and parcel of the politics of knowledge in a society where knowledge is the basis of status and power. Thus, Hopi prophecy is intimately bound up with clan identity and clan ideology which defines individual identity within a network of political and social relationships.

Other characteristics of Hopi prophecies are that they are collective, which means that there are prophecies but no prophets; they are located in a simultaneous continuum of present perfect, past perfect, and future perfect tenses, where the historical present is a repetition of the mythical past and the past is in the present. The speaker can choose to define him/herself in any moment on that continuum. They are fatalistic and simultaneously find their cause and end in the moral codes of the *pöts-kwani,* which are inculcated during the socialization process consciously and effectively with the result that the end of the world rests solely on the immorality of humanity–and thus the end is unavoidable. And finally, they reflect political, social, and ideological contexts.

The documents at our disposal clearly show that the importance and meaning of Hopi prophecy is not to be found in its "prophetic" claims (which are constantly changing), but in its functions as mechanisms for incorporating contemporary affairs into the framework of traditional religious values, for evaluating those affairs in terms of conceived tradition, and for interpreting and judging those affairs on the authority of conceived tradition. Seen in this light, prophecy is primarily a rhetorical device that is authoritative, conditional, open-ended (metaphorical), reflective (interpretive), inflective (changeable, malleable), and emotive.

More importantly, Hopi prophecy is viewed here as pivotal to social and political strategies. It is therefore useful to characterize the ways prophecies are used, identify interest groups who use them, and identify themes that are meaningful to these groups. Thus, I presented six strategies that formed a point of reference for this study: On the Hopi side, to establish or maintain ethnic identity and/or internal sociopolitical structures, to resist White society, to attract subversive interest groups in the White society, and to recreate stability and meaning; and, on the Euro-American side, the use of Hopi myths to define one's own identity and to resist one's own society. Thus, in our examination of changing interpretations we must pay attention not only to the motives of the narrator, but also to the way the narratives have been used and interpreted by Whites and Hopis alike.

In arguing my two proposals in the Introduction, I contended that tradition and prophecy are a way of thinking, a way of speaking, and a way of acting which articulate the webs of significance produced by human culture. Prophecy is not prediction, even though it purports to be so. Prophecy is a thread in the total fabric of meaning, in the total worldview. In this way it can be seen as a way of life and of being. It is discourse transmuted into social praxis. Prophecy is tradition that is spoken by someone to someone else for specific purposes whether for moral, ideological, or political reasons. Prophecy is not static; it is and always has been used in response to internal and external conditions. It is a way of articulating and defining contemporary events within the context and language of "tradition."

In chapter 1 the main emphasis was on the human dimensions of Hopi prophecy. It spanned the centuries of Hopi history, linking current events with Hopi conceptions of the past and with the historical sources at our disposal. It demonstrated how two leaders separated by time and space, yet confronted by similar problems, chose to solve their hermeneutical problems. In comparing their different solutions it became evident that the tapestry of meaning is creative and contingent. I concluded that their story presented us with two significant variables: 1) that there may be indigenous factors of deliberate cultural change whose form and impact we have difficulty measuring and evaluating; and 2) that of the many narratives at our disposal, only a handful are authoritative.

In chapter 2, I identified the core narrative as the emergence myth. My description of the narrative indicated that there are variables even in the core account and that those variables are also related to the prophecies. These include how Maasaw is to return, what the signs of his coming will be, what the role and significance of the stone tablets are, and what role the White Brother will play in the apocalypse.

Chapters 3 and 4 attempted to discover what influence the medium of communication has on the rates and kinds of change prophecy undergoes. I distinguished between three basic contexts: prose narrative, ethnopoetic narrative, and modern prose narrative. The prose narrative context concerns myth and ritual speech. Hopi myth is a formalized, stylistic, repetitive prose genre that serves as the source which informs the other genres. It is a restricted, collective, cultural treasure. It was noted that this type of narrative leaves only minimal possibilities for change over shorter periods of time. The changes that occur are restricted to details. The ethnopoetic narrative context concerns ritual song. Songs seem to have been an important source of prophetic detail. They are highly formalized in structure, but allow greater possibilities for individual innovation than myths do. At the same time, songs are filled with metaphorical and other poetic techniques that invite a great deal of creative interpretation on the part of the listener. Since it is a highly visible medium that potentially can reach the ears of hundreds of participants, it may be assumed that individual innovation would be restricted to the standardized details worked out during the consensual dialogues at brotherhood meetings. When the song is one that has simply been passed on from one singer to another, it can be assumed that any significant changes would immediately be noticed and commented on.

Before moving on to the third narrative context, it would be useful to summarize what we know about the possibilities for change in Hopi oral tradition:

1. There is an indigenous tradition of secret, directed cultural change.
2. Narratives have varying degrees of authority and authenticity. Each clan has its own stories best known to the older, initiated members

of central lineages. Each clan tradition has its place in a phratry and village hierarchy, and thus any panclan matters are, in principle, only known or best known by important leaders. Narratives are reinterpreted and redefined in an environment of negotiation.
3. The point at which various traditions disagree most is in the area of prophetic detail.
4. Prophetic traditions are influenced by social and political factors.
5. Prophetic traditions are influenced by such factors as linguistic style, genre, and media.

The modern, prose narrative context concerns casual conversations, speeches, eyewitness accounts, letters to the editor, newspaper interviews, propaganda literature, letters, books, radio, and so on. This context has expanded the possibilities of change more than any other. In focusing on the written medium, I argued that there is no evidence of any cognitive change in the transition from orality to literacy, but plenty of evidence for other kinds of change.

As it turns out, the Traditionalists were the first to formulate Hopi prophecy in the new media, and they therefore became active partners in acculturation–albeit in other ways–together with their political opponents, the Tribal Council. The various generative factors are as follows:

A. Acculturative factors:

1. English was adopted as the lingua politica, thus reproducing Hopi prophecies in a foreign medium. The disparate traditions were transformed into an unprecedented cohesive body. The change of language also brought a change of audience. Prophecies began to appear in new genres: letters, petitions, statements, and affidavits.
2. The problem of storage and retrieval helped change the habits of a strictly oral environment.

B. Factors which influenced the degree of availability of knowledge:

1. The use of the written media created a greater impact in the national arena. It provided the possibility of bypassing lower echelons and addressing a prophetic monologue directly to the highest officials. It provided the possibility of conceiving political legitimacy in apocryphal terms.
2. The use of the written media led to a greater degree of extramural dialogue. It brought outside support, but it also made Hopi tradition more vulnerable to generative factors. The use of the mass media provided effective propaganda devices which

by definition implies the manipulation of information for political ends.

3. The use of the written media led to a greater degree of intramural dialogue. This gave Hopi youth alternative paths to knowledge. It allowed opposing parties the possibility of public confrontation. It served to construct a common ground for the development of a pan-Hopi consensus.

C. Literacy has frozen prophetic tradition into texts that have carried that tradition beyond the reach, understanding, and control of its bearers.

1. What was once restricted to formalized and ritualized indigenous contexts became accessible to a broader public.
2. The publication of Hopi prophecies invited contention, especially because of indelible proof of constant manipulation and change.

Against the background of this kaleidescope of factors, I embarked on a series of descriptive and interpretive chapters which attempted to characterize the political, social, religious, and historical factors that have influenced the development and use of Hopi prophecy.

Chapter 5 contextualized all prophetic statements between 1858 and 1961. These statements were presented both in their historical contexts and were also catalogued in a typology which allowed them to be subjected to comparative evaluation as well as potential quantification. This chapter documented that no recorded prophecy can be shown to predate the event and that the prophecies clearly reflect contemporaneous concerns. The Hopis have experienced an increasing fragmentation and individualization in the face of cultural disintegration, but the chapter ends with a discussion of how they now have begun to turn the tables and reassert the *collective* meaning and function of prophecy. Once again, prophecies have changed in the process.

Chapter 6 investigated the stone tablets and the theme of the White Brother. The investigation explored the political factors at play in the use and interpretation of Hopi prophecy. It also illustrated how prophecies are interwoven with the politics of knowledge. The fact that there are many chiefs and several (but not enough) tablets as well as a wide range of interpretations of their meaning provides contending political groups with a natural focal point around the question of *who* has the *true* tablet. The chapter revealed that the Hopis are in dispute concerning just about everything about the tablets: their number, who owns them, their origins, what is on them, what they signify, and what role they play in the apocalypse. My main conclusion was that since the stones are symbols of chiefly authority and legitimacy, they constitute a highly significant, strategic resource. Legitimation was shown to be a question of the competitive construction of meaning, or, a battle of meanings in changing arenas.

I then embarked on a series of chapters that established my second proposal, namely, that the rhetoric of traditionalism is not equivalent to the reality it portrays. I moved from the analysis of a religious phenomenon in chapter 6 to the analysis of a religious leader, namely, Dan Qötshongva in chapters 7 and 8. In following Qötshongva's career, we were afforded the opportunity to follow the rise and decline of the Traditionalist Movement as well.

Qötshongva's career illustrated how the Traditionalists attempted to reformulate their religion and prophecies. This reformulation departed from the central focus of agricultural concerns and reinterpreted Hopi religion as a universal, salvific one.

What is fascinating about the Traditionalist Movement is that its appeal differed according to the audience. The movement can be understood as a "millenarian" movement with modifications. Whereas its appeal on the reservation was completely political, its appeal to Euro-Americans was primarily religious. The former appeal can be labeled a "resistance" movement and the latter appeal a "revival" or "renewal" movement. Its status as a resistance movement held sway on the reservation only for as long as its leaders actually possessed reasonably legitimate claims to political authority. These claims ceased in Hotevilla with the death of Qötshongva. Together with the increasing popularity and importance of the Tribal Council in Hopi affairs, Monongya and Banancya had no other choice but to put their energy into the "revival" aspect, an aspect that had greater appeal to non-Hopis than to Hopis. There are many reasons for this peculiar situation, but briefly I would suggest the following:

1. Hopi prophecies have been a legitimate and integrated facet of Hopi ceremonialism probably as far back as—if not before—the Spanish confrontation.
2. These prophecies specifically address the issue of cultural confrontation and have therefore provided an interpretive framework for all Hopis at all times.
3. These two factors bear the consequence that the Traditionalist Movement had little to offer to their own people that was "new" in terms of religious meaning.
4. Their position was further weakened by several factors: The Traditionalists had no control over the resources that attracted many Hopis, nor over the ideological discipline required to reject Ameri-

can goods; they were unable to establish clearcut boundaries between their and the Tribal Council's analyses, goals, and methods; they were notorious for making up and/or changing their prophecies from audience to audience; and they addressed non-Hopis more than Hopis on religious matters and were therefore under constant suspicion of revealing secrets to Whites.

5. Still, Hopi prophecies have always carried political connotations because they address the issue of cultural confrontation. Therefore, it can be argued that the political savvy and at times tactical finesse the Traditionalists possessed had their greatest appeal on the reservation in times of political turbulence such as the split of Oraibi in 1906 and the establishment of District Six in 1936 (during the pre-Traditionalist "Hostile" period) and World War Two, the reestablishment of the Tribal Council in 1951, and the coal-mining scandals of the early 1970s (during the Traditionalist period).
6. The political appeal lost impetus as a correlate to changing political needs, the growing sophistication and prominence of the Tribal Council, the increasing discreditability of the Traditionalist leaders, and the growing impression that Traditionalist policies under Monongya's leadership were traitorous.
7. The revivalistic aspect appealed to non-Hopis during periods of cultural dissonance and stress (the dissatisfaction of the cold war 1950s and early 1960s, the profound existential revolution of the 1960s, and the religious revival of the 1970s) where the interest was not so much in helping the Hopis to revitalize, but in using Traditionalist revival rhetoric in order to pursue one's own revivalistic interests.
8. The millenarian aspect appealed most to non-Hopis because Euro-American history is a history of millenarianism, and because Hopi apocryphal thought harmonized well with the ecology and peace movements.

The latter two points are specifically addressed in chapters 9 and 10. In chapter 10 the evidence on the petroglyph etched on "Prophecy Rock" was examined in detail. The investigation provided an opportunity to gain insight into the style and methods of "second-generation" Traditionalists and especially the role of the movement's new secular leadership. Both chapters indicate that the greatest changes in Hopi prophetic statements occurred during this time and that these changes occurred primarily through the dialogue which Thomas Banancya was carrying on with non-Hopis. I have shown especially that the language and concerns of ecology movements and New Age groups have crept into Banancya's prophetic corpus, thus contributing to the dialectical nature of Traditionalist theology. But, I have also shown that the dwindling support of non-Hopi interest groups has moved the few remaining Traditionalists to change their tactics by addressing a primarily Hopi audience and by reformulating their prophecies along more "traditional" lines.

I have consistently argued that Traditionalist prophecies are not the same as "traditional" prophecies. This is because Traditionalist prophecies are a summary of different clan traditions, they were formulated in a foreign language to a foreign audience, and that audience has influenced the content of the prophecies. It is also a fact, however, that "traditional" prophecies were subject to change and reinterpretation. And although these changes were due to similar historical mechanisms, there is at least a sociopolitical difference between "traditional" and "Traditionalist" prophecies which any knowledgeable Hopi can distinguish immediately. Superficially, the differences seem to consist of stylistic matters, but in Hopi social reality they consist of matters of political legitimacy.

FACTORS OF CONTINUITY

In the face of the overwhelming evidence of changing audiences changing meanings at the edges of competing worldviews, are there any factors of continuity in Hopi prophetic "tradition"? I have argued that there are.

We can use the same methods of comparison and historical criticism that exposed factors of change to expose factors of continuity. Comparisons of all the documents over a period of about 140 years indicate the striking stability and homogeneity of the emergence myth. This homogeneity is not only evident in the redundancy of the core narrative in all versions, but also in the indigenous, abbreviated versions that narrators have presented to the public on such occasions as the BIA hearings in 1955.

In chapter 3 I identified the main elements of the emergence myth in terms of episodes and stories. This method allowed the possibility for evaluating the relative degrees of variance in different versions of the myth. The method also allowed the possibility of determining what kind of variation has occurred.

It was noted that 1) the basic narrative structure remains unchanged, 2) the basic message remains the same, 3) the narrative provides a model for and is reciprocally reinforced by social and religious domains, and 4) the narrative serves as a coherent framework for the production of meaning.

Concerning the first point, I observed that most of the stories not only follow a standard structure, but also evince standard contents. It seems that where significant variation in detail occurs, we can expect to find the reason in political motivation. Whether it is the result of disagreements between political rivals or of the accommodation of contemporary political exigencies or of individual clan traditions, these variations are made identifiable and explanable through comparative lenses.

Concerning the second point, our main problem in the study of Hopi prophecy is that it is specifically in the realms of prophecy that we find some of the greatest variation. And yet, again, the basic message remains the same. The emergence myth is a story about the human capacity for evil and the effects this capacity has on the human environment. Since the human environment is perceived as being intimately linked with the ecological and superhuman environments, human intentions and actions influence those environments as well. But the basic message is even more specific than that. It entails the confrontation between god and man in primordial times as well as in a coming time. Maasaw owns the fourth world. He gave humanity permission to join him on the condition that they follow his humble way. Humanity arrived and, as could be expected, nothing changed. Maasaw, therefore, only allowed them temporary residence, told them that they still had to realize their evil capacities, and that he would return to cleanse or punish them. All versions agree on this.

They also agree that there were two brothers, one White and the other Hopi. They shared a tablet, or a set of tablets, and they knew that their ways were to part, but not forever. The Older Brother would return one day from the east, whether to help or to punish his Younger Brother, the versions cannot agree. They all agree, however, that the tablet or tablets will match and that the matching of the tablets will cause worldwide repercussions.

The third area of disagreement is that of the clan migration legends, although all agree that the clans spread out after the emergence in order to find their final residence and to fulfill their destiny. They also agree that each clan established reciprocal relationships with specific geographical locations and with certain nonhuman or superhuman beings during their migrations. And they agree on the standard procedure of admission to the village. What is most important is that they agree that the relationships to places and beings and the order of arrival determine contemporary social, political, and religious order.

Concerning the third point, I argued in chapter 3 that the core narrative is enhanced, mobilized, and reiterated in hundreds of ways in social praxis. But, it is equally important to realize that the narrative serves as a *model for* social praxis. Whether the one came before the other is irrelevant here. The fact remains that the Hopis themselves believe that the narrative provides a model for social and organizational praxis. This belief is in itself a significant factor of continuity. That social and religious praxis continually reconfirms both the narrative and its model further strengthens its significance as a factor of continuity.

Concerning my fourth point, the narrative serves as a coherent framework for the production of meaning, despite variations in detail. This is due, among other things, to the fact that the narrative is the superstructure within which clan tradition unfolds itself. Thus, the panclan narrative attains significance in a hierarchy of significance: the individual defines his or her identity in terms of lineage tradition; the lineage defines itself in terms of clan tradition, especially in terms of the migration legends; the clan defines itself in terms of important stories and the order of arrival; and the whole conglomeration is given meaning in terms of the emergence myth. The emergence myth *is* the story of the Hopi people. What better place can there be for the individual to find meaning?

A MODEL OF CONTINUITY AND CHANGE IN HOPI PROPHECY

My hypothesis concerning continuity and change in Hopi prophecy is inspired by Robert LeVine's characterization of the properties of culture. LeVine defined culture as "a shared organization of ideas that includes the intellectual, moral, and aesthetic standards prevalent in a community and the meanings of communicative actions" (1984:67). LeVine argued that four of the main characteristics of culture are:

1. its collective nature, i.e., "that culture represents a consensus on a wide variety of meanings among members of an interacting community" (ibid.:68);
2. its organized nature, i.e., that the beliefs, norms, values, and social actions are "connected and comprehensible only as parts of a larger organization" (ibid.:72);
3. its multiplex nature, i.e., that the organization of shared meanings consists of both explicit and implicit dimensions as well as rational and nonrational elements, and that "some meanings are more explicit than others, for reasons having to do with the pragmatics of social life and their history for a given society" (ibid.:77); and
4. its variability across human populations, i.e., that economic, organizational, and communicative patterns vary, that cultural standards vary, and that cultures even in the modern age resist homogenization (ibid.:80).

LeVine's third characteristic is the one I find most relevant here. I argued in the Introduction that myth is a conceptualized symbol system that organizes experience around a culture's "core symbols" and thus serves as a socially imposed interpretive mechanism for producing meaning. This process of experiencing and interpreting is not always (or even usually) deliberate. There are even whole areas where ethnographers have discovered regularities that informants cannot easily explain or consider to be self-evident. Thus, LeVine raised the important point that:

> Many ethnographers arrive at the conclusion that what informants find difficult to verbalize is more important, more fundamental, in the cultural organization of ideas than what they can verbalize. They argue that the more general ideas–basic assumptions–are less accessible to verbal formulation because the social consensus in a community protects them from challenge and shifts the focus of discourse to more specific points that are at issue in normal social life. (ibid.:76)

The Hopi context seems to confirm LeVine's observations. The Hopis expend enormous energy in arguing about prophetic detail. This can be understood as "shifting the focus of discourse" to the specifics. What is never challenged in Hopi tradition is the core narrative. The Hopis argue about *what* Maasaw said, but not about *whether* he ever said anything at all. They disagree on the identity of the White Brother and on what he will do, but never on whether he exists at all. The clans squabble over the details of their arrival, but never over whether it has any relevance to social reality.

In other words, my hypothesis is that the core narrative is a constant factor, even over long periods of time, and that the flux of detail represents a graduated structure of meanings and signs which take on increasing polyvalence the further removed they are from the core. These outer structures, or "buffer" zones, create easily accessible matters for discussion, disagreement, debate, and deliberation, but keep critical, agnostic attention away from the core and source of these levels of meanings and signs.

This study has attempted to prove that variables in Hopi prophecy are dependent on political, historical, and social concerns in changing contemporaneous situations, but that the core remains unchanged.

My theory of zones of increasing polyvalence can be illustrated in the accompanying model, figure 25, which illustrates the total narrative. The central zone contains the emergence myth as the core narrative (nos. 1, 2, 3, 6). The second zone contains prophetic and other politically significant detail (nos. 4, 6). The third zone contains clan-specific detail (nos. 5, 6). Each zone demonstrates increasing multiplexity as well as varying degrees of "buffer" rationale.

Each of the stories in the emergence myth can also be mapped out in the same manner. For instance, figure 26 illustrates story no. 1. The first

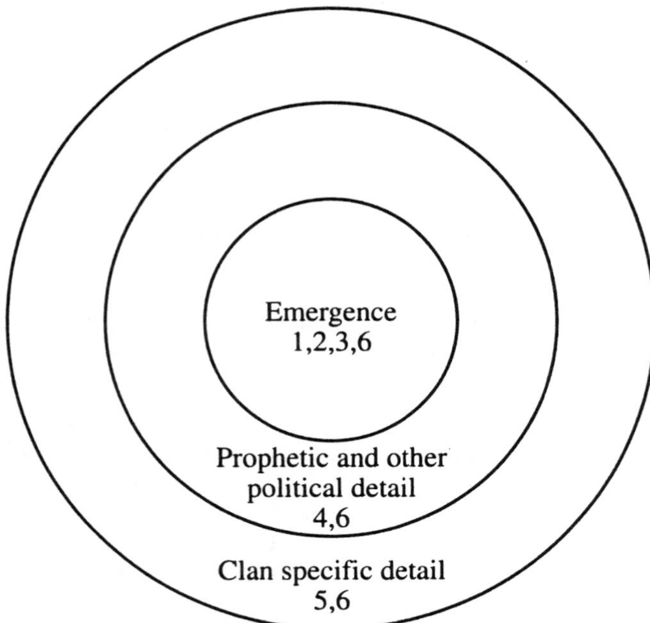

Figure 25. Zones of increasing polyvalence:
The narrative model.

zone contains the standard narrative structure, i.e., the third world is in chaos, the chiefs hold council and create and send some birds on their way, and contact is made with Maasaw, who grants permission to them. Variations in detail are in the second zone and concern the identity of the society that first contacted Maasaw. Complications arise in the third zone especially when comparing the versions of political opponents. The words of Maasaw are specifically aimed at discrediting and/or criticizing the other factions.

The model can also be applied to the details of each episode. Figure 27 illustrates the episode concerning the confrontation with Maasaw either in story no. 4 or no. 6. Again, we find an escalating scale of disagreement in detail for each zone. The first zone contains universal agreement on the fact that the Hopis met with Maasaw, who denied them ownership of the land and who refused to become their chief. They also agree that he will return to punish them. The second zone concerns other details in his speech: Did he say anything about mining the land or about the allotment program? The third zone is the zone of grand speculation concerning the signs of his immanent return.

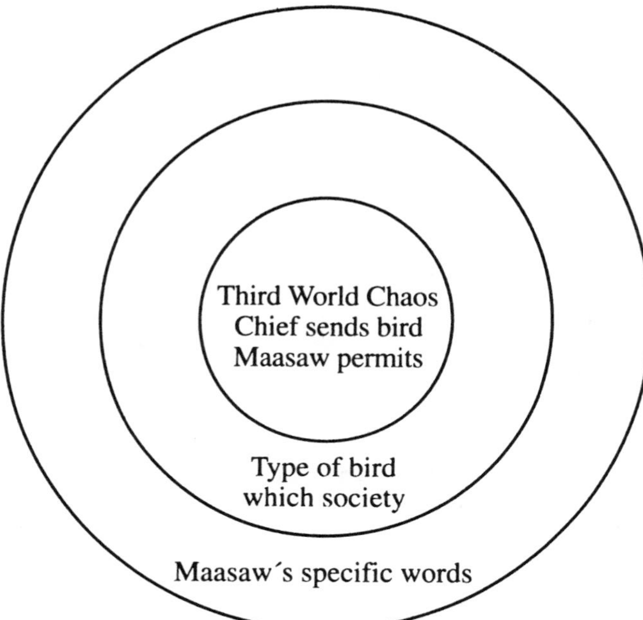

Figure 26. Zones of increasing polyvalence:
The story model.

This model implicitly assumes a center-periphery orientation. I have argued in chapter 8 that there are good reasons to believe that the center-periphery model is relevant in exploring Hopi reality. The model is seldom formulated explicitly in Hopi discourse and yet it seems to show up everywhere: in myth, social organization, village planning, and ritual activity.

Although it may seem superfluous to mention it, it should be pointed out that my model is only a heuristic device. It is not reality. The "map is not territory" (Smith 1978). The historian of religions Peter Slater applied a similar model to the dynamics of religion in general arguing that the phenomenon of "centering" is an important mechanism for individuals or groups in securing identity in a changing pattern of faith, and that it can conveniently serve as a model for organizing our data and approaching our problems. In his opinion the key to the model "is the concept of a master story in each tradition, which retains the same central symbol as an identifying reference, but changes meaning as its pattern of auxiliary symbols develops" (1978:11).

Slater operated with a model of symbols clustered in stories in much

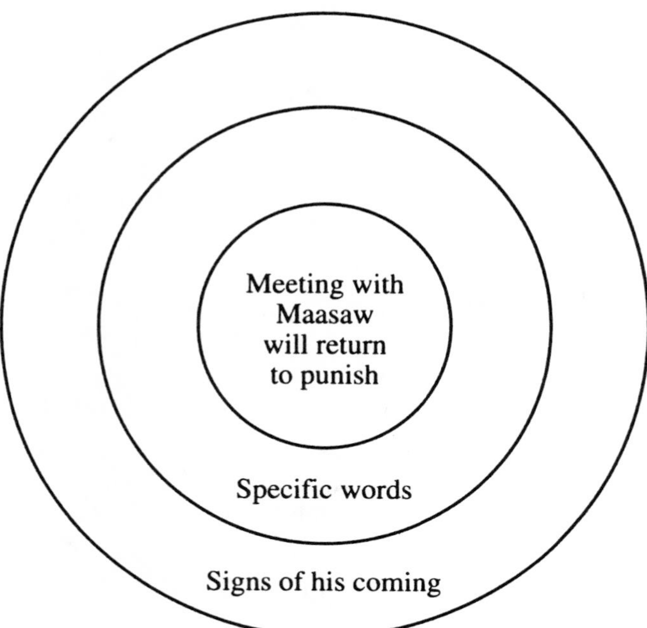

Figure 27. Zones of increasing polyvalence:
The episode model.

the same way that I have done. He stressed the transfiguring impact that symbols have on perception and on putting situations and roles in perspective (ibid.:27). Some symbols are more central than others. Those symbols which are "primary" have the greatest impact in the development of a particular religious tradition (ibid.:29) and promote a stronger sense of continuity. This does not mean that they are static. The meaning of the symbols shifts in relation to new frames of reference. It is in the interactions between the central symbol and the changing constellations of primary, secondary, and tertiary symbols that we can define a particular religion at a given moment in history (ibid.:34). It is this whole cycle of stories and symbols which Slater tries to account for in his model.

Slater applied his model to a number of comparative goals: to discover the pattern of symbols in the tradition of one religion, to compare changing emphases in common traditions shared by different religions, or to compare patterns of faith in different religions. The model also provides an instrument for understanding both changes in a religious tradition, fundamental change in or even the loss of a tradition, and individual transformations (ibid.:90–113ff).

The master story expresses the way of life associated with the central symbol. Besides this, the story must have the following characteristics:

> [It] must have a plot which brings its central figures to "salvation" or healing or wholeness. It must communicate some affirmation of identity with integrity, some hope of personal fulfillment or self-realization, which enables its characters to transcend the negativities of existence. (ibid.:58)

Dealing with things cultural as we are, we might rightfully ask in what sense the Hopis "control" the Whites through symbolization. The most obvious answer is that explanatory adequacy is perhaps a universal far more compelling—and therefore far more effective in social reality—than, for example, military might. The Hopis have had several military confrontations with the Spaniards and the Americans and, except for a few extraordinary cases, quickly capitulated with little loss of human life. And yet, they have applied such ingenious political tactics against the White presence that they stand in a unique position in contemporary U.S.-Indian affairs (Whiteley 1988:11–28). It has not been easy for the Hopis, however, and this is a problem often addressed by Hopi prophecies. The White Brother clearly changes character in the history of Hopi prophecy (cf. chapter 5).

I will not press the point too much. One thing is strategy, another is social efficacy. But in the realm of cognitive affairs, I have argued that it is useful to stress the role of symbolization. Anthropologist Roy Wagner has argued in the course of several of his books that "the necessity of a culture, or its members, to substantiate and confirm, to invent, a particular reality" (1975:149) expresses itself through the activity of symbolization. All meaningful symbolizations "compel," in Wagner's opinion, the innovative and expressive force of metaphors into new contexts and thus new constructions (1972; 1975:xiv). For Wagner, myth manifests itself in the cognitive, emotional, and volitional realms of human reality. Through myth people reflect on experience and generate what Victor Turner called "metasocial commentaries" (Wagner 1978:7). Myth is in this sense innovative (Wagner 1978:252).

In a preface to Wagner's study (1978:7) Victor Turner interpreted Wagner's complicated theory in the following manner:

> In myth, certain speech forms "kill"; they do not spread out discursive understanding at the cognitive level. They aim, in fact, to undermine ("obviate") such surface understandings, to bring the members of the cultures in which they play a vital part to an encounter with the ontological curvatures of their experience with others and with their own reflexive solitudes—not

> unknown even in "tribal" societies. For Roy Wagner, myth is by no means an expression or reflection of cognitized economic or political social "reality"; rather it is a liberation, through destruction, "lethal speech," from that world, a continuous exploration of alternative modes of doing things, personally and socially.

For Wagner, myth can be understood as being "a single constructive event" which constitutes a "cosmic dislocation, a metaphor (reversible in some cases) of one part of the human experiential world through the terms of another. It is an event in the conventional ordering of this world" (ibid.:256).

Hopi mythology is not as tropic, metaphorical, obviating, or transformative as the Daribi mythology Wagner studied evidently is. The complexity of Hopi prophecy is not to be found in the mythological realm, rather in the subtleties and machinations of the social and political contexts. Thus, my interest in the symbolization process is more geared to those contexts. In other words, symbolization has social efficacy insofar as it informs and motivates social action.

I have argued that myth is used by the Hopis to define themselves in relation to other peoples; to normalize actual, historical relationships; to differentiate between human types; and to assimilate dangerous peoples into Hopi cosmic thought. Thus, the Euro-American presence is conceptualized within the conditional logic of Hopi argument and is contrasted with Hopi ethnic identity. It is, in fact, claimed here that Hopi prophecy mobilizes ethnic identity in terms of cultural confrontation, thus assimilating and ultimately defusing the effects of such confrontation. It is this theory that offers possible alternatives to personal and corporate social action.

CONCLUSION

I have argued that tradition is both change and continuity. Tradition must change in order to retain meaning in the face of changing social and political circumstances. It must draw on the central narrative to account for change. It must objectify and symbolize agents of change whether foreign peoples or ideas, internal mechanisms, or factional interests, in order to identify and ultimately assimilate these agents in terms of indigenous theory.

The main assumption of this work has been that humanity has prophesied the end of the world ever since it began. There is nothing new about present worldwide fears of ecological disaster. And there is nothing new about the proposed cause of it. In all cases, everywhere in human history, the cause of the end of the world is attributed to humanity itself. Whether due to immorality or other affronts to superhuman agents, or to thoughtless industrial waste, humanity is constantly on the path to its own apocalypse.

I have argued throughout that prophecy has little to do with precognitions about historical events or with actual, physical cataclysms. Instead, it has much to do with constructed worlds and constructed realities which are, after all, card houses exposed to every wind.

The idea of the end of the world is a strategy for living *in* the world. It is often connected with the idea of a primordial golden age. Where once was purity, the apocalypse will help reinstate it. Between these two extremes, human cultures find meaning by reworking the symbols which dominate just before and just beyond human ken.

The end of the world is often horrifying to think about. It gives form and substance to collective fears, and it serves to keep the straying flocks within the malleable boundaries of invented worlds. But, it is also a strategy of hope in face of the fact that humans seldom improve.

Maasaw will indeed return to the Hopis. He is already doing it in their dreams, their strategies, and their most private whisperings.

Appendices

APPENDIX A

A Bilingual Version of the Emergence Myth with Commentary

There are many versions of the emergence myth. In my 1984 article I noted twelve versions which all originated from Third Mesa alone. Other versions have been published since that time, and there are several more versions in *Hopi Hearings* (Bureau of Indian Affairs 1955). Already in 1948, E. S. Goldfrank (1948) demonstrated that the versions all contain political implications. With few exceptions, all of the published versions were told by village chiefs, their relatives, or other leaders who were responsible for the split of Oraibi and the subsequent founding of Hotevilla in 1906.[1] This is normal considering the equivalence which is placed between secret knowledge and political power (cf. chapter 6).

Remarkably, none of the published versions has appeared in the original Hopi text. A Hopi version just recently appeared in Malotki and Lomatuway'ma (1987*b*), but it seems to be a mosaic from several consultants and unfortunately only contains a portion of the whole story. The myth presented below shows how one person, from one particular clan or society, tells the story in his or her idiom in extenso. And as the narrative clearly shows, the emergence myth is a natural prelude to the migrations of the various clans.

1. The following list of data was first published in my 1984 article as note 19. Since it contains useful information, it is reproduced here with additional information. The references note the chiefs and leaders involved, their village of origin, the date recorded and publication data: Talay'ima, Oraibi, 1883, Cushing 1924 [reproduced in Appendix B of this book; see chapter 5 for arguments concerning the identity of Cushing's informant]; Yukiwma, Oraibi, later chief of Hotevilla, 1903 or 1904, Voth 1905:16–26 [reproduced in Appendix B]; Yukiwma, 1911, Scott 12-5-1911 [reproduced in Appendix B; an abridged version was published in Crane 1925:163–167]; Tawakwaptiwa, chief of Oraibi, 1933 (a condensed version of his uncle Chief Loololma's narrative), Titiev 1944:73–74; Tawa-

THE PIIKYASNGYAM VERSION OF THE EMERGENCE OF HUMANITY AND THE GREAT MIGRATIONS[2]

The narrative itself can be divided into the following subsections: activities and conditions in the third world prior to the emergence (paragraphs 1–33), the actual emergence (paragraphs 34–38), the post-emergence creation of the heavenly bodies (paragraph 39); the meeting with Maasaw, who foretells the prophecy (paragraphs 40–41), the migrations of certain clans (paragraphs 42–72), the settlement at Oraibi (paragraphs 73–90), and conclusions drawn by the narrator (paragraphs 91–92).

1. We did not live here. We used to reside somewhere down below where there was a Hopi settlement. Then we became as we are (today).[3] We live in that same manner today. We carry on that sort of life today. They led a chaotic life.[4] Even though they were not going to perform a (social) dance, they kept company with young women in their kivas. (As time went on) they also had (sex with) women with children. The fathers of these youngsters tended them all night without sleep.

2. The leader there was of the Bow clan. He was very unhappy. He did not know how to control his children (the villagers), and, desiring to

kwaptiwa, the late 1930s, James 1940:9–12 (published in more detail in James 1974:2–8); Dan Qötshongva, functioning chief of Hotevilla, 1955, Bureau of Indian Affairs 1955:23–26 [reproduced in Appendix B]; Qötshongva 1956, Bentley 1956:3–6 [reproduced in Appendix B]; Qötshongva, 1970, Skidmore 1970 [reproduced in Appendix B]; Qötshongva, 1970, Katchongva 1973:3–15 (also published in Tarbet 1972) [reproduced in Appendix B]; David Monongya, Hotevilla, leader of the Traditionalist Movement after Qötshongva, 1955, Bureau of Indian Affairs 1955:44–46 [reproduced in Appendix B]; Tuwaletstiwa, Kykotsmovi, chief of the Bow clan, 1955, Bureau of Indian Affairs 1955: 171–173; Thomas Banancya, Kykotsmovi, interpreter for the Traditionalist Movement, Banyacya 1-12-1961 [the original letter published in part in Appendix B]. The version told by Don Talayesva to Simmons (Simmons 1942:418–420) is most likely taken from Voth, a trick Talayesva used in several other places in Simmon's book. The only version that does not belong to the political figures named above and which is accepted here as Third Mesa evidence is the Oraibi version collected in 1870 by Powell (1875:24–25). Waters' version (1963) is rejected on the grounds that it is a synthetic, panmesa retelling concocted by Waters, Oswald White Bear Fredericks and Otto Pentiwa (cf. A. W. Geertz 1983, 1987*b*, 1990*b*). Waters' version is completely atypical for Hopi mythology in almost every way, but particularly because there is no emergence from the third world. Courlander's version (1971) is equally unacceptable because it is a synthetic retelling of versions from all three mesas and from various clans. There are other versions scattered throughout *Hopi Hearings* (Bureau of Indian Affairs 1955) which are not listed here.

2. The following text, which I recorded in Hotevilla in 1982, was related by a Piikyas consultant, transcribed by Michael Lomatuway'ma, and translated by me.

3. Words in parentheses indicate the gist of the Hopi term.

4. *Pas qa unangwtalyay*, "they were very distracted."

send them to a place (of refuge) he went about seeking someone (to help him). He was considering someone to explore the place above. He would summon someone. It seemed that someone inhabited this (present) place.[5]

3. Having this in mind, he first approached the members of the Wuwtsim Society. He may have been a member of the Wuwtsim Society. Possessing the knowledge of the Wuwtsim Society, he summoned his fellow kiva members to gather. Thus, they congregated at their particular kiva. They probably had a strong one,[6] and they sent him on that mission; but he failed to reach this place in the attempt. So he encountered no one. He traveled so far, then tired, and returned without having fully ascended to this place. He alighted upon his return and informed them that he didn't succeed, and so did not find anyone (up there). "How truly unfortunate," they lamented.

4. Thus, it was to be that others were to make an attempt. So they delegated this task to another kiva group, informing them that they should take on this mission. Thereupon they also tried, but as with the others, they found no one.

5. It was another group's turn to try before they finally encountered someone. They also undertook this assignment but to no avail. So they passed this matter on to the members of the Kwan Society. Thus, they were to make an attempt at it.

6. They now summoned their strong one, and, after successfully bringing him to their presence (i.e., creating him), he asked them, "All right, what is it that needs my immediate attention?"

7. "Yes, (they answered) we, the leaders here, are preparing for something, and we want someone to go to the (world) above. It is certain that someone lives there. Whoever reaches that place should plead on our behalf. We want to get away from this place and go there. If that person permits us (to do so), we will come to him. Our village chief wishes to send his children there to safety. We are in a state of chaos. He has no solution to (supressing) their evil behavior. He doesn't know how to stop it. This is what he has in mind, and that is why we urgently summoned you. Thus, you should give it a try. Let us attempt this thing." They then held

5. Readers who are not familiar with Hopi cosmography, should refer to my 1984 article. Briefly stated, the present world is one of several worlds, all of which are cosmographically situated one upon the other. Note the temporal and spatial frame of the tale itself: The narrator jumps continually from present to past and from the surface of this present world to the depths of the primordial underworld.

6. This refers to the bird that was magically created by the brotherhood and which was sent up to the upper world in order to find Maasaw and ask permission for the people to emerge onto his world.

a vigil. They did not sleep. They smoked ritually throughout the night, handing it (the pipe) over to their strong one.[7]

8. While the sun was rising the following morning, their strong one perched on top of the ladder (to the kiva hatchway), and they instructed him to fly directly in the direction where the sun appeared. Upon arriving at this site he was to circle it. He was to make four circuits and then fly straight upwards. There was an opening into this (present) world similar to a kiva hatchway. This opening would resemble exactly a kiva hatchway. He would undoubtedly find it.

9. And so he did it. When the sun appeared over the horizon, he flew directly in that direction. Upon his arrival he flew circling this place four times, then, upon gaining great height, he flew straight upwards. As he flew along, he apparently discovered the kiva opening, and he entered this world through it.

10. They had provided him with additional information. There was darkness here. No one was there. But it was inevitable that someone would be here somewhere. Thus, if a campfire became visible, he was to fly to it.[8]

11. He arrived at this place. He then sat there observing the area. A fire became visible, and so he flew towards it. The fire was barely visible. Small flames were flickering out. Proceeding towards it, he finally arrived.

12. Someone was seated there by the fire. He possessed very little. He embraced all that he had. Then he spoke to him, "Sit down, stranger; you are about. Have a seat; who are you that you are about? No one has ever come here before. What is your reason for coming around?" he inquired of him.

13. "Yes, I have been sent on an errand, that is why I have come here."

14. "Why did you come?" he then asked. "Which group are you from?"

15. He told him that he was from the Kwan group. "I'm from the Kwan Society," he replied.

16. "I see, so you're from that group. You are from the right ones. I've been awaiting their arrival," he answered. "What is it that they ask you (to do)?"

17. "Yes, upon your granting them permission, they will come."

7. On the pipe ritual see Titiev 1937, Bradfield 1973, II:284–286, A. W. Geertz 1986:50, 1987*a*:11–12, A. W. Geertz and Lomatuway'ma 1987:65–68, 162–163.

8. Note the use of predetermination here, mentioned in chapter 2 as a key theme in Hopi lore.

18. "How very sad, I possess nothing of value. I live here just as you see me now. I don't have any light. I don't have anything of value. I own no treasures. The very least possession which I own is the land here," he declared. "But it's up to you. Come on, if you're willing. There is nothing propitious anywhere here," he avowed. "This is all there is to me. This is all I hold. This is it," he said.

19. "Therefore, it is up to you. If you have the courage to come up (then do so). But you cannot come for the sake of coming. So I want you to tell them. Tell them to initiate their young men. They are to plan an initiation ceremonial. Set a date after you have roasted corn. When you have determined a date, then teach your children the rituals on that day. Then on "hair-washing" day,[9] come here (begin your ascent). You are to return on that very day, and we will tend the people. Together we will help them. So all of you come on that day," he instructed him.

20. "Very well," he complied.

21. "I want you to do a survey here. How much of an area do I occupy? I don't even know myself. I have no knowledge of the length and breadth of the realm I inhabit," he told him.

22. Thereupon he headed in a southerly direction. Doing this, he repeated what he had done earlier. He flew in a circular path four times, then proceeded straight upwards, and, after reaching the firmament, he returned. He went back to that person. Back to Maasaw.[10]

23. "You've returned?" he inquired.

24. "Yes," he answered.

25. "All right, what did you find out?"

26. "The space (here) approximates that of down below," he reported. "It appears that there will be room for us. The area is about the same as below," he said. "The depth is also about equal," he said.

27. "Very well," he said, "very well. Now, do as I have instructed. Take my message back."

28. So he headed back to the kiva opening, and then flew down, making a straight course, and, just as evening was approaching, he made a full descent. Arriving in the evening, he entered the kiva. He flopped over on the north side of the firepit. He rested there.

29. "You have arrived?" they inquired. "Thank you for returning."

30. He sat there panting. Only after catching his breath did he come

9. *Astotokya*, "hair-washing day", is the initiation day. See A. W. Geertz 1986:50–51, 1987*a*:11–13, and A. W. Geertz and Lomatuway'ma 1987:59–61 on the ceremonial day count.

10. Positive identification first comes at this late stage of the story. Everybody knows who the narrator is talking about, but for the sake of dramatic appeal, his identity is avoided as long as possible.

over to them and give them his account. He related to them what he had discovered. "There is nothing of value to be found anywhere. That one (above) informed me there was nobody to emit light–he only sits by his campfire. There is nothing to be treasured."

31. "That is right, he lives there under those conditions," someone interjected. They then smoked ritually.

32. "He told me that we are to do the following. He asked me to convey the following to you." He then divulged the directives he had been given.

33. "Very well, we will do that," they agreed. "We'll be sure to carry this out."

34. And so they did it. When they had roasted their corn, they arranged a date to hold the initiation. They then pursued that date.[11] Having set the date, they harvested their crops. After completing their harvest, they began storing the produce. As they concluded this, the appointed time arrived. So then they began their ceremonial. They took their children (the novices) into the kivas. Then they made it to the "hair-washing" day. On the "hair-washing" day, he (the bird) went up to check on things and thus made another ascent.

35. During this time, the members of the Kwan Society planted a spruce tree. The tree had reached the firmament, but it bent over at the top without penetrating the heavens. So then they planted the reed. As it grew it reached the top. It was this (plant) that pierced through to the other side. It had gone through the kiva opening, and so they made their preparations.

36. Then they chanted the "emerging song" as they emerged.[12] They emerged through the reed.

37. People became aware of what was taking place and informed one another, "Our elders are going (away) somewhere." In some places people woke up and started to follow them. All this was taking place in the middle of the night. They all wanted to come along. (But) they had no intentions of taking anyone evil along. But those people entered it (the reed) and accompanied them (anyway). It was evidently all sorts of people (clans or races) who did this.

38. While they were continuing onwards, the song ended, whereupon they kicked at the reed, and it toppled over. There must have been quite a few people still in it (the reed). When they felled the reed, not many escaped from inside it. Only certain members of some clans. Various clans emerged (safely) and entered this place.

11. See my comments on Hopi attitudes towards future events in chapter 2.

12. The song sung as the Katsinas emerge from the kiva hatchway in order to perform a Katsina dance.

39. Nothing of value was found anywhere. Now it was up to the Kwan men. The Kwan members hastened to create things, and they made the sun. And the moon too. A being known as Kwan Old Woman,[13] carrying a sackful of stars, (came along with them) and was decorating the skies. While she was decorating with them, the Coyote quickly opened her sackful of stars, it being his nature to be curious. (Prior to this) she was taking them out one at a time and adorning the heavens when he opened it, which resulted in the stars flying out and scattering haphazardly across the sky. Consequently they are now in this position. She had completed only the Star Sling (Ursa Minor), the Bow, the Dipper—the Star Dipper (Ursa Major), and those Strung Up Ones (Orion's Belt), when he caused this to happen.[14] She had also just drawn the Milky Way. It was due to Coyote's meddling that the stars became aimlessly strewn across the heavens. Thus, only these few were nicely placed in the sky.[15]

40. This they (the elders) also tell us. Then we people lived there, (near) the place of our emergence. They settled there when they came up.

41. They informed Maasaw when the time came to sow their seeds. Thus, he was supposed to give them his land. He was to mete out land to them so that they might till the soil and sow it. When they went to ask him, he answered, "No, farm whatever parcel of land you feel will suit your needs. After that, whenever a person does not wish to use the land again, it will revert back to me. Because if I give you the land, I'll never get it back. If I do not give it to you, whoever doesn't use it further will give it back to me. If a person does not sow that plot, it will become mine again. You have emerged to this place having great plans. You emerged from down below with evil schemes. You have grand visions. That is why I cannot turn it over to you. Whenever something happens to you I will regain its possession. You will progress into the future wishing for different ways (of life),[16] at which time you will meet your fate,[17] and I will get the land back. You will turn my land over to me at that time. I will then get the land back," he informed them. Consequently he did not (permanently) yield up his land, and they tilled it and they sowed their crops on it.

13. According to the narrator's daughter, it was Kookyangwso'wuuti, "Spider Grandmother."

14. Cf. Malotki 1983*b*:443–450.

15. See variant texts in Malotki and Lomatuway'ma 1985:17–19. This and Malotki and Lomatuway'ma 1984 provide interesting folkloristic materials on the Coyote in Hopi religious thought. See A. W. Geertz 1987*d* for more information.

16. Meaning: "different than the lifeway commanded by Maasaw."

17. Literally: "you (will) arrive at your something."

42. They had evidently spent a good number of years there, whereafter they were to migrate to Oraibi. They were to make preparations prior to their setting out for Oraibi. The Kwan men instructed the young men to go on a hunt. "Go out and hunt. Hunt for all kinds of game. We'll have our fill of food. We'll have a thanksgiving (dinner)[18] and then set out."

43. So they went out hunting and, after bagging their game, they baked the meat. And they stewed some of it. They also prepared fresh green corn in a variety of dishes. There was not a dish they had not prepared. As a matter of fact, they had a great feast. They feasted, and four days later they proceeded on their journey.

44. "Now, let's set out. I, Maasaw, am going ahead. I am going before you. I will be going and will await your arrival at Oraibi." Thus, he set out for that location.

45. Then they followed after him. He preceeded them as they commenced towards Oraibi. Because they were to follow him, some said, "We won't accompany the Kwan members. They will not be able to find a way for us, and they won't be able to find food. They won't bring anything worthwhile to us. We'll go to Kawestima," some decided and proceeded to Kawestima.[19]

46. But we were to follow them (the Kwaakwant). The Parrot clan, the clan that owns the corn (Piikyas clan), and the Bear clan, only these few clans followed the Kwan Society to Oraibi. These were the only followers they had when they migrated towards Oraibi. Meanwhile the various other clans went on to Kawestima.

47. "We will go with them. We have brought along something good. We have an old woman. Because we have Maasaw, we will somehow endure. So we will travel with the Kwan Society," they said, and then they went on. Only those few went with them. There weren't many that went along. The others followed those who did not take anything of value along.

48. Now they continued on their journey. They established settlements as they went along. Those who proceeded to Kawestima arrived there. They were to plant crops upon their arrival at Kawestima. They arrived there around planting time and were just about to do that, but the weather did not warm up. The Spider clan had a cicada as their clan "pet" (or "totem"), and the poor thing chirped constantly.[20] It was his

18. She uses the English term: tenskiving-lalwat, "(we) will make a thanksgiving."

19. One of the major settlements along the aboriginal boundary. The site is known as Betatakin ruins. See A. W. Geertz 1982*a*:173.

20. Concerning Hopi totemism, see A. W. Geertz and Lomatuway'ma 1987:138, nn. 80 and 81.

chirping that brought about the warmth. It was he who possessed the ability to produce heat. But he was unable to overcome (the cold). The poor thing froze to death.

49. The people then retreated from there. They were angered. Surely the others lived prosperously. And due to this prosperity, they had most likely reached their destination, and so they pursued them.

50. Now Old Spider Woman went to spy on them. As she went out in search of them, she finally caught up with them. It was true, they *were* living comfortably. They were very happy living like this. Witnessing this, she became angry and said, "We shouldn't have gone there (to Kawestima)", she said and returned home. She was jealous over this. She was upset. They were living a good life.

51. Someone from the Kwan Society became aware of this and said, "Someone was here last night. A person was about last night. Therefore we will have to go on," he suggested. "Let's go."

52. On his recommendation, they made preparations. "Some people will overtake us at some time. Thus, we will have to move on," he commented, and therefore they moved on.

53. They had traveled a far distance, then founded a settlement where they resided. Building a village, they colonized that place. They had been there for quite a spell when the Kwan Society instructed them. They were to excavate a site where the Kwan kiva was situated. They were not to go off taking another route. They told them they were to go along beneath the earth burrowing their way along. "The enemy is sure to overtake us."

54. Thus, they did as they were directed. This they were doing, excavating this kiva. They proceeded along underground and, after traveling a good distance, they surfaced and then continued along (above ground). Then they (stopped and) inhabited another location.

55. Of course the enemy caught up with them. It was the Castillians. The Old Spider Woman had created them. They were the ones who were pursuing them. But their rations became depleted, and they had no other alternative but to return. She provided them with more rations, and they continued their pursuit and discovered the site where they had surfaced. From this place they continued their chase and, after overtaking them, they devastated them when they raided them. They say this occurred at Palatkwapi. This took place there, whereupon the clans went on their separate ways never to find one another again.

56. Only the people of the Bear clan went along with them while the owners of the corn went this way. They evidently took a route along the north making their way (to Hopiland). But the Piikyas clan settled at another place called Masaatuyqa. There they lived. There they have a ruin. The Piikyas clan has a ruin there.

57. Once more, the foe overtook them and chased them to this place. Into this place where there is a huge overhang near Flagstaff, where a ruin is situated into the wall. It is said that this was the former home of the Corn clan.[21] When they attacked them, the entire group ascended up to this settlement where the enemy raised a siege against them. This band dug their way upwards along a crevice and, after accomplishing this, they escaped.

58. They had already escaped when those (the foe) below settled down permanently. They had made their exit long ago while the enemy were still camping down there. A good amount of time had elapsed and no one had come out from this place, so their pursuers made their way up there. They had surmised that those up there had perished and that's why no one ever peeped out. "Perhaps we have killed them. Maybe we have starved them to death. Perhaps they have died and that's why they haven't come out," they speculated.

59. A long time had now gone by and they were still camping there. Then one of them ascended. They must have fashioned some sort of a ladder so he was able to go up, and, on entering, he discovered that they were long gone. They had abandoned this place a long time ago. "No one is here! They've gone off quite a while ago!"

60. Then the entire group went up and discovered their escape route. They had chopped down a juniper tree, propped it up against the ceiling, then made their way up and out. Once more they followed them. But when they lost their tracks after some time, they abandoned the pursuit. This is the way they tell it.

61. They headed alone towards Oraibi. We then went through here. We who own the corn were said to have gone through Moenkopi. First they established a settlement on the west side of (upper) Moenkopi. They resided there. They descended from there and moved to the edge of the bluff where a church is now situated and also inhabited that place. They spent an unknown number of years there, then moved to a location east and above Moenkopi.

62. They lived there for a while and then were again going to move on. At that time someone known as Corn Grandmother said, "Wait! Wait until I tend to something, and then we'll move on. I have been burdened with carrying these[22] around, and I am tired. However, the large flow of water here is suitable. And by using them we will make our mark. With them we'll hold title to this place. Perhaps by the time we have arrived at Oraibi there will be no land left to farm. We will probably be the

21. Another name for the Piikyas clan.

22. For an explanation of what she is carrying, see paragraph 64.

last to arrive there. So I will fashion our marker with these. So you strong young men go about and seek out a home for them. But take me along as you go."

63. So they made their way down and searched about. Somewhere on the west side beneath a promontory there was a huge cavern and one of the young men entered this place. This was to be the place. "I have found it," he shouted from there.

64. Now the old woman took tadpoles which were mates, in addition to frogs, into this place. These were the beings the elderly woman was carrying about in her container. She had been toting them on her back. "Let it be like this. We will hold the deed to this place in this manner and with these creatures. There is a large flow of water down here which makes this place very suitable. Clearly the land here is valuable. With these beings we will hold on to this (land). It is apparent that we will be the last ones (to complete our migration)."

65. Thus, by using those creatures they left their mark. It was as if they had left their (clan) inscription. Then they proceeded to the higher ground and moved onward along the rims of the canyons. This is the way the (Piikyas) people tell it.

66. The route which those who made these migrations followed was determined by that particular group. They also chose the time that they would approach Oraibi. This is how they relate this to us. Thus, we possess this knowledge.[23]

67. They also tell us about it, those of our (Piikyas) clan. This old matron, Talangöysi, would say, "We belong together with the members of the Kwan Society. So don't push them aside. We were not to forsake them. Truly, we are with them. We were (destined) to arrive at Oraibi in their company. The Piikyas clan was to converge on Oraibi with them, but those evil ones (the enemy) routed us, and so we didn't arrive together. They also left a ruin above Savutuyqa."

68. [Jr. interrupts with the following:] Which route did we actually take?

69. Through there. Along there are eagle aeries. Since they went through there it now belongs to us. They left ruins there along the top. We traveled through the vicinity of Pavi'ovi. While going through Pavi'ovi we took a westerly route and, coming back from there, we also went to Mongwu. From there we traveled far to the east. We advanced north of Pangwu, made a circuit along the east, and then arrived there (at Savutuyqa).

70. After we arrived and settled up at Savutuyqa, it was probably our

23. The term used here for knowledge is *navoti*.

leader who was on the lookout and discovered a light (way) over there. For this reason we are not supposed to use that as fuel, these things which belong to the White Man, that which emits smoke. With smoke people let others who are far away become aware of things (their presence).

71. "Don't use that as fuel as the others." See, they forbade us to do many things. "Don't use electricity as the others do.[24] Use wood for fuel. You make your presence known by smoke. They can communicate in this way too."

72. It's a fact that smoke rises just when they build fires in the morning. "Someone is living there. Therefore smoke is visible there," they say. "So don't use that for light like the others," they tell each other. So because we know these things we won't light our place with it. It's due to the fact that we fear it.

73. While he (the leader) reconnoitered, he discovered the smoke coming from Oraibi and sent his nephew there. "Check that place out. Go and seek permission so that we may enter there."

74. As he commenced from there, he went along and arrived at his destination. It seems that when one arrives, that person utters prayers there below the mesa. After he had done so, someone came down and approached him. He greeted him very warmly. He cordially accepted the fellow from Savutuyqa, the nephew and descendent of Ahooli,[25] "You have arrived at long last? I have been waiting for your arrival," he said. And he was evidently one of the Bear clan. "I have been waiting for you, but you took a long time coming. There are people arriving here, and so I have many inhabitants," he disclosed.

75. "That is excellent," he replied.

76. "I have been waiting for you but you took some time coming," he repeated.

77. "Yes, he (my uncle) gave me instructions last night, so I came here."

78. "Come tomorrow, without delay. But dress Ahooli according to the way that he is costumed. Dress him in the way he is dressed. He knows how, so have him dress like that. Then bring him along dressed like that. And, in turn, I will prepare myself and wait for you," he instructed him.[26]

24. The term used here is *talwiipiki*, "lightning, or electricity." I am not quite sure what RN is referring to here, since the rule against talwiipiki as well as the command to use wood just do not seem to solve the problem of being discovered.

25. Ahooli is the tutelary of the Piikyas clan. On Ahooli see Titiev 1944:62–63, 114ff, 201, 224–225, and Wright 1973:19.

26. Note here how the use of ritual garb by the proper individuals performing the proper commemorative actions bridges the gaps between past and present as well as between humans and superhumans.

79. And so he received this good bit of news. Prior to his departure, the man told the youth, "Bring these words to them," and the lad returned from there. They were elated when he came bearing this information.

80. The following day, after having their morning meal, they commenced with the preparations. They dressed themselves. Ahooli began costuming himself and, after finishing, their clan ancestor told them, "All right, let's go. Follow me with happy hearts." Ahooli led the procession as the others followed.

81. [Jr.:] Where did he dress and then proceed onwards?

82. There, at the house. Above Savutuyqa. That was where they resided. Now they went to the west side and proceeded along the edges of the mesas. Thus, they also own the area along there. So those people established a settlement on our land. See, that eagle nesting place belongs to us. Therefore they went directly past Putsngasonvi. They went along there and neared Masaatuyqa, headed north, and then arrived at Oraibi. Thus, the Piikyas people traveled as far as Masaatuyqa and made a groove, a marker, there.

83. [Jr.:] Then why did Julius come to us recently and was complaining to us? When we took eaglets from there. Why did he have something to say about it?

84. That's because they don't want us to have it. They don't want anyone to have it. That's just their nature. Because that person told me this, and I in turn reiterated it to him. We shouldn't be unwilling to share it. That's what I also told him.[27]

85. Thus, they went along and were approaching Oraibi. They took a direct route and, after coming to Kykotsmovi, they went to Kwitangöntaqa and arrived at this place.

86. Ewtoto was present at this place.[28] Ewtoto was dressed up. After preparing himself, he descended to this place. Another person accompanied him. It was an elderly man. "You have arrived?" he inquired.

87. "Yes, we have," he answered.

88. "Very well, follow me." He was evidently the person who granted the others permission (to join the village). At that point he drew a path of cornmeal, and from there they began ascending. This person led them.

89. When they had come up to Oraibi, they went along the east side. "Go ahead into the village," he instructed them. "Take this path. And

27. Here is a clear example of clan negotiations in action.

28. Ewtoto is the tutelary deity of the Bear clan. On Ewtoto see Titiev 1944:62, 114ff, 120, 128, 225–226, 234–235, 253–254 and Wright 1973:18.

we'll enter this way. I'll accompany your clan ancestor. We will repeat our arrival in exactly the same way (in the future)," he commented.

90. "We will follow you," they said. "We too will follow the path on which you lead him." Thus, they formed a line behind him. They went along the mesa edge and came to that place, and, heading toward the west side, they approached the village from the south. He probably led them along the west side of the old mission. Then he took them into the village. This was the route by which he brought them there.

91. This is how they tell it to us. Our grandmother relates it in this way. Yukiwma also narrates it in this manner. So don't trouble the Kwan men. Don't bother them. Be thankful that you are with them. They won't cause trouble. They are foremost. They are knowledgeable in many ways and in many things. They certainly will not cause any agitation. They won't push anyone aside. They are kind to all people. They lead all people.

92. And yet we bear all sorts of falsehood against them. Listen, they predicted this, and we are surely like that. People dislike us. They have done this to all of us. This is constantly related to us, and that is how we people arrived here.[29]

THE HOPI TEXT

1. Itam hapi qa yep as yeese. Itam haqam atkyahaqam hopiikiningwuniqw pep as itam yesngwu. Pu' itam yantoti. Itam pu' paavan yeese. Itam pu' paavan qatsiy'yungwa. Pu' puma pephaqam pas qa unangwtalya. Pu' pay puma as qa tiivanikyangw pay puma sutsep mamantuy kivaapeq tangay'yungwa. Niikyangw pu' puma imuy momoymuy okiw timuy'yungqamuy enangtota. Okiw pumuy tsaatsakwmuy namat amumum qa tokngwu.

2. Pu' pep hak aawatwungwa kikmongwi. Pu' yaw pam okiw qa haalayti. Pam yaw kur pumuy timuy hintsanniqe pu' pam pumuy haqami as waa'oyaniqe pu' pam oovi haqami hakiy heeva. Niikyangw yuk oomi pam yaw as pan wuuwankyangw yaw pam as hakiy heeviy'ta. Hakiy pam pew ayataniqey. Pay yaw as hak yep pas qatu.

3. Pu' yaw pam pan wuuwantaqe pu' pam oovi mooti wuwtsimtuy tuwa. Sen pi pam hak oovi wuwtsimwimkya. Wuwtsimuy pam tuwiy'taqe pu' pam put pan tunatyawtaqe pu' yaw pam oovi pumuy soosokmuy kivasngwamuy tsovala. Pay puma oovi haqam kivay'yungqe puma oovi pep tsovalti. Pu' puma son pi hakiy qa hongvi'ayay'yungqe pu' puma oovi put pew ayatotaqw pu' pam pewhaqami as pan wupnikyangw pu' pay qa pew

29. See my interpretation of the political motives behind this support of the Kwan Brotherhood in A. W. Geertz and Lomatuway'ma 1987:119–127, 138–139, 141.

wuuvi. Pay qa hakiy pam oovi tuwa. Pay pam haqami maanguy'qe pay pam oovi qa pew oomi pitut pu' pay piw ahoy haawi. Pu' pam oovi ahoy hawqe pu' pam pumuy amumi pangqawu yaw qa pew pituuqe oovi qa hakiy tuwaaqey. "Is ohi antsa'ay," kitota.

4. Yaw tur hakim tuwatyani. Niiqe pu' puma oovi hiituywatuy kivaptuy amumi pangqaqwa puma yaw tuwatyani. Pu' puma oovi piw tuwat pantotikyangw pay yaw puma piw qa hakiy tutwa.

5. Puma qa hakiy tutwaqw paasat pu' yaw piw peetu tuwatya. Pu' puma yaw as piw tuwatyakyangw pay yaw puma piw qa hakiy tutwa. Paasat pu' yaw puma imuy kwaakwantuy amumi pangqaqwa. Paasat pu' yaw puma oovi tuwatyani.

6. Paasat pu' yaw puma put hongvi'ayay wangwayyaqe pu' put pitsinayaqw pu' yaw pam pumuy amumi pangqawu, "Ta'ay, ya uma hintiqw pas nuy kyeteynanawaknay?" kita yaw pam pumuy amumi.

7. "Owiy, pay as itam yep momngwit hintsatskyaniqw hak as itamungem yuk oominiy. Pephaqam as hak sumataq qatuy. Noq hak as pangsonen put hakiy aw pite' pu' hak as itamungem put aw maqaptsitaniy. Itam hapi yangqw as pangsoyaniy. Noq pu' pam hak itamuy nakwhanaqw pu' itam paasat awyaniy. I' itaakikmongwi as pangso peetuy timuy waa'oyaniqey naawaknay. Itam hapi yep pas qa unangwtalyay. Pam kur hin yaw pumuy powatani. Hin kur pumuy qe'tapnani. Yan pam wuuwantaqw oovi antsa itam ung pas kyeteynanawaknay. Noq kur oovi um tuwantani. Kur itam tuwatyani." Paasat pu' yaw puma oovi pepeq toktay'yungwa. Qa tookya puma. Tookyep yaw puma tsootsonglalwa put hongvi'ayay taviy'kyaayangw.

8. Qavongvaqw pu' yaw taawa yamaktoq pu' yaw pam pumuy hongvi'aya'am put saaqat atsveq qatuptuqw pu' yaw puma put aw pangqaqwa haqaqw pam taawa kuyvaqw pu' yaw pam suupangsoq warikni. Pu' yaw pam pangsoq pitukyangw pu' yaw pam pepeq qöniwmani. Epeq qöniwmakyangw pu' naalös pan qöniltikyangw pu' su'omiqni. Pay yaw pangso oomi kivaytsiwa. Pay yaw kivat angqw hin oomiq hötsiningwuniqw pay yaw pangsoq put su'an hötsiniiqat puma put aw pangqaqwa. Pay yaw sonqa tuwani.

9. Paasat pu' yaw pam oovi panti. Pu' angqaqw yaw taawa kuyvaqw paasat pu' yaw pam put su'aqwwat puuyalti. Niiqe pu' yaw pam oovi pangsoq pituuqe pu' yaw pam oovi pepeq naalös qöniltikyangw pu' yaw pam pas oovehaqtit paasat pu' yaw pam su'omiti. Panmakyangw pu' yaw pam antsa pephaqam kivaytsiwat tuwaaqe pu' yaw pam pewwat yama.

10. Noq pu' yaw puma put aw piw pangqaqwa. Yaw yep qa taala. Qa haqam yaw himu. Niikyangw so yaw hak haqam qa qatuni. Noq oovi yaw haqam qööhi maatsiwtaqw pangso yaw pamni.

11. Pu' yaw pam oovi yuk pitu. Niiqe pu' yaw pam pep haqam yankyangw yaw angqe' taynuma. Noq antsa yaw haqam qööhi maatsiwtaqw

pu' yaw pam oovi pangso. Hihin yaw pam haqam mamatsila. Angqaqw yaw pam hihin uwta. Paasat pu' yaw pam pangso put awniiqe pu' yaw pam put aw pitu.

12. Noq yaw himu ep qatu. Qa hiita yaw pam hinta. Pay yaw putsa pam mavokoy'ta. Pu' yaw pam put aw pangqawu, "Qatu'uy, um hak waynumay," yaw aw kita. "Qatu'u, um hak waynuma? Qa hisat hak yangqaqw pew'i. Noq um hintiqw piw hak waynuma?" yaw pam put aw kita.

13. "Owiy, pay nuy angqw ayaytotaqw oovi nu angqöy."

14. "Ya um hiituy angqöy?" pu' aw kita. "Um hakimuy angqöy?"

15. Pay yaw pam kwaakwantuy angqw. "Kwaakwantuy nu' angqöy," yaw aw kita.

16. "Kur antsa'ay, kur um pumuy angqöy. Kur um pas pumuy angqöy. Pumuy hapi nu' nuutaytay," pu' yaw aw kita. "Ya hiita ung ayatotay?"

17. "Owiy, pay yaw as ung hin lavaytiqw puma angqwyaniy."

18. "Is ohi okiway, pay qa himu inuupe nukngwa. Pay nu' pas panis yankyangw yep qatu. Nu' qa hiita taalay'ta. Nu' qa hiita nukngwat himuy'ta. Qa haqam inuupe himu nukngwa. Pay nu' itsa itutskway ep yantaqe pay nu' ngas'ew putsa himuy'ta," yaw aw kita. "Noq pay pi uma piyani. Suutaq'ewye' angqwyani. Qa haqam hapi himu nukngwa," pu' yaw aw kita. "Pay nu' panis yanta. Itsa nu' mavokoy'ta. Pay nu' panis yanta," pu' yaw aw kita.

19. "Pay pi oovi uma piyani. Suutaq'ewye' pi angqwyani. Niikyangw pay son uma paysoq angqwyani. Noq oovi um tuu'awvani. Um tuu'awvaqw uma tsaatsakwmuy tangatotani. Uma natngat tunatyaltotini. Tu'tsaye' uma tiingapyani. Uma tiingapye' pu' uma umuutimuy tangatotani. Uma pumuy tangatotaqw pu' uma ason astotokpe pu' uma angqwyani. Pu' um ep piw angqwniqw pu' itam sinmuy tumaltani. Itam naamaniikyangw pumuy tumaltani. Noq oovi ep uma angqwyani," yaw pam put aw kita.

20. "Kur antsa'a," yaw pam kita.

21. "Noq um tur piw oovi yep ang pootani. Hiisaqhaqam pi nu' yep qenit ep qatu. Pay nu' qa navotiy'ta. Hiisaq nu' ep qatuuqey, hin hö'it ep qatuuqey nu' qa navotiy'ta," pu' yaw pam put aw kita.

22. Paasat pu' yaw pam piw suutatöq wari. Suutatöq warikqe pu' yaw pam piw anti. Ang yaw pam poniwmakyangw pu' piw naalös qöniltikyangw pu' su'omiqniiqe pu' tokpelat tupoq pituuqe pu' pam pangqw piw ahoy put awi. Paasat pu' yaw pam piw put aw ahoy pitu. Put maasawuy awi.

23. "Ya um pitu?" yaw aw kita.

24. "Owiy," yaw kita.

25. "Ta'a, um hin navota?"

26. "Pay kur atkyaniiqat aasaqhaqam qeniy," yaw aw kita. "Pay itam

son kur qa qeniptuniy. Atkyaniiqat pay aasaqhaqam qeni," yaw kita. "Pu' piw pay aasavohaqam hö'i," yaw aw kita.

27. "Kur antsa'ay," yaw kita, "kur antsa'a. Ta'a, noq oovi uma panhaqam hintotini. Yanhaqam um tuu'awvani."

28. Paasat pu' yaw pam piw kivaytsiwat awniiqe pu' pam pay paasat pas suwip su'atkyamiq puuyawmakyangw panmakyangw su'aw yaw oovi tapkiwmaqw pu' yaw pam pas soosok haawi. Tapkiqw pu' pituuqe pu' yaw aqw kivamiq paki. Pu' yaw pam it qöpqöt akwniwi piqamti. Pangso yaw pam qatuptu.

29. "Ya um pitu?" yaw aw kitota. "Kwakwhay um pituu."

30. Pu' yaw pam pep qatuwkyangw hiikwislawu. Pas yaw pam oovi hikwsut pu' yaw pam amuminiiqe pu' yaw pam yanhaqam amumi lavayti. Hin pam navotqey put yaw pam pumuy amumi lavayti. "Qa himu yaw haqam nukngwa. Qa himu yaw haqam talniy'taqw pay yaw pam oovi qööhiysa aw qatu. Qa himu haqam nukngway."

31. "Hep owiy, pay pam pantaqat ep qatuy," yaw pam hak kita. Pu' yaw puma tsootsonglalwa.

32. "Noq oovi yanhaqam yaw itam hintotiniqat kita inumi'i. Niiqe yan nuy ayata." Pu' yaw pam put aw hin tutaptaqat put pu' yaw pam pumuy amumi lalvaya.

33. "Ta'a, pay itam pantotini," yaw kita. "Pay itam sonqa pantotini."

34. Pu' yaw puma oovi pantoti. Pu' yaw puma oovi put kwasinayaqe pu' yaw puma oovi put natngat tiingapya. Tiingapyaqe pu' yaw puma put angk hoyoyota. Pu' puma kya pi oovi höhöqya put tiingaviy'kyaakyangw. Pu' yaw puma oovi höqyukuyaqe pu' puuvut tangalalwa. Su'aw yaw puma oovi put soosok tangatotaqw pu' yaw puma tiingaviy angk öki. Paasat pu' yaw puma yungya. Pu' yaw puma pumuy timuy tangatota. Pu' yaw astotokyayamuy aqw hoyoyota. Pu' yaw oovi ep astotokpe pu' yaw pam piw aw pootatoqe pu' yaw pam piw aw oomi wuuvi.

35. Noq paasat pu' yaw puma kwaakwant yaw it salavit uu'uyya. Pu' yaw pam as pay aqw oomiq pitukyangw pay yaw pam epeq ooveq qa aw oomi yamakt pay yaw pam ngölölti. Paasat pu' yaw puma piw paaqavitwat uu'uyya. Paasat pu' yaw pam wungwiwmakyangw pu' yaw aqw oomiq pitu. Niiqe pu' yaw pam aqwhaqami yamakma. Aw oomiq kivaytsiwat ang yamakqw paasat pu' yaw puma yuuyahiwta.

36. Paasat pu' yaw puma it nöngantawit akw nöönganta. Paasat pu' yaw puma put paaqavit ang nöönganta.

37. Pu' pay yaw kur sinom nanaptaqe pu' yaw pangqaqwa, "Itanam haqamiya," yaw puma kitota. Pu' peetu pay yaw angqe' taatayayaqe pu' paasat pay yaw puma pumuy amungkya. Noq puma pi yaw suutokihaq pantsatskya. Puma hapi yaw pay peetuysa awiniy'kyaakyangwyaqe oovi. Puma hapi yaw qa imuy nuunukpantuy enang pangso tsamyaniqe oovi.

Pu' pay yaw sinom pumuy amumum put ang yungqe pu' pay yaw pumuy amumumya. Pu' pay puma kya pi soosoy hiitu pantoti.

38. Pu' pay yaw puma naat haqe'yaqw pu' pay yaw pam taawi so'tiqw pu' pay yaw puma put paaqavit aw horakyaqw pu' pay yaw wa'ö. Son pi sinom put ang naat qa wukotangawta. Put puma wa'öknayaqw paasat pu' pay ima sinom qa pas wuuhaqniiqam pang nönga. Pay yaw oovi himungyamsa. Hiihiituy amungaqw ngyam nöngakqe yaw antsa panhaqam hintaqat aw nönga.

39. Qa haqam yaw himu nukngwa. Pu' yaw puma kwaakwant paasat pu' yaw paptsiwyungwa. Puma kwaakwant yaw pisoqtotiqe pu' yaw puma hiita hintotiqe pu' yaw puma taawat yukuya. Pu' piw muuyawuy. Pu' yaw i' himu kwanso'wuuti yaw imuy sootuy moktaqe pu' yaw pam pumuy oova akw penta. Naat yaw pam oovi pumuy akw pangqe pentaqw pay yaw iisaw hiita ningwuniiqe pu' yaw put mookiyat aqw suuhöta, pumuy sootuy aqwa. Naat yaw pam pumuy suskomuy ipwankyangw akw oovaqe pentaqw pay yaw pam pumuy amumiq hötaqw pu' pay yaw puma pangqw nöngnangaykuqe pu' pay puma naanap hin pangqe aatsavalti. Niiqe paniqw yaw puma oovi pu' pangqe naanap hin hin panyungwa. Panis i' sootuviipiniqw, awtaniqw, kuyapi, sookuyapi, pu' mima hotomqam, pumuysa naat pam yukuqw pay pam panti. Pu' soongwuqat pam naat pu' angqe tuuwuha. Pu' pam iisaw pantiqw pu' pay puma sootu naanap hin pangqe aatsavalti. Pay yaw pumasa oovi pangqe pan nukwangwvey'yungwa.

40. Yanhaqam it enang yu'a'atotangwu. Pu' itam sinom pay paasat pepeq yeese, haqam nöngakqey. Haqam nöngkqey pu' pay puma oovi pepeq kya pi yeese.

41. Noq pu' yaw puma uu'uyaniqe pu' yaw puma put maasawuy aw pangqaqwa puma yaw uu'uyyani. Noq yaw pam oovi pumuy tutskway maqani. Pumuy yaw pam put huytaqw pu' yaw puma pastote' pu' yaw ang uu'uyyani. Yaw kitota puma put awniqw pu' yaw pam pumuy amumi pangqawu, "Qa'e, pay hak naap haqam pan aw wuuwante' pay hak pep pastamantani. Pay hak naap pante' pu' ason hak hisat qa ep uymantaniniqw pu' pay pam ahoy ihimuniwtimantani. Taq nu' umuy put maqe' nu' son put ahoy naaptini. Pu' nu' pay qa umuy put maqaqw pu' pay hak qa ep mongvasnen pu' pay paasat piw inumi ahoy put no'amantani. Qa ep uyniniqw pam pay ahoy ihimuniwtimantani. Taq uma a'ni hiita tunatyawkyaakyangw pew nönga. Pay uma hiita qa lomatunatyawkyaakyangw pew nönga. Uma a'ni naat hiita tunatyawyungwa. Noq oovi nu' son umuy naat put maqani. Pay umuy hintotiqw pay nu' naap putni. Uma yep hiihin naawakinwiskyaakyangw uma hiita aw ökiqw pu' pay nu' paasat put naaptini. Pay uma paasat piw inumi itutskway no'ayani. Pay nu' put soosok ahoy naaptini," pu' yaw pam amumi kita. Niiqe pay yaw

pam oovi pumuy put tutskway qa maqaqw pu' pay yaw puma oovi put tutskwayat paslalwakyangw pu' paasat ang uylalwa.

42. Pay kya pi puma oovi pepehaq wuuhaq yaasangwnayat paasat pu' puma yaw oraymiyani. Oraymiyaniqw pu' puma oovi pangso nankwusaniqw pu' yaw puma oovi hiita yukuyat pu'yani. Noq paasat pu' yaw puma kwaakwant pumuy tootimuy mak'ayatota. "Uma maqwisniy. Uma soosok hiituy maqwisni. Noq itam naanasnani. Itam tengskivinglalwat pu' itam nankwusani."

43. Pu' yaw puma maqwisqe pu' yaw puma qöqyaqw pu' yaw puma pumuy tuupeya. Pu' yaw peetuy kwipya. Pu' yaw hiihiita samit puuvut yaw aw hinwat noovatota. Qa hiita yaw qa noovatota. Noq antsa yaw puma naanasna. Naanasnat pu' aapiy nalöstalnayat pu' yaw puma nankwusa.

44. "Ta'a, itam nankwusani. Nu' maasaw hapi payni. Nu' hapi umuusavo payni. Nu' paynen umuy orayvehaqam nuutaytani." Paasat pu' pay yaw pam nakwsuqe pu' pay pangsohaqami.

45. Paasat pu' yaw puma put angkya. Pu' yaw puma oraymiyaniqw pu' yaw pam pangso oraymi pumuy amuusavo. Pu' yaw puma put angk awyaniqw pu' yaw puma peetu pangqaqwa, "Itam pay qa imuy kwaakwantuy amumumyani. Pay pi ima son haqe' itamungem hiita qenit, nöösiwqat tuway'wisni. Son ima haqam itamuy hiita nukngwat aw ökinayani. Itam pay kawestimay aqwyani," kitota puma peetuniiqe pu' yaw puma oovi pay pangsoqwatya.

46. Pu' yaw itam pay tuwat pumuy amumumyani. Pu' panis kyarngyam, pu' qaa'öt himuy'yungqam, pu' ima honngyam, panis puma paasa'niiqam yaw pangso oraymi pumuy kwaakwantuy amumumya. Panis yaw paasa'niiqamuy sinomuy'kyangw pangqw nankwusa. Pu' puma soosoy hiitungyam pangsoq kawestimay aqwhaqamiya.

47. "Itam pay imuy amumumyani. Ima pi pay pas nukwangwhiita hinwisa. So'wuutiy'wisa. Maasawuy'wisqe ima pay son hin haqam qa yesni. Itam oovi pay imuy kwaakwantuy amumumyani," yaw puma kitotaqe pu' yaw puma pangsoqhaqamiya. Panis paasa'niiqam oovi puma pumuy amumumya. Qa himu pas yaw pumuy amumum. Pu' pay mimawat pumuy qa hiita pas nukngwat hinyungqamuy amumumya.

48. Paasat pu' yaw puma oovi pangqw nankwusa. Pu' puma oovi pangqw panwiskyaakyangw pu' pangqw kiy'tiwisa. Pu' puma kawestimay aqwyaqam pu' puma pepeq öki. Kawestimay epeq ökiiqe pu' yaw puma as uu'uyani. Uyismi kya pi puma ökiqw pu' yaw puma as uu'uyaniqw yaw qa kwangqatti. Pu' yaw ima kookyangwngyam it maahut pookoy'yungqw pu' yaw pam as okiw sutsep leelena. Pam pi yaw leelenqw pu' yaw kwangqattingwu. Pam pi yaw it mumkiwuy tuwiy'ta. Niiqe pay yaw pam put qa angwuy'numa. Niiqe pay yaw pam oovi okiw tusungwmoki.

49. Pu' pay yaw puma paasat pangqw ahoyya. Pu' yaw puma itsivutoti. Nanalt pi yaw puma son haqe' qa qatsituway'numya. Haqe' qatsituway'-numyaqe pay yaw son aw haqami qa ökiiqat yaw puma kitotaqe pu' yaw puma pangqw pumuy amungkyaqe pu' yaw puma pumuy ngöytota.

50. Noq pu' yaw mi' kookyangwso'wuuti pumuy amungk poota. Pam yaw pumuy heptoqe pu' yaw pam pumuy haqam amungk pitu. Antsa yaw puma qatsiy'yungwa. Pu' yaw pam haqam amumi pituqw yaw antsa qatsiy'yungwa. Nanalt yaw puma qatsiy'yungqe yaw haalayya. Yan yaw pam yorikqe pu' yaw pam itsivutiqe pu' yaw pam paasat pangqawu, "Naapi kur itam pangsoqhaqamiya," kitat pu' yaw pam angqw nimaaqe pu' yaw paasat pitu. Pu' yaw pam put ep qa naani. Itsivuti yaw pami. Nanalt yaw puma qatsiy'yungwa.

51. Pu' yaw pay kur hak pumuy kwaakwantuy amungaqw navotqe pu' yaw pam pumuy amumi pangqawu, "Pay tooki hak pituy," pam yaw kwaaniy'taqa yaw pumuy amumi kita. "Tooki hak pituy. Noq oovi itam payyaniy," yaw kita. "Itam payyani."

52. Yaw pumuy amumi kitaqw pu' yaw puma oovi yuuyahiwta. "Pay son hisat itamungk hiitu qa ökiniy. Pay sonqa ima tuwqam hisat itamungk qa ökiniy. Itam oovi payyaniy," yaw kitaqw pu' yaw puma oovi pay pangqaqw nankwusa.

53. Niiqe pu' yaw puma haqami haq'urtotit pu' puma pay piw pepehaq kitsoktotaqe pu' puma oovi piw pepehaq kiy'yungwa. Pay kitsoktotaqe pu' puma piw pepehaq yesva. Pu' yaw puma oovi piw pepeq hiisavo yesqw pu' yaw pam kwaaniy'taqa pumuy amumi pangqawu. Pay yaw puma pumuy kwaakwantuy kivayamuy ep hangwayani. Pay yaw puma qa aye'haqe' nankwusani. Pay yaw puma pang hangwanwiskyaakyangw pay yaw puma pang atkye' hötsiy'wisniqat yaw pam pumuy amumi kita. "Pay sonqa tuwqam itamungk ökini."

54. Pu' yaw puma pepeq pantoti. Pantsatskya, haqam put kivay yaahantota. Pu' yaw puma pang aatö'yakyangw pu' yaw puma pay pas yaaptotit paasat pu' yaw puma haqam pookwakyaqe pu' yaw puma piw aapiytota. Pu' yaw puma haqamwat piw yesva.

55. Noq pay yaw antsa puma tuwqam pumuy amungk öki. Ima kastiilam. Pumuy yaw kur i' kookyangwso'wuuti yuku. Puma yaw kur pumuy amungkya. Niikyangw pay yaw puma pumuy qa tutwa. Pay yaw puma nitkyasoswaqe pu' yaw pay nawus ahoyya. Pu' yaw pam piw pumuy amungem nitkyataqw pu' yaw puma piwyakyangw pu' yaw puma pepeq haqam pookwakyaqw put pu' yaw puma tutwa. Paapiy pu' yaw puma pumuy amungkyaqe pu' haqam pu' yaw puma pumuy amungk ökiiqe pu' yaw puma pepeq pumuy tatslaknaya amumi kiipokqe. Noq palatkwapit epeq pam paniwtiqat pangqaqwangwu. Pepeq haqam puma pumuy pantotiqw pu' pay pumangyam naanahoyyaqe pu' pay aapiy qa piw naatutwa.

56. Pay mimasa honngyam pay pumasa pumuywatuy amumumyaqw pu' i' qaa'öt himuy'taqa pu' pay pam yukyiqwat. Niiqe pam pay oovi kwiningyaqeeqe kur peqw hinma. Niiqe pu' puma ayahaq pu' piw yesva, ayaq masaatuyqaveq. Pepeq puma oovi yesva. Pepeq oovi puma kiiqöy'-yungwa. Pepeq oovi kya pi himu piikyaswungwa kiiqöy'ta.

57. Pu' pay piw amungk ima tuwqam ökiiqe pu' pangso pumuy laalayya. Ayoq pösömiq aqw yukyiq wukotuusöt, ayaq nuvatukya'oviy yepehaq ura ang tuupelaq kiiqö. Pam hapi yaw pumuy qa'öngyamuy kiiqö'am. Noq pu' pumuy amumi kiipoq pu' puma pangsoq suuvoq ayoq pösömiq kiihut aqw yayvaqw pangsoq pu' ima tuwqam pumuy tsöngqöyantota. Paasat pu' yaw puma aqw oomiq porokinkyaakyangw pu' haqe' kya pi siisikyaniqw pang pu' yaw puma pangsoq oomiq poroknayaqe pu' yaw puma oovi pangsoq nönga.

58. Pangsoq nöngakqw pu' paasat puma pangqw atkyaqw pumuy amumiq sutsepyesva. Pay yaw puma hisat nöngaqw naat yaw puma pepeq panyungwa. Pay yaw pas aapiy hisattiqw pas yaw qa hak pangqaqw yamakqw pu' yaw puma aqw yayva. Pay kya pi yaw puma so'q oovi pas yaw qa hisat himu angqw kukuyqat yaw kitota. "Pay kya itam pumuy qöqya. Pay kya itam tsöngqöqya. Pay kya so'qe oovi qa nönga," yaw kitota.

59. Pu' yaw pay nuwu wuuyavotiqw puma yaw pumuy amumiq pepeq yeese. Pu' yaw oovi suukyawa aqw wuuvi. Son pi qa hiita aqw saqtotaqw pu' yaw pam aqw wupqe pu' yaw aqw pakiqw pay yaw kur puma hisat haqamiya. Pay yaw kur puma hisat pangqw haqamiya. "Pay qa hak qatuy. Pay kur puma hisat haqamiya."

60. Pu' yaw puma aqw yayvaqe pu' yaw puma pumuy oovi angqe' hepnumyakyangw pay yaw puma put tutwa haqe' yaw kur puma nöngakqw. Hohut yaw kur puma tukuyaqe pu' yaw puma kur put pangsoq wunuptsinayat pu' put ang aqw nönga. Pu' yaw puma pumuy piw ngööngöya. Niikyangw pay yaw puma hisattiqw pumuy qa kuktutwaqe pay yaw puma pangso pumuy maatatve. Yan it yu'a'atotangwu.

61. Pu' puma nanalt pangqw oraymiq hoyta. Pu' itam paasat yangqeya. Ima qaa'öt himuy'yungqam yaw yangqe mungqapaqeya. Pu' puma munqapiy yangqw taavangqöyngaqw mooti yaw kiiqötota. Pepeq yaw puma yesngwu. Nit pu' yaw angqw hanqe pu' yaw yuk ayo' ep tsiisaski, put yuk tumpo yaw pumayaqe pep puma piw yesngwu. Pu' yaw puma oovi piw pep hiisakis yaasangwnayat pangqw pu' yaw puma ayo' mungqapiy hoopo oomi yayva.

62. Pep pu' yaw puma piw yeskyaakyangw pu' yaw puma piw nankwusani. Paasat pu' yaw pam hak qa'öso'wuuti pangqawu, "Haaki, ason nuy mooti hiita hintiqw pu' itamyani. Nu' imuy naamangw'iwnumqe nu' maangu'i. Noq yepeq hin'ur paahuniiqe nukngwa. Noq oovi itam pay yepeq imuy akw tuvoylatotani. Itam it akw yepeq it nguy'yungwni. Pay

sen itam oraymi ökiqw sen pay paasat qa himu haqam paasani. Pay pi itam sonqa nuutungk aw ökini. Pay nu' oovi it akw tuvoylatani. Oovi uma tootim hohongvit angqe' amungem kiihepyani. Niikyangw uma nuy wikkyaakyangw hanni."

63. Pu' yaw puma oovi aqw atkyamiq hanqe pu' pangqe' yannumya. Pu' haqam yaw pepeq taavangqöyveq it tuyqat aqw atpikyaqe aqwhaqami hin'ur hötsiniqw pu' yaw suukyawa pangsoqhaqami paki. Noq pay yaw sonqa pepeqni. "Pay nu' tuway," pu' yaw pam angqaqw kita.

64. Paasat pu' yaw so'wuuti pangsoq pumuy paavawkyamuy naanawuutimuy pu' piw imuy paavakwtuy oya. Pumuy yaw kur pam qa'ösowuuti tangay'numa. Pumuy yaw pam iikwiwnuma. "Yantani. Yan itam imuy akw it yepeq nguy'yungwni. Yang hapi atkyamiq hin'ur paahuniiqe nukngwa. Sumataq yepeq nukngwa tutskwa. Itam imuy akw yepeq it nguy'yungwni. Itam hapi pay susmataq nuutungktotini."

65. Pu' yaw puma oovi pepeq pumuy akw tuvoylatota. Songyawnen epeq peenaya. Paasat pu' yaw puma pangqw nankwusaqe pu' yaw puma aqw oomiqyat pu' pay puma pang tuutupqat ang hinwisa. Yan it lavaytangwu sinom.

66. Pu' pay haqe' pi hakim hinwisngwuniqw pam pay paasat pumuy sinmuy epe. Hisat hakim aw oraymi ökingwu. Yan it itamumi yu'a'atotangwu. Pay itam yan pi oovi it navotiy'yungwa.

67. Niiqe oovi hakimuy puma piw amumi pangqaqwangwu, itamuyngyamuy amumi. Pam so'wuuti hak talangöysi pangqawngwu, "Itam hapi pas kwaakwantuy amumumya. Uma oovi qa pumuy ayo' no'iy'yungwni. Itam yaw qa pumuy maatatveni. Pay itam pas yaw pumuy amumumya. Itam yaw as pumuy amumum oraymi ökini. I' himu piikyaswungwa yaw as put amum oraymi pituniqw pay puma nuunukpant itamuy tatslaknayaqw oovi itam pay qa pumuy amumum aw öki. Pu' puma piw ayaq savutuyqat ooveq piw kiiqöy'yungwa.

68. Noq itam haqe' pas suyan nankwusa?

69. Hep yang'a. Pang pi pay kwaatipkya. Pay puma pang nankwusaqe oovi pang put himuy'yungwa. Ang atsva pi pay son oovi qa kiiqötiwisa. Noq pay pi itam pavi'oviy pangqe' hintsakwisa. Pavi'oviy pangqe' kya pi itam hintsakwiskyangw pu' pay hihin teevenge kya pi yantotiqe pu' yangqw peqw kya pi oovi ökit paasat pu' yaw ayoq mongwumiq piwya. Pang pu' piw itam hoopoqhaqamiya. Pu' pay pangwuy itam kwiningye' panwiskyaakyangw pu' pangqe hopkyaqe poniwwiskyangw pu' pangsoq öki.

70. Savutuyqat oomiqniiqe pu' pepeq huruutotiqw pu' pangqw pu' pam son pi qa kikmongwi taytaqw pu' yaw pepeq qööhiwtangwu. Noq oovi paniqw yaw itam qa pas soosoyam put qööhiy'yungwmantani, it hiita pahanhiita, kwiikwitsqat. Put pay kwiitsingwuy akw ima sinom pas haqami hiita aawintotangwu.

71. "Uma oovi qa nuutum put qööhiy'yungwni." Meh, soosok hiita itamuy meewantota. "Uma qa nuutum talwiipikit qööhiy'yungwni. Pay uma kohot qööhiy'yungwni. Put kwiitsingwuy akw pay haqami hiita hakimuy aawintota. Put akw pay piw naa'awintota."

72. Antsa naat pu' talavay qööyaqw angqw kwiikwitsngwu. "Kur hak pepehaq qatu. Oovi pangqw kwiikwitsi," kitotangwu. "Oovi uma qa nuutum put qööhiy'yungwni," kitotangwu hakimuy amumi. Noq pu' itam pay it navotiy'taqe oovi son pi put nuutum qööhiy'tani. Put pi pay nu' mamqasqe oovi.

73. Pu' pam pangqw taykyangw pu' pam put kwiitsingwuy pangso oraymi tuwaaqe pu' pam put hakiy tiw'ayay pangso ayata. "Kur um aw pootani. Kur um awnen ep maqaptsitaqw itam awyani."

74. Paasat pu' pam pangqw nakwsuqe pu' pay pam pang haqe' hinmakyangw pu' pam aw pitu. Pu' kya pi hak pangso pite' pu' yaw hak ayaq atkyaq naawaknangwu. Pu' yaw pam oovi naawaknaqw pu' yaw pam hak put aw haawi. Niiqe pam yaw put aw haalayti. Put savutuyqangaqw ahoolit taahay'taqat, wu'yay'taqat pam yaw aw haalayti, "Ya uma nawis'ewtiqw peqw öki? Umuy nu' hapi nuutayta," pu' yaw aw kita. Noq pam yaw kur hak honwungwa. "Umuy nu' nuutaytaqw pas uma nuwu qa ökiy. Pay ep ökiwtaqw oovi pay nu' a'ni sinotay," yaw aw kita.

75. "Pay tsangaw piy," yaw aw kita.

76. "Noq nu' umuy as nuutaytaqw pas uma nuwu qa ökiy," pu' yaw aw kita.

77. "Owiy, pam tooki inumi pangqawlawqw oovi nu' pu' angqöy."

78. "Noq uma qaavo pay angqwyaniy. Niikyangw oovi hin pam ahooli pas yuwsiy'tangwuniqw uma put pan yuwsinayaniy. Hin yuwsingwuqey pan yuwsiniy. Pay pi tuwiy'taqe pay pan yuwsini. Noq pu' uma put pangqw pantaqat wikyani. Noq pu' nu' ason tuwat yuwsit pu' nu' pay yep umuy nuutaytaniy," yaw pam put aw kita.

79. Paasat pu' yaw pam oovi yan suunukwangwnavota. Pu' yaw pam oovi pangqw ahoy nakwsuniqw pu' yaw pam put aw pangqawu, "Yan oovi um ep tuu'awvaniy," yaw pam put aw kitaqw pu' yaw pam pangqw ahoy. Pu' yaw pam yan tuu'awvaqw pay yaw puma haalaytoti.

80. Pu' yaw qaavotiqw pu' yaw puma nöönösat pu' yaw puma yuuyahiwta. Pu' yaw puma oovi yuwsiya. Pu' yaw pam ahooli yuuyuwsiqe oovi yukut paasat pu' yaw pam wu'ya'am ahooli pangqawu, "Ta'ay, tumaa. Uma haalaykyaakyangw inungk kwilalatotani." Pu' yaw pam ahooli oovi motiy'maqw pu' yaw puma angkya.

81. Haqam pam yuwsit pu' pam nakwsu?

82. Epeq kiihut epeq. Pepeq savutuyqat ooveq. Pepeq pi puma piw kiy'yungwa. Paasat pu' puma kya pi oovi pangqw aatavangqöymiq hanqe pangqw pu' puma nankwusaqe pu' pay puma oovi yang hihin tuphaykye'ya. Niiqe pay pi puma oovi piw pang put himuy'yungwa. Puma pi pay

oovi put itaatutskway ep kiitota, mima. Meh, pam pi pay kwaatipkya itaahimu. Niiqe puma kya pi oovi aye' putsngasonvay ang iikye' aqw teevengeya. Pay puma put ang hinwiskyaakyangw pangsoq masaatuyqamiq peep ökit pang pu' puma kwiniwiyaqe pu' pay pangqeyaqe pu' aqw oraymiq öki. Niiqe oovi pam pangsoq masaatuyqamiq paasavo kya pi pam piikyaswungwa nakwsuqw oovi pangqw piw yaw pam oovi hövawta, tuvoyla'iwta.

83. Noq hintiqw oovi pu' hisat Julius yepeq pituuqe pangqawlawu itamumi? Pumuy itam pangqw kwaatuy kwusuyaqw. Hintiqw piw pam put ep hingqawlawu?

84. Ispi puma pi pay put itamumi kyaakyawnayaqe'e. Puma pay puuvut kyaakyawnaya. Puma pi pay panyungwni. Noq pam mi' pi pay piw itamumi pangqaqw oovi nu' aw pangqawu. Itam qa naanami put kyaakyawnayaniqat. Nu' pi oovi pay piw aw kita.

85. Pu' yaw puma oovi pay pangqe hinwiskyaakyangw pu' puma yaw aqw oraymiq ökiwisa. Pangqw pu' pay yaw puma suwip aqwyaqe pu' puma aw kiqötsmomi ökit paapiy pu' puma ayo' kwitangöntaqay awyaqe pu' aw öki.

86. Noq pephaqam yaw pam ewtoto. Ewtoto yaw kur pan yuwsi. Pan yaw yuwsit pu' pangso haawi. Noq pu' yaw piw hak suukyawa amum yawi. Hak wuuyoqa taaqa. "Uma öki?" yaw pam amumi kita.

87. "Owiy, itam ökiy," yaw kita.

88. "Ta'ay, uma pay inungkyaniy." Pam kya pi hak tuuyayvantoynaqa. Paasat pu' yaw pumuy amungem homvöötaqw pangqw pu' yaw puma yayvanta. Pam pu' yaw pumuy wiikiy'ma.

89. Pu' yaw puma aw oraymi yayvaqe pu' yaw puma angqe hopkyaqeeqeya. "Pay uma aw kiimiyaniy," kita yaw pam pumuy amumi. "Yang pay uma awyaniy. Pu' itam pay yangqeeqeyani. Nu' pay it umuuwu'yay wiikiy'maniy. Noq pay itam hin aw pituuqey pay itam sonqa pan aw pituniy," kita pami.

90. "Pay pi itam sonqa umungkyaniy," yaw kitota. "Pay um haqe' it wiikiy'maqw pay itam sonqa umungkyani." Pay yaw puma oovi pangqe put angk leetsiwta. Pangqeeqe puma tumkyaqeeqe yanwiskyangw aqw ayoq ökit pu' pangqw pu' puma paasat taavangqöymiq haykyalayat pangqw pu' puma tatkyaqw aw ökiwisa. Son pi qa santikit aatavangqöyvahaqe' pam pumuy wiikiy'ma. Pu' yaw pam pangso kiimi pumuy pitsina. Yanhaqam yaw pam pumuy aw ökina.

91. Yan hapi puma it itamumi yu'a'atotangwu. Itaaso yan it itamumi yu'a'atangwu. Pu' piw yukiwma pay piw yan it itamumi yu'a'atangwu. Noq oovi uma hapi pumuy kwaakwantuy qa hintsaatsanyani. Uma hapi qa pumuy hintsaatsanyani. Tsangaw uma pumuy amumumya. Puma hapi pay qa hintsatskyani. Puma hapi pas moopeqya. Puma hapi ii'it hiihiita

tuwiy'yungwa. Puma hapi oovi pay pas qa hintsatskyani. Puma pay qa hakiy ii'ingyalya. Puma soosokmuy sinmuy paasya. Puma soosokmuy pumuy tsaamiy'wisa.

92. Noq itam yep hapi pay pumuy hiihiita akw a'tsalalwani. Meh, yan it yu'a'atotangwuniqw pay itam antsa panyungwa. Noq pu' pay itamuy okiw pay pi qa himuya. Soosokmuy itamuy yantsatsna. Yan hapi it itamumi yu'a'atotangwuniqw pangqaqw pi oovi itam pew öki, sinom.

APPENDIX B

Selected Versions of the Emergence Myth

Narrated by Hostiles and Traditionalists

The original misspellings, orthographic inconsistencies, punctuation practices, and other such matters have been preserved here. These myths should be read in conjunction with the analysis presented in this book. This collection is meant to illustrate to what extent the Traditionalist mythology has changed—even in accounts given by the same narrator. The myths also demonstrate to what extent they deviate from the more traditional emergence myths such as the one reproduced in Appendix A.

Narrator: Talay'ima
Date: 1882
Source: Cushing (1924)

I. When the world was new, men and the creatures lived not and things were not on the top of the earth, but below. All was black darkness as well above as below. There were four worlds, this world (the top of the earth), and three cave worlds, one below the other. No one of the cave worlds was large enough to contain all living creatures and men, for they increased in the lowest first cave world so as to overfill it. They were poor and knew not whither to turn in the black darkness, and when they moved, they jostled one another. The place was filled with the filth and dung of those who dwelt in it. No man could turn to spit but he spat on another, or cast slime from his nose but it fell upon another. The people filled the place with their complainings and exclamations of disgust.

II. It was said by the masters (gods?), "Being thus it is not well," and, "How can it be made better?" and, "Let it be tried and seen!" Two boys, the older brother and the younger, said, "Yes, let it be tried and seen and it shall be well; by our wills shall it be well," said "The Two" to the masters and to the priest-chiefs of the dwellers in the cave world. "The Two" pierced the roofs of the caves and descended to the dark abode of men and beings. They then planted one after the other all the plants which grew, hoping that one of them would grow up to the opening through which they had descended, yet have the strength to bear the weight of men and the beings; and that by climbing it they might deliver themselves into the second cave world. At last, after many many trials, the cane (*arundinaria*) was found so tall that its top grew through and so strong that men could climb on it to the top. It was jointed that it might be like a ladder readily ascended, and ever since then the cane has grown in joints as we see it today along the Colorado.

III. Up this cane many men and creatures climbed to the second cave world. When a part of the number had climbed out, fearing that the second cave world–which was so dark that they could not see how large it was–would prove too small, they shook the cane ladder so that those who were coming up, fell back. Then they pulled the ladder quite out, preventing the others from ascending. It is said that those who were left, ultimately came out. They are our brothers to the westward.

IV. After a long time the second cave became filled with men and the beings, as had been the first. Wrangling and complainings were heard as in the beginning. Again the cane was placed under the roofvent, and thus once more men and the creatures found deliverance, yet those who were slow to climb out, were shaken back or left, as had been a part of the number in the first cave world. Though larger, the third cave was as dark as were the others. Fire was found by "The Two" with which torches were set ablaze, and by the light of these men built their huts and *kivas* or traveled from place to place.

V. Times of evil came while the creatures and men dwelt in this third world. Women became crazed. They neglected all things for the dance. They even forgot their babes. Wives became mixed with wives so that husbands knew not their own from others. Then there was no day, but one night. Throughout this night women danced in the kivas, ceasing only to sleep. Whereupon fathers became mothers to the neglected little ones. When these little ones cried of hunger, the fathers carried them to the *kivas* where the women were dancing. The mothers, hearing their cries, came and suckled them, then, again forgetting them, left them to be cared for by the fathers, to rejoin the dance.

VI. These troubles caused men to long for light and to seek again deliverance. They ascended to the fourth world which was this world. But when they came out, they found it as dark as it had been below, for the earth was closed in by the sky, as had been the cave worlds by their roofs. Men went abroad and did their doings only by the light of torches and fires. They found the tracks of only one being, of the single ruler of the unpeopled world, the tracks of Corpse Demon or Death. They led eastward and the people sought to follow them, but the world was damp and men knew not what to do in the darkness; for waters seemed to surround them everywhere and the tracks to lead out into the waters.

VII. There were with men—who came forth with other creatures from the cave worlds—five beings, Spider, Vulture, Swallow, Coyote and Locust. The people and these beings consulted together, that they might make light. Many, many attempts were made, but without success. It was decided that Spider should first try. She spun a mantle of pure white cotton. It gave some light, but still not enough. She is therefore our grandmother. So the people procured and prepared a very white deerskin which had nowhere been pierced. Of this they formed a shield-case, which they painted with turquoise paint. Lo, it shed forth such brilliant light when they had done that it illuminated the whole world. In its light the cotton mantle light faded. So they sent the shield-light to the east where it became the sun, and the mantle-light they sent to the west where it became the moon. Now down in the cave world Coyote had stolen a jar which was very heavy, so heavy that Coyote was weary of carrying it. He therefore decided to leave it, but he was curious to see what it contained. So now that it was light he opened it, whereupon many shining fragments and sparks flew out and upward, singeing his face in their passage. Hence the coyote has a black face to this day. These became the stars.

VIII. By these lights it was found that the world was indeed very small and surrounded on every side by waters which made it damp. The people appealed to Vulture who spread his wings and fanned the waters, that they flowed away to the east and west until mountains began to appear. Across these "The Two" cut channels through which the waters rushed away, wearing their courses deeper and deeper, thus forming the great canyons and valleys of the world. The waters have kept on flowing for ages, until the world has grown and is still growing drier and drier. Now that it was light and land appeared, the people easily followed the tracks of Death whither they led toward the eastward. Hence Death is our greatest father and master (God), for we followed his tracks from the exit of the cave worlds, and he was the only being that awaited us on the great world of waters where now is this world. Although all the waters had flowed away, all the earth was damp and soft, hence it is that we may see to this day, between this place toward the westward and the place whence we came out, the tracks of men and of many strange creatures;

for the earth has since changed to stone and all the tracks are preserved as when they were first made.

IX. Now men had proceeded but a short distance in the tracks of Corpse Demon, when they overtook him. There were two little girls. One was the daughter of a great priest (*cacique*) and was most beautiful. The other was only the child of somebody-or-other. She was not of such beauty as the daughter of the priest, and was jealous of her. So (with the aid of Corpse Demon) she caused her death. Now this was the first death. When the people saw that the maiden slept and could not be awakened, that she grew cold and that her heart had ceased beating, the great priest grew angry. He loudly cried to all his children, asking who had caused his daughter to become thus; but the people only looked at one another. Then said the priest, "I will make a ball of sacred meal which I will cast into the air, and which in descending will strike some-one on the head. This one shall I know as the one whose magic and evil art have brought my calamity upon me." He made a ball of sacred flour and pollen. This, when he had cast it into the air, fell upon the head of the little girl (the daughter of somebody-or-other). When the priest saw this, he exclaimed, "Aha! so you have caused this thing." He then called a council of the people, and they tried the girl. They had killed her, had she not cried out for mercy and a little time. Then she begged the priest and his children to return to the hole whence they had all come and look down, promising that she would willingly die should they, after looking, still wish to destroy her. Thus persuaded, the people returned and looked down. Lo! Amid plains of beautiful flowers, in a land of everlasting summer and fruitfulness, they saw her wandering, so happy that she heeded them not nor longed to return. "Look!" said the girl who had caused the death of the priest's daughter, "Thus shall it be with the children of men." "When we die then," said the people to one another, "we are to return to the world whence we have come out and be happy! Why should we fear to die or resent death?" Hence they did not kill the little girl, but suffered her to live. Her children became the powerful wizards and witches of the world, increasing with other men. Her children still live and have the most wonderful and dreadful of all powers. (As you Americans will find out, if you attempt to meddle with us, for we are, some of us, *they*.)

X. Then the people journeyed once more eastward. As they went, they discovered in their company Locust. They asked him whence he came from. He replied that he came out with the other beings. Then they asked him why he accompanied them, and he replied, that he might be useful. "Ha!" said the people to one another, "can such a creature be useful?"—"No, of course not," said others. So they commanded Locust to return whence he had come, but he would not obey them. This so enraged the people that they ran arrows through him, even through his heart, so that his blood all oozed out of his body and he died. Yet after a long time he came to life again and ran about, looking as he had before, save that the blood had dried, turning his coat black. Then the people said to one another, "Ha! although we have pierced him through and through, yet here he lives again. Useful indeed shall he be, and with us preciously journey, for who so possesses the wonderful power of renewing his life? Possesses he not the medicine for the renewal of the lives of others? Therefore shall he become the medicine of mortal wounds and of war." Hence the locust is at first white, as was the first locust who came forth with the ancients. And, like him, he dies, and after he has been dead a long time, he comes to life again, only he is black. (He is our father, too, for having his medicine, we are the greatest of men. Have we not still his medicine? Even though you Americans bring soldiers and slay us, we can defy you, for the locust medicine heals mortal wounds.)

XI. After man had journeyed a great distance, eating nothing but flesh, they became woefully hungry. They had, in their anxiety to get away from the cave worlds, forgotten to bring seed. There was much lamenting, much discussing, until the God of Dew sent the chimney-swallow back to bring the seed of corn and other foods. When the swallow returned, the God of Dew planted in the ground the seed. Incantations knew the God of Dew. By their power he caused the corn to grow and ripen in a single day. So, for a long time the people in their journey carried no seed with them for food, only such as served for planting. They depended upon their father, the God of Dew, to raise for them in a single day abundance of corn and other things. This father taught even the children of men his power and gave them seed which should grow and ripen in a single day. To the Corn people (clan) he gave this seed, and they were long able to accomplish the raising of corn in a marvelously short time; but the time has kept growing longer and longer, until now sometimes our corn does not have time to grow old (ripen) in the ear, or our other foods to ripen. Had it not been for the children of the little girl whom the ancients let live, even now we would not need to watch cornfields whole summers through or carry heavy food on journeys! (You see by this the wonderful powers of our wizards and witches. Teaches it you not fear?)

XII. As the people journeyed on, these children of the little girl thought they would try their powers, and caused other troubles. And other troubles met the people on their way, for they found men and creatures who had come out before them. These people made war because they were stirred up by the magicians. The people warred, too, with one another, until it became necessary that they should, wherever they ceased their journeyings, build their houses on high mountains with but one road leading up to them, or in caves with but one path down to them, or in the sides of deep canyons. Thus only could they sleep with easy thoughts. Now among these people who had come out before our ancients, was the great warrior, the Navaho. He was made and sent up that he might protect all men, therefore he was from the beginning a great warrior. But when he saw how powerful he was, he became bad, and turned against those he had been sent to protect. Then all men turned against him. This is the reason why he is today the enemy of all men, and the most foolish of nations.

XIII. The Mexican, long before men reached their journey's end, was made of clay and breathed upon until he came to life. But he had a bad color; so he was washed, yet they had to wash him so hard that his outside skin and much of the substance of his flesh came off, hence he became whiter than were our ancients. Of this skin and substance the horse and the burro were made, and on them the Mexican rode away so far that he disappeared for a long time. At last he came back, but he insisted that all men should be washed as he had been, and do as he did. These are the reasons why the Mexican is always accompanied by the horse, mule, and burro; and why he insists on washing (baptising) everybody. Therefore we did not look kindly upon him, and he became our enemy, as did the Navajo and all other men. But still we live!

XIV. Among those who came out from the cave worlds first were the Americans, so said our ancients. Now while we were yet journeying, before we settled where now we get being, our older brother left us and journeyed toward the land of the sun. (So said our ancients). And when our older brother (the Americans) separated from his younger brother (the Oraibi) the younger brother commanded him, saying, "Brother Older, you go toward the country whence comes out the sun. Toward the country of great rivers and great trees you go. There you will find a home. Many men's ages shall pass while we are apart. Your children shall increase, and mine. Your children shall fill the world whither you go. Then you shall turn back to the place of your birth, seeking a country more spacious wherein to dwell. It is then that you will meet me again. You will find me poor, while you will return in the grandeur of plenty, and in the welfare of good food. You will find me hungry and offer me nourishment; but I will cast your morsels aside from my mouth. You will find me naked and offer me garments of soft fabrics, but I will rend your raiments and trample them under my feet. You will find me sad and perplexed, and offer me speeches of consolation and advice; but I will spurn your words, I will reproach, revile, and despise you. You will smile upon me and act gently; but I will scowl upon you and cast you aside as I would cast filth from my presence. Then will you rise and strike my head from my neck. As it rolls in the dust you will arrest it and sit upon it as upon a stool-rock. Then, nor until then, may you feed my belly or clothe my body. But a sorry day will it be for you when you sit upon my head as upon a stool-rock, and a glad day for me. For on that day you will but divide the trail of your own life with the knife which severs my head from my body, and give to me immortal life, liberty, and surcease from anxiety."

Narrator: Yukiwma
Date: 1903–1904
Source: Voth (1905)

A very long time ago they were living down below. Everything was good there at that time. That way of living was good down there. Everything was good, everything grew well; it rained all the time, everything was blossoming. That is the way it was, but by and by it became different. The chiefs commenced to do bad. Then it stopped raining and they only had very small crops and the winds began to blow. People became sick. By and by it was like it is here now, and at last the people participated in this. They, too, began to talk bad and to be bad. And then those who have not a single heart, the sorcerers, that are very bad, began to increase and became more and more. The people began to live the way we are living now, in constant contentions. Thus they were living. Nobody would listen any more. They became very bad. They would take away the wives of the chiefs.

The chiefs hereupon became angry and they planned to do something to the people, to take revenge on them. They began to think of escaping. So a few of the chiefs met once and thought and talked about the matter. They had heard some sounds away up, as of footsteps, as if somebody was walking there, and about that they were talking. Then the Kíkmongwi, who had heard the sounds above, said that they wanted to investigate above and see how it was there, and then if the one above there wanted them, they wanted to try to go out. So the others were willing too that they wanted to find out about that, and then if they were permitted they wanted to move up there. So they were now thinking who should find out. So they made a Pawáokaya, sang over it, and thus brought it to life. "Why do you want me?" the bird said. "Yes," the chief said, "we are not living well here, our hearts are not light, and they are troubling us here, and now I have been thinking about these few children of mine here and we want to see whether we can find some other way of living. Away above there somebody seems to be walking, and now we thought maybe you could go up there and see about that and find out for us, and that is the reason why we want you." "All right," the Pawáokaya said, "all right, I shall go up there and find out about it." Hereupon the chief planted a lööqö (species of pine or fir), but they saw that it did not reach up, but that its point was turning downward. Hereupon they planted a reed by the side of the pine and that reached up. They then told the Pawáokaya to go up now and if he should find anybody to tell him and then if he were willing they would go.

So the Pawáokaya ascended, flying in circles upward around these two ladders. When he came up to the top he found an opening there, through which he went out. After he came out he was flying around and around, but did not find anybody, so he returned to the opening again and came down. As he was very tired he fell down upon the ground before the chiefs. When he was somewhat revived they asked him, "Now, what have you found out?" "Yes," he said, "I went through there and there was a large space there, but I did not find anybody. When I did not find anybody I became hungry and thirsty and very tired, so I have come back now." "Ishohi! (Oh!)" they said. "Very well, now who else will go?" and they were thinking. "Somebody else shall go," they said, and they kept thinking about it.

So they made another one, but this time a small one, and when they were singing over it it became alive. When it had become alive they saw that it was a Humming-bird (Tóhcha), which is very small, but very swift and strong. "Why do you want me?" the bird said. "Yes," they said, "our children here are not with good hearts. We are not living well here; we are living here in trouble. So we want you to go up there for us and see what you can find out, and if the one up there is kind and good, we think of going up there, and that is the reason why we want you. So you go up there; you hunt somebody, and if he is gentle and kind, we shall go up there." So the Tóhcha flew upward, circling around the two trees, went through the opening and flew around and around, and not finding anybody also became tired and came back. He flew lower and lower and alighted in front of the chiefs, exhausted. When he had somewhat revived, they asked him: "Now, then, what have you heard, what have you found out?" "Yes," he said, "yes, I flew around there that way and became tired and exhausted and have come back." "Ishohí!" they said again, "now then, we shall send somebody else."

They then created another one, and sang over it. But this time they had made a larger one, and when they had chanted their song over it, it became alive and it was a Hawk (Kisha). "Why do you want me?" the Hawk also said. "Yes," they replied, "yes, these our children do not listen to us, they worry us, and we are living in trouble here, and that is why we want you. You go up there and find out for us and inform us." So the Hawk flew up also, passed through the opening, and circled around for some time in the space above the opening. But he also became tired and returned, exhausted. So when he was somewhat revived, they asked him: "What did you find out?" and he told them the same as the others had, that he had not found any one. "Ishohi!" they said, "We shall try it once more."

So they made another one, and sang over it again. While they were singing over it it became alive, and it was the Mótsni. "Why do you want me?" the latter asked. "Yes," they said, "our children here do not listen to us, they have hard hearts, and we are living in trouble here. So we have been thinking of leaving here, but these here have not found anybody there, so you go up too, and you find out for us. And, if you find some one there who is kind and gentle and has a good heart, why you tell us and we shall go up there." So he flew up too, and having passed through the opening, he kept flying around and looking about, as he was very strong. Finally he found the place where Oraibi now is, but there were no houses there yet, and there somebody was sitting, leaning his head forward, and as the Mótsni came nearer he moved it to the side a little. Finally he said: "Sit down, you that are going around here, sit down. Certainly you are going around here for some reason. Nobody has seen me here yet." "Yes," the Mótsni said, "down below we are not living well, and the chiefs there have sent me up here to find out, and now I have found you, and if you are kind, we have thought of coming up here, since I now have found you. Now you say, you tell me if you are willing, and I shall tell them so, and we will come up here." This one whom the Mótsni had found was Skeleton (Másauwuu). "Yes," he said, "now this is the way I am living here. I am living here in poverty. I have not anything; this is the way I am living here. Now, if you are willing to live here that way, too, with me and share this life, why come, you are welcome." "All right," the Mótsni said, "whatever they say down there, whatever they say. Now, I shall be off." "All right," Skeleton said, whereupon the Mótsni left.

So he returned and descended to where the chiefs were sitting, but this one did not drop down, for he was very strong, and he came flying down to them. "What have you found out?" they asked the bird. "Yes," he said, "I was up there and I have found him away off. But it is with you now; he also lives there poorly, he has not much, he is destitute. But if you are satisfied with his manner of living, why you are welcome to come up there." "All right," they said, and were happy. "So that is the way he is saying, so he is kind, we are welcome, and we are going."

At that time there were all kinds of people living down there, the White Man, the Paiute, the Pueblo; in fact, all the different kinds of people except the Zuñi and the Kóhonino, who have come from another place. Of all these people some whose hearts were not very bad had heard about this, and they had now assembled with the chiefs, but the greater part of the people, those whose hearts were very bad, were not present. They now decided that they would leave. The chief told them that in four days they were to be ready to leave. So during the four days those who knew about it secretly told some of their friends whose hearts also were at least not very bad, that after four days they were going to leave. So the different chiefs from the different kinds of people assembled with small parties on the morning of the fourth day, after they had had their morning meal. They met at the place where they were appointed to meet, and there were a good many. "We are a great many," the chief said, "may be there will be some here among them whose heart is not single. Now, no more must come, this is enough." So they commenced to climb up the reed, first the different chiefs, the Village chief (Kík-mongwi), who was also at the same time the Soyál-mongwi, the Flute chief (Lán-mongwi), Horn chief (Al-mongwi), Agave chief (Kwán-mongwi), Singer chief (Táo-mongwi), Wúwuchim chief (Kél-mongwi), Rattle-snake chief (Tcú-mongwi), Antelope chief (Tcöb-mongwi), Maraú chief (Maraú-mongwi), Lagón chief (Lagón-mongwi), and the Warrior chief (Kaléhtak-mongwi or Pöokong). And then the people followed and a great many went out. By this time the people in the lower world had heard about this, and they now came crowding from all sides towards the trees. When the Kík-mongwi above there saw that so many were coming he called down to stop. "Some of those Pópwaktu," he said, "are going to come up too, I think, so that is enough, stop now!" He then commenced to pull up the reed so that a great many people that were still on it dropped back.

So they now moved on a little bit to the rim or edge of the opening, and there they gathered, and there were a great many of them. The Kík-mongwi now addressed them and said: "Now this many we have come out, now we shall go there, but we want to live with a single heart. Thus long we have lived with bad hearts. We want to stop that. Whatever that one there (referring to the Mótsni) tells us, we want to listen to, and the way he says we shall live. Thus he instructed them.

In a little while the child of the chief, a small boy, became sick and died. "Ishohí!" the chief said, "A Powáka has come out with us," and they were thinking about it. Then he made a ball of fine meal and threw it upward, and it alighted on the head of a maiden. So he went there and grabbed her, saying: "So you are the one. On your account my child has died. I shall throw you back again." He then lifted her to the opening. "I am going to throw you down here," he said, "you have come out with us and we shall now live in the same way here again." But she did not want to. "No," she said, "you must not throw me down, I want to stay with you, and if you will contend with one another again I shall always talk for you (be on your side). Now, you go and look down there and you will see your child going around down there." So he looked down and there he saw his child running around with the others. "That is the way it will be," the maiden said to the chief; "if any one dies, he will go down there and he will remain there only four days, and after the four days he will come back again and live with his people." Hereupon the chief was willing that she should remain and he did not throw her down, but he told her that she could not go with them right away. When they should leave, when they had slept, after the first day she might follow them. So she remained there near the opening.

Hereupon Pöokong looked around all over and he found out that towards one side it was always cold. It was at this time dark yet, so Spider Woman (Kóhkang Wuhti) took a piece of white native cloth (ówa) and cut a large round piece out of it on which she made a drawing. She was assisted by the Flute priest. They sang some songs over it, and Spider Woman then took the disk away towards the east. Soon they saw something rise there, but it did not become very light yet, and it was the moon. So they said they must make something else. Spider Woman and the Flute priest then took a piece of buckskin, cut a circular piece out of it, and made on it a drawing of the sun symbol, as is still used by the Flute priest to-day. They sang over this, whereupon Spider Woman took that away and in a little while something rose again, and now it became light and very warm. But they had rubbed the yolks of eggs over this sun symbol and that is what makes it so very light, and that is why the chickens know when it is light and yellow in the morning, and crow early at the sunrise, and at noon, and in the evening, and now they know all about the time. And now the chief and all the people were happy because it was light and warm.

The chiefs now made all different kinds of blossoms and plants and everything. They now thought of starting and scattering out. The language then spoken was the Hopi language. This language was dear and sacred to the Hopi chief, and he wanted to keep it alone to himself and for the Hopi, but did not want the people who would scatter out to take this language along, and so he asked the Mocking-bird (Yáhpa), who talks everything, to give to the different people a different language. This the Mocking-bird did, giving to one party one language, to another party another language, and so on, telling them that these languages they should henceforth speak. Hereupon they sat down to eat a common meal, and the chief laid out a great many corn-ears of different lengths which they had brought from the under-world. "Now," he said, "you choose of these corn-ears before you start." So there was a great wrangle over these corn-ears, every one wanting the longest ears, and such people as the Navaho, Ute, Apache, etc., struggled for and got the longest corn-ears, leaving the small ones for the Hopi, and these the chief took and said: "Thanks, that you have left this for me. Upon this we are going to live. Now, you that took the long corn-ears will live on that, but they are not corn, they will be kwáhkwi, láhu, and such grasses that have seed." And that is the reason why these people rub out the tassels of those grasses now and live on them; and the Hopi have corn, because the smaller ears were really the corn.

The chief had an elder brother, and he selected some of the best foods that tasted well, such as nöokwiwi, meats, etc. They were now ready to start, and then the chief and his elder brother talked with each other and agreed that the elder brother should go with a party ahead towards the sunrise, and when he would arrive there he should touch the sun, at least with his forehead, and then remain and live there where the sun rises. But they should not forget their brethren, they should be looking this way, towards the place where they would settle down. A So Wuhti (old woman, grandmother) went with each party. Each party also took a stone upon which there were some marks and figures, and that fitted together. They agreed that if the Hopi should get into trouble again, and live again the same way as they did in the lower world, the elder brother should come back to them and discover the Powákas who caused the trouble, and cut off their heads.

The elder brother and his party started first, and they became the White Men as they traveled eastward. The chief and his party started next, both taking a southern route. The maiden that had been found to be a Powáka, and who had been left behind at the opening, followed these two parties after they had left.

The people hereupon formed different parties, each party following a certain chief, and all traveling eastward. They usually stopped for longer or shorter periods at certain places, and then traveled on again. For this reason there are so many ruins all over the country. The Pueblo Indians also passed through about here where the Hopi now live. The White Men were more skillful than the others and got along better. Spider Woman, who was with them, made horses and burros for them, on which they traveled when they got tired, and for that reason they went along much faster. The party that brought Powák-mana with them settled down at Palátkwapi, where they lived for quite a while, and these did not yet bear a particular clan name.

The other parties traveled different routes and were scattered over the country, each party having a chief of its own. Sometimes they would stay one, two, three, or four years at one place, wherever they found good fields or springs. Here they would raise crops so that they had some food to take with them when they continued their journeys, and then moved on again. Sometimes when they found good fields but no water they would create springs with a báuypi. This is a small perforated vessel into which they would place certain herbs, different kinds of stones, shells, a small balölöokong, bahos, etc., and bury it. In one year a spring would come out of the ground where this was buried. During this year, before their spring was ready, they would use rainwater, because they understood how to create rain. When they continued their journeys they usually took such a báuypi out of the ground and took it with them.

Before any of the parties had arrived at the place where the Hopi now live they began to become bad. Contentions arose among the parties. They began to war against each other. Whenever a certain party possessed something, another party would attack and kill them on account of those possessions. For that reason some of them built their villages on top of the bluffs and mesas, because they were afraid of other parties. Finally some of them arrived at Múenkapi. These were the Bear clan, Spider clan, Hide Strap clan, Blue-bird clan, and the Fat Cavity clan; all of which had derived their names from a dead bear upon which these different parties had come as they were traveling along.

While these parties lived near Múenkapi for some time another party had gone along the Little Colorado river, passed by the place that is now called the Great Lakes, and arrived at Shongópavi, where they started a village at the place where now the ruins of old Shongópavi are, east of the present village. These people were also called the Bear clan, but they were different Bear people from those living at Múenkapi about that time. Shongópavi was the first village started. When these Bear people arrived at Shongópavi, Skeleton was living at the place where Oraíbi now is, where he had been living all the time. The clan that had stopped northeast of Múenkapi soon moved to the place where Múenkapi now is, but did not remain there long. The Bear clan, the Hide Strap clan, and the Blue-bird clan soon moved on towards Oraíbi. When the Spider clan arrived at Múenkapi they made marks or wrote on a certain bluff east of Múenkapi, saying that this place should always belong to the Hopi, that no one should take it away from them, because there was so much water there. Here the Hopi should always plant.

Soon after the Spider clan had moved on towards Oraíbi the Snake clan arrived. When these Snake people saw the writing on the bluff they said, "Somebody has been writing here that they wanted to own this. Let us write also that we want to own this here, too." So they wrote the same thing on the bluff. After they had left the place, the Burrowing Owl clan arrived, and they also wrote the same thing on the bluff. But they all had heard that Skeleton was living where Oraíbi now is, and so they all traveled on towards Oraíbi. When the Bear clan arrived at Nátuwanpika, a place a very short distance west of Kuiwánva, Skeleton came to meet them there. "We have arrived here," the Hón-wungwa said, "we would like to live here with you, and we want you to be our chief. Now, what do you think about it? Will you give us some land?" But Skeleton replied, "No, I shall not be chief. You shall be chief here, you have retained your old life. You will be the same here as you were down in the under-world. Some one that is Powáka has come out with you and it will be here just the same as it was down there when he comes here. But when the White Man, your elder brother, will come back here and cut off the heads of the bad ones, then I shall own all this land of mine myself. But until then you shall be chief. I shall give you a piece of land and then you live here."

Hereupon he stepped off a large tract of land, going east of where they were, and then descending the mesa west of Köqöchmovi, then towards the present trail towards Oraíbi, up the trail, past the present village site, down the mesa on the west side, along the trail towards Momóshvavi, including that spring, and back up the mesa. This piece of land he allotted to the Bear clan. The leader of the Bear clan now asked him where he lived. He said he lived over there at the bluff of Oraíbi, and that is where they should live also. So this clan built its houses right east of the bluff of Oraíbi where there are now the ruins.

The Bear clan brought with them the Soyál cult, the Aototo, and the Soyál Katcínas. Soon other clans began to arrive. When a clan arrived usually one of the new arrivals would go to the village and ask the village chief for permission to settle in the village. He usually asked whether they understood anything to produce rain and good crops, and if they had any cult, they would refer to it and say, "Yes, this or this we have, and when we assemble for this ceremony, or when we have this dance it will rain. With this we have traveled, and with this we have taken care of our children." The chief would then say, "Very well, you come and live in the village." Thus the different clans arrived: First, the Hide Strap clan, the Blue-bird clan, the Spider clan, etc. While these different clans were arriving in Oraíbi, other clans were arriving in Wálpi and Mishóngnovi, and settling up those villages. When a new clan arrived, the village chief would tell them: "Very well, you participate in our cult and help us with the ceremonies," and then he would give them their fields according to the way they came. And that way their fields were all distributed.

One of the first clans to arrive with those mentioned was the Bow clan, which came from the south-west. When the village chief asked the leader of this clan what he brought with him to produce rain, he said, "Yes, I have here the Sháalako Katcinas, the Tangík Katcinas, the Túkwunang Katcina, and the Sháwiki Katcina. When they dance it usually rains." "Very well," the village chief said, "you try it." So the Aoatwungwa arranged a dance. On the day before the dance it rained a little, and on the last day when they had their dance it rained fearfully. All the washes were full of water. So the village chief invited them to move to the village and gave them a large tract of land. He told them that they should have their ceremonies first. This was the Wúwuchim ceremony, the chief of the Bow clan being the leader of this ceremony. So this ceremony was the first one to take place.

Then followed the Soyál ceremony, in charge of the village chief. And then in the Báho month the Snake and the Flute ceremonies, which change about every two years. The Snake cult was brought by the Snake clan, the Antelope cult by the Blue-bird clan, and the Flute cult by the Spider clan. The Lizard, which also arrived from the north-west, brought the Maraú cult, and the Parrot clan the Lagón cult. Others came later. Small bands living throughout the country when they could hear about the people living in Oraíbi would sometimes move up towards Oraíbi and ask for admission to live in the village. In this way the villages were built up slowly.

At that time everything was good yet. No wicked ones were living in the village at that time. When the Katcinas danced it would rain, and if it did not rain while they danced, it always rained when the dance was over, and when the people would have their kiva ceremonies it would also rain. But at that time they had not so many Katcinas. There were only the Hopi Katcinas, which the Hopi brought with them from the under-world. They were very simple but very good. People at that time lived happily, but by this time the Pópwaktu had increased at Palátkwapi. The one Powáka maiden that had come with these people from the under-world had taught others her evil arts. And so these wicked ones had increased very much until finally Palátkwapi was destroyed by a great water produced by the Bálölöokongs. Nearly all the people were destroyed, but a few succeeded in reaching dry land in the flood and they were saved.

They traveled northeastward and finally came to Matövi, and from there to Wálpi. From Wálpi they scattered to the different villages, teaching their evil arts to others. They would put sickness into the people so that the people contracted diseases and died. They also turned the Ute Indians and the Apache, who used to be friends of the Hopi, into their enemies, so that after that these tribes would make wars on the Hopi. They also caused contentions among the Hopi. The Navaho also used to be friends of the Hopi, but these Pópwaktu would occasionally call the Ute and the Apache to make raids on the Hopi. They also turned the Navaho into our enemies, and then the White Men came and made demands of the Hopi. The White Men are also called here by these Pópwaktu, and now the White Men are worrying the Hopi also.

But the Hopi are still looking towards their elder brother, the one that arrived at the sunrise first, and he is looking from there this way to the Hopi, watching and listening how they are getting along. Our old men and ancestors (wúwuyom) have said that some White Men would be coming to them, but they would not be the White Men like our elder brother, and they would be worrying us. They would ask for our children. They would ask us to have our heads washed (baptized), and if we would not do what they asked us they would beat us and trouble us and probably kill us. But we should not listen to them, we should continue to live like the Hopi. We should continue to use the food of the Hopi and wear the clothes of the Hopi. But those Pópwaktu of the Hopi would help the White Men, and they would speak for the White Men, because they would also want to do just the same as those White Men would ask them to do. And now it has come to that, our forefathers have been prophesying that. We are now in trouble. Our children are taken away from us, and we are being harassed and worried.

Narrator: Yukiwma
Date: 1911
Source: Scott (12-5-1911)

The Hopis used to live down in the underworld, down in the earth. There the Hopis had their chiefs and their villages. But the Hopis had too much love for a good time, and finally ran into a rut, refusing to recognize their chiefs. They gave social dances to the exclusion of religious rites and ceremonies. The chiefs attempted vainly to guide them. First the girls, next, the women, and then all the Hopi People began to come under this degenerate influence; they forgot everything else. At last the wives of the chiefs of all the clans neglected their religion and practiced the social dancing.

Then the heads of all the tribes of the vast underworld met and held a large council. Not liking the way their people were living, they decided to look for another world. For anything asked for will be given to good chiefs and priests. They debated on how they were to move to the next world. So they planted tall pine trees, and then through religious ceremonies, they started the growth of these trees. Such things were done only by the chiefs. The pine trees grew up into the sky against a high roof which they did not pierce; they bent over and spread. Thus was the plan of the pine trees abandoned.

Then the chiefs planted sharp pointed reeds, and these reeds grew tall and pierced the sky. The next question was where to live. So they sent birds as messengers; humming-birds out through the holes in the sky to look for a land where the good people. They told the birds that the people were disobedient to the chiefs and priests and said they would move to the place which the birds would report to them. The birds flew upward, circling around the tall reeds and resting thereon when fatigued by the long ascent, but the undertaking was far too great, and exhausted, they fell to the earth. A chicken hawk was then sent up, which could fly much better than the first birds. He ascended in a similar manner, but exhausted fell to the earth. The swallow was sent but could not reach the top of the reeds. One more religious fraternity, the Quoguan,[1] was yet to send a messenger. This fraternity sent a bird (probably a cat-bird) which flew with a jerky motion. The chiefs were sure that somebody lived above them. Everyone thought that this bird was doomed to failure like the others, but he reached the top, flew through a hole in the sky and came to Oraibi. Here he found the red-headed ghost, or spirit sometimes imitated at harvest time. The ghost asked the bird his mission. Then the bird told his story and asked permission for the underworld people to

1. Kwaakwant.

come up and live there. The ghost was willing that they should and so the bird went back to the underworld and delivered his message.

Most of the people were still busy with their social dances, but the village chiefs and all the other chiefs rushed to the tall reeds and began to climb them. In this they were aided by the two gods of hard substances, who made the reeds firm. Finally all the people had crawled through the hole in the sky, the chief watching and keeping out those who had given up their time to social dances. When he saw two of these people coming up the reed, he shook it loose and dropped them back to the ground, and stopped up the hole.

A search for the new home was then commenced, but the chief's daughter died and he decided that some of the powerful witches had come up with them so he called his people together and threw up some sacred bread made of corn meal, saying that the meal would fall on the witch's head. It fell on a girl's head. He then decided to throw her back through the hole into the underworld. But upon looking through the hole the chief saw his daughter who had just died, playing in the underworld like their little children. Thereby the chief knew that everyone went to the underworld after death. The witch told him that if he would let her live with him that his own daughter would before long return. She also said that she would keep him out of all difficulties. On these terms, the girl was spared.

It was utter darkness when the Hopis arrived on earth. They counciled and attempted to create light. They cut out a round piece of buckskin which they had brought with them from the underworld, and took bits out of the hearts of all the people, birds and beasts put them into the buckskin and told it to give light. But this was not sufficient. So taking white cotton cloth, they put the bits of hearts on it and put it in the east for the sun. Thus the sun gave light for every living thing, each of which welcomes the rising of the sun. They placed corn on the ground and told the people to pick that up which they wished for food. Each person picked up an ear of corn. After the people had picked up the food, the shortest ear was left for the chief. He was thankful for the short ear for it would provide him with food in any land. The chief cautioned the people who were to go to Oraiba, to live as the ghost wished them to live. Each band went in a different direction. The older brother of the chief was told to go to where the sun rises and stay there. The younger brother was to send for the older in time of trouble. The chief then called the mocking bird and told him to give each band a language, written on a piece of stone. The older brother received the first language, which was to be the language of the white man. The chief who came to Oraiba received also a plate. If the older brother upon being sent for should come and find the Oraiba tribe backsliding into their old ways of life in the underworld, he (the older brother) should cut off the head of the Oraiba chief. The older brother's name was Väläkän.[2] When the older brother went east, the chief told him not to be baptized into any fraternity.

The mocking-bird gave out several more different languages, and then the clans went to their respective lands. Ukeoma belongs to the ghost clan. They put the witch girl behind so that she could not get to Oraiba first and be the ruler. The chief led the ghost people to Oraiba, carrying their seeds. They travelled for a while; stopped and raised a crop and proceeded again on their journey. The brother who went east, travelled faster than the chief. Sometimes they would stop at one place two or three years. The ruling clan was the Oraiba clan, the clan which the witch followed. The corn clan travelled along south with the Cochina Clan. All the clans came out of the ocean to the far west. The bear clan was headed for Oraiba, followed by the ghost clan, then came the witch. The ghost clan finally arrived at Tuba (thirty miles N.W. of Oraiba), and saw that some other clan had been there. So they went on. The smoke clan, ghost clan and spider clan came together at Tuba. After living there a few years, they found a part of the Bear Clan. The real chief of the Bear Clan came to Chimopovy where he found out that it was not Oraiba. He moved to Oraiba where the ghost, Smoke and Spider Clans later found him. Transients from various clans came in and built up Oraiba. As the ghost clans were coming to Oraiba, they met the red-headed ghost about two miles west of Oraiba. The ghost was very kind to them. The ghost clan immediately asked the Red headed ghost to become their chief. He refused saying that they will go to the bad again. The ghost let the old chief rule. They asked the ghost to set aside some land for them. He did so, allotting it right around the point of the Mesa at Oraiba. He then told them to move on the mesa at Oraiba. The ghost himself lived off the mesa, just west of Oraiba. The ghost clan settled around a large boulder called Oraiba. While they were settled at this place, the Bear Clan came and settled under the cliff to the South of Oraiba. When they became stronger, they ascended the Mesa and settled with the Ghost and Smoke and Spider clans. In the ghost clan were two parties;—one known as the Ghost and bird, and the other the ghost clan proper. Ukeoma's clan was the Ghost and Bird clan which came after Oraiba was settled. They first settled at the foot of the Mesa. The chief would not consent that they should come up at first. They were known as the Bravery clan, being a guard to the Bear Clan. Then the Oraiba People went back to their bad underworld ways; the witches ran things, making people sick etc. The Utes, Navajos, Apaches, and other warriors came in and fought the Bear Clan at Oraiba. The ghost clan, though in

2. Paalölöqangw.

great difficulty, would not ask the Ghost-and-Bird Clan up. Finally when the enemies were lined up for attack, the chief went down and implored the Ghost-and-Bird Clan to come up and fight for him. The ghost invited them up. The Ghost gave his clan power to defeat the hostile warriors. Two of the bravest of the Ghost Clan, with explosives, in pottery, went out into the enemies ranks and threw these explosives. The Oraibans defeated the Piutes, through the power of the Red-headed Ghost. They chased them from the village, and scattered them out over a large territory. The ghost guided the clans. He stopped the fight three or four miles north of Hotivilla. Here an irregularly shaped tree grew. The Ghost and Bird Clan told the other Oraiba clans that they no longer wished to be regarded as the Braves. From then on the Ghost and Bird Clan lived at Oraiba. Here they lived in peace for a time. They were taken into the sacred fraternities, and were recognized as fighters. Tradition runs that a stronger people will come to the Hopis and try to get them to adopt their ways of living. The Hopis will be attacked by all the Navajos etc. The ruling clan at Oraiba, the Bear Clan, will yield to some stronger clan. The Navajos at first guarded the Hopis, but when the Hopis went to the bad, the Navajos attacked them.

The Oraiba chief betrayed his own people. The Spaniard came and fought, coming from the South. They were here four years and then attempted to make the Hopi adopt their ways. The Bear Clan yielded up to the stronger people. Then the Spider clan yielded, and then the warriors, but the Ghost and Bird Clan did not yield. The stronger people in an unpretentious and quiet way forced their ways upon the people. The native police are examples of a stronger people gradually forcing their ways upon the Hopis.

When the Spaniard (Priests) came to live at Oraiba, the ruling clan wanted to yield to them. After four years, the priests would have them baptized. That caused trouble. Their tradition was against such. The fighting men were unwilling to assist the ruling clan because they had already yielded to the Spanish. They thought the sea would swallow up the land if they yielded. The ghost and bird clan had kept the traditions. The Bear Clan gave up to the Ghost and Bird Clan, in order to prevent the Sea from swallowing up the land. Finally the Badger Clan killed the Priests. This killing made the Navajos hostile. So the Navajos, together with the Spaniards attacked the Hopis. The last fight was between the Oraibans on one side and the first and second Mesa People and the Navajos and Spanish on the other. The GHOST and Bear Clan assisted the Oraibans, who won the fight, driving the enemy off of the Mesa onto skull flat, so named because of the heads piled up there. They drove the people onto the 2nd mesa. Then the Oraibans drew a line at the edge of the second mesa and returned home. Upon their home-coming, the Ghost and Bird Clan again gave notice to the Oraibans, that they were to be warriors no longer. They recorded the number killed by inscribing it on the large boulder at the foot of their Mesa. The Oraibans recognized the Ghost and Bird Clan as the saviors of their people, having saved them from destruction in the sea. The Oraibans grew in number and lived in peace for a time.

Ukeoma says that again they will be urged to yield up. Probably the present coming of soldiers indicates this fact. The Spider clan yielded next. The Oraiba people have taken up new ways taught them by the government. The ghost and bird clan would not take up government ideas. The Chief of the Oraibans wanted the Ghost and Bird Clan to take up Government ways, which caused trouble and Ukeoma was told to take the Ghost and Bird Clan away from Oraiba. This he did and settled at Hotivilla in 1905.[3] Ukeoma regards the Oraibans as traitors. The big brothers across the sea will soon come and send a messenger to Santa Fe, then a second one to the Pacific. These messengers are to report everything to the whites across the sea. The Oraibans have received the whites, and sent for soldiers, and taken members of the Ghost and Bird Clan prisoners. The Hopi Policemen also assist the whites. Finally all the enemies will combine and do harm to the Ghost and Bird people unless they conform to the new ideas and ways of living. All of these things must happen. Ukeoma can't help it.

The soldiers from the West will do the capturing and will take them east as prisoners or West to death. Ukeoma must not depart from his traditions. Only will his people yield when removed and put under another chief. If the whole band moves East, by chance, they are not to be harmed, but will be more likely, if moved West. Soldiers are meaner if from the West than they are if from the East. Ukeoma blames the Oraibans for receiving aid from the Government in securing land and asking for soldiers to force the Hotivillos into government schools.

[Seven pages of script follow describing the split of Oraibi in detail.]

Ukeoma does not like to send children to school because his ancestors said he should not do so. The right kind of people will not force them to be baptized and send children to school. Sometime, a good people will come to whom the Hopis will yield, but they will not require the baptizm of the children nor schools.

Ukeoma says all the white men's talk is incited by the witches. These troubles have been predicted by his ancestors. He is to suffer at the hand

3. This is incorrect. The date was 1906.

of the whites and Navajos. The government is guilty of wrongdoing in troubling him more than four times. He wears white people's clothes because he buys and pays for them. He is chief and will not send children to school for if he does, he will no longer be chief. White men buy things from soldiers and soldiers buy white men's things, a legitimate business, not against traditions, sending children to school is against Hopi Traditions.

Ukeoma says white people treat him kindly in beginning but do not encourage him in his own way of living. Commissioner at Washington told him it was impossible that the children be brought up according to Hopi ways, and that soldiers would be sent for his children. Col. Scott is giving made-up arguments to Ukeoma. It is true that the white man will finally usurp all the Indian's Country, but the Indians will not be beggars, the white men will not harm the Indians. The only way for the white brother to rule is to cut Ukeoma's head off. This act will bring his people to different life, the life of the stronger people. If the Oraiba chief is bad, cut his head off; if Ukeoma is good, do not cut his head off. All the Hopis who have deserted their traditions are progressing.

The witches right hand man must have his head cut off. After this is done, all tribes will go the same way. Traditions say that he must hold to the Hopi way. Finally the troubles will end and all will be peace. Oceans will swallow up the land unless Hopi traditions be observed. At Oraiba, the chief has a square stone plate representing the earth. A serpent is carved on one side and a man's figure on the other. The serpent represents the ocean which is swallow up the land. The other figure, the white brother who is to come and cut off the heads of the bad people. The Oraiba Chief will fall and Ukeoma will triumph over all the tribes.

Oraiba holds a stone plate brought from the underworld and it gives him the right to the country. If soldiers come, Ukeoma will not resist. If Ukeoma consents to his children being taken without force, it means that he yields to the government. Ukeoma thinks Col. Scott has been hurried by Ukeoma's enemies, because letters were handed to Col. Scott in the Kiov[4] this morning and right away he left, and now he has quit listening to Ukeoma's story, and has gone to questioning him about schools. In answer to the idea of being laughed at by his enemies, Ukeoma says a chief must suffer ridicule but friends will not laugh at him. Some of Ukeoma's people have taken up government ways and called themselves progressives. Some Bocali,[5] government friends, live in Ukeoma's village. These will not need to be forced. Why do you hesitate to cut off Ukeoma's head, if you think he is wrong? Tradition says somebody's head must be

4. Kiva.
5. Bacavi.

cut off before the trouble is ended. The evil spirit goes around at night in the form of an animal or a bird of some kind. The right hand man of this bad spirit must have his head cut off. If the Oraiba chief be the right hand man, let his head be cut off. If Ukeoma, be the bad man, led his head be cut off. Ukeoma doesn't want soldiers at all. If soldiers care to come, Ukeoma is no longer friend to the whites. Let them go their way, and let Ukeoma go his way. The chief will not do anything. Some of his own people may have given up to Col. Scott, or they may have told him they would fight, but Ukeoma will not fight. Ukeoma says somebody has agreed to give up to the government. If the children's parent agree to let the children go, they may go, but he asks that they may not be taken forcefully. Spare the children of the chief, the children of the chief's close friends to the Hopi ways. Ukeoma does not always wear white mens clothes. Ukeoma doesn't think he is the real chief of all the people. Some of them have probably turned away from him, and they may get their children, but leave Ukeoma's alone. Ukeoma will not agree to anything. He wants no trouble. (Ukeoma here presented two slabs of rock on which he said was inscribed the tradition. The red-headed ghost gave them to his people upon their arrival at Oraiba.)

Narrator: Qötshongva
Date: 1935
Source: Kotchongva (1936)

There was a lot of wickedness down below this earth somewhere, where my people used to live and some of their wise leaders anxiously looked ahead for the people. These people with their wise leaders have been told way far back, for hundreds of years that there was another earth to come to, which was this earth we are now on. They knew someone was on this earth as they heard his footsteps above them, and realized that only through a marvelous performance would they be able to find some way of penetrating through from the world below.

The chief of these wise leaders had cultivated the friendship of various kinds of birds. He made the birds as messengers to the man who was already here to gain his permission to come to the earth. The man on the earth told the Bird Messenger to take back the message that he had nothing here that was very good; his life was hard; he was very poor and that they would not like to live as he had to do. The leaders of the people said they wanted to come anyway. They wanted to live here just as he had been living, as they were willing to live under any hard circumstances to get away from the wicked two-hearted people—people, who have two hearts, one for good and one for evil.

When these leaders found a way to come, they desired not to bring any wicked people to this earth, as that was the main idea of getting away from the place where they were.

Somehow one of these two-hearted deceivers came with them, unseen by anyone. He was discovered by the chief almost as soon as they got here. The people, being very disappointed, decided to throw this young boy back to the world below, but hesitated as they listened to his pleadings to be allowed to stay. Finally winning them over, he was allowed to stay upon the earth, with the understanding that he must shift for himself, and would not be taken among them or cared for by anyone, hoping that he could not survive. Allowing him to remain proved to be their first mistake, as this brought Evil and Death into the world.

Their leader had always taught them not to be greedy or to seek after gaining large amounts of food in a selfish way, but to be satisfied in humble living. One night this leader left his people unseen, seeking the owner of the earth. He was rewarded by finding the place and the man of his search. The man, extending him a hearty welcome, placed all kinds of nice things to eat before him, things that he did not have very often. As everything looked so good to him, without thinking he went ahead and ate up everything that was put before him. He then went back to his people. After he got back he felt the stomach-ache was coming upon him. He had made a mistake by grabbing at first sight. For this reason it has ever since been a Hopi's belief, that any sweet or fresh food will always give one a stomach-ache. The chief's two sons scolded their father over what he had done.

The leader feeling that his part was played, resigned his leadership in favor of his two sons, but they waited until the old chief was dead before becoming the leaders. After his death, the younger son said, "All right, it is up to us to carry on."

According to their beliefs it is the son's place to carry on what the father has begun. The younger brother told the older brother to go ahead and in a hurry; told him to go up to where the sun rises, that he must not stop there very long. He must get there to touch his forehead to the Sun and then come back, otherwise he would be so late he would hold a lot of things back.

This older brother went along the edges of the ocean, along the edges of the Gulf of Mexico, and probably around by California. As he was going along, he was told that he was going to be a white man and become a wonderful man and could perform any kind of great things he might wish. With this power, he made a horse to help carry his burdens. He had a lot of provisions to carry along. The rest of the people had some things to carry too, but since this brother had to go in a hurry, he needed a horse to help him along. The younger brother, leader of the people, knew where this brother was going. The rest of the people thought only of their quest to find the Man who owned the earth.

Everybody was in a big rush to get to this Person. They were all rushing to see who could get to His place first, where the Bird Messengers had found Him. This is the way they started off. They divided into small groups or clans under the leadership of the person who was the head of one of their sacred ceremonial dances, and went out in different directions. According to their beliefs, they were able to receive the blessings of raising their crops for food through their devotion to their sacred dances, which they brought with them to this earth from the world before.

Some of these people were moving along from place to place with but one thought in mind, that of living worthily enough to find this Man, and did not think much of their history or of trying to gain wealth. They went along slowly, not greedily but humbly, building their homes, raising crops, making their clothing, and filling their other needs. They were always looking forward to finding the Man at the center of this world. Therefore, they would abandon their homes and move again a little farther, always looking forward to finding the Man. They were anxious at all times to live peaceably and humbly, to be sincere in their prayers and sacred dances, and faithful always to the teachings of their prophets and high priests, that they might be acceptable to the Man, who owned the earth.

We see the track of these people right now in the ruins all over the country. These faithful people are called Hopis. They moved slowly from place to place over a long period of time until they came to the place which is called Moencopie. All the clans which now make up the Hopi nation did not come together at one time. The three clans, Spider Clan, Snake Clan, and Spirit Clan arrived first at this place, being very careful to examine things carefully. They saw that the land was good. Deciding to put up a landmark at this place, Moencopie, they had a record written in some form of hieroglyphics on the wall of the cliff, stating that this good land would be held for the humble but poor people among them. This record was to be a landmark for their poor from generation to generation and has been held sacred by these people.

Leaving Moencopie, they traveled southeast coming to the north end of the village now known as Oraibi. At this place they were rewarded in their long search, for there was the Man for whom they had been looking. Having been expecting them for several days, he often stayed very late at this meeting place. The Spirit Clan led by the younger brother was the first to reach Him. They asked this Man where he lived to which he answered, "Just south of here on a hill."

Then they asked Him the name of the place. Hesitating at first, he finally told them it was Oraibi, which was the first place named or pronounced by this Man. Their first understanding was that He lived at this place called Oraibi, but later learned that it was only His resting-place, where He comes to rest under a big rock, later going away home to somewhere, nobody knows. It was at one of these times of rest that He was found by these Indians. He told them they might build their houses at this place and He would be with them except in the evening, when He would go home, somewhere. This Spirit was known to the Indians as Mausauu and was the Man who owned the earth.

After they had settled for awhile at the place called Oraibi, they decided to find some way of governing their people. Since this place belonged to the Mausauu they asked this spirit to be the chief of them all, but this man, Mausauu refused, telling them that their leader, who had brought them over, should be the chief among his own people. After they counseled over the leadership for four days, Mausauu still told them he could not do it. He told the leader of the people to look over the land and whatever he could use he could put his people on and make use of it, but the Mausauu could not be their leader at this time. He told them that they had many ambitions and plans for the future in their own minds, which they would have to experience, such as the things they are doing now-a-days, before he could be their leader. They must work out their own ideas for themselves and after they had gone through this period under their own leadership He could return to lead them. But if he did it at this time, He would do it out of His place, as it was not the time for Him to be their leader.

Mausauu left the village, circled around and came back, then told the people, "All right, I have finished marking out the land for you. I have fixed it for you at this time."

He meant that all this land from ocean to ocean belongs to Him and that He was going to make them guardians over it, until He could come to be their leader. He could not give them title to it or divide it up individually into small pieces, such as so many acres, but they could live on it and make use of it. The humble, valiant Spirit Clan, who had come to him first and who had proved their faithfulness, were to be next to Him in authority and were to have charge of his sacred trusts.

In this manner Mausauu fixed the land which is held sacred by the Hopi Indians today; it is never to be forgotten by them. They are going to be faithful to the trust placed upon them by the Mausauu who will bless them at His return, if they hold this land for Him and not turn it over to any other people. When Mausauu fixed the land this way He did not make any mistake.

This Spirit Clan, who lived with Him before He disappeared and the people, who are still staunch believers, are seeing him and their leaders in the fires. While this Spirit, Mausauu, was still with them, they held a ceremony of different sacred religious dances. They began to talk over how they were going to make a plan to live together and govern all the people, what would be the best for the world, and which clan would be the one to govern. They wished to find the best plan that would help them live righteously enough to fulfil the trust the Mausauu had placed upon them. The leaders of the sacred dances, counseling together looked back upon their lives to see how they were able to get to this place and to raise their crops. They know that they had lived according to the laws of right living and that by their faithfulness to their prayers and ceremonials expressed in their sacred dances they could still make their living in this land.

With these thoughts in mind each clan gave a performance of its own sacred dance. In different months throughout different seasons of the year, the Hopis today put on these sacred dances in humble thanksgiving. These dances are ceremonies or dance-dramas commemorating the coming of each clan to the place of the Mausauu, Oraibi Village.

While they were counseling and dancing Mausauu looked upon their leaders in admiration. The only time they would eat was after the sun went down—in the afterglow. He considered these people as most important people, because of their sincere devotion as expressed in their sacred dances. This is the way we Hopis feel toward one another in our desire to prove true to our beliefs.

As the Mausauu watched their dances, He saw that their devotion had enabled them to go far ahead of what he had done. Intending to give them more than they now had, He showed them His ceremonial dance. He made preparation for His dance by fasting sixteen days, only eating a small portion of cornmeal soup in the middle of the night. This soup was made with a small measure of His own, of equal parts of cornmeal and soup, this measure is still in the hands of the Hopis today. When His great day came all the people watching eagerly, learned much more than they had ever known. This still proved that the Mausauu had more powers and more knowledge than they had and was still their leader. Today the Hopi Indians perform the sacred dance in memory of the Mausauu's great day and the instructions He gave them which they are never to forget.

After His performance, he told them that he could not live among them any longer at this time. He gave them instructions to remember while He was away. He said they had many things on their minds which they wanted to accomplish and that many things would happen during His absence. He chose the Spirit Clan, otherwise known as the Mausauu Clan, to be next to Him in authority. He left in their care a sacred record which was in the form of a pink marble tablet, or plate, upon which was a map of his land and they were charged to protect it until the White Brother, who had gone to touch his forehead to the sun, would return and translate it for them. They were to fight against any people taking possession of the land. He would tell them what the map meant.

He charged them to be faithful to this sacred trust until the day of the White Brother, which was to be when a road is made in the sky. Their faithfulness to this sacred trust would cause them to go through many hardships; people would strike them; they would wipe tears out of their eyes, as they went along trying to uphold what they have been told and waiting for their White Brother to come to their relief. But they were told to hold on courageously to what they believed, not to strike back or to commit violence or bloodshed, but staunchly to defend their religious beliefs and the trust of the sacred tablet throughout whatever came. When the White Brother came, He would cure all these evil things and we would all be more brotherly. That is what the Hopi Indians are looking forward to today.

Narrator: Qötshongva
Date: 1955
Source: Bureau of Indian Affairs (1955)

We the Hopi people are the first on this land, and in these villages we are following certain live pattern which we obtained from Massua from whom we came when we first came upon this land. The Hopi people met Massua and asked permission to live on this land with him, and it was only after obtaining his permission that we entered this land. If he had not given his permission we would not be here today. We actually came face to face with him and talked to him. This took place at a point just a couple of miles north of Old Oraibi around the bend in the road, and he took us over to Oraibi and the people who met with him. They asked him if he would be their leader. From there on Massua being a great spirit. So our hearts and our intentions, and he said he will not be our leader until we fulfill all the things that we as people wish to do in this land.

He gave us a life principle and told us to always keep those instructions and remain fast to this so that we will not lose our way or cause trouble to come upon our life in this new land, because we came here when the life of the people in other lands were destroyed because of some trouble, and there we have decided that we will put all those wicked ways aside and live according to the teachings or instructions of Massua. And the Hopis have made an oath to follow that and never to abandon it. So he told the people that whoever brought you here as your leader will continue to be your leader until you have traveled this life and fulfilled your own desires or intentions. Then I will come back and be your leader from there on. So he gave us a stone tablet which contains the instructions and on which was written all the life plan of the Hopi people. And looking into the future if this life becomes disrupted again and if the Hopis remain fast to it it will be settled because of the stone tablet and because of some people who have the courage and the strong faith that they have kept to the instructions that were handed down to them by the Spirit Massua.

Each group leader was appointed to uphold certain part of the life pattern for all Hopi people and all people in this land, and each leader has special duties which they perform throughout the year in order that this life will not be destroyed and that they will not forget Massua. He told us if we doubted and lost it, we will bring trouble upon ourselves, and we were told then that there will be a person coming to us, a very intelligent person, a person who will bring many things to us that may not be right or in accordance with the teachings of Massua. You must be strong. You must be up at dawn each day, run to the fields or the springs and take cold showers so that you will be strong, so that when trouble comes in later days you will not be afraid. When the time comes for the Great Spirit to take over there will be a great purification day which will not be a small thing. It will be a big event. If you are strong in heart you may be saved, but because of fear you might die. He left this stone tablet with certain clan leaders of the Hopi people, and they are to take charge of this for all of us. Then there were certain clan leaders appointed to lead the people in each village or wherever they happen to settle and always take care of this life pattern for all the Hopi people. But if these leaders fail, then another group behind them will take it up and carry it on, and if this second group fail, then there are another group of people who are following them who would not have the high position as those ahead of him, but they will have to take it up and carry the duties that were placed upon the leaders who failed.

We were told we will pass through three great stages of life, and if we made a mistake then we will be faced with this confusion of life and the beginning of the disruption of the privileged live we obtained from Massua who will being us to the purification day.

We were told that another person will come to us, and he will do many things to us. There will be a man of white skin who will come to us, and the life will be very hard because he will do many things to us—things that you do not have no knowledge of because you are following a certain life pattern given to us by Spirit Massua. But there may be someone of strong heart who will carry on this life for all of us–one strong man of good heart, and he will be found in that day, and he will work for all people in this land and for all life on this earth. Today we are witnessing many of those things which we are fully aware of because of these instructions and the prophecies which were passed on down to us by our forefathers. We were told in our tradition that there will be two men among us too who will steal things from us. There will be a white man with white skin and another man of your own people—today we call them Navajos. They will be the ones that bring all these troubles upon you and eventually lead you to disrupt your life. Our future is all well known to us what will take place if we made a mistake. We are both striving–the white man and the Hopi and also other Indian people are all striving for the same goal–a good life, a peaceful life, an everlasting life. But there will be a purification day where all those who have done wrong or committed great sins will be punished at that time. And to face his Spirit Massua he must remain to his instructions because if we go along and anything goes wrong or any happenings take place in this life, we will begin to blame each other because of someone doing things. We must adhere to these teachings so that we will not destroy this life, and we were warned never to cut up our land in any manner because this whole land was given to guard for all Indian people. This is our home.

If we ever doubt these instructions we may make a mistake by cutting it up, and we will lose that life and land. We all know there are two people, one of one heart and other of two hearts. The people following the ways of two hearts will always work to disrupt this life pattern of Massua and they will do anything to gratify their own selfishness and desires and will cause many hardships upon the good people of one heart, and this will lead us to many wars. The Hopi only knows of three great wars to take place. The third war will be the one to take place at purification time upon this land. Therefore, the Hopi, knowing all this, did not consent to any of these wars anywhere. He was especially warned never to allow himself to go to foreign countries to make wars upon other people because this is our home land. Here we must stay and take care of it. Because we are still waiting for someone–a brother of the Hopi–who will come to prove this land for us. So he will continue to follow instructions of Massua and waiting for the time of our brother to come to prove this land. We have our stone tablet with us here today which was given by him when we first came here. Our brother will come and look for this stone tablet when placed side by side which will show whoever comes to this land to purify this land for us and will be recognized as our true brother. It is toward this goal we are working, therefore, I will not take part in any wars. You have already heard many of the hardships brought upon the Hopi after these were the things prophecied to us, and it seems we are at the very last end of our life plan because all these things are being fulfilled every day. So it is up to all of us Hopi people, knowing this to work toward that goal so that we will not make a mistake. We are not only working for the Hopi people but for all people here with us because this trust was placed upon the Hopi. We will look to our father the Sun who travels above us every day taking care of all of us, and it is he who is the highest, and in all of our religious ceremonies we take care of him in our own way so that he will continue to perform his duty in taking care of our life on this land. We also prepare certain prayer offerings for the Spirit Massua who gave us this land and life and are still carrying on this same life which we have been told to adhere to so that we will not make a mistake.

Narrator: Qötshongva
Date: 1956
Source: Bentley (1956)

At the beginning time when the first Indian people came upon this land with the proper admission of the Great Spirit, we lived on this land happily and were very well taken care of by Him.

This land was here long before any human being set foot upon this earth, but there was Great Spirit living on it alone and I will call His name Maasauu. . . .

Somewhere the human race began, but I will not be able to go into that at this time, and we came to this land after asking permission from the Great Spirit, Maasauu. It was ONLY after obtaining His consent that we came and settled with Him on this land. THAT IS ONE OF THE MOST IMPORTANT PRINCIPLES UPON WHICH THE HOPI BASES HIS LIFE; that is, that we must obtain permission or consent from other people before we do things on our land. This same principle was well known to all the Indian people at the time when we were given permission to settle here and live with the Great Spirit, Maasauu. It is a principle worth remembering today.

After we all arrived on this land Maasauu showed us the boundary of this continent. He Himself showed us the land and the life of the people and their leaders. Then Maasauu marked out the boundaries for each group until they covered the whole continent, after which, each group was given an individualized Life Plan with certain religious beliefs, and, the way to worship, the way to live, the food to eat, and languages for each group. The one thing I want to bring out to all the world's people is that Maasauu gave us the different truths of the land, and gave us our way-of-life, food, and language. His final instructions were, "Now LIVE and never lose faith in what I have given you. Because if you lose faith and turn away from this Life Plan I gave you, you will be lost and you will later bring trouble upon yourselves. DO NOT EVER LOSE FAITH AS YOU GO OUT OVER THIS LAND.". . .

Now to begin: There are many things I would like to bring out which lead up to the time we met our Great Spirit, but unfortunately it would take many days to tell the complete story. Therefore I will just tell you now that He waited for us at a certain spot when we came to the place now called Oraibi.

The first group that actually met Maasauu gathered with Him and asked Him to be their Highest Leader. But by being a spirit He could see within the hearts of those group leaders and He saw that they had many personal ideas, intentions, and hopes as to what they wished to bring about in this land, and so, in order to give them full freedom, He told them He would not be their Leader at that time but wished to recommend that whoever had brought the group into that area should be the leader. Then, after they had fulfilled everything in their desiring hearts, He would return and be their Great Leader again. This liberty was given in order that each group could have the responsibility to follow the Life Pattern and see if they could remember to be a faithfull people to the end. It was done to see what we would do with His Life Plan. If the Great Spirit had consented to be the Great Leader at that time, when one group would disobey and make a mistake they would point their finger and say, "And now you have caused us a wrong," and they would blame the Great Spirit. He saw ahead and knew that we would blame each other for the mistakes at these times, instead of looking into our own hearts. But these are not the Great Spirit's mistakes, rather they are the mistakes of all of us who have obtained these instructions from the Great Spirit and insist on disobeying them. We must today find that Life Pattern again and be ready for the Great Spirit when He comes. We must not follow those little personal things which WE think must be done. We must follow the Great Spirit and NOT make these mistakes again. There is a great warning given to us as to what will happen to this land and human race if we turn away from the Life Pattern He gave us.

These matters are of no small value, this is not a little thing. Instead, this is the very foundation of all of us humans who are living on this land. Our common life together is based on the Life Plan our Great Spirit has given to us. It is a Life Plan with strong instructions and serious warning that we must never lose faith—no matter how difficult that may be. WE MUST NEVER LOSE FAITH! for if we do, we will also lose our Great Spirit and we will once again destroy both Life and Land as was done before. . . .

In ancient times it was prophesied by our forefathers that this land would be occupied by the Indian people and then from somewhere a white man will come. He will come either with a strong faith and righteous religion which the Great Spirit has also given to him, or he will come after he has abandoned that Great Life Plan and fallen to a faith of his own personal ideas which he invented before coming here. It was known that the white man is an intelligent person, an inventor of many words, a man who knows how to influence people because of his sweet way of talking and that he will use many of these things upon us when he comes. We knew that this land beneath us was composed of many things that we might want to use later such as mineral resources. We knew that this is the wealthiest part of this continent, because it is here the Great Spirit lives. We knew that the white man will search for the things that look good to him, that he will use many good ideas in order to obtain his hearts desire and we knew that if he had strayed from the Great Spirit, he would use ANY means to get what he wants. These things we were warned to watch and we today know these prophesies were true because we can see how many new and selfish ideas and plans are being built up before us. Many of them I do not understand in a white man's way, but we know that if we accept these things we will lose our land and give up our very lives. . . .

A clear pattern of life has been laid out for all of us. The Hopi have, in following that Life Pattern ever since the Great Spirit gave it to us, obtained many prophesies. One of the things that was told to us was that the white man will come and be a very intelligent man, bringing to us many things that he will invent. One of the inventions that our forefathers talked about was a machine or object that would move on the land with animals pulling it. Untill the wagon came along we didn't know what this prophesy meant. Our forefathers spoke also of a machine which would afterwards move with nothing pulling it, and when we saw the automobile we knew what they were talking about. Then they told us that the land would be cut up and that there would be many roads, and today we see the pavement all over the land. Then later on there would be a road in the sky. How could anyone build a road in the sky?, we wondered. But when we see airplanes going back and forth over us we know what they were talking about. We were told that there would be something that would be shiny and would run through our land and look like a path of water glittering. We found this to be refering to the roads which have been built on our land, because when we go down these roads we see they DO look like water ahead.

These signs all tell us that we are nearing the end of our Life Patterns, that man will soon have to be judged. We call that Great Day the Purification Day, the white man calls it the Judgement Day. We look forward to it with great joy and the white man with horror and fear; and rightly so for both of us know that on that day each will be dealt with according to what he justly deserves. And when we see the airplanes we know that we are that much closer to the end of the Life Plan, for we know of the things which will take place as this Life Plan is being fulfilled.

Another prophesy that has been passed down to us is that there will be three great wars which will take place on this earth. Someone will start the war and it will go a little way and it will come to an end; another person will start it again and then it will stop for a little while; then the third one will come and it will not stop untill everything is purified on this earth and the wicked ones destroyed.

As to these wars, we have been warned that if anyone comes to try to force His Chosen into war, the Hopi must not allow himself to take part. If we once do so, it is very uncertain whether we will be saved at the Purification Day. Therefore, because we are still waiting for our True Brother to come and purify this land, we Hopi never participate in any war effort. Because we know who are true, that a purifier will have a greater power and authority than us when He comes to this land, it is up to the Hopi and other religious organizations to NOT participate in war. It is the only way one can be right with the Great Spirit. If we turn loose our bow and arrow on anyone, we will receive an even greater tragedy than our victim.

I am sure that all other Indian people on this land know these same teachings and they too are awaiting that White Brother of ours who will come upon this land, who will not steal, lie, or take our land from us or destroy our beliefs but will restore His land and Life and belief. It is He who will punish those who have caused harm to these first people, the very people whom the Great Spirit has planted on this earth. As I have said, the Hopis call it Purification Day, the day that all good people will be allowed to continue on into everlasting life–the bad people will be destroyed.

Narrator: Qötshongva
Date: 1970
Source: Skidmore (1970)

This text is exactly the same as Banancya (Banyacya 1–12–1961) and will therefore not be repeated here. I refer the reader to the Banancya text following. This text is important for comparative purposes because it is so radically different from Qötshongva's other texts.

Narrator: Qötshongva
Date: 1970
Source: Tarbet (1972)

The Beginning of Life

Somewhere down in the underworld we were created by the Great Spirit, the Creator. We were created first one, then two, then three. We were created equal, of oneness, living in a spiritual way, where the life is everlasting. We were happy and at peace with our fellow men. All things were plentiful, provided by our Mother Earth upon which we were placed. We did not need to plant or work to get food. Illness and troubles were unknown. For many years we lived happily and increased to great numbers.

When the Great Spirit created us, he also gave us instructions or laws to live by. We promised to live by his laws so that we would remain peaceful, using them as a guideline for living happily upon that land where he created and placed us. But from the beginning he warned us that we must not be tempted by certain things by which we might lose this perfect way of life.

Of course we had advantage of many good things in this life, so by and by we broke the Creator's command by doing what he told us not to do. So he punished us by making us as we are now, with both soul and body. He said, "From now on you will have to go on your own. You will get sick, and the length of your life will be limited."

He made our bodies of two principles, good and evil. The left side is good for it contains the heart. The right side is evil for it has no heart. The left side is awkward but wise. The right side is clever and strong, but it lacks wisdom. There would be a constant struggle between the two sides, and by our actions we would have to decide which was stronger, the evil or the good.

We lived in good ways for many years, but eventually evil proved to be stronger. Some of the people forgot or ignored the Great Spirit's laws and once again began to do things that went against his instructions. They became materialistic, inventing many things for their own gain, and not sharing things as they had in the past. This resulted in a great division, for some still wanted to follow the original instructions and live simply.

The inventive ones, clever but lacking wisdom, made many destructive things by which their lives were disrupted, and which threatened to destroy all the people. Many of the things we see today are known to have existed at that time. Finally immorality flourished. The life of the people became corrupted with social and sexual license which swiftly involved the Kikmongwi's (chief's) wife and daughters, who rarely came home to take care of their household duties. Not only the Kikmongwi but also the high religious leaders were having the same problem. Soon the leaders and others with good hearts were worried that the life of the people was getting out of control.

The Kikmongwi gathered the high priests. They smoked and prayed for guidance toward a way to solve the corruption. Many times they gathered, until finally someone suggested that they move, find a new place, and start a new life.

Emergence into the Present World

Now they had often heard certain thumping sounds coming from above, so they knew that someone might be living there. It was decided that this must be investigated. I will describe this briefly, for the whole story would take much space.

Being gifted with wisdom, they created birds for this purpose. I will name three. Two which are known for their strength and swiftness are the *kisa* (hawk) and the *pavowkaya* (swallow). The third was a *moochnee* (related to the mockingbird). His flight is awkward, but he is known to be wise. They were each created at separate times by magic songs, tobacco smoke and prayers, from dirt and saliva, which was covered by a white cape (*ova*). Each was welcomed respectfully and given instructions for his mission, should he succeed. The first two failed to reach the top side of the sky, but the third one, *moochnee*, came through the opening into this world.

The new world was beautiful. The earth was green and in bloom. The bird observed all his instructions. His sense of wisdom guided him to the being he was instructed to seek. When he found him it was high noon, for the being, Maasauu, the Great Spirit, was preparing his noon day meal. Ears of corn lay beside the fire. He flew down and lit on top of his *kisi* (shady house) and sounded his arrival.

Maasauu was not surprised by the visitor, for by his wisdom and sense of smell he already knew someone was coming. Respectfully he welcomed him and invited him to sit down. The interview was brief and to the point. "Why are you here? Could it be important?" "Yes," said Moochnee, "I was sent here by the underworld people. They wish to come to your land and live with you, for their ways have become corrupted. With your permission they wish to move here with you and start a new life. This is why I have come." Maasauu replied bluntly, but with respect, "They may come."

With this message the bird returned to the underworld. While he was gone the Kikmongwi and the leaders had continued to pray and wait for his successful return. Upon his return with the good news of the new world and Maasauu's permission for them to come, they were overjoyed.

Now the question was how they were to get to the top, so again they smoked and prayed for guidance. At last they agreed to plant a tree that would grow to the top and serve as a pathway. They planted the seed of a *shalavee* (spruce tree), then they prayed and sang magic songs. The tree grew and grew until it reached the sky, but its branches were so soft and so many that it bent under the heavy earth pressure from the top, so it did not pierce the sky. They planted another seed, this one to be a *louqu* (pine). It grew as they sang their magic songs. This tree was stout and strong. "Surely this one will go through," they thought. But it was unsuccessful, for its branches also bent upon contact with the solid object. Again they planted a seed. This time it was a *pakave* (reed). Since it had a pointed end it pierced the sky up into the new world.

Meanwhile all of this had been kept secret. Only proper righteous and one-hearted people were informed of the plans to leave the corrupt world. They were prepared to move out, so as soon as they knew it was successful they started to come up on the inside of the plant, resting between the joints as they worked their way up to the opening.

When they got to this world, everything was beautiful and peaceful. The land was virgin, unmolested. They were very happy. They sang and danced with joy, but their joy was shortlived, for that night the chief's daughter died suddenly. Everyone was sad and worried. People looked at one another suspiciously. An evil spell had been enacted. This caused great concern that a witch or two-hearted person might be among them.

Now the Kikmongwi had great power which he must use to settle the concern of his people. He made a small ball out of cornmeal which he tossed up above the group of people. The one upon whose head it landed would be the guilty one. It landed upon the head of a girl. A quick decision was made to throw her back through the opening into the underworld. The wickedness must be gotten rid of, for they wished to live peacefully in this new land. But the witch girl cried out for mercy, telling them that on their long journey they would face many obstacles and dangers of every description, and that her services would become useful, for she had power to fight evil. She invited the Kikmongwi to look back down into the underworld. He looked and saw his child playing happily with the other children in the underworld, where upon death we will all return. She was spared, but they left her there alone, perhaps hoping that she would perish by some unknown cause.

The First Meeting with the Great Spirit in This World

It was here that the Great Spirit first appeared to them on this earth, to give them the instructions by which they were to live and travel. They divided into groups, each with its selected leader. Before them he laid ears of corn of various lengths. They were each instructed to pick one ear of corn to take with them on their journey, for their subsistance and their livelihood. One by one they greedily picked out the longest and most perfect-looking ears until only the shortest was left. They did not realize that this was a test of wisdom. The shortest ear was picked by the humblest leader. Then the Great Spirit gave them their names and the languages by which they would be recognized. The last picker of short corn was named *HOPI*.

HOPI means not only to be peaceful, but to obey and have faith in the instructions of the Great Spirit, and not to distort any of his teachings for influence or power, or in any way to corrupt the Hopi way of life. Otherwise the name will be taken away.

He then gave them instructions according to which they were to migrate for a certain purpose to the four corners of the new land, leaving many *footprints*, *rock writings* and *ruins*, for in time many would forget that they were all one, united by a single purpose in coming up through the reed.

Now that we were on top we were each to follow our own leaders, but so long as we did not forget the instructions of the Great Spirit we would be able to survive. We were now bound by a vow to live by these instructions and to complete our pattern of migration. Maasauu told us that whoever would be the first to find him would be the leader of those who were to follow, then he disapppeared.

An Act of Prophetic Consequence

We migrated for many years to every corner of this continent, marking our claim as we travelled, as these markings clearly testify up to the present day. On our way we stopped for rest near the great river now known as the Colorado. We had travelled far and gained a great deal of knowledge, not forgetting our instructions. The group leader was of the Bow Clan, a great chief with wisdom. But it was here that this great chief disappeared into the dark night. After putting his family to sleep he left in search of the Earth Center, where clever, ingenious people from all nations meet to plan the future. By some means he found the place, and was welcomed with respect. It was a beautiful place with all manner of good things. Good food was laid before him by most beautiful girls. It was all very tempting.

Until today we did not know the significance of this action. It had to do with the future. By this action he caused a change to occur in the pattern of life as we near the end of the life cycle of this world, such that many of us would seek the materialistic world, trying to enjoy all the good things it has to offer before destroying ourselves. Those gifted with the knowledge of the sacred instructions will then live very cautiously, for they will remember and have faith in these instructions, and it will be on their shoulders that the fate of the world will rest. The people will corrupt the good ways of life, bringing about the same life as that from which we fled in the underworld. The sacred body of the female will no longer be hidden, for the shield of protection will be uplifted, an act of temptation toward sexual license, which will also be enjoyed. Most of us will be lost in all the confusion. An awareness that something extraordinary is happening will develop in most of the people, for even their leaders will be confused into polluting themselves. It will be difficult to decide whom to follow.

The Hopi knew all this would come about. All these aspects of today's life pattern were planned. So today we must stand firmly on our belief in order to survive. The only course is to follow the instructions of the Great Spirit himself.

The Mission of the Two Brothers

This Bow Clan chief had two grown sons. When they learned of their father's misdeed they were very sad. Their knowledge of the teachings which they had received from him was all in order. Now they were left alone to lead their people, for the very next day their father died.

They asked their mother to permit them to carry out the order of their instructions for an event of this nature. She replied that it was up to them, for their knowledge was complete. Upon agreement, the younger brother was to continue in search of Maasauu, and to settle where he found him. There he would await the return of his older brother, who was to travel eastward toward the rising sun, where he would rest briefly. While resting, he must listen for the voice of his younger brother, who would expect him to come to his aid, for the change in the life pattern will have disrupted the way of life of his people. Under the pressure of a new ruler they will surely be wiped off the face of the earth unless he comes.

So today we are still standing firmly of the Great Spirit's instructions. We will continue to look and pray toward the East for his prompt return.

The younger brother warned the elder that the land and the people would change. "But do not let your heart be troubled," he said, "for you will find us. Many will turn away from the life plan of Maasauu, but a few of us who are true to his teachings will remain in our dwellings. The ancient character of our *heads*, the shape of our *houses*, the layout of our villages, and the type of *land* upon which our village stands, and our *way of life*. All will be in order, by which you will find us.

Before the first people had begun their migrations the people named Hopi were given a set of stone tablets. Into these tablets the Great Spirit inscribed the laws by which the Hopi were to travel and live the good way of life, the peaceful way. They also contain a warning that the Hopi must beware, for in time they would be influenced by wicked people to forsake the life plan of Maasauu. It would not be easy to stand up against this, for it would involve many good things that would tempt many good people to forsake these laws. The Hopi would be led into a most difficult position. The stones contain instructions to be followed in such a case.

The older brother was to take one of the stone tablets with him to the rising sun, and bring it back with him when he hears the desperate call for aid. His brother will be in a state of hopelessness and despair. His people may have forsaken the teachings, no longer respecting their elders, and even turning upon their elders to destroy their way of life. The stone tablets will be the final acknowledgement of their true identity and brotherhood. Their mother is Sun Clan. They are the children of the Sun.

So it must be a Hopi who travelled from here to the rising sun and is waiting someplace. Therefore it is only the Hopi that still have this world rotating properly, and it is the Hopi who must be purified if this world is to be saved. No other person anyplace will accomplish this.

The older brother had to travel fast on his journey for there was not much time, so the horse was created for him. The younger brother and his people continued on in search of Maasauu.

On their way they came to a land that looked fertile and warm. Here they marked their clan symbols on the rock to claim the land. This was done by the Fire Clan, the Spider Clan, and the Snake Clan. This place is now called Moencopi. They did not settle there at that time.

While the people were migrating, Maasauu was waiting for the first ones to arrive. In those days he used to take walks near the place where he lived, carrying a bunch of violet flowers (*du-kyam-see*) in his belt. One day he lost them along the way. When he went to look for them he found that they had been picked up by the Hornytoad Woman. When he asked her for the flowers she refused to give them back, but instead gave him her promise that she would help him in time of need. "I too have a metal helmet," she told him, (possibly meaning that certain people with metal helmets would help the Hopi when they get into difficulty).

Often Maasauu would walk about a half mile north of his *du-pa-cha* (a type of temporary house) to a place where there lay a long rock which formed a natural shelter, which he must have picked as the place where he and the first people would find each other. While waiting there he would amuse himself by playing a game to test his skill, the name of which (*Nadu-won-pi-kya*) was to play an important part later on in the life of the Hopi, for it was here that the knowledge and wisdom of the first people was to be tested. Until recent times children used to play a similar game there, something like "hide-and-seek." One person would hide, then signal by tapping on the rock, which would transmit the sound in a peculiar way so that the others could not tell exactly where the tapping was coming from. (Some years ago this rock was destroyed by government road builders.) It was here that they found Maasauu waiting.

The Meeting with Maasauu Near Oraibi

Before the migrations began Maasauu had let it be known, though perhaps not by direct instructions, that whoever would find him first would be the leader there. Later it became clear that this was a procedure by which their true character would be specified.

When they found him the people gathered and sat down with him to talk. The first thing they wanted to know was where he lived. He replied that he lived just north of there at a place called *Oraibi*. For a certain reason he did not name it fully. The full name is *Sip-Oraibi*, meaning something that has been solidified, referring to the fact that this is the place where the earth was made solid.

They asked permission to live there with him. He did not answer directly, for within them he saw evil. "*It's up to you,*" he said. "*I have nothing here. My life is simple. All I have is my planting stick and my corn. If you are willing to live as I do, and follow my instructions, the life plan which I shall give you, you may live here with me, and take care of the land. Then you shall have a long, happy, fruitful life.*"

Then they asked him whether he would be their leader, thinking that thus they would be assured a peaceful life. "*No,*" he replied, "*the one who led you here will be the leader until you fulfill your pattern of life,*" (for he saw into their hearts and knew that they still had many selfish desires). "*After that I will be the leader, but not before, for I am the first and I shall be the last.*" Having left all the instructions with them, he disappeared.

The Founding of Oraibi Village

The village of Oraibi was settled and built in accordance with the instructions of the Great Spirit. The Bow Clan chief was the father of the ceremonial order. They remained under the leadership of the Bow Clan for some time, perhaps until corruptions set in. As you recall, the Bow Clan chief of the past had contaminated his standing by taking part in the changing of the life pattern.

Later the Bear Clan took over. This might have been because the bear is strong and mighty. There may have been other reasons too, such as a prophecy which told that a bear, sleeping somewhere in the northern part of what is now called Europe, would awaken at a certain time and walk to the northern part of this country, where he would wait. This group is called Bear Clan because they came across a dead bear at the place of the shield symbol. Most of the important people claimed to be of the Bear Clan, including the Bluebird and Spider Clan people.

For some reason the Coyote Clan, who migrated from Sh-got-kee near Walpi, were considered bad people, though very clever. At first they were not permitted to enter but, in accord with our custom, on the fourth request they were admitted, on agreement that they would act as a protection and in time speak for the chief should difficulties arise. But they were warned to be cautious, though faithful ones might remain true to the last. So it is with all clans, for along the way most of us will deceive our leaders for glory, which will tend to pollute our ways and jeopardize our beliefs.

The last group to be permitted into Oraibi was the Grey Eagle Clan. When they had finished their migrations, they first settled in what is now called New Mexico. Being warlike and troublemakers, they were evicted by the Pueblo Indians. When they came to this area, they first settled in Mushongnovi on Second Mesa, on the agreement that they would not cause trouble. Should they break their agreement, they were to leave without resistance.

They made trouble in Mushongnovi so they left as promised. They went by way of Oraibi, where they asked to be admitted. After several attempts they finally gained entry, promising as they had in the other village that they would leave voluntarily should they create trouble. According to this agreement the chief of Mushongnovi would then consider whether to receive them again at Second Mesa, or send them back to New Mexico, where the Pueblo people could deal with them as they saw fit.

The vow which we made with the Great Spirit obligated us to follow his way of life. He gave the land to us to use and care for through our ceremonial duties. He instructed us and showed us the road plan by which we must govern our lives. We wrote this pattern on a rock so that we would always be reminded to follow the straight road. The Hopi must not drift away from this road or he will take this land away from us. This is the warning given to us by Maasauu.

Oraibi village was settled firmly. Migrating people were now gathering there and asking to be admitted into the village. The Kikmongwi and the high priests would always consider their request and base their judgment upon their character and wisdom. Those who showed signs of boastfulness were turned away and told to go to the south mesas where their kind of people lived. Only good people, humble and sincere in their prayers, were admitted.

Among the ceremonies of each group the prayer for rain was important in order for the crops to grow and produce an abundance of food. The people depended on this for their livelihood. Boastful people were not admitted so that the prayers would not be polluted.

Oraibi was now firmly established. The pattern of the religious order was established. Cycle by cycle we paid respect to our Mother Earth, our Father Sun, the Great Spirit, and all things through our ceremonials. We were happy for we were united as one.

The Arrival of Another Race Foretold

Time passed on, people passed on, and the prophecies of things to come were passed from mouth to mouth. The stone tablets and the rock writing of the life plan were often reviewed by the elders. Fearfully they waited as they retold the prophecy that one day another race of people would appear in their midst and claim our land as his own. He would try to change our pattern of life. He would have a "sweet tongue" or a "fork tongue," and many good things by which we would be tempted. He would use force in an attempt to trap us into using weapons, but we must not fall for this trick, for then we ourselves would be brought to our knees, from which we might not be able to rise. Nor must we ever raise our hand against any nation. We now call the people *Bahanna*.

The Forces of Purification

We have teachings and prophecies informing us that we must be alert for the signs and omens which will come about to give us courage and strength to stand on our beliefs. Blood will flow. Our hair and our clothing will be scattered upon the earth. Nature will speak to us with its mighty breath of wind. There will be earthquakes and floods causing great disasters, changes in the seasons and in the weather, disappearance of wildlife, and famine in different forms. There will be gradual corruption and confusion among the leaders and the people all over the world, and wars will come about like powerful winds. All of this has been planned from the beginning of creation.

We will have three people standing behind us, ready to fulfill our prophecies when we get into hopeless difficulties: the *Meha Symbol* (which refers to a plant that has a long root, milky sap, grows back when cut off, and has a flower shaped like a *swastika*, symbolizing the four great forces of nature in motion), the *Sun Symbol*, and the *Red Symbol*. Bahanna's intrusion into the Hopi way of life will set the *Meha Symbol* in motion, so that certain people will work for the four great forces of nature (the four directions, the controlling forces, the original force) which will rock the world into war. When this happens we will know that our prophecies are coming true. We will gather strength and stand firm.

This great movement will fall, but because its subsistance is milk, and because it is controlled by the four forces of nature, it will rise again to put the world in motion, creating another war, in which both the *Meha* and the *Sun Symbol* will be at work. Then it will rest in order to rise a third time. Our prophecy fortells that the third event will be the decisive one. Our road plan fortells the outcome.

This sacred writing speaks the word of the Great Spirit. It could mean the mysterious *life seed* with two principles of tomorrow, indicating one, inside of which is two. The third and last, which will it bring forth, purification or destruction?

This third event will depend upon the *Red Symbol*, which will take command, setting the four forces of nature (*Meha*) in motion for the benefit of the *Sun*. When he sets these forces in motion the whole world will shake and turn red and turn against the people who are hindering the Hopi cultural life. To all these people Purification Day will come. Humble people will run to him in search of a new world, and the equality that has been denied them. He will come unmercifully. His people will cover the Earth like red ants. We must not go outside to watch. We must stay in our houses. He will come and gather the wicked people who are hindering the red people who were here first. He will be looking for someone whom he will recognize by his *way of life*, or by his *head* (the special Hopi haircut), or by the shape of his *village* and his *dwellings*. He is the only one who will purify us.

The Purifier, commanded by the *Red Symbol*, with the help of the *Sun* and the *Meha*, will weed out the wicked who have disturbed the way of life of the Hopi, the true way of life on Earth. The wicked will be beheaded and will speak no more. This will be the Purification for all righteous people, the Earth, and all living things on the Earth. The ills of the Earth will be cured. Mother Earth will bloom again and all people will unite into peace and harmony for a long time to come.

But if this does not materialize, the Hopi traditional identity will vanish due to pressure from Bahanna. Through the whiteman's influence, his religions, and the disappearance of our sacred land, the Hopi will be doomed. This is the Universal Plan, speaking through the Great Spirit since the dawn of time.

Narrator: Monongya
Date: 1955
Source: Bureau of Indian Affairs (1955)

I want to bring out this Hopi life which is followed since he first came to Oraibi. It was at Oraibi here the Great Spirit who gave this life plan to us, and here we established our first village. Here all these life patterns are being told to the various religious orders which were established at that time, and all are for the future of the Hopi people and all those who are with him here. In Oraibi we obtained this life pattern of the Hopi which has been told until things took place that cause people to not teach their young people of this life pattern, and many of them knowing this failed to pass on down to their children, but some of us would obtain these life patterns from our forefathers and have remembered them and are striving to keep within this life pattern of the Hopi which life is for all of us.

[Illustrates with a map or drawing of the Life Plan]

This is one of the life patterns of the Hopi which I believe he has copies from a rock east of Old Oraibi and which tells of the Hopi from the time he came to this land. We all know that from the beginning we came from the Lower World. We came to this person who after obtaining his permission we were allowed to enter this new land, and from the very beginning we have passed through great stages of life or cycles until we came into Old Oraibi, knowing where we have traveled, what has happened in the past, and why we have settled in this land.

This land at first glance appears to be of no value, mostly rock and sand, hardly any trees, hardly any water, but we came to this person who will take care of us if we follow his life plan, and all will be provided for us with many things around us. The land underneath us are many natural resources which the Hopi knows long before he came here to live and knows that this part is really the home of the Massua, and that he must hold fast to this life pattern. If he does not then we may make a mistake of going off on the wrong road. If we did make a mistake we will trail off on another road which will cause us all kinds of trouble. The Spanish first came here, and they tried every way to have the Hopi people follow them and showed these signs, but it turns out that his life will lead us to corruption and destroy our life plan. So they had to be taken out in order that this life will continue on. Here while we settled we were traveling on one road, but we also know from our tradition that something will happen and cause us to go on another road. But we also know that this is the wealthiest part, that we must never allow that to be used for any purpose or wars, but for the peaceful use of all people in this land, and that if other people begin to come and dig out these things, we must not allow that because they will use it for destroying other lives. This we must never allow to happen because we also know from our tradition which speaks of three great wars to take place. When all this land has been purified then we will allow these natural resources to be taken out so that all people will have some benefit out of it, but not for destroying life and property. We have already passed two great wars.

The third war we have been told that nothing will stop it, and if we do not want to destroy ourselves, we must never take part in it, but hold this land for all people and not destroy this land for ourselves, our children and own people who live here, but we want to strive to remain on this life pattern as we were instructed to do.

This is the life plan of the Hopi and this is what we are standing on in bringing these things out so that all people will know. This life pattern is known to all Hopi people in every village, but many of us doubted this life plan of the Hopi, and to some perhaps it sounds funny or just something to try to scare people into. We both met here with some beliefs in us but in different ways, yet we are under the same Supreme Being, and the Hopi must not destroy this. So we want to go on to continue this life for all of us to everlasting life toward which the Hopi is striving. Here we have come to face with these problems created another road which will only lead to other troubles, but this road leads on to everlasting life. If we go this way and do not make a mistake of letting this life plan go, we will live to a ripe old age. We all know when you get old you have to have a cane, and then if you go on you have to get so you bend over a little more and getting older you get a shorter cane, and you go on down until you become very old, because your life has been good and clean and because you have followed the teachings which were handed down, and if you are pure in heart your life will enter everlasting life. These are the things that we are striving for and must never let go of. These are the teachings and beliefs that the Hopi has and is working toward it because we were told these things from our fathers and forefathers.

Now here if we made a mistake and take this other road which is the road of evil being. If we follow that then our life will be hard. We will run into many troubles. We will go this way and that way, and that way will have many problems. And perhaps we might go up very high in life and become wealthy or we might be in a very high position in any life, but because someone continues to follow this somewhere his mistakes will cause him to come down again, and he will fall bumping here and there, and there is no way out for him. These figures up here represent a man without a head. These are the wicked people because wicked people cause other people hardship and do all manner of wickedness in this life, and if we follow them up to purification time which we all know from our tradition, all wicked people will be beheaded. Everyone of us knows these teachings so many of our Hopi people are holding fast to this life. Let us look back to our own teachings and see that we do not destroy this life and hold fast to it.

Narrator: Banancya
Date: 1961
Source: Banyacya 1-12-1961

Briefly Hopi Ancient Teachings and Prophecy:

Hopi believed that human race has passed thru three stages of life since its origin. Three being a Sacred Number. At the end of each stages human life has to be purified or punished by certain Acts of The Great Spirit due mainly to the corruption, greed and turning away from the Great Spirit's Teachings. The last Great Destruction was by FLOOD which destroyed all but a few Faithful Ones. Before this happens these few Faithful Ones asked and received a PERMISSION from the Great Spirit to live with Him in this new land. Great Spirit said: "It is up to you, if you are willing to live my poor, humble and simple life. It is hard but if you are willing to live according to my Teachings and Instructions and will NEVER loose faith in the life I shall give you, you may come and live with me." The Hopi and all who were saved from the Great Flood made a Sacred Covenant with the Great Spirit. They made an oath that they will never turn away from Him.

To the Hopi The Great Spirit is ALL Powerful, being a Spirit, can change into any shape or form. Sometime he appears as a handsome man, or a frightful looking man or being. He is said to be a very large man, a Red Man. He appeared to the first people as a man and talked with them. He taught them how to live, to worship, where to go and what food to carry. He, in order to safeguard his land and life made a set of Sacred Stone Tablets into which He breathe all Teachings, Instructions and Prophecies and Warnings. This was done with the help of a Spider Woman and Her two Grandsons all of whom were most intelligent and powerful as helpers of the Great Spirit. Before the Great Spirit hid himself He placed before the leaders of different group different colors and sizes of corn for them to choose and which shall be their food in this world. Hopi waited last and picked up the smallest one. By this means Hopi showed himself to the Great Spirit as intelligent. Thereupon Great Spirit said, "It is well done you have obtained the real corn for all others are imitations inside of which are hidden seeds of different plants. You have shown to me as intelligent for this reason I will place in your hands this Stone Tablets, Tiponi, symbol of Power and Authority over All Land and Life to guard, protect and hold in trust for me until I shall return to you in a later days for I am the First and I am the Last."

Now the Great Chieftain who lead the Faithful One to this new land and life was a BOW CLAN and he had Two Sons who were of the same mother. Their father fell into Evil Ways and died. The two sons, the two brothers scold their father for the mistake he had made and after he died they took over the responsibilities of Leadership. It was to these TWO BROTHERS a set of Sacred Stone Tablets were given and both were instructed to carry them to a place the Great Spirit had instructed them. The Older Brother was to go immediately to East, to the Rising and upon reaching his destination must immediately start back to look for his younger brother who shall remain in the land of the Great Spirit. His mission was to help his younger brother to bring about Purification Day at which time all wicked or wrong doers shall be punished or destroyed after which Real Peace, Brotherhood and Everlasting Life shall be brought about. He will restore all land back to his brother from whom the Evil One among White man shall have taken from him. He will come also to look for Sacred Stone Tablets and to fulfill the Sacred Mission given him by The Great Spirit.

The Younger Brother was instructed to cover all land, to mark well his footprints as he goes about in this land. Both of the brothers were told that a great White Star will appear in the sky as the people moved about in this land and in other lands. They were told that when that happened ALL people shall know that Older Brother has reached his destination and there upon all people were to settle wherever they may happened to be at that time. They were to settle permanently until his Older Brother who went East returned to him. It is said that the Older Brother after many years may change in color of skin which may become white but his hair will remain black. He will also have the ability to write things down and will therefore be the only one to read the Sacred Stone Tablets. When he returns to this land and find his younger brother these Stone Tablets will be placed side by side to show to all the world that they are TRUE BROTHERS. Then great judgement and punishment will take place for he will help his younger brother to bring about real justice for all Indian Brothers who have been mistreated since the coming of the white man upon our motherland.

Many prophecies concerning the time of his coming is well known to the Hopi leaders few of which (there) are when the lives of all people in this land are so corrupted, people turning to material things and not to spiritual teachings and when the evil ones among white race about to destroy the land and life of Hopi and other Indian Brothers. When the Road in the Sky has been fulfilled and when the inventing of something, in Hopi tongue, a gourd of ashes, one of which when fall upon the earth will boil everything within great area of land where no grass will grow for many years. When leaders turned to evil one instead of Great Spirit. Many ways this life may be destroyed if and when the THREE who were commissioned by the Great Spirit to bring about the Purification Day failed to fulfill their duties.

Every Hopi Village have some knowledge of this prophecy. It was in this manner Oraibi and Shungopavy were settled permanently in this area which is a desert without any water to irrigate his land for in this way the Hopi will never forget the Teachings and Instructions of the Great Spirit.

It is known that our TRUE WHITE BROTHER when he comes will be all powerful and he will wear RED CAP OR RED CLOAK. He will be large in population, belongs to no religion but his very own. He will bring with him the Sacred Stone Tablets. Great will be his coming. None will be able to stand against him. All power in this world will be placed in his hand and he will come swiftly and in one day get control of this whole continent. Hopi has been warned never to take up arms.

With him there will be TWO GREAT ONES both very intelligent and powerful one of which will have a symbol or sign of SWASTIKA (Figure 28a) which represent PURITY and is a Male. Also he will have this symbol or sign (Figure 28b) which also represent PURITY and is a Female, a producer of Life, the red lines in between the sign represent lifeblood of a woman. It also known that he will wear a cap similar to the back of Horned Toad (Figure 28c). One of the Grandsons of Spider Woman wears a cap which is still in use is this (Figure 28d). The Third One or the Second One of the two helpers to our True White Brother will have a sign of a symbol of SUN. He, too, will be many people and very intelligent and powerful. We have in our sacred Kachina Ceremonies a gourd rattle which is still in use today and upon which painted a sign of these two powerful helpers of our True Brother. It looks something like this (Figure 28e).

This the Hopi say represent the world and that when the time of Purification Day is near those with these signs, Swastika and Sun, will shake the earth first for a short period of time in preparation for the final day of Purification. They will shake the Earth two times then it will fall upon the Third One with whom these two will join and together they will come as ONE to bring on Purification Day and to help his younger Brother who waits in this land.

It is also prophecied that if these Three failed to fulfill their mission then the ONE from the WEST will come like a big storm. He will be many, many people, and unmerciful One. When he comes he will cover the land like ants. The Hopi people have been warn not to get up on house tops to watch as he will come to punish all people. We do not yet know who this man is from the West only that he will have a very large population.

Then if none of these fulfill their mission in this life the Hopi Leaders will place their prayer-feathers to the four corners of the Earth in an appeal to the Great Spirit he will cause the lightning to strike the Earth

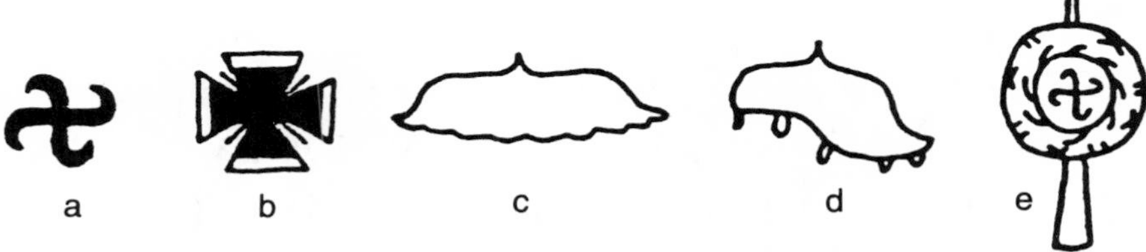

Figure 28. Drawings accompanying Thomas Banancya's letter to Muller-Fricken. From left to right: symbol of the swastika; symbol of female purity; a cap resembling the back of the horned toad; the cap of one of the grandsons of Spider Woman; and the symbol of the sun on the Powamuy rattle. SOURCE: Banyacya 1-12-1961.

People. Only the Righteous Ones will revive. Then if all People turned away from the great Spirit (He will cause) the Great Waters to cover the Earth again. We, humans, shall have lost the chance to enter Everlasting Life. They say the ANTS may inhabit the Earth after that.

But if the Three fulfill their sacred mission and if ONE or TWO or Three Hopi remained fast to the last on these Ancient Teachings or Instructions then the Great Spirit, Massau'u, will appear before all that will be saved and the THREE will lay out a new Life Plan which leads to Everlasting Life. This Earth will become new as it was from the beginning. Flowers will bloom again, wild games will come home and there will be abundance of food for all. Those who are saved will share everything equally. They will all recognize Great Spirit and they may intermarry and may speak ONE TONGUE. A New Religion will be set up if the people desire it.

This is what the Hopi knows and wait for by adhering to his way of life and in spite of hardship they have been faithful up to this day. For they are upholding this land and life for all Righteous people.

Now the evil White Man is about to take away our last remaining homeland. We are still being denied many things including the right to be as Hopis and to make our livelihood in accordance with our Religious Teachings. The Hopi Leaders have warned leaders in White House and the leaders in Glass House but they do not listen. We now stand at a cross road, whether to lead ourselves into Everlasting Life or total destruction! The Hopi still holds the Sacred Stone Tablets and is now await for the coming of his TRUE WHITE BROTHER.

APPENDIX C

A Catalogue and Typology of Hopi Prophecies, 1858–1961

THE WHITE BROTHER

1.0.0. White men are awaited. [Oraibi consultant; 1858, Little 1881: 62.]

1.0.1. The White men will come from the west. [Oraibi consultant, 1858; Little 1881:62.]

1.0.2. The White men will bring the Hopis great blessings. [Oraibi consultant, 1858; Little 1881:62.]

1.1.0. The White chief will protect the Hopis against their enemies. [Müauwutaka, Walpi, 1883; Stephen 1929:72.]

1.2.0. The White chief will give the Hopis many things, implements to dig and to break wood and stones with. [Müauwutaka, Walpi, 1883; Stephen 1929:72.]

1.3.0. The White Older Brother travels to the place of the sunrise from the place of emergence, flourishes, and will turn back towards the west in search of more spacious country. [Talay'ima?, Oraibi, 1883; Cushing 1924:169–170.]

1.4.0. The White Older Brother will return in grandeur and find the Hopis to be poor, hungry, naked, sad, and perplexed, and will offer nourishment, garments, consolation and advice, and friendship, all of which will be violently rejected by the Hopi Brother, whereupon the White Older Brother will behead his Hopi Brother and sit upon the head as upon a stool-rock. [Talay'ima?, Oraibi, 1883; Cushing 1924:169–170.]

1.4.1. When the White Older Brother sits upon the severed head of the Hopi Brother, the trail of life of the White Older Brother will be divided, and the Hopi Brother will gain immortal life, liberty, and surcease from anxiety. [Talay'ima?, Oraibi, 1883; Cushing 1924:169–170.]

1.5.0. When one of the migrating parties reached the sunrise, many stars would fall from the sky and all should settle where they are. The White people reached the east first. [Lomavantiwa, Shipolovi, 1903–1904; Voth 1905:15.]

1.6.0. If those who did not reach the place of the sunrise should ever be molested by enemies, the ones who did reach the east will come and help them. [Lomavantiwa, Shipolovi, 1903–1904; Voth 1905:15.]

1.7.0. The Elder Brother should touch the sun with his forehead, remain there, and look towards the west. The Elder Brother became the White men. [Yukiwma, Oraibi, 1903–1904; Voth 1905:21.]

1.8.0. If the Hopis get into trouble again, as in the lower world, the Elder Brother will come back to them, find the sorcerers who caused the trouble, and cut off their heads. [Yukiwma, Oraibi, 1903–1904; Voth 1905:21.]

1.9.0. Some White men will be coming who are not the Elder Brother. They will baptize, beat, trouble, and kill the Hopis, and take their children away. [Yukiwma, Oraibi, 1903–1904; Voth 1905:25–26.]

1.9.1. Hopi sorcerers will join these White men and try to be like them and speak on their behalf. [Yukiwma, Oraibi, 1903–1904; Voth 1905:25–26.]

1.9.2. But Hopis should not listen to them; they should continue to live as Hopis, wearing Hopi clothes, and eating Hopi food. [Yukiwma, Oraibi, 1903–1904; Voth 1905:25–26.]

1.10.0. The Bear clan stayed with the Americans in the east and learned English. The Americans sent them west and said that if any sorcerers treated them badly and caused their children to die, the Americans would come and cut the sorcerers' heads off. [Wikvaya, Oraibi, 1903–1904; Voth 1905:28.]

1.11.0. The Hopis are waiting for the White Brother who lives near the ocean where the sun rises, is dressed and wears hair like the Whites, but is not baptised. [Yukiwma, Oraibi, 1905; Voth n.d.: 2–3; quoted in Whiteley 1988:270–271.]

1.11.1. When the White Brother hears about the Oraibi trouble, then he will come and behead the bad ones. [Yukiwma, Oraibi, 1905; Voth n.d.:2–3; quoted in Whiteley 1988:271.]

1.11.2. When he comes, he will ask for the chief and many will claim they are the chief; and he will behead them. [Yukiwma, Oraibi, 1905; Voth n.d.:2–3; quoted in Whiteley 1988:271.]

1.11.3. Then he will ask who wrote to him, who are the ones that want to follow the old ways and resist the Americans. [Yukiwma, Oraibi, 1905; Voth n.d.:2–3; quoted in Whiteley 1988:271.]

1.11.4. Then Yukiwma will probably be made chief. [Yukiwma, Oraibi, 1905; Voth n.d.:2–3; quoted in Whiteley 1988:271.]

1.11.5. Yukiwma will show his stone tablet to the White Brother, and the White Brother will interpret it for him and make him chief since Yukiwma represents Maasaw. [Yukiwma, Oraibi, 1905; Voth n.d.: 2–3; quoted in Whiteley 1988:271.]

1.12.0. If the Hopis ever get into trouble, they will be rescued by their White Brother who lives in the east where the sun rises. [Yukiwma, Oraibi, 1906; Leupp 1907:120.]

1.13.0. The chief who departs from the Hopi way should be beheaded (by the Americans). [Yukiwma, Hotevilla, 1906; Lemmon 10-25-1906.]

1.14.0. White men will come to Hopi country and persuade the Hopis to leave their ways and accept the good things they bring. [Yukiwma, Hotevilla, 1910; Lawshe 12–19–1910.]

1.14.1. The Hopis are free to take and use the good things but should never leave the Hopi way. [Yukiwma, Hotevilla, 1910; Wilson 1910.]

1.14.2. If the Hopis follow the White man's ways, it would be the end of the Hopis, but if they keep to the Hopi way, all would be well with them. [Yukiwma, Hotevilla, 1910; Wilson 1910.]

1.15.0. A stronger people will come upon the Hopis and try to get them to adopt new ways of living. The Bear clan will yield to them. [Yukiwma, Hotevilla, 1911; Scott 12–5–1911:6.]

1.15.1. If Hopi traditions are not observed, the oceans [Paalölöqangw] will swallow up the land. [Yukiwma, Hotevilla, 1911; Scott 12–5–1911:7.]

1.15.2. If Yukiwma accepts the White ways, Paalölöqangw will turn over and the sea will rush in. [Yukiwma, Hotevilla, 1911; Crane 1925: 166.]

1.16.0. Sometime a good people will come, and they will not require baptism or forced schooling. [Yukiwma, Hotevilla, 1911; Scott 12–5–1911:16.]

1.16.1. To them the Hopis will yield. [Yukiwma, Hotevilla, 1911; Scott 12–5–1911:16.]

1.17.0. The Older Brother (named Paalölöqangw) was to go to the east and wait there until his Younger Brother sends for him in times of trouble. [Yukiwma, Hotevilla, 1911; Scott 12–5–1911:4.]

1.17.1. He is living across the sea and receives messages and will soon come. [Yukiwma, Hotevilla, 1911; Scott 12–5–1911:7.]

1.17.2. If he returns to find the people fallen into their former evil ways, then the Oraibi chief will be beheaded. [Yukiwma, Hotevilla, 1911; Scott 12-5-1911:4.]

1.17.3. Whoever is the partner of the witch or bad spirit (Maasaw) will be beheaded. If it is Oraibi, he will be beheaded. But if it is Yukiwma, then he will be beheaded. [Yukiwma, Hotevilla, 1911; Scott 12-5-1911:17, 18.]

1.17.4. He must hold onto the Hopi way and then all troubles will end and there will be peace. [Yukiwma, Hotevilla, 1911; Scott 12-5-1911:17.]

1.18.0. If the sorcerer who slipped out during the emergence teaches his evil ways to others, the Americans will return and cut his head off and put a stop to the evil. [Sun Clan consultant, Shongopovi, 1912; Wallis 1936:12.]

1.18.1. If the American does not behead the bad people, then Paalölöqangw will rise up, shake the world, and turn it upside down. He will do this four times. [Sun clan consultant, Shongopovi, 1912; Wallis 1936:12.]

1.18.2. If the Hopis become baptized, Paalölöqangw will cause earthquakes and turn the world upside down. [Sun clan consultant, Shongopovi, 1912; Wallis 1936:12.]

1.18.3. If the bad ones are beheaded, then perhaps the Hopis and Americans will intermarry. [Sun clan consultant, Shongopovi, 1912; Wallis 1936:12.]

1.19.0. If ever the Pahaana and the Hopis are to meet and show their respective stone tablets, they will treat each other as brothers. [Tawakwaptiwa, Oraibi, 1933; Titiev 1972:68.]

1.20.0. The Pahaana will travel to the east and keep an eye on his Hopi Brother, and if the Spider Woman makes trouble (witchcraft), he will return and cut her head off. [Tawakwaptiwa, Oraibi, 1933-1934; Titiev 1944:74.]

1.21.0. When the White Brother, who had gone to touch his forehead to the sun, returns, he will translate the stone tablet which Maasaw left in their keeping. [Qötshongva, Hotevilla, 1935; Kotchongva 1936:118.]

1.21.1. The Hopis will be subjected to hardships, violence, and sadness in their faithfulness. [Qötshongva, Hotevilla, 1935; Kotchongva 1936:118.]

1.22.0. The White Brother will return when a road is made in the sky. [Qötshongva, Hotevilla, 1935; Kotchongva 1936:118.]

1.22.1. When the White Brother returns, he will come to their relief and cure all the evil things which are to happen to the Hopis. [Qötshongva, Hotevilla, 1935; Kotchongva 1936:118.]

1.22.2. Then they will be more brotherly. [Qötshongva, Hotevilla, 1935; Kotchongva 1936:118.]

1.23.0. The White Brother will return when the winters become very cold, the summers very dry, when earthquakes and other signs of nature come, when men become uneasy and restless in their minds, and when a road is made in the sky. [Qötshongva, Hotevilla, 1935; Kotchongva 1936:118.]

1.23.1. All men will then know that they must live better lives. [Qötshongva, Hotevilla, 1935; Kotchongva 1936:118.]

1.23.2. And the White Brother will return and make everything right. [Qötshongva, Hotevilla, 1935; Kotchongva 1936:118.]

1.23.3. If men do not heed these warnings and live better and more humbly, they will be destroyed when the White Brother comes. [Qötshongva, Hotevilla, 1935; Kotchongva 1936:118.]

1.23.4. The world will be cured of evil through the destruction of the wicked. [Qötshongva, Hotevilla, 1935; Kotchongva 1936:118.]

1.24.0. After the destruction, the righteous White people and the Indians will be as brothers. [Qötshongva, Hotevilla, 1935; Kotchongva 1936:118.]

1.24.1. They will share equally a land of rich treasures, and they will live as White people do. [Qötshongva, Hotevilla, 1935; Kotchongva 1936:119.]

1.24.2. They will speak but one language, which will be Hopi, although it might be the White people's language. [Qötshongva, Hotevilla, 1935; Kotchongva 1936:119.]

1.24.3. Living as brothers and sisters, no one will object to intermarriage. [Qötshongva, Hotevilla, 1935; Kotchongva 1936:119.]

1.25.0. The one who reaches the sun first, to see if the sun is their god, will settle down and look forward to meeting his brother, and he will come with wisdom and truth and teach the true religion of god. [Nequatewa, Shongopovi, 1936; Nequatewa 1936:29.]

1.25.1. Others will come with the true Brother who will try to cheat the Hopis out of their land. [Nequatewa, Shongopovi, 1936; Nequatewa 1936:34.]

1.25.2. If the Pahaana is willing to teach his religion, and it resembles Hopi religion, then he will be the true Pahaana. [Nequatewa, Shongopovi, 1936; Nequatewa 1936:50.]

1.26.0. The Pahaana will bring great knowledge and many benefits. [Nequatewa, Shongopovi, 1936; Nequatewa 1936:50.]

1.27.0. The Pahaana will recognize the sorcerers and he will come and make peace and do away with all evil. [Nequatewa, Shongopovi, 1936; Nequatewa 1936:50.]

1.28.0. A time will come when other people will settle in the Hopi area and be undesirable–fighters, thieves, or robbers; these are the Navajos. [Peter Nuvamsa, Shongopovi, 1939; Commissioner of Indian Affairs 1939:2.]

1.28.1. At that time the Hopis must make laws or regulations which are to remove these people. [Peter Nuvamsa, Shongopovi, 1939; Commissioner of Indian Affairs 1939:2.]

1.28.2. Another party will come to the rescue of the Hopis and protect their interests; this is the U.S. government. [Peter Nuvamsa, Shongopovi, 1939; Commissioner of Indian Affairs 1939:2.]

1.29.0. The Pahaana will come to behead the sorcerers and destroy them completely. [Qötshongva, Hotevilla, 1940; Simmons 1942: 379.]

1.29.1. Only then will Hopis and Whites be united as one people, live in peace and prosperity, such as once existed in the underworld. [Qötshongva, Hotevilla, 1940; Simmons 1942:379.]

1.29.2. Hitler is the chosen White Brother. [Qötshongva, Hotevilla, 1940; Simmons 1942:379.]

1.30.0. Some day a White Brother will come who will be able to read the stone tablet and to tell its true meaning. [Qötshongva and Pongyayawma, Hotevilla, 1941; Anonymous 1941.]

1.30.1. When he comes, the Hopis will know him and he will enable all people to share equally in the wealth given to humanity. [Qötshongva and Pongyayawma, Hotevilla, 1941; Anonymous 1941.]

1.31.0. The White man will divide against himself, but the Hopis must not take sides. [Qötshongva and Pongyayawma, Hotevilla, 1941; Anonymous 1941.]

1.32.0. At the most critical time in the history of mankind, the Hopis and Whites will meet at the crossroads of their respective lives. [Traditionalists, 1949; Hopi Empire 3–28–1949.]

1.33.0. The White Brother went east with the understanding that he will return to the Hopis with his stone tablet. [Traditionalists, 1949; Hopi Empire 3–28–1949.]

1.33.1. If the stone tablets fit together, it will prove to the whole world that this land belongs to the Hopis and that the Hopis and the White Brother are true brothers. [Traditionalists, 1949; Hopi Empire 3–28–1949.]

1.33.2. Then the White Brother will restore order and judge all the people in Hopi land who have been unfaithful to their traditional and religious principles and who have mistreated his people. [Traditionalists, 1949; Hopi Empire 3–28–1949.]

1.34.0. Maasaw warned that when the White man comes, he will enforce his will on the Hopis and cause them to change their way of life. [Hermequaftewa, Shongopovi, 1953; Hermequaftewa 1953:6.]

1.34.1. If the Hopis abandon their way of life and religion, disaster will follow, and they will not be allowed to live with Maasaw. [Hermequaftewa, Shongopovi, 1953; Hermequaftewa 1953:6.]

1.35.0. Some day the White man will come and do many things to the Hopis so that they do not lose their life plan. [Nasewiseoma, Hotevilla, 1955; Bureau of Indian Affairs 1955:12.]

1.36.0. A person is coming, a very intelligent person, who will bring many things to the Hopis that may not be right or in accordance with Maasaw's teachings. [Qötshongva, Hotevilla, 1955; Bureau of Indian Affairs 1955:24.]

1.36.1. This person is of white skin and he will make life hard for the Hopis. [Qötshongva, Hotevilla, 1955; Bureau of Indian Affairs 1955:25.]

1.36.2. There will come two men who will steal from the Hopis: a White man and a Navajo. [Qötshongva, Hotevilla, 1955; Bureau of Indian Affairs 1955:25.]

1.36.3. They will lead the Hopis to disrupt their lives. [Qötshongva, Hotevilla, 1955; Bureau of Indian Affairs 1955:25.]

1.36.4. One strong Hopi of good heart will work for the good of the people and for all life on earth, and if the Hopis adhere to the teachings, they will not be destroyed. [Qötshongva, Hotevilla, 1955; Bureau of Indian Affairs 1955:25.]

1.37.0. The White Brother will come looking for the stone tablet and when the two tablets are placed side by side, then he will be recognized as the true Brother. [Qötshongva, Hotevilla, 1955; Bureau of Indian Affairs 1955:25.]

1.38.0. Someone will come and try to reorganize Hopi life; this must have been Oliver LaFarge. [Qötshongva, Hotevilla, 1955; Bureau of Indian Affairs 1955:58.]

1.39.0. A White man will come, and if he does things that are not right, which may destroy Hopi ways and break up Hopi lands, then the leaders must prevent it. [Hermequaftewa, Shongopovi, 1955; Bureau of Indian Affairs 1955:75.]

1.39.1. If they forsake the teachings and duties, they will face a severe punishment. [Hermequaftewa, Shongopovi, 1955; Bureau of Indian Affairs 1955:82.]

1.40.0. The White man will arrive with great plans, he will subject the people, deceive them, scare them, pretend to be a sympathizer; he will claim all the land, come with "metal instruments of power";

he will change the laws according to his own designs; but the Hopis must resist confusion and not give in. [Hermequaftewa, Shongopovi, 1955; Bureau of Indian Affairs 1955:86–87.]

1.41.0. The White Brother is to look for the Hopi Brother and find out whether he is still living his way of life; if not, then he will punish the Hopis and destroy them; if so, then he will give them everlasting life. [Ralph Selina, Shongopovi, 1955; Bureau of Indian Affairs 1955:99.]

1.42.0. The White Brother will come and correct the wrongs being done to the Hopis. [Earl Pela, Shongopovi, 1955; Bureau of Indian Affairs 1955:105.]

1.43.0. Many other tribes will claim that they are Hopis—the Navajos and the Whites will claim this; but when the truth becomes evident, all will recognize the land as Hopi land. [Viets Lomaheftewa, Shongopovi, 1955; Bureau of Indian Affairs 1955:116.]

1.44.0. The Brother will return to take the place of his Brother and defend him. [Guy Kootshaftewa, Mishongovi, 1955; Bureau of Indian Affairs 1955:124.]

1.45.0. There will be wars among nations, the world will be turned upside down, the Hopi way will be underneath and the White man's way on top. [Tuwaletstiwa, Kykotsmovi, 1955; Bureau of Indian Affairs 1955:173.]

1.46.0. There will come a time when another person will come upon the Hopis, write things down, use his ways upon them, and tie them up with those ways. [Ralph Hotewa, Kykotsmovi, 1955; Bureau of Indian Affairs 1955:210.]

1.47.0. When the White man comes he will have many good things, and the Hopis must work hard to get them. [Pahongva, Hotevilla, 1955; Bureau of Indian Affairs 1955:240.]

1.48.0. The Hopis are waiting for the White Brother who will be looking for the person who has held on to his traditions. [Qötshongva, Hotevilla, 1955; Bureau of Indian Affairs 1955:262.]

1.49.0. A time will come when the Hopis and Whites will meet to discuss matters of a controversial nature. [Ned Nayatewa, Walpi, 1955; Bureau of Indian Affairs 1955:327.]

1.50.0. The White Brother will return and show the Hopis how to live a new life. [Lomavaya, Walpi, 1955; Bureau of Indian Affairs 1955:344.]

1.50.1. But if the Hopis do not give up their sinful ways, they will be punished, and blood will flow. [Lomavaya, Walpi, 1955; Bureau of Indian Affairs 1955:344.]

1.51.0. The White Brother will have everything that is pleasant and pure, and he will purify both animals and enemies. [Lomavaya, Walpi, 1955; Bureau of Indian Affairs 1955:344.]

1.52.0. The White man will come either with a righteous religion or he will come after having fallen from the faith; if the latter, he will use any means to get what he wants. [Qötshongva, Hotevilla, 1956; Bentley 1956:7.]

1.53.0. The White man will bring inventions: a machine which moves on land and is pulled by animals; a machine which is propelled without the help of animals; the land will be cut up by many roads; there will be a road in the sky; something shiny will run through the land (reflections on the roads)—these are signs of the end of the world and the coming purification day. [Qötshongva, Hotevilla, 1956; Bentley 1956:8.]

1.54.0. The White Brother will punish the enemies and persecutors of the Hopis on purification day. [Qötshongva, Hotevilla, 1956; Bentley 1956:9.]

1.55.0. The wicked Whites will drop a gourd full of ashes and destroy many lives. [Monongya, Hotevilla, 1956; Bentley 1956:10.]

1.56.0. When purification day comes, Whites will be allowed to live in Hopi land again—only a few, and maybe none, will be saved. [Monongya, Hotevilla, 1956; Bentley 1956:10.]

1.57.0. The White man will come and try to get control of the land. [Hermequaftewa, Shongopovi, 1956; Bentley 1956:13.]

1.58.0. A White man will come one day and make the Hopis live a drunken life. [Qötshongva, Hotevilla, 1956; Bentley 1956:20–21.]

1.59.0. The True Brother will purify the land, and if the Whites have tried to right their wrongs, the U.S. may be saved, if not they will not be allowed to live on Hopi land. [Qötshongva, Hotevilla, 1956; Bentley 1956:21.]

1.60.0. The True White Brother will purify the land, behead the wicked, and help the Hopis; then they can intermarry and speak one language (probably Hopi); he will take the minerals out and divide them equally; there will be no sickness, there will be happiness, abundance, and everlasting life. [Ralph Tawangyawma, Hotevilla, 1956; Bentley 1956:23–24.]

1.61.0. If no Hopi will help spread the word, then a Paiute may; if not, then a Navajo may; if not, then another Indian tribe may; if not, then maybe a White person will. [Qötshongva, Hotevilla, 1956; Bentley 1956:26.]

1.62.0. As the day of purification approaches, the chief must knock on the door of the White House, and if the door is not opened, then he must knock on the door of the United Nations and tell about all the problems brought upon the Hopis by the White man. [Qötshongva, Hotevilla, 1958; Katchongva 1958.]

1.63.0. The White man must clean his own house before the true White Brother comes to judge, punish, and destroy all evil and wicked people on the day of purification. [Qötshongva, Hotevilla, and Hermequaftewa, Shongopovi, 1960; Katchongva and Hermequaftewa 9-20-1960.]

1.64.0. When the land of the Hopis and other Indians are about to be taken away from them and their way of life destroyed by evil White men and evil Indians, then the Hopi leaders must go to the "House of Glass or Mica" (U.N. building), where great leaders from many lands are gathered to help people who are in trouble, to look for the true White Brother, to seek justice for all good people, and to warn the great leaders of the coming purification day. [Banancya, Oraibi, 1961; Banyacya 1-12-1961.]

1.64.1. When the Hopis do this at least one, two, or three leaders or nations will hear and understand, and will immediately correct all the wrongs being done to the chosen race, i.e. the Indian. [Banancya, Oraibi, 1961; Banyacya 1-12-1961.]

1.64.2. If the door to the U.N. is closed, then the Hopis will know that the great leaders of the Glass House are working for the evil ones; and they must rejoice because on that day the White race will have severed itself from the Hopis thereby having led themselves to the greatest punishment on the day of purification—thus it has been decreed by Maasaw and it cannot be changed. [Banancya, Oraibi, 1961; Banyacya 1-12-1961.]

1.65.0. The Older Brother was to go to the east and, after reaching that place, to immediately start back in order to look for his Younger Brother, since his mission is to help his Younger Brother bring about the purification day, during which all the evil ones will be punished or destroyed and real peace, brotherhood, and everlasting life will be brought about. [Banancya, Oraibi, 1961; Banyacya 1-12-1961.]

1.66.0. After many years the Older Brother may change the color of his skin to white, but he will still have black hair. [Banancya, Oraibi, 1961; Banyacya 1-12-1961.]

1.67.0. The Older Brother will restore all land back to his Brother which the Evil One among White men had taken. [Banancya, Oraibi, 1961; Banyacya 1-12-1961.]

1.67.1. The Older Brother will also look for the stone tablets and when their tablets are placed side by side, it will show the world that they are true Brothers. [Banancya, Oraibi, 1961; Banyacya 1-12-1961.]

1.67.2. Then great judgment and punishment will take place, for he will help his Younger Brother to bring about real justice for all Indian Brothers who have been mistreated by the Whites. [Banancya, Oraibi, 1961; Banyacya 1-12-1961.]

1.68.0. There will be many signs concerning the time of the coming of the Older Brother: People's lives will become corrupted and materialistic, the evil Whites will nearly destroy land and life for Hopis and other Indians, a road will be built in the sky, a gourd of ashes will fall on the earth and boil everything within a great area and no grass will grow for many years, and the leaders will turn to evil instead of to Maasaw. [Banancya, Oraibi, 1961; Banyacya 1-12-1961.]

1.69.0. The true White Brother will be all powerful, wearing a red cap or cloak, being large in population, and having his own religion. [Banancya, Oraibi, 1961; Banyacya 1-12-1961.]

1.69.1. He will bring the tablets, none will be able to stand against him, he will come swiftly and take over the whole continent in one day, and all power in this world will be placed in his hands. [Banancya, Oraibi, 1961; Banyacya 1-12-1961.]

1.69.2. The Hopis must never take up arms. [Banancya, Oraibi, 1961; Banyacya 1-12-1961.]

1.70.0. Two great ones will be with the White Brother. [Banancya, Oraibi, 1961; Banyacya 1-12-1961.]

1.70.1. One will have the symbol of the swastika and the iron cross, and he will be wearing a cap similar to the back of a horned toad. [Banancya, Oraibi, 1961; Banyacya 1-12-1961.]

1.70.2. The second helper will have the symbol of the sun, and he will be numerous. [Banancya, Oraibi, 1961; Banyacya 1-12-1961.]

1.70.3. These two will shake the earth two times in final preparation for the day of purification. [Banancya, Oraibi, 1961; Banyacya 1-12-1961.]

THE MORMONS

2.0.0. Hopis must not cross the Colorado River to live with the Mormons until the three prophets who took them into Hopi land should visit them again. [Oraibi consultant, 1858; Little 1881:62.]

2.0.1. The Mormons will settle in the country south of Hopi land. [Oraibi consultant, 1858; Little 1881:62.]

INTERNAL AFFAIRS

3.0.0. If the Hopis ever contend with one another, as in the lower world, the witch at the Sipaapuni will be allied with the chief. [Yukiwma, Oraibi, 1903–1904; Voth 1905:20.]

3.1.0. It was prophesied that each faction at Oraibi will want the other to leave. [Yukiwma?, Oraibi, 1906; Keith 9-16-1906; quoted in Whiteley 1988:109.]

3.2.0. The split was prophesied. Whichever party was vanquished, they are to leave the village and go to Kaawestima as told in the songs. [Tawakwaptiwa, Oraibi, 1906; Lemmon 9-9-1906; quoted in Whiteley 1988:265.]

3.3.0. All the enemies will combine against the Kookop clan unless they conform to the new ideas and ways of living. [Yukiwma, Hotevilla, 1911; Scott 12-5-1911:8.]

3.3.1. If the soldiers who capture the Kookops take them west, they will die; if east, then they will be imprisoned. [Yukiwma, Hotevilla, 1911; Scott 12-5-1911:8.]

3.3.2. Yukiwma must not depart from his traditions. [Yukiwma, Hotevilla, 1911; Scott 12-5-1911:8.]

3.3.3. The Oraibi chief will fall and Yukiwma will triumph over all the clans. [Yukiwma, Hotevilla, 1911; Scott 12-5-1911:17.]

3.4.0. The Spider clan and Bear clan will come together, but the Spider Woman will draw away the followers of the Bear clan. [Tawakwaptiwa, Oraibi, 1933–1934; Titiev 1944:95.]

3.4.1. Tawakwaptiwa will lose his entire following, keep his Soyalangw while all other rites and ceremonies will be abandoned, followed by a great famine, after which the full ceremonial calendar will be revived once more. [Tawakwaptiwa, Oraibi, 1933–1934; Titiev 1944:95.]

3.5.0. This condition was prophesied: The people of Oraibi will be scattered, they will have too many chiefs. [Tawakwaptiwa, Oraibi, 1933; Titiev 1944:251.]

3.6.0. Tawakwaptiwa will be deserted by his followers and he will remain alone with his Soyalangw. Another war will destroy civilization by atomic bomb, after which man will begin his struggle toward civilization clad only in leaves. [Tawakwaptiwa, Oraibi, 1946–1948; Brandt 1954:32.]

3.7.0. If the Hopis lose faith in their life pattern, then they will fight and quarrel and hate each other, and this will lead them to war. [Monongya, Hotevilla, 1955; Bureau of Indian Affairs 1955:49.]

3.8.0. The Hopis were warned never to take part in the Tribal Council;

if they do, then it would break up the Hopi life pattern. [Monongya, Hotevilla, 1955; Bureau of Indian Affairs 1955:51.]

3.9.0. If the Hopis follow those who have left the traditional path, then they will drive the Hopis to their death. [Hermequaftewa, Shongopovi, 1955; Bureau of Indian Affairs 1955:87.]

3.10.0. The Hopis were told not to follow the Tribal Council. [Hermequaftewa, Shongopovi, 1955; Bureau of Indian Affairs 1955:88.]

3.11.0. The younger people will appoint themselves as leaders without the rights of inheritance; this organization will last for four years and then die out; if it is reorganized, it will mean the destruction of Hopi life. [George Nasoftie, Shongopovi, 1955; Bureau of Indian Affairs 1955:102.]

3.12.0. When one of the great leaders changes the writing on the stone tablet and drops or neglects his duties, he will not be able to be chief again. [Qötshongva, Hotevilla, 1955; Bureau of Indian Affairs 1955:258.]

3.12.1. When this happens, Qötshongva must take over the leadership. [Qötshongva, Hotevilla, 1955; Bureau of Indian Affairs 1955: 258.]

3.13.0. The time will come when the Hopis will fight among themselves and, while doing this, things will disappear for them. [Samuel Shing, Moenkopi, 1955; Bureau of Indian Affairs 1955:312.]

MAASAW AND THE PURIFICATION DAY

4.0.0. Maasaw would not become chief, and said that the Hopis will become as they were in the underworld, and when the White man comes back to cut off the heads of the bad ones, then Maasaw will own all of his land again. [Yukiwma, Oraibi, 1903–1904; Voth 1905:23.]

4.1.0. Maasaw would not become chief because the Hopis have many ambitions and plans to experience (such as they do today), after which he will return and be their leader. [Qötshongva, Hotevilla, 1935; Kotchongva 1936:116.]

4.2.0. After the destruction, the faithful people will be rewarded with a place to live, and the righteous White people and the Indians will be as brothers. [Qötshongva, Hotevilla, 1935; Kotchongva 1936:118.]

4.3.0. There will come a time when there will be great trouble involving many nations, but the Hopis must stay out of the fight. [Qötshongva and Pongyayawma, Hotevilla, 1941; Anonymous 1941.]

4.3.1. The fight which will be brought by the White man will bring equality. [Qötshongva and Pongyayawma, Hotevilla, 1941; Anonymous 1941.]

4.4.0. If the Hopis forsake Maasaw's instructions, as inscribed on the stone tablet, then they will lose their permission to live on his land; if they obey, then they will not fail. [Banancya, Oraibi, 1941; Anonymous 1941.]

4.5.0. The judgment day is going to take place and be completed in the Hopi Empire. [Traditionalists, 1949; Hopi Empire 3-28-1949.]

4.6.0. Maasaw told the Hopis that there will be trouble and confusion if they forsake his instructions, but if the Hopi way is followed, people may be able to settle everything properly. [Hermequaftewa, Shongopovi, 1953; Hermequaftewa 1953:4, 6.]

4.7.0. On the day of purification, all people will be judged according to their conduct. [Monongya, Hotevilla, 1955; Bureau of Indian Affairs 1955:22.]

4.7.1. Some will be punished, but because of one, two, or three men and their strong faith, the good people will be saved and a new everlasting life will be brought into this life, and humanity will not destroy itself. [Monongya, Hotevilla, 1955; Bureau of Indian Affairs 1955:22.]

4.8.0. Maasaw will not become chief until the Hopis have fulfilled their desires or intentions, and then he will come back and be the chief. [Qötshongva, Hotevilla, 1955; Bureau of Indian Affairs 1955:24.]

4.9.0. If life becomes disrupted, it will be settled because of the stone tablet and because of some people who have the courage and faith to remain faithful to Maasaw's instructions. [Qötshongva, Hotevilla, 1955; Bureau of Indian Affairs 1955:24.]

4.10.0. When Maasaw is to take over, there will be a great purification day. [Qötshongva, Hotevilla, 1955; Bureau of Indian Affairs 1955:24.]

4.10.1. Those who are strong in heart may be saved, those who are afraid may die. [Qötshongva, Hotevilla, 1955; Bureau of Indian Affairs 1955:24.]

4.11.0. Three great wars will take place. The third will be at the time of purification. [Qötshongva, Hotevilla, 1955; Bureau of Indian Affairs 1955:25.]

4.12.0. Three great wars will take place. We have already passed two great wars. The third will come—it cannot be stopped—and the Hopis must not take part in it. [Monongya, Hotevilla, 1955; Bureau of Indian Affairs 1955:45.]

4.13.0. If the Hopis stick to their traditional lifeway, the road will lead to everlasting life. [Monongya, Hotevilla, 1955; Bureau of Indian Affairs 1955:46.]

4.13.1. If the Hopis choose the other road, that of evil being, then life will be very hard and troubled, since the evil ones will be beheaded at the purification. [Monongya, Hotevilla, 1955; Bureau of Indian Affairs 1955:46.]

4.14.0. As long as the Hopis adhere to the teachings of the tablet, Paalölöqangw will withhold the punishment, but if they forsake the "stone map" and the Hopi life pattern, life in Hopi land will be wiped out. [Secquaptewa, Hotevilla, 1955; Bureau of Indian Affairs 1955:55.]

4.15.0. A beheading might have to take place because the evil man must choose. [Secquaptewa, Hotevilla, 1955; Bureau of Indian Affairs 1955:55.]

4.16.0. If the Hopis forsake Maasaw's instructions as inscribed on the stone tablets, then they will cause destruction of all life. [Hermequaftewa, Shongopovi, 1955; Bureau of Indian Affairs 1955:81.]

4.16.1. If the Hopis stick to the traditional way, they will attain everlasting life. [Hermequaftewa, Shongopovi, 1955; Bureau of Indian Affairs 1955:87.]

4.17.0. The purifier will come with his tool, but if the Hopis have not forsaken their life patterns, then he will have no use for the tool and will only strike an old can or throw up an old shoe. [Hermequaftewa, Shongopovi, 1955; Bureau of Indian Affairs 1955:88.]

4.18.0. If the Hopis participate in the wars of others, they will meet hardship and be severely punished when the White Brother comes. [Ralph Selina, Shongopovi, 1955; Bureau of Indian Affairs 1955:101.]

4.19.0. One day a (stock) reduction will occur, and the Hopi's food will be taken from them. [Tuwaletstiwa, Kykotsmovi, 1955; Bureau of Indian Affairs 1955:173.]

4.20.0. When two or four persons die in Oraibi, the villagers will be scattered and will live in old ruins until they return to Oraibi and find ceremonial costumes and other important things thrown around, and they will not know what those things are. [Tuwaletstiwa, Kykotsmovi, 1955; Bureau of Indian Affairs 1955:173–174.]

4.21.0. Hopi religion will destroy its people, and they are to follow the Holy One. [Tuwaletstiwa, Kykotsmovi, 1955; Bureau of Indian Affairs 1955:174.]

4.22.0. A time of confusion will come. [Ralph Hotewa, Kykotsmovi, 1955; Bureau of Indian Affairs 1955:210.]

4.23.0. If the Hopis ever forget Maasaw's teachings, they will bring great troubles on themselves. [Ralph Hotewa, Kykotsmovi, 1955; Bureau of Indian Affairs 1955:210.]

4.24.0. There will come a time of great strife, but the Hopis should not be discouraged, and they will witness many great things. [Julius Doopkema, Bacavi, 1955; Bureau of Indian Affairs 1955:222.]

4.24.1. There will come a time when there will be a road in the sky, traveled on by many types of vehicles, and there will be broad roads graded upon the land. [Julius Doopkema, Bacavi, 1955; Bureau of Indian Affairs 1955:222.]

4.25.0. The time will come when Hopi ceremonies will cease–Katsina ceremonies will be the last. [Julius Doopkema, Bacavi, 1955; Bureau of Indian Affairs 1955:224.]

4.26.0. There will be four wars after many roads are built on the earth and in the air and water. [Lewis Numkena, Moenkopi, 1955; Bureau of Indian Affairs 1955:286.]

4.26.1. The "Reds" will be the last, and there will be a rain of bombs and bullets, and a river of blood will flow upon the earth, and the earth will be burned. [Lewis Numkena, Moenkopi, 1955; Bureau of Indian Affairs 1955:286.]

4.27.0. If the Hopis lose faith, they will lose Maasaw and destroy life and land. [Qötshongva, Hotevilla, 1956; Bentley 1956:6.]

4.28.0. There will be three great wars, the last will end when everything is purified and the wicked ones are destroyed. [Qötshongva, Hotevilla, 1956; Bentley 1956:8.]

4.28.1. If the Hopis participate in any way, they will not be saved. [Qötshongva, Hotevilla, 1956; Bentley 1956:8.]

4.29.0. Maasaw will return and take over leadership, and he will purify the land. [Monongya, Hotevilla, 1956; Bentley 1956:9.]

4.29.1. Maasaw will judge according to who has kept his way of life; the good will be saved, the evil will be punished. [Monongya, Hotevilla, 1956; Bentley 1956:10.]

4.30.0. Signs from Maasaw that the Hopis are straying are: drought, grass drying up, people doing things that will not bring rain, and people being mistreated by false leaders. [Monongya, Hotevilla, 1956; Bentley 1956:10.]

4.30.1. If the signs are not heeded, there will be great punishment: severe droughts, floods, earthquakes, lightening striking people, big winds, and great sickness. [Monongya, Hotevilla, 1956; Bentley 1956:10.]

4.31.0. Only after the purification day can the minerals be taken out of the earth, because then they will not be used to harm others, and they will be evenly divided. [Monongya, Hotevilla, 1956; Bentley 1956:30.]

4.32.0. Maasaw gave the Hopis the symbols of power and authority over all land and life (i.e. stone tablets and tiiponi) to guard, protect, and hold in trust until he returns in the latter days. [Banancya, Oraibi, 1961; Banyacya 1-12-1961.]

4.33.0. Maasaw commissioned three to bring about the purification day: the true White Brother, one with the swastika symbol, and one with the sun symbol. [Banancya, Oraibi, 1961; Banyacya 1-12-1961.]

4.33.1. If these three fail, then one from the west will come like a big storm and cover the land like ants—they are many and unmerciful. [Banancya, Oraibi, 1961; Banyacya 1-12-1961.]

4.33.2. The Hopis must not get on their house tops to watch him, as he will come to punish all people. [Banancya, Oraibi, 1961; Banyacya 1-12-1961.]

4.33.3. If all of these fail, then the Hopi leaders will ask Maasaw to strike people with lightening, and only the righteous will revive. [Banancya, Oraibi, 1961; Banyacya 1-12-1961.]

4.33.4. If none revive, then Maasaw will send a flood, and humanity will have lost the chance to acquire everlasting life. Then only ants will inhabit the earth. [Banancya, Oraibi, 1961; Banyacya 1-12-1961.]

4.33.5. If the three succeed, and if one, two, or three Hopis remain faithful to the ancient traditions, then Maasaw will appear before all those who will be saved, and the three will lay out a new life plan which will lead to everlasting life. [Banancya, Oraibi, 1961; Banyacya 1-12-1961.]

4.33.6. The earth will be renewed, flowers will bloom, the wild game will return, and there will be abundance for all. [Banancya, Oraibi, 1961; Banyacya 1-12-1961.]

4.33.7. Those who are saved will share equally, recognize Maasaw, intermarry, and speak one tongue. [Banancya, Oraibi, 1961; Banyacya 1-12-1961.]

4.33.8. A new religion will be established if the people so desire. [Banancya, Oraibi, 1961; Banyacya 1-12-1961.]

THE EMERGENCE MYTH

5.0.0. If the emergence myth is forgotten, disaster will occur: Perhaps the stars will fall into the ocean and turn it into oil, and the sun will set fire to it, and the conflagration will consume everyone.

Or perhaps an earthquake will kill everyone. [Sun clan consultant, Shongopovi, 1912; Wallis 1936:16–17.]

THE LAND

6.0.0. If the Hopis hold on to Maasaw's land and not turn it over to any other people, Maasaw will return and bless them. [Qötshongva, Hotevilla, 1935; Kotchongva 1936:116.]

6.1.0. The Hopis are to fight against any people trying to take possession of the land. [Qötshongva, Hotevilla, 1935; Kotchongva 1936:118.]

6.2.0. After the destruction, the faithful Indians and the righteous Whites will share a land filled with treasures. [Qötshongva, Hotevilla, 1935; Kotchongva 1936:119.]

6.3.0. Maasaw told the Hopis that the Pahaana will try to claim all the lands for himself even though the leader who sent him instructed him to respect all peoples found living there. [Hermequaftewa, Shongopovi, 1953; Hermequaftewa 1953:4.]

6.4.0. The Hopis were warned never to cut up the land in any manner because it is to be guarded for all Indian people, and it is the home of the Hopis. [Qötshongva, Hotevilla, 1955; Bureau of Indian Affairs 1955:25.]

6.5.0. The Hopis have two roads they can follow. Something will happen to cause the Hopis to choose the other road which contains the mineral wealth of the earth. [Monongya, Hotevilla, 1955; Bureau of Indian Affairs 1955:45.]

6.5.1. The Hopis must never allow that wealth to be used for any purposes or wars because it will be used for destroying other lives. [Monongya, Hotevilla, 1955; Bureau of Indian Affairs 1955:45.]

6.5.2. When the land has been purified, then the natural resources may be taken out for the benefit of all people. [Monongya, Hotevilla, 1955; Bureau of Indian Affairs 1955:45.]

6.6.0. Someone will come and attempt to cut up Hopi land, and if this ever happens, Hopis are to support those who stand for the traditional life pattern. [Monongya, Hotevilla, 1955; Bureau of Indian Affairs 1955:53.]

6.7.0. The White man will come and try to take the land, so the Hopis must not accept anything from the White man or they will lose both life and land. [Otis Polelonema, Shongopovi, 1955; Bureau of Indian Affairs 1955:103.]

6.8.0. The White man will offer the Hopis a lot of money for the land, and if they accept it, the money will be gone in a few years and the Hopis will have no land to make their livelihood from, but the White man will immediately make the same amount overnight. [Otis Polelonema, Shongopovi, 1955; Bureau of Indian Affairs 1955:105.]

6.9.0. Other peoples will crowd in on the Hopis, but the Hopis must never give up their claims which are fixed by distant shrines. [Earl Pela, Shongopovi, 1955; Bureau of Indian Affairs 1955:106.]

6.10.0. The Hopis must never divide the land up. [Ralph Hotewa, Kykotsmovi, 1955; Bureau of Indian Affairs 1955:211.]

6.11.0. The Navajos will try to get Hopi land. When this is found out, the government will find a document at the bottom of the piles of documents in Washington D.C. which will prove that the land belongs to the Hopis. [Qötshongva, Hotevilla, 1956; Bentley 1956:21.]

APPENDIX D

Letter to President Harry Truman from Representatives of the Hopi Indian Empire

Hopi Indian Empire
Oraibi, Arizona
March 28, 1949

The President
The White House
Washington, D.C.

To the President:

We, the hereditary Hopi Chieftains of the Hopi Pueblos of Hotevilla, Shungopovy, and Mushongnovi humbly request a word with you.

Thoroughly acquainted with the wisdom and knowledge of our traditional form of government and our religious principles, sacredly authorized and entrusted to speak, act, and to execute our duties and obligations for all the common people throughout this land of the Hopi Empire, in accordance with the fundamental principles of life, which were laid down for us by our Great Spirit, Masau'u and by our forefathers, we hereby assembled in the Hopi Pueblo of Shungopovy on March 9, 13, 26, and 28 of this year 1949 for the purpose of making known to the government of the United States and others in this land that the Hopi Empire is still in existence, its traditional path unbroken and its religious order intact and practiced, and the Stone Tablets, upon which are written the boundaries of the Hopi Empire are still in the hands of the Chiefs of Oraibi and Hotevilla Pueblos.

Firmly believing that the time has now come for us the highest leaders of our respective pueblos to speak and to reexamine ourselves, our sacred duties, our past and present deeds, to look to the future and to study carefully all the important and pressing policies that are coming to us from Indian Bureau at the present time, we met here.

What we say is from our hearts. We speak truths that are based upon our own tradition and religion. We speak as the first people in this land you call America. And we speak to you, a white man, the last people who came to our shores seeking freedom of worship, speech, assembly and a right to life, liberty and the pursuit of happiness. And we are speaking to all the American Indian people.

Today we, Hopi and white man, come face to face at the crossroad of our respective life. At last our paths have crossed and it was foretold it would be at the most critical time in the history of mankind. Everywhere people are confused. What we decide now and do hereafter will be the fate of our respective people. Because we Hopi leaders are following our traditional instructions, we must make our position clear to you and we expect you to do the same to us.

Allow us to mention some of the vital issues which have aroused us to action and which we recognized them to be the last desperate move on the part of the leaders in Washington, D.C. They are as follows:

1. From the Land Claims Commission in Washington, D.C. a letter requesting us to file in our claim to land we believed we are entitled to before the five-year limit beginning August 13, 1946 is expired. We were told that after the five-year limit is expired we can not file any claim.
2. We are being told by the Superintendent at Keams Canyon Agency about leasing of our land to some Oil Companies to drill for oil. We are told to make the decision on whether to lease out our land and control all that goes with it or we may refuse to do so. But, we were told if we refused, then these Oil Companies might send their smart lawyers to Washington, D.C. for the purpose of inducing some Senators and Congressmen to change certain laws that will take away our rights and authority to our land and placing that authority in another department where they will be leasing out our land at will.
3. We've heard that a $90,000,000 is being appropriated for the purpose of carrying out the provisions of the Act No. S.2363 which read: To promote the rehabilitation of the Navajo and Hopi Tribes of Indians and the better utilization of the resources of the Navajo and Hopi Reservation, and for other purposes.
4. Recently we were told about the Hoover Commission's proposal to Congress the launching of a program to convert the country's 400,000 Indians into "full, tax-paying citizens" under state jurisdiction.

5. Now we heard about the North Atlantic security treaty which would bind the United States, Canada, and six European nations to an alliance in which an attack against one would be considered an attack against all.

Now these vital issues coming to us from Washington touches the very core of the Hopi life, a peaceful life. By this we know it is time for us to speak and act. It is now time for us as highest leaders of our respective people to come to a definite understanding of our positions before we go forward into the future and before you embark upon your new program. We want the people everywhere to know our stand, the Hopi people. It is of utmost importance that we do this now.

The Hopi form of government was established solely upon the religious and traditional grounds. The divine plan of life in this land was laid out for us by great Spirit, Masau'u. This plan cannot be changed. The Hopi life is all set according to the fundamental principles of life of this divine plan. We can not do otherwise but to follow this plan. There is no other way for us. We also know that the white people and all other races everywhere are following certain traditional and religious principles. What have they done with them? Now we are all talking about the judgment day. We all are aware of that fact because we are all going to that same point no matter what religion we believed in. In the light of our Hopi prophecy it is going to take place here and will be completed in the Hopi Empire. So for this reason we urge you to give these thoughts your most careful consideration and to reexamine your past deeds and future plans. Again we say let us set our house in order now.

This land is a sacred home of the Hopi people and all the Indian Race in this land. It was given to the Hopi people the task to guard this land not by force of arms, not by killing, not by confiscating of properties of others, but by humble prayers, by obedience to our traditional and religious instructions and by being faithful to our Great Spirit Masau'u. We are still a sovereign nation. Our flag still flies throughout our land (our ancient ruins). We have never abandoned our sovereignty to any foreign power or nation. We've been selfgoverning people long before any white man came to our shores. What Great Spirit made and planned no power on earth can change.

The boundaries of our Empire were established permanently and was written upon Stone Tablets which are still with us. Another was given to his white brother who after emerging of the first people to this new land went east with the understanding that he will return with his Stone Tablet to the Hopis. These Stone Tablets when put together and if they agree will prove to the whole world that this land truly belongs to the Hopi people and that they are true brothers. Then the white brother will restore order and judge all people here who have been unfaithful to their traditional and religious principles and who have mistreated his people.

Now, we ask you Mr. President, the American people and you, our own people, American Indians, to give these words of ours your most serious considerations. Let us all reexamine ourselves and see where we stand today. Great Spirit, Masau'u has granted us, the Indians, the first right to this land. This is our sacred soil.

Today we are being asked to file our land claims in the Land Claims Commission in Washington, D.C. We, as hereditary Chieftains of the Hopi Tribe, can not and will not file any claims according to the Provisions set up by Land Claims Commission because we have never been consulted in regards to setting up these provisions. Besides we have already laid claim to this whole western hemisphere long before Columbus's great, great grandmother was born. We will not ask a white man, who came to us recently, for a piece of land that is already ours. We think that white people should be thinking about asking for a permit to build their homes upon our land.

Neither will we lease any part of our land for oil development at this time. This land is not for leasing or for sale. This is our sacred soil. Our true brother has not yet arrived. Any prospecting, drilling and leasing on our land that is being done now is without our knowledge and consent. We will not be held responsible for it.

We have been told that there is a $90,000,000 being appropriated by the Indian Bureau for the Hopi and Navajo Indians. We have heard of other large appropriations before but where all that money goes we have never been able to find out. We are still poor, even poorer because of the reduction of our land, stock, farms, and it seems as though the Indian Bureau or whoever is planning new lives for us now is ready to reduce us, the Hopi people, under this new plan. Why, we do not need all that money, and we do not ask for it. We are self-supporting people. We are not starving. People starve only when they neglect their farms or when someone denies them a right to make a decent living or when they become too lazy to work. Maybe the Indian Bureau is starving. Maybe a Navajo is starving. They are asking for it. True, there are the aged, the blind and the crippled need help. So we will not accept any new theories that the Indian Bureau is planning for our lives under this new appropriation. Neither will we abandon our homes.

Now we cannot understand why since its establishment the government of the United States has taken over everything we owned either by force, bribery, trickery, and sometimes by reckless killing, making himself very rich, and after all these years of neglect of the American Indians have the courage today in announcing to the world a plan which will "convert the country's 400,000 Indians into 'full, tax-paying citizens' under state jurisdiction." Are you ever going to be satisfied with all the wealth you have now because of us, the Indians? There is something terribly wrong with your system of government because after all these years, we the Indians are still licking on the bones and crumbs that fall to us from your tables. Have you forgotten the meaning of Thanksgiving Day? Have the American people, white people, forgotten the treaties with the Indians, your duties and obligations as guardians?

Now we have heard about the Atlantic security treaty which we understood will bind the United States, Canada and six other European nations to an alliance in which an attack against one would be considered an attack against all.

We, the traditional leaders want you and the American people to know that we will stand firmly upon our own traditional and religious grounds. And that *we will not bind* ourselves to any foreign nation at this time. Neither will we go with you on a wild and reckless adventure which we know will lead us only to a total ruin. Our Hopi form of government is all set and ready for such eventuality. We have met all other rich and powerful nations who have come to our shores, from the Early Spanish Conquistadors down to the present government of the United States all of whom have used force in trying to wipe out our existence here in our own home. We want to come to our own destiny in our own way. We have no enemy. We will neither show our bows and arrows to anyone at this time. This is our only way to everlasting life and happiness. Our tradition and religious training forbid us to harm, kill and molest anyone. We, therefore, objected to our boys being forced to be trained for war to become murderers and destroyers. It is you who should protect us. What nation who has taken up arms ever brought peace and happiness to his people? All the laws under the Constitution of the United States were made without our consent, knowledge, and approval, yet we are being forced to do everything that we know are contrary to our religious principles and those principles of the Constitution of the United States.

Now we ask you, American people, what has become of your religion and your tradition? Where do we stand today? The time has now come for all of us as leaders of our people to reexamine ourselves, our past deeds, and our future plans. The judgement day will soon be upon us. Let us make haste and set our house in order before it is too late.

We believe these to be truths and from our hearts and for these reasons we, Hopi Chieftains, urge you to give these thoughts your most earnest considerations. And after a thorough and careful consideration we want to hear from you at your earliest convenience. This is our sacred duty to our people. We are,

Sincerely yours,
Chief Talahaftewa, Village Chief, Bear Clan, Shungopovy
Basevaya, Adviser, Katchin Clan, Shungopovy
Andrew Hermequaftewa, Adviser, Blue Bird Clan, Shungopovy
Chief Sackmasa, Village Crier, Coyote Clan, Mushongnovi
Chief James Pongyayawma, Village Chief, Kokop Clan (Fire), Hotevilla
Chief Dan Katchongva, Adviser, Co-ruler, Sun Clan, Hotevilla

Interpreters
Thomas Banyacya, (Formerly Thomas Jenkins), Oraibi
Herbert Talahaftewa, Shungopovy
George Nasafatie, Shungopovy
Roy Kuchinhongva, Mushongnovi

Others
Lewis Tewanima, (Antelope Priest), Shungopovy; Namorstewa, Mushongnovi; Naquahongva, Mushongnovi; Sacklestewa, Mushongnovi; Seyestewa, Mushongnovi; Masayesva, Mushongnovi; Nuvanyinewa, Shupawlavi; Starlie Lomayaktewa, Mushongnovi; Andy Seletstewa, Mushongnovi; Will K. Mase, Mushongnovi; Taylor Wazzie, Shungopovy; Tawameunewa, Shungopovy; Glen Josytewa, Shungopovy; Otis Polehonema, Shungopovy; Wadsworth Nevayoungtewa, (Snake Chief), Shungopovy; Franklin Coochestewa, (Kwan Chief), Shungopovy.

APPENDIX E

Hopi Names and Terms with Corrected Orthography

Except for the names of the villages, which follow the orthography of the Tribal Council, all names and terms are followed in parentheses using the orthographic system developed by Ekkehart Malotki.

A'losaka (Aalo'saka)
Aguatubi (Awat'ovi)
Aototo (Ewtoto)
Aoatwungwa (Aawatwungwa)
Awatobi (Awat'ovi)
Awatovi (Awat'ovi)
Bacabi (Bacavi)
Bahana (Pahaana)
Bahanna (Pahaana)
baho (paaho)
Balölöokong (Paalölöqangw)
Banyacya (Banancya)
Banyayca (Banancya)
báuypi (paa'uypi)
Bocali (Bacavi)
Bohanna (Pahaana)
Chimopovy (Shongopovi)
cochina (katsina)
diingavi (tiingavi)
du-kyam-see (tukyamsi)
du-pa-cha (tupatsa)
Hotevillay (Hotevilla)
Hotivilla (Hotevilla)
Jenkins, T. (Banancya)
Johnson, K. (Nasewytewa)
Johnson, K. T. (Tuwaletstiwa)
Kochhongva (Qötshongva)
kachina (katsina)
kahopi (qahopi)
Kaléhtak-mongwi (Qaleetaqmongwi)
Katchgonva (Qötshongva)
Katchongua (Qötshongva)
Katchongva (Qötshongva)
katcina (katsina)
kikmoñwi (kikmongwi)
Ki'oma (Kiy'oma)
kiov (kiva)
kisha (kiisa)
Kóhkang Wuhti (Kookyangwwuuti)
Kokop (Kookop)
Köqöchmovi (Kykotsmovi)
Kotchongva (Qötshongva)
kwáhkwi (kwaakwi)
Kyakotsmovi (Kykotsmovi)

Lagón (Lakon)
Lololama (Loololma)
Lololoma (Loololma)
Loloma (Loololma)
louqu (löqö)
Maasau (Maasaw)
Maasauu (Maasaw)
Ma'cawa (Maasaw)
Maraú (Maraw)
Masauu (Maasaw)
Masau'u (Maasaw)
Masauwu (Maasaw)
Másauwuu (Maasaw)
Másaw (Maasaw)
Masawu'u (Maasaw)
Massau'u (Maasaw)
Massua (Maasaw)
Matcito (Matsito)
Mausauu (Maasaw)
meha (möha)
Moencopi (Moenkopi)
Moencopie (Moenkopi)
Moki (Hopi)
Monongye (Monongya)
moochnee (motsni)
Moqui (Hopi)
mótsni (motsni)
Múenkapi (Moenkopi)
Mushongnovi (Mishongovi)
New Oraibi (Kykotsmovi)
nöokwiwi (nöqkwivi)
Oraiba (Oraibi)
Ozaivi (Oraibi)
Pahana (Pahaana)
Pahána (Pahaana)
pakave (paaqavi)
pavowkaya (pavawkya)
pawáokaya (pavawkya)
pbutsquani (pötskwani)
Pikyas (Piikyas)
Pongonyuma (Pongyayawma)
Pongyayouma (Pongyayawma)
Ponyoinyowma (Pongyayawma)
Pöokong (Pöqangwhoyat)
pópwaktu (popwaqa)
powáka (powaqa)
Powák-mana (powaqmana)
powako (powaqa)
Quoguan (Kwaakwant)
Sewaemanewa (Suwuminewa)
Sháalako Katcina (Sa'lakwkatsina)
shalavee (salavi)
Sháwiki Katcina (Saaviki katsina)
Shipaulovi (Shipolovi)
Shongópavi (Shongopovi)
Shumopovi (Shongopovi)
Shungopavi (Shongopovi)
Shungopavy (Shongopovi)
Shupawlavi (Shipolovi)
So Wuhti (So'wuuti)
Spider Grandmother
(Kookyangwso'wuuti)
Spider Woman (Kookyangwwuuti)
Tangík Katcina (Tangiktsina)
Tawaquaptewa (Tawakwaptiwa)
Tawaqwaptiwa (Tawakwaptiwa)
Tcöb-mongwi (Tsöpmongwi)
Tcú-mongwi (Tsu'mongwi)
Tewaquaptewa (Tawakwaptiwa)
tiponi (tiiponi)
tóhcha (tootsa)
Túkwunang Katcina (Tukwunangw)
Ukeoma (Yukiwma)
Väläkän (Paalölöqangw)
Wuwuchim (Wuwtsim)
Wúwuchim (Wuwtsim)
wúwuyom (wuuwuyom)
yáhpa (yaapa)
Yokeoma (Yukiwma)
Yokioma (Yukiwma)
Youkeoma (Yukiwma)
You-kew-ma (Yukiwma)
Yukioma (Yukiwma)
Yukiuma (Yukiwma)

BIBLIOGRAPHY

Abruzzi, William S.
1989 "Ecology, Resource Redistribution, and Mormon Settlement in Northeastern Arizona." *American Anthropologist* 91:642–655.

Adolph, Jonathan
1988 "What Is New Age?" In *The 1988 Guide to New Age Living*, 4–14, 120. Brighton: New Age Journal 1988.

Agar, Michael
1980 "Hermeneutics in Anthropology: A Review Essay." *Ethos* 8 (3): 253–272.

Aidala, Angela A.
1984 "Worldviews, Ideologies and Social Experimentation: Clarification and Replication of 'The Consciousness Reformation.'" *Journal for the Scientific Study of Religion* 23 (1):44–59.

Albert, Roy, and David Leedom Shaul, compilers
1985 *A Concise Hopi and English Lexicon*. Amsterdam: John Benjamins.

Albrecht, Mark
1981 "New Age Spirituality–A General Overview." *Up-Date* 5 (2):2–5.

Allen, Michael, ed.
1981 *Vanuatu: Politics, Economics and Ritual in Island Melanesia*. Sydney: Academic Press.

Alli, Antero
1988 "When the Light Hits. . . . A Post-convergence Interview with Jose Arguelles." *Magical Blend* 18:17–20.

Almagor, Uri
1987 "The Structuration of Meaning in a 'Primitive Religion'." In Shaked, Shulman, and Stroumsa 1987, 11–34.

Alston, William P.
1967 "Religion." In *The Encyclopedia of Philosophy*, volume 7, 140–145. New York: Macmillan and the Free Press.

Andrews, Lynn V.
1981 *Medicine Woman*. New York: Harper and Row.

Anonymous
1941 "Hopi Claim Religion is Bar to Service." *Arizona Republic*, May 23, 1941. Special Collections, The University of Arizona, Tucson.

Anonymous
1961 Minutes of a meeting at Shungopavy, May 6–7, 1961. An unsigned manuscript typescript from files to Thomas Banancya. 13 pp. Special Collections, The University of Arizona, Tucson.

Anonymous
1963 Interview with Chief Dan Katchongva of Hotevilla, Independent Hopi Nation, Arizona, May 8, 1963. An unsigned manuscript typescript. 4 pp. Special Collections, The University of Arizona, Tucson.

Anonymous
1969 "Harmony with Nature is Key to Life, Says Leader." *Winslow Mail*, June 5, 1969. Special Collections, The University of Arizona, Tucson.

Anonymous
1970*a* "Hopi Chief Arrives for Saucer Contact." *Prescott Courier*, August 10, 1970. Genealogy Library, Department of Library, Archives and Public Records, Phoenix.
1970*b* "UFO Sightings to End—Solem." *Prescott Courier*, August 18, 1970. Genealogy Library, Department of Library, Archives and Public Records, Phoenix.

Anonymous
1972 "When They Have Eyes: The Hopi Vision." *Clear Creek: The Environmental Viewpoint* 13:32–39.

Anonymous
1978 "The Selling of Our Earth Mother." *Techqua Ikachi* 12 (January-February):1–2.

Anonymous
1980 "Hopis Condemn Smoki for Performing Dances." *Qua' Töqti*, September 11, 1980.

Ardener, Edwin
1980 "Some Outstanding Problems in the Analysis of Events." In Foster and Brandes 1980, 301–363.

Argüelles, José
1987 *The Mayan Factor: Path Beyond Technology*. Santa Fe: Bear and Company.

Aronoff, Myron J.
1983 "Conceptualizing the Role of Culture in Political Change." In Aronoff, ed. 1983, 1–18.

Aronoff, Myron J., ed.
1983 *Political Anthropology Volume 2: Culture and Political Change*. New Brunswick: Transaction Books.

Baal, Jan van
1971 *Symbols for Communication: An Introduction to the Anthropological Study of Religion*. Assen: Van Gorcum.

1981 *Man's Quest for Partnership: The Anthropological Foundation of Ethics and Religion*. Assen: Van Gorcum.

Baal, Jan van, and W. E. A. van Beek
1985 *Symbols for Communication: An Introduction to the Anthropological Study of Religion*. 2nd rev. ed. of van Baal 1971. Assen: Van Gorcum.

Baaren, Th. P. van
1984 "The Flexibility of Myth." In Dundes 1984, 217–224.

Bailey, Frederick George
1960 *Tribe, Caste, and Nation: A Study of Political Activity and Political Change in Highland Orissa*. Manchester: Manchester University Press.

Baird, Robert D.
1971 *Category Formation and the History of Religions*. The Hague: Mouton.

Banton, Michael, ed.
1966 *Anthropological Approaches to the Study of Religion*. London: Tavistock.

Banyacya, Thomas
1-12-1961 Letter to M. Muller-Fricken (White Star), Frankfurt/Main, Germany. Hotevilla: Independent Hopi Nation. Special Collections, The University of Arizona, Tucson.
1-31-1961 Letter to Herbert C. Holdridge. 1 p. Oraibi. Special Collections, The University of Arizona, Tucson.
8-4-1970 Letter to President Richard M. Nixon. On Behalf of Mina Lansa, Claude Kawangyama, Starlie Lomayaktewa, and Dan Katchongva. 1½ pp. Special Collections, The University of Arizona, Tucson.
1975 "The Hopi Prophecy." *East West Journal* 5 (12):36–39.

Barol, Bill, and Pamela Abramson
1987 "The End of the World (Again). Preparing for the Harmonic Convergence." *Newsweek*, August 17:50–51.

Barth, Fredrik
1966 *Models of Social Organization*. London: Royal Anthropological Institute.
1975 *Ritual and Knowledge among the Baktaman of New Guinea*. New Haven: Yale University Press.
1987 *Cosmologies in the Making: A Generative Approach to Cultural Variation in Inner New Guinea*. Cambridge: Cambridge University Press.

Bates, Elizabeth
1979*a* "On the Evolution and Development of Symbols." In Bates ed. 1979, 1–32.
1979*b* "Intentions, Conventions, and Symbols." In Bates ed. 1979, 33–68.

Bates, Elizabeth, ed.
1979 *The Emergence of Symbols: Cognition and Communication in Infancy*. New York: Academic Press.

Baudet, Henri
1959 *Het Paradijs op Aarde*. Amsterdam: Royal Van Gorcum. Eng. transl. New Haven, 1965.

Beaglehole, Ernest
1936 "Hopi Hunting and Hunting Ritual." *Yale University Publications in Anthropology* 4:3–26.

Beaglehole, Ernest, and Pearl Beaglehole
1935 *Hopi of the Second Mesa.* Memoirs of the American Anthropological Association 44. Menasha: George Banta.
Beckford, James A.
1985 *Cult Controversies: The Societal Response to the New Religious Movements.* London: Tavistock.
1987 "New Religions: An Overview." In *The Encyclopedia of Religion*, volume 10, 390–394. New York: Macmillan.
Bellah, Robert N.
1976 "New Religious Consciousness and the Crisis in Modernity." In Glock and Bellah 1976, 333–352.
Bellman, Baryl Larry
1984 *The Language of Secrecy: Symbols and Metaphors in Poro Ritual.* New Brunswick: Rutgers University Press.
Bendix, Reinhard
1968 "Weber, Max." *International Encyclopedia of the Social Sciences*, volume 16, 493–502. New York: Macmillan and the Free Press.
Bendix, Reinhard, and Guenther Roth
1971 *Scholarship and Partisanship: Essays on Max Weber.* Berkeley: University of California Press.
Bentley, Wilder, ed.
1956 *Hopi "Meeting of Religious People."* Hotevilla: Hopi Indian Nation.
Berger, Peter L., and Thomas Luckmann
1966 *The Social Construction of Reality: A Treatise in the Sociology of Knowledge.* Garden City: Doubleday 1966, Harmondsworth: Penguin Books Ltd. 1987.
Berkhofer, Robert F., Jr.
1978 *The White Man's Indian: Images of the American Indian from Columbus to the Present.* New York: Vintage Books.
Bharati, Agehananda
1976 *The Light at the Center: Context and Pretext of Modern Mysticism.* Santa Barbara: Ross-Erikson.
Bianchi, Ugo
1972 "The Definition of Religion (On the Methodology of Historical-Comparative Research)." In Bianchi, Bleeker, and Bausani 1972, 15–34.
1975 *The History of Religions.* Leiden: E. J. Brill.
Bianchi, Ugo, C. Jouco Bleeker, and A. Bausani, eds.
1972 *Problems and Methods of the History of Religions: Proceedings of the Study Conference Organized by the Italian Society for the History of Religions on the Occasion of the Tenth Anniversary of the Death of Raffaele Pettazzoni, Rome, 6th to 8th December 1969.* Leiden: E. J. Brill.
Billington, Ray Allen
1981 *Land of Savagery, Land of Promise: The European Image of the American Frontier.* New York: W. W. Norton.

Bindell, Stan
1989 "Caleb Johnson Wants the Chairman's Post." *The Navajo-Hopi Observer*, September 27, 1989.

Binsbergen, Wim van, and Matthew Schoffeleers, eds.
1985 *Theoretical Explorations in African Religions*. London: Routledge and Kegan Paul.

Birnbaum, N.
1964 "Religion." In Gould and Kolb 1964, 588–589.

Black, Mary E.
1984 "Maidens and Mothers: An Analysis of Hopi Corn Metaphors." *Ethnology* 23:279–288.

Bloch, Maurice
1974 "Symbols, Song, Dance and Features of Articulation." *European Journal of Sociology* 25:55–81.
1977 "The Past and the Present in the Present." *Man* 12 (2):278–292.
1980 "Ritual Symbolism and the Nonrepresentation of Society." In Foster and Brandes 1980, 93–102.

Boissiere, Robert
1986 *Meditations with the Hopi*. Santa Fe: Bear and Company.

Booth, Wayne
1979 *Critical Understanding: The Power and Limits of Pluralism*. Chicago: University of Chicago Press.

Boster, James Shilts
1985 "'Requiem for the Omniscient Informant': There's Life in the Old Girl Yet." In Dougherty 1985, 177–198.

Bourke, John G.
1884 *The Snake-Dance of the Moquis of Arizona: Being a Narrative of a Journey from Santa Fe, New Mexico, to the Villages of the Moqui Indians of Arizona, with a Description of the Manners and Customs of This Peculiar People, and Especially of the Revolting Religious Rite, the Snake-Dance*. London: Sampson Low, Marston, Searle, and Rivington.

Bowerman, Melissa
1980 "The Structure and Origin of Semantic Categories in the Language-Learning Child." In Foster and Brandes 1980, 277–299.

Bradfield, Richard M.
1973 *A Natural History of Associations: A Study in the Meaning of Community*. 2 volumes. New York: International Universities Press.

Brand, Stewart
1988 "Indians and the Counterculture, 1960s–1970s." In Washburn 1988, 570–572.

Brandt, Elizabeth
1980 "On Secrecy and the Control of Knowledge: Taos Pueblo." In Tefft 1980, 123–146.

Brandt, Richard B.
1954 *Hopi Ethics: A Theoretical Analysis*. Chicago: University of Chicago Press.

Brannigan, Augustine
1981 *The Social Bases of Scientific Discoveries.* New York: Cambridge University Press.
Brew, John O.
1949 "Spaniards at Awatovi." In Montgomery, Smith, and Brew 1949, 3–43.
1979 "Hopi Prehistory and History to 1850." In Ortiz 1979, 514–523.
Brewer, William F.
1985 "The Story Schema: Universal and Culture-Specific Properties." In Olson, Torrance, and Hildyard 1985, 167–194.
Brewer, William F., and Edward H. Lichtenstein
1981 "Event Schemas, Story Schemas, and Story Grammars." In Long and Baddeley 1981, 363–379.
Brice, Calvin N.
11-5-1970 Letter to Thomas Banyacya. United States Department of the Interior, Bureau of Indian Affairs, Washington, D.C. 1 p. Special Collections, The University of Arizona, Tucson.
Bromley, David G., and James T. Richardson, eds.
1983 *The Brainwashing-Deprogramming Controversy: Sociological, Psychological, Legal and Historical Perspectives.* New York: Edwin Mellen.
Broms, Henri, and Rebecca Kaufmann, eds.
1988 *Semiotics of Culture: Proceedings of the 25th Symposium of the Tartu-Moscow School of Semiotics, Imatra, Finland, 27th–29th July, 1987.* Helsinki: Arator.
Bruner, Edward M.
1986*a* "Experience and Its Expressions." In Turner and Bruner 1986, 3–30.
1986*b* "Ethnography as Narrative." In Turner and Bruner 1986, 139–155.
Bullard, Thomas E.
1989 "UFO Abduction Reports: The Supernatural Kidnap Narrative Returns in Technological Guise." *Journal of American Folklore* 102:147–170.
Bureau of Indian Affairs, Phoenix Office, Hopi Agency
1955 *Hopi Hearings, July 15–30, 1955.* Keams Canyon: Hopi Agency.
Burridge, Kenelm
1969 *New Heaven New Earth: A Study of Millenarian Activities.* Oxford: Basil Blackwell.
1985 "Millennialisms and the Recreation of History." In Lincoln 1985, 219–235.
1987 "Revival and Renewal." In *The Encyclopedia of Religion,* volume 12, 368–374. New York: Macmillan.
Byrne, Peter
1988 "The Theory of Religion and Method in the Study of Religion in the *Encyclopedia of Religion.*" *Religious Studies* 24 (1):3–10.
Campbell, Colin, and Shirley McIver
1987 "Cultural Sources of Support for Contemporary Occultism." *Social Compass* 34 (1):41–60.

Carpenter, Craig

3-20-1961 To Whom It May Concern. Statement, St. George, Utah. ½ p. Special Collections, University of Arizona, Tucson.

Carroll, John B., ed.

1956 *Language, Thought, and Reality: Selected Writings of Benjamin Lee Whorf.* Cambridge: M.I.T. Press 1956, 1976.

Castaneda, Carlos

1968 *The Teachings of Don Juan: A Yaqui Way of Knowledge.* Los Angeles and Berkeley: University of California Press.

1971 *A Separate Reality: Further Conversations with Don Juan.* New York: Simon and Schuster.

1972 *Journey to Ixtlan: The Lessons of Don Juan.* New York: Simon and Schuster.

1974 *Tales of Power.* New York: Simon and Schuster.

1977 *The Second Ring of Power.* New York: Simon and Schuster.

1981 *The Eagle's Gift.* New York: Simon and Schuster.

1984 *The Fire from Within.* New York: Simon and Schuster.

1988 *The Power of Silence: Further Lessons of Don Juan.* New York: Simon and Schuster.

Castile, George Pierre, and Gilbert Kushner, eds.

1981 *Persistent Peoples: Cultural Enclaves in Perspective.* Tucson: University of Arizona Press.

Chiappelli, Fredi, Michael J. B. Allen, and Robert L. Benson, eds.

1976 *First Images of America.* 2 volumes. Berkeley: University of California Press.

Claessen, Henri J. M.

1979 "Introduction." In Seaton and Claessen 1979, 7–28.

Clemhout, Simone

1964 "Typology of Nativistic Movements." *Man* o.s. 64, 14–15.

1966 "The Psycho-Sociological Nature of Nativistic Movements and the Emergence of Cultural Growth." *Anthropos* 61:33–48.

Clemmer, Richard O.

1969 "The Fed-up Hopi: Resistance of the American Indian and the Silence of the Good Anthropologists." *Steward Anthropological Society* 1 (1):18–40.

1972 "Resistance and the Revitalization of Anthropologists: A New Perspective on Cultural Change and Resistance." In Hymes 1972, 213–247.

1977 "Hopi Political Economy: Industrialization and Alienation." *Southwest Economy and Society* 2 (2):4–33.

1978*a* "Black Mesa and the Hopi." In Jorgensen et al. 1978, 17–34.

1978*b* *Continuities of Hopi Cultural Change.* Ramona: Acoma Books.

1979 "Hopi History, 1940–1970." In Ortiz 1979, 533–538.

Clemmer, Richard O., et al.

1989 "Anthropology, Anthropologists, and the Navajo-Hopi Land Dispute: Reply to Washburn." *American Anthropologist* 91:743–753.

Clifford, James

1980 "Fieldwork, Reciprocity, and the Making of Ethnographic Texts: The Example of Maurice Leenhardt," *Man* 15 (3):518–532.

1986 "Introduction: Partial Truths." In Clifford and Marcus 1986, 1–26.

1988 *The Predicament of Culture: Twentieth-Century Ethnography, Literature, and Art*. Cambridge: Harvard University Press.

Clifford, James, and George E. Marcus, eds.

1986 *Writing Culture: The Poetics of Ethnography*. Berkeley: University of California Press.

Clifton, James A.

1968 "Factional Conflict and the Indian Community: The Prairie Potawatomi Case." In Levine and Lurie 1968, 184–211.

Cohen, Ira J.

1987 "Structuration Theory and Social *Praxis*." In Giddens and Turner 1987, 273–308.

Colby, Benjamin N., and Michael Cole

1973 "Culture, Memory and Narrative." In Horton and Finnegan 1973, 63–91.

Colby, Benjamin N., James W. Fernandez, and David B. Kronenfeld

1981 "Toward a Convergence of Cognitive and Symbolic Anthropology." *American Ethnologist* 8 (3):422–450.

Collins, Allan, and Dedre Gentner

1987 "How People Construct Mental Models." In Holland and Quinn 1987, 243–265.

Colson, Elizabeth

1953 *The Makah Indians: A Study of an Indian Tribe in Modern American Society*. Manchester: Manchester University Press.

Colton, Harold S.

1949 *Kachina Dolls: With a Key to their Identification*. Albuquerque: University of New Mexico Press.

Comaroff, John L., and Simon Roberts

1981 *Rules and Processes: The Cultural Logic of Dispute in an African Context*. Chicago: University of Chicago Press.

Commissioner of Indian Affairs

1939 *Minutes of Conference on Hopi Extension Area held April 24, 1939*, Washington, D.C., Doc. 60471. Special Collections, The University of Arizona, Tucson.

Courlander, Harold

1971 *The Fourth World of the Hopis*. Greenwich: Fawcett.

Courlander, Harold, ed.

1982 *Hopi Voices. Recollections, Traditions, and Narratives of the Hopi Indians*. Albuquerque: University of New Mexico Press.

Cox, Bruce A.

1970 "What Is Hopi Gossip About? Information Management and Hopi Factions." *Man* 5 (1):68–98.

Crane, Leo
1925 *Indians of the Enchanted Desert*. Boston: Little, Brown, 1925. Glorieta: Rio Grande Press, 1972.

Crick, Malcolm
1982 "Anthropological Field Research, Meaning Creation and Knowledge Construction." In Parkin 1982, 15–38.

Crossley-Holland, Peter, ed.
1968 *Proceedings of the Centennial Workshop on Ethnomusicology held at the University of British Columbia, Vancouver, June 19 to 23, 1967*. Vancouver: The Government of the Province of British Columbia.

Curtis, Edward S.
1922 *The North American Indian: Being a Series of Volumes Picturing and Describing the Indians of the United States, the Dominion of Canada, and Alaska*. Cambridge: University Press, 1922. New York: Johnson Reprint, 2nd rpr., 1975, volume 12.

Cushing, Frank Hamilton
1922 "Oraibi in 1883." *American Anthropologist* 24 (3):253–268.
1924 "Origin Myth from Oraibi." *Journal of American Folklore* 36 (140): 163–170.

Dagnal, Cynthia, and Leigh Jenkins
1985 *Katsi. Happiness, Health and Peace: Report of the 1984 Fourth Annual Hopi Mental Health Conference*. Kykotsmovi: Hopi Health Department, The Hopi Tribe.

D'Andrade, Roy G.
1984 "Cultural Meaning Systems." In Shweder and LeVine 1984, 88–122.

Deloria, Vine, Jr.
1969 *Custer Died for Your Sins: An Indian Manifesto*. New York: Macmillan.

Dewanyema, Ray Rutherford
12-12-1911 Letter to President William Taft. Shongopavy, Arizona. 5 pp. In File: "Re: Delegation of Moqui Indians Coming to Washington." Record Group 75. National Archives. Washington, D.C.

Dockstader, Frederick J.
1954 *The Kachina and the White Man: The Influences of White Culture on the Hopi Kachina Cult*. Cranbrook Institute of Science Bulletin 35, 1954, rev. and enlarged ed. Albuquerque: University of New Mexico Press, 1985.
1979 "Hopi History, 1850–1940." In Ortiz 1979, 524–532.

Donaldson, Thomas
1893 *Moqui Pueblo Indians of Arizona and Pueblo Indians of New Mexico*. 11th Census of the United States. Extra Census Bulletin. Washington: United States Census Printing Office.

Donner, Florinda
1985 *The Witch's Dream*. New York: Pocket Books.

Dorsey, George A., and Henry R. Voth
1901 "The Oraíbi Soyal Ceremony." *Field Columbian Museum Publication 55, Anthropological Series* 3 (1):1–59.

Doty, William G.
1986 *Mythography: The Study of Myths and Rituals.* University: University of Alabama Press.
Dougherty, Janet W. D., ed.
1985 *Directions in Cognitive Anthropology.* Urbana: University of Illinois Press.
Drees, Wim B.
1990 "Extraterrestrial Persons." In Kippenberg, Kuiper, and Sanders 1990, 383–392.
Drummond, Lee
1981 "The Serpent's Children: Semiotics of Cultural Genesis in Arawak and Trobriand Myth." *American Ethnologist* 8 (3):633–659.
Duerr, Hans Peter, Hrsg.
1987 *Authentizität und Betrug in der Ethnologie.* Frankfurt am Main: Suhrkamp Verlag.
Dundes, Alan, ed.
1984 *Sacred Narrative: Readings in the Theory of Myth.* Berkeley: University of California Press.
Dunn, Anthony T.
1987 Review of *The Mayan Factor,* by Jose Arguelles. *Shaman's Drum* 10, (Fall):52–54.
Edgerton, Robert B.
1985 *Rules, Exceptions, and Social Orders.* Berkeley: University of California Press.
Edwards, Steven
1986 "Liz Joins Midnight Cowboy in Bizarre Indian Prophecy." *Star Magazine,* August 19, 1986.
Eggan, Fred
1950 *Social Organization of the Western Pueblos.* Chicago: University of Chicago Press.
1967 "From History to Myth: A Hopi Example." In Hymes and Bittle 1967, 33–53.
Eisenstadt, S. N.
1966 *Modernization: Protest and Change.* Englewood Cliffs: Prentice-Hall.
1973 *Tradition, Change, and Modernity.* New York: John Wiley and Sons.
Eister, Alan
1974 *Changing Perspectives in the Scientific Study of Religion.* New York: John Wiley and Sons.
Eliade, Mircea
1949 *Le Mythe de l'éternel retour: archetypes et répétition.* Paris: Librairie Gallimard.
1965 *The Myth of the Eternal Return or, Cosmos and History.* Translation of 1949, revised and enlarged by the author. Princeton: Princeton University Press, 2nd pr. with corrections 1965, Bollingen paperback ed. 1971.

1976 *Occultism, Witchcraft, and Cultural Fashions: Essays in Comparative Religions.* Chicago: University of Chicago Press.

Ellwood, Robert S., Jr.
1979 *Alternative Altars: Unconventional and Eastern Spirituality in America.* Chicago: The University of Chicago Press.

Evens, T. S. M.
1977 "The Prediction of the Individual in Anthropological Interactionism." *American Anthropologist* 79:579–597.

Fabian, Johannes
1969 "Charisma and Cultural Change: The Case of the Jamaa Movement in Katanga (Congo Republic)." *Comparative Studies in Society and History* 11:155–173.
1979*a* "The Anthropology of Religious Movements: From Explanation to Interpretation." *Social Research* 46 (1):4–35.
1979*b* "Text as Terror: Second Thoughts about Charisma." *Social Research* 46 (1):166–203.
1983 *Time and the Other: How Anthropology Makes Its Object.* New York: Columbia University Press.
1985 "Religious Pluralism: An Ethnographic Approach." In van Binsbergen and Schoffeleers 1985, 138–163.

Fabian, Johannes, ed.
1979 *Beyond Charisma: Religious Movements as Discourse. Social Research* 46 (1):1–203.

Fairchild, Hoxie Neale
1928 *The Noble Savage: A Study in Romantic Naturalism.* New York: Columbia University Press.

Fallers, L. A.
1961 "Ideology and Culture in Uganda Nationalism." *American Anthropologist* 63:677–686.

Fardon, Richard
1985 "Secrecy and Sociability: Two Problems of Chamba Knowledge." In *Power and Knowledge: Anthropological and Sociological Approaches.* Ed. R. Fardon, 127–150.

Ferguson, Marilyn
1980 *The Aquarian Conspiracy.* Los Angeles: J. P. Tarcher.

Fernandez, James W.
1964 "African Religious Movements—Types and Dynamics." *Journal of Modern African Studies* 2:428–446.
1978 "African Religious Movements." *Annual Review of Anthropology* 7:198–234.
1982 *Bwiti: An Ethnography of the Religious Imagination in Africa.* Princeton: Princeton University Press.

Festinger, Leon, Henry W. Riecken, and Stanley Schachter
1956 *When Prophecy Fails: A Social and Psychological Study of a Modern Group that Predicted the Destruction of the World.* New York: Harper and Row.

Fewkes, Jesse Walter

1893 "A-wá-to-bi: An Archaeological Verification of a Tusayan Legend." *American Anthropologist* o.s. 6 (4):363–375.

1898 "Archaeological Expedition to Arizona in 1895." *Seventeenth Annual Report of the Bureau of American Ethnology to the Secretary of the Smithsonian Institution 1895–96*, Washington, 519–744.

1900 "Tusayan Migration Traditions." *Nineteenth Annual Report of the Bureau of American Ethnology to the Secretary of the Smithsonian Institution 1897–98*, Washington, part 2, 573–634.

1922 "Oraibi in 1890." *American Anthropologist* 24 (3):268–283.

Fienup-Riordan, Ann

1988 "Robert Redford, Apanuugpak, and the Invention of Tradition." *American Ethnologist* 15 (3):442–455.

Finnegan, Ruth

1970 *Oral Literature in Africa*. Oxford: Oxford University Press.

Firth, Raymond E.

1957 "Introduction: Factions in Indian and Overseas Indian Societies." *British Journal of Sociology* 8:291–295.

Fiske, Donald W., and Richard A. Shweder, eds.

1986 *Metatheory in Social Science: Pluralisms and Subjectivities*. Chicago: University of Chicago Press.

Fogelson, Raymond D.

1985 "Interpretations of the American Indian Psyche: Some Historical Notes." In Helm 1985, 4–27.

Foster, Mary LeCron

1980 "The Growth of Symbolism in Culture." In Foster and Brandes 1980, 371–397.

Foster, Mary LeCron, and Stanley H. Brandes, eds.

1980 *Symbol As Sense: New Approaches to the Analysis of Meaning*. New York: Academic Press.

Foucault, Michel

1976 *The Archaeology of Knowledge*. Translation of the French 1969 edition. New York: Harper and Row.

Freeman, Linton C., A. Kimball Romney, and Sue C. Freeman

1987 "Cognitive Structure and Informant Accuracy." *American Anthropologist* 89:310–325.

French, David H.

1962 "Ambiguity and Irrelevancy in Factional Conflict." In Sherif 1962, 232–243.

Fu, Charles Wei-hsun, and Gerhard E. Spiegler, eds.

1987 *Movements and Issues in World Religions: A Sourcebook and Analysis of Developments Since 1945: Religion, Ideology, and Politics*. New York: Greenwood Press.

Gardner, Howard

1984 "The Development of Culturally Defined Domains: A Preliminary Framework." In Shweder and LeVine 1984, 257–275.

Garfinkel, Harold
1967 *Studies in Ethnomethodology*. Englewood Cliffs: Prentice-Hall.
1968 "The Origin of the Term 'Ethnomethodology.'" In Hill and Crittenden 1968, 5–11.

Garment, Leonard
9–22–1970 Letter to Thomas Banyacya. The White House, Washington, D.C. Special Collections, The University of Arizona, Tucson.

Geertz, Armin W.
1977 "Fundamental Methodological Problems with Particular References to Cults and Myths Associated with the Investigation of the Religion of the Hopi Indians." Ph.D. diss. University of Aarhus, Denmark.
1982*a* "The Sa'lakwmanawyat Sacred Puppet Ceremonial among the Hopi Indians in Arizona: A Preliminary Investigation." *Anthropos* 77:163–190.
1982b *Hotevilla Village and "Adoration Is Not Appreciated."* Aarhus: University of Aarhus.
1983 "Book of the Hopi: The Hopi's Book?" *Anthropos* 78 (3/4):547–556.
1984 "A Reed Pierced the Sky: Hopi Indian Cosmography on Third Mesa, Arizona." *Numen* 31 (2):216–241.
1986 "A Typology of Hopi Indian Ritual." *Temenos* 22:41–56.
1987*a* *Hopi Indian Altar Iconography*. Leiden: E. J. Brill.
1987*b* "Hopi-Forschung, literarische Gattungen und Frank Waters' *Das Buch der Hopi*." In Duerr 1987, 111–136.
1987*c* "Prophets and Fools: The Rhetoric of Hopi Indian Eschatology." *European Review of Native American Studies* 1 (1):33–45.
1987*d* "Hopi Coyote: Trickster, Corpse, or God?" *History of Religions* 27 (1):89–92.
1989*a* "The Great God Maasaw: A Hopi Deity." *European Review of Native American Studies* 2 (2):56–57.
1989*b* "A Container of Ashes: Hopi Prophecy in History." *European Review of Native American Studies* 3 (1):1–6.
1989*c* "Kalabasbomben og 'Unidentified Flying Objects': Apokalyptik og ideologi hos hopi-indianerne." *Chaos* 12:45–57.
1989*d* "Ethnosociology and the Study of the Hopi." *European Review of Native American Studies* 3 (2):59–60.
1989*e* "The Second Warsaw Conference on Methodology and Theory." *Temenos* 25:107–108.
1990*a* "Hopi Hermeneutics: Ritual Person among the Hopi Indians of Arizona." In Kippenberg, Kuiper, and Sanders 1990, 309–336.
1990*b* "Reflections on the Study of Hopi Mythology." In Vecsey 1990, 119–135.
1990*c* Review of William G. Doty, *Mythography*. *Temenos* 25:174–177.
1990*d* "The Study of Indigenous Religions in the History of Religions." In Tyloch 1990, 30–43.
1991 "Hopi Prophecies Revisited: A Critique of Rudolph Kaiser." *Anthropos* 86 (3/4):199–204.

1993 "Theories on Tradition and Change in Sociology, Anthropology, History, and the History of Religions." In Martin 1993, 323–347.

Geertz, Armin W., and Jeppe Sinding Jensen, eds.

1990 *Religion, Tradition and Renewal*. Aarhus: Aarhus University Press.

Geertz, Armin W., and Michael Lomatuway'ma

1987 *Children of Cottonwood: Piety and Ceremonialism in Hopi Indian Puppetry*. Lincoln: University of Nebraska Press.

Geertz, Clifford

1957 "Ethos, World View, and the Analysis of Sacred Symbols." In C. Geertz 1973*a*, 126–141.

1966*a* "Person, Time, and Conduct in Bali." In C. Geertz 1973*a*, 360–411.

1966*b* "Religion as a Cultural System." In Banton 1966, 1–46, and C. Geertz 1973*a*, 87–125.

1972 "Deep Play: Notes on the Balinese Cockfight." In C. Geertz 1973*a*, 412–453.

1973*a* *The Interpretation of Cultures: Selected Essays*. New York: Basic Books.

1973*b* "Thick Description: Toward an Interpretive Theory of Culture." In C. Geertz 1973*a*, 3–30.

1974 "'From the Native's Point of View': On the Nature of Anthropological Understanding." In C. Geertz 1983, 55–70.

1975 "Common Sense as a Cultural System." In C. Geertz 1983, 73–93.

1976 "Art as a Cultural System." In C. Geertz 1983, 94–120.

1977 "Centers, Kings, and Charisma: Reflections on the Symbolics of Power." In C. Geertz 1983, 121–146.

1983 *Local Knowledge: Further Essays in Interpretive Anthropology*. New York: Basic Books.

1986 "Making Experience, Authoring Selves." In Turner and Bruner 1986, 373–380.

Giddens, Anthony

1976 *New Rules of Sociological Method*. London: Hutchinson.

Giddens, Anthony, and Jonathan H. Turner, eds.

1987 *Social Theory Today*. Cambridge and Oxford: Polity Press and Basil Blackwell.

Gipper, Helmut

1972 *Gibt es ein sprachliches Relativitätsprinzip? Untersuchungen zur Sapir-Whorf-Hypothese*. Frankfurt am Main: S. Fischer Verlag.

Glock, Charles Y., and Robert N. Bellah, eds.

1976 *The New Religious Consciousness*. Berkeley: University of California Press.

Gluckman, Max

1963 "Gossip and Scandal." *Current Anthropology* 4 (3):307–316.

Gluckman, Max, and Fred Eggan, eds.

1965 *Political Systems and the Distribution of Power*. London: Tavistock.

Goffman, Erving

1959 *Presentation of Self in Everyday Life*. Garden City: Doubleday.

1969 *Strategic Interaction*. Philadelphia: University of Pennsylvania Press.

Goldfrank, Esther S.
1948 "The Impact of Situation and Personality on Four Hopi Emergence Myths." *Southwestern Journal of Anthropology* 4:241–262.

Goody, Jack
1961 "Religion and Ritual: The Definitional Problem." *The British Journal of Sociology* 12:142–164.

Gould, Julius, and William L. Kolb, eds.
1964 *A Dictionary of the Social Sciences.* London: Tavistock.

Grant, Richard E.
n.d. The Hopi Traditionalists Indexed from *The Navajo Times.* 2 pp. Special Collections, The University of Arizona, Tucson.

Graves, Florence, ed.
1988 "Editorial Statement." In *The 1988 Guide to New Age Living,* pub. by *New Age Journal* April 30, 1988, 3.

Green, Rayna
1976 "The Pocahontas Perplex: The Image of Indian Women in American Culture." *The Massachusetts Review* 16:698–714.
1988 "The Tribe Called Wannabee: Playing Indian in America and Europe." *Folklore* 99 (1):30–55.

Gross, Bertram M.
1968 "Political Process." In *International Encyclopedia of the Social Sciences,* volume 12, 265–273. New York: Macmillan.

Gulliver, P. H.
1979 *Disputes and Negotiations: A Cross-cultural Perspective.* New York: Academic Press.

Guthrie, Stewart
1980 "A Cognitive Theory of Religion." *Current Anthropology* 21 (2):181–203.

Hadden, Jeffrey K., and Anson Shupe, eds.
1986 *Prophetic Religions and Politics: Religion and the Political Order.* New York: Paragon House.

Hallowell, A. Irving
1963 "American Indians, White and Black: The Phenomenon of Transculturation." *Current Anthropology* 4 (5):519–531.

Hammond, George Peter
1957 *Navajo-Hopi Relations, 1540–1956.* 3 vols. Mimeograph. Special Collections, University of New Mexico Library, Albuquerque.

Haviland, John Beard
1977 *Gossip, Reputation, and Knowledge in Zinacantan.* Chicago: University of Chicago Press.

Helm, June, ed.
1965 *Essays in Economic Anthropology: Proceedings of the 1965 Annual Spring Meeting of the American Ethnological Society.* Seattle: University of Washington Press.
1985 *Social Contexts of American Ethnology, 1840–1984.* Washington, D.C.: American Ethnological Society.

Heritage, John

1984 *Garfinkel and Ethnomethodology*. Oxford: Polity Press.

Hermequaftewa, Andrew

1953 *The Hopi Way of Life Is the Way of Peace*. Santa Fe: Hopi Friendship Association, 7th pr. 1968. Special Collections, The University of Arizona, Tucson.

Herskovits, Melville Jean

1937*a* *Acculturation: The Study of Culture Contact*. New York: Alfred A. Knopf.

1937*b* *Life in a Haitian Valley*. New York: Alfred A. Knopf.

Herskovits, Melville Jean, and Frances S. Herskovits

1947 *Trinidad Village*. New York: Alfred A. Knopf.

Herzfeld, Michael

1981 "An Indigenous Theory of Meaning and Its Evaluation in Performative Context." *Semiotica* 34 (1/2):113–141.

Hieb, Louis Albert

1972 "The Hopi Ritual Clown: Life as It Should Not Be." Ph.D. diss., Princeton University.

1979 "Hopi World View." In Ortiz 1979, 577–580.

Hill, Richard J., and Katherine Stones Crittenden, eds.

1968 *Proceedings of the Purdue Symposium on Ethnomethodology*. Lafayette, Indiana: Purdue University.

Hinde, Robert A., Anne-Nelly Perret-Clermont, and Joan Stevenson-Hinde, eds.

1985 *Social Relationships and Cognitive Development: A Fyssen Foundation Symposium*. Oxford: Clarendon Press.

Hodge, Carle

1980 "The Hopi Prophecies: A Vast and Complex Liturgy." *Arizona Highways* 56 (9):43–44.

Hoekema, Anthony A.

1963 *The Four Major Cults: Christian Science, Jehovah's Witnesses, Mormonism, Seventh-day Adventism*. Exeter: The Paternoster Press, Ltd. 1963, 1st paperback ed. 1969, 3rd impr. 1975.

Holland, Dorothy, and Naomi Quinn, eds.

1987 *Cultural Models in Language and Thought*. Cambridge: Cambridge University Press.

Holy, Ladislav

1986 *Strategies and Norms in a Changing Matrilineal Society: Descent, Succession and Inheritance among the Toka of Zambia*. Cambridge: Cambridge University Press.

Holy, Ladislav, and Milan Stuchlik

1981 *The Structure of Folk Models*. London: Academic Press.

1983 *Actions, Norms and Representations: Foundations of Anthropological Inquiry*. Cambridge: Cambridge University Press.

Honko, Lauri, ed.

1979 *Science of Religion: Studies in Methodology. Proceedings of the Study Conference of the International Association for the History of Religions, Held in Turku, Finland August 27–31, 1973*. The Hague: Mouton.

Hopi Empire
3-28-1949 Letter to the President, Hotevilla: The Hopi Empire. Special Collections, The University of Arizona, Tucson.

Hopi Health Department
n.d. *Hopi Mental Health Conference Report.* (Report of the First Hopi Mental Health Conference, January 26-27, 1981, Oraibi, Arizona.) Kykotsmovi: The Hopi Health Department, The Hopi Tribe.

Hopi House
3-4-1967 Letter to President Lyndon B. Johnson. Special Collections, The University of Arizona, Tucson.

Hopi Independent Nation
3-2-1967 Letter to President Lyndon B. Johnson. Special Collections, The University of Arizona, Tucson.

Hopi Lands, Office of
1984 *Chronology of Events and Court Cases Leading to the Relocation of the Navajo and Hopi Indians.* Kykotsmovi: The Hopi Tribe.
1988 *The Taking of Hopi Land: A Hopi Perspective.* Kykotsmovi: The Hopi Tribe.

Hopi Tribe
1967 Resolution No. H-9-67. Kykotsmovi: The Hopi Tribe. Special Collections, The University of Arizona, Tucson.
1987 *Hopi-Tunayt'ya: Hopi Comprehensive Development Plan. A Summary.* Kykotsmovi: The Hopi Tribe.

Hoppál, Mihály
1987 "Proxemic Patterns, Social Structures, and World View." *Semiotica* 65 (3/4):225-247.
1988 "Ethnosemiotics and Semiotics of Culture." In Broms and Kaufmann 1988, 17-33.

Horton, Robin
1967 "African Traditional Thought and Western Science." *Africa* 37:50-71, 155-187.

Horton, Robin, and Ruth Finnegan, eds.
1973 *Modes of Thought: Essays on Thinking in Western and Non-Western Societies.* London: Faber and Faber.

Howard, James H.
1955 "Pan-Indian Culture of Oklahoma." *Scientific Monthly* 18 (5):215-220.

Hunter, James Davison, and Stephen C. Ainlay, eds.
1986 *Making Sense of Modern Times: Peter L. Berger and the Vision of Interpretive Sociology.* London: Routledge and Kegan Paul.

Hurst, Jane, and Joseph Murphy
1987 "New and Transplanted Religions." In Fu and Spiegler 1987, 215-242.

Hymes, Dell, ed.
1972 *Reinventing Anthropology.* New York: Random House.

Hymes, Dell, and W. Bittle, eds.
1967 *Studies in Southwestern Ethnolinguistics: Meaning and History in the Languages of the American Southwest.* The Hague: Mouton.

Jahoda, Gustav, and I. M. Lewis, eds.
1988 *Acquiring Culture: Cross-cultural Studies in Child Development*. London: Croom Helm.

James, Harry C.
1940 *Haliksai! A Book of Hopi Legends of the Grand Canyon Country as told to Harry C. James*. El Centro: The Desert Magazine.
1974 *Pages From Hopi History*. Tucson: University of Arizona Press.

Janzen, John M.
1985 "The Consequences of Literacy in African Religion: The Kongo Case." In van Binsbergen and Schoffeleers 1985, 225–252.

Jarvie, Ian C.
1963 "Theories of Cargo Cults: A Critical Analysis." *Oceania* 34 (1):1–31, 34; (2):109–136.
1972 *Concepts and Society*. London: Routledge and Kegan Paul.

Jenkins, Leigh, and Merwin Kooyahoema, eds.
1984 *Report of the Third Hopi Mental Health Conference: "Prophecy in Motion."* Kykotsmovi: Hopi Health Department, the Hopi Tribe.

Jorgensen, Joseph G.
1985 "Religious Solutions and Native American Struggles: Ghost Dance, Sun Dance and Beyond." In Lincoln 1985, 97–128.

Jorgensen, Joseph G., et al., eds.
1978 *Native Americans and Energy Development*. Cambridge: Anthropology Resource Center.

Kaiser, Rudolf
1989 *Die Stimme des grossen Geistes: Prophezeiungen und Endzeiterwartungen der Hopi-Indianer*. München: Kösel-Verlag.
1991 *The Voice of the Great Spirit: Prophecies of the Hopi Indians*. Trans. Werner Wünsche. Boston: Shambhala.

Kammer, Jerry
1980 *The Second Long Walk: The Navajo-Hopi Land Dispute*. Albuquerque: University of New Mexico Press.

Kaplan, Martha
1990 "Meaning, Agency and Colonial History: Navosavakadua and the *Tuka* Movement in Fiji." *American Ethnologist* 17 (1):3–22.

Katchongva, Dan
1958 "Message Delivered to Albuquerque Indian Meeting, 1958." Hotevilla: Hopi Indian Nation, March 21, 1958. Special Collections, The University of Arizona, Tucson.
7–15–1968 Letter to Superintendent, Hopi Indian Agency. Hotevilla: Hopi Independent Nation. Special Collections, The University of Arizona, Tucson.
1973 *Hopi: A Message for All People*. Rooseveltown: Akwesasne Notes.

Katchongva, Dan, and Andrew Hermequaftewa
9–20–1960 Letter to Honorable Frederick B. Hanley, U.S. Court of Appeals, San Francisco, California. Hotevilla: Hopi Sovereign Nation. Special Collections, The University of Arizona, Tucson.

Katz, Elihu
1977 "Can Authentic Cultures Survive New Media?" *Journal of Communication* 27 (2):113–121.
Katz, Elihu, and George Wedell
1977 *Broadcasting in the Third World: Promise and Performance.* London: Macmillan.
Keesing, Felix M.
1953 *Culture Change: An Analysis and Bibliography of Anthropological Sources to 1952.* Stanford: Stanford University Press.
Keesing, Roger M.
1974 "Theories of Culture." *Annual Review of Anthropology* 3:73–97.
1985 "Conventional Metaphors and Anthropological Metaphysics: The Problematic of Cultural Translation." *Journal of Anthropological Research* 41 (2):201–217.
1987 "Models, 'Folk' and 'Cultural': Paradigms Regained?" In Holland and Quinn 1987, 369–393.
1989 "Exotic Readings of Cultural Texts." *Current Anthropology* 30 (4):459–479.
Keith, Christine
1984 "Simple Ceremonies." *Arizona* (July 15):4, 12, 14.
Keith, Miltona M.
9-16-1906 Letter to Superintendent Matthew M. Murphy. In "Oraibi Troubles," File I. Record Group 75, National Archives. Washington, D.C.
Kennard, Edward A.
1937 "Hopi Reactions to Death." *American Anthropologist* 39:491–496.
1938 *Hopi Kachinas by Edwin Earle: Text by E. A. Kennard.* New York: Museum of the American Indian. Heye Foundation, 2nd rev. ed. 1971.
1965 "Post-war Economic Changes among the Hopi." In Helm 1965, 24–32.
1972 "Metaphor and Magic: Key Concepts in Hopi Culture and Their Linguistic Forms." In Smith 1972, 468–473.
1975 Review of *The Hopi Indians of Old Oraibi*, by Mischa Titiev. *American Anthropologist* 77:109–110.
Kerr, Howard, and Charles L. Crow, eds.
1983 *The Occult in America: New Historical Perspectives.* Urbana: University of Illinois Press.
Kertzer, David I.
1983 "The Role of Ritual in Political Change." In Aronoff 1983, 53–74.
Khatri, Tek Bahadur
1976 *Mass Communications in Nepal.* Kathmandu: Department of Information.
Kippenberg, Hans G., Yme B. Kuiper, and Andy F. Sanders, eds.
1990 *Concepts of Person in Religion and Thought.* Berlin: Mouton de Gruyter.
Kotchongva, Dan
1936 "Where is the White Brother of the Hopi Indian." *The Improvement Era* 39 (2):82–84, 116–119.

Kraus, Joe

1970 "Prophecy Told at Friday's Sightings." *Prescott Courier* (August 9, 1970), 1–2. Genealogy Library, Department of Library, Archives and Public Records, Phoenix.

1974 "The Smoki Dancers." *Desert* (July 1974), 32–35.

Krutz, Gordon V.

1973 "The Native's Point of View as an Important Factor in Understanding the Dynamics of the Oraibi Split." *Ethnohistory* 20 (1):77–89.

Kurtz, Donald V.

1979 "Political Anthropology: Issues and Trends on the Frontier." In Seaton and Claessen 1979, 31–62.

La Barre, Weston

1971 "Materials for a History of Studies of Crisis Cults: A Bibliographic Essay." *Current Anthropology* 12 (1):3–44.

Laird, W. David

1977 *Hopi Bibliography: Comprehensive and Annotated.* Tucson: University of Arizona Press.

Lakoff, George

1987 *Women, Fire, and Dangerous Things: What Categories Reveal About the Mind.* Chicago: University of Chicago Press.

Lakoff, George, and Mark Johnson

1980 *Metaphors We Live By.* Chicago: University of Chicago Press.

Lamendella, John T.

1980 "Neurofunctional Foundations of Symbolic Communication." In Foster and Brandes 1980, 147–174.

Laughlin, Charles D., Jr., and Christopher D. Stephens

1980 "Symbolization, Canalization, and *P*-Structure." In Foster and Brandes 1980, 323–363.

Lawshe, A. L.

12-19-1910 Letter to the Commissioner of Indian Affairs. *Keam's Canyon Letterbooks.* Hopi Indian Agency, Keam's Canyon: Arizona.

Lawson, E. Thomas, and Robert N. McCauley

1990 *Rethinking Religion: Connecting Cognition and Culture.* Cambridge: Cambridge University Press.

Leach, Edmond R.

1961 *Pul Eliya: A Village in Ceylon.* London: Cambridge University Press.

Lemmon, Theodore G.

9-9-1906 Letter to the Commissioner of Indian Affairs. In "Oraibi Troubles," File I. Record Group 75, National Archives. Washington, D.C.

10-25-1906 Letter to the Commissioner of Indian Affairs. *Keams Canyon Letterbooks.*

Lent, John A.

1975 *Asian Mass Communications: A Comprehensive Bibliography.* Philadelphia: Temple University School of Communications and Theater. Supplement 1978.

1977 *Third World Mass Media and Their Search for Modernity: The Case of Commonwealth Caribbean, 1717–1976*. Lewisburg: Bucknell University Press.

Leuba, J. H.
1912 *A Psychological Study of Religion*. New York: Macmillan.

Leupp, Francis E.
1907 "Disturbances among the Hopi." In *Annual Reports of the Department of the Interior, 1906: Indian Affairs*, 118–125. Washington, D.C.: U.S. Government Printing Office.

Levine, Donald N.
1986 "The Forms and Functions of Social Knowledge." In Fiske and Shweder 1986:271–283.

LeVine, Robert
1984 "Properties of Culture: An Ethnographic View." In Shweder and LeVine 1984, 67–87.

Levine, Stuart, and Nancy Oestreich Lurie, eds.
1968 *The American Indian Today*. Deland, Florida: Everett/Edwards.

Lewis, Gilbert
1980 *Day of Shining Red: An Essay on Understanding Ritual*. Cambridge: Cambridge University Press.

Lewis, Ioan M., ed.
1977 *Symbols and Sentiments: Cross-cultural Studies in Symbolism*. London: Academic Press.

Lincoln, Bruce, ed.
1985 *Religion, Rebellion, Revolution: An Interdisciplinary and Cross-cultural Collection of Essays*. Houndmills: Macmillan.

Lindstrom, Lamont
1984 "Doctor, Lawyer, Wise Man, Priest: Big-men and Knowledge in Melanesia." *Man* 19:291–309.

Linton, Ralph
1943 "Nativistic Movements." *American Anthropologist* 45:230–240.

List, George
1968 "The Hopi as Composer and Poet." In Crossley-Holland 1968:43–53.

Little, James A.
1881 *Jacob Hamblin*. Salt Lake City: Deseret News, 1881, Bookcraft Inc., 1969.

Loeffler, Jack
1972 "A Crystal of Many Windows: The Southwest as Symbol." *Clear Creek: The Environmental Viewpoint* 13:10–12.

Loewenstein, Karl
1966 *Max Weber's Political Ideas in the Perspective of Our Time*. Amherst: University of Massachusetts Press.

Lomayaktewa, Starlie
5-14-1971 Statement of Hopi Religious Leaders. Exhibit A in Hopi Indians v. Rogers C. B. Morton. Washington, D.C. 1½ pp. Special Collections, The University of Arizona, Tucson.

Long, John, and Alan Baddeley, eds.
1981 *Attention and Performance IX: Proceedings of the Ninth International Symposium on Attention and Performance, Jesus College, Cambridge, England, July 13–18, 1980*. Hillsdale: Laurence Erlbaum Associates.

Long, Theodore E.
1986 "Prophecy, Charisma, and Politics: Reinterpreting the Weberian Thesis." In Hadden and Shupe 1986, 3–17.

Lord, Albert S.
1960 *The Singer of Tales*. Cambridge: Harvard University Press.

Lummis, Charles F.
1903 *Bullying the Moqui*. Edited with an introduction by Robert Easton and Mackenzie Brown. Flagstaff: Prescott College Press 1968.

Lurie, Nancy Oestreich
1988 "Relations Between Indians and Anthropologists." In Washburn 1988, 548–556.

Lutz, Catherine
1987 "Goals, Events, and Understanding in Ifaluk Emotion Theory." In Holland and Quinn 1987, 290–312.

MacCannell, Dean
1979 "Ethnosemiotics." In Winner and Umiker-Sebeok 1979, 149–171.

MacCannell, Dean, and Juliet Flower MacCannell
1982 *The Time of the Sign: A Semiotic Interpretation of Modern Culture*. Bloomington: Indiana University Press, 1985.

McCauley, Robert N.
1986 "Problem Solving in Science and the Competence Approach to Theorizing in Linguistics." *Journal for the Theory of Social Behaviour* 16 (3):299–312.

Machalek, Richard
1977 "Definitional Strategies in the Study of Religion." *Journal for the Scientific Study of Religion* 16:395–401.

McClintock, James H.
1921 *Mormon Settlement in Arizona: A Record of Peaceful Conquest of the Desert*. Tucson: University of Arizona Press 1985.

McLoughlin, William G.
1978 *Revivals, Awakenings, and Reform: An Essay on Religion and Social Change in America, 1607–1977*. Chicago: University of Chicago Press.

MacQueen, Graeme
1988 "*Whose* Sacred History? Reflections on Myth and Dominance." *Studies in Religion* 17 (2):143–157.

Mallery, Garrick
1886 "Pictographs of the North American Indians. A Preliminary Paper." In *Fourth Annual Report of the Bureau of Ethnology to the Secretary of the Smithsonian Institution 1882–83*, Washington 1886, 3–256.

Malotki, Ekkehart
1979 *Hopi-Raum: Eine sprachwissenschaftliche Analyse der Raumvorstellungen in der Hopi-Sprache*. Tübingen: Gunter Narr Verlag.

1983*a* "The Story of the 'Tsimonmamant' or Jimson Weed Girls: A Hopi Narrative Featuring the Motif of the Vagina Dentata." In Swann 1983, 204–220.

1983*b* *Hopi Time: A Linguistic Analysis of the Temporal Concepts in the Hopi Language.* Berlin: Mouton.

Malotki, Ekkehart, and Michael Lomatuway'ma

1984 *Hopi Coyote Tales: Istutuwutsi.* Lincoln: University of Nebraska Press.

1985 *Gullible Coyote Una'ihu: A Bilingual Collection of Hopi Coyote Stories.* Tucson: University of Arizona Press.

1987*a* *Stories of Maasaw, a Hopi God.* Lincoln: University of Nebraska Press.

1987*b* *Maasaw: Profile of a Hopi God.* Lincoln: University of Nebraska Press.

Manning, Frank

1981 "Celebrating Cricket: The Symbolic Construction of Caribbean Politics." *American Ethnologist* 8 (3):616–632.

Manser, Walter

4-8-1981 Letter to Ms. Sally BigPond. Memorandum Document, Village of Hotevilla, 4-24-1981. 2 pp.

Maranda, Pierre, ed.

1972 *Mythology. Selected Readings.* Harmondsworth: Penguin Books.

Marcus, George E.

1980 "Rhetoric and the Ethnographic Genre in Anthropological Research." *Current Anthropology* 21 (4):507–510.

Marcus, George E., and Dick Cushman

1982 "Ethnographies as Texts." *Annual Review of Anthropology* 11:25–69.

Martin, Luther H., ed.

1993 *Religious Transformations and Socio-Political Change: Eastern Europe and Latin America.* Berlin: Mouton de Gruyter.

Maruyama, Magoroh

1980 "Mindscapes and Science Theories." *Current Anthropology* 21 (5):589–608.

Mbelolo ya Mpiku

1972 "Introduction à la littérature KiKongo." *Research in African Literatures* 3 (2):117–161.

Melton, J. Gordon

1986 *Encyclopedic Handbook of Cults in America.* New York: Garland.

Michaels, Eric

1986 *Aboriginal Television: Central Australia 1982–6.* Canberra: Australian Institute of Aboriginal Studies.

Mille, Richard de

1976 *Castaneda's Journey: The Power and the Allegory.* Santa Barbara: Capra Press.

Mille, Richard de, ed.

1990 *The Don Juan Papers: Further Castaneda Controversies.* Belmont: Wadsworth Publishing Company.

Miller, Jay, and Carol M. Eastman, eds.

1984 *The Tsimshian and their Neighbors of the North Pacific Coast.* Seattle: University of Washington Press.

Miller, Peggy J., and Barbara Byhouwer Moore

1989 "Narrative Conjunctions of Caregiver and Child: A Comparative Perspective on Socialization through Stories." *Ethos* 17 (4):428–449.

Miller, Peggy J., et al.

1990 "Narrative Practices and the Social Construction of Self in Childhood." *American Ethnologist* 17 (2):292–311.

Mills, C. Wright

1959 *The Sociological Imagination*. New York: Oxford University Press.

Mindeleff, Victor.

1891 "A Study of Pueblo Architecture: Tusayan and Cibola." *Eighth Annual Report of the Bureau of Ethnology to the Secretary of the Smithsonian Institution 1886–'87*, Washington 1891, 4–228.

Mommsen, Wolfgang J.

1974 *The Age of Bureaucracy: Perspectives on the Political Sociology of Max Weber*. Oxford: Basil Blackwell.

Monongye, David

1976 Address Given at the 70th Anniversary of Hotevilla Village. *Techqua Ikachi* 8 (August-September):2–3.

Montgomery, Ross Gordon, Watson Smith, and J. O. Brew

1949 *Franciscan Awatovi: The Excavation and Conjectural Reconstruction of a 17th-Century Spanish Mission Establishment at a Hopi Indian Town in Northeastern Arizona*. Papers of the Peabody Museum of American Archaeology and Ethnology, Harvard University 36. Cambridge: The Museum.

Moone, Janet R.

1981 "Persistence with Change: A Property of Sociocultural Dynamics." In Castile and Kushner 1981, 228–242.

Moore, R. Laurence

1986 *Religious Outsiders and the Making of Americans*. New York: Oxford University Press.

Murphy, W. P.

1980 "Secret Knowledge as Property and Power in Kpelle Society: Elders Versus Youth." *Africa* 50:193–207.

Myerhoff, Barbara

1979 *Number Our Days*. New York: Dutton.

Nadel, Siegfried Frederick

1951 *The Foundations of Social Anthropology*. Glencoe: Free Press.

1954 *Nupe Religion*. London: Routledge and Kegan Paul.

Nader, Laura, and Harry F. Todd, Jr., eds.

1978 *The Disputing Process—Law in Ten Societies*. New York: Columbia University Press.

Nagata, Shuichi

1968 "Political Socialization of the Hopi 'Traditional' Faction." Paper Read at the 8th Annual Meeting of the Northeastern Anthropological Association, Hanover, New Hampshire, April 6, 1968. 32 pp. Special Collections, The University of Arizona, Tucson.

1970 *Modern Transformations of Moenkopi Pueblo*. Urbana: University of Illinois Press.
1977 "Opposition and Freedom in Moenkopi Factionalism." In Silverman and Salisbury 1977, 146–170.
1978 "Dan Kochhongva's Message: Myth, Ideology and Political Action among the Contemporary Hopi." *Yearbook of Symbolic Anthropology* 1:73–87.

Native American Rights Fund
5-14-1971 News Release. Berkeley, California. 1½ pp. Special Collections, The University of Arizona, Tucson.

Needham, Rodney
1985 *Exemplars*. Berkeley: University of California Press.

Nequatewa, Edmund
1936 *Truth of a Hopi: Stories Relating to the Origin, Myths and Clan Histories of the Hopi*. Flagstaff: Museum of Northern Arizona. 1936, 2nd pr., 1967.

Nicholas, Ralph W.
1965 "Factions: A Comparative Analysis." In Gluckman and Eggan 1965, 21–61.
1966 "Segmentary Factional Political Systems." In Swartz, Turner, and Tuden 1966, 49–60.

Nisbet, Robert A.
1969 *Social Change and History: Aspects of the Western Theory of Development*. Oxford: Oxford University Press.

Noel, Daniel C., ed.
1976 *Seeing Castaneda: Reactions to the "Don Juan" Writings of Carlos Castaneda*. New York: G. P. Putnam's Sons.

Noonan, Eddie
1981 "A Random Sampling: A Brief Survey of 20 New Age Groups from the Festival of Mind, Body and Spirit." *Up-Date* 5 (2):6–21.

Ochs, Elinor, and Bambi B. Schieffelin
1984 "Language Acquisition and Socialization: Three Developmental Stories and Their Implications." In Shweder and LeVine 1984, 276–322.

O'Dea, Thomas F.
1957 *The Mormons*. Chicago: University of Chicago Press.

Ohnuki-Tierney, Emiko
1981 "Phases in Human Perception/Conception/Symbolization Processes: Cognitive Anthropology and Symbolic Classification." *American Ethnologist* 8 (3):451–467.

O'Keefe, Daniel
1979 "Ethnomethodology." *Journal for the Theory of Social Behaviour* 9: 187–219.

Olson, David R., Nancy Torrance, and Angela Hildyard, eds.
1985 *Literacy, Language, and Learning. The Nature and Consequences of Reading and Writing*. Cambridge: Cambridge University Press.

Ortiz, Alfonso, ed.

1979 *Southwest*. Handbook of North American Indians 9. Washington: Smithsonian Institution.

Ortner, Sherry B.

1973 "On Key Symbols." *American Anthropologist* 75:1338–1346.

1984 "Theory in Anthropology Since the Sixties." *Comparative Studies in Society and History* 26:126–166.

Pagden, Anthony

1982 *The Fall of Natural Man: The American Indian and the Origins of Comparative Ethnology*. Cambridge: Cambridge University Press.

Paine, Robert

1967 "What Is Gossip About? An Alternative Hypothesis." *Man* n.s. 2: 278–285.

1968 "Gossip and Transaction." *Man* n.s. 3:305–308.

Parker, Charles Franklin, and Kitty Joe Parker Nelson

1964 "When the Smoki Dance." *Arizona Highways* 40 (April):36–41.

Parkin, David, ed.

1982 *Semantic Anthropology*. London: Academic Press.

Parsons, Elsie Clews

1927 "Witchcraft among the Pueblos: Indian or Spanish?" *Man* 27 (70 and 80), 106–112, 125–128.

1933 *Hopi and Zuni Ceremonialism*. Memoirs of the American Anthropological Association 39. Menasha: George Banta.

1939 *Pueblo Indian Religion*. 2 volumes. Chicago: University of Chicago Press.

Parsons, Elsie Clews, ed.

1922 "Contributions to Hopi History." *American Anthropologist* 24 (3):253–298.

1925 *A Pueblo Indian Journal 1920–1921*. Memoirs of the American Anthropological Association 32. Menasha: George Banta.

1936 *Hopi Journal of Alexander M. Stephen*. New York: Columbia University Press.

Parsons, Elsie Clews, and Ralph L. Beals

1934 "The Sacred Clowns of the Pueblo and Mayo-Yaqui Indians." *American Anthropologist* 36 (4):491–514.

Parsons, Talcott

1963 "Introduction." In Weber 1963, xix–lxvii.

Pearce, Roy Harvey

1953 *Savagism and Civilization: A Study of the Indian and the American Mind*. Baltimore: Johns Hopkins University Press.

Pelc, Jerzy

1982 "Semiotic and Nonsemiotic Concepts of Meaning." *American Journal of Semiotics* 1 (4):1–19.

Pentikäinen, Juha

1979 "Taxonomy and Source Criticism of Oral Tradition." In Honko 1979, 35–52.

Peterson, Charles S.
1971 "The Hopis and the Mormons 1858–1873." *Utah Historical Quarterly* 39 (2):179–194.
Polkinghorne, Donald E.
1988 *Narrative Knowing and the Human Sciences*. Albany: State University of New York Press.
Popenoe, Cris, and Oliver Popenoe
1984 *Seeds of Tomorrow: New Age Communities that Work*. New York: Harper and Row.
Pouillon, Jean, and Pierre Maranda, eds.
1970 *Échanges et Communications: Mélanges Offerts à Claude Lévi-Strauss à l'Occasion de son 60ème Anniversaire*. 2 volumes. The Hague: Mouton.
Powell, J. M.
1977 *Mirrors of the New World: Images and Image-Makers in the Settlement Process*. Kent: W. Dawson.
Powell, John Wesley
1875 *The Hopi Villages: The Ancient Province of Tusayan*. Wild and Wooly West Books 21. Palmer Lake: Filter Press. Reprinted 1972.
Powers, William K.
1988 "The Indian Hobbyist Movement in North America." In Washburn 1988, 557–561.
Pritchard, Linda K.
1976 "Religious Change in Nineteenth-century America." In Glock and Bellah 1976, 297–330.
Quasthoff, Uta H.
1986 "Ethnomethodology." In Sebeok 1986, vol. 1, 231–233.
Quinn, Naomi, and Dorothy Holland
1987 "Culture and Cognition." In Holland and Quinn 1987, 3–40.
Radford, Colin
1985 "Must Knowledge—or, '*Knowledge*'—Be Socially Constructed?" *Philosophy of the Social Sciences* 15:15–33.
Ricoeur, Paul
1962 "The Hermeneutics of Symbols and Philosophical Reflections." *Philosophical Quarterly* 2:191–218.
Robbins, Thomas
1988 *Cults, Converts and Charisma: The Sociology of New Religious Movements*. London: Sage.
Robbins, Thomas, William C. Shepherd, and James McBride, eds.
1985 *Cults, Culture, and the Law: Perspectives on New Religious Movements*. Chico: Scholars Press.
Robin, Robert
1983 *Report of the Second Hopi Mental Health Conference: Crossroads of Cultural Change*. Kykotsmovi: Hopi Health Department, the Hopi Tribe.
Rose, Wendy
1984 "Just What's All This Fuss about Whiteshamanism Anyway?" In Schöler 1984, 13–24.

Roszak, Theodore

1969 *The Making of a Counter Culture: Reflections on the Technocratic Society and Its Youthful Opposition*. Garden City: Anchor Books.

Roth, Paul A.

1989 "Ethnography without Tears." *Current Anthropology* 30 (5):555–569.

Rubinstein, Robert L.

1981 "Knowledge and Political Process on Malo." In Allen 1981, 135–172.

Ruppert, Ray

1969 "Harmony with Nature Is Key to Life, Says Hopi Leader." *The Seattle Times*, May 10.

Rushton, Mary

1970 "Do Flying Saucers Indicate Truth of Hopi Prophecy?" *Independent*, October 27, 1 and 12. Cline Library, Special Collections Department, Northern Arizona University, Flagstaff.

Sabin, Edwin Legrand

1935 *Kit Carson Days, 1809–1868*. New York: Press of the Pioneers.

Sangren, P. Steven

1988 "Rhetoric and the Authority of Ethnography: 'Postmodernism' and the Social Reproduction of Texts." *Current Anthropology* 29 (3):405–435.

Satin, Mark

1978 *New Age Politics: Healing Self and Society: The Emerging New Alternative to Marxism and Liberalism*. West Vancouver: Whitecap Books.

Saum, Lewis O.

1965 *The Fur Trader and the Indian*. Seattle: University of Washington Press.

Sawyer, Jesse, ed.

1971 *Studies in American Indian Languages*. Berkeley: University of California Press.

Schlegel, Alice

1973 "The Adolescent Socialization of the Hopi Girl." *Ethnology* 12 (4): 449–462.

1977 "Male and Female in Hopi Thought and Action." In Schlegel 1977, 246–269.

1979 "Sexual Antagonism among the Sexually Egalitarian Hopi." *Ethos* 7 (2):124–141.

Schlegel, Alice, ed.

1977 *Sexual Stratification: A Cross-cultural View*. New York: Columbia University Press.

Schöler, Bo, ed.

1984 *Coyote was Here: Essays on Contemporary Native American Literary and Political Mobilization*. Aarhus: University of Aarhus.

Schutz, Alfred

1967 *The Phenomenology of the Social World*. Translated by George Walsh and Frederick Lehnert from the German 1932 edition. Chicago: Northwestern University Press.

Schwartz, Hillel
1976 "The End of the Beginning: Millenarian Studies, 1969–1975." *Religious Studies Review* 2:1–15.
1987 "Millenarianism: An Overview." In *The Encyclopedia of Religion*, volume 9, 521–532. New York: Macmillan.
Schwartz, Theodore, ed.
1975 *Socialisation as Cultural Communication*. Berkeley: University of California Press.
Schweidlenka, Roman
1987 "Eberhard Kohler: Ein christlicher Esoteriker legitimiert den Völkermord." *Informationsdienst Indianer heute* 4:29–31.
Scott, Colonel Hugh L.
12-5-1911 Letter to the Secretary of the Interior, including enclosure: "The Story of Ukeoma, Chief of the Hotivillos, a Village of the Hopi." 4 pp. letter and 18pp. enclosure, typescript. In File "Re: Delegation of Moqui Indians Coming to Washington." Record Group 75, National Archives. Washington, D.C.
Seaton, S. Lee, and Henri J. M. Claessen, eds.
1979 *Political Anthropology. The State of the Art*. The Hague: Mouton.
Sebeok, Thomas A., ed.
1986 *Encyclopedic Dictionary of Semiotics*. 3 volumes. Berlin: Mouton de Gruyter.
Sekaquaptewa, Emory
1972 "Preserving the Good Things of Hopi Life." In Spicer and Thompson 1972, 239–260.
Sekaquaptewa, Wayne
1976 "Three Score and Ten Years Later." *Qua' Töqti*, September 9.
1978 "Project Waterlog is Waterlogged." *Qua' Töqti*, May 18.
Selina, Ralph
10-2-1968 Letter to President Lyndon B. Johnson. Hopi Independent Nation, Shongopavy. 1½ pp. Special Collections, The University of Arizona, Tucson.
Shaffer, Carolyn R.
1987 "Dr. Leslie Gray, Bridge between Two Realities," *Shaman's Drum* 10: 21–28.
Shaked, Shaul, David Shulman, and Gedaliahu G. Stroumsa, eds.
1987 *Gilgul: Essays on Transformation, Revolution and Permanence in the History of Religions: Dedicated to R. J. Zwi Werblowsky*. Leiden: E. J. Brill.
Sharrock, Wes, and Bob Anderson
1986 *The Ethnomethodologists*. Chichester: Ellis Horwood.
Sheppard, Gerald T., and William E. Herbrechtsmeier
1987 "Prophecy: An Overview." In *The Encyclopedia of Religion*, vol. 12, 8–14. New York: Macmillan.
Sherif, Muzafer, ed.
1962 *Intergroup Relations and Leadership: Approaches and Research in Industrial, Ethnic, Cultural, and Political Areas*. New York: John Wiley and Sons.

Sherzer, Joel F.
1987 "A Discourse-centered Approach to Language and Culture." *American Anthropologist* 89:295–309.

Shils, Edward
1958 "The Concentration and Dispersion of Charisma: Their Bearing on Economic Policy in Underdeveloped Countries." *World Politics* 11: 1–19.
1961 "Centre and Periphery." In *The Logic of Personal Knowledge.* Glencoe: The Free Press, 117–130.
1965 "Charisma, Order, and Status." *American Sociological Review* 30 (April): 199–213.
1968 "Charisma." In *International Encyclopedia of the Social Sciences,* volume 2, 386–390. New York: Macmillan.
1971 "Tradition." *Comparative Studies in Society and History* 13 (2):122–159.
1975 *Center and Periphery: Essays in Macrosociology.* Chicago: University of Chicago Press.

Shupe, Anson D., Jr., and David G. Bromley
1981 *Strange Gods: The Great American Cult Scare.* Boston: Beacon Press.

Shupe, Anson D., Jr., David G. Bromley, and Donna Garland Oliver
1984 *The Anti-Cult Movement in America: A Bibliography and Historical Survey.* New York: Garland Press.

Shweder, Richard A., and Robert A. LeVine, eds.
1984 *Culture Theory: Essays on Mind, Self, and Emotion.* Cambridge: Cambridge University Press.

Sider, Gerald
1987 "When Parrots Learn to Talk, and Why They Can't: Domination, Deception, and Self-deception in Indian-White Relations." *Comparative Studies in Society and History* 29 (1):3–23.

Siegel, Bernard J., and Alan R. Beals
1960*a* "Pervasive Factionalism." *American Anthropologist* 62:394–417.
1960*b* "Conflict and Factionalist Disputes." *Journal of the Royal Anthropological Insitute* 90 (1):107–117.
1966 *Divisiveness and Social Conflict.* Stanford: Stanford University Press.

Siikala, Jukka
1982 *Cult and Conflict in Tropical Polynesia: A Study of Traditional Religion, Christianity and Nativistic Movements.* Helsinki: Academia Scientiarum Fennica.

Silverman, Maryland, and Richard F. Salisbury, eds.
1977 *A House Divided? Anthropological Studies of Factionalism.* St. Johns: Memorial University of Newfoundland.

Simmons, Leo W., ed.
1942 *Sun Chief: The Autobiography of a Hopi Indian.* New Haven: Yale University Press 1942, 14th pr. 1974.

Singer, Milton
1971 "Beyond Tradition and Modernity in Madras." *Comparative Studies in Society and History* 13 (2):160–195.

Skidmore, Nonnie S.
1970 *Chief Dan Katchongva's Message: Hopi Prophecy*. Hotevilla: Hopi Independent Nation.

Slater, Peter
1978 *The Dynamics of Religion: Continuity and Change in Patterns of Faith*. New York: Harper and Row.

Smart, Ninian
1969 *The Religious Experience of Mankind*. New York: Charles Scribner's Sons.
1973 *The Science of Religion and the Sociology of Knowledge. Some Methodological Questions*. Princeton: Princeton University Press.
1983 *Worldviews: Crosscultural Explorations of Human Beliefs*. New York: Charles Scribner's Sons.

Smith, Frank
1985 "A Metaphor for Literacy: Creating Worlds or Shunting Information?" In Olson, Torrance, and Hildyard 1985, 195–213.

Smith, Jonathan Z.
1978 *Map Is Not Territory: Studies in the History of Religions*. Leiden: E. J. Brill.

Smith, M. Estellie, ed.
1972 *Studies in Linguistics in Honor of George L. Trager*. The Hague: Mouton.

Smith, Marian W.
1959 "Towards a Classification of Cult Movements." *Man* o.s. 59:8–12.

Smith, Michael G.
1960 *Government in Zazzau: 1800–1950*. Oxford: Oxford University Press.

Smoki People
1937 *Smoki Ceremonials and Snake Dance: Official Program*. 34 pp. Special Collections, The University of Arizona, Tucson.

Spangler, David
1980 *Explorations: Emerging Aspects of the New Culture*. Forres, Scotland: Findhorn Publications.

Spencer, Jonathan
1989 "Anthropology as a Kind of Writing." *Man* 24 (1):145–164.

Sperber, Dan
1974 *Le symbolisme en général*. Paris: Hermann.
1985 "Anthropology and Psychology: Towards an Epidemiology of Representations." *Man* 20 (1):73–89.

Sperber, Dan, and Deirdre Wilson
1986 *Relevance: Communication and Cognition*. Oxford: Basil Blackwell.

Spicer, Edward H.
1961 "Types of Contact and Processes of Change." In Spicer 1961, 517–544.
1962 *Cycles of Conquest: The Impact of Spain, Mexico, and the United States on the Indians of the Southwest, 1533–1960*. Tucson: University of Arizona Press. 6th pr. 1976

1971 "Persistent Cultural Systems: A Comparative Study of Identity Systems that Can Adapt to Contrasting Environments." *Science* 174: 795–800.

1972 "Plural Society in the Southwest." In Spicer and Thompson 1972, 21–76.

Spicer, Edward H., ed.

1961 *Perspectives in American Indian Culture Change*. Chicago: University of Chicago Press.

Spicer, Edward H., and Raymond H. Thompson, eds.

1972 *Plural Society in the Southwest*. New York: Interbook.

Spiro, Melford E.

1966 "Religion: Problems of Definition and Explanation." In Banton 1966, 85–126.

Staat, Wim

1990 "Interactive Meaning Representation of Audiovisual Texts: A Peircean Approach." *Semiotica* 79 (1/2):51–78.

Stanner, W. E. H.

1958 "On the Interpretation of Cargo Cults." *Oceania* 29 (1):1–25.

1959 "Continuity and Schism in an African Tribe." *Oceania* 29 (4):208–217.

Stedman, Raymond W.

1982 *Shadows of the Indian: Stereotypes in American Culture*. Norman: University of Oklahoma Press.

Stephen, Alexander M.

1929 "Hopi Tales: With Preface and Notes by E. C. Parsons." *Journal of American Folklore* 42:1–72.

Stipe, Claude E.

1980 "Anthropologists versus Missionaries: The Influence of Presuppositions." *Current Anthropology* 21 (2):165–179.

Stone, Donald

1976 "The Human Potential Movement." In Glock and Bellah 1976, 93–115.

Street, Brian V.

1984 *Literacy in Theory and Practice*. Cambridge: Cambridge University Press.

Suderman, John P.

n.d. *A Hopi Indian Finds Christ: The Experience of Mr. K. T. Johnson and His Judgment on Idolatry*, Oraibi.

Swan, Jim

1987 "Harmonic Convergence Celebrated Around World." *Shaman's Drum* 10 (Fall):6.

Swann, Brian, ed.

1983 *Smoothing the Ground*. Berkeley: University of California Press.

Swanson, Earl H., Jr., ed.

1970 *Languages and Cultures of Western Northern America: Essays in Honor of Sven Liljeblad*. Pocatello: Idaho State University Press.

Swartz, Marc J., Victor W. Turner, and Arthur Tuden, eds.
1966 *Political Anthropology*. Chicago: Aldine.

Tanner, George S., and J. Morris Richards
1977 *Colonization on the Little Colorado: The Joseph City Region*. Flagstaff: Northland Press.

Tarbet, Thomas V., Jr.
1975 "The Hopi: At the Heart of the World." *East West Journal* 5 (7):13–15.

Tarbet, Thomas V., Jr., ed.
1972 *From the Beginning of Life to the Day of Purification: Teachings, History and Prophecies of the Hopi People as told by the late Dan Katchongva, Sun Clan (c. 1865–1972)*. Translated by Danaqyumptewa. Los Angeles: Committee for Traditional Indian Land and Life. Rev. ed. 1977.

Taylor, Colin F.
1988 "The Indian Hobbyist Movement in Europe." In Washburn 1988, 562–569.

Tedlock, Dennis
1983 *The Spoken Word and the Work of Interpretation*. Philadelphia: University of Pennsylvania Press.

Tefft, Stanton K., ed.
1980 *Secrecy: A Cross-Cultural Perspective*. New York: Human Sciences Press.

Thompson, Laura
1950 *Culture in Crisis: A Study of the Hopi Indians*. New York: Harper and Brothers.

Titiev, Mischa
1937 "The Use of Kinship Terms in Hopi Ritual." *Museum Notes of the Museum of Northern Arizona* 10 (3):9–11.
1943 "Notes on Hopi Witchcraft." *Papers of the Michigan Academy of Science, Arts, and Letters* 28:549–557.
1944 *Old Oraibi: A Study of the Hopi Indians of Third Mesa*. Papers of the Peabody Museum of American Archaeology and Ethnology, Harvard University 22 (1). Cambridge: The Museum.
1972 *The Hopi Indians of Old Oraibi: Change and Continuity*. Ann Arbor: University of Michigan Press.

Turner, Brian S.
1981 *For Weber*. London: Routledge and Kegan Paul.

Turner, Harold W.
1977 *Bibliography of New Religious Movements in Primal Societies*. Volume I: *Black Africa*. Boston: G. K. Hall.
1978 *Bibliography of New Religious Movements in Primal Societies*. Volume II: *North America*. Boston: G. K. Hall.
1979 *Religious Innovation in Africa. Collected Essays on New Religious Movements*. Boston: G. K. Hall.

Turner, Jonathan H.
1987 "Analytical Theorizing." In Giddens and Turner 1987, 156–194.

Turner, Victor W.
1957 *Schism and Continuity in an African Society*. Manchester: Manchester University Press.

1969 *The Ritual Process: Structure and Anti-structure.* New York: Aldine.

1974 *Dramas, Fields, and Metaphors.* Ithaca, N.Y.: Cornell University Press.

1986 "Dewey, Dilthey, and Drama: An Essay in the Anthropology of Experience." In Turner and Bruner 1986, 33–44.

Turner, Victor W., and Edward M. Bruner, eds.

1986 *The Anthropology of Experience.* Urbana: University of Illinois Press.

Turner, Victor W., and Edith Turner

1978 *Image and Pilgrimage in Christian Culture: Anthropological Perspectives.* New York: Columbia University Press.

Tyler, Hamilton A.

1964 *Pueblo Gods and Myths.* Norman: University of Oklahoma Press, 1964, 2d pr. 1972.

1975 *Pueblo Animals and Myths.* Norman: University of Oklahoma Press.

Tyler, Stephen A.

1978 *The Said and the Unsaid: Mind, Meaning, and Culture.* New York: Academic Press.

1987 *The Unspeakable: Discourse, Dialogue, and Rhetoric in the Postmodern World.* Madison: University of Wisconsin Press.

Tyloch, Witold, ed.

1990 *Studies on Religions in the Context of the Social Sciences: Methodological and Theoretical Relations.* Warsaw: Polish Society for the Science of Religions.

Udall, Louise, ed.

1969 *Me and Mine: The Life Story of Helen Sekaquaptewa as told to Louise Udall.* Tucson: University of Arizona Press.

Upham, Steadman

1982 *Polities and Power: An Economic and Political History of the Western Pueblo.* New York: Academic Press.

Valentine, Robert Grosvenor

1911 Conference between the Commissioner of Indian Affairs and Yukeoma, Hopi Indian. March 28, 1911. 16 pp. typescript. In File "Re: Delegation of Moqui Indians Coming to Washington." Record Group 75, National Archives. Washington, D.C.

3-30-1911 Letter to Chief Yukeoma, c/o Supt., Moqui Reservation. 1 p. typescript. In File "Re: Delegation of Moqui Indians Coming to Washington." Record Group 75, National Archives. Washington, D.C.

Van Maanen, John

1988 *Tales of the Field: On Writing Ethnography.* Chicago: University of Chicago Press.

Vansina, Jan

1961 *De la tradition orale; essai de méthode historique.* Tervuren: Musée Royal de l'Afrique Centrale, Eng. transl. 1965.

Varenne, Hervé

1984 "Collective Representation in American Anthropological Conversations: Individual and Culture." *Current Anthropology* 25 (3):281–299.

Vecsey, Christopher
1983 "The Emergence of the Hopi People." *American Indian Quarterly* 1983 (Summer):69–92.
Vecsey, Christopher, ed.
1990 *Religion in Native North America*. Moscow: University of Idaho Press.
Victor, Frances Fuller
1870 *The River of the West: Life and Adventures in the Rocky Mountains and Oregon; Embracing Events in the Life-time of a Mountain-man and Pioneer: With Early History of the North-western Slope*. Hartford: R. W. Bliss.
Voegelin, Charles F.
1959 "The Notion of Arbitrariness in Structural Statement and Restatement I: Eliciting." *International Journal of American Linguistics* 25 (4): 207–220.
Voegelin, Charles F., and Florence M. Voegelin
1960 "Selection in Hopi Ethics, Linguistics, and Translation." *Anthropological Linguistics* 2:48–78.
1970*a* "Hopi Names and No Names (With Reference to Households in Social Organization)." In Swanson, Jr. 1970, 47–53.
1970*b* "Cross-cultural Typologies and Folk Taxonomies." In Pouillon and Maranda 1970, vol. 2, 1132–1147.
1971 "The Autonomy of Linguistics and the Dependence of Cognitive Culture." In Sawyer 1971, 303–317.
Voget, Fred W.
1959 "Towards a Classification of Cult Movements: Some Further Contributions." *Man* o.s. 59:26–28.
Voigt, Vilmos
1986 "Ethnosemiotics." In Sebeok 1986, vol. 1, 235–237.
Voth, Henry R.
n.d. Interview with Yukioma. Mennonite Library and Archives. Bethel College, North Newton, Kansas.
1905 *The Traditions of the Hopi*. Field Columbian Museum Publication 96, Anthropological Series 8. Chicago: Field Columbian Museum.
Wagner, Roy
1972 *Habu: The Invention of Meaning in Daribi Religion*. Chicago: University of Chicago Press.
1975 *The Invention of Culture*. Chicago: University of Chicago Press 1975, rev. and expanded 1981.
1978 *Lethal Speech: Daribi Myth as Symbolic Obviation*. Ithaca: Cornell University Press.
1979 "The Talk of Koriki: A Daribi Contact Cult." *Social Research* 46 (1): 140–165.
1986 *Symbols that Stand for Themselves*. Chicago: University of Chicago Press.
Wahlström, Bertel
1981 "The Indefinability of Religion." *Temenos* 17:101–115.
Wallace, Anthony F. C.
1956 "Revitalization Movements: Some Theoretical Considerations for their Comparative Study." *American Anthropologist* 58:264–281.

Wallgren, Jane Bennett
1973 *The Juniper Tree as a Symbol of Transformation among the Hopi Indians.* Ph.D. diss., Carl G. Jung Institute, Zürich, Switzerland.

Wallis, Wilson D.
1936 "Folk Tales from Shumopovi, Second Mesa." *Journal of American Folklore* 49:1–68.

Walls, Andrew
1987 "Primal Religious Traditions in Today's World." In Whaling 1987, 250–278.

Washburn, Wilcomb E.
1971 *Red Man's Land/White Man's Law: A Study of the Past and Present Status of the American Indian.* New York: Charles Scribner's Sons.
1976 "The Historical Context of American Indian Legal Problems." *Law and Contemporary Problems* 40 (1):12–24.
1979 "On the Trail of the Activist Anthropologist: Response to Jorgensen and Clemmer." *Journal of Ethnic Studies* 7 (1):89–99.
1985 "Ethical Perspectives in North American Ethnology." In Helm 1985, 51–64.
1989 "Anthropological Advocacy in the Hopi-Navajo Land Dispute." *American Anthropologist* 91 (3):738–743.

Washburn, Wilcomb E., ed.
1988 *History of Indian-White Relations.* Handbook of North American Indians 4. Washington: Smithsonian Institution.

Waters, Frank
1963 *Book of the Hopi.* New York: Viking Press. New York: Ballantine Books 1963. 4th pr. 1971.
1969 *Pumpkin Seed Point.* Chicago: The Swallow Press. 2nd pr. 1970.
1975 *Mexico Mystique. The Coming Sixth World of Consciousness.* Chicago: Sage Books.
1987 "Kokopilau: The Humpbacked Flute Player." *Shaman's Drum* 10 (Fall): 17–20.

Weber, Max
1911–1913 *Wirtschaft und Gesellschaft: Grundriss der verstehenden Soziologie,* Tübingen: J. C. B. Mohr. 1ste Aufl. 1921, 5te, rev. Aufl. 1972, 1976.
1963 *The Sociology of Religion.* Translation of "Religionssoziologie" from Weber 1911–1913. Boston: Beacon Press. 1963. Paperback 1964.

Weigle, Marta
1989 "From Desert to Disney World: The Santa Fe Railway and the Fred Harvey Company Display the Indian Southwest." *Journal of Anthropological Research* 45 (1):115–137.

Werblowsky, R. J. Zwi
1975 "On Studying Comparative Religion: Some Naive Reflections of a Simple-minded Non-philosopher." *Religious Studies* 11:145–156.
1976 *Beyond Tradition and Modernity: Changing Religions in a Changing World.* London: Athlone Press.

Werbner, Richard P.
1985 "The Argument of Images: From Zion to the Wilderness in African Churches." In van Binsbergen and Schoffeleers 1985, 253–286.

West, James
1945 *Plainsville, U.S.A.* New York: Columbia University Press.

Whaling, Frank, ed.
1987 *Religion in Today's World: The Religious Situation of the World from 1945 to the Present Day*. Edinburgh: T. and T. Clark.

White, Hayden
1973 *Metahistory: The Historical Imagination in Nineteenth Century Europe*. Baltimore: Johns Hopkins University Press.

Whiteley, Peter M.
1985 "Unpacking Hopi 'Clans': Another Vintage Model Out of Africa?" *Journal of Anthropological Research* 41 (4):359–374.
1986 "Unpacking Hopi 'Clans' II: Further Questions About Hopi Descent Groups." *Journal of Anthropological Research* 42 (1):69–79.
1987 "The Interpretation of Politics: A Hopi Conundrum." *Man* 22:696–714.
1988 *Deliberate Acts: Changing Hopi Culture Through the Oraibi Split*. Tucson: University of Arizona Press.
1992 "Burning Culture: Auto-da-fé at Oraibi." *History and Anthropology* 6 (1):46–85.

Wilson, John H.
1910 Letter to the Commissioner of Indian Affairs. *Keams Canyon Letterbooks* 13:430.

Winner, Irene Portis, and Jean Umiker-Sebeok, eds.
1979 *Semiotics of Culture*. The Hague: Mouton.

Wisdom, J. O.
1973 "The Phenomenological Approach to the Sociology of Knowledge." *Philosophy of the Social Sciences* 3:251–266.

Wittgenstein, Ludwig
1953 *Philosophical Investigations*. Translated by G. E. M. Anscombe. New York: Macmillan.

Worth, Sol, and John Adair
1973 *Through Navajo Eyes: An Exploration in Film Communication and Anthropology*. Bloomington: Indiana University Press.

Wright, Barton
1973 *Kachinas: A Hopi Artist's Documentary. Original Paintings by Cliff Bahnimptewa*. Flagstaff, Arizona: Northland Press.

Wuthnow, Robert
1986 "Religion as Sacred Canopy." In Hunter and Ainlay 1986, 117–135.
1987 *Meaning and Moral Order: Explorations in Cultural Analysis*. Berkeley: University of California Press.

Yaiva-BigPond, Sally
4-24-1981 Letter to Mr. Walter Manser. Memorandum Document, Village of Hotevilla, 4-24-1981. 9 pp.

Yava, Albert

1978 *Big Falling Snow: A Tewa-Hopi Indian's Life and Times and the History and Traditions of His People.* Edited and annotated by Harold Courlander. Albuquerque: University of New Mexico Press 1978, 1982.

Young, M. Jane

1987 "'Pity the Indians of Outer Space': Native American Views of the Space Program." *Western Folklore* 46:269–279.

INDEX

Designer: U.C. Press Staff
Compositor: Prestige Typography
Text: 10/12 Baskerville
Display: Baskerville
Printer: Braun-Brumfield, Inc.
Binder: Braun-Brumfield, Inc.